Erratalist to *The Epistle of J*

Page v (Preface), line 16: for "prof. em."

Page vi (Preface), line 21: for "Manuscripts" read "manuscripts."

Page 4, note 7: for "*katholischen*" read "*Katholischen.*"

Page 19, line 14: for "pre- Harklean" read "pre-Harklean."

Page 24, note 107: for "xviii" read "35*."

Page 55, line 13: for "be best" read "be the best."

Page 61, note 36: substitute second comma for parenthesis.

Page 80, line 15: for "this" read "these."

Page 105, line 24: for "recent" read "recently."

Page 105, line 26: for "1274b" read "1274b [=2822]."

Page 118, line 11: for "is" read "are."

Page 125, line 26: remove comma after σπιλάδες.

Page 125, line 39: remove punctuation before ὅτι.

Page 126, between line 18-19 insert new line: "v. 18: τοῦ (*ECM:* omit)."

Page 129, line 11: for "adresses" read "adressees."

Page 170, line 1: remove first comma after σπιλάδες.

Page 188, line 3: remove punctuation before ὅτι.

Page 240, line 18: for "came in" read "came into."

Page 243, note 25: for "they" read "the."

Page 247, line 5: for "lenghty" read "lengthy."

Page 260, line 12: for "Patristic," read "patristic."

Page 271, line 21: for "twice in Jude" read "including Jude 7."

Page 271, line 22: for "the Majority reading of Jude 7" read "Jude 3 and 20."

Page 301, line 11: for "before", read "after."

Page 334, note 385: for "05C" read "06C."

Page 367, reference to "5:6" move from 2 Peter to 1 Peter.

Plates

Plate II (𝔓72), transcription on facing page, line 17: for "σοφον" read "ζοφον."

Plate VI (𝔓72), transcription on facing page, line 13: for "ζατε" read "σατε."

Plate VIII-IX (𝔓78), transcription on facing page: for "Fol. 2, *recto*" read "Fol. 2, *verso*"; for "Fol. 2, *verso*" read "Fol. 2, *recto.*"

Description of MS. Garrett 8 (1799), last line: for "XII-XIII" read "XV-XVI."

The indicated ISBN-13 number (on the cover and in the frontmatters) is incorrect. The final digit should be 9 (not 0).

CONIECTANEA BIBLICA • NEW TESTAMENT SERIES 43

CB

CONIECTANEA BIBLICA
NEW TESTAMENT SERIES
43

Present editors:
Bengt Holmberg (Lund) and Kari Syreeni (Uppsala)

The Epistle of Jude:
Its Text and Transmission

TOMMY WASSERMAN

Almqvist & Wiksell International
Stockholm, Sweden

2006

Abstract

Wasserman, Tommy. 2006. The Epistle of Jude: Its Text and Transmission. Coniectanea Biblica. New Testament Series 43. xvi + 368 pp. + xvi plates. ISBN-10 91-22-02159-0. ISBN-13 978-91-22-02159-0.

This study treats the textual tradition of the Epistle of Jude. After an introductory survey of earlier text-critical research, the two main purposes of this investigation are formulated: to gather and to analyze the complete textual evidence of the Epistle of Jude.

The first task, to gather the evidence, involves the collation of all Greek continuous text MSS of the *Epistle of Jude*. The evidence of 560 Greek MSS, including dozens of lectionaries, is presented in an exhaustive critical apparatus. The major part of these textual witnesses have not received the attention they deserve. Now, for the first time, all these MSS have been examined in a complete book of the NT. The full collation has brought many new readings to light, some of which were only known through ancient versions, and previously known and important readings have gained additional support.

The second task is to analyze the evidence from different perspectives. The pursuit of the traditional goal of textual criticism, i.e., the reconstruction of the history of the text, and, ultimately, the "original text" (or "initial text" as here defined), is reflected in the adopted critical text of Jude. An accompanying textual commentary explains the rationale behind the various text-critical decisions in over 100 passages. An innovation is the employment of a new rating system of a more descriptive nature than counterparts.

The history of the text is also the history of scribes who read and re-created their texts for various reasons. Hence, there is a constant focus on individual manuscripts and interesting manuscript readings throughout the study. Every manuscript has a unique story to tell about the ancient copyists, owners and users. In particular, the two earliest papyrus witnesses to Jude, $\mathfrak{P}^{72}$ and $\mathfrak{P}^{78}$ (ca. 300 C.E.), are studied in detail. Plates of these and other selected MSS are published in the volume along with descriptions and transcriptions.

The study also includes a treatment of the literary and text-critical relationship between 2 Peter and Jude. It is argued that the Epistle of Jude has literary priority. Further, the textual traditions of the two writings show that scribal harmonization between the parallel accounts occurs relatively infrequently. Two significant witnesses, $\mathfrak{P}^{72}$ and Codex Vaticanus (B 03), lack such harmonization altogether.

Key words

Bible, New Testament, Catholic Epistles, Catholic Letters, *Apostolos*, Epistle of Jude, Letter of Jude, Jude, 2 Peter, Second Peter, literary relationship, 1 *Enoch*, textual criticism, papyrology, paleography, codicology, manuscript, papyrus, codex, Bodmer, Bodmer Miscellaneous Codex, Papyrus 72, P72, Papyrus 78, P78, uncial, minuscule, lectionary, magic, amulet, apparatus, initial text, textual commentary, textual variant, variation-unit, reading, external evidence, internal evidence

© Tommy Wasserman
Published by Almqvist & Wiksell International, Stockholm
Printed by Media-Tryck, Lund 2006

ISBN-10 91-22-02159-0
ISBN-13 978-91-22-02159-0
ISSN: 0069-8946

Cover image: Dumbarton Oaks MS 3, Dumbarton Oaks, Byzantine Photograph and Fieldwork Archives, Washington, DC

Preface and Acknowledgements

Once upon a time, when I was a graduate student preparing a subject for an exam paper, I decided to embark on the study of New Testament textual criticism. Through a scholarly discussion list of biblical textual criticism, the tc-list, I came in contact with several renowned scholars working in the field. One of these scholars, Prof. Maurice A. Robinson, offered me to participate in a research project which involved a visit to the Institute for New Testament Textual Research in Münster. Here I was to examine Greek New Testament manuscripts on a large scale for the first time. The work was successful, and eventually led to the publication of my first article in textual criticism.

I owe great thanks to Robinson for introducing me to the world of New Testament manuscripts, and for being a splendid discussion partner in text-critical matters over the years.

After completing a Master of Theology degree (Örebro Theological Seminary/Uppsala University), I contacted prof. em. René Kieffer, who had approved of my previous text-critical work. He encouraged me to pursue further research—especially since very few Swedish scholars, apart from himself, had been involved in textual criticism. The research board of the Faculty of Theology at Lund University accepted my proposal—an exhaustive examination of the manuscript tradition of the Epistle of Jude—and granted me a research post as Predoctoral Fellow. I am indebted to the faculty for accepting the proposal and for granting me a scholarship during four years.

Assoc. Prof. Walter Übelacker was willing to be the supervisor of this dissertation. I am grateful for his interest and support, not only in relation to the research as such, but also in regard to all sorts of practical matters of importance for a Ph.D. student.

In this connection, I must also express my thanks to the Senior New Testament Seminar Group at Lund University. Apart from Übelacker and Kieffer, I wish to thank all the participants of the seminar for the many stimulating and useful discussions of the material at various stages, in particular Prof. Bengt Holmberg, who also proofread parts of the manuscript and offered many helpful suggestions, Prof. em. Birger Olsson, Assoc. Prof. Lars Rydbeck, Dr. Runar M. Thorsteinsson, my fellow Ph.D. students Per Rönnegård and Lisa Buratti, and Mr. Bent Groth-Hansen.

In addition, I express my thanks to all of the colleagues at Örebro Theological Seminary, in particular to the department of Old and New

Testament Exegesis, and to my former teacher, Dr. Sune Fahlgren who first introduced me to the Greek New Testament.

During the recent years of manuscript research, I have had the opportunity to visit the Institute for New Testament Textual Research in Münster many times, in order to examine their almost complete microfilm collection of Greek New Testament manuscripts. The staff of the institute has always welcomed me heartily. My gratitude goes to the former director Prof. Barbara Aland, to the current director Prof. Holger Strutwolf, to Dr. Klaus Wachtel, Dr. Klaus Witte, Dr. Beate Köster, and to the other staff at the institute.

I am also grateful for the invitation by Prof. David C. Parker to the Institute for Textual Scholarship and Electronic Editing at Birmingham University. During this visit in May 2006, I had the opportunity to present my research in a special seminary, where I received valuable input.

My acknowledgements also go to Koninklijke Brill N.V., and to Cambridge University Press for granting me permission to republish slightly revised material (chs. 2-3). Special thanks to the Martin Bodmer Foundation, the Egypt Exploration Society, the Pierpont Morgan Library, Dumbarton Oaks, and Princeton University Library for granting me permission to publish plates of their priceless treasures, Greek New Testament Manuscripts.

Then I would like to thank the editors Prof. Bengt Holmberg and Prof. Kari Syreeni for accepting the monograph in the series ConBNT.

Finally, above all I thank my precious family, my wife Camilla who has stood by my side, my three children Joel, Rebecka and Sara, and the rest of my family. I deeply regret that my father Richard Wasserman was not able to share this moment with me, but I believe he is smiling at me from heaven.

Μόνῳ θεῷ σωτῆρι ἡμῶν διὰ Ἰησοῦ Χριστοῦ τοῦ κυρίου ἡμῶν δόξα μεγαλωσύνη κράτος καὶ ἐξουσία πρὸ παντὸς τοῦ αἰῶνος καὶ νῦν καὶ εἰς πάντας τοὺς αἰῶνας, ἀμήν.

Örebro, October 19, 2006

Tommy Wasserman

Table of Contents

Plates

Sammanfattning (Swedish Summary)

List of Plates

The plates are placed at the back of the volume (unpaginated). The two papyri and the uncial (Plates I-XI) are accompanied by transcriptions on facing pages. The minuscules are accompanied by short descriptions.

Tables

Abbreviations

Abbreviations follow the list of abbreviations in *The SBL Handbook of Style: For Ancient Near Eastern, Biblical, and Early Christian Studies* (ed. Patrick H. Alexander et al.; Peabody: Hendrickson, 1999). Abbreviations of the Greek papyri follow the *Checklist of Editions of Greek and Latin Papyri, Ostraca and Tablets* (ed. J. F. Oates, et al.; 4th ed.; BASPSup 7; Atlanta: Scholars Press, 1992). In addition, the following abbreviations are used:

ASE	*Annali di storia dell'esegesi*
ARWAW	Abhandlungen der Rheinisch-Westfälischen Akademie der Wissenschaften (Opladen)
CBGM	Coherence-Based Genealogical Method
CSNTM	Centre for the Study of New Testament Manuscripts
CPM	Claremont Profile Method
ECM	*Novum Testamentum Graecum Editio Critica Maior*
ESV	English Standard Version
FThSt	Freiburger Theologische Studien
Gr.-Al.	Gregory-Aland (list of NT MSS)
HDB	*Hasting's Dictionary of the Bible*
IGNTP	International Greek New Testament Project
INTF	Institut für neutestamentliche Textforschung (Münster)
KNT	Kommentar till Nya testamentet
Liste	*Kurzgefasste Liste der griechischen Handschriften des Neuen Testaments*
Lm	*Novum Testamentum Graece.* Edited by Karl Lachmann. Berlin, 1831.
MPER	Mitteilungen aus der Papyrussammlung der Österreichischen Nationalbibliothek
NIVAC	The New International Version Application Commentary
NTGM	*New Testament Greek Manuscripts: Variant Readings Arranged in Horizontal Lines against Codex Vaticanus.* Edited by Reuben J. Swanson.
PapyCol	Papyrologica Coloniensis
Td⁷	*Novum Testamentum Graece.* Edited by Constantin von Tischendorf. 2 vols. 7th ed. Leipzig: Hinrichs, 1856-1859.
Td⁸	*Novum Testamentum Graece.* Edited by Constantin von Tischendorf. 3 vols. 8th ed. Leipzig: Hinrichs, 1869-1894.
Tr	*The Greek New Testament.* Edited by S. P. Tregelles. London: Samuel Bagster & Sons, 1857-72.
TENT	Texts and Editions for New Testament Study
TuT	*Text und Textwert*

Part I

Prolegomena

Chapter One

Introduction

1. Survey of the Textual Research on the Epistle of Jude

1.1 Introduction

The Epistle of Jude contains only twenty-five verses, and yet the number of text-critical problems are both relatively numerous and complicated as compared to other books of the NT.[1] However, this textual complexity has not been reflected in the amount of factual textual research on Jude, as compared to other parts of the NT. This lack of attention is perhaps not so surprising in light of the fact that this book has been largely neglected in the history of exegesis in general, and even treated with contempt on the part of some scholars.[2] However, there has been major progress in recent years, and in the following I shall briefly treat the most significant textual studies of Jude.

In this brief description of previous research I will not treat the long history of printed editions of the NT with their varying ranges of manuscript evidence for the Epistle of Jude, although some words about the most recent and extensive edition of Jude, the *Editio Critica Maior* (*ECM*), are in place.[3] Nor does space permit a thorough discussion of the text-critical work found in numerous exegetical commentaries, the studies of textual problems in individual verses of Jude, and studies on single manuscripts containing Jude. With a few exceptions works from these categories will be cited and commented on in the textual commentary in chapter nine.

---

[1] Cf. Joseph B. Mayor who states, "[T]he text is in a less satisfactory condition than that of any other portion of the NT" (*The Epistle of St. Jude and the Second Epistle of St. Peter* [London: Macmillan, 1907], clxxi). B. F. Westcott and F. J. A. Hort suggest four conjectures in this short epistle—the same number as for the eight chapters of the Petrine Epistles and the 44 chapters of the Gospels of Matthew and Mark (*The New Testament in the Original Greek* [2 vols.; London: Macmillan, 1881-1882]).

[2] Cf. D. J. Rowston, "The Most Neglected Book in the New Testament," *NTS* 21 (1975): 554-63.

[3] Barbara Aland, Kurt Aland, Gerd Mink and Klaus Wachtel, eds., *Novum Testamentum Graecum Editio Critica Maior*. Vol. IV: *The Catholic Letters*. Installment 4: *The Second and Third Letter of John, The Letter of Jude* (Stuttgart: Deutsche Bibelgesellschaft, 2005). For a detailed survey of Jude in printed editions up to 1960, see C. A. Albin, *Judasbrevet: Traditionen, Texten, Tolkningen* (Stockholm: Natur och Kultur, 1962), 153-316.

1.2 Bernhard Weiss: The Dominance of the Early Uncials

In 1892 Bernard Weiss' published a study of the Catholic Epistles in which he presented a critical text, the manuscript evidence of seven majuscules (ℵ A B C K L P), along with comments on their various readings.[4] This publication came out only a few years after the groundbreaking work of B. F. Westcott and F. J. A. Hort, *The New Testament in the Original Greek*, which had signaled the end of the dominance of the Textus Receptus.[5] Westcott and Hort had basically accepted as original the readings of ℵ B (representing their "Neutral text") unless strong internal evidence was found to the contrary.[6] In Weiss' reconstruction of the text of the Catholic Epistles he depended upon an evaluation solely of the majuscules, disregarding the remaining textual evidence (minuscules, versional and patristic evidence), which, as he argued, was only significant for the history of the text.[7] From that starting point he then used an eclectic method, based on internal criteria, which in practice resulted in a text heavily dependent on codex B—in this regard he at times even surpassed Westcott and Hort.[8] Nevertheless, one of the great values with Weiss' study is the detailed attention he pays to the textual features of the individual majuscules.

1.3. J. de Zwaan and J. D. M. Brown: Early "Reasoned Eclectics"

Weiss was followed in 1909 by J. de Zwaan's study of 2 Peter and Jude in which he presented a critical text with apparatus, a textual commentary, and a classification of some of the minuscules in families.[9] His extensive critical apparatus did not represent independent work with the manuscripts, but was based on the published material of others, mainly Constantin von Tischendorf's *Editio octava critica maior*.[10] Unfortunately, de

---

[4] Bernhard Weiss, *Die Katholischen Briefe* (Textkritische Untersuchungen und Textherstellung 8/3; Leipzig: Hinrichs, 1892).

[5] B. F. Westcott and F. J. A. Hort, *The New Testament in the Original Greek* (2 vols.; London: Macmillan, 1881-1882).

[6] Ibid., 2:225.

[7] Weiss, *Die katholischen Briefe*, iv.

[8] Cf. A. Jülicher, "[I]m Vertrauen auf B überbietet Weiss die Engländer noch erheblich" (*Einleitung in das Neue Testament* [5-6th ed.; Tübingen: Mohr Siebeck, 1931], 573). However, Albin points out that this tendency is not observable in the Epistle of Jude (*Judasbrevet*, 253, n. 294).

[9] J. de Zwaan, *II Petrus en Judas. Textuitgave met inleidende Studiën en textueelen Commentaar* (Ph.D. diss., University of Leiden, 1909). He later modified some of his manuscript classifications in "Minuskelgruppen in 2 Petri und Judas," *ZNW* 12 (1911): 76-82.

[10] Constantin von Tischendorf, *Novum Testamentum Graece* (3 vols.; 8th ed.; Leipzig: Hinrichs, 1869-1894).

Zwaan's apparatus contains a large number of errors.[11] His overall method of reconstructing the text of Jude could perhaps be described in modern terms as a kind of reasoned eclecticism. Curiously, however, he displayed a very radical eclecticism at places, in that he suggested a large number of conjectures without any support in the Greek manuscript tradition![12]

A few years later, in 1912, J. D. M. Brown devoted a study to the Epistle of Jude, in which he presented a critical text and brief apparatus to some selected passages in Jude, along with a textual commentary.[13] Brown's apparatus, like de Zwaan's, was based on various critical editions, and contains some serious errors in spite of its brevity.[14] Brown mainly resorts to internal criticism (especially intrinsic probability) in trying to solve some of the "most vital problems" in Jude.[15]

1.4 Hermann von Soden: Gathering and Classifying the Evidence

During the years between 1902-1913, Hermann von Soden's monumental four-volume text-critical work, *Die Schriften des Neuen Testaments in ihrer ältesten erreichbaren Textgestalt hergestellt auf Grund ihrer Textgeschichte*, appeared.[16] Von Soden and his colleagues had collated numerous Greek manuscripts, which were presented in the edition with comments on various readings. Moreover, he classified nearly all Greek MSS known at the time (including some 1260 minuscules).

However, von Soden's venture proved to be a failure in several respects: first, his theoretical presuppositions regarding the text-types proved to be false, as did many of his manuscript classifications, especially in regard to his so called *I*-text.[17] Secondly, his very complicated system of symbols

---

[11] See Albin, *Judasbrevet*, 258-63, esp. n. 312-316.

[12] De Zwaan suggests the following conjectures in Jude: v. 1: καὶ ἐν Ἰησοῦ Χριστῷ τετηρημένοις; v. 4: δεσπότην καὶ τὸν κύριον; v. 7: omit ἑτέρας; v. 11: omit μισθοῦ; v. 12: omit δὶς ἀποθανόντα ἐκριζωθέντα; v. 18: omit τῶν ἀσεβειῶν; v. 22: omit διακρινο-μένους/διακρινόμενοι; v. 23: οὓς δὲ ἐκ πυρὸς ἁρπάζετε; v. 23: omit ἐν φόβῳ.

[13] J. D. M. Brown, "The Text of the Epistle of Jude. Studies in Textual Criticism," *Lutheran Church Review* 31 (1912): 53-64, 295-307, 474-84.

[14] In Jude 15, for example, the evidence in Brown's apparatus for the inclusion or omission of λογῶν after περὶ πάντων τῶν σκληρῶν is the wrong way round.

[15] Ibid., 55. In this regard it is remarkable that Brown does not treat the notoriously difficult text in Jude 22-23!

[16] Hermann von Soden, *Die Schriften des Neuen Testaments in ihrer ältesten erreichbaren Textgestalt hergestellt auf Grund ihrer Textgeschichte* (2 parts in 4 vols.; 2d unchanged ed.; Göttingen: Vandenhoeck & Ruprecht, 1911-1913).

[17] In regard to Jude, Sakae Kubo tested von Soden's classification by using more recent methodology (see further below). Kubo analyzed 37 MSS, including 31 MSS that had been classified by von Soden, and concluded concerning the purported *I*-text, "The large number of manuscripts classified under I by von Soden cannot be distinguished from the manuscripts

representing manuscripts, as well as his divided apparatuses has provoked much misunderstanding.[18] Finally, the information in the apparatus is often incomplete and unreliable, so that the attestation of its readings needs constant verification elsewhere.[19]

Notwithstanding, von Soden is counted among the giants of NT textual criticism, as being a pioneer in collecting the evidence from a large number of hitherto unknown manuscripts, especially minuscules. Moreover, remarkably many of von Soden's genealogical classifications in sub-groups have actually been confirmed by more recent methods.[20] In conclusion, his work still remains important for its genealogical studies, and for the wealth of variant readings, including comments.[21] As for his critical text, the deciding factor was often the *I*-text, which in the Catholic Epistles had to be reconstructed from relatively late MSS, so that the resultant critical text in modern terms is rather akin to the Byzantine text.

---

of the K text" ("Textual relationships in Jude," in *Studies in New Testament Language and Text* [ed. J. K. Elliott; NovTSup 44; Leiden: Brill, 1976], 280). Cf. J. Tim Gallagher, "A Study of von Soden's H-Text in the Catholic Epistles," *AUSS* 8 (1970): 97-119; and W. L. Richards, "A Critique of a New Testament Text-Critical Methodology: the Claremont Profile Method," *JBL* 96 (1977): 555.

[18] Indeed von Soden's edition is almost impossible to use without keys and transposition tables, such as are available in Friedrich Krüger, *Schlüssel zu von Soden's die Schriften des Neuen Testaments in ihrer ältesten erreichbaren Textgestalt hergestellt* (Göttingen: Vandenhoeck & Ruprecht, 1927), and in Kurt Aland, Michael Welte, Beate Köster and Klaus Junack, eds., *Kurzgefasste Liste der griechischen Handschriften des Neuen Testaments* (2d rev. and enl. ed; ANTF 1; Berlin/New York: de Gruyter, 1994), 390-427. Von Soden's own notes on format and apparatus are not sufficient. A brief introduction to the edition is available in Kurt Aland and Barbara Aland, *The Text of the New Testament: An Introduction to the Critical Editions and to the Theory and Practice of Modern Textual Criticism* (trans. Erroll F. Rhodes; 2d rev. and enl. ed.; Grand Rapids: Eerdmans, 1995), 40-43.

[19] A quite illustrative example is Albin's report of 11 errors in von Soden's account for Codex Ψ (044) in Jude alone (Albin, *Judasbrevet*, 275, n. 345). Cf. Wayne A. Blakely, "Manuscript Relationships As Indicated by the Epistles of Jude and II Peter" (Ph.D. diss., Emory University, 1964), 5-6.

[20] Eldon J. Epp offers a brief description and a summary of the results utilizing the Claremont Profile Method (CPM) for the IGNTP project and concludes: "On the other hand, many of von Soden's groupings and classifications have been strikingly confirmed, including designations of groups, subgroups and individual MSS" ("The Claremont Profile Method For Grouping New Testament Minuscule Manuscripts," in Eldon J. Epp and Gordon D. Fee, *Studies in the Theory and Method of New Testament Textual Criticism* [SD 45; Grand Rapids: Eerdmans, 1993], 220).

[21] The parts of special relevance for Jude are found in von Soden, *Die Schriften*, 2:657-60 (text and apparatus of Jude) and 1:1840-98 (a survey of the text-types in the Catholic Epistles).

1.5 The Discovery of 𝔓⁷²: The Oldest Extant Witness to Jude

In the 1950s the Swiss collector and patron of the arts, Martin Bodmer, acquired a collection of ancient Egyptian papyri in Greek and Coptic. Among these very important manuscripts known as the Bodmer papyri was 𝔓⁷², published by Michel Testuz in 1959, which contains the entire text of 1-2 Peter and Jude.[22] Dated to around 300 C.E. this is the earliest known MS of these epistles.[23] The discovery of the Bodmer papyri, including 𝔓⁷², stimulated a number of articles and studies.[24] The latter category includes Sakae Kubo's dissertation of 1964, "A Comparative Study of 𝔓⁷² and the Codex Vaticanus."[25] Kubo compares 𝔓⁷² with numerous Greek MSS in over 300 variation-units, and concludes that it stands closest to Codex Vaticanus (B 03).[26] Then he uses the new papyrus to re-examine the long-assumed superiority of Vaticanus in 1-2 Peter and Jude. Where the two

---

[22] Michel Testuz, ed., *Papyrus Bodmer VII-IX* (Cologny-Geneva: Bibliotheca Bodmeriana, 1959). For the text of 𝔓⁷², see Klaus Junack and Winfried Grunewald, eds., *Das Neue Testament auf Papyrus*. I: *Die Katholischen Briefe* (ANTF 6; Berlin/New York: de Gruyter, 1986), 159-71.

[23] For a comprehensive discussion of the dating of 𝔓⁷² and other issues in regard to the codex of which it forms a part, see Tommy Wasserman, "Papyrus 72 and the Bodmer Miscellaneous Codex," *NTS* 51 (2005): 137-54. In addition, the fragmentary manuscript 𝔓⁷⁸ (containing a few verses of Jude) is dated to the 3rd-4th centuries, and may thus be earlier than 𝔓⁷².

[24] The following are devoted particularly to the text of Jude in 𝔓⁷²: Edouard Massaux, "Le texte de l'épître de Jude du Papyrus Bodmer VII (𝔓⁷²)," in *Scrinium Lovaniense: mélanges historiques historische opstellen Étienne van Cauwenbergh* (ed. Jozef Vergote, et al.; Gembloux: J Duculot, 1961), 108-25; J. Neville Birdsall, "The Text of Jude in 𝔓⁷²," *JTS* 14 (1963): 394-99; Marchant A. King, "Notes on the Bodmer Manuscript," *BSac* 121 (1964): 54-57; M. Mees, "Papyrus Bodmer VII (𝔓⁷²) und die Zitate aus dem Judasbrief bei Clemens von Alexandrien," in *Miscelánea Patristica; Homenaje al Angel C Vega* (ed. T. Alonso; Madrid: Real Monasterio de El Escorial, 1968), 133-41; Tobias Nicklas, "Der 'lebendige Text' des Neuen Testaments. Der Judasbrief in 𝔓⁷² (*P.Bodmer* VII)," *ASE* 22 (2005): 203-222.

[25] Sakae Kubo, "A Comparative Study of 𝔓⁷² and the Codex Vaticanus" (Ph.D. diss., University of Chicago, 1964). The main part of Kubo's dissertation was later published as *𝔓⁷² and Codex Vaticanus* (SD 27; Salt Lake City: University of Utah Press, 1965).

[26] In an analysis of MSS in 1 Peter, Jean Duplacy and Christian-Bernard Amphoux grouped 𝔓⁷² with ℵ, A, B, C, 044 ("À propos de l'histoire du texte de la première épître de Pierre," in *Études sur la Première Lettre de Pierre* [ed. C. Perrot; LD 102; Paris: Cerf, 1980], 155-73). The authors came to the same result as Kubo in regard to the affinity with B, "Leur parenté est nette ou assez nette, mais pas très forte: 𝔓⁷² et B.03 sont les seuls à présenter un pourcentage d'accord supérieur à 70% (75,7%)" (ibid., 162); see also Terry Robertson, "Relationships Among the Non-Byzantine Manuscripts of 2 Peter," *AUSS* 39 (2001): 47. Birdsall's characterization of 𝔓⁷² is open to misunderstanding—he did not say that 𝔓⁷² is "Western," but only drew a parallel between the "wild" but ancient and widespread text of 𝔓⁷² and the "Western" text of the Gospels and Acts (Birdsall, "The Text of Jude in 𝔓⁷²," 396; cf. Mees, "Papyrus Bodmer," 134).

MSS agree (246 times), Kubo concludes that their common text is almost always superior, and where they disagree (94 times), he thinks that $\mathfrak{P}^{72}$ preserves more genuine readings (60) than Codex Vaticanus (34).[27] In his analysis, Kubo comments in detail on some 25 variation-units in Jude.[28]

1.6 C. A. Albin, Wayne A. Blakely, and Sakae Kubo: Collations and Classifications of MSS

In 1962, the dissertation of C. A. Albin was published.[29] It is a very large work written in Swedish (with a German summary). This is probably one of the reasons why this text-critical work has remained fairly unknown on the international arena.[30] The great accomplishment of Albin is his first hand work with the Greek MSS—he collated and presented the transcriptions of over 200 MSS in Jude in great detail, and generally with a high degree of accuracy.[31] Albin did not attempt to classify these manuscripts

---

[27] Idem, *$\mathfrak{P}^{72}$ and Codex Vaticanus*, 154.

[28] Ibid., 48, 57-59, 85-92, 140-47; Kubo also presents a brief analysis of the scribal characteristics of the scribe of $\mathfrak{P}^{72}$, which is now largely superseded by the more comprehensive study of the scribal habits in the six extensive papyri from before the 4th century by James R. Royse, "Scribal Habits in Early Greek New Testament Papyri" (Th.D.diss., Graduate Theological Union, 1981), esp. 450-511 (dealing with $\mathfrak{P}^{72}$). Royse specifically criticizes Kubo for providing inaccurate data of the singular readings of $\mathfrak{P}^{72}$ (ibid., 453-54, 493-94, n. 24).

[29] C. A. Albin, *Judasbrevet: Traditionen, Texten, Tolkningen* (Stockholm: Natur och Kultur, 1962).

[30] There are of course some exceptions: Bruce M. Metzger once referred to Albin's work as being "an encyclopedic survey of all known textual evidence for the Epistle of Jude" (*Manuscripts of the Greek Bible* [New York/Oxford: Oxford University Press, 1981], 118). (Metzger's statement is, nevertheless, an exaggeration, since Albin collated less than half of the known MSS.) Further, Albin's study is mentioned in various surveys of research: Richard J. Bauckham, "The Letter of Jude: An Account of Research," *ANRW*, Part II, vol. 25/5, ed. W. Haase (Berlin/New York: de Gruyter, 1988), 3792; idem, *Jude and the Relatives of Jesus in the Early Church* (Edinburgh: T. & T. Clark, 1990), 134-35; Bauckham cites explicitly only from the German summary (*Jude and the Relatives*, 150, 153-57); Roman Heiligenthal, "Der Judasbrief: Aspekte der Forschung in den letzten Jahrzehnten," *ThR* 51 (1986): 117. In addition, a few articles refer to Albin's work: Carroll D. Osburn, "The Text of Jude 5," *Bib* 62 (1981): 111; William Whallon, "Should We Keep, Omit, Or Alter the Hoi in Jude 12," *NTS* 34 (1988): 158, n. 3. In his recent text-critical study of Jude, Charles Landon has used limited parts of Albin's work. He states right in the introduction that Albin's study is incomplete, at least from the perspective of an eclectic approach, since Albin's comments on variants are extremely brief (Charles Landon, *A Text-Critical Study of the Epistle of Jude* [JSNTSup 135; Sheffield: Sheffield Academic Press, 1996], 13, esp. n. 2).

[31] The transcriptions are found in Albin, *Judasbrevet*, 344-421. In order to access such a vast range of Greek MSS, Albin had to order photographic material from over 50 institutions worldwide. In my independent examination of all the MSS included in Albin's study, I have found relatively few errors. One drawback, however, is Albin's failure to indicate uncertain words and letters at numerous places.

genealogically, beyond making a major division corresponding to two textual recensions, Alexandrian text ("AT") and Byzantine text ("BT"), respectively. He expressed as one of his main tasks the establishment of these two texts in all their difference.[32] The other main task, of course, was the presentation of a critical text and apparatus, including all the Greek MSS, supplemented with versional and patristic evidence, along with extremely brief textual comments on noteworthy variants.[33] Albin's critical text follows almost wholly his reconstructed Alexandrian text, and, thus, diverges from e.g., NA[27] only a few times.[34]

Just two years later, Wayne A. Blakely published his dissertation on manuscript relationships in 2 Peter and Jude.[35] Apparently, Blakely was not aware of Albin's work, and he refers only to the apparatuses of Tischendorf and von Soden. In Jude, Blakely collated 113 MSS, including eight lectionaries. He presented the textual evidence in a detailed apparatus of practically all types of variation distributed in Jude among 123 units of variation.[36] He then used a computer in order to calculate manuscript relationships by comparing all MSS with every other MS in the units of variation. This was a rather new methodology at the time, and is still a common procedure—earlier the standard method to deduce manuscript relationships was to count their common deviations from the TR. However, Blakely's methodology is seriously flawed for two other reasons: first, Blakely includes all kinds of variation even such as is genealogically insignificant (e.g., orthographic variance), which seriously obscures genealogical relationships.[37] Secondly, Blakely's selected variation-units,

---

[32] Ibid., 318-27, esp. 319.

[33] Ibid, 590-631. In his comments to vv. 2, 6, 7-11, 17, 19-20, 24, Albin states categorically that "no text-critical problem exists" (my translation). However, in a summary of the text-critical problems of "current interest" in Jude, he provides a list that includes 39 problems in vv. 3-7, 12-16, and 20-25, whereas he lists 55 other problems as "already solved and out of date" (ibid. 147-52; citations in my translation).

[34] The differences between Albin's critical text and NA[27] are as follows: v. 5: ειδοτας υμας απαξ παντα οτι κυριος λαον (Albin); ειδοτας [υμας] παντα οτι [ο] κυριος απαξ (NA); v. 15: ελεγξαι παντας τους ασεβεις (Albin); ελεγξαι πασαν ψυχην (NA; a rare reading attested in 𝔓[72] ℵ 1852); v. 16: αυτων (Albin); εαυτων (NA; the manuscript attestation is evenly divided); v. 23: σωζετε εκ πυρος (Albin; only attested in B) ους δε σωζετε εκ πυρος (NA).

[35] Wayne A. Blakely, "Manuscript Relationships As Indicated by the Epistles of Jude and II Peter" (Ph.D. diss., Emory University, 1964).

[36] Ibid., 49-149. On the whole, I have found Blakely's apparatus to be less accurate than that of Albin.

[37] Apparently, Blakely was well aware of this problem. In his Master's thesis published in 1958 he used the same method, and there he stated, "In the determination of manuscript relationships, the variation of a single letter, even a -ν movable, or an itacistic spelling, was adequate to produce a separate reading. This . . . tended to make manuscripts having a

albeit normally of suitable length for the presentation of evidence in his apparatus, actually often comprises more than one unit of genealogically significant variation.[38] This means that an agreement between two MSS in one part of the unit is not counted, since they diverge in another part of the unit. In conclusion, whereas Blakely's collations are valuable, the genealogical analysis is practically useless.

In the appendix of Sakae Kubo's dissertation from the same year, he also attempted to classify manuscripts in Jude.[39] This study was modified and published in a later article, in which the author examined the textual relationship of 37 MSS in Jude, based upon comparisons in 65 variation units.[40] In his analysis, Kubo used the quantitative method of E. C. Colwell and E. W. Tune.[41] The MSS were selected in order to test the earlier classifications of von Soden and, thus, represented twelve of his proposed main- and sub-groups for the Catholic Epistles. Kubo was able to assign the MSS to either of the two major groups today known as the Byzantine and Alexandrian, but, as mentioned above, his analysis disproved the integrity of von Soden's *I*-text.[42]

1.7 The INTF: Preparation for an *Editio Critica Maior* of the Greek New Testament

Of particular importance in relation to the whole corpus of the Catholic Epistles is the extensive work performed over the years at the Institute for

---

number of such readings appear to be less closely related to the other manuscripts in their general text type" ("The Text of the Epistle of Jude, A Critical Study" [Master Thesis, Emory University, 1958], 28).

[38] On this topic, see esp. Eldon J. Epp, "Toward the Clarification of the Term 'Textual Variant'," in Eldon J. Epp and Gordon D. Fee, *Studies in the Theory and Method of New Testament Textual Criticism* (SD 45; Grand Rapids: Eerdmans, 1993), 47-61; and Gordon D. Fee, "On the Types, Classification, and Presentation of Textual Variation," in ibid., 62-79.

[39] Kubo, "A Comparative Study," 259-91.

[40] Kubo, "Textual Relationships in Jude." Some years earlier Kubo had examined six Greek lectionaries in the Catholic Epistles, "The Catholic Epistles in the Greek Lectionary: A Preliminary Investigation," *AUSS* 1 (1963): 65-70. In this study Kubo used the older methodology, which meant that relationships between MSS were formed on the basis of their percentages of agreement against the TR.

[41] Ernest C. Colwell and Ernest W. Tune, "The Quantitative Relationships Between MS Text types," in *Biblical and Patristic Studies in Memory of Robert Pierce Casey* (ed. J. Neville Birdsall and Robert W. Thomson; Freiburg/Basel/New York: Herder, 1963), 25-32.

[42] Kubo's results further removed Codex P from von Soden's *H* group, the Alexandrian, but added MSS 5, 323, 623, 1611, and 1739 (all from von Soden's various *I* groups), together with ℵ, A, B, C, Ψ, and 33. Previously unclassified MSS, 𝔓72 and 2412 were also assigned to the Alexandrian group—𝔓72 was found to be related most closely to Codex B, but "apparently not a strong Alexandrian witness in Jude"—while the rest of the examined MSS belonged more or less to the Byzantine group ("Textual Relationships in Jude," 280).

New Testament Textual Research (henceforth INTF) in Münster. Therefore, I will describe their work at some length. The goal of the method used at the institute has been briefly summarized by Kurt and Barbara Aland:

> (1) The determination and exclusion of all *eliminandi*, i.e., discovering and excluding from consideration those manuscripts [particularly Byzantine minuscules] which have simply been copied from others; (2) The identification of those MSS that deserve closer examination and are to be included in an *editio critica maior* of the GNT; (3) The examination of these remaining MSS for their interrelationships, establishing families and groups among them where possible.[43]

In order to classify the Greek manuscripts and obtain the above goals without having to do full collations, the institute selected test passages in the whole NT (*Teststellen*). In the Catholic Epistles, practically all known manuscripts (540 MSS) were collated in 98 such test passages (11 in Jude).[44] It remains unclear exactly how the test passages were selected, but it was a trial-and-error process in which these particular passages were found particularly suitable, since the manuscripts "show their colours" in them, which primarily means that they contain Byzantine readings that differ significantly from older ones.[45]

The total number of agreements between witnesses in all passages as well as the number of agreements between witnesses in all of the non-Majority readings were computed and accounted for in different tables and lists.[46] Eventually, the results were summarized for each MS, in that it was ascribed a textual value (*Textwert*) according to a ranking system, which can be conveniently displayed in a set of numbers.[47] Every MS was then placed in one of five categories according to its proportion of agreement with the "original text," or else of peculiar readings (i.e., non-Byzantine and important for the establishment of the original text, or otherwise for the history of transmission).

---

[43] Aland and Aland, *The Text of the New Testament*, 318.

[44] Kurt Aland ed., *Text und Textwert der griechischen Handschriften des Neuen Testaments*. I: *Die Katholischen Briefe* (3 vols.; ANTF 9-11; Berlin/New York: de Gruyter, 1987). The test passages and the manuscript support in each passage are accounted for in 1:15-229.

[45] Aland, *Text und Textwert*, I, 2: vii. Cf. W. L. Richards, "An Analysis of Aland's Teststellen in 1 John," *NTS* 44 (1988): 29.

[46] Aland, *Text und Textwert*, I, 1-2. A "Majority reading" is the reading of the majority of MSS in a variation unit (i.e., a quantitative category). Since the text of the great majority of extant MSS is Byzantine (a historical category), all Majority readings are necessarily Byzantine readings; but not all Byzantine readings are Majority readings, since at many places the Byzantine tradition is split into two or more streams.

[47] See ibid., vol. 3.

The method used at the INTF (henceforth the Teststellen-method) has been criticized by several scholars, and I will briefly mention some of the objections. First, Frederik Wisse has pointed out the difficulty connected with establishing what is the "Byzantine reading," since in the same variation-unit there may be several different Byzantine readings, and Aland's statistics will ignore this aspect in that it counts only the Majority-reading.[48]

Secondly, the problem with the "fish-net" procedure of the Alands, i.e., the examination of MS readings in ready-made test passages instead of all known variations is the danger of not detecting unique readings that will link small groups of MSS with common descent, which is a very important task in writing the history of textual transmission.

Thirdly, some manuscripts display so-called block mixture, which arises when the scribe has made use of multiple exemplars (or an exemplar with mixture) when copying the text, and, thus, may result in a sudden shift of text-type within a corpus.[49] A good example in the Catholic Epistles is MS 1175, which was classified as a Category I manuscript by the Alands.[50] However, W. L. Richards has demonstrated that this MS is Alexandrian in 1-2 Peter and James, but purely Byzantine (i.e., Category V) in 1-3 John and Jude.[51] In another study, Richards compared the classification of 109 MSS *in Text und Textwert* against his own data in the Johannine Epistles, and concluded that 90 MSS had been assigned the same classification, but that

---

[48] Frederik Wisse, *The Profile Method for the Classification and Evaluation of Manuscript Evidence as Applied to the Continuous Greek Text of the Gospel of Luke* (SD 44; Grand Rapids: Eerdmans, 1982), 21. Nevertheless, the vast information included in the published volumes of *Text und Textwert* (*TuT*) allows the reader to study the complete distribution of MS support in every test passage without presuppositions.

[49] It is to be noted that all MSS have a more or less "mixed" text in terms of text-types, but as long as the mixture is evenly spread a sampling method using test passages may produce reliable results (provided that the sample is large enough). The more mixed a manuscript, however, the greater is the need for a larger sample of text.

[50] Aland and Aland, *The Text of the New Testament*, 134.

[51] W. L. Richards, "Gregory 1175: Alexandrian or Byzantine in the Catholic Epistles," *AUSS* 21 (1983): 155-68. Klaus Wachtel provides another example in MS 1799, "Dort erweist sich 1799 für Jak-1Joh eindeutig als Zeuge für den Text der Gruppe HK. In den letzten drei Briefen des Corpus reproduziert die Handschrift jedoch, soweit sie erhalten ist, weitgehend den Byzantinischen Text" (*Der byzantinische Text der Katholischen Briefe: eine Untersuchung zur Entstehung der Koine des Neuen Testaments* [ANTF 24; Berlin/New York: de Gruyter, 1995], 62, n. 18). A third significant example is 𝔓[72], which in 1 Peter shows a connection with the Sahidic (F. W. Beare, "The Text of 1 Peter in Papyrus 72," *JBL* 80 [1961]: 260), but not in Jude (Kubo, *𝔓[72] and Codex Vaticanus*, 26). The text of 𝔓[72] is characterized by the Alands as "normal" in 1-2 Peter, and "free" in Jude (Aland and Aland, *The Text of the New Testament*, 100).

the remaining 19 were classified differently.[52] This may in part be due to incompatible definitions, but Richards did attempt to follow the methods of the INTF and for each MS indicate its "probable Aland Category."[53] The main reason for the different classification seems to be the selection of text under examination (1-3 John as opposed to 98 testpassages in the Catholic Epistles). This should remind us of Colwell's suggestion that text-types in the NT be studied "book by book or section by section." [54] In regard to the Catholic Epistles, I would even suggest that the examination of the textual tradition book by book is crucial, since the different parts of this section seem to have a unique textual tradition (see below). However, since smaller books of the NT (like Jude) may result in a sample too small to be statistically significant, a slight modification of Colwell's dictum is in place; texts or text-types should be studied book by book *and* section by section.[55]

Finally, in regard to Alands' five different categories to which MSS are eventually assigned, Bart Ehrman has identified "a problem of textual circularity" in the criteria for the categories, "By agreement with the 'original text' the Alands mean the 'Standard' text—i.e., the text reconstructed by the five editors of the UBS Greek NT (of which Kurt Aland was one) and used by the Alands for the NA[26] edition."[56]

Nevertheless, the Teststellen-method appeared to have worked well in the elimination of the mass of Byzantine MSS from further consideration, i.e., full collations and inclusion in the textual apparatus of the *ECM*, and to some degree the procedure of using carefully chosen test passages reminds one of the urging of Colwell and Tune that readings be "weighed" rather than merely counted, since some variants are of more significance than others.[57]

---

[52] Richards, "An Analysis," 35. In the abstract of the article, it is stated that the total number for comparison was 112 MSS, but Richards then says he was unable to find data on 3 MSS (1522 1799 1845).

[53] Ibid., 36-38 (Table 1).

[54] Ernest C. Colwell, "Method in Grouping New Testament Manuscripts," in Ernest C. Colwell, *Studies in Methodology in Textual Criticism of the New Testament* (NTTS 9; Leiden: Brill, 1969), 21; repr. from *NTS* 4 (1958).

[55] Cf. Kurt Aland's statement that a final judgment of the character of a manuscript rests with a full collation (*Text und Textwert*, I, 2:xi).

[56] Bart D. Ehrman, "A Problem of Textual Circularity: The Alands on the Classification of New Testament Manuscripts," *Bib* 70 (1989): 383.

[57] Ernest C. Colwell and E. W. Tune, "Method in Establishing Quantitative Relationships," 56.

1.8 Genealogical Survey of the Manuscript Tradition of the Catholic Epistles

The Teststellen-method is but one example of the recent methodological developments in the genealogical classification of manuscripts.[58] Through the years there have been a number of efforts to classify MSS in various Catholic Epistles apart from those described above.[59] Various groups and families of textually related MSS have been identified. However, in terms of the broader category of "text-types" only the Byzantine and Alexandrian text-types have received general acceptance in the Catholic Epistles, whereas attempts to import labels such as "Western" or "Caesarean" have been largely unsuccessful. For example, Muriel Carder suggested that MS 1243 could be "Caesarean" in 1 Peter and the Johannine Epistles, because of its high proportion of Alexandrian and "Western" readings.[60] However, Kurt Aland strongly opposed Carder and proved that both her method and

---

[58] For a brief overview in this area, see T. C. Geer, Jr., "Analyzing and Categorizing New Testament Greek Manuscripts: Colwell Revisited," in *The Text of the New Testament in Contemporary Research: Essays on the Status Quaestionis* (ed. Bart D. Ehrman and Michael W. Holmes; SD 46; Grand Rapids: Eerdmans, 1995), 253-67.

[59] Muriel M. Carder, "An Enquiry into the Textual Transmission of the Catholic Epistles" (Th.D. diss., Victoria University, 1968). Carder classified 25 MSS in 1 Pet, and 1-3 John; W. L. Richards, *The Classification of the Greek Manuscripts of the Johannine Epistles* (SBLDS 35; Missoula, MT: Scholars Press, 1977). Richards classified 81 MSS in the Johannine Epistles; Joel D. Awoniyi, "The Classification of the Greek Manuscripts of the Epistle of James" (Th.D. diss., Andrews University, 1979). Awoniyi classified 86 MSS in James; Jean Duplacy and Christian-Bernard Amphoux, "À propos de l'histoire du texte de la première épître de Pierre," 155-73. The authors classified 85 MSS in 1 Peter and compared their classifications with von Soden's. They confirmed his *H*- and *K*-texts, but not the *I*-text, which was made up of several distinct groups; for example, von Soden's *Ib*[1], *Ic*[1-2] was labeled "gr(oupe) 2138" (ibid., 162, 171); Christian-Bernard Amphoux, "Le Texte des épîtres catholiques" (Ph.D. diss., Paris Sorbonne University, 1981); idem, "Quelques témoins grecs des formes textuelles les plus anciennes de l'Épître de Jacques: le groupe 2138 (ou 614)," *NTS* 28 (1982): 91-115; Kenneth K. Yoo, "The Classification of the Greek Manuscripts of 1 Peter with Special Emphasis on Methodology" (Ph.D. diss., Andrews University, 2001). Yoo classified 106 MSS in 1 Peter; Terry Robertson, "Relationships," 41-59. Robertson classifed 150 MSS in 2 Peter; Matthew Spencer, Klaus Wachtel and Christopher J. Howe, "The Greek Vorlage of the Syra Harclensis: A Comparative Study on Method in Exploring Textual Genealogy," *TC: A Journal of Biblical Textual Criticism* [http://purl.org/TC] 7 (2002), pars. 1-46. The authors analyzed 164 MSS in James primarily in order to isolate and further examine the manucript members of the so-called "Harclensis Group" (HK group) through two methods of stemma reconstruction. For an extensive study of the Greek lectionaries in the Catholic Epistles, see Klaus Junack, "Zu den griechischen Lektionarien und ihrer Überlieferung der Katholischen Briefe," in *Die alten Übersetzungen des Neuen Testaments, die Kirchenväterzitate und Lektionare* (ed. Kurt Aland; ANTF 5; Berlin/New York: de Gruyter, 1972), 498-591.

[60] Muriel M. Carder, "A Caesarean Text in the Catholic Epistles?," *NTS* 16 (1970): 252-70.

results were seriously flawed.[61] Christian-Bernard Amphoux and Bernard Outtier have developed Carder's suggestions and they see a "Caesarean" text in "Family 1739" (primarily in 1739 and about ten other minuscules, including 1243), the text of which is also related to the first Georgian version.[62]

In Amphoux' view, the text of Family ("groupe") 1739 contains elements that go back to a pre-recensional period.[63] Similar elements are present in Family ("groupe") 2138, identified by Duplacy and Amphoux.[64] Amphoux subsequently labeled it as a "Western" text.[65] However, there is no good reason for that label, first because the main Greek witness for the "Western" text, Codex Bezae (D 05), is not extant in the Catholic Epistles (apart from a Latin fragment in 3 John), and, secondly, the "Western" text is generally difficult to identify among the Old Latin witnesses in the Catholic Epistles (and in the Paulines).[66] Instead, Klaus Wachtel has argued persuasively that the distinct text of Family 2138 represents the early stages in the development of the Byzantine text (see below).[67] Actually, Amphoux

---

[61] Kurt Aland, "Bemerkungen zu den gegenwärtigen Möglichkeiten text-kritischer Arbeit aus Anlass einer Untersuchung zum Cäsarea-Text der Katholischen Briefe," *NTS* 17 (1970): 1-9. Aland's main objection is that only MSS related to either Origen or Eusebius in critical places could rightfully be labeled "Caesarean," and, surprisingly, Carder did not address this question at all (ibid., 4, 7).

[62] Christian-Bernard Amphoux and Bernard Outtier, "Les leçons des versions géorgiennes de Jacques," *Bib* 65 (1984): 365-76.

[63] Jean-Paul Bouhot and Christian-Bernard Amphoux, "Lecture liturgique et critique textuelle des Épitres Catholiques," in *La lecture liturgique des Épîtres catholiques dans l'Église ancienne* (ed. Jean-Paul Bouhot and Christian-Bernard Amphoux; HTB 1; Lausanne: Éditions du Zèbre, 1996), 289-90.

[64] Duplacy and Amphoux, "À propos de l'histoire du texte de la première épître de Pierre," 162.

[65] Amphoux, "Le Texte," 244.

[66] For a general summary of the problems, see Jean Duplacy, "Le texte occidental des Épitres Catholiques," *NTS* 16 (1970): 397-99. In regard to the Latin version of the NT, see Jacobus H. Petzer, "The Latin Version of the New Testament," in *The Text of the New Testament in Contemporary Research*, 113-30, esp. 124-25 (in regard to the relationship to the Greek text of the Catholic Epistles). Walter Thiele, who has worked with the Vetus Latina edition of the Catholic Epistles, does acknowledge a "Western" text in the Catholic Epistles (*Epistula Catholicae* [Vetus Latina 26/1; Freiburg im Breisgau: Herder, 1956-1969], 98-99); cf. idem, *Die lateinischen Texte des 1. Petrusbriefes* (GLB 5; Freiburg im Breisgau: Herder, 1965), 27-34, 50-54, 83-87, 104-8; and idem, "Beobachtungen zum Comma Iohanneum (1 Joh 5, 7f.)," *ZNW* 50 (1959): 61-73, esp. 64ff. However, Thiele is mostly concerned with the inner-Latin variations and does not pursue the further implications for the textual history of the Greek NT. In fact, most of the typical "Western" variants Thiele has identified in the Catholic Epistles have no counterpart in the Greek textual tradition (cf. idem, "Probleme der Versio Latina in den Katholischen Briefen," in *Die alten Übersetzungen des Neuen Testaments*, 111).

[67] Wachtel, *Der byzantinische Text*, 56-57, 188-89.

himself says of the "Western" text, "this text is not a type of text, rather it contains several types. Indeed under the term 'Western' are grouped witnesses which are acknowledged to be heterogeneous."[68]

Until very recently, however, there has been a consensus regarding the major textual groupings in the Catholic Epistles: there are the Alexandrian and Byzantine texts or text-types and then there are various clusters, families or groups with a mixed text, whether Byzantine, Alexandrian or "pre-recensional" (e.g., "Family 2138" and "Family 1739"). The exact nature of the relationship between these various smaller groupings and how to correctly label them according to their place in the historical and geographical schema of textual transmission is a controversial issue.

Recently, one of the editors of the *ECM*, Gerd Mink has developed a new method, "Coherence-Based Genealogical Method" (CBGM), in order to survey the genealogical structure of the manuscript tradition. In brief, Mink attempts to draw up as many local stemmata of variants as possible in order to trace the overall "predominant textual flow" and draw up the most probable global stemma and reconstruct the initial text ("Ausgangstext") of the NT.[69] The method is still under development, but it is already affecting the evaluation of external evidence in the *ECM*.[70] The new method has also made the conception of text-types problematic. The traditional recensional hypothesis makes sharp distinctions between text-types and their corresponding geographic locations. However, these notions seem incompatible with the new results of the CBGM: first, manuscripts from different text-types show up in stemmatic diagrams in unexpected places, indicating textual interaction and ancestry beyond the traditional borders of the text-types.[71] Secondly, the relationship between the versional evidence and the Greek manuscript tradition has proven

---

[68] Leon Vaganay and Christian-Bernard Amphoux, *An Introduction to New Testament Textual Criticism* (trans. Jenny Read-Heimerdinger; 2d rev. and enl. ed.; New York: Cambridge University Press, 1991), 110; cf. ibid., 96. More surprising is the fact that Amphoux actually assumes the priority of the "Western" text, which he views as a "pre-recensional text form," and the closest surviving witness (in spite of its diversity) to the "first written text" of the New Testament (ibid., 94).

[69] Cf. Gerd Mink, "Problems of a Highly Contaminated Tradition: The New Testament. Stemmata of Variants As a Source of a Genealogy for Witnesses," in *Studies in Stemmatology II* (ed. Pieter van Reenen, August den Hollander and Margot van Mulken; Amsterdam: John Benjamins, 2004), 13-85. For Mink's definition of "initial text" as opposed to "autograph" and "archetype," see pp. 25-27.

[70] Barbara Aland, Kurt Aland, Gerd Mink and Klaus Wachtel, eds., *Novum Testamentum Graecum Editio Critica Maior*. Vol. IV: *The Catholic Letters*. Installment 2: *The Letters of Peter*. Part 1: *Text* (Stuttgart: Deutsche Bibelgesellschaft, 2000), 23-24*.

[71] Note, for example, the respective positions of the Byzantine uncials 018, 020, 025 and 049 in Mink's stemma of "predominant textual flow" (Mink, "Problems," 47).

more complex then previously thought, which makes it difficult to assign the traditional text-types to any geographical location.[72]

Thus, the CBGM gives priority to the role a witness plays in the genealogy of the text rather than its pre-concieved text-type. In practice, however, the traditional external evaluation of well-known witnesses still plays a certain role in the initial stage of the procedure, not only in the prior exclusion of a large number of MSS applying the Teststellen-method, but also when local stemmata of the selected MSS are drawn up. Thus, Mink states:

> [T]here is a circular argument typical of textual criticism: witnesses are good because of their good variants, variants are good because of their good witnesses. This circle cannot be avoided, but it has to be controlled. We need a method, therefore, which can provide an overall view of the consequences of all the decisions we take, so that also the overall plausibility of what we are doing can be examined. In the present method [CBGM] this is done through an iterative process, especially designed to perform this examination.[73]

In this connection, it should be noted that the utilization of the new method for the *ECM* has not led to many changes of the critically reconstructed text as such in relation to the NA[27] text.[74]

1.9 Klaus Wachtel: The Byzantine Text in the Catholic Epistles

A major investigation of one of the texts or text-types in the Catholic Epistles saw the light in 1995, when, on the basis of previous work at the INTF, Klaus Wachtel, a member of the staff, published his dissertation on the Byzantine text in the Catholic Epistles.[75] Wachtel's main thesis is that the common view prevailing from the days of Westcott and Hort of the

---

[72] Cf. Franz-Jürgen Schmitz who says of the Coptic versions, "Die koptischen Übersetzungen galten bisher immer als Zeugen des griechischen sog. 'alexandrinischen Textes', diese Annahme muss nun revidiert werden. Die Vorlagetexte für die meisten koptischen Übersetzungen sind nicht etwa mehr oder minder 'alexandrinisch', sondern vielschichtiger als bisher vermutet wurde. . . . Für die neutestamentliche Textkritik bedeutet dies, dass ein koptischer Textzeuge jetzt nicht mehr a priori als ein Vertreter des griechischen gemeinhin als 'alexandrinisch' bezeichneten Textes gewertet werden darf" (*Das Verhältnis der koptischen zur griechischen Überlieferung des Neuen Testaments* [ANTF 33; Berlin/New York: de Gruyter, 2003], 595).

[73] Mink, "Problems," 25.

[74] One of the editors, Klaus Wachtel, admits this fact without mentioning the element of circularity in partial dependence on traditional external criteria as one possible factor: "The text of ECM has been criticized for showing relatively few differences from that of NA27. The reason is that the NA[27] text, being the condensation of textual research done in over 200 years since Griesbach, is not that bad" (Klaus Wachtel and D. C. Parker, "The Joint IGNTP/INTF Editio Critica Maior of the Gospel of John: Its Goals and Their Significance for New Testament Scholarship" [paper presented at the SNTS meeting, Halle, August 15, 2005]).

[75] Wachtel, *Der byzantinische Text.*

origin of a uniform Byzantine, or *Koine*, text resulting from a recension in the fourth century is an oversimplification.[76] Instead it arose over a long period, in a process of smoothing and normalization, extending from the fourth century into the ninth century when it achieved a relatively fixed form (albeit later revised in the 12th century).[77] In order to establish his thesis Wachtel analyses the so-called majority-readings, by definition present in the majority of witnesses, and, thus, always present in the majority of Byzantine MSS, but occasionally attested also in early MSS of other text-types.[78] Drawing from the data in *Text und Textwert*, he examines the majority-readings from two perspectives, namely their character and historical development.

In terms of textual character, Wachtel distinguishes three types of majority-readings: (1) typical majority-readings such as normalize, clarify, or polish the text (this is the largest category); (2) untypical majority-readings such as plain errors or clumsy efforts to improve the text; and (3) majority-readings which have a good claim of being original, or at least very early, especially judging from internal criteria (few readings belong in this last category).[79]

In tracing this historical development and growth of the Byzantine text, the so-called Harklean version, completed in 616 C.E. by Thomas of Harqel becomes a vital key for Wachtel.[80] Barbara Aland and Andreas Juckel at the INTF had been able to successfully reconstruct the Greek *Vorlage* of the Harklean (HK[gr]) in their work on the Syriac transmission of

---

[76] Ibid., 10.

[77] Ibid., 199-201. In some ways his thesis was anticipated in Barbara Aland's discussion on the uncial MSS of the Pauline Epistles from the 4-10th centuries: "Die Majuskelüberlieferung als ganze lehrt uns, die Textgeschichte des 4-10. Jahrhunderts als einen allmählichen Entwicklungsprozeß zu verstehen, dessen Ausgangspunkte durch die unterschiedlichen und teilweise recht frei kopierten Handschriften des 2. und 3. Jahrhunderts gegeben waren" (foreword in Klaus Wachtel and Klaus Witte, *Das Neue Testament auf Papyrus*. II.2: *Die Paulinischen Briefe* [ANTF 22; Berlin/New York: de Gruyter, 1994], xxx).

[78] Wachtel himself consistently avoids the term "text-type," since it is normally associated with recensional-hypotheses (*Der byzantinische Text*, 201). He prefers to use terms more easily associated with his process theory, e.g., "Traditionssträngen" (ibid., 199). Thus, he says, "Es ist an der Zeit, eine Theorie der Überlieferung des Neuen Testaments zu formulieren, die auf das relativ bequeme Konzept der 'Texttypen' verzichtet und die Textgeschichte als ein Kontinuum begreift" (ibid., 23). In my view, this perspective is preferable, and therefore I have attempted to avoid the term in the current study.

[79] Ibid., 73-84.

[80] In the Catholic Epistles, we lack the commentary-based textual witness of Chrysostom or the Gothic version to the 4th century Byzantine tradition, as well as the Byzantine imperial purple MSS of the 6th century. The earliest surviving Byzantine witnesses (apart from the HK) are from the 9th century (MSS 018, 020, 025, 049, 1862, and 1895).

the NT.[81] In his work, Wachtel underlines the importance of HK[gr] for the understanding of the history of the Byzantine text.[82] Since Thomas' translation represented an attempt to produce a translation as close as possible to the contemporary orthodox Greek text in the 7th century, it is therefore on the whole a witness to the Byzantine text of the time. Significantly, the textual character of the Harklean version in the Catholic Epistles is rather divergent from the later Byzantine text, which became dominant in the 9th century, and so it allows us to view the earlier stages of the Byzantine text-type.

Thus, Wachtel appeals to the textual evidence in general, and the HK[gr] in particular, as he identifies three different strata of majority-readings (typical or untypical), in turn representing three phases in the historical development of the Byzantine text in the Catholic Epistles: (1) majority-readings with early pre- Harklean attestation (observable in non-Byzantine witnesses like A, ℵ and C), representing a stratum that stems from the 4-6 centuries; (2) majority-readings of which the Harklean is the earliest witness (stratum of the 7-8 centuries); (3) majority-readings with no manuscript support from before the 9th century (post 8th century).[83]

Significantly, the existence of untypical as well as typical majority-readings in all of the three strata (originating from different times) contradicts the theory of a homogenous Byzantine text resulting from a recension at a certain point, done according to firm principles, and instead confirms Wachtel's thesis of a continuing growth process.[84]

The second half of Wachtel's dissertation is a textual commentary on each of the 98 test passages in *TuT*.[85] In this part, Wachtel follows the local-genealogical method of evaluating the extant variants in each variation-unit and reconstructing the original text and its later development

---

[81] Barbara Aland and Andreas Juckel, eds., *Das Neue Testament in syrischer Überlieferung*. I: *Die großen Katholischen Briefe* (ANTF 7; Berlin/New York: de Gruyter, 1986), 41-90. Through the use of computers Aland and Juckel identified a close relationship of their back-translation and the group of Greek MSS, known as Family 2138 (ibid., 52-72). Thus, Family 2138 could function as a further guide in the reconstruction of HK[gr] (see the collation of the core members in ibid., 271-75). Christian-Bernard Amphoux had described this family and the relationship with the Harklean version earlier ("La parenté textuelle du sy[h] et du groupe 2138 dans l'épître de Jacques," *Bib* 62 [1981]: 259-71).

[82] Wachtel, *Der byzantinische Text*, 188-89.

[83] Ibid., 192.

[84] Ibid., 199-200.

[85] Ibid., 205-419. Wachtel's commentary on the 11 test passages of the epistle (ibid., 343-79, 412-419) is considered in detail in the textual commentary below.

in a particular passage.[86] Here he is able to draw from the results of the former part, especially in regard to the history and (most often secondary) character of the Byzantine text, when evaluating external and internal criteria for each variation-unit.[87] The discussions in the textual commentary are valuable not only for text-critics, but for any exegete who will find in them a treasure of information on these particular variants that goes well beyond other textual commentaries.

1.10 Charles Landon: Radical Eclecticism Applied to Jude

A year later, in 1996, Charles Landon's dissertation on the textual problems in the Epistle of Jude appeared.[88] Just like Wachtel's dissertation it contains a large textual commentary, but Landon chooses a different approach in that he represents the so-called "thoroughgoing," or "radical," eclectic school of textual criticism (pioneered mainly by G. D. Kilpatrick and J. K. Elliott). In an introductory chapter, he outlines the history of thoroughgoing eclecticism, and sets out to define and substantiate the approach.[89] Being a radical eclectic, Landon disregards all external criteria and proposes instead an evaluation of individual readings exclusively on the basis of internal criteria.[90] However, he hardly succeeds to defend the theoretical bases of the approach, since he devotes the major part of the introduction to a practical demonstration of the method in work.[91]

The main bulk of the study is the examination of the Epistle of Jude in 95 variation-units. In each unit, Landon offers a limited sample of manuscript evidence in an apparatus derived from secondary sources (as far back as Tischendorf and von Soden).[92] Thus, unchecked errors in

---

[86] For a description of the local-genealogical method as applied by Wachtel, see especially ibid., 44-48.

[87] This ambition is also made explicit, "Eine detallierte Beschreibung der *Internal Evidence* der 'syrischen' Gruppe anhand ihrer Lesarten gibt Hort—im Vertrauen auf *Genealogical Evidence*— nicht. Sie für die Katholischen Briefe beizubringen, ist ein Ziel dieser Arbeit. Die Ergebnisse sollen für die Anwendung der lokal-genealogischen Methode genutzt werden" (ibid., 43-44). Cf. ibid., 202.

[88] Charles Landon, *A Text-Critical Study of the Epistle of Jude* (JSNTSup 135; Sheffield Academic Press, 1996).

[89] Ibid., 14-26.

[90] Cf. Landon's attempt to formulate a definition of his position, "Thoroughgoing eclecticism is a text-critical methodology which aims to reconstruct the original text of the New Testament from extant New Testament MSS by relying mainly on internal evidence to choose the best reading whenever the MSS divide, which places minimal reliance on external evidence, and which places minimal reliance upon conjectural emendation" (ibid., 25).

[91] Ibid., 26-45.

[92] See ibid., 45-46 for an account of sources for Landon's apparatus.

Landon's sources are perpetuated.[93] Apart from the import of old errors, Landon adds numerous new errors and inconsistencies to his apparatus, which at times also affect the subsequent discussions.[94] Another problem is his decision to offer only a limited sample of manuscript evidence in each unit, which means that he omits the support from important witnesses for several readings, and that he even omits many readings altogether—the latter of which is clearly a problem considering that Landon is a radical eclectic.[95] As for his actual text-critical decisions, I often find myself in complete disagreement with Landon, especially in regard to his line of argumentation behind the decisions.[96]

---

[93] A blatant example is Landon's dependence on Edouard Massaux's collation of the text of Jude in 𝔓[72], which, for Landon, "proved to be a valuable reservoir of variants" (ibid., 45). James R. Royse has demonstrated how Massaux's work ("Le Texte") is rendered worthless because of its high rate of error (Royse, "Scribal Habits," 451-53 [with footnotes]). Hence, Landon repeats Massaux's erroneous word order in the apparatus of Jude 6 and says that "ἀϊδίοις δεσμοῖς in 33 2344 runs contrary to word order tendencies in Jude," and then he continues to describe the adjectival word order tendencies in Koine Greek and in Jude, without realizing that there is actually no extant MS with the unnatural word order in the first place (*Text-Critical Study*, 81). In his treatment of Jude 5 several errors have been imported from Carroll D. Osburn's apparatus, "The Text of Jude 5," 108, e.g., the very significant variant ἅπαξ πάντα ὅτι ὁ κύριος (927 1245) which, in fact, is not extant in any MS.

[94] For example, Landon thinks C* omitted the whole phrase σόδομα καὶ γόμορρα καί in Jude 7, "motivated by doctrinal reasons, in this case a prudish avoidance of the mention of two such notorious towns" (*Text-Critical Study*, 84), when in fact C*, according to Tischendorf, has omitted only αἱ (although not in my view; nor according to the *ECM*). Probably Landon misinterpreted Tischendorf's apparatus at this point. In this same unit we find another type of inconsistency in Landon's apparatus, in regard to the extent of a variation unit. Since Landon does not indicate with a base text the extent of the variation unit, one may get the impression that the second καί (which Landon thought was omitted in C*) is not present in any other of the ten witnesses accounted for, when in fact the word is present in all extant witnesses of Jude. The following are some other plain errors I have found in Landon's apparatus (textual witnesses in parentheses are wrongly cited): variation unit 0.1 (P); 1.2 (322 323 add πατρι); 5.3 (𝔓[72] C 623ᶜ 927 1245); 6.5 (33 2344); 7.1 (C*); 9.1: (vg); 9.2 (632); 9.3 (241 250; Ψ should read υπενεγκειν); 12.3 (𝔓[72] ℵ B K L 049 should read αγαπαις; Syrᵖʰ; 424;); 13.2 (απαφριζοντα is misspelled and the reading μεταφριζουτα is not extant in any MS); 14.3 (104 378—the latter cited twice, but wrongly both times); 15.3 (𝔓[72]); 18.1 (226 639 641); 20.2 (the reading of 𝔓[72] misspelled); 22-23.1 (ℵ*).

[95] Only eight MSS are cited consistently (𝔓[72] ℵ A B K L Ψ 049) and four more are cited frequently (𝔓[74] 𝔓[78] C P). Landon thinks that this selection is "wide enough to allow a comparative evaluation of the internal quality of MSS of different text types and antiquity," and, at the same time, he states that his apparatus "attempts to represent as many internally interesting readings as possible" (ibid., 45).

[96] See my textual commentary below.

Landon claims that "assumptions about impressive MSS have in the present work been replaced by arguments for impressive readings."[97] In practice, however, he manages to agree with B in 70 out of 95 readings, and with A in 69, whereas he agrees fewer times with Byzantine witnesses (e.g., L 64/95; 049 62/95 and K 58/95).[98] Hence, in the end A and B turn out to be the most "impressive" witnesses.[99]

In a final chapter Landon summarizes his results and includes an evaluation of the text in the UBS Greek New Testament (UBS⁴) to see to what extent it is "eclectic." He concludes that "GNT4 does not always satisfy the ideal of thoroughgoing eclecticism."[100] It is perhaps surprising to see that Landon agrees with the UBS⁴ 73 out of 95 times (77%), considering the two very different approaches. Nevertheless, Landon proposes twenty-two improvements to the edition, many of which have slim manuscript support—one is in fact a plain conjecture not reflected in any Greek MS![101] Nevertheless, some of Landon's suggestions make valuable contributions to existing arguments. Most significantly, he uses the criteria of the writer's style and vocabulary to good effect, based on the assumption that Jude has a consistent and distinctive style (drawing mainly from the rhetorical analysis of J. Daryl Charles), i.e., the frequent use in Jude of *hapax legomena*, triadic illustration, repeated catchwords, synonymous parallelism, paronomasia, contrast or antithesis, set expressions, and consistent word order.[102]

1.11 The *Editio Critica Maior*: A Milestone in the History of Textual Criticism

One of the main goals of the Alands and the INTF, as stated above, was to

---

[97] Landon, *Text-Critical Study*, 134.

[98] Ibid., 148 (the figure given for the "correct readings" of K is incorrect, and should be 58).

[99] In light of the fact that Landon cites many singular readings and misspellings of 𝔓⁷² and ℵ, it is perhaps even more significant that he agrees with these witnesses 57 times, respectively. In the opinion of most scholars, singular readings and errors are not genealogically significant, i.e., they most probably reside with the individual scribe and do not reflect the exemplar, and should therefore not be counted at all when judging the relative quality of the text represented in an individual witness.

[100] Ibid., 143.

[101] Ibid., 145-47. Landon claims only twenty-one improvements, but forgets to count variation-unit 14.3. In Jude 6 Landon proposes the conjecture based only on Latin citations from "Lucifer Speculum" (cf. ibid., 82-84). The unclear reference gives the impression of one source (author and work); the citations are found in Pseudo-Augustine (*Spec. 33*) and Lucifer (*De non conv.* 15).

[102] See especially Landon, *Text-Critical Study*, 78-79, 93-94, 111-12, 114-19, 125-27, 134-35, 137. Cf. J. Daryl Charles, *Literary Strategy in the Epistle of Jude* (Scranton: University of Scranton Press, 1993).

produce a major critical edition, *Editio Critica Maior* (*ECM*) and the first part for publication, the volume of the Catholic Epistles, is nearly complete.[103] We have already considered some of the preparatory steps for the *ECM* done over the years through the various enterprises of the INTF. But the groundwork and method of selecting and gathering the textual data is one thing, the presentation in an *apparatus criticus* another, and perhaps an even more challenging aspect of the task. In his review of the first installment of the *ECM*, William L. Petersen describes the challenge with an apt choice of words:

> An apparatus is obliged to be a butterfly and an elephant at the same time: an elephantine amount of information must be conveyed in an exquisite minimum of space. The apparatus must be instantly accessible to the user and understandable, transparent in its clarity, without ambiguity. It must also be entirely accurate, convey all of the readings of all of the manuscripts, Fathers, versions, and apocryphal works collated; nothing can be omitted.[104]

In successfully meeting most of these requirements, the publication of the *ECM* meant a major breakthrough; the highly acclaimed new edition has become a milestone in the history of textual criticism, and has revolutionized the setting out of an *apparatus criticus*, not only for its unprecedented presentation of a wide range of textual data with great thoroughness and precision, but also for its clarity of presentation in text and apparatus, achieved through a number of innovative and splendid features.[105]

The most recent installment includes the Johannine Epistles and Jude.[106] For the edition of Jude, 134 Greek continuous text MSS and six lectionary MSS were fully collated and selected for inclusion in the apparatus, only a few of which represent a pure form of the Byzantine text as represented in the majority of extant minuscules. The critical text was reconstructed in

---

[103] Barbara Aland, Kurt Aland, Gerd Mink and Klaus Wachtel, eds., *Novum Testamentum Graecum Editio Critica Maior*. Vol. IV: *The Catholic Letters* (Stuttgart: Deutsche Bibelgesellschaft, 1997–).

[104] William L. Petersen, "Some Remarks on the First Volume (The Epistle of James) of the Novum Testamentum Graecum Editio Critica Maior," *TC: A Journal of Biblical Textual Criticism* [http://purl.org/TC] 3 (1988): par. 5.

[105] Presentations of the edition by the editors, and several scholarly reviews are available in *TC: A Journal of Biblical Textual Criticism* [http://purl.org/TC] 3 (1998). See J. K. Elliott, review of Barbara Aland, et al., eds., *Novum Testamentum Graecum Editio Critica Maior*. Vol. IV: *The Catholic Letters. Installment 1: James. Part 1: Text*, *NovT* 40 (1998): 195-204, and idem, "The Petrine Epistles in the *Editio Critica Maior*," *NovT* 42 (2000): 328-39.

[106] Barbara Aland et al., eds., *Novum Testamentum Graecum Editio Critica Maior*. Vol. IV: *The Catholic Letters*. Installment 4: *The Second and Third Letter of John, The Letter of Jude* (Stuttgart: Deutsche Bibelgesellschaft, 2005).

two stages following the CBGM method, described above. First, local stemmata of variants were drawn up in a high number of passages where the genealogical relationship was relatively clear, by using usual philological methods of internal and external critieria, the latter with "grave reservations," since the role of most witnesses in the history of transmission is largely unknown.[107] In the second stage, an optimal global stemma was constructed to be as compatible as possible with the relationships of the witnesses in the local stemmata of variants, which in turn were subject to revision following the iterative process of the CBGM.

In this process, the editors made a trial evaluation of the genealogical data for all three epistles together (2-3 John and Jude), and compared it with an evaluation of each epistle taken separately. Significantly, the results showed that each epistle must be evaluated separately, since their conditions of transmission are so different. In Jude, then, the editors list the following MSS, which they considered to be particularly significant for the reconstruction of the text, divided into three classes:[108]

1. The witnesses that were considered to have the initial text as their closest related potential ancestor: $\mathfrak{P}^{72}$, 01, 02, 03, 04, 020, 044, 81, 88, 307, 326, 431, 436, 442, 453, 808, 1739, 2200.
2. The witnesses considered to have the initial text as their next most closely related potential ancestor: 18, 33, 35, 323, 621, 623, 630, 665, 915, 1067, 1409, 1836, 1837, 1845, 1852, 1875, 2374.
3. The witnesses with the initial text as third to fifth most closely related potential ancestor: 5, 6, 61, 93, 254, 468, 1243, 1292, 1735, 1846, 1881, 2186, 2298, 2344, 2805, 2818.

The editors express their surprise over the large number of witnesses with the initial text as their closest related potential ancestor, and over the fact that a large number of witnesses in general have a high agreement with the initial text, which "conforms with the assumption that the initial text has been preserved with but little variation in a corresponding number of witnesses."[109]

Those MSS having the highest degree of agreement with the initial text in Jude, according to the editors, are 81 (96.9%) and 03 (95.4%). Of course, these data must be carefully interpreted, because they are based on relatively few variants (204 in Jude). Thus, in my opinion, the following

---

[107] Ibid., xviii.
[108] Ibid., 36*.
[109] Ibid., 36-37*.

statement is somewhat misleading: "03 loses its exceptional position in Jd, and *A* [initial text] is no longer its sole potential ancestor. This distinction now goes to 81."[110]

As noted above, the critical text of the *ECM* generally differs little from the NA[27], and Jude is no exception; in relation to NA[27], there are three changes in the new edition, two of which are very minor involving the removal of words that were already in square brackets in NA[27] (ὅτι and τοῦ in v. 18). The third change in the difficult passage in v. 5 is substantial, and apparently involved intense discussions on the part of the editors (see the textual commentary on v. 5 below). (There are no changes to the text in 2-3 John.)

2. Purpose, Outline and Preliminary Observations

2.1 The Desiderata: A Complete Collation and Analysis of the Evidence

At least in one regard, the new *ECM* does not satisfy the needs; the edition does present *all* of the readings, but only those attested in all the *selected* MSS, not in all *extant* MSS. Therefore, the introduction to volume four, installment one, promises too much in that it states that the selection of included MSS "guarantees reliably that the critical apparatus contains all the known readings which have appeared in the history of the text from its earliest beginnings through the formation and final establishment of the Byzantine text."[111]

Following any method of selection of MSS, one cannot know if all of the readings, whether early or late, have been located until it is confirmed by full collations. For this reason, Thomas C. Geer Jr. issues a plea towards the end of an article treating the analysis and categorization of NT Greek MSS:

> For too long in our discipline, too much has been based on too little. The time has come for full collations of MSS to enable us to write confidently about the history of the NT text. . . . How many more centuries must we wait before we deal with this, the major desideratum of NT textual criticism? I issue a plea that while we use as productively as possible what the Alands, the Claremont Profile Method, and others have provided based on sampling methods and test passages, we not allow ourselves to stop so short of our ultimate goal. Rather, these preliminary methods must urge us on to a complete study of the witnesses to the NT text.[112] *

---

[110] Ibid., 36*.
[111] Barbara Aland, Kurt Aland, Gerd Mink and Klaus Wachtel, eds., *Novum Testamentum Graecum Editio Critica Maior*. Vol. IV: *The Catholic Letters*. Installment 1: *James*. Part 1: *Text* (Stuttgart: Deutsche Bibelgesellschaft, 1997), 12*.
[112] Thomas C. Geer, Jr., "Analyzing and Categorizing New Testament Greek Manuscripts: Colwell Revisited," in *The Text of the New Testament in Contemporary Research: Essays on the Status*

Such full collations will probably not help us getting much closer to the original text.[113] However, the complete data will enable us to better understand the history of textual transmission, where the minuscules play a critical role. A comprehensive history of the text will also improve the external criteria used to access readings.[114]

Furthermore, the history of the text is also the history of scribes who read and re-created their texts for various reasons. The recent developments in NT textual criticism have brought forward a renewed interest not only in individual manuscripts and their environment, but in the whole history of the text and its relationship to the wider historical context.[115]

2.2 Purpose and Outline of the Present Study

In the current work, I have attempted to fulfill some of the needs and interests described above. In the first part (*Prolegomena*), I survey the history of research on the Catholic Epistles and the Epistle of Jude, and describe the purpose and outline of the present study. Then I devote two chapters to special studies of the early papyri of Jude ($\mathfrak{P}^{72}$, $\mathfrak{P}^{78}$), placing them in their contemporary setting. In a subsequent chapter the literary relationship between 2 Peter and Jude is examined. A survey of the history of transmission of the two books in relation to each other concludes the first part.

The second part (*Editio*) commences with an exhaustive list of all the manuscripts included in the study with short descriptions and bibliographic notes. The list is followed by an introduction to the apparatus, including a few notes on the reconstruction of the text. The introduction also includes a comparison with the *ECM*, with an overview of the points of differences between the editions. Then, the critical text and apparatus provide a reconstruction of the initial text of Jude, based on the collation data of all extant Greek continuous text MSS of the epistle, as recorded in the

---

Quaestionis (ed. Bart D. Ehrman and Michael W. Holmes; SD 46; Grand Rapids: Eerdmans, 1995), 265-66. Cf. W. J. Elliott, "The Need for an Accurate and Comprehensive Collation of all Known Greek NT Manuscripts," in *Studies in New Testament Language and Text* (ed. J. K. Elliott; NovTSup 44; Leiden: Brill, 1976), 137-43.

[113] That this is true in relation to the work at the INTF is evident from the fact mentioned above, that the reconstructed text of the Catholic Epistles in the *ECM* differs very little from the text of the recent 27th Nestle-Aland edition.

[114] Cf. Barbara Aland and Klaus Wachtel, "The Greek Minuscule Manuscripts of the New Testament," in *The Text of the New Testament in Contemporary Research: Essays on the Status Quaestionis*, 56.

[115] See Eldon J. Epp, "Issues in New Testament Textual Criticism," in *Rethinking New Testament Textual Criticism* (ed. David A. Black; Grand Rapids: Baker, 2002), 52-70.

apparatus.[116] Appended to the apparatus is an errata-list and a lacuna-list of the Greek MSS. There is also an errata-list containing the plain errors, which I have identified in the *ECM*, and another list with some further differences between the two editions, regarding the interpretation of the manuscript evidence.[117] The actual transcriptions of the manuscripts will be distributed electronically on the Internet and on a CD-ROM/DVD-ROM, as planned for the future.

In the third part (*Commentarius*), I offer a textual commentary, in which I cite the most significant evidence and account for my text-critical decisions. Here I am concerned with the question of the initial text as well as its further development, and I attempt to pay some attention to the reception history of Jude as reflected both in the manuscript tradition of Jude and 2 Peter.

2.3 Preliminary Observations

The complete collation of all MSS as recorded in the apparatus has yielded significant results in terms of variant readings and corresponding manuscript support. Thus, numerous previously unknown readings have come to light. Let me take an example from the very opening of the letter in the author's address to those *in God the Father*. The *ECM* accounts for three variants at this point:

1. εν θεω πατρι
2. εν θεω και πατρι
3. πατρι

---

[116] Because of limitations of time I was prevented from collating all of the extant Greek lectionary MSS. For the same reason, the Greek patristic and versional evidence in this study is partly dependent on other sources, and will be cited only in the textual commentary. The reader is encouraged to consult these sources for verification and further information. The material for a full presentation of the Greek patristic evidence has been collected, but not yet evaluated and worked into the apparatus, so that will have to await a future edition. Nevertheless, I have sometimes felt compelled to correct and supplement the data found in other editions, as noted in the textual commentary. For example, the crucial citations of Jude 5 by Cyril of Alexandria (*Thesaurus de sancta consubstantiali trinitate* 302), and Jude 22-23 by Clement of Alexandria (*Stromata* 6.8.65) are missing altogether in the *ECM*, whereas the citation of Didymus, *De Trinitate* 1.27 in Jude 4 is based upon a misunderstanding. Moreover, I have added the evidence from a commentary, *Expositio in epistolam S. Judae Apostoli* (PG 126:85-104), ascribed to Theophylact of Ochrid (ca. 1075), since it is based on a edition superior to that of the practically identical commentary, *Catholica epistola Judae Apostoli* (PG 119:703-22), ascribed to Pseudo-Oecumenius, the evidence of which is included in the *ECM*.
[117] Some of the errors or discrepancies are explicable by the fact that I have worked with different photographic material (so in the case of MSS 0316, 252 and 1799).

The complete collation has uncovered an additional four readings:

4. εν πατρι θεω
5. εν θεω πατρασιν
6. εν τω πατρι
7. εν χριστω πατρι

Further, previously known and significant readings have gained new manuscript support. For example, the rare spelling χάριτα in Jude 4 attested by 𝔓⁷² 02 03 is supported also by 38. The agreement is probably coincidental, but interesting. On the other hand, the marginal readings of 2627 (not in the *ECM*) are more significant; in Jude they occur only in v. 3: τοῦ γράφειν ὑμῖν (𝔓⁷² 01 044 2627Z) and ἡμῶν σωτηρίας καὶ ζωῆς (01 044 2627Z). A collation of all marginal readings of this MS is higly desirable and would probably yield valuable results. In other cases, a Greek equivalent to a versional reading has now come to light, e.g., προφερόμεναι in v. 12 (1509 **K:**S), or τέλος in v. 21 (462 **S:**Hᴹ).

Many new readings will not contribute much to the reconstruction of the initial text, but, nonetheless, they will shed light on the history of interpretation. Perhaps the best example is the creative scribe of 044, whose text presents an original solution to a well-known crux in Jude—the unknown apostolic prophecy in v. 18—which he seems to identify with the predicted judgment in Jude 4 and Jesus' words according to the apostle Matthew about "this evil generation": ἄνδρες Νινευῖται ἀναστήσονται ἐν τῇ κρίσει μετὰ τῆς γενεᾶς ταύτης καὶ κατακρινοῦσιν αὐτήν, ὅτι μετενόησαν εἰς τὸ κήρυγμα Ἰωνᾶ (Matt 12:41). The peculiar text of 044 in Jude 4 and 18 seems to allude to this passage: προγεγραμμένοι εἰς τοῦτο τὸ κήρυγμα ἀσεβεῖν (v. 4); ἐπ᾽ ἐσχάτου χρόνου ἀναστήσονται ἐμπαῖκται (v. 18; singular reading).

Another good example is the obscure text of vv. 22-23 that caused an interesting interpretative expansion on the part of one scribe: οὓς δὲ ἐν φόβῳ σῴζετε ἐκ πυρὸς ἁρπάζοντες τὸν ἑαυτῶν ἁμαρτιῶν κεκηλιδωμένον βίον (1744), which reflects the influence of a patristic comment on these verses. Newly discovered readings may also support the interpretations of modern commentators; for example, E. E. Kellett has suggested that the phrase τοὺς μὴ πιστεύσαντας, "those who did not believe," in Jude 5 could refer to the Amorites who Joshua destroyed.[118] Interestingly, the same interpretation is reflected in MS 615, where the phrase is replaced with

---

[118] E. E. Kellett, "Note on Jude 5," *Expository Times* 15 (1903-1904): 381.

τοὺς ἐκεινῶν ἐχθρούς, "their enemies." In a few cases, some known readings, labeled as errors in the *ECM*, are reinterpreted as sensible variants in the current edition. For example, MS 1501 reads ἐπαφρίζοντα τοὺς ἑαυτῶν αὐχένας in Jude 13, the noun and article of which are labeled as errors in the *ECM*. In my opinion, the reading makes perfect sense in the context, and even makes the text smoother.

The complete collation will also reveal that a number of MSS, not included in other editions, have a considerable number of significant readings. Certainly, new manuscript witnesses will be added to previously known textual groupings. However, the attempt to classify the MSS of the Epistle of Jude on the basis of all genealogically significant variation will have to await a future study. Because of the small statistical sample this brief writing can offer, the results of such an analysis should preferably be used in comparison with earlier and future classifications of MSS in Jude and in the Catholic Epistles.

In this regard, it would be interesting to construct an extensive global stemma for the complete textual tradition of Jude using the CBGM, in order to compare the results with the global stemma as constructed for the *ECM*, based on the selection of 134 MSS. The results would show to what degree the selection based on the Teststellen-method is warranted.[119] This trial, however, should preferably be conducted by the scholars at the INTF, in order to avoid distortion of the results.

---

[119] In this connection, it should be noted that the Teststellen were not evenly spread over the Catholic Epistles; there were relatively many in Jude (11 out of 95), so the results are not immediately applicable to other books.

Chapter Two

Papyrus 72 and the
*Bodmer Miscellaneous Codex**

Introduction

In the 1950s, the Swiss collector and patron of the arts Martin Bodmer acquired a collection of ancient Egyptian papyri in Greek and Coptic. As these manuscripts were published their tremendous historical value was soon acknowledged.[1] Most biblical scholars are familiar with the Bodmer Papyri, which were to give NT textual study a new boost; $\mathfrak{P}^{66}$ (around 200), $\mathfrak{P}^{72}$ (3rd-4th century), $\mathfrak{P}^{74}$ (7th century), $\mathfrak{P}^{75}$ (early 3rd century) and $\mathfrak{P}^{73}$ (a tiny fragment from the 7th century).

$\mathfrak{P}^{72}$ contains the entire text of 1-2 Peter and Jude and is the earliest known manuscript of these epistles.[2] However, these biblical texts designated as $\mathfrak{P}^{72}$ are bound with other works into a single codex (henceforth called the *Bodmer codex* for convenience). Unfortunately, NT scholars have tended to focus only on the text of $\mathfrak{P}^{72}$, disregarding the rest of the codex. Something similar has been true for the other works contained in the codex as well. In fact, when we consider the history of this codex as a whole, a consistent pattern of division and specialization is observable, a pattern that conceals the comprehensive picture of the historical context in which the codex once existed. First, the codex has been disassembled; second, today the manuscript is divided between Geneva and the Vatican; third, it took decades before the provenance of the discovery was made known; fourth, the texts of the codex were given nine different designations (*P.Bodmer* V, *P.Bodmer* VII, etc.), edited and dispersed in five different publications; and, finally, the specialization among scholars of different fields and interests has made the situation worse.

---

* This chapter is a revised version of an article with the same title, published in *NTS* 51 (2005): 137-54.

[1] From 1954 onwards, the University of Geneva has published a number of these MSS in the series *Bibliotheca Bodmeriana*.

[2] In addition, a few verses of Jude are extant in a fragment, $\mathfrak{P}^{78}$, dated to the 3rd-4th centuries.

Few scholars have attempted to examine the codex as a whole in order to get as complete a picture as possible of its historical context. Therefore my aim will be to examine the codex from several aspects—codicological, palaeographic, text-critical, literary, and theological—and, it is hoped, this investigation will allow us to get a glimpse of that context; the scribes involved in the production, the person(s) who collected the different writings of the codex, the kind of purpose it served, and in what kind of community it existed. From considerations of space, however, an extensive examination of the theological themes of the codex is treated elsewhere.[3]

1. The Context of the Bodmer Codex

Today, the Bodmer codex is disassembled, but originally it must have comprised at least 190 written pages in an almost cubic format, 15.5-16 x 14-14.5 cm.[4] The small format along with other clues led the first editor of the majority of the texts, Michel Testuz, to conclude that it was originally produced by Egyptian Christians for private use, probably for the private library of a rich member of the community, rather than for public reading in the church.[5] Testuz also found evidence in $\mathfrak{P}^{72}$ (specifically in 1-2 Peter) that made him attribute it to a Christian Coptic scribe working in the neighbourhood of Egyptian Thebes. The scribe had added marginal notes in 1-2 Peter in rather haphazard Greek, usually summarizing the meaning of the text, introduced with the preposition περί followed by a variety of cases (mostly the nominative and not the required genitive).[6] On one occasion, in 2 Pet 2:22, the note is in Coptic where the scribe has glossed the word αληθου with the Coptic word ΠΜΕΪ.[7] Moreover, there are particular orthographic features—in particular the interchange of γ and κ—which indicate sound confusions by a Coptic ear, such as were common

---

[3] See Tobias Nicklas and Tommy Wasserman, "Theologische Linien im *Codex Bodmer Miscellani?*" in *New Testament Manuscripts: Their Texts and Their World* (ed. Thomas J. Kraus and Tobias Nicklas; TENT 2; Leiden: Brill, 2006), 161-88.

[4] The *Apology of Phileas* is quite fragmentary, and some other leaves from the codex are missing. Today only 172 pages are extant (Klaus Junack and Winfried Grunewald, eds., *Das Neue Testament auf Papyrus.* I: *Die Katholischen Briefe* [ANTF 6; Berlin/New York: de Gruyter, 1986], 17; Michel Testuz, ed., *Papyrus Bodmer VII-IX* [Cologny-Geneva: Bibliotheca Bodmeriana, 1959], 8).

[5] Testuz, *Papyrus Bodmer VII-IX*, 9-10.

[6] The Coptic has numerous loanwords from the Greek in the nominative. There are no case endings in Coptic. Cf. Bruce M. Metzger, *The Early Versions of the New Testament* (Oxford: Clarendon, 1977), 141-52.

[7] Testuz refers to another marginal note in 2 Pet 2:8, ορασις that may count as Coptic here, since, unlike the word it glosses, βλεμματι, the same word is used in Coptic (Testuz, *Papyrus Bodmer VII-IX*, 33).

around Thebes.[8] G. D. Kilpatrick, however, was more cautious since he found sound changes typical of other parts of southern Egypt, e.g., Panopolis, and, thus, he suggested a less precise localization somewhere between Panopolis and Thebes.[9]

James M. Robinson devoted much effort to tracing the provenance of the Bodmer Papyri, to which this codex belongs. He found that the manuscripts had apparently passed through the hands of numerous intermediaries before they arrived at Geneva.[10] Robinson eventually learned that they were part of a find of manuscripts stuffed in a jar that was discovered in 1952 about 5.5 km north-west of the town Dishna in Egypt (between the ancient Panopolis and Thebes). The jar, found within a stone's throw of the Pachomian headquarters (situated at the foot of the mountain Jabal Abu Mana), contained a collection of some 50 MSS, among which were several copies of Pachomius' letters. Hence, Robinson identified the find as a "Pachomian monastic library."[11] Apart from Pachomian letters, this library consisted of various biblical and Christian writings, literary works such as Homer and Menander, and non-literary material, for example a school-boy's Greek exercises, a Greek grammar, and a Greek-Latin lexicon for deciphering Pauline epistles. According to the records of the monastery, funeral processions moved from the monastery up to higher ground where the monks buried their dead; apparently, they had also secreted their library here. Today, this original find is referred to as the *Dishna Papers* and the material is scattered among eight different repositories, of which the Bodmer Library and the Chester Beatty Library are the most important.[12]

---

[8] Ibid., 30-33. For the specific location of Thebes, Testuz reports Rodolphe Kasser's opinion that the sound errors can be localized to this region. A "sound" error does not necessarily mean that the scribe took the text from dictation, since he or she may have read the text aloud (contra F. W. Beare, "Some Remarks on the Text of I Peter in the Bodmer Papyrus [𝔓72]," in *Studia Evangelica* 3. Part 2: *The New Testament Message* [ed. F. L. Cross; TU 88; Berlin: Akademie-Verlag, 1964], 263). Numerous corrections of the same scribe point to a written original for 𝔓72.

[9] G. D. Kilpatrick, "The Bodmer and Mississippi Collection of Biblical and Christian Texts," *GRBS* 4 (1963): 34.

[10] James M. Robinson, *The Pachomian Monastic Library at the Chester Beatty Library and the Bibliothèque Bodmer* (Occasional Papers of the Institute for Antiquity and Christianity 19; Claremont: Institute for Antiquity and Christianity, 1990).

[11] It will be noted that the oldest MSS among the discovery predate the Pachomian Order and must have entered the library from outside (this would also explain the several non-Christian texts in the monastic library).

[12] For a full list of the contents of the discovery and current location, see Robinson, *The Pachomian Monastic Library*, 19-21.

2. The Contents of the Codex

The codex contains eleven writings, which were copied by a number of different scribes. Testuz included a useful overview (here somewhat modified) of the contents:[13]

Table 1: The contents of the Bodmer miscellaneous codex

TEXT	COPYIST	PAGINATION[14]	LINK[15]
1. *Nativity of Mary* (*P.Bodmer* V)	A	1-49	certain
2. *Apocryphal Correspondence* (X) (between Paul and the Corinthians = *3 Corinthians*)	B	50-57	certain
3. 11th *Ode of Solomon* (XI)	B	57-62	certain
4. Jude (VII)	B	62-68	certain
5. Melito's *Homily on the Passion* (XIII)	A	1-63	certain
6. A fragment of a liturgical hymn (XII)	A	64	uncertain
7. *Apology of Phileas* (XX)	C	129-146?[16]	certain
8. LXX Psalms 33:2-34:16 (IX)	D	147-151?	uncertain
9. 1-2 Peter (VIII)	B	1-36	

---

[13] Testuz, *Papyrus Bodmer VII-IX*, 8.

[14] The codex contains three or four different (ancient) pagination complexes. Testuz supposed that the *Apology of Phileas* and Psalms 33-34 continued complex 1 (pp. 1-68) and complex 2 (1-64), but that the scribe made a miscalculation starting the *Apology* with p. 129 instead of p. 133—or p. 132, since there is a pagination error within the *Ode of Solomon* (Testuz, *Papyrus Bodmer VII-IX*, 9). See below.

[15] "Link" refers to the establishing of a codicological connection between the different writings so as to decide the order of the writings in the final form of the codex (a work of reconstruction since the codex is disassembled). For example, the link between the 11th *Ode of Solomon* and Jude is certain since the same scribe (B) concludes the *Ode* on the same page as Jude commences.

[16] Page numbers are found in one folio of the *Apology* which enable a reconstruction backwards.

3. The Production of the Codex

The question of how the codex reached its final form has been a matter of controversy, and the answer will have implications for a number of aspects, such as dating, isolation of scribal tendencies and detection of possible motifs behind the collection of these particular texts. Regarding the specific dating of $\mathfrak{P}^{72}$, it is necessary to look for evidence beyond the copyist's (or copyists') handwriting, because of its very personal and informal character. Moreover, it should be pointed out that the *Apology of Phileas* offers a *terminus post quem*, since this work has been securely dated to the first decade of the 4th century—the trial against Phileas took place somewhere between 303-307 C.E. The date for this text, however, may have different implications depending on the identification of its links with the other texts. The discussion to the present time may be summarized by three different viewpoints, represented in turn by Testuz, Eric G. Turner and Winfried Grunewald:[17]

1. Depending on his identification of four scribes at work, and the links between the writings (see Table 1), Testuz argued that the codex contains three different collections that once existed separately, corresponding to the scribes A, B (both dated to the 3rd century by Testuz) and, finally, the combination C+D (!), dated to the 4th century (post 304-307), when the codex reached its final form. Testuz found traces of two sets of binding throughout the whole codex.[18] Moreover, he argued that the scribe of the *Apology* and the Psalms (the latest writings) was responsible also for the pagination of the fragment of a hymn, and that the pagination of this section was a continuation of the two preceding pagination complexes. Hence, Testuz assumed that the Epistles of Peter, constituting a new pagination complex, concluded the codex. In his reconstruction, he stated that a blank folio followed the last numbered page of this complex. The blank folio had, apparently, served as an outer protection.

2. Turner identified six hands behind the texts: hand 1: the *Nativity of Mary*; hand 2: the *Apocryphal Correspondence* (= 3 *Cor.*), the 11th *Ode* and Jude; hand 3: Melito's *Homily on the Passion*; hand 4: the *Apology of Phileas*; hand 5: Psalms 33-34 (LXX); hand 6: 1-2 Peter (information is missing about the hymn fragment). Turner concluded that (a) the codex was probably produced within a short period of time, not much earlier than the 4th

---

[17] Testuz, *Papyrus Bodmer VII-IX*, 8-9; Eric G. Turner, *The Typology of the Codex* (Pennsylvania, PA: University of Pennsylvania Press, 1977), 8, 79-80; Junack and Grunewald, *Die Katholischen Briefe*, 16-25.

[18] Cf. the plate (not paginated) in Michel Testuz, ed., *Papyrus Bodmer XIII* (Cologny-Geneva: Bibliotheca Bodmeriana, 1960).

century; (b) all of the links between the texts were certain (except that between Jude and Melito) and; (c) the parts of this "composite codex" were probably copied intentionally in the above order—especially so, according to Turner, if scribe B really had copied $\mathfrak{P}^{72}$, found in two separate sections. Behind Turner's designation *composite* lies his suspicion that scribes did not care to waste any writing material and would wish to fill any free pages left over at the end of a codex. According to Turner, this gradual process of growth explained the existence of codices like "P. Bodmer Composite," containing "heterogeneous material." The composite codex would be distinguished from the *miscellany* in which several texts of different authors, but more or less homogenous (e.g., sharing a common theme), would be organized in a single container.[19]

Turner did express some hesitation, since one section of the codex, *P.Bodmer* XIII+XII, is 0.5 cm larger in size compared to what would have been earlier and later sections, thus giving impression of what could have been an earlier and distinct collection. However, Turner allowed for this discrepancy in size, since "in c. iv A.D. in such an ancient papyrus book small differences in page or sheet sizes were readily tolerated."[20] Another apparent problem with Turner's assumption of gradual growth over a short period of time is the odd pagination.

It is important to bear in mind that the Bodmer Library, to Turner's great regret, did not give him the opportunity to examine the physical codex, so he had to account for evidence derived from Testuz, whose information was incomplete in several aspects, e.g., the palaeographic evidence for his identification of scribes. Turner came to his different conclusions after examining the very few photographic reproductions of the codex (approximately one plate per book).[21]

3. Grunewald could offer a correction of Turner's analysis after a correspondence with the current holders of the codex, the Bodmer Library (except for 1-2 Peter, today kept in the Vatican Library in Rome). The new

---

[19] For definitions and discussion of the composite and miscellaneous book, see Armando Petrucci, *Writers and Readers in Medieval Italy: Studies in the History of Written Culture* (New Haven, CT: Yale University, 1995), 1-2.

[20] Turner, *Typology*, 8. It will be noted that many of the pages are damaged especially at the top of the page. Kurt Aland estimates the reconstructed format as 16 x 14.5 cm (*Repertorium der griechischen christlichen Papyri*. I: *Biblische Papyri: Altes Testament, Neues Testament, Varia, Apokryphen* [PTS 18; Berlin/New York: de Gruyter, 1976], 303). Naturally, the edges of the larger section would be more liable to damage.

[21] Earlier, Jean Duplacy had also questioned Testuz' identification of the same scribal hand at work in Jude and 1-2 Peter ("Bulletin de critique textuelle du NT," *RSR* 50 [1962]: 253).

codicological data had to do with the make-up of the quires.[22] Grunewald concluded that the link between Jude and Melito was certain (contra Turner) and thus belonged to "series I." In this connection, however, it should be pointed out that the last gathering of series I concludes with a folio containing the end of Jude (verso) and an unpaginated page (recto) with only the title, Μελιτωνος περι πασχα.[23] The actual text of the *Homily* begins in the next gathering, of which the two first pages are now lost. There is, therefore, the possibility that the *Homily* once constituted an independent section, which, at a later stage, was placed after Jude—the new pagination and the different size favor this possibility.[24]

To continue with Grunewald's view, the *Apology of Phileas* and the Psalms formed a distinct set of quires ("series II"), as did also the Epistles of Peter ("series III"). In Turner's reconstruction, on the other hand, he had assumed a secure link between Melito and the *Apology*, since he reckoned that the title of the latter appeared on the last leaf of the preceding quire. To be sure, there are traces of text below the end of the hymn, but the defective state of this text makes Turner's assumption uncertain, which perhaps is indicated by his own question mark in the table displaying his reconstruction.[25] (As we have seen, the different size of this section also caused him to express some hesitation.)

In a similar way, Turner had indicated a secure link between the Psalms and the Epistles of Peter, since he assumed that the text of 1 Peter began in the same quire as the Psalms (although he put a question mark here too). Grunewald could not receive decisive information from Geneva concerning this part of the codex, since it is now in Rome, but he pointed to an important "Material-Beweis," mentioned by Testuz, which disproved Turner's reconstruction of the quires, and favored Testuz' original view of an uncertain link: "Bei den Petrusbriefen ist noch teilweise der Faden der Heftung vorhanden, ebenso in der Mitte jeder Lage ein Pergamentstreifen zum Schutz gegen die Heftung; auch im Judasbrief ist ein solcher in der Lagenmitte (zwischen Seite 65 und 66) noch zu sehen."[26] Here I may add that a similar parchment strip is visible in the only plate of the *Apocryphal Correspondence* in the *editio princeps*, which is that of page 50 (in the first

---

[22] A quire refers to a papyrus (or parchment) gathering. First, a sheet was folded, producing two leaves and four pages (*bifolium*). Then, the *bifolia* could be sewn together in gatherings, two forming a *binio*, three a *ternio*, four a *quaternio* (the most common), and so forth.

[23] See the first plate (not paginated) in Testuz, *Papyrus Bodmer XIII*.

[24] See the last plate in Testuz, *Papyrus Bodmer XIII*.

[25] Turner, *Typology*, 79-80 (Table 12).

[26] Junack and Grunewald, *Die Katholischen Briefe*, 20. Cf. Testuz: "Au centre de chaque cahier, se trouve une petite bande de renforcement en parchemin" (*Papyrus Bodmer VII-IX*, 29).

pagination complex of the codex)—also found in the middle of a quire.[27] Nevertheless, the report from Dr Braun of the Bodmer Library made Grunewald question Testuz' reconstruction of the last gathering of the Epistles of Peter (pp. 31ff. of this pagination complex). Testuz had assumed that two single sheets followed after the two first quaternions, i.e., four quires making up a total of 40 pages (16 + 16 + 4 + 4). (The first two pages of the first gathering are lost and do not belong to the pagination complex.) As mentioned above, Testuz had found a blank folio, which he assumed had been a protective cover and he placed it at the end of the last gathering. According to Braun and Grunewald, however, pages 31ff. (= pp. 33ff. including the first two pages that are lost) must have been a "Mehrblattslage," i.e., a quaternion, or at least a ternion. If we consult the facsimile edition of Carlo M. Martini, it is possible to decide by looking at the fibre-direction of the pages.[28] If Testuz had been correct, pages 32-33 would have been the inside of a single folded sheet with the fibres running in the same direction. However, since this is not the case I must confirm the conclusion of Braun and Grunewald. Although Grunewald was not explicit on the matter, this state of affairs means that another text, now lost, probably followed 2 Peter. Furthermore, the blank folio that Testuz placed right after the last paginated page of this gathering must have belonged elsewhere—it may still have been at the end of the last gathering but not immediately after 2 Peter.[29]

The established distinction of three series seems to speak in favor of Testuz' hypothesis of earlier collections brought together. On the other hand, Grunewald pointed out that the separation of series I and III is disturbing for Testuz: why would a later collector separate the works of the same scribe (Testuz' "B") and squeeze in a distinct later collection? (Turner would have interpreted this as conclusive evidence that the whole codex was produced in a short period of time, had he agreed with Testuz' identification of scribe B.) Do we have to assume a different scribe for 1-2 Peter, then? Grunewald offers an alternative explanation. He sees the *Apology* and the Psalms as originally part of another collection (thus the odd pagination), and this detached part came to form the nucleus of a new collection, so that the other seven texts of scribes A and B, written at a later

---

[27] Michel Testuz, ed., *Papyrus Bodmer X-XII* (Cologny-Geneva: Bibliotheca Bodmeriana, 1959) (unpaginated after p. 6).

[28] Carlo M. Martini, ed., *Beati Petri Apostoli Epistulae ex papyro bodmeriana VIII transcriptae* (Milan: ex Hamilcaris Pizzi officina libraria, 1968). Martini's transcription is accompanied by a replica of $\mathfrak{P}^{72}$ (1-2 Peter).

[29] Cf. Junack and Grunewald, *Die Katholischen Briefe*, 19-20.

stage, were then grouped around this nucleus in a conscious order for certain theological-dogmatic reasons.[30]

It is true that theological motivations could explain any order in the final collection, and scholars have indeed found evidence of theological motivation behind the collection (see below). However, we must first ask ourselves: is there any evidence for the assumption that the writings of the codex followed in the actual order originally suggested by Testuz, and accepted by other scholars like Turner and Grunewald? Grunewald presented conclusive evidence that there were three separate sections, but his data says nothing of the original order of these sections—in this regard, he seems to take Testuz' reconstruction for granted, and the position of section II, separating $\mathfrak{P}^{72}$, was one of the main reasons for his "nucleus theory." But, in fact, Grunewald questioned two of Testuz' very reasons for this order, i.e., first, the assumption that the pagination of the *Apology* and Psalms (section II) was a continuation from section I (with a miscalculation of four pages), and, secondly, Testuz' reconstruction of the last gathering of the codex.[31] We know that the blank folio that Testuz placed at the end of the codex did not follow immediately upon the last page of the Epistles of Peter, but it could still have been present at the end of the codex. On the other hand this unpaginated folio may represent the two missing pages at the beginning of the Epistles of Peter, since the pagination starts on the page where the text commences. This folio could still have functioned as a protective cover—at the beginning of 1-2 Peter. It would be interesting to know more about the state in which the codex reached Geneva before it was disassembled. However, Victor Martin's description of *P.Bodmer* XX (*ed.pr.*) confirms that section II was combined by Testuz with the other sections found among the material at the Bodmer Library in the first place, solely because of the similar format and because of his theory concerning the pagination.[32]

In conclusion, it is not necessary to retain the reconstructed order of section I-III. On the contrary, there are signs that connect sections I and

---

[30] Ibid., 23-24.

[31] "Überzeugender [than a miscalculation] ist aber die Ansicht, daß die Phileas-Apologie Teil eines anderen ‚Sammelcodex' gewesen ist, dessen Reste wir nicht mehr haben" (ibid., 18).

[32] Victor Martin, ed., *Papyrus Bodmer XX* (Cologny-Geneva: Bibliotheca Bodmeriana, 1964), 8-9. Martin did express some hesitation: "La liaison de plusieurs d'entre eux est assurée par des indices physiques. Toutefois, précisément pour l'Apologie de Phileas, cette certitude fait defaut." Nevertheless, he identified a theological connection between all of the writings, and he pointed out that the odd pagination did not have to be original and that an extensive work like the *Apology* would more naturally comprise a codex of its own had its inclusion in the collection not been conscious.

III, and it is likely that they followed in sequence, whereas section II was placed either at the beginning or the end in the final collection. The first and obvious connection is 𝔓⁷², provided that it was produced by one and the same scribe—a question to which we will return. However, there is another piece of evidence in the remarkably similar colophons in some of the writings, the *Nativity*, Melito's *Homily* (both section I) and 1-2 Peter (section III), while the *Apology* (section II) has a distinct and more common colophon:

ειρηνη τω γραψαντι και τω αναγινωσκοντι (the *Nativity*, 1 and 2 Peter)
ιρηνη τω γραψαντι και τω αναγινωσκοντι και τοις αγαπωσι τον κ͞υ (Melito's *Homily*)
ιρηνη τοις αγειοις πασει (the *Apology of Phileas*)

These colophons strengthen the impression of section II (the *Apology* and the Psalms) as being a "Fremdkörper" (to use Grunewald's designation) and, at the same time, the difference speaks against Turner's hypothesis of one single production. If section II with the *Apology* were the nucleus of the collection (so Grunewald), one would perhaps have expected assimilation to the colophon in the *Apology* on the part of the other scribes. Moreover, Grunewald's hypothesis is open to another important reservation—Testuz stated that he had found traces of two different bindings in the entire codex, not only in Grunewald's series II, and, if this is true, it follows that the other seven texts had formed at least one, but possibly two or three, earlier collections (three if the title-page of Melito's *Homily* was not original). Of course, there is also the possibility that a second binding represents a repair of a damaged original binding.

Hence, according to my view, sections I and III were probably produced over a short period of time, and included in sequence in the final codex (possibly also in an earlier collection). At the end of section I we find a fragment of a hymn that gives the impression of being unfinished, or demanding some sort of continuation (other than Phileas' *Apology*).[33] Below line 6, where the text ends, we find traces of what Turner interpreted as the title of the *Apology*. If we then turn to the beginning of section III, Grunewald confirms Testuz' reconstruction of the first gathering (a quaternion) of *P.Bodmer* VIII. The text of 1 Peter commences on the third page of the reconstructed gathering (a quaternion), but with a new pagination, and the two preceding pages, now lost, could have contained

---

[33] Cf. Othmar Perler, *Ein Hymnus zur Ostervirgil von Meliton?* (Freiburg: Universitätsverlag Freiburg, 1960), 9: "Die 6 Zeilen geben einen vollständigen Sinn, der aber eine Fortsetzung verlangt."

another short text, perhaps a psalm (so Testuz).[34] If section III followed section I, it would be possible that the text below the short hymn was a title of another hymn or psalm that followed in Grunewald's section III (within the same pagination complex?).[35]

There is another important clue that connects section I and III; there is a liturgical connection between the 11th *Ode*, Melito's *Homily*, the hymnal fragment and 1 Peter.[36] This is not to say that the Bodmer codex was actually used in church services. The strong liturgical connections between some of the writings could be explained by the fact that these texts were transmitted in a liturgical context and, therefore, could have been brought together earlier in the manuscript tradition and continued to travel as a unit within the stream of transmission.[37]

In conclusion, we may at this stage firmly reject Turner's gradual-growth view and accept a collection-hypothesis. As to section II, the odd pagination, traces of two bindings and the different colophon suggest that it was once part of a different collection. At some point this section was probably added to another collection (section I and III), possibly at the beginning of the codex. Hence, this explanation enables an earlier dating of $\mathfrak{P}^{72}$ (3rd century), but the question remains open when exactly this part of the codex was produced. However, the hands of the other scribes who copied the *Nativity* and Melito's *Homily* cannot be dated much earlier than 300 C.E.

From the text-critical point of view one could look for possible harmonization on the part of the scribes, which could reveal dependence in any direction: 1 Peter contains citations and allusions from Ps 33 (LXX), and there are also citations of and allusions to both Jude and 1-2 Peter in

---

[34] Testuz, *Papyrus Bodmer VII-IX*, 29. Cf. Junack and Grunewald, *Die Katholischen Briefe*, 19.

[35] It will be noted that this sequence would exclude the possibility that the title-page of Melito was originally empty. If that were the case, the sequence III-I-II seems more likely.

[36] Significantly, another papyrus codex, originally belonging to the Dishna Papers, the Coptic Crosby-Schøyen codex, contains Melito of Sardis' *Homily on the Passion*; 2 Macc 5:27-7:41 (a martyrology section); 1 Peter; Jonah; and a homily or hymn. This codex is the only comparable item to our Bodmer codex among the Dishna Papers; it is approximately of the same cubic format, 15 x 15 cm; it has been identified as the oldest Christian liturgical MS; and it would be defined as a miscellany since at least the four first texts probably have a common denominator in the theme of Easter. For a description, see James E. Goehring, ed., *The Crosby-Schøyen Codex MS 193 in the Schøyen Collection* (CSCO 521; Leuven: Peeters, 1990).

[37] Cf. Petrucci's observation: "It [the miscellaneous book] was influenced by the liturgical model, characterized by a succession of different passages handsomely laid out in sequence for uses extraneous to their origins (homiliaries, Gospels, etc). In short, the miscellaneous book corresponded to a conception of texts that was both global and hierarchical, in whose circle the individual textual segments, rather than being considered autonomous, were seen as parts of a whole" (*Writers and Readers*, 9).

the *Nativity* and Melito (the latter also cites LXX Ps 34).[38] However, a survey of these passages shows that there are no overall traces of textual harmonization on the part of the scribes in any direction. On the other hand, the rich amount of scriptural cross-references and common theological themes in the codex does support the notion of a consciously theologically motivated collection, even on the part of the final collector.

Theological reasons for the composition of the codex were suggested at an date by Martin in the introduction to his edition of the *Apology of Phileas*, where he pointed to the theological and apologetic character of the writings.[39] Recently, however, Kim Haines-Eitzen expressed a slight dissatisfaction with Martin's "rather general explanation" of the motive behind the collection, and she singled out the theme of the *body* as "perhaps the most pervasive" in the texts of the codex and offered several examples from the texts.[40] The body is certainly an important theme in the codex; however, one may well hesitate to call it "the most pervasive." Since the final codex is probably made up of earlier collections, an identification of one single pervasive theme seems problematic. The final collector may have had one particular theme in mind, but more probably this person somehow found a common denominator in the texts. In any case, the texts in question apparently filled an important purpose for the collector(s), who probably belonged to an Egyptian proto-Orthodox community (it is impossible to identify any particular group), since several characteristics typical of incipient orthodoxy are prominent in practically all of the texts, especially in the area of Christology.[41] This not only applies to the writings themselves, but is also an observable tendency even on the level of scribal transmission, as far as singular readings can be identified (especially in $\mathfrak{P}^{72}$—see below). For example, Jesus is typically identified as God, which means both that Jesus as pre-existent worked in the history of Israel, and, conversely, that it was God who suffered on the cross (see e.g., the *Nativity of Mary* 15:4; *3 Cor.* 3:15; Jd 5; the *Apology of Phileas* cols. 7-8; Melito's *Homily on the Passion* 96; 1 Pet 1:11; 5:1).

It is clearly impossible to know who the final collector was. If all of the writings were first part of earlier collections, it would not necessarily have

---

[38] 1 Pet 2:3 (LXX Ps 33:9), 3:10-12 (LXX 33:13-17); *Nativity of Mary* 3:2 (2 Pet 2:12; Jude 10), 7:2 (2 Pet 3:3), 9:2 (Jude 11), 15:4 (1 Pet 5:6), 25:1 (2 Pet 3:15); Melito's *Homily on the Passion* 12 (1 Pet 1:19), 22 (LXX Ps 34:5), 68 (1 Pet 2:9), 72 (LXX Ps 34:12).

[39] Martin, *Papyrus Bodmer XX*, 9.

[40] Kim Haines-Eitzen, *Guardians of Letters: Literacy, Power, and the Transmitters of Early Christian Literature* (Oxford: Oxford University Press, 2000), 103-4.

[41] See further Nicklas and Wasserman, "Theologische Linien im *Codex Bodmer Miscellani?*" in *New Testament Manuscripts*, 185-88.

to be any of the scribes involved. However, there is at least one good candidate among them: as we shall see, the scribe of 𝔓⁷² has been ascribed a theological (or Christological) tendency, and this could well be in line with those theological reasons, that may have led him to collect all of the writings in the codex (it would, of course, imply a later dating of 𝔓⁷², post Phileas' *Apology*. In the following, I will limit myself to a detailed examination of 𝔓⁷², since the result will have a number of implications for the question of the origin of the codex and its parts.

4. The Production of 𝔓⁷²

The first question we must deal with is the number of scribes responsible for 𝔓⁷². We have seen that Turner argued for two different scribes. If he is correct, it would of course enable a differentiation of the dating of 𝔓⁷², and, moreover, the question of the origin of the codex would be even more complex. Haines-Eitzen devotes a chapter in her study to an analysis of this codex.[42] She refers to Turner's description of the codex and provides some more arguments for his identification of six scribes in all. In her own examination of the handwriting and textual characteristics she notices significant differences between the *Nativity of Mary*, on the one hand, and Melito's *Homily* and the fragment of a hymn on the other hand (the different style of sigmas and omicrons, differences in the abbreviations of *nomina sacra* and in punctuation, etc.). Secondly, she adduces similar arguments in favor of different scribes for Jude and the Epistles of Peter. However, Haines-Eitzen admits that she, like Turner, has worked from the few photographic reproductions that Testuz provides for these texts, and that they are more problematic than for the *Nativity* and Melito since "the one plate provided of the Epistles of Peter is one in which the original hand was traced over."[43]

It is not necessary to doubt the judgment concerning different scribes for the *Nativity of Mary* and Melito.[44] However, in the following, I shall examine more closely Haines-Eitzen's arguments concerning different scribes for

---

[42] Haines-Eitzen, *Guardians*, 96-104.

[43] Ibid., 98. In n. 87 she mentions her failed effort to obtain a microfilm of the texts from the Bodmer Library, but that they planned a full photographic reproduction—one that has now appeared: *Bibliotheca Bodmeriana: La collection des papyrus Bodmer* (ed. Martin Bircher; 10 vols. Munich: K. G. Saur, 2000).

[44] Testuz himself later admitted this: see Èmile de Strycker, *La Forme la plus ancienne du protévangile de Jacques: Recherches sur Le Papyrus Bodmer 5 avec une édition critique de texte grec et une traduction annotée* (Subsidia Hagiographica 33; Brussells: Société des Bollandistes, 1961), 22, n. 4.

Jude and the Epistles of Peter. Haines-Eitzen had complained that she could not obtain microfilms of the texts from Geneva, but that is unnecessary since the part containing 1-2 Peter has been kept in the Vatican since the early 1960s. In 1968 a facsimile edition of the Epistles of Peter was published along with a transcription of the text edited by C. M. Martini.[45] Moreover, Michael Lattke published a facsimile edition of *P.Bodmer* XI (the 11th *Ode of Solomon*; same scribe as Jude).[46] These two publications provide sufficient material for a detailed palaeographic analysis.

4.1 The Hand of the Scribe

Firstly, Haines-Eitzen starts with a description of Jude's hand that "tends toward cursive," while "by contrast, the Epistles of Peter are written in a hand that attempts to avoid (quite painstakingly) cursively formed letters and ligatures."[47] For example, α, υ and η are made in one stroke, whenever possible, in Jude, and ligatures like λη or αι appear frequently. In the Epistles of Peter, on the other hand, she finds multistroke letters, e.g.,in the formation of υ (the standard uncial form Υ is used), and ligatures like those in Jude are absent.

Haines-Eitzen is quite correct in her analysis, except for one thing: she refers to the palaeographic data of "the Epistles of Peter" although she had access to only one plate. However, if we consult Martini's facsimile edition we find a gradual shift towards an increasingly cursive hand, and the scribe does indeed use the same type of ligatures (λη, αι, etc.) and letters (e.g., not only the uncial Υ) as in Jude. Significantly, this gradual shift corresponds to the error rate of the scribe (see below). The varying form of individual letters, ligatures and other textual features gives an overall impression of an inexperienced and careless scribe displaying all sorts of irregularities. Hence, the informal and personal character of this hand makes a

---

[45] Martini, *Beati Petri*; a plate showing the last page of 1 Peter is also available in F. V. Filson, "More Bodmer Papyri," *BA* 25 (1962): 53, and in Kurt Aland and Barbara Aland, *The Text of the New Testament: An Introduction to the Critical Editions and to the Theory and Practice of Modern Textual Criticism* (trans. Erroll F. Rhodes; 2d rev. and enl. ed.; Grand Rapids: Eerdmans, 1995), 92 (plate 25).

[46] M. Lattke, *Die Oden Salomos in ihrer Bedeutung für Neues Testament und Gnosis* (4 vols.; OBO 25; Göttingen: Vandenhoeck & Ruprecht, 1979-1998) 1980 (note that this is vol. 1a).

[47] All citations in this discussion are from Haines-Eitzen, *Guardians*, 98-99. In an earlier chapter Haines-Eitzen refers to only one copyist of 𝔓[72]. This probably reflects an earlier stage of her research, and at this point she wrongly attributed the edition of the text to Victor Martin (ibid., 67, 159, n. 78).

comparison with dated papyri difficult and in itself allows any date ranging from the second to the fourth centuries.[48]

4.2 The Orthography

In her discussion of the orthography, Haines-Eitzen states that the itacisms are different, for example the interchange of ι/ει in the title of Jude, ιουδα επειστολη, does not occur in the Epistle of Peter: "the title appears (four times!) as πετρου επιστολη (at the beginning and end of the first and second Epistles). The consistency with which these scribes spell the titles is significant." We can assume that Jude and 1-2 Peter were copied on two different occasions (also indicated by the codicological evidence), and we do not know how much time elapsed between the occasions, but a simple explanation is that the scribe made a single error in Jude. During the period that he or she was copying the Epistles of Peter the scribe consistently spelled επιστολη correctly. However, in a number of places the scribe still has general difficulty with the interchange of ει/ι: αρτει (1 Pet 1:8), περει x 2 (1 Pet 1:10), επειθυμειαις (1 Pet 1:15), πειστειν (1 Pet 1:21) and τεις (1 Pet 2:19); θιας (2 Pet 1:3), διγμα (2 Pet 2:6) and δι (2 Pet 3:11, for δεῖ). Other examples of itacisms include the interchange of αι/ε, χερειν (3 *Cor.* 1:1), κε (3 *Cor.* 3:32, for καί), παλε (Jude 4), Εγυπτου (Jude 5), κε (1 Pet 1:17, for καί), ε (1 Pet 3:1, for αἱ), βεβεαν (2 Pet 1:10) (more rarely αι for ε).

I could go on and list a number of other orthographic features, some of which are isolated and others that occur regularly, but that would make this discussion too long. However, we must consider Haines-Eitzen's argument that the particular orthographic features that indicate a Coptic scribe are only applicable to 1-2 Peter, not to Jude. She explicitly mentions the sound confusion between γ and κ, but this type of error does occur in Jude 5 (εγ for εκ), although it is certainly more frequent in the Epistles of Peter. In any case, the different frequency of certain sound confusions can be due to all sorts of factors surrounding the different occasions on which the texts were copied.

4.3 Errors and Corrections

According to James Royse, who studied the scribe of $\mathfrak{P}^{72}$, there are 52 corrections, most of which are misspellings and obvious blunders, only two

---

[48] Cf. Kurt Aland's description: "unliterarische Hand mit Unregelmässigkeiten in den Abständen der litt und auch der Zeilenführung; Tendenz zur Kursive; gegen Ende der Briefe grössere Nachlässigkeit der Schrift" (*Repertorium*, 1:303).

of which appear to be by a hand other than the scribe's (2 Pet 1:8; 3:9).[49] Regrettably, Royse did not examine the other two writings copied by the same scribe, i.e., the *Ap. Corr.* (= 3 *Cor.*) and the 11th *Ode.* This symptom, as described earlier, is true also of the latter two works, but in examinations of scribal tendencies scholars have tended to focus exclusively on the writing that has caught their particular interest.[50]

There are approximately a dozen corrections in the *Ode*, and about as many in 3 *Cor.* Missing letters are placed supralinearly, while the scribe has either marked superfluous letters/words by supralinear dots, e.g., in οναυτος, εντυπον (3 *Cor.* 1:6; 3:7), κυματα (Jude 13), κοσκμος (2 Pet 3:6), or else they are bracketed, erased, crossed out or overwritten—there is absolutely no regular system, (cf. the word αντιτασσεσται in 1 Pet 5:5 marked with both dots and a bracket). Two corrections involving larger omissions (in Jude 16 and *Ode Sal.* 11:16) are marked with a so-called "ancora," a small arrow in the margin of the line and again at the bottom of the page, followed by the missing words. Most of the time, however, the errors are left uncorrected, some of which are irregular and others consistent, e.g., ζοη for ζωή (Jude 21; 1 Pet 3:10; 2 Pet 1:3, *Ode Sal.* 11:6) and even more significant, ζοη εωνιου (1 Pet 3:7) and ζοη εωνιας (*Ode Sal.* 11:16).

Royse, in his study of the singular readings of 𝔓[72], noted that "the significant percentage of nonsense readings in 𝔓[72] and the very large percentage of singulars resulting from non-standard spelling show that the scribe of 𝔓[72] was extraordinarily careless" but that the scribe "can also be seen to have increased the rate of production of nonsense as he went farther with his copying."[51] This textual pattern is true for both the Epistle of Jude and the Epistles of Peter, and it actually corresponds to the palaeographic data—the hand is more careless towards the end of each epistle.

4.4 *Nomina sacra* and Non-Greek Proper Names

Haines-Eitzen also appeals to the difference in *nomina sacra*: "in Jude, Ἰησοῦ Χριστοῦ is always abbreviated as ιηυ χρυ; by contrast at the very opening of

---

[49] James R. Royse, "Scribal Habits in Early Greek New Testament Papyri" (Th.D. diss., Graduate Theological Union, 1981), 476.

[50] Besides the *editio princeps* for each work, cf. Lattke, *Die Oden*, 1:10-23 (the 11th *Ode*); Vahan Hovhanessian, "Third Corinthians: Reclaiming Paul for Christian Orthodoxy" (Ph.D. diss., Fordham University, 1998), 211-27; Junack and Grunewald, *Die Katholischen Briefe*, 20-23 (𝔓[72]); Royse, "Scribal Habits," 470-510 (𝔓[72]).

[51] Royse, "Scribal Habits," 475.

1 Peter, the scribe offers ιῡ χρῡ (1 Pet 1:1, 2)." However, in the light of the fact that either ιηυ or ιης occur at all other places in 1-2 Peter (17 times), this argument loses its force completely. More significantly, in both Jude and the Epistles of Peter we find that certain non-Greek proper names are marked with a stroke that does not cover the whole width of the name: Ενῶχ (Jude 14), Σαρρα, Αβρααμ (1 Pet 3:6), Νῶε (1 Pet 3:20).[52] Other names are marked with an apostrophe or left unmarked.

4.5 Diaeresis, Apostrophe, Spiritus and Punctuation

Some other textual features are regular and not isolated to any of the scribe's writing, e.g., the diaeresis used mostly over initial vowels ι and υ, or the apostrophe utilized to separate two similar neighbouring letters (mostly γ'γ or γ from a guttural). On the other hand, there are rare features like the apostrophe after a Hebrew name (only in 3 *Cor.* 3:32; 2 Pet 2:7, 15). There is virtually no punctuation (only in *Ode Sal.* 11:1; Jude 20; 1 Pet 4:9; 2 Pet 1:16). Hence, when Haines-Eitzen mentions that there are no breathing marks in Jude while such appear with some frequency in 1-2 Peter, this could be readily explained by reference to the irregularity of the scribe.

4.6 The Marginal Notes

In my estimate, Haines-Eitzen's strongest argument for a differentiation of the scribes is the existence of marginal notes in 1-2 Peter only, and in particular those notes that are introduced with a περί and serve to highlight themes in the text. Apparently they have nothing to do with the later use of *kephalaia*, and, like many other features described above, they occur irregularly. We have already mentioned that the preposition περί is often not followed by the genitive, which could be explained either by reference to the case in which the word is found in the text, or by the fact that we have to do with a Coptic scribe.[53] More surprising is the difference in spelling on a number of occasions when the same word occurs in the note and in the text, e.g., ιερατευμα (1 Pet 2:5, 9; ειερατευμα in the text), βασιλιον (1 Pet 2:9), ψεδοδιδασκαλοι (2 Pet 2:1). Why did the scribe not attempt to correct the discrepant spelling in the text? Most likely, the marginal notes were added at a later stage when the scribe read the text and formulated a proper thematic note, and this was simply not the time for proofreading and making additional corrections. We do not know why

---

[52] The overlines in standard *nomina sacra* always cover the whole width of the words; the indication of an overline over the second letter only, e.g., ιῡυ, follows the general transcription convention of this study, and is not an indication of a partial overline in the manuscript.

[53] Testuz, *Papyrus Bodmer VII-IX*, 33.

such marginal notes were not added to the other writings; perhaps these particular notes had something to do with the use of these epistles (didactic, apologetic?), or perhaps the scribe simply did not find an occasion to add marginal notes elsewhere.

4.7 The Theological and Liturgical Tendencies of the Scribe

Finally, we must consider the text itself. Marchant A. King commented upon three unique readings in $\mathfrak{P}^{72}$, one in each of the epistles, "giving evidence of the fullest acceptance of the deity of Christ by the scribe (or one of his predecessors) and the church in his area."[54] These are Jude 5b, 1 Pet 5:1a, and 2 Pet 1:2b. In Jude 5b, the usual reading is "the Lord" (who saved the people from Egypt), some MSS have "Jesus" (02 03 33C 81 88 323 424C 665 915 1739 *pc* **L:V K:S**) or "God" (04C2V 442 621 623 1845 *pc* **L:TV**mss **S:Ph**), while $\mathfrak{P}^{72}$ reads θεος χριστος ("God Christ"). This cannot be a conflation since no MS reads Χριστός." Moreover, in 1 Pet 5:1, $\mathfrak{P}^{72}$ reads "the sufferings of God" (instead of Christ) and in 2 Pet 1:2 it omits "and" after "God" so that the resulting text reads "in the knowledge of God our Lord Jesus." This could be a mere omission but fits very well with the two previously discussed readings, so that we have here a conscious theological change through which Jesus is identified as God.

Haines-Eitzen was well aware of these textual data since she refers to these particular changes in another chapter under the heading "singular readings indicating ideological modifications."[55] Bart Ehrman (who was the supervisor of Haines-Eitzen's dissertation on the same subject) has described these changes of $\mathfrak{P}^{72}$ under the heading "anti-adoptionistic corruptions."[56] We may well ask ourselves if it is justified to speak of a *Tendenz* if the scribe of Jude did not copy 1-2 Peter. It is of course possible that a specific theological tendency was shared by two scribes in the same community which led them both to modifications of their texts—this possibility is increased when we recall that the very collection of the codex seems to have been theologically motivated. However, if we apply the principle of Occam's razor, the simplest explanation is a theological tendency on the part of one singular scribe. In addition to the unique theological or, more specifically, Christological readings mentioned by King, one may also note Jude 25, where all other witnesses (with textual variation) attest to a single doxology (to God through Christ). In $\mathfrak{P}^{72}$,

---

[54] Marchant A. King, "Notes on the Bodmer Manuscript," *BSac* 121 (1964): 57.

[55] Haines-Eitzen, *Guardians*, 113.

[56] Bart D. Ehrman, *The Orthodox Corruption of Scripture: The Effect of Early Christological Controversies on the Text of the New Testament* (New York/Oxford: Oxford University Press, 1993), 85.

however, glory is ascribed to God and to Christ in a two-fold doxology, accentuating the divine glory and honour of Christ: μόνῳ θεῷ ἡμῶν αὐτῷ δόξα κράτος τίμη διὰ Ἰησοῦ Χριστοῦ τοῦ κυρίου ἡμων αὐτῷ δόξα καὶ μεγαλωσύνη.[57] The unique expansion in 𝔓[72] was perhaps indirectly inspired by other early Christian doxologies where the same nouns appear together with μεγαλωσύνη (Rev 5:13; *1 Clem.* 64:1; 65:2), but evidently it adheres to the pattern of Christological readings. Further, the reading of 𝔓[72] in 1 Pet 2:3 should be noted: ει εγευσασθαι [itacism] επειστευσατε οτι χ̅ρ̅ς̅ ο κ̅ς̅. The substitution Χριστός for χρηστός is shared by other witnesses (018 019 049 33 *al*), and is in line with a common wordplay in early Christianity, i.e., the referring of LXX quotations in which God is called χρηστός to Christ. 𝔓[72] further inserts ἐπιστεύσατε, which specifies the "tasting" as believing in Christ. In this way the scriptural allusion is now turned into a confessional formula, "Christ is Lord," that is to be believed. (Note also the use of the *nomen sacrum* in this passage in 𝔓[72].)

Another category of singular readings in 𝔓[72] that Haines-Eitzen discusses is that of harmonization.[58] Surprisingly, she has not drawn any conclusion on the question of the number of scribes for 𝔓[72] from this discussion, which in turn builds on Royse's aforementioned study.[59] Having stated that scribes of the early papyri harmonized their texts *infrequently*, she appeals to a high and significant frequency of harmonization in 𝔓[72]: "What is particularly striking in this copy [𝔓[72]] is the number of harmonizations that appear to be influenced by 'liturgical' usage of 'texts'." She then refers to a number of readings that Royse had isolated as harmonizations to remote parallels, in contrast to the more common harmonization to the immediate context. For example, in Jude 24a the scribe of 𝔓[72] has replaced φυλαξαι with the στηριξαι found in the doxology of Romans 16:25. In this case, however, Royse (and Haines-Eitzen) mistakenly regarded στηριξαι as a singular reading, since the word is transmitted in other witnesses, although the papyrus attests to a different word order (see my textual commentary on Jude 24). In 1 Peter 3:7c the scribe replaces ζωης with ζοης εωνιου (we have noted that this combination and spelling occurs also in *Ode Sal.* 11:16), and the latter expression was embedded within the liturgical hymns and

---

[57] Cf. Tobias Nicklas, "Der 'lebendige Text' des Neuen Testaments: Der *Judasbrief* in 𝔓[72] (*P.Bodmer* VII)," *ASE* 22 (2005): 220.

[58] Haines-Eitzen, *Guardians,* 72-73.

[59] Royse, 'Scribal Habits,' 481-83. In the 11th *Ode of Solomon* and the *Apocryphal Correspondence,* it is difficult to identify any scribal tendencies since these texts have been preserved in very few textual witnesses and, in Greek, we have only the texts in this codex.

prayers of the early church. Furthermore, in 2 Peter 1:20 the scribe writes προφητια και γραφη for προφητεία γραφῆς, which Haines-Eitzen suggests is an influence from literary and liturgical customs to make the distinction "prophets and scripture." Haines-Eitzen thus finds support for an identification of the scribe as "a member of a Christian community, whose participation in church services is evident in the text."[60]

Likewise, Barbara Aland points out that most of the harmonizations in 𝔓[72] stem from the "paraenetic language," which the scribe evidently masters well. However, she suggests that the particular reading in 2 Peter 1:20, προφητια και γραφη, was theologically motivated and reflects the conviction that both the prophetic Old Testament as well as the testimony of Christ in the New Testament, spoken of as γραφή by this time (3rd-4th centuries), were inspired by the Holy Spirit (cf. *3 Cor.* 3:10).[61]

In connection with the question of harmonization, one may also note the interesting fact that there is no apparent harmonization in any direction between the parallel accounts of Jude and 2 Peter in 𝔓[72] (see chapter 6).

5. Conclusions

The Bodmer codex was discovered at a site near the town of Dishna, in Egypt, and was probably part of a Pachomian monastic library. The codex contains eleven writings that probably stem from several earlier collections. Three independent sections have been identified, and there is reason to believe that the original order of the writings as suggested by Testuz is wrong. There are strong connections between sections I and III and they probably followed in sequence. The most significant connection is the fact that one single scribe is responsible for the copying of 𝔓[72].

This same scribe displays examples of liturgical/paraenetic harmonization, a trait that places him in the context of community life and church worship. On the other hand, the informal and personal character of the scribe's hand, and the many errors and irregularities in his text, suggest that at least these parts of the codex were probably produced for private, rather than liturgical, use. Moreover, the scribe of 𝔓[72] displays a theological

---

[60] Cf. also the reading of 𝔓[72] in Jd 20b: προσευχομενοι εαυτοις, possibly referring to communal prayer.

[61] Barbara Aland, "Welche Rolle spielen Textkritik und Textgeschichte für das Verständnis des Neuen Testaments? Frühe Leserperspektiven," *NTS* 52 (2006): 307-8. Aland also cites other variant readings of 𝔓[72] in 2 Pet 2:12 (om. γεγεννημενα); 2 Pet 2:14 (om. μεστους); 2 Pet 3:10 (ευρεθησεται; add λυομενα), which reflect an ability of the scribe to create intelligent solutions to difficulties and cruxes in the exemplar, which in turn should make us expect similar conscious modifications of the text elsewhere (ibid., 307, n. 14).

tendency, and this, in fact, qualifies him or her as a good candidate for the person responsible for the whole collection. Several scholars have suggested that there were certain theological reasons for the composition, and, indeed, the texts of the codex betray the influence of incipient orthodoxy, but to single out one specific theme is problematic, since the codex is made up of several earlier collections. I have proposed a liturgical connection between some of the writings. These texts were probably brought together earlier in the manuscript tradition (c.f. the Crosby-Schøyen codex), so, again, it is not necessary to conclude that the codex or its parts were actually used in church services.

Chapter Three

$\mathfrak{P}^{78}$ (*P. Oxy.* XXXIV 2684):
The Epistle of Jude on an Amulet?*

Introduction

In the *editio princeps* of *P. Oxy.* XXXIV 2684, known among biblical scholars as $\mathfrak{P}^{78}$, the first editor, P. J. Parsons, suggested, that "most probably we have to do with an amulet."[1] However, he pointed out that the textual content of this double leaf preserving four verses from the Epistle of Jude, is an odd choice of text for an amulet. During the years to follow, several scholars have concurred with the judgment that the MS was probably an amulet, but there has been disagreement about the range of verses in relation to the number of quires once extant; Kurt Treu concluded that the Epistle of Jude was too long for a single-quire codex, but, on the other hand, the whole text would not be necessary for an amulet.[2] However, Kurt Aland assumed that it was a single-quire codex and stated, "[Der Codex] diente vermutlich als Amulett, umfaßte aber wohl den ganzen Judasbrief."[3] Winfried Grunewald, in his work on the papyrus witnesses of the Catholic Letters, also agreed that $\mathfrak{P}^{78}$ could be an amulet, but, like the first editor, he expressed his surprise of the fact that this particular text would have been used for the purpose in question.[4] It was perhaps for this reason that he suggested the alternative function of a "Schmuckcodex."[5] An amulet could of course be worn for both purposes. However, the very

---

* This chapter is a revised version of an essay with the same title, published in *New Testament Manuscripts: Their Texts and Their World* (ed. Thomas J. Kraus and Tobias Nicklas; TENT 2; Leiden: Brill, 2006), 137-60.

[1] L. Ingrams, P. Kingston, P. J. Parsons and J. R. Rea, eds., *The Oxyrhynchus Papyri XXXIV* (Graeco-Roman Memoirs 49; London: Egypt Exploration Society, 1968), 5.

[2] Kurt Treu, "Christliche Papyri IV," *APF* 22 (1973): 373. In regard to the choice of this text for an amulet, Treu stated: "Der Abschnitt nicht ganz abwegig, wenn auch eher apotropäisch" (ibid.).

[3] Kurt Aland, ed., *Repertorium der griechischen christlichen Papyri*. I: *Biblische Papyri: Altes Testament, Neues Testament, Varia, Apokryphen* (PTS 18; Berlin/New York: de Gruyter, 1976), 314 (NT 78).

[4] "Überraschend is jedoch die Tatsache, daß überhaupt der Text oder Textteile gerade dieses Briefes, für einen solchen Zweck ausgewählt sind" (Klaus Junack and Winfried Grunewald, *Das Neue Testament auf Papyrus*. I: *Die Katholischen Briefe* [ANTF 6; Berlin/New York: de Gruyter, 1986], 29).

[5] Ibid.

mundane nature of this particular item speaks in favor of the religious or magical purpose rather than the decorative. One should of course also note the possibility that the function of a manuscript may shift over time.

In this study, I will first describe the manuscript itself—its physical and textual features—and then very briefly the historical context in which it once filled its function, probably as an amulet. Finally, I will attempt to offer an explanation as to why this particular text was chosen for the occasion. Why would an individual, the scribe or someone else, want to produce and carry around an amulet with verses from the Epistle of Jude? Can the text itself offer any explanation as to its specific function?

1. Description of 𝔓⁷⁸

1.1 Codicological and Paleographical Description
The extant portion of the manuscript, today kept in the Sackler Library in Oxford, consists of a *bifolium*, a double leaf, from a papyrus codex with one column per page. The size and especially the proportions of this miniature codex are unusual as it is much broader than high (5.3 x 2.9 cm).[6] There is a visible fold in the middle with two small holes approximately 7 and 9 mm from the upper edge.[7] The presence of visible folds is a characteristic feature of amulets, since they were often single sheets rolled or folded into compact form and worn upon the person.[8] However, in this case we have to do with a codex, and, therefore, the evidence is inconclusive, since there is always a folding in the middle of a codex. The two holes probably carried a thread for binding. It is impossible to say if there was a pair of holes in the corresponding area at the foot, since this part is broken away. Sometimes amulets of a single sheet were provided with a string used to

---

[6] Eric G. Turner reserved the term "miniature" for codices less than 10 cm broad (*The Typology of the Early Codex* [Philadelphia: The University of Pennsylvania Press Press, 1977], 25). In his list of miniature codices (Table 1, group 11), which needs an updating, there are no comparable items (ibid., 22; cf. Colin H. Roberts, "The Codex," *Proceedings of the British Academy* 40 [1954]: 198-99). For recent discussions of the terms involved, see M. J. Kruger, "P. Oxy. 840: Amulet or Miniature Codex?," *JTS* 53 (2002): 81-94; and Thomas J. Kraus, "*P.Oxy.* V 840—Amulett oder Miniaturkodex? Grundsätzliche und ergänzende Anmerkungen zu zwei Termini," *ZAC* 8 (2005): 485-97.

[7] On the facsimile it looks like there are three holes, but Parsons indicates two holes (Parsons et al., *The Oxyrhynchus Papyri*, 4).

[8] The compact form is applicable also in the case of miniature codices used as amulets; cf. Leiv Amundsen, "The reasons for using the diminutive book may be partly economical; it may, however, be considered too, that such a tiny volume was a handy thing to carry along in one's pocket, and also easy to conceal if necessary (cf. the μαντική and the amulet!)" ("Christian Papyri from the Oslo Collection," *SO* 24 [1945]: 128).

hang, for instance, around the neck of the owner.[9] However, in this case involving several sheets (see below), the function of binding is the most natural explanation of the presence of the holes.[10]

The hand has been described as "leisurely half-cursive" (Parsons) or "semi-uncial with elements of cursive" (Grunewald) and the manuscript has been dated to the 3rd or 4th century.[11] The form and size of the letters are consistent, but the number of lines are irregular; folio 1 has three lines on recto and verso, whereas folio 2 has five lines on verso; on the fifth line only the last three letters of ενύπνειαδομενοι followed by a middle stop are squeezed underneath the word to be completed that way.[12] The recto has four lines. Of lectional signs are found only the *diaeresis* (fol. 1↓, line 4 and 5; fol. 2↓, line 4) and the middle stop (fol. 1↓, line 4; fol. 2↓, line 5). *Nomina sacra* occur in usual forms: ιῆν, κῡ, χρ̄ν (fol. 1→, line 3). The orthography reflects common itacisms: ι for ει (fol. 1→ line 1); ει for ι (fol. 2↓, line 4; fol. 2→, line 7); and ε for αι (fol. 1↓, line 6).[13] However, the confusion of δ and ζ (fol. 2↓, line 4) is quite remarkable. The extraordinary format, the strange spelling, the remarkable layout and the irregular hand give the impression of an untrained scribe.

All margins are intact and the two leaves must have contained at least 176 letters. The leaves are not consecutive—ca. 335 letters (without punctuation) from the text of Jude are missing between them.[14] In the following, I shall try to reconstruct the possible extent of the missing leaves of the codex. This can only be an approximation, due to the irregularity of writing and format, and to the fact that we do not know exactly the textual

---

[9] See e.g., Chrysostom, *Stat.* 19.14 (*NPNF*[1] 9:470).

[10] Grunewald thinks that the two holes were used for both purposes; first he refers to them as "eine wichtige Angabe für die Zweckbestimmung. . . . Das Format und das Vorhandensein der beiden Löcher am oberen Rand (van Haelst, s.o.), durch die ein Faden gezogen werden konnte, lassen den Schluß zu, daß es sich bei 𝔓78 um ein Amulett bzw. einen Schmuckcodex handelt, der um den Hals getragen wurde." Secondly, he refers to "zwei kleine Löcher in dem Knick, die wohl für die Heftung bestimmt waren" (*Die Katholischen Briefe*, 28-29).

[11] Parsons assigns it to the third or earlier fourth century C.E. (ibid.); Grunewald points out that a specific date is difficult to indicate because of the very individual outlook of the hand, but he finds the nearest equivalents in 𝔓9 (3rd century), and 𝔓17 (4th century), and so dates the MS to the 3rd-4th centuries (*Die Katholischen Briefe*, 29).

[12] Perhaps this was done in order to avoid a possible confusion, had the last three letters begun a new page, with νοι, the dative form of νοῦς, "mind," as opposed to the next word σαρκα, "flesh."

[13] Cf. Edwin Mayser, *Grammatik der griechischen Papyri aus der Ptolemäerzeit. Band I: Laut- und Wortlehre. 1. Teil: Einleitung und Lautlehre* (2d ed.; revised by H. Schmoll; Berlin: de Gruyter, 1970) §8.3; §9.2-3; §14.3.

[14] For convenience' sake, the text of the standard edition of the Greek New Testament (NA[27]) is used in the reconstruction of the missing portions.

character and extent of the missing parts of the original manuscript.

> Fol. 1, recto (Jd 4) contains three lines and 35 letters (12 + 11 + 12)
> Fol. 1, verso (Jd 4-5) contains three lines and 39 letters (13 + 12 + 14)
> Fol. 2, verso (Jd 7-8) contains five lines and 56 letters (12 + 15 + 14 + 12 +3)
> Fol. 2, recto (Jd 8) contains four lines and 46 letters (10 + 13 + 13 + 10)

We do not know which portions of Jude were copied in the original codex, but since the text on the first folio commences in the middle of a word and sentence in v. 4 (the itacistic γιαν, in ἀσέλγειαν), we may conclude that there was at least one leaf on the outer side of the extant leaf, or possibly in another preceding quire. Moreover, v. 5 breaks off in the middle of a sentence (before εἰδότας) and commences again in the end of v. 7 (αιωνιου), so we can conclude that there was at least one leaf on the inside of the extant leaf. As mentioned above, the missing portion of text in between (Jd 5-7) consists of ca. 335 letters, which would occupy two double leaves. These leaves would then contain an average of 42 letters per page, which makes good sense if we consider the tendency of the scribe to increase the number of lines and letters progressively. Possibly, the scribe had to condense his text in consideration of the extent of his writing material (especially if the codex was made up of one single quire, which is likely, and brought forward by Parsons in the *editio princeps*).

It seems reasonable to assume that there was more than one leaf on the outer side, or another preceding quire with several leaves, since the complete sentence of v. 4 would require at least two leaves—there are ca. 125 letters from παρεισεδυσαν to [ασελ]γιαν. If Jude was copied from the very beginning, it would require approximately six outer leaves (12 pages), or three leaves in a preceding quire (12 pages), since there are ca. 390 letters in the missing portion of vv. 1-4. This would make an average of ca. 33 letters per page, which is consistent with the pattern above. However, six outer leaves would not be enough to hold the latter part of Jude, provided that we have to do with a single quire codex—thus, Kurt Aland's assumption of a single-quire codex holding all of the text is wrong.[15] From [βλ]ασφημουσιν to the end of the letter there are ca. 1,450 letters, and six outer leaves would only hold about enough space for vv. 8-13, i.e., ca. 600 letters, which means ca. 50 letters per line (12 pages), in consistence with the pattern above.

Thus three main possibilities remain:

---

[15] Aland's assumption could still be correct if the MS contained some other text preceding Jude, but this fact was not expressed, nor can it be evidenced. Cf. Aland, *Repertorium*, 314.

(a) the letter was copied in more than one quire (the whole letter would require 13-14 leaves);
(b) another text (e.g., a prayer) preceded Jude, if the complete text was copied in a single quire;
(c) only a part of Jude was copied, possibly vv. 1-13 considering both the pattern of the extant leaf in terms of letters per line, and the natural sense divisions of the letter.

The first alternative is least attractive, since it does not explain the described tendency on the part of the scribe to increase the number of lines, and letters per line. The choice between the two latter alternatives is best resolved by appealing to Occam's razor; the second alternative brings in the notion of another text, of which there is no extant evidence, and, therefore, the last alternative seems to be best explanation.[16]

1.2 Transcription
For the benefit of the reader, I include a transcription of the text:[17]

Fol. 1→			Fol. 1↓		
v. 4	γιαν και τον μο	1	v. 5	αρνουμενοι· ὑπο	4
	νον δεσποτην			μνησαι δε ὕμας	
	κ̄ν̄ ημων ιη̄ν χρ̄ν	3		βουλομε αδελφ[	6

Fol. 2↓			Fol. 2→		
v. 7	αιωνιου δικην	1	v. 8	σαρκα μεν μι	6
v. 8	επεχουσαι ομοιως			αινουσιν κυρει	
	μεντοι και αυτοι			οτητα δε αθετου	
	ενὕπνειαδομε			σιν δοξαν δε [..	9
	νοι·	5			

It will be noted that my transcription differs slightly from that found in the *editio princeps*, as far as uncertain or extant letters are concerned.[18]

---

[16] The fact that only a part of Jude would have been copied cannot be used as evidence for or against the last alternative, since many amulets record short extracts from works of various lengths. If this MS was used as an amulet, it is perhaps even easier to imagine that only the first part of the epistle was copied (see below).

[17] See also plate and transcription at the end of this volume.

[18] Differences from Parsons' transcription (*The Oxyrhynchus Papyri XXXIV*, 5): v. 4: δεσποτην; ημων (uncertain letters not indicated by Parsons); v. 5 αδελφ[(the ending is not visible and could be either -οι or -ε as indicated by Parsons in a note; ibid. 6); v. 8 αθετουσιν (uncertain letters not indicated); δοξαν (final *nu* is visible); δε[.. (there is room for two letters, the first of which there is a trace). Differences from Junack and Grunewald, *Die Katholischen Briefe*, 60-63:

1.3 Peculiar Readings

Parsons indicated "two unique" and "three rare readings" (repeated by Treu with the remark "ohne kritisches Gewicht") in the four extant verses of Jude, whereas Grunewald indicated that five readings deviated from NA[26], three of which were "Singulärlesarten."[19] Actually, there is only one singular reading (ἀδελφοί in v. 5) and four other rare readings.[20] Below is a selective apparatus showing these five peculiar readings, in which $\mathfrak{P}^{78}$ constitutes the base text (in the left margin):

v. 4: δεσπότην κύριον ἡμῶν Ἰησοῦν Χριστόν: so 38
　　　δεσπότην καὶ κύριον ἡμῶν Ἰησοῦν Χριστόν 01 02 03 04 81 326T
　　　326Z2 424C 431 436 442 453* 808 1739 *al*
　　　δεσπότην θεὸν καὶ κύριον ἡμῶν Ἰησοῦν Χριστόν 020 044 𝔐
　　　δεσπότην θεὸν καὶ κύριον Ἰησοῦν Χριστόν 88 915 1836 1875 *pc*
　　　δεσπότην καὶ θεὸν καὶ κύριον ἡμῶν Ἰησοῦν Χριστόν 424* *pc*
　　　ἡμῶν δεσπότην καὶ κύριον Ἰησοῦν Χριστόν ἡμῶν $\mathfrak{P}^{72}$
　　　θεὸν καὶ κύριον ἡμῶν 378 2147 2652 L593

v. 5: ἀδελφ[οί
　　　omit *rell*

v. 7: δίκην ἐπέχουσαι: so 630 1505 1611 2138 2200 *pc*
　　　δίκην ὑπέχουσαι $\mathfrak{P}^{72}$ 03 04 020 044 81 88 307 326 431 436 442
　　　453 808 1739 𝔐
　　　δίκην ὑπερέχουσαι 02 2718
　　　δίκην ὑπέχουσιν 01C2
　　　δίκην οὐκ ἔχουσιν 01*

---

v. 4: the letter π in δεσπότην is visible; v. 5: αδελφ[(the ending is not visible and could be either -οι or -ε); v. 8: ενϋπνειαδομενοι (the letter ε is only partly visible but can be nothing else); δοξαν (final nu is visible); δε (ε is partly visible and can be nothing else).

[19] Parsons, *The Oxyrhynchus Papyri XXXIV*, 5; Treu, "Christliche Papyri," 373; Junack and Grunewald, *Die Katholischen Briefe*, 29.

[20] Ernest C. Colwell, "Method in Evaluating Scribal Habits: A Study of $\mathfrak{P}^{45}$, $\mathfrak{P}^{66}$, $\mathfrak{P}^{75}$," in Ernest C. Colwell, *Studies in Methodology in Textual Criticism of the New Testament* (NTTS 9; Leiden: Brill, 1969), 106-24, was the first to use singular readings in order to isolate the scribal tendencies in individual MSS. See also Eldon J. Epp, "Toward the Clarification of the Term 'Textual Variant'," in *Studies in the Theory and Method of New Testament Textual Criticism* (ed. Eldon J. Epp and Gordon D. Fee; SD 45; Grand Rapids: Eerdmans, 1993), 47-61; and James R. Royse, "Scribal Tendencies in the Transmission of the Text of the New Testament," in *The Text of the New Testament in Contemporary Research. Essays on the Status Quaestionis* (ed. Bart D. Ehrman and Michael W. Holmes; SD 46; Grand Rapids: Eerdmans, 1995), 239-52. Royse describes Colwell's method and results and gives examples of a number of more recent studies based upon his method.

v. 8: αὐτοί: so 1735 1885T
　　　omit 142
　　　οὗτοί *rell*

v. 8: δόξαν: so 5 631 636 1799 1831 2865 *pc*
　　　δόξας *rell*

It may be argued that a discussion of the text proper does not belong in a paleographical description as such. However, the singular reading in v. 5 deserves a brief comment here, since it has bearing on my judgment on the original range of verses of the MS: the address in the nominative (vocative), αδελφ[οι] is superfluous—especially if the personal pronoun ὑμᾶς was repeated a second time as in some witnesses, which is impossible to say, since the text is not extant—and may be an indication that the manuscript did not contain v. 3, where Jude has used the address, ἀγαπητοί (as in v. 17). However, the address in v. 5 is more likely an influence from 2 Pet 1:10 (ἀδελφοί, σπουδάσατε), which is a parallel to Jude 3, (ἀγαπητοί, πᾶσαν σπουδὴν ποιούμενος), in which case 𝔓⁷⁸ probably included v. 3 with the same substitution. The scribe might then have repeated the word a second time in order to create a greater sense of immediacy or gravity to the warnings.

Nevertheless, it is clear from the relatively large number of peculiar variants in only four verses, that we have to do with an "eccentric text," to use Parsons' words.[21] This feature may be due to the inexperience and carelessness of the scribe, but it can also be interpreted in connection with the purpose and function of the MS.

In regard to the question of the purpose and function of 𝔓⁷⁸, we must return to another important issue briefly touched in the introduction; is it possible that the function of this manuscript shifted over time? G. H. R. Horsley has offered a detailed reconstruction of the prehistory of another manuscript, *P. Vindob.* G 29831.[22] The manuscript is another double leaf of

---

[21] Parsons, *The Oxyrhynchus Papyri XXXIV*, 5. The text of 𝔓⁷⁸ is categorized by the Alands as "free text, category I." Cf. Kurt Aland and Barbara Aland, *The Text of the New Testament: An Introduction to the Critical Editions and to the Theory and Practice of Modern Textual Criticism* (trans. Erroll F. Rhodes; 2d rev. and enl. ed.; Grand Rapids: Eerdmans, 1995), 101. The textual categorization of this MS is of course somewhat problematic due to its fragmentary nature. For a general critique of the Alands' categories, see Bart D. Ehrman, "A Problem of Textual Circularity: The Alands on the Classification of New Testament Manuscripts," *Bib* 70 (1989): 377-88.

[22] G. H. R. Horsley, "Reconstructing a Biblical Codex: the Prehistory of MPER *n.s.* XVII. 10 (*P. Vindob.* G 29831)," in *Akten des 21. Internationalen Papyrologenkongresses, Berlin, 13.-19.8.1995* (ed. B. Kramer et al.; 2 vols.; APF Beihefte 3; Stuttgart/Leipzig: Teubner, 1997), 473-81.

a presumed miniature codex (without Gr.-Al. number), originally devoted to the Gospel of John (presumably John 1:1-18), and the extant portion contains a passage from John 1:5-6 on the first folio and an amulet formula on the second folio. In his reconstruction Horsley suggests that the arrangement of sheets was binary, and that the scribe, after completing John 1:1-5 on two sheets (not surviving), took out a third (the surviving leaf) by mistake and proceeded with the rest of v. 5—possibly because he was used to working with larger gatherings (ternions, quaternions etc.)—and realized his error only after having copied the full folio on both sides. Since this sheet did not fit into the codex and he did not want to waste his effort, he reused it by adding a standard amulet formula on the second folio (which is written in the same hand). Horsley's suggestion is tempting, but there are of course other possibilities.[23]

As a "preliminary investigation," Horsley also appended a list of other potential manuscripts intended for codices but then reused as amulets.[24] Interestingly, he included 𝔓[78] in the list of items. However, the possibility that the extant folio of 𝔓[78] represents a sheet, intended for a codex, but rejected because of erroneous copying in relation to the arrangement of the gatherings can be firmly excluded: 𝔓[78] comprises text from Jude on both folios, which means that the copying process was not interrupted in the

---

[23] Significantly, the point of departure for Horsley is the question what relevance the content of this passage (John 1:5-6) would have for the wearer, since the content does not speak of health or safety, nor is a text of the popular kind such as LXX Ps 90. This rather contradicts Horsley's own conclusion—that the scribe after having realized his mistake, did see the text as fit for an amulet, even in spite of the fact that the text is broken off in mid-phrase at the end (v. 6). Moreover, Horsley does not mention the fact that Gospel incipits, sometimes extended to more than the initial verse, were very common on amulets and were often copied in sequences where other incipits would precede John (cf. University of Chicago MS 125 which contains Mark 1:1-8; Luke 1:1-7; John 1:1-17; and some other texts), which could be the case here. For example, if the codex was made up of binions, a number of preceding gatherings could have contained other incipits, plus the missing part of John 1:1-5, and inside the extant leaf there could have been another one perhaps containing John 1:5-8 (ca. 70 letters per folio), thus forming the concluding binio. There is also the possibility that the extant manuscript does not preserve the complete amulet formula—it ends somewhat abruptly with ἐπὶ τὸν φοροῦντα τοῦτο (the existence of any punctuation is not mentioned by Horsley). Horsley suggests that τὸ φυλακτήριον is implied, which is of course possible, but the more common version of the formula explicitly includes τὸ φυλακτήριον; cf. Roy Kotansky, *Greek Magical Amulets. The Inscribed Gold, Silver, Copper, and Bronze "Lamellae": Text and Commentary. Part I: Published Texts of Known Provenance* (ARWAW PapyCol 22.1; Opladen: Westdeutscher Verlag, 1994), 345. A presumed longer formula continuing into another folio would of course open up further possibilities. Cf. Kurt Treu and Johannes M. Diethart, eds., *Griechische literarische Papyri christlichen Inhalts II* (MPER N.S. 17; Vienna: Hollinek, 1993), 23: "Obwohl der Text auf IIv 12 (Folio 2, verso l. 12; Anm. d. Verf.) mitten im Satz abbricht, folgte vielleicht nicht mehr."

[24] See G. H. R. Horsley, "Reconstructing," 480-81.

same way as Horsley tried to demonstrate in the case of *P.Vindob.* G 29831. There are of course other ways of reusing a manuscript. Recently, Peter Arzt-Grabner and Michael Ernst have convincingly demonstrated how *P.Bingen* 16 (= *P.Vindob.* G 39205) was once part of a parchment codex, but then cut or torn out and reused as an amulet.[25] However, this possibility too can be excluded in the case of 𝔓78, since the margins are intact and the text continues from fol. 1 recto to verso (vv. 4-5), and fol. 2 verso to recto (vv. 7-8), which means that the format is original.

In conclusion, a theory of reuse in the case of 𝔓78 is unnecessary, since it demands additional and purely hypothetical explanations. The evidence suggests that our manuscript was intended for the use of an amulet in the first place. Nevertheless, the main question remains: why was this text chosen for an amulet?

2. Magic and the Use and Function of Amulets in Early Christianity

"Magic" is a very difficult word to define. In many societies magic is an integral part of religious thought and behavior, whereas in others, especially in the Western world, it is generally thought of as mere superstition. Traditionally, it has been thought to mark a distinction between so-called primitive and advanced cultures, or even between non-Christian and Christian religions. In the 19th century it was common among scholars to contrast magic with religion as well as science.[26] Today, however, there is a consensus, in particular among anthropologists and sociologists, that the old dichotomy between magic and religion is false; magic is increasingly acknowledged as being a general substructure of all religions.[27] However, it is still possible to distinguish magic and religion, if not in essence, at least in the empirical sense. Sociologists regard religion, including magic, as a social fact; while religion is a collective practice, there

---

[25] Peter Arzt-Grabner and Michael Ernst, "*P.Bingen* 16. *Ps.*, 43, 21-24.27 und *Ps.*, 44, 1-2 LXX," in *Papyri in Honorem Johannis Bingen Octogenarii* (ed. Henri Melaerts et al.; Studia Varia Bruxellensia 5; Leuven: Peeters, 2000), 79-84 (+ plate 9).

[26] So the early and influential anthropologists Edward B. Tylor (1832-1917) and James G. Frazer (1854-1941); see for example Edward B. Tylor, *Primitive Culture: Researches into the Development of Mythology, Philosophy, Religion, Language, Art, and Custom* (London: John Murray, 1871); James G. Frazer, *The Golden Bough: A Study in Magic and Religion* (abr. ed.; London: Macmillan, 1922).

[27] E. E. Evans-Pritchard, also an anthropologist, was among the first to criticize the theories of Tylor and Frazer, and dismissed the view of "magic" and "religion" as mutually exclusive phenomena capable of clear definition. See his *Theories of Primitive Religion* (Oxford: Clarendon, 1965).

being no religion without a "church," magic is an individual affair unauthorized by the religious collectivity, and often regarded as abnormal or at least suspect.[28] Indeed, as we shall see, such a negative attitude was prevalent towards amulets on the part of the early church and its official representatives.

From the second through the fifth century C.E., magic increased in popularity within all cults in the Roman Empire, and early Christianity rapidly developed a distinct form of magic in coherence with its reality construction. In this process it absorbed magical traditions from Judaism as well as the surrounding Graeco-Roman world. The Oriental peoples, including the Jews, were especially addicted to the practice of wearing amulets.[29] With their absorption into the Roman Empire the use became equally common among the population in the West.[30] Plutarch's description well reflects the contemporary attitude towards amulets and magic:

> As people with chronic diseases, when they have despaired of ordinary remedies and customary regimens turn to expiations and amulets and dreams, . . . it is necessary to try those [accounts] that are more out of the way and not scorn them but literally to chant over ourselves the charms of the ancients and use every means to bring the truth to test.[31]

---

[28] The French Sociological School pioneered this view; see Émile Durkheim, *Les formes élementaires de la vie religieuse: le système totemique en Australie* (Paris, 1911); Lucien Lévy-Bruhl, *Les fonctions mentales dans les societés inférieures* (Paris: F. Alcan, 1910); Henri Hubert and Marcel Mauss, "Esquisse d'une théorie génerale de la magie," *Année sociologique* 7 (1904): 1-146. In his study of magic in early Christianity, David E. Aune offers a non-dichotomous, sociological definition of the nature and function of magic in relation to religion: "[M]agic is defined as that form of religious deviance whereby the individual or social goals are sought by means alternate to those normally sanctioned by the dominant religious institution" ("Magic in Early Christianity," *ANRW* 23.2:1515. For similar discussions and definitions, see J. N. Bremmer, "The Birth of the Term 'Magic'," *ZPE* 126 (1999): 1-12, esp. 9-12; Georg Luck, *Arcana Mundi: Magic and the Occult in the Greek and Roman World. A Collection of Ancient Texts* (Baltimore: Johns Hopkins University, 1985), 3-61, esp. 7-9; 46-53; and F. A. M. Wiegemann, "Magie I," *RGG* 5:661-62.

[29] See, for instance, Brigitte Kern-Ulmer, "The Depiction of Magic in Rabbinic Texts: The Rabbinic and the Greek Concept of Magic," *JSJ* 27 (1996): 289-303; Meir Bar-Ilan, "Between Magic and Religion: Sympathetic Magic in the World of the Sages of the Mishnah and Talmud," *Review of Rabbinic Judaism* 5 (2002): 383-99.

[30] Although there is no word in the Hebrew Bible denoting "amulet," objects of this kind seem to be implied at various places. Possibly, the golden ear-rings, out of which the molten calf was made, were amulets (Exod 32:2-3). The ornaments worn by women and condemned in Isa 3:16-26 were of this nature (the Hebrew word used in v. 20, *lehashim*, is actually rendered "amulets" in many translations, e.g., RV, RSV, NRSV, NASB, ASV). Cf. Exod 13:16; Deut 6:8; 11:18; Prov 6:21; 2 Macc 12:40.

[31] Plutarch, *Fac.* 920B (Cherniss and Helmbold, LCL).

In the NT period amulets were probably regarded as among the magic arts and their use was strongly condemned (cf. Acts 19:17-20).[32] However, from the second century onwards popular Christianity showed an increasing interest in amulets and by the time of the fourth century, when Christianity had won imperial favor, the use of amulets and devotional emblems had become so common that the official church through its bishops, synods and church fathers had to inveigh strongly against it.[33] The Council of Laodicea even issued a separate canon (36) prohibiting the manufacture and use of amulets: "They who are of the priesthood, or of the clergy, shall not . . . make what are called amulets, which are chains for their own souls. And those who wear such, we command to be cast out of the Church."[34] Another way of dealing with such practices of religious deviance was to "christianize" them. Several ancient Christian authors mention the custom of carrying portions of the Scripture as amulets.[35] However, the custom, especially persistent among the lower strata of society, seems to have been accepted by the official church rather reluctantly.[36] The fact that magical practices in general were associated with the lower strata of society is also reflected in the unpretentious common language of magical texts.

---

[32] The incident recorded in Acts 19 took place in the town of Ephesus, infamous for its abundance of sorcery in ancient times. The practice of wearing written charms, the so-called Ἐφέσια γράμματα, in little leather bags is attested as early as the 4th century B.C.E. See Campbell Bonner, *Studies in Magical Amulets* (Ann Arbor: The University of Michigan Press, 1950), 5. Aune's discussion of the magical use of the name of Jesus by some NT authors, and his references to Paul's use of amulet imagery in Gal 6:17 ("the marks of Jesus") and the name of Jesus functioning as a charm or amulet in Rev 14:7 is problematic (see Aune, "Magic in Early Christianity," 1545). The metaphorical language does not indicate a positive attitude to amulets as such on the part of these authors.

[33] See the synods in Elvira (303 or 313 C.E.) can. 6; Ancyra (315 C.E.) can. 24; and Laodicea (ca. 360 C.E.) can. 34-36. For the critical attitude of the church fathers, see Augustine, *Doctr. chr.* 2.24 (*NPNF*[1] 2:547-48); Chrysostom, *Hom. 1 Cor.* 4.11 (*NPNF*[1] 12:21); see further discussion and references in Matthew W. Dickie, "The Fathers of the Church and the Evil Eye," in *Byzantine Magic* (ed. Henry Maguire; Washington D.C.: Dumbarton Oaks Research Library and Collection, 1995), 9-34.

[34] *The Seven Ecumenical Councils* (*NPNF*[2] 14:151).

[35] In Jewish tradition we notice a similar development, whereby the ancient pagan practice of wearing amulets was infused with new significance and a worthier motive in consistence with the dominant religion of Jahweh; it was namely common among Jews to wear small rolls of parchments (Heb. *tefillin*, Gr. *phylakterion*) in leather boxes, containing scriptural portions from the Law (the practice persists to this day). This was done according to Mosaic instruction (Exod 13:9, 16; Deut 6:8; 11:18).

[36] Apparently, both Chrysostom (*Stat.* 19.14 [*NPNF*[1] 9:470], and Augustine (*Tract. Ev. Jo.* 7.12 [*NPNF*[1] 7:52]) accepted the practice, but they were careful to stress the importance of the inner faith of "heart" and "mind" in God's word, rather than the external efficacy of an amulet itself. Cf. Reiner Kaczynski, *Das Wort Gottes in Liturgie und Alltag der Gemeinden des Johannes Chrysostomus* (FThSt 94; Freiburg: Herder, 1974).

While the vast majority of amulets employed in the Graeco-Roman world has perished, archaeologists have discovered thousands of items that have survived.[37] Naturally, there is a wealth of extant amulets made of durable material, such as stone and metal.[38] However, these necessarily held briefer inscriptions than another class of amulets written on small pieces of papyrus, of which a considerable number have survived in the dry heat of Egypt.[39] Some of these items contain biblical citations, prayers, or liturgical portions etc., and can therefore be provisionally defined as Jewish or Christian amulets.[40] A brief survey of the extant texts on these amulets reveals the fact that Psalms or extracts from Psalms, or Odes were very popular and in this regard Ps 90 (LXX) holds an exceptional place.[41] The reason for the extensive use of this particular psalm is obvious from the

---

[37] For an extensive, though somewhat dated, description of amulets in the Graeco-Roman world including many examples and a voluminous bibliography, see H. Leclercq, "Amulettes," *DACL* 1:1784-1860.

[38] The most important survey of stone and metal amulets is Campbell Bonner, *Studies in Magical Amulets*.

[39] Many items are described in Joseph van Haelst, *Catalogue des papyrus littéraires juifs et chrétiens* (Série "Papyrologie" 1, Université de Paris IV; Paris, Sorbonne: Publications de la Sorbonne, 1976). Van Haelst listed 118 amulets in his index (items no. 967 and no. 1006 were not included in the index, but described as amulets). Information about more recent items can be accessed through the *Leuven Database of Ancient Books* (LDAB), at http://ldab.arts.kuleuven.ac.be, and the *Advanced Papyrological Information System* (APIS; A part of the *Columbia University Digital Library Projects*), at http://columbia.edu/cgibin/cul/resolve?ATK2059.

[40] It is tempting to assume that all amulets with biblical citations, etc., must be either Jewish or Christian, but in some cases it is difficult to prove that the wearer of an amulet was a follower of the religion indicated by the amulet, especially since the field of magic in this era was characterized by syncretism; the latter is especially evident in the magical papyri. See Karl Preisendanz and Albert Henrich, eds., *Papyri Graecae Magicae: Die griechischen Zauberpapyri* (2 vols.; 2d rev. ed.; Stuttgart: Teubner, 1973-1974); and H. D. Betz, ed., *The Greek Magical Papyri in Translation Including the Demotic Spells* (2 vols.; 2d ed.; Chicago/London: University of Chicago Press, 1992); henceforth *PGM*; see also Robert W. Daniel and Franco Maltomini, eds., *Supplementum Magicum* (2 vols.; ARWAW PapyCol 16.1-2; Opladen: Westdeutscher Verlag, 1990-1992). The danger of misinterpretation is of course decreased in regard to items with exclusively Jewish or Christian features and of larger extent than single names or phrases.

[41] Thomas J. Kraus has described some 75 items (papyri and parchment MSS, medallions, rings, bracelets, wooden tablets, etc.) that contain the psalm or parts of it ("Septuaginta-Psalm 90 in apotropäischer Verwendung: Vorüberlegungen für eine kritische Edition und [bisheriges] Datenmaterial" [paper presented at *The 24th International Congress of Papyrology*, Helsinki, August 2, 2004]. For psalms on amulets in general, see Paul Collart, "Psaumes et amulettes," *Aegyptus* 14 (1934): 463-67. For a discussion of other passages, see Edwin A. Judge, "The Magical Use of Scripture," in *Perspectives on Language and Text: Essays and Poems in Honor of Francis I. Andersen's Sixtieth Birthday* (ed. Edgar W. Conrad and Edward G. Newing; Winona Lake: Eisenbrauns, 1987), 339-49; and A. Biondi, "Le citazione bibliche nei papiri magici cristiani greci," *SPap* 20 (1981): 93-127.

contents, suggesting an apotropaic use.[42] The phenomenon of using verses from the Scripture in a magic context often derives from their liturgical prominence.[43] Therefore it is not surprising to find that the Lord's prayer (Matt 6:9-13) is the most cited passage from the NT on extant amulets. Next in place comes Gospel *incipits*, often all four in a sequence.[44]

Without going into more detail concerning particular texts, it is important to note in regard to magical texts and amulets in general, that there is often a direct connection between the text and the particular function of the amulet, particularly in cases when they contain *historiolae*, i.e., narratives, very often divine precedents, which would comprise the main point of reference for the mobilization and development of the particular magical action desired. In the Christian context, the desired action most often involved healing and protection against evil forces and, thus, some amulets contain healing narratives, or texts about God's protection (cf. LXX Ps 90).[45] Perhaps more surprising, we also find examples of *historiolae* in the context of love and fertility, and even in connection with cursing—if not on many extant amulets, at least amply in the magical texts from Christian Egypt.[46] Ernst von Dobschütz classified the ancient charms with their functions into three main categories, which are more or less applicable to amulets: *Defensive charms* (apotropaic, counter

---

[42] For the continuing apotropaic use of Ps 91 (masoretic) in Jewish tradition, cf. the passage in *bŠebu.* 15b, which says that it is permitted to recite Ps 91:1-9 as a protection against approaching evil (but not in order to heal a wound). Cf. also *y. Šabb.* VI 8b.

[43] Cf. Joseph Naveh and Shaul Shaked, *Magic Spells and Formulae* (Jerusalem: The Magnes Press, 1993), 24.

[44] The incipit represented the whole Gospel in question, which in turn was perceived as having a special power for protection, exorcism or healing. In *P.Rain.* 1, for example, the wearer of the amulet commands different types of fever to flee by appealing to the four Gospels of the Son (ὁρκίζω ὑμᾶς κατὰ τῶν τεσσάρων εὐαγγελίων τοῦ υἱοῦ κτλ.).

[45] For example, several amulets contain the passage in Matt 4:23-24, which records a summary statement of how Jesus went about in Galilee, preaching the Kingdom of God, curing all kinds of diseases including demon possession. Significantly, *P.Oxy.* VIII 1077 presents this text under a heading that expressly indicates its function, ιαματικον ευαγγελιον κατα Ματθαιον ("Curative Gospel according to Matthew").

[46] Sexual spells in magical texts of Christian character involve references to the Annunciation (London Hay 10376) and, in regard to desired fertility, to the remarkable pregnancy of Sarah, with citation of the divine promise in Gen 18:10 of an offspring (*P.Morgan Copt.* M662B 22). A sample of magical texts belonging to the category of malevolent magic includes references to the curse mentioned in Zech 5:3 (*P.Berlin* inv. 10587; this item also refers to Gnostic traditions); to "the curses of the Law and Deuteronomy" (*P. Mich.* inv. 3565); the curse of Cain (London Or. 5986; *P.Lichačev*); the curse of Sodom and Gomorrah (Florence, Museo Arch., inv. 5645—this text is written on a human bone [!]; *P.Lichačev*). *P.Vindob.* G. 19929 is an amulet from the sixth century that contains an appeal to the Lord for vengeance (without *historiola*).

charms, curative, detective); *Productive charms* (fertility, weather charms, birth and capacity, love charms); and *Malevolent charms* (cursing).[47] Perhaps we should here add a fourth category, that of *divination*.[48]

3. The Epistle of Jude on an Amulet?

Practically all of the biblical citations on the extant amulets indicate that Jewish and Christian amulets generally had either an apotropaic or a curative function, and, judging from the text of Jude, there is reason to believe that $\mathfrak{P}^{78}$ belongs to the former category of apotropaic amulets. A malevolent function of a Christian amulet, on the other hand, seems paradoxical, since it would contradict Christian doctrine in general, and Jesus' command to love one's enemies in particular. However, as mentioned above, there are examples of malevolent magic in a Christian context, and such a function of $\mathfrak{P}^{78}$ cannot *a priori* be excluded, especially if one considers the pronounced polemical character of Jude, which comes to expression in a fierce and violent judgment language, indirectly aimed at human adversaries.[49] If $\mathfrak{P}^{78}$ contained only a portion of Jude breaking off somewhere in the middle, e.g., vv. 1-13 (leaving out the final exhortations), the latter part would indeed form an effective verbal climax suitable for a malevolent purpose; apart from judgmental *historiolae* and a pejorative characterization of the antagonists, we find the repeated formulaic phrase, οὗτοί/οὗτοί εἰσιν (vv. 8, 10, 12), marking the transition from "text" to interpretation, which in this case would mean the transition from *historiolae* to immediate application on to some contemporary adversaries.[50] In v. 11

---

[47] Ernst von Dobschütz, "Charms and Amulets (Christian)," *Encyclopedia of Religion and Ethics*, 3:416-21.

[48] For studies on the practice of fortune-telling in the ancient world, see e.g., T. C. Skeat, "An Early Medieval 'Book of Fate': The Sortes XII Patriarcharum. With a Note on 'Books of Fate' in General," *Mediaeval and Renaissance Studies* 3 (1954): 41-54. For divination in connection with NT MSS, see Bruce M. Metzger, "Greek Manuscripts of John's Gospel with 'Hermeneia'," in *Text and Testimony: Essays on New Testament and Apocryphal Literature in Honour of A. F. J. Klijn* (ed. Tjitze Baarda et al.; Kampen: Pharos, 1988), 162-69.

[49] Cf. Tobias Nicklas who says concerning $\mathfrak{P}^{78}$ and the choice of text for this amulet: "Soll die im Text angedrohte Strafe abgewendet werden? Geht es um einen Bann übelgesonnener Menschen oder wie auch immer gearteter dämonischer Kräfte?" ("Zur historischen und theologischen Bedeutung der Erforschung neutestamentlicher Textgeschichte," *NTS* 48 [2002]: 149).

[50] The peculiar reading in v. 8, αὐτοί for οὗτοι, if not due to a simple scribal error, may lend some support for this notion, since an original demonstrative pronoun might have rendered difficult an anaphoric reference to adversaries "outside" the text on the part of the scribe. Moreover, we recall the insertion of the superfluous ἀδελφοί in v. 5, in this case perhaps to increase the exigency and immediateness. The same address was probably present at least in v. 3 (and maybe in v. 17) in $\mathfrak{P}^{78}$ instead of the normal address of Jude, ἀγαπητοί—again

we find the powerful performative utterance of a "Woe!" against the evil enemies, οὐαὶ αὐτοῖς, and, finally, the pronouncement of their eternal damnation in v. 13, which would be a forceful climactic conclusion of such an amulet.

Interestingly, a Coptic papyrus from the 4th-5th centuries C.E., *P.Lichačev*, presents several parallels in this regard; the speaker in the text calls upon God in the heavenly throne-room among the angels (Michael, Gabriel, etc.) urging him to bring judgment against people who have committed violence against him (or someone else), and in doing so he appeals to several of the OT examples of God's judgment, as referred to in Jude. In the case of this text—the work of a Coptic Christian—it is not unlikely that the influence actually goes via the Epistle of Jude.[51]

However, there are still other features in the Epistle of Jude to be considered before we can make a final judgment as to the original function of our MS. One very prominent feature in contemporary magic in general was the appeal to Jewish or Christian divine names and titles (e.g., "Iao," "Adonai," "Sabaoth," "Eloi," "God of Abraham, Isaac, and Jacob," "Jesus the God of the Hebrews," and all kinds of transcriptions of the *Tetragrammaton*, etc.).[52] In particular, the belief in the magical power of the name of Jesus is attested from the earliest times of Christianity (cf. Acts 19:13).[53] Significantly, in Jude we note an abundance of divine and angelic references, particularly in connection with Jesus.[54]

---

perhaps enhancing the application in a context of magic, whether apotropaic or "malevolent," by downplaying the exhortative features of the original letter and laying more stress on the communal factor (perhaps the amulet was even used in public); the strength of brotherly unity against evil. Consider also the passage in 1 Cor 5:3-5, where we note the appeal to the name of the Lord Jesus, and the factor of unity in the curselike action, in this case turning an immoral person over to Satan. Cf. Adolf Deissmann, *Light from the Ancient East* (transl. L. R. M. Strachan; New York: George H. Doran Co., 1927), 302-3.

[51] " . . . As you cursed Somohra and Komohra through the anger of your wrath, [cf. Jd 7] you must curse the one who has committed this act of violence. You must bring the vengeance of Enoch against them [cf. Jd 14-15]. As the blood of Abel called out to Cain his brother [cf. Jd 11], the blood of this miserable man will call out, until you bring judgment on his behalf. . . ." Translation by Marvin W. Meyer and Richard Smith, *Ancient Christian Magic: Coptic Texts of Ritual Power* (Princeton: Princeton University Press, 1999), 190-91. The text starts and ends with a staurogram.

[52] See further samples in *PGM*.

[53] See Wilhelm Heitmüller, *Im Namen Jesu: Eine sprach- und religionsgeschichtliche Untersuchung zum Neuen Testament, speziell zur altchristlichen Taufe* (FRLANT 2; Göttingen: Vandenhoeck & Ruprecht, 1903). Cf. Aune, "Magic in Early Christianity," 1545-49.

[54] Concerning the appeal to divine names in the context of Jewish, Christian and pagan magic, Aune states, "The fundamental significance of the magical use of the names of divinities, supernatural beings or great men of the past is the supposition that such names

Possibly, two of the peculiar readings of 𝔓⁷⁸ may be explained as accentuated expressions of the divinity and glory of Jesus Christ, perhaps occasioned by a magical purpose:⁵⁵ In v. 4, the text as it stands in NA²⁷, τὸν μόνον δεσπότην καὶ κύριον ἡμῶν Ἰησοῦν Χριστόν, can be interpreted as two parallel references, to God and to Jesus.⁵⁶ However, it is also possible to interpret the whole phrase as a reference entirely to Jesus, and so the author of 2 Peter interpreted Jude 4, provided that Jude is prior.⁵⁷ This ambiguity may have led scribes to append θεόν (attested by the majority of witnesses) in order to clarify that the divine title, δεσπότης, refers to God.⁵⁸ However, 𝔓⁷⁸ most clearly attributes the title to Jesus by dropping the conjunction καί.⁵⁹ Likewise, the rare reading, δόξαν, in the context in v. 8, may likewise be interpreted as a Christological reference, "they set aside the majesty of the Lord [or simply "they set aside the Lord"], they blaspheme his glory."⁶⁰

Thus, in 𝔓⁷⁸ it is made clear right at the beginning that "the Lord" in the text refers to Jesus; hence, it was Jesus who acted mightily both in the history of Israel and in the history of the entire cosmos; he saved the people out of Egypt, but destroyed those who did not believe; he sent the fallen angels to be kept under darkness for judgment; and he punished Sodom and Gomorrah and the cities around them with eternal fire!⁶¹ References to

---

share the being and participate in the power of their bearers; to possess a name is to possess power over the one who bears the name" ("Magic in Early Christianity," 1546).

⁵⁵ Cf. Michael Mees, "𝔓⁷⁸ ein neuer Textzeuge für den Judasbrief," *Orient-Press* 1 (1970): 10.

⁵⁶ The absence of the article before κύριον does not resolve the issue, since it is often omitted before κύριος.

⁵⁷ The passage in 2 Peter 2:1b, describing the opponents, reads καὶ τὸν ἀγοράσαντα αὐτοὺς δεσπότην ἀρνούμενοι. ἐπάγοντες ἑαυτοῖς ταχινὴν ἀπώλειαν.

⁵⁸ The title δεσπότης ("Master") attributed to God is widely attested in Judaism as well as in early Christian usage. In the NT, we find this divine title ascribed to Christ only in Jude 4 and 2 Peter 2:1.

⁵⁹ Cf. the discussion in Thomas J. Kraus, *Sprache, Stil und historischer Ort des zweiten Petrusbriefes* (WUNT 2.136; Tübingen: Mohr Siebeck, 2001), 76-78.

⁶⁰ A few witnesses read the plural, κυριότητας (ℵ Ψ 1845 1846), probably referring to classes of angels (cf. Eph 1:21; Col 1:16) in analogy with δόξας in the latter part of the verse. The singular, δόξαν (𝔓⁷⁸ *pc*), probably reflects the Greek equivalent in LXX of the Hebrew *kabod*, originally used in reference to God, especially in the majesty of his historical acts of salvation and judgment.

⁶¹ Jarl E. Fossum argues for the originality of the reading Ἰησοῦς in Jude 5 (not extant in our MS), and suggests that Jude 5-7 presents Jesus as the Angel of the Lord, since the acts described in vv. 5-7 were all attributed to the Angel of the Lord in pre-Christian tradition, and among later church fathers. The Angel of the Lord was said to share God's Name (Exod 23:21) and could even be designated by the Tetragrammaton or the Greek equivalent, κύριος ("Kyrios Jesus as the Angel of the Lord in Jude 5-7," *NTS* 33 [1987]: 226-43).

divine acts of salvation were generally common in contemporary apotropaic magic, and in this regard the Exodus held a prominent place, being the great shining salvific event of the Hebrew Bible. More significantly, however, the specific reference in Jude 6 to an action by the Lord in the angelic realm definitely speaks in favor of an apotropaic function. In this connection, I would like to draw the attention to another Greek papyrus amulet, *P.Fouad* inv. 203 (1), dated to the 1st or 2nd century C.E.. In my view, the fragmentary text mainly suggests an apotropaic function of the amulet. However, there is some ambiguity, which is perhaps reflected in the title of the article by Pierre Benoit, who edited the fragment, "Fragment d'une prière contre les spirits impurs?"[62]

> . . . the glorious name [cf. Deut 28:58] and you are impure [addressing the demons]. May he send [cf. LXX Ps 19:2] his angel [probably Michael] who has led this people through the exodus, who revealed himself [cf. Jos 5:13-15] for Jesus [Joshua], son of Naoum [Nun], especially since he has plunged us [Benoit's conjecture, "you"] into the Abyss, into the place of destruction and covered you in Chaos [cf. *1 En.* 10:5; Jd 6; *PGM* IV. 1247]. This is why you will not appear any more and not become present in order to commit evil against any living soul. Honor and praise to the Lord forever, to the One invoked, to [. . .], and for all who are near him and present.[63]

Here we find several interesting parallel features and conceptions in relation to Jude; first, the appeal to the divine name; secondly, the reference to God's act of salvation in the Exodus event, here through an angelic agent, probably Michael; thirdly, the reference to his action against the impure spirits in throwing them into the Abyss (ἄβυσσος), again executed by an angelic agent in accordance with the tradition in *1 En.* 10:4-6, 11-12 (here Raphael and Michael are mentioned).[64] In early Judaism and in the NT the Abyss is thought of as the place in which the rebellious angels, or spirits, are confined in darkness (*Jub.* 5; *1 En.* 10; Jude 6; 2 Pet 2:4; Rev 9:1; 20:1, 3).[65] Hence, we see an example of how these same *historiolae* in question apparently filled an apotropaic function,

---

[62] Pierre Benoit, "Fragment d'une prière contre les esprits impurs?," *RB* 59 (1951): 549-65.
[63] My translation after the Greek original and Benoit's reconstruction in French (ibid., 552-60).
[64] The concept of the rebellious angels, or spirits, has its roots in Gen 6:1-4, a classical passage for the explanation of the origins of evil on earth. In turn, the story was elaborated first in the so-called 'Book of Watchers' of *1 Enoch* (probably dated to the third century B.C.E.), and then used frequently in Jewish-Christian literature of the period 200 B.C.E.-300 C.E.; in the NT in 2 Peter 2:4, Jude 6, and perhaps 1 Pet 3:19-20 (cf. Rick Strelan, "The Fallen Watchers and the Disciples in Mark," *JSP* 20 [1999]: 73-92).
[65] See further Joachim Jeremias, "ἄβυσσος," *TDNT* 1:9.

whether the fragment is Jewish or Christian.[66] The main difference in relation to Jude is of course the direct confrontation of the unclean spirits in a vocative reference, which may suggest an exorcistic function of the text, but, on the other hand, the fact that the spirits are said to have been plunged into the Abyss and that they, therefore, are not to appear any more, indicates a primarily protective function.[67]

The usage of the same traditions is attested also in the incantatory texts of Qumran, particularly in 11Q11, which is a collection of at least three non-canonical incantation psalms followed by a version of Ps 91.[68] Esther Eshel has treated the incantation texts of this scroll extensively.[69] She highlights a number of interesting features of 11Q11 and the other incantation texts from Qumran, which have parallels in Greek and Aramaic magical papyri, such as the invocation of the name of the Lord, references to deeds of God on earth, the direct address of the spirits, and, significantly, "the most popular threat being that they [the spirits] will be sealed in the abyss with iron chains."[70] Eshel also notes the call in 11Q11 for help by a powerful angel, with the epithet "the chief of the army of YHWH," who will bring the evil spirit to the Abyss, and she refers to the parallel in *P.Fouad* inv. 203.[71] Note, however, that in 11Q11 the angelic action is in the future, which confirms Eshel's judgment of this text as being primarily "exorcistic."[72]

---

[66] Cf. Benoit, "Fragment," 564-65.

[67] Cf. Benoit, "Fragment," 564: "Il ne s'agit pas d'un 'exorcisme' au sens restreint du mot, car il n'est pas question de chaser des demons d'un corps humain qu'ils posséderaient."

[68] The script of this scroll is dated to the 1st century; see the edition in Adam S. van der Woude, "11QApocryphal Psalms," in *Qumran Cave 11. II: 11Q2-18, 11Q20-31. 11Q2-18, 11Q20-31* (ed. Florentino García Martínez, Eibert C. J. Tigchelaar and Adam S. van der Woude; DJD 23; Oxford: Clarendon, 1998), 181-205.

[69] E. Eshel, "Genres of Magical Texts in the Dead Sea Scrolls," in *Die Dämonen. Demons* (ed. Armin Lange, Hermann Lichtenberger and K. F. Diethard Römheld; Tübingen: Mohr Siebeck, 2003), 394-415.

[70] Eshel, "Genres," 403-404. In 11Q11 there is no specific reference to iron chains, but there is a similar threat that the angel will "shut the bronze gates through which no light penetrates" (ibid., 399).

[71] Eshel, "Genres," 405. Cf. also Kotansky, who cites the text of a magical tablet from Beirut, "The Great Angelic Hierarchy" (Paris, Musée du Louvre inv. M.N.D. 274), from the 4th century C.E., where the demons are addressed in a command to flee to a place under the springs and the Abyss, φύγετε . . . ὑποκάτω τῶν πηγῶν καὶ τῆς ἀβύσσου ("Greek Magical Amulets," 295).

[72] Whereas Eshel takes the "main body" of incantation texts to be "exorcistic," she classifies the concluding Ps 91 as an "apotropaic hymn" (ibid., 398). Hermann Lichtenberger, who treats Ps 91 in the collection, points out that the concluding psalm is integrated with the other texts, not only in terms of content, but also by liturgical responsory phrases, and so concludes: "Durch die Einbeziehung in die Sammlung von Exorcismen wird Ps 91 selbst zu einem

A similar conception is reflected in the magical papyrus text *PGM* IV. 1227-64 (*Bibl. Nat. suppl. gr.* 574; the so-called "Great Magical Papyrus of Paris"). In this extensive manual for exorcism from the 4th century, the practitioner, after the expulsion of the demon, is instructed to drape an amulet around the person, which contains magical words ending with "protect him, NN." Significantly, the incantation used for the exorcism proper concludes: "I deliver you into the black chaos in perdition" (*PGM* IV. 1247), which surely reflects the threat of the demon returning unless properly confined.[73] Hence, the desired magical action in appealing to the *historiola* in Jude 6 would arguably be to ensure that any threatening demons stay imprisoned, "kept in eternal chains under darkness." Unfortunately, this verse is no longer extant in 𝔓78, so we cannot look for signs of any special treatment of the verse, but the apotropaic conception in question may have influenced the scribe in the very next verse, recording the parallel judgment of the cities of Sodom and Gomorrah: practically all witnesses read δίκην ὑπέχουσαι, "undergoing punishment" (or "judgment"), whereas our MS reads δίκην ἐπέχουσαι, "staying in punishment."[74]

If we now return to the notion of angelic agents appealed to in Jewish-Christian magic, we find that Michael stands in a class for himself.[75] In the elaborate angelology that emerged in Judaism during the Hellenistic period, Michael is an archangel (*1 En.* 20:1-7; 71:3; *2 En.* 22:6; cf. Jude 9), present along with Raphael, Gabriel and Phanuel before the throne of God (*1 En.* 9:1; 40; 54:6; 71:8-9, 13). He is often represented as the leader of the archangels (*Asc. Isa.* 3:16), and as patron angel of Israel (Dan 10:23; 12:1; *1 En.* 20:5; 1QM 17:6-8). In the NT, Michael is the leader of the angels who battles against Satan and his angels, and causes their fall from heaven. Michael's role in the angelic warfare against Satan and his demonic forces leads us on to the next "proof-text" in Jude 9, where Michael contends with Satan for the body of Moses, and here we find elements very suitable for apotropaic purposes: the kernel and climax of the story is the powerful utterance by Michael against the devil, ἐπιτιμήσαι σοι κύριος. The whole

---

solchen Beschwörungstext." ("Ps 91 und die Exorzismen in 11QpsApᵃ," in *Die Dämonen Demons*, 420). In my view, the manifest unity of the collection in spite of the diversity of its parts does not exclude a combined exorcistic and apotropaic function.

[73] Cf. Matt 12:43-45; Luke 11:24-26; Rev 9:1-2; Josephus, *Ant.* 8:47.

[74] The verb in the sense of *staying* is intransitive (often accompanied by a time reference in the accusative; cf. Acts 19:22), and therefore δίκην is problematic, since it cannot be an object of the verb. Perhaps it can be interpreted as an accusative of respect ("staying, so as to be punished with eternal fire"). See also Mees, "𝔓78," 9.

[75] This fact can easily be deduced by looking in the index of personal names in any edition of contemporary magical texts.

episode in Jude may be directly dependent on the *Assumption of Moses*, or, more likely, as Richard Bauckham has argued, a lost ending of the *Testament of Moses*.[76] Nevertheless, Michael's utterance is definitely an echo of Zech 3:2 where Satan is likewise rebuked by the Lord (or the angel of the Lord).[77]

Significantly, Joseph Naveh and Shaul Shaked state that this very passage is perhaps the most commonly used verse in Jewish magic texts.[78] Howard C. Kee has attempted to show that the Aramaic verb גער underlying ἐπιτιμάω in Zech 3:2 and other passages in the LXX, became a technical term used for exorcism in sectarian Judaism (see e.g., 1QSA 20:28) and the oldest layers of the gospel tradition (Mark 1:25 and 9:25 with par.) signifying "the word or command that brought the hostile powers under control."[79] Be that as it may, there is no doubt that at least in Zech 3:2, and in Jude 9, the term occurs in a context of struggle between God and Satan.[80] Demonstrably, the powerful divine (or angelic) utterance was used frequently in Jewish incantations, and this may be another reason for the choice of Jude as text for our amulet, provided that the verse was once extant in 𝔓78, as I have argued. The attested connection of the verb with exorcism, and the very distinct and direct address of Satan in this verse implicate that there is no sharp division between defensive and offensive magic.

4. Conclusions

In this examination of 𝔓78, I have attempted to describe both the physical and textual features of the extant manuscript, and to reconstruct the codex of which it once was part. The reconstruction suggests that the codex once contained a larger portion of Jude, arguably vv. 1-13, and that it was produced, not reused, for the purpose of an amulet. Moreover, I have tried to answer the crucial question posed at the outset of the examination: why

---

[76] Richard J. Bauckham, *Jude and the Relatives of Jesus in the Early Church* (Edinburgh: T. & T. Clark, 1990), 235-80.

[77] Many editors of the Hebrew Bible prefer the Syriac reading, "angel of Yahweh," for reasons of consistency within the verse and the vision scene as a whole. The rebuke formula in Zech 3:2 may in turn reverberate the primal "Cursed are you" of Gen 3:14.

[78] Naveh and Shaked, *Magic Spells*, 25. Cf. Charles D. Isbell, *Corpus of Aramaic Incantation Bowls* (Missoula: Scholars Press, 1975), 195; Christa Müller-Kessler, *Die Zauberschalentexte in der Hilprecht Sammlung, Jena* (Wiesbaden: Harrassowitz Verlag, 2004), 69.

[79] Howard C. Kee, "The Terminology of Mark's Exorcism Stories," *NTS 14* (1968): 232-46. Kee's overall attempt is deemed "unsuccessful" by Aune, "Magic in Early Christianity," 1530-31, esp. note 106.

[80] Kee finds that the verb is used in the same context of struggle between God and Satan in rabbinic literature, e.g., *b. Qidd.* 81b ("Terminology," 239).

would someone choose this text for an amulet to carry around on his or her body? The text itself may hint at an answer since there is often a clear connection between the text of an amulet and its particular function. Some examined features of the Epistle of Jude, for example the violent polemic against the adversaries, may suggest an amulet for a malevolent purpose, directed against other human beings. However, an apotropaic usage is more likely, not only because such a function is more common for amulets in general, but also for the fact that the text in question seems very appropriate for such a purpose.

First, we find several divine and angelic references, particularly in connection with Jesus, such as were common in magic texts in general. Moreover, there are a number of references to particular divine acts of judgment and salvation, which evidently functioned as *historiolae* in apotropaic texts, as attested elsewhere. For example, in Jude 6 it is said that the Lord sent the fallen angels to be kept under darkness for judgment. Apparently, this and similar notions play an important role in Jewish as well as Christian magic, both curative (exorcistic) and apotropaic. The reference to the bound angels in Jude is expressed as a past event (cf. *P.Fouad* inv. 203), rather than a direct threat such as occurs in exorcistic texts (e.g., 11Q11). This points to an apotropaic function, i.e., a prophylactic measure because of the perceived threat of the unclean spirits escaping from their prison and returning to torment human beings. Another reference in Jude, very appropriate for the purpose, is the story of the dispute between the archangel Michael and the devil in Jude 9, where we find a powerful angelic command directed against the devil, echoing Zech 3:2, a text used very frequently in Jewish incantations.

In regard to the text of 𝔓[78], I have also considered a number of peculiar readings, some of which may have been occasioned by the specific purpose of the manuscript. This is difficult to determine, but in any case the eccentric text in itself reflects the heavy influence of the context in which it was reproduced, and does strengthen the overall impression that we have to do with an amulet. For this reason it might be argued that the manuscript, although valuable for the historian as a fingerprint of real existing people in antiquity and their reception and usage of the text, is of no value for the text-critic in the reconstruction of the text of Jude, and, therefore, should not have been included in the list of "New Testament papyri" in the first place.[81] However, the text-critical value of any extant

---

[81] Possibly, it was Kurt Aland's assumption that the codex once contained the whole continuous text of Jude that led to its inclusion in the 𝔓-list of so-called "New Testament papyri" (see above). Cf. Thomas J. Kraus, "'Pergament oder Papyrus?' Anmerkungen zur

manuscript can never be anything other than relative, in that it is more or less influenced by the context in which it was copied. Stuart R. Pickering discusses the value of non-continuous NT texts and says:

> [I]t would clearly be fallacious to argue that they [school exercises or magical texts] can *never* transmit a passage according to the wording which one would expect from a continuous text. . . . The question of textual value goes beyond the merely verbal level. A manuscript is of text-critical value not only in the individual words which it contains, but in the evidence it provides for the scribal approaches which influenced the wording. In this respect, an alleged weakness of noncontinuous texts—the likely extent of scribal interference—turns out to be one of their great strengths for New Testament text-critical purposes.[82]

This way of reasoning actually bridges the gap between the text and its transmission and use in a particular historical context. It points to the necessity to consider all the evidence for the New Testament text, not only continuous texts. Moreover, it underlines the importance of methodological integration and interaction between all the different disciplines with an interest in ancient manuscripts, such as archaeology, codicology, papyrology, palaeography, textual criticism, and, in extension, theology. It is my hope that this study of $\mathfrak{P}^{78}$ will prove to be an example of such interaction.

Signifikanz des Beschreibstoffes bei der Behandlung von Manuskripten," *NTS* 49 (2003): 425-32, where the author deals with some inconsistencies of the Gregory-Aland list (where some items, designated "amulet," or "school exercise" are included and, while other items of the same kind are excluded).

[82] Stuart R. Pickering, "The Significance of Non-Continuous New Testament Textual Materials in Papyri," *Studies in the Early Text of the Gospels and Acts. The Papers of the First Birmingham Colloquium on the Textual Criticism of the New Testament* (ed. D. G. K. Taylor; Texts and Studies 3.1; Birmingham: University of Birmingham Press, 1999), 125.

Chapter Four

The Literary Relationship between
2 Peter and Jude:
Criteria and Probability

Introduction

From the earliest times of research scholars have acknowledged the close relationship that exists between 2 Peter and Jude. The major resemblances are found in 2 Peter 2:1-18; 3:1-3 and Jude 4-13, 16-18, and the degree of verbal correspondence seems to require the existence of a literary relationship between the two epistles. This relationship has further implications, not least for the text-critical evaluation; the reconstructed text of the primary writing must be one from which the other writing might have resulted.

1. The Literary Relationship: An Open Question

In Richard J. Bauckham's account of the research on 2 Peter, he outlines five possible explanations and provides ample reference to the respective adherents:[1] (1) Jude is dependent on 2 Peter; (2) 2 Peter is dependent on Jude; (3) 2 Peter in its present form is dependent on Jude. However, the passages that show this dependence are interpolations into the original 2 Peter; (4) Both works are dependent on a common source; (5) Both works were written by the same author. The first explanation (Jude is dependent on 2 Peter) prevailed before the late 19th century, but the second explanation (2 Peter is dependent on Jude) has become the most widely accepted among modern scholars.[2] The other three possible explanations

---

[1] Richard J. Bauckham, "2 Peter: An Account of Research," *ANRW* 25.5:3714-15.
[2] Cf. Lauri Thurén, "The Relationship between 2 Peter and Jude: A Classical Problem Resolved?" in *The Catholic Epistles and the Tradition* (ed. Jacques Schlosser; BETL 176; Leuven: Leuven University Press/Peeters, 2004), 451-60. Some scholars from the 20th century and onwards have argued for the priority of 2 Peter. See for example Charles Bigg, *A Critical and Exegetical Commentary on the Epistles of St. Peter and St. Jude* (ICC; Edinburgh: T & T Clark, 1901), 216-24; R. C. H. Lenski, *The Interpretation of The Epistles of St. Peter, St. John and St. Jude* (Columbus: The Wartburg Press, 1945), 597-99; Richard Wolff, *A Commentary on the Epistle of Jude* (Grand Rapids: Zondervan, 1960), 26-27; Douglas J. Moo, *2 Peter and Jude* (The NIV Application Commentary; Grand Rapids: Zondervan, 1996), 17-18, 28; Anders Gerdmar,

outlined above are generally more complicated than the hypothesis of direct dependence.[3] These explanations have received relatively little support and will not receive any further consideration here.

It is appropriate to first consider the question of methodology. What methods have been, and should be used in order to resolve the problem of literary dependence? Traditionally, extrinsic arguments played a decisive role. Most importantly, Petrine authorship of 2 Peter was long taken for granted and, consequently, it was difficult to imagine how the great apostle Peter could have borrowed material from the lesser-known Jude. As scholarship assumed a more sophisticated historical understanding of the two writings, the arguments gradually shifted in character; some scholars still defend 2 Peter as authentic, but generally supply other arguments for the priority of 2 Peter.[4] Nevertheless, the standard approach among modern commentators is to assume the priority of Jude, and to discuss the parallel passages in the two works more or less in detail, and thereby demonstrate how 2 Peter has adapted the material.[5] However, it is clear that even full scale stylistic comparisons cannot resolve the question in any final way, since the results obviously have led scholars to take opposite positions.

From the 1970s, redaction-critical methodology was applied to the investigation of the literary relationship between the two epistles. The examinations of Tord Fornberg, Jerome H. Neyrey and Richard Bauckham have challenged the assumption that the writings, containing so much common material, have to reflect a similar background.[6] Typically,

---

Rethinking the Judaism-Hellenism Dichotomy: A Historiographical Case Study of Second Peter and Jude (CBNTS 36; Stockholm: Almqvist & Wiksell International, 2001), 116-23.

[3] For example, Bo Reicke suggests that the parallels originate from a common sermonic pattern, possibly oral, formulated to resist the threat against the church (*The Epistles of James, Peter, and Jude* [AB 37; New York: Doubleday, 1964], 148, 189-90). However, J. N. D. Kelly raises the fatal objection that "the parallels are not confined to the denunciatory blocks" and, therefore, "the supposed common source must have been to all intents and purposes identical with Jude" (*A Commentary on the Epistles of Peter and Jude* [BNTC; London: A. & C. Black, 1969], 226). Kelly uses the same argument in favor of the priority of Jude, but this is more open to debate (see the discussion of the criterion of brevity below). The last alternative, that both works were written by the same author, is difficult in several regards, not least for stylistic and linguistic reasons.

[4] Cf. Donald Guthrie, *New Testament Introduction* (Leicester: Intervarsity Press, 1970), 820-48.

[5] Joseph B. Mayor provides one of the earliest, and yet most elaborate discussions to this effect (*The Epistle of St. Jude and the Second Epistle of St. Peter*. London: Macmillan, 1907), i-xxv.

[6] Tord Fornberg, *An Early Church in a Pluralistic Society: A Study of 2 Peter* (CBNTS 9; Lund: CWK Gleerup, 1977), 33-59; Jerome H. Neyrey, "The Form and Background of the Polemic in 2 Peter" (Ph.D.diss., Yale University, 1977), 119-67; idem, *2 Peter, Jude* (AB 37C; New York: Doubleday, 1993); Richard J. Bauckham, *Jude, 2 Peter* (WBC 50; Waco: Word Books, 1983).

the epistles had been labeled as products of "Frühkatholizismus."[7] Fornberg, Neyrey and Bauckham, in turn, concluded that 2 Peter and Jude, albeit of similar polemic nature, nevertheless derive from quite different historical situations in which the respective author combated different adversaries by using the common material in his own way.

A central theme of the opponents' teaching that comes to surface in 2 Peter is an eschatological skepticism (see esp. 3:4, 9a). The opponents scoffed at the predictions of a final coming and denied God's eschatological judgment, which would eliminate evil and establish a world of righteousness (2:3b). Neyrey identifies this skepticism as an expression of popular polemic against theodicy.[8] The opponents' negative attitude to eschatology was the result of a denial of God's sovereignty and providence. Such an attitude was usually associated with "atheists" such as the Epicureans. Hence, the attack on the prophecy of the Parousia in 1:16 is a denial, not only of a future judgment and of God's providence, but a denial of prophecy as such, and in extension a denial of a God who created the world and who could predict future events.

In Jude, it is more difficult to say anything about the specific nature of the teaching or doctrines that the opponents brought into the church. Jude concentrates on the opponents themselves, and brands them as evil heretics who indulged in immoral behavior, probably sexual misconduct (vv. 6-8, 10). They too denied the Lord (v. 5), which may or may not include a denial of future judgment. In general, the opponents have been regarded as in some sense Gnostics. Usually, scholars refer to the beginnings of Gnosticism, and few today would ascribe to them clearly second-century Gnostic features. Bauckham is very careful in this regard: "In the absence of cosmological dualism it is probably misleading to speak of Gnosticism at all. At most the antinomianism of Jude's opponents was one of the streams which flowed into later Gnosticism."[9]

All of the redaction-critical studies mentioned above have assumed the priority of Jude as a working hypothesis, and, hence, they have offered

---

[7] Ernst Käsemann was among the first to describe the theological character of 2 Peter, "Denn der 2. Petrusbrief ist vom Anfang bis zum Ende ein Dokument frühkatholischer Anschauung und wohl die fragwürdigste Schrift des Kanons" ("Eine Apologie der urchristlichen Eschatologie," *ZTK* 49 [1952]: 272). Cf. Fornberg, *An Early Church*, 3-6; Bauckham, *Jude, 2 Peter*, 8-11, 151-54.

[8] Neyrey, *2 Peter, Jude*, 124-27.

[9] Bauckham, "The Letter of Jude: An Account of Research," *ANRW* 25.5:3811. It will be noted that the question of the opponents is intertwined with a number of other questions such as the date of the epistle. Bauckham has argued for an early date, plausibly in the 50s ("Jude, Epistle of," *ABD* 3:1101).

plausible explanations of how 2 Peter has adapted the material in Jude to new circumstances.[10] However, it will be noted that these scholars disagree over many of 2 Peter's assumed redactional alterations of Jude. Bauckham rightly criticizes Fornberg for being too optimistic in his claim to have "refuted" the theory of the priority of 2 Peter, since Fornberg has only tested and argued convincingly for the hypothesis of Jude's priority.[11] One cannot *a priori* exclude an equally plausible explanation of Jude's use of 2 Peter. To simplify the matter: adaptations of material in 2 Peter which have been explained on the basis of a certain redactional interest on the part of the author may be interpreted in the opposite way, as adaptations in Jude due to a different redactional interest, such as may have caused the author to excise from, or add certain elements to the common material.[12] Hence, the question of literary dependence between 2 Peter and Jude has not fully been resolved and remains an open question.

2. Criteria and the Balance of Probability

It will be clear by now that scholars have approached the data with a different presupposition of the direction in which literary dependence lies, and both sides have adduced reasonable arguments in support of their position. In my opinion, one way forward is a more conscious discussion of valid criteria on which a judgment should eventually be based. This is not to say that there has been a lack of criteria or good arguments in scholarly discussions hitherto, but I think that a larger consciousness and explicitness in the application of different criteria, redaction-critical, linguistic, stylistic, theological, etc., would be welcome.[13] In this connection, one may look to

---

[10] Cf. the recent attempt by Terrance Callan ("Use of the Letter of Jude by the Second Letter of Peter," *Bib* 85 [2004]: 42-64). In the abstract Callan states, "Assuming that 2 Pet 2,1-3,3 is dependent on Jude 4-18, this essay describes in detail the way the author of 2 Peter has used Jude's material. It is clear that the author of 2 Peter has not simply incorporated Jude, as is sometimes asserted." Indeed, Callan's latter conclusion confirms the fact that he has worked with an "assumption."

[11] Fornberg, *An Early Church*, 58; Bauckham, *Jude, 2 Peter*, 143.

[12] Bauckham outlines the task as follows: "Redaction criticism could demonstrate the priority of Jude only by considering at each point the relative plausibility of a redaction of Jude by 2 Peter and of a redaction of 2 Peter by Jude, and then calculating the overall relative plausibility of the two possibilities. But this would be a very complex task, because there is a great deal of room for differing interpretations of redactional changes" (*Jude, 2 Peter*, 143).

[13] Michael J. Gilmour offers an insightful discussion of criteria for determining the value of parallels between 2 Peter and other writings (*The Significance of Parallels between 2 Peter and Other Early Christian Literature* [Academia Biblica 10; Atlanta: Society of Biblical Literature, 2002], 47-80). In the specific treatment of the relationship of Jude to 2 Peter (pp. 83-91), he repeats a number of common arguments for the different positions, and Gilmour's accomplishment, in my view, consists in the refutation of several secondary arguments.

other areas of exegetical research for analogies, for example, the so-called "canons of criticism" which are applied in textual criticism, or the criteria for judging authentic material in the Gospels in the quest for the historical Jesus.

However, terms like *criteria* or *canons* should not be misunderstood as functioning in a mechanical fashion to decide priority—in reality they are measures of probability, which generate complementary or even competing arguments for priority. At the same time, the arguments will be of varying force, more or less relevant to a given context. Thus, the specific nature of the problem in question must be the final guide as to the formulation of adequate criteria to be applied—the validity of the criteria is displayed only in the analytic interaction with the texts themselves.

As mentioned above, Anders Gerdmar is among the few modern scholars who have argued for the priority of 2 Peter, and his arguments have gained some acceptance in the contemporary discussion.[14] Gerdmar applies "reversed heuristics" on the two epistles, which, in this case, means that he assumes the priority of 2 Peter and attempts to demonstrate how Jude could have redacted 2 Peter. In my view, however, his attempt is unsuccessful; his procedure illustrates the application of criteria which are not relevant to the particular context, i.e., criteria rendered invalid by contextual factors. Therefore, my own analysis below will respond mainly to Gerdmar as being representative in several regards. My point is that judgments should ideally be based on criteria that are suited to the particular context, so as to generate arguments as unequivocal as possible. Then other kinds of criteria can generate supportive arguments, reinforcing a prior verdict. After all, it is always a matter of probability, weighing one argument against the other—everything is possible, but not everything is likely.

---

[14] For example, Thomas J. Kraus states, "[Ü]ber Bauckham und Kelly hinaus gibt es weitere Argumente, wie sie von Anders Gerdmar vorgetragen wurden . . . die auch den umgekehrten Fall—2Pet als Vorlage von Jud—möglich erscheinen lassen, selbst wenn ich die erste Relation für richtig halte" (Thomas J. Kraus, review of S. J. Kraftchick, *Jude, 2 Peter*, n.p. [published 15 May 2004]. Online: *http://www.bookreviews.org/pdf/3126_3436.pdf*). See further Thomas J. Kraus, *Sprache, Stil und historischer Ort des zweiten Petrusbriefes* (WUNT 2.136; Tübingen: Mohr Siebeck, 2001).

3. Criteria in the Current Debate
Under this heading I will list only a few examples of criteria, to which scholars have appealed:[15]

3.1 The Criterion of the More Difficult Reading
This criterion plays a decisive role in Gerdmar's attempt to prove the priority of 2 Peter. He explicitly declares his dependence on the principles of textual criticism, specifically the criteria of internal evidence as outlined in Metzger's *Textual Commentary*:

> I regard it probable that the more difficult or syntactically less clear the reading, as well as the use of unfamiliar words; or the use of odd, faulty or less elegant grammatical forms and Semitisms, the more likely it is to be altered by a redactor, because a redactor may add pronouns, conjunctions, and expletives or anything that may enhance the flow.[16]

I am inclined to agree with Gerdmar that a redactor is likely to "enhance the flow" and make a passage more comprehensive. However, this criterion must be used with greatest caution; the more general a principle, or "canon of criticism," the more it is liable to improper use. General principles, in particular, are often in need of qualification, and, as pointed out above, must not be applied in a mechanical fashion.[17] In fact, another traditionally venerable text-critical canon, "prefer the shorter reading" (*lectio brevior potior*), has proven to be in such need of qualification that some regard it as relatively useless.[18] Hence, a general principle must often give way to a more specific principle that is applicable to the specific textual problem. One specific factor in the particular case of literary dependence between 2

---

[15] Guthrie provides an extensive list of similar arguments for the priority of Jude and 2 Peter, respectively but leaves the question unresolved (*New Testament Introduction*, 920-25). However, Thurén points out that Guthrie's list of arguments is unhelpful and that there are "more weighty aspects to be considered in this issue" ("The Relationship between 2 Peter and Jude," in *The Catholic Epistles and the Tradition* [ed. Schlosser], 451).

[16] Gerdmar, *Rethinking*, 118 (cf. notes 16, 21); cf. Bruce M. Metzger, *A Textual Commentary on the Greek New Testament* (2d ed.; Stuttgart: Deutsche Bibelgesellschaft, 1994), 12-14.

[17] Cf. Bertil Albrektson, "'Difficilior Lectio Probabilior'—A Rule of Textual Criticism and Its Use in Old Testament Studies," in *Remembering All the Way* (ed. Bertil Albrektsson; Oudtestamentische Studiën 21; Leiden: Brill, 1981), 5-18. See also, Kurt Aland and Barbara Aland who specifically reject a mechanical function for the rules of the harder reading, the shorter reading, and harmonization (*The Text of the New Testament: An Introduction to the Critical Editions and to the Theory and Practice of Modern Textual Criticism* [trans. Erroll F. Rhodes; 2d rev. and enl. ed.; Grand Rapids: Eerdmans, 1995], 280-81).

[18] See e.g., Michael W. Holmes, "Reasoned Eclecticism in New Testament Textual Criticism" in *The Text of the New Testament in Contemporary Research: Essays on the Status Quaestionis* (ed. Bart D. Ehrman and Michael W. Holmes; SD 46; Grand Rapids: Eerdmans, 1995), 343.

Peter and Jude is the extensive use of traditional material. Therefore the criterion of the harder reading may be rendered invalid if, in a specific passage, a redactor betrays independent influence from other sources or traditions; what may at first glance look like a more difficult, and therefore original, reading may be a redactor's adaptation of the material by use of another source or tradition (see below).

Of course, another reason for being cautious in the identification of "the more difficult reading" is the fact that it is not easy for a modern reader to identify what difficulties an ancient redactor would perceive in a text. It should be noted that harmonization to parallel passages in the manuscript tradition of 2 Peter and Jude may indicate perceived difficulties on the part of the ancient scribes, who might have turned to a parallel passage in order to resolve such difficulties. However, this data is ambiguous and can only be used as a supportive argument. On the other hand, the preferred view of literary priority should subsequently affect the way one regards the textual variation in parallel passages.

3. 2 The Criterion of Brevity

Since Jude is the briefer document of the two, some scholars have argued that it is more probable that it is the source for 2 Peter. Guthrie considers this to be a strong argument for the priority of Jude:

> There would be an obvious point in an enlargement of an earlier work where the additions would enable the author to append his own special features. But the opposite is less easy to imagine, especially when the briefer epistle appears merely to extract a portion of the longer and append little more than a salutation and a doxology. There seems to be no adequate reason for the publication of the shorter epistle at all if 2 Peter already exists, and still less [under] so obscure a name as Jude.[19]

This argument is of course very attractive at first sight. However, as pointed out above, the usefulness in textual criticism of the principle of preferring the shorter text has been called into question.[20] A scribe or a redactor may either shorten or expand his text, and it is evident that the redactor—whether the author of Jude or 2 Peter—has done both things with his material. Moreover, it needs to be pointed out that the unique material of Jude constitutes more than merely "a salutation and a doxology." The appeal of v. 3 expresses the main purpose of the epistle,

---

[19] Guthrie, *New Testament Introduction*, 920.
[20] Cf. Gerdmar who in this debate likewise questions the validity of this criterion by appealing to Josephus' redaction of the Letter of Aristeas as a telling example, where the priority of Aristeas is a given: "Josephus alternatively shortens and expands Aristeas: he adds, omits, and corrects" (*Rethinking*, 117).

further elaborated in the exhortations of vv. 20-23, which constitute the climax of the epistle.[21] The common material found in the pesher-exegesis of vv. 4-19 forms only a background to the appeal, which is the main point of the epistle.

3.3 The Criterion of Use (or Non-Use) of Apocryphal Sources

The use of the apocryphal books *1 Enoch* and the *Assumption of Moses* (or, more appropriately, the *Testament of Moses*) in Jude apparently caused some church fathers to doubt its status as Scripture.[22] It is commonly suggested that the author of 2 Peter omitted these direct quotations because of their unorthodox character, and, evidently, he does express concern for "all scriptures" and their correct interpretation (2 Pet 1:19; 3:16).[23] On the other hand, doubts about *1 Enoch* seem to have become common only in the 4th century. Earlier, in the 2nd century, the book was one of the most popular in the Christian church.[24] Perhaps the author of 2 Peter was simply unfamiliar with this other works that are used in Jude, or else he assumed his readers would be unfamiliar with them, possibly because they were not yet in wide circulation in the church. Besides, the author of 2 Peter did not disapprove of Jewish apocryphal works in general, since he probably made use of another Jewish apocryphal source in 3:4-13, cited in *1 Clem.* 23:3 and *2 Clem.* 11:2-4, which dealt with the issue of eschatological delay.[25]

3.4 The Linguistic Criterion

W. F. Howard has characterized the author of Jude as "quite at home in Hellenistic idiom," whereas he ascribed to the author of 2 Peter "an

---

[21] So Bauckham, "Jude, Epistle of," 1098. In his rhetorical-critical analysis of Jude, D. F. Watson identifies the main point of the epistle in the comparatively brief *narratio* of v. 4 (which has a parallel in 2 Pet 2:1-3): "It [*narratio*] describes the exigence and the points upon which the rhetor would like the audience to render judgment" (*Invention, Arrangement, and Style: Rhetorical Criticism of Jude and 2 Peter* [SBLDS 104; Atlanta: Scholars Press, 1988], 43). In my view, however, Bauckham's identification of the structure and genre of the epistle is based on a sounder method. In his works on Jude, Bauckham has convincingly shown the massive influence from Jewish tradition and exegetical methods, whereas Watson is too heavily dependent upon Greco-Roman rhetorical handbooks.

[22] See e.g., Jerome, *Vir. ill.* 4 (PL 23:613); Didymus the Blind, in his commentary on Jude, mentions that some doubted the authority of the epistle on these grounds (*Enarrat. Ep. Cath.* [PL 34:1815]).

[23] See e.g., Guthrie who states, "It is significant, that 2 Peter contains no reference to the book of Enoch, which Jude formally cites" (*New Testament Introduction*, 921-22).

[24] For a list of second-century writers that freely use *1 Enoch*, see Bauckham, *Jude, 2 Peter*, 139.

[25] The origin of this "prophetic word" (*2 Clem.* 11:2) or "scripture" (*1 Clem.* 23:3) is unknown. Cyril C. Richardson refers to the lost apocalypse of *Eldad and Modad*, of which there is only one positively identified fragment in *Herm. Vis.* 2:3:4 (Cyril C. Richardson, ed., *Early Christian Fathers* [New York: Macmillan, 1979], 55). Cf. Bauckham, *Jude, 2 Peter*, 140, 284-85.

artificial dialect of high-sounding words learnt from rhetoricians or books and employed with the uneasy touch of one who acquired language in later life."[26] Consequently, one may suggest that the polished language of Jude has been obscured by the author of 2 Peter, in his parallel words and phrases of a more awkward character.[27] As pointed out above, however, scholars reasoning from the principle of preferring the harder reading will opt for the priority of 2 Peter for the same reason—this is a typical case where two kinds of criteria, applied to one and the same feature in the text, generate contradictory arguments.[28]

4. Contextually Defined Criteria: A Proposal

In the interaction with the texts in some of the parallel passages, I shall propose three contextually defined criteria.

4.1 The Criterion of Redactional Purpose

Elements in parallel passages that fit the polemic context and the author's general interest, but at the same time refer to, or prepare for passages that treat other subject matters, are more likely to have been added in a redaction. On the other hand, the opposite possibility, that such attractive elements were excised, requires a specific reason. In short, the more attractive an element in terms of the redactor's purpose, the less is the likelihood that he would remove that same element.

---

[26] James H. Moulton and W. F. Howard, *Accidence and Word Formation with an Appendix on Semitisms in the New Testament* (vol. 2 of *Grammar of New Testament Greek*; eds. James H. Moulton, W. F. Howard and Nigel Turner; Edinburgh: T. & T. Clark, 1920), 27-28. Gerdmar uses a part of this reference in order to show that 2 Peter is regarded as having "high literary Greek" and after his own investigation he concludes, "the dominant picture of 2Peter having good literary Greek is highly debatable" (*Rethinking*, 30, 62). However, I think that Gerdmar has misrepresented W. F. Howard's evaluation of 2 Peter. Moreover, I feel somewhat uncomfortable with Gerdmar's description of the "dominant picture of 2Peter;" cf. Thurén who says, "scholars have assessed the style in 2 Peter in different ways. In many studies, it is characterized in a negative way" ("The Relationship between 2 Peter and Jude," in *The Catholic Epistles and the Tradition* [ed. Schlosser], 453). Thurén himself has tried to show that 2 Peter is consistent with Asian style in contrast to Attic style ("Style Never Goes Out of Fashion—2 Peter Reconsidered," in *Rhetoric, Scripture and Theology* [ed. Stanley E. Porter and Thomas H. Olbricht; JSNTSup 131; Sheffield: Sheffield Academic Press, 1996], 341-47).

[27] So F. H. Chase, "Jude, Epistle of," *HDB*, 2:803.

[28] This phenomenon occurs frequently in textual criticism, where the two types of internal evidence, (a) intrinsic evidence based upon considerations of what the author was more likely to have written, and (b) transcriptional evidence based upon consideration of the habits of scribes, are often contradictory.

In Jude 5-7, 11, and 2 Peter 2:4-8, 15-16 we encounter examples from the OT of ancient punishments and salvation. Below is a list of these examples:

Jude	2 Pet 2
The desert generation (v. 5)	
The angels who sinned (v. 6)	The angels who sinned (v. 4)
	The Flood: punishment of the old world
	Salvation of Noah (v. 5)
Sodom and Gomorrah (v. 7)	Sodom and Gomorrah (v. 6)
	Salvation of Lot (vv. 7-8)
Cain, Balaam and Korah (v. 11)	Balaam (vv. 15-16)

As is apparent, Jude contains elements not found in 2 Peter, and vice versa, so in this case the redactor has excised some elements and added others. Either the author of Jude has omitted the reference to the Flood, to Noah (Gen 6:5-8:22) and to Lot (Gen 19), but added the reference to the desert generation (Num 14:26-38), Cain (Gen 4:3-16), and Korah (Num 16:1-35), or else, the author of 2 Peter has done the opposite. Which scenario is the most probable? All of the examples of divine punishments in the OT fit the immediate polemic context—the opponents will likewise be judged by God.

In 2 Peter, the theme of judgment is coupled with a theme of salvation, both of which are neatly summed up in 2 Pet 2:9: "[T]he Lord knows how to rescue godly men from trials and to hold the unrighteous for the day of judgment" (NIV). However, Fornberg identifies another dimension in the references in 2 Peter 2, which is missing in Jude at this point, namely the eschatological.[29] He identifies the water-fire pattern in the sequence of the Flood and Sodom and Gomorrah, which prepares for the eschatological statement in 2 Pet 3:6-7: "By these waters also the world of that time was deluged and destroyed. By the same word the present heavens and earth are reserved for fire, being kept for the day of judgment and destruction of ungodly men" (NIV). Moreover, Fornberg points out that the author of 2 Peter is dependent on a tradition contained in Luke 17:26-30, where Noah and Lot are clearly eschatological figures (the only other occurrence of these characters in direct combination). In this way, Fornberg has provided a very compelling motive for the author of 2 Peter to add these elements— they are in line with his particular eschatological interest.

---

[29] Fornberg, *An Early Church*, 41.

Hence, the scoffers' position in 2 Pet 3:4 is formulated so as to fit the defense arguing from the example of Noah and the Flood in 2:4, regardless of whether he is using a specific Jewish apocalyptic source or not (see above). Evald Lövestam draws a similar conclusion in his examination of the argumentation against the scoffers in 2 Pet 3:3-13:

> Seen within the framework of the composition of 2 Pet it is likely that the specific reference to the *dor* [Heb. generation] of the Flood has been made primarily with the exposition in chap. 3 in view. . . . The very point of departure in 2 Pet shows considerable similarity to the situation before the Flood according to ancient Jewish picture. The people . . . turned their backs on God and lived according to their own desires. They did not listen to the warnings of the righteous Noah. . . . In some passages in early Jewish literature it is also said that the people used ridicule as a weapon (cf. 2 Pet 3:4). It can thus be seen that the presentation in 2 Pet 3:3-13 moves in a motif and conceptual sphere which was related to the *dor* of the Flood and the catastrophe of the deluge.[30]

The question now remains whether Jude displays no interest in eschatological salvation. If so, it then could be argued that he omitted the references to Noah and Lot, because they constituted an element of salvation and the aim of his epistle was only to condemn the adversaries, focusing on their judgment. But that is not the case. In the salutation, the recipients are addressed as "those who have been called, who are loved by God the Father and kept by Jesus Christ" (NIV). There is much to suggest that the second participial clause, Ἰησοῦ Χριστῷ τετηρημένοις κλητοῖς, should be interpreted in an eschatological sense, "kept for Jesus Christ" (cf. 1 Thess 5:23; 1 Pet 1:4; and φυλάσσω in Jude 24). In v. 21 the addressees are told to "wait for the mercy of our Lord Jesus Christ"—an eschatological expectation of mercy for God's people to be revealed in the Parousia, to which Jude also refers in his Christological interpretation of *1 En.* 1:9 in vv. 14-15. Finally, in the textually corrupt passage in vv. 22-23 the author continues on the theme of perseverance and salvation. The latter verse even speaks about snatching persons from the fire (and the presence of these words in the original is undisputed), and an association to the story of Lot's rescue from Sodom and Gomorrah would not seem farfetched.[31]

---

[30] Evald Lövestam, *Jesus and "this Generation"* (CBNTS 25; Stockholm: Almqvist & Wiksell International, 1995), 107-109. Cf. Anton Vögtle, "Petrus und Paulus nach dem Zweiten Petrusbrief," in *Kontinuität und Einheit, Festschrift für Franz Mussner* (ed. Paul-Gerhard Müller and Werner Stenger; Freiburg: Herder, 1981), 230.

[31] Cf. Amos 4:11 (LXX): κατέστρεψα ὑμᾶς, καθὼς κατέστρεψεν ὁ θεὸς Σοδομα καὶ Γομορρα, καὶ ἐγένεσθε ὡς δαλὸς ἐξεσπασμένος ἐκ πυρός· καὶ οὐδ' ὡς ἐπεστρέψατε πρός με, λέγει κύριος.

On the other hand, it may be argued that the particular aim of the section in vv. 4-19 in Jude, a kind of apocalyptic *pesher*-exegesis of types and prophecies from the OT and *Jewish Pseudepigrapha*, is exclusively devoted to show that both the false teachers and their condemnation by God was predicted long ago (v. 4); and that, for this reason, all elements of salvation in these verses have been excised in redaction. However, there are implicit elements of salvation in these verses too, e.g., in v. 5 where the author says that "the Lord delivered his people out of Egypt, but later destroyed those who did not believe." The implied warning of divine punishment seems to have a clear connection to the positive appeal to God's people, in v. 3, to "contend for the faith which was once delivered unto the saints."

What is far more significant, however, is the absence of a reference to the Flood in Jude. The Flood is one of the main examples of punitive judgment in Jewish literature and, as in 2 Pet 2:5-6, it was sometimes linked to the destruction of Sodom and Gomorrah as the two prime examples of divine judgment.[32] It is very difficult to imagine why Jude should have omitted this reference if he adapted the material from 2 Peter, since he clearly displays a strong interest in eschatological judgment.[33] Some clear examples include the reference to "judgment on the great Day" (v. 6) and, further, in vv. 14-15 in which *1 En.* 1:9 is quoted, "See, the Lord is coming with thousands upon thousands of his holy ones to judge everyone, and to convict all the ungodly of all the ungodly acts they have done in the ungodly way, and of all the harsh words ungodly sinners have spoken against him."[34]

---

[32] Cf. Jacques Schlosser, "Les Jours de Noé et de Lot: A Propos de Luc, XVII, 26-30," *RB* 80 (1973): 13-14, 23-24; Olle Christoffersson, *The Earnest Expectation of the Creature. The Flood Tradition As Matrix of Romans 8:18-27* (CBNTS 23; Stockholm: Almqvist & Wiksell International, 1990), 47-93.

[33] Gerdmar says of the eschatology of Jude that it focuses on judgment, as part of the pragmatic strategy of the epistle. Then he goes on to identify and discuss the eschatological statements in vv. 6, 7, 13, 14-15, 18, 21, 23(?), 25 (*Rethinking*, 184).

[34] Fornberg implies that the passage was omitted by the author of 2 Peter, since the aorist form in Jude 14 (ἦλθεν) cannot be read as future and, therefore, it "could not be used against those who denied the parousia of Christ" (*An Early Church*, 47). It is possible that the author of 2 Peter did find the verb form disturbing. However, the aorist represents an Aramaic prophetic perfect in the original (cf. Dan 7:27; see also GKC 312-13), and it is almost certain that Jude intended the citation as a reference to the future—he even specified the subject of the verb as κύριος. The explicit reference to the Lord is neither found in the original Aramaic of *1 Enoch*, nor in the Ethiopic or Greek translations, and, thus, it probably represents Jude's Christological interpretation referring to the Parousia. There are other explanations for the omission in 2 Peter. We have already considered the possibility that *1 Enoch* was unknown to the author of 2 Peter, or among his addressees.

Finally, we must ask the reverse question concerning the absence of references in 2 Peter to the desert generation (Jude 5), and Cain and Korah (Jude 11): is there any reason why the author of 2 Peter should have omitted these references to OT judgments? Fornberg offers a compelling argument for the omission of the former in 2 Peter, in that "it was wrongly placed in terms of chronology [in Jude], and could not exemplify the pattern of destruction of water and fire respectively, which was used in 2 Pet 3:5-7."[35] The same awkward chronology is true of the three references in Jude to Cain (Gen 4), Balaam (Num 31), and Korah (Num 16) both in regard to their sequence and in relation to previous references. In this case, the principle of the harder reading evidently points in the same direction.

4.2 The Criterion of Source Development

If certain passages where there is relatively high verbal agreement between the two epistles contain elements that can be traced back to a particular identifiable source, then it is possible to identify a line of development; the redactor who adapts the material is likely to remove the text farther from its underlying source. This is especially true if he or she is unfamiliar with the source in question, or else, if the redactor thinks that the readers will be unfamiliar with it.

I shall examine two parallel passages more closely, in order to identify the underlying sources and traditions of the respective accounts, and consider the implications for the question of literary dependence.

a) Jude 6 and 2 Pet 2:4

Jude 6	2 Pet 2:4
ἀγγέλους τε τοὺς μὴ τηρήσαντας τὴν ἑαυτῶν ἀρχὴν ἀλλὰ ἀπολιπόντας τὸ ἴδιον οἰκητήριον εἰς κρίσιν μεγάλης ἡμέρας δεσμοῖς ἀϊδίοις ὑπὸ ζόφον τετήρηκεν	Εἰ γὰρ ὁ θεὸς ἀγγέλων ἁμαρτησάντων οὐκ ἐφείσατο ἀλλὰ σειραῖς ζόφου ταρταρώσας παρέδωκεν εἰς κρίσιν τηρουμένους

In Gerdmar's application of the principle of the harder reading to this passage, he states, "Jude uses ζόφος in a more comprehensible way: ὑπὸ ζόφον; *dark chains* σειραῖς ζόφου [in 2 Pet 2:4] is more difficult to understand."[36] Before proceeding, we should note the presence of a textual

---

[35] Fornberg, *An Early Church*, 46.
[36] Gerdmar, *Rethinking*, 118-19. Admittedly, σειραῖς is more rare than δεσμοῖς. Mayor points out that several of 2 Peter's more rare forms are due to his apparent sensitiveness to euphony

variant in 2 Peter, σιροῖς ζόφου ("in pits of darkness"), attested by 01 **L**:T (02 03 04 81: σειροῖς). The UBS Committee adopted σειραῖς, since it is the oldest and most widespread reading, attested by 𝔓[72] 044 33 1739 1881, as well as many versional witnesses, some patristic witnesses and almost all minuscules.[37] Nevertheless, the external evidence is apparently ambiguous, and the internal evidence, in my view, is balanced; scribes may have changed an original σειραῖς to σιροῖς under the influence of pagan Greek usage where the word refers to an underground pit, or they could have made the opposite change, harmonizing to δεσμοῖς in Jude. (Any of the changes could occur via the itacism σειροῖς attested in important witnesses.) As noted above, one must beware of a circular reasoning; it is true that the question of literary priority affects how one regards the variants in this and other parallel passages. In this case, the priority of Jude would definitely favor an original σειραῖς in 2 Peter, being the adaptation of the author (not a scribe) to δεσμοῖς in Jude.[38] On the other hand, these textual variants cannot be used in any way to determine the priority of either Jude or 2 Peter.

Gerdmar goes on to suggest that it is easier to explain that Jude added μεγάλης ἡμέρας to κρίσιν (the "great day of judgment," or "the judgment of the great day") than the opposite procedure.[39] However, Gerdmar offers no such explanation, and he does not consider that Jude in the whole passage, rather than modifying 2 Peter, is largely dependent upon the account of the fallen angels in *1 En.* 6-19 (particularly ch. 10). In *1 En.* 10:4-6 God commands Raphael, "'Bind Azaz'el hand and foot (and) throw him into the darkness!' And he made a hole in the desert which was in Duda'el and cast him there; he threw on top of him rugged and sharp rocks. And he covered his face in order that he may not see light; and in order that he

---

and rhythm, which could well be the case here (*The Epistle of St. Jude*, lxii). Gerdmar suggests that Wis 17:16, which speaks of ἀλύσει σκότους, may lie behind 2 Peter, but if that is true, the author still formulated a more peculiar phrase than that found in his source.

[37] Gerdmar also notes the alternate reading σιροῖς, but the discussion is unclear in several regards (*Rethinking*, 138, esp. n. 73). Gerdmar mistakenly thinks that only 03 has the spelling σειροῖς (attested by 02 03 04 81 *al*). He mentions that "the itacism could confuse σειροῖς and σιροῖς," but the main point is the possible confusion (in any direction) of σιροῖς and σειραῖς via the itacism σειροῖς. Furthermore, he misrepresents Klaus Wachtel, who favors the reading σιροῖς (*Der byzantinische Text der Katholischen Briefe: eine Untersuchung zur Entstehung der Koine des Neuen Testaments* [ANTF 24; Berlin; New York: W. de Gruyter, 1995], 103, n. 56). Wachtel does not suggest that "σειραῖς can be 2Peter's adjustment to Jude's δεσμοῖς." On the contrary, Wachtel is referring to the adjustment of scribes.

[38] The priority of 2 Peter would probably imply that the author of Jude had access to a MS reading σειραῖς.

[39] Gerdmar, *Rethinking*, 119.

may be sent into the fire on the great day of judgment."[40] Some manuscripts have the whole passage in the imperative, and add after "rocks," "Cover him with darkness and let him abide there forever." Furthermore, in 10:12, preserved in the Aramaic fragment 4QEn[b] (1:4:11), God commands Michael to bind the fallen angels "for seventy generations in the valleys of the earth, until the great day of their judgment."[41] The phrase "until the great day of judgment" occurs also in *1 En.* 22:11 and 84:4. In this connection, it is also possible to appeal to the linguistic criterion as a supportive argument—why would the author of Jude, with evident command of the Greek language, add μεγάλης ἡμέρας to κρίσιν and, thus, create a very awkward phrase in Greek if not due to his heavy reliance on *1 Enoch* in the first place.[42] Semitisms are not prominent in his epistle, yet some are found in his formal quotation of *1 Enoch* in vv. 14-15, which, significantly, is a decisive evidence of his dependence on and familiarity with this Jewish source.[43]

The context in *1 En.* 10 further suggests that the phrase "forever" (in Greek MSS, εἰς τοὺς αἰῶνας/εἰς τὸν αἰῶνα) in 10:5 refers to the duration of the world until the great day of judgment. Hence, the same source accounts for the notion of δεσμοῖς ἀϊδίοις ("everlasting chains") in Jude 6, which Gerdmar takes as the more comprehensible in comparison with σειραῖς ζόφου ("dark chains"). I would argue that the expression in Jude is just as difficult without resort to the source in *1 Enoch*, as is evident especially from the patristic and versional evidence, which display various substitutions or the omission of the adjective attributive altogether; how

---

[40] Translation and textual apparatus in E. Isaac, ed., "1 (Ethiopic Apocalypse of) ENOCH," in *The Old Testament Pseudepigrapha* (ed. James H. Charlesworth; 2 vols.; London: Darton Longman & Todd, 1983-1985), 1:5-89.

[41] There are many other signs that Jude uses *1 Enoch* in its original Aramaic form rather than in Greek translation. See further the textual commentary on vv. 14-15.

[42] An appeal to the case of Luke and his purported "septuagintal style" is not warranted; Albert Wifstrand has argued that Luke consciously imitated the style of the Septuagint ("Lukas och den grekiska klassicismen," *SEÅ* 6 [1941]: 243-62). However, William G. Most suggests that Luke's style is the result of his having used documentary source material written in that style ("Did St Luke Imitate the Septuagint?," *JSNT* 15 [1982]: 30-41). Cf. the recent contribution of Loveday Alexander, "Septuaginta, Fachprosa, Imitatio: Albert Wifstrand and the Language of Luke-Acts," in *Die Apostelgeschichte und die hellenistische Geschichtsschreibung: Festschrift für Eckhard Plümacher zu seinem 65. Geburtstag* (ed. Cilliers Breytenbach et al.; Leiden/Boston: Brill, 2004), 1-26. Regardless of the cause behind the feature in Luke, Most's explanation is clearly applicable to Jude, where the author's deviations from good Greek style are limited to the passages where he is evidently dependent on source material.

[43] The allusion in Jude 7 to the angels' sexual intercourse with women further confirms the dependence on the account in *1 Enoch* (*1 En.* 6:1-2). For further connections with *1 Enoch*, see Bauckham, *Jude, 2 Peter*, 52-53.

would the notion of everlasting chains be reconciled to that of eschatological judgment?

Finally, Gerdmar considers it significant that in v. 6 "Jude avoids the rare ταρταρόω" found in 2 Pet 2:4.[44] Why would 2 Peter make Jude's text more difficult with this rare word? There is a simple explanation: the verb, meaning "to cast into Tartarus," was first used with reference to the early Greek theogonic myths, in which the Cyclopes and Titans were imprisoned in Tartarus. However, the thought of "Tartarus" as the place where divine punishment was meted out occurs, not only in Greek literature, but in Israelite apocalyptic as well, and even a couple of times in the LXX.[45] Apparently, several Hellenistic Jewish authors even connected the Titans of the Greek myth with the Watchers or their sons. Hence, we may safely attribute the choice of the word in 2 Pet 2:4 to common Hellenistic Jewish practice.

It should be pointed out that Gerdmar is well acquainted with this and other sources and traditions behind the two epistles. In my opinion, he successfully proves one of his main theses—that the "Jewish" features in 2 Peter have been largely neglected in the history of NT exegesis. However, his source-critical insights have not enough influenced his discussion of literary dependence. In his discussion of the passage in 2 Pet 2:4, and the common suggestion that the author shows signs of influence from the Greek myth of the Titans in Hesiod's *Theogony*, Gerdmar points out that there are even more apparent verbal similarities between Jude and Hesiod, which have been largely overlooked.[46] The author of Jude uses the same words for "chains," δεσμοῖς (*Theogony* 717), and "darkness," ὑπὸ ζόφον (ὑπὸ ζόφῳ, *Theogony* 729). However, these verbal parallels are quite insignificant in light of the prominence of the motif of the chains in the tradition of the fall of the Watchers in *1 Enoch* (cf. 13:1; 14:5; 54:3-5; 56:1-4; 88:1). Admittedly, the phrase ὑπὸ ζόφον is not found in the Greek Enoch, but this phrase alone is not enough evidence to suggest that Jude is dependent on Hesiod.[47] Possibly, the author betrays some influence from Greek literature—the phrase is commonly used for the underworld in Greek

---

[44] Gerdmar, *Rethinking*, 119.

[45] The noun τάρταρος occurs in Prov 30:16; Job 40:20; 41:24 (41:32). For the corresponding verb, see BDAG, s.v. ταρταρόω.

[46] Gerdmar, *Rethinking*, 170. In this connection, Gerdmar discusses the word ταρταρόω in detail and concludes, "[T]he imagery of Tartaros-darkness was so broadly established as to be a description of the underworld that no connection to the Titan myth [in 2 Pet 2:4] needed to be implied."

[47] Especially so in light of the fact that the section in vv. 4-19 is dominated with quotations of and allusions to Jewish sources, *1 Enoch* in particular.

poetry (e.g., Homer, *Il.* 21:56; *Od.* 11:57, 155; 20:356). In conclusion, it is clear that Jude is *directly* dependent on *1 Enoch*, whereas 2 Peter is drawing from various traditions. Gerdmar seems to agree with this general observation:

> A closer background [than Hesiod's *Theogony*] to 2Peter 2:4 is, e.g. in *1En* 10:4-6, 18:11-21:10, which in turn may be influenced by Hesiod. . . . Yet, there are too few verbal similarities between 2Peter and *1En* to suggest a *genetic* connection. . . . This affinity is large enough to suggest a *common dependence* on the part of *1En* and 2Peter upon traditions of the fall of the angels, whereas the *literary* affinities are greater between Jude and *1En*. As suggested above, a borrowing from Jude does not suffice to explain this. Here, 2Peter is congruent with Jewish tradition as evidenced in Ps 116:3, Wis 17:16.[48]

Wis 17:16 refers to the Egyptian plague of darkness, and describes how the Egyptians were bound with one and the same chain of darkness (μιᾷ ἁλύσει σκότους). Clearly, it is possible that this passage influenced the author of 2 Peter. However, Gerdmar goes one step further and suggests that Jude was unaware of this tradition and therefore inserted the modifier ἀϊδίοις to δεσμοῖς.[49] This explanation completely disregards Jude's close affinity to *1 En.* 10. Also, 2 Peter reminds of ideas in *1 Enoch* but draws on several different traditions. In Sir 16:7-10 the phrase οὐκ ἐφείσατο is found in the context of a traditional schema that describes God's judgment of both the fallen giants of Gen 6, the fellow inhabitants of Lot and the desert generation (cf. the double use of the phrase in 2 Pet 2:4-5).[50] In Ps 116:3 the psalmist says, "The cords of death entangled me, the anguish of the grave [Heb. *Sheol*] came upon me" (NIV). Hence, Gerdmar is correct to the extent that a borrowing from Jude *alone* does not suffice to explain the language of 2 Peter. The author draws from a rich reserve of tradition. Thus, on the whole, Gerdmar successfully demonstrates how the "Jewish" features in 2 Peter have been neglected, and he concludes that the author of 2 Peter is an independent "'aggadic exegete' with clear apocalyptic Jewish profile."[51] However, in his excursus on the intertextuality between 2 Peter and Jude, he allows the principle of the more difficult reading to overshadow this and other important factors.

To sum up, there are a number of common elements in 2 Peter and Jude that stem from an identifiable source (sinning/fallen angels, chains of darkness/everlasting chains under darkness, being kept for judgment/kept

---

[48] Ibid., 171.
[49] Ibid., 118.
[50] For similar lists of examples that suggest an underlying paraenetic tradition, see Sir 16:6-14; 3 Macc 2:4-7; CD 2:17-3:12; Jude 5-7.
[51] Ibid., 160.

for the great day of judgment). We have seen that one particular source, *1 Enoch*, can account for the presence of all of these elements in Jude (including others that are unique to him), whereas the author of 2 Peter shows signs of influence from several sources and traditions in relation to these elements, as well as others that are unique to him. Hence, the line of development of the common elements most likely originates in *1 Enoch*, goes via Jude into 2 Peter, whose account on the whole is farther removed from this source, and blended with other traditions. The opposite scenario is very unlikely, and would imply that Jude has isolated elements in 2 Peter that are present also in *1 Enoch*, and then brought his whole account closer to this particular source, while excising other elements from the same streams of aggadic traditions.[52]

b) 2 Peter 2:10b-11 and Jude 8b-9.

Jude 8b-9	2 Pet 2:10b-11
8b. . . . δόξας δὲ βλασφημοῦσιν.	10b. τολμηταὶ αὐθάδεις, δόξας
9. Ὁ δὲ Μιχαὴλ ὁ ἀρχάγγελος,	οὐ τρέμουσιν βλασφημοῦντες,
ὅτε τῷ διαβόλῳ διακρινόμενος	11. ὅπου ἄγγελοι ἰσχύϊ καὶ
διελέγετο περὶ τοῦ Μωϋσέως	δυνάμει μείζονες ὄντες οὐ φέ-
σώματος, οὐκ ἐτόλμησεν κρίσιν	ρουσιν κατ' αὐτῶν παρὰ κυρίου
ἐπενεγκεῖν βλασφημίας ἀλλὰ	βλάσφημον κρίσιν.
εἶπεν· ἐπιτιμήσαι σοι κύριος.	

Both accounts refer to the opponents who are said to insult/slander (βλασφημέω) the "glorious ones" (δόξας). There is widespread agreement that δόξας in both epistles refer to angelic powers (cf. *T. Jud.* 25:2; *T. Levi* 18:5). In Jude they are good angels insulted by the false teachers; in 2 Peter they are either evil angels (and then κατ' αὐτῶν refers back to them—not even the good angels slander the evil ones as do the false teachers); or they are good angels, identical with ἄγγελοι, and then κατ' αὐτῶν refers to the

---

[52] The evident reliance on *1 Enoch* in Jude yields more examples where the suggested criterion applies. For example, Caroll D. Osburn suggests that *1 En.* 80:2-8 provides the essential framework for Jude's metaphors in Jude 12-13 ("waterless clouds," "autumn trees," "wild waves," and "wandering stars") ("1 Enoch 80:2-8 [67:5-7] and Jude 12-13," *CBQ* 47 [1985]: 296-303). Three out of four metaphors occur in *1 En.* 80:2-8 in the same order as in Jude, and in a section that treats the impending punishment of the ungodly. (Osburn suggests that the third metaphor is from *1 En.* 67:5-7.) Again, the parallel in 2 Peter 2:17 is farther removed from the underlying source. Further, Jude 15b-16 is clearly connected to *1 En.* 5, whereas 2 Peter 2:18 preserves identifiable traces from the same source.

false teachers; i.e., the false teachers do not hesitate to insult the good angels, but these in turn refrain from insulting the false teachers.

Jude then refers to the story of the archangel Michael's dispute with the devil. The original story, which he must have known from an apocryphal source, probably the lost ending of the *Testament of Moses*, is no longer extant. However, there are later stories that describe a debate between Michael and the devil over the body of Moses. Bauckham has collected a number of these versions in order to reconstruct the story that Jude knew.[53] It is unnecessary to go into detail here; it suffices to outline some of the elements of the reconstructed story: there was a verbal dispute between Michael and the devil concerning Moses' right to an honorable burial. The devil charged Moses with murder because he smote the Egyptian. But his accusation was considered slander (βλασφημία) against Moses. Michael, therefore, answered the devil with the words from Zech 3:2, "May the Lord rebuke you, devil!" The devil fled and Michael removed Moses' body and buried it with his own hands, so that no human saw the burial of Moses.

Thus, in light of the source of Jude, the reference to βλασφημία in Jude 9 probably refers to the devil's accusation against Moses, not an insult against angels corresponding to v. 8. In that case, the triple catchwords of vv. 8-10 (βλασφημοῦσιν, βλασφημίας, βλασφημοῦσιν) create a verbal rather than a conceptual link. The point that the author of Jude would be making is that no one, not even an archangel, is a law to himself; no one can dismiss accusation and despise authority, God alone is the judge of all. Without knowledge of the source of Jude, however, it is natural to understand the phrase κρίσιν ἐπενεγκεῖν βλασφημίας as a "slanderous accusation," which Michael refrained from making. That would make the expression synonymous to 2 Peter, βλάσφημον κρίσιν. In fact, most commentators have understood Jude in this way, especially since the phrase then would represent the Greek translation of an ordinary Semitic construction, but that does not do justice to the point of the story.[54]

Regardless of the exact meaning of the expression in Jude, there is a striking similarity between the parallels: first, the subject in Jude is ὁ Μιχαὴλ ὁ ἀρχάγγελος, whereas it is ἄγγελοι in 2 Peter. In Jude it is said that Michael did not dare, οὐκ ἐτόλμησεν, to bring judgment, whereas the opponents in 2 Peter are quite daring, τολμηταί. The negated verb phrase, οὐκ ... κρίσιν ἐπενεγκεῖν βλασφημίας in Jude corresponds to, οὐ φέρουσιν ... βλάσφημον κρίσιν in 2 Peter. The implied indirect object in Jude, τῷ διαβόλῳ,

---

[53] Bauckham, *The Relatives*, 235-80.
[54] Cf. Bauckham, *Jude, 2 Peter*, 61.

corresponds to the prepositional phrase κατ᾽ αὐτῶν in 2 Peter. Finally, Michael's utterance, ἐπιτιμήσαι σοι κύριος, makes the point of the story clear—the judgment is ultimately God's concern and this corresponds to the awkward phrase, παρὰ κυρίου in 2 Peter, making the same point. Here, one should note a point of textual variation in 2 Peter, regarding the phrase παρὰ κυρίου, attested by 𝔓⁷² 0142 330 918 1241 *al* **L**:T **S**:HᴬPhᵐˢˢ. The reading, παρὰ κυρίῳ is attested in other important witnesses (01 03 04 025 88 915 945 1175 1739 𝔐) and some significant witnesses omit the prepositional phrase altogether (02 044 33 81 614 630 1505 1881 2464 *al*). The reading παρὰ κυρίου is clearly the most difficult in that it attributes a "slanderous judgment" to God, and it could well have caused scribes to either modify or omit the phrase. However, the phrase is explicable as an equivalent of Michael's utterance in Jude, if we assume the priority of Jude (although the explanation does not in any way prove the latter point).

Gerdmar treats this parallel rather differently. He sees "considerable differences between Jude and 2 Peter, which cannot be explained from dependence in either direction."[55] He notes that "the devil is not mentioned [in 2 Peter]; the scene is less clear than in Jude, who probably explicated this by using the aggadah on Michael."[56] Gerdmar also thinks that the story about the dispute between Michael and the devil provided the author of Jude with a solution for the difficult notion of a "slanderous judgment," βλάσφημον κρίσιν, originating from God—in Jude, βλασφημίας is the reason for the judgment.[57]

Nevertheless, Gerdmar acknowledges the fact that the scene is one and the same in both accounts—the heavenly courtroom scene.[58] As for 2 Peter, Gerdmar does not refer to any particular literary source behind the courtroom scene. Instead he merely describes the roles in the judgment scene in the respective account, and makes the daring suggestion that humans take on the prosecuting role in 2 Peter![59]

---

[55] Gerdmar, *Rethinking*, 180.

[56] Ibid., 179. In n. 79 he states, "There is no indication in 2Peter of a belief in devils, but of evil angels."

[57] Ibid., 119-20. Gerdmar also appeals to the textual variation in 2 Peter 2:11 (although giving reference to 2:10) indicating the difficulty of the notion of a "slanderous judgment of the Lord," which Jude is said to avoid by providing "an alternative explication."

[58] ὅπου in 2 Pet 2:11 is thus interpreted in the local sense.

[59] Gerdmar appeals to 1 Cor 6:3, where Paul says that the Christians will judge angels, which, as he suggests, may have a background in Jewish apocalypticism, e.g., *1 Enoch* (cf. *1 En.* 48:9), and he concludes, "Against this background in Paul and 1 Enoch, it is conceivable that believers . . . could be regarded superior to angels and in position to judge them at least in an eschatological setting, and it need not have been intrinsically wrong to judge. But the context implies that judging certain powers was reserved for the Lord" (ibid., 178). Further, Gerdmar

The depictions of the heavenly council in Job 1:6-12, 2:1-7 and Zech 3:1-7 reveal the beginnings of the development of the figure of the Satan ("the adversary"), who brings accusations before Yahweh.[60] In the courtroom scene in Zech 3:1-7, Satan accuses the high priest Joshua, but is rebuked by Yahweh.[61] The text of LXX reads καὶ εἶπεν κύριος πρὸς τὸν διάβολον ἐπιτιμήσαι κύριος ἐν σοί, διάβολε (Zech 3:2). There is much to suggest that Michael's utterance in Jude 9, the echo from Zech 3:2, is the very kernel of Jude's source. In Zech 3 there is also a verbal dispute in a legal context (the courtroom before God), where the Lord (or the "angel of Yahweh") replies with these words against an accusation from Satan. Hence, we see that Jude is dependent upon a particular, identifiable source, where the same point is made—judgment belongs to the Lord. Regardless of whether κρίσιν βλασφημίας in Jude is perceived as "slanderous judgment," as in 2 Peter, or of "judgment on account of slander," the literary contrast provides an antithesis to the opponent's arrogant mockery of the spiritual realm—even the archangel Michael was aware of the fact that he was not the judge, judgment is from the Lord.

Gerdmar's solution implies that the author of 2 Peter has created a courtroom scene far removed from the traditional, and without a particular source or parallel (which is all the more surprising, since he goes far to demonstrate the clear apocalyptic Jewish profile of the author), whereas the author of Jude has found "a solution" to several difficulties by adapting the material to an attested traditional courtroom scene, while retaining a correspondence between many of the elements in the parallel, making the same basic point—judgment is from the Lord.

In my opinion, a line of development starting in the underlying source is much more probable. The author of Jude uses the apocryphal story as his source, in order to make his point (the same as in the story). Subsequently, the author of 2 Peter, possibly unaware of the particular source, adapts elements from the story to his particular situation. In conclusion, the notion of "a slanderous judgment from the Lord" is indeed difficult; in a courtroom scene where, according to tradition, the devil is the slanderer, it seems too difficult, not only for copyists (see above), but for the very author

---

finds a parallel in *1 En.* 46:6-7 to the phenomenon of people exceeding their authority by judging angels ("the stars of heaven") (ibid., 178-79). This parallel is interesting, but the context of the judgment scene in *1 En.* 46 is definitely not the heavenly courtroom.

[60] The development of specialized functions and figures such as Satan became even more apparent toward the intertestamental period (cf. *Jub.* 49:2; CD 4:13; 5:18; 8:2; 1QS 1:18, 23-24).

[61] Many editors prefer the Syriac reading, "angel of Yahweh," for reasons of consistency within the verse and the vision scene as a whole.

to have conceived. While it is perfectly legitimate to appeal to the principle of the harder reading, in order to explain the textual variation in the manuscript tradition of 2 Peter, the same principle cannot be applied automatically to the relationship between 2 Peter and Jude; the lack of an explanation provided by an existing parallel to 2 Peter (other than Jude) greatly increases the difficulty to the point of impossibility (there is often a thin line between a difficult and a non-sensical reading).[62] However, the account of Jude, based on an identifiable tradition, well explains the difficult phrase in 2 Peter.

4.3 The Criterion of Structural Elements

If an element is found in both parallel passages, where there is relatively high verbal agreement, and this element has a more complex function in one composition in terms of co-ordination and integration with the discourse as a whole, then it more probably stems from the author of that composition.

E. Earle Ellis was the first to characterize the careful composition of Jude 5-19 as "midrash."[63] This genre classification plays a central role in Bauckham's interpretation of Jude, although he has offered some minor modifications of Ellis' analysis.[64] For Bauckham, the acknowledgement of

---

[62] The priority of 2 Peter in this case possibly would increase the likelihood that the reading παρὰ κυρίῳ is original. Scribes could have changed an original dative case to the genitive under influence of the slightly more common construction of παρά with the genitive, without perceiving the theological difficulties. In any case, the absence of the prepositional phrase is definitely the least difficult reading; the parallel in Jude makes no mention of the presence of the Lord and could have caused scribes to omit the phrase. Moreover, it would be hard to imagine that angels would pronounce a judgment in the Lord's presence (παρὰ κυρίῳ); rather they act as mediators. This latter point reflects a balance between transcriptional evidence in favor of, and intrinsic evidence against the phrase in the dative. However it is not necessary to interpret the dative in the local sense; the phrase may indicate quality or standard, i.e., angels do not make slanderous judgments "by God." Metzger prefers the reading without a prepositional phrase in view of external evidence, but this is questionable due to the overwhelming external support of a prepositional phrase as such (*Textual Commentary*, 633). Notably, the *ECM* editors accept the reading παρὰ κυρίῳ. It has to be admitted that, in this case, the difficult phrase with the genitive in 2 Peter cannot be used decisively in the chain of evidence for the priority of Jude, since the priority of 2 Peter would decrease the probability of its originality. On the other hand, the complete picture still speaks in favor of the priority of Jude.

[63] E. Earle Ellis, *Prophecy and Hermeneutic in Early Christianity: New Testament Essays* (WUNT 18; Tübingen: Mohr Siebeck, 1978; repr., Grand Rapids: Eerdmans, 1978), 221-36.

[64] In his later works Bauckham does not use the term "midrash" since it has a potential for misunderstanding. Instead he uses the term "exegesis" or "commentary" and prefers to talk about the formal similarities to the thematic pesher exegesis of Qumran ("The Letter of Jude: An Account of Research," 3801-3; *Jude and the Relatives*, 179-86).

the elaborate composition of Jude has a direct bearing on the question of literary dependence.[65]

One of the traits that led Ellis to identify the midrashic character of Jude was the distinctive form in which the "texts" and their interpretation were alternated.[66] The commentary sections are marked by a shift in tense to the present, where Jude makes his application of the historical types and prophecies to the opponents. Moreover, the commentary sections are consistently introduced by the repeated formula οὗτοι (8, 10) or οὗτοι εἰσιν (12, 16, 19). The ample use of catchword connections between "texts" and expositions, of which we have seen examples, is another hallmark of the midrashic procedure.[67] What interests us here is the repeated use of the word or phrase, οὗτοι/οὗτοι εἰσιν, since the constructions occur also in 2 Peter 2:12, 17. The phrases in Jude resemble the use of exegetical formulae in Jewish exegesis, where they likewise mark the transition from "text" to interpretation; the pronoun refers to that which is to be interpreted, or to the persons to whom the interpretation applies (cf. Gal 4:24; 2 Tim 3:8). The interpretations of apocalyptic dreams and visions are often introduced by a similar formula (Dan 5:25-26; Zech 1:10; *1 En.* 46:3). The so-called "thematic pesharim" of Qumran offer another parallel to this feature in Jude (e.g., 4QFlor 1:2-3, 11, 17-18; 2:1).[68]

---

[65] Bauckham, *Jude, 2 Peter*, 142.
[66] Ellis, *Prophecy*, 225.
[67] Cf. Bauckham, *Jude, 2 Peter*, 5.
[68] A "thematic pesher" is a commentary on various biblical verses organized around a single or several themes, in contrast to the "continuous pesher," which provides a running commentary on a single biblical text. The designation "pesher" derives from the frequent use of the same term, meaning "interpretation, realization," to introduce an interpretation of a biblical text. The occurrence of the term in the text is important, but not indispensable; in Jude as well as in some instances in 4QFlor, the demonstrative explanations are used to the same effect.

Jude 8, 10, 12, 16, 19 and 2 Pet 2:10, 12-13 and 17:

Jude 8, 10, 12-13, 16, 19	2 Pet 2:10, 12-13, 17
8. Ὁμοίως μέντοι καὶ <u>οὗτοι</u> ἐνυπνιαζόμενοι σάρκα μὲν μιαίνουσιν κυριότητα δὲ ἀθετοῦσιν δόξας δὲ βλασφημοῦσιν.	10. μάλιστα δὲ τοὺς ὀπίσω σαρκὸς ἐν ἐπιθυμίᾳ μιασμοῦ πορευομένους καὶ κυριότητος καταφρονοῦντας. τολμηταὶ αὐθάδεις, δόξας οὐ τρέμουσιν βλασφημοῦντες,
10. <u>Οὗτοι</u> δὲ ὅσα μὲν οὐκ οἴδασιν βλασφημοῦσιν, ὅσα δὲ φυσικῶς ὡς τὰ ἄλογα ζῷα ἐπίστανται, ἐν τούτοις φθείρονται.	12. <u>Οὗτοι</u> δὲ ὡς ἄλογα ζῷα γεγεννημένα φυσικὰ εἰς ἅλωσιν καὶ φθορὰν ἐν οἷς ἀγνοοῦσιν βλασφημοῦντες, ἐν τῇ φθορᾷ αὐτῶν καὶ φθαρήσονται
12-13. <u>Οὗτοί εἰσιν</u> οἱ ἐν ταῖς ἀγάπαις ὑμῶν σπιλάδες συνευωχούμενοι ἀφόβως, ἑαυτοὺς ποιμαίνοντες, νεφέλαι ἄνυδροι ὑπὸ ἀνέμων παραφερόμεναι ... ἀστέρες πλανῆται οἷς ὁ ζόφος τοῦ σκότους εἰς αἰῶνα τετήρηται.	13. ... σπίλοι καὶ μῶμοι ἐντρυφῶντες ἐν ταῖς ἀπάταις αὐτῶν συνευωχούμενοι ὑμῖν,
16. <u>Οὗτοί εἰσιν</u> γογγυσταὶ μεμψίμοιροι κατὰ τὰς ἐπιθυμίας ἑαυτῶν πορευόμενοι, καὶ τὸ στόμα αὐτῶν λαλεῖ ὑπέρογκα	17. <u>οὗτοι εἰσιν</u> πηγαὶ ἄνυδροι καὶ ὁμίχλαι ὑπὸ λαίλαπος ἐλαυνόμεναι, οἷς ὁ ζόφος τοῦ σκότους τετήρηται.
19. <u>Οὗτοί εἰσιν</u> οἱ ἀποδιορίζοντες, ψυχικοί, πνεῦμα μὴ ἔχοντες.	18. ὑπέρογκα γὰρ ματαιότητος φθεγγόμενοι δελεάζουσιν ἐν ἐπιθυμίαις σαρκὸς ἀσελγείαις τοὺς ὀλίγως ἀποφεύγοντας τοὺς ἐν πλάνῃ ἀναστρεφομένους

There is much more to be said about the elaborate exegetical techniques and hermeneutics of Jude.[69] However, the main point here is that the word or phrase οὗτοι/οὗτοι εἰσιν takes on another significance in Jude, in that it functions as an effective and indispensable structuring element for the discourse as a whole, as compared to the more occasional usage in 2 Peter. It is natural to attribute the conscious usage and the complex function of this element in Jude to the author's ingenuity, whereas a dependence on 2

---

[69] For an extensive treatment of Jude's exegesis, see Bauckham, *Jude and the Relatives*, 179-234.

Peter is very unlikely. A reference to other textual features, unique to Jude, which enhance the complexity of the structure, is not an effective argument for the priority of Jude, since the author of 2 Peter is not inferior in regard to style.

5. Conclusions

In this chapter I have first reviewed the history of research into the question of the literary relationship between 2 Peter and Jude. Although a clear majority of modern scholars have taken a position in favor of the priority of Jude, the question has not yet been fully resolved. The standard method among exegetes has been to assume the priority of one epistle (mostly Jude) and account for the way in which it was redacted by the author of the other epistle. Admittedly, redaction-critical methodology has brought many new insights to the research of the literary relationship, but some scholars still defend the priority of 2 Peter.

There have been a lot of "good arguments" in the debate. The problem is that many of these arguments are based on too general criteria, which are not relevant to the context. The nature and validity of these criteria are seldom discussed, or made explicit in scholarly accounts. I have listed some traditional examples of criteria, which, in my view, are not useful for the estimation of probability in this particular context. Then, I have proposed three contextually defined criteria and applied them to a number of parallel accounts in Jude and 2 Peter.

First, I have attempted to display the possible motives behind the redaction of common material, which would explain why one of the authors, the redactor, has excised some elements and added others. I have concentrated on such elements as ought to have been attractive for both of the authors in terms of their shared polemic purpose. In the parallel accounts in Jude 5-7, 11 and 2 Peter 2:4-8, 15-16, there is an evident motive for a redaction of Jude on the part of the author of 2 Peter. The latter clearly displays an eschatological interest throughout his epistle, which in the parallel account in question is embodied in the chronological sequence of God's judgments, in particular in the pattern of destruction by water and fire respectively (i.e., the reference in 2 Peter to the Flood and to Sodom and Gomorrah). This chronological and eschatological pattern explains perfectly well both the additions and the omissions in 2 Peter, whereas it is very difficult to explain why the author of Jude would omit a prime example of God's judgment (the Flood), and construct a non-chronological sequence from the *Vorlage* in 2 Peter. (In this case the principle of *lectio difficilior* corroborates the conclusion.)

Secondly, I have proposed that the respective parallel accounts in Jude 6; 2 Pet 2:4, and in Jude 8-9; 2 Pet 2:10-11 most likely represent a line of development that goes from a particular source via Jude into 2 Peter, whose account on the whole is farther removed from the underlying source in question, blended with other traditions, or preserving only vague, but identifiable, traces of the particular source.

Finally, I have argued that the word or phrase οὗτοι/οὗτοι εἰσιν, also occurring in 2 Peter, takes on another significance in Jude, where it functions as an effective and indispensable structuring element for the discourse as a whole. Hence, I suggest that the phrase most likely originates from the author of Jude, and was borrowed by the author of 2 Peter.

After having applied these contextually defined criteria to the parallel texts in Jude and 2 Peter, I must conclude that the balance of probabilities clearly favors the priority of Jude. The plausibility of this conclusion is confirmed by an appeal to traditional criteria, as is evident both from the current analysis, but, more significantly, from the history of scholarly research in the area.

Chapter Five

Scribal Harmonization in the Textual Tradition of 2 Peter and Jude

Introduction

In light of the close literary relationship between Jude and 2 Peter, it is not surprising that scribes at certain times would harmonize the wordings to the parallel account. However, I have found that such instances of harmonization are strikingly few, and that they go in both directions. In the following, I will list the apparent examples of harmonization. These are found in 2 Pet 2:13, 17; 3:2-3 and Jude 12-13, 17-18—I have omitted ambiguous cases that occur elsewhere. Because of the incomplete textual data on 2 Peter, this survey cannot be exhaustive, and therefore I have selected for consideration only those MSS which are included in the *ECM* for 2 Peter and Jude, in order not to bias the picture.[1]

1. Harmonization to Parallel Accounts in 2 Peter/Jude

2 Pet 2:13: ἐν ταῖς ἀπάταις αὐτῶν
Jude 12: ἐν ταῖς ἀγάπαις ὑμῶν

In some witnesses ἀπάταις in 2 Pet 2:13 is changed to ἀγάπαις (02C 03 044 5 623 1243 1611 1827 2464 2718 2805 **L**:CS V **K**:SB **S**:PhH) in harmony with Jude 12. Two of these witnesses and one version also replace αὐτῶν with ὑμῶν (1243 2718 **G**). On the other hand, some witnesses in Jude read ἀπάταις ὑμῶν (02*V 04V 88 104 459 915 1243 1842 1845 1846 2492)—a combination not to be found in 2 Peter. It is very unlikely that Jude would ascribe the deceitfulness (ἀπάτη) to the addressees and not to the enemies as in 2 Pet 2:13—only one witness to Jude reads ἀπάταις αὐτῶν (02C).[2] Thus, the presence of the word in Jude can only be explained as an assimilation to 2 Peter or a mistake in copying. A misreading of ΑΓΑΠΑΙΣ as ΑΠΑΤΑΙΣ on the part of the author of 2 Peter may also explain its apparent original presence there. Thus, the reading in Jude, ἀγάπαις ὑμῶν, best explains the

---

[1] The abbreviations and symbols follow the *ECM*.
[2] Cf. Charles Landon, *A Text-Critical Study of the Epistle of Jude* (JSNTSup 135; Sheffield: Sheffield Academic Press, 1996), 105.

origin of all variants, including those in 2 Peter, even if there has been subsequent harmonization in both directions.

2 Pet 2:13: συνευωχούμενοι ὑμῖν
Jude 12: σπιλάδες συνευωχούμενοι

Many witnesses in Jude supply ὑμῖν (04 6 88 93 252 323 467 665 915 996 1241 1243 1270 1297 1501 1595 1609 1661 1739 1845 1846 1881 2298 2492 2718 L921 L938 L1141 **A G**:A1 **SI**:ChMSiS), which is in harmony with 2 Peter where no witness omits the word. One witness in 2 Peter adds σπιλάδες (04) from Jude.

2 Pet 2:17: οὗτοί εἰσιν πηγαὶ ἄνυδροι καὶ ὁμίχλαι ὑπὸ λαίλαπος ἐλαυνόμεναι
Jude 12: οὗτοί εἰσιν ... νεφέλαι ἄνυδροι ὑπὸ ἀνέμων παραφερόμεναι

The majority of witnesses in 2 Pet 2:17 add νεφέλαι from Jude at various places between ἄνυδροι and ὑπὸ λαίλαπος (048V 88 104 206 218 254AV 429 431 459 467 522 629 630 720C 808 876 996 1127 1292f 1359 1448 1490 1501 1563 1611 1661 1718 1751 1799 1831 1832 1838 1842 1848 2138 2200 2243 2374 2544 **Byz** [2423V] PsOec **S**:Ph^mss). However, the word is absent from the most important witnesses (𝔓⁷² 01 02 03 04 025 044 5 33 69 81 94 181 254T 307 321 323 378 398 436 442 453 614 621 623 720* 915 918 945 1067 1175f 1241 1243 1409 1505 1524 1678 1735 1739 1852 1875 1881 2147 2298 2344 2412 2464 2541 2652 2718 2805 2818 L596 **L**:VT **S**:H).

2 Pet 2:17: οἷς ὁ ζόφος τοῦ σκότους τετήρηται
Jude 13: οἷς ὁ ζόφος τοῦ σκότους εἰς αἰῶνα τετήρηται

Many witnesses in 2 Peter add εἰς αἰῶνα/εἰς τὸν αἰῶνα/εἰς αἰῶνας after σκότους in harmony with Jude (02 04 020 025 049 0142 1 5 6 18 33 35 43 61 69 81 88 93 94 104 180 181 206 218 252 254 307 319 321 323 326 330 365 378 398 400 424 429 431 436 442 453 459 467 468 522 607 614 617 621 623 630 642 720 808 876 915 918 945 996 1067 1127 1241 1270 1292 1297 1359 1409 1448Z 1490 1501 1524 1563 1595 1609 1611 1661 1678 1718 1729 1735 1739 1751 1799 1827 1831 1832 1837 1838 1842 1845 1848 1852 1874 1875 1881 1890 2138 2147 2186 2200 2243 2298 2344 2374 2412 2423 2464 2492 2541 2544 2652 2774 2805 2818 L590 L596 L938 L1141 L1281 PsOec **K**:B^ms **A SI**). However, the phrase is missing in several important witnesses ($\mathfrak{P}^{72}$ 01 03 044 048 629 1175 1243 1448T 1505 2718 **L**:VT **K**:SB **S**:PhH **G Ä**).

2 Pet 3:2: τῶν προειρημένων ῥημάτων
Jude 17: τῶν ῥημάτων τῶν προειρημένων

In 2 Peter there is no variation of the word order, but in Jude many witnesses follow the word order of 2 Pet (02 6 323 378 424C 630 876 1241 1270 1292 1297 1448 1501 1505 1595 1611 1739 1832 1881 2138 2147 2200 2243 2298 2374 2412 2652).

2 Pet 3:2: ὑπὸ τῶν ἁγίων προφητῶν καὶ τῆς τῶν ἀποστόλων
Jude 17: ὑπὸ τῶν ἀποστόλων

One Greek MS in 2 Peter repeats the epithet ἁγίων a second time in front of ἀποστόλων (2344 **K**:S^mss), whereas a few MSS in Jude, under the influence of the parallel, similarly insert the epithet in front of ἀποστόλων (617 L921 L1281).

2 Pet 3:3: ἐλεύσονται ἐπ' ἐσχάτων τῶν ἡμερῶν
Jude 18: ἐπ ἐσχάτου τοῦ χρόνου ἔσονται

Many witnesses in Jude read ἐλεύσονται in harmony with 2 Peter (01Z2 02 04C2 5 6 33 61 81 93 94 307 321 323 326 378 424Z 431 436 453 617 623 629 665 918 1067 1241 1409 1501 1735 1739 1751 1837 1881 2147 2186 2298 2344 2412 2652 2805 2818 L1281/2 Cyr Did **K**:B^mss). However, ἔσονται, which is not present among the witnesses to 2 Peter, is attested by practically all other witnesses in Jude. One witness also replaces τοῦ χρόνου in Jude with τῶν ἡμερῶν (1881).

2. Conclusions

This brief survey shows that scribal harmonization between 2 Peter and Jude on the whole is relatively infrequent, and where it does occur it often concerns the addition of a word or phrase, or the choice of a more natural word or expression drawn from the parallel account. There seems to be about as many instances of harmonization in both of the traditions, but in terms of the number of witnesses attesting probable harmonization, it is more common in the tradition of 2 Peter. This may be due to the relative popularity of the respective writing; possibly, the least popular writing would be more likely to become subject to harmonization. In this case, however, it is difficult to say if one epistle was more popular than the other; both epistles are cited relatively infrequently by patristic authors, but Jude, being the shorter epistle, is cited slightly more often in regard to the amount of text.

Only at one point in the parallel accounts (2 Pet 2:13/Jd 12) does harmonization seem to go in both directions (ἀγάπαις/ἀπάταις); in this particular case, there is probably an indication of accidental change. Significantly, harmonization between the two epistles occurs in several early witnesses, most frequently in 02, as well as in a broad spectrum of minuscules. On the other hand, two of the most important MSS, 𝔓⁷² and 03, do not display harmonization in any direction.[3] Harmonization between the epistles is evidently rare also in the Majority Text.

---

[3] James R. Royse, suggests that the reading of 𝔓⁷²C in 2 Pet 2:6b, εἰς τὸ δεῖγμα, is an assimilation to Jude 7 (δεῖγμα) ("Scribal Habits in Early Greek New Testament Papyri" [Th.D. diss., Graduate Theological Union, 1981], 481). In my opinion, Royse is clearly wrong; the original writing is unclear, but the text seems to read υτοδιγμα (ὑπόδειγμα accidently copied and, thus, wrongly corrected to εἰς τὸ δεῖγμα).

Part II

Editio

Chapter Six

Manuscript Witnesses to the Epistle of Jude

The lists below in Tables 2-3 indicate the MSS included (or not included) in this edition. In Table 4 those MSS are listed which contain various parts of the Catholic Epistles except the Epistle of Jude (i.e., not included). The notes and descriptions are based on my own data, and the standard reference sources, in particular the main register of Greek New Testament manuscripts, Kurt Aland, Michael Welte, Beate Köster and Klaus Junack, eds., *Kurzgefasste Liste der griechischen Handschriften des Neuen Testaments* (ANTF 1; 2d rev. and enl. ed; Berlin/New York: De Gruyter, 1994), hereafter *Liste*, and the continuous update of the *Liste* on the website of the INTF; online: http://www.uni-muenster.de/INTF/KgLSGII06_03.pdf. Further, I have made use of the almost exhaustive list of MSS of the Catholic Epistles in Kurt Aland, ed., *Text und Textwert der griechischen Handschriften des Neuen Testaments*. I: *Die Katholischen Briefe* (3 vols.; ANTF 9-11; Berlin/New York: De Gruyter, 1987), 1:2-14, hereafter *TuT*. There are some discrepancies between the *Liste* and *TuT*, and in most cases the more recent *Liste* is to be trusted, since circumstances are constantly changing; MSS have been relocated, new identifications have been made and new manuscripts have come to light.[1] However, there are still some errors and incomplete or outdated data in both the *Liste* and *TuT*, some of which I account for in the endnotes to Tables 2-4 at the end of this chapter.[2]

Whenever there is more than one date indicated for a manuscript in the *Liste*, the date (or dates) here given refers to the portion containing the Epistle of Jude, as far as I could find out. When a manuscript is divided between two or more locations (or catalogue numbers), only the part containing Jude is listed. Sometimes a MS is bound together with one or several other MSS, in which cases I have indicated the folio numbers of the MS in question. The MSS in parenthesis in Table 2 have not been

---

[1] To take a telling example, MSS 1518 and 1522, earlier in London, were thought to have disappeared by the time *TuT* was published. However, the two MSS eventually were identified as 1896 and 1890, respectively (in *TuT* these were listed as four separate MSS).

[2] The most significant notes and corrections will be published as "Some Bibliographic Notes on Greek New Testament Manuscripts" in *Novum Testamentum* (forthcoming).

collated, and are not included in the study, and the reasons are apparent from the notes in the right hand column.

My aim has been to include all extant evidence from the Greek manuscript tradition, and I have succeeded to collate practically all extant continuous text MSS. However, the restraint of time prevented me from collating all available lectionary MSS. The selection of lectionaries rests upon several considerations: I thought it very important to collate all lectionaries that are also published in the *ECM* of Jude (L156, L596, L921, L938, L1141 and L1281). Secondly, I included several lectionaries cited in the *ECM* of James (where readings from Jude were extant). Thirdly, some lectionaries were selected on the basis of Klaus Junack's study of the Greek lectionaries in the Catholic Epistles.[3] Fourthly, L585 (synaxarion and menologion) was one of the lectionaries collated by Wayne A. Blakely, and it had an interesting text.[4] Finally, I tried to cover the lectionaries up to the 12th century. I should add that there are approximately 400 Greek Apostolos lectionaries. However, in my estimation readings from the Epistle of Jude occur in only half of them.[5]

In conclusion, my study includes 560 manuscript witnesses to the Epistle of Jude. A large collection of microfilms of MSS was available to me in the University Library of Lund (donated to the library by the late C. A. Albin). For the most part, however, I accessed the MSS through the almost complete collection of microfilms at the INTF. In a few cases I managed to acquire some additional MSS from various institutions, including some of the most recent registered MSS. As a result, this study includes several MSS that, to my knowledge, have never been examined by the INTF (613, 823, 1274b, 1834, plus 90a, seemingly not noticed before). As a by-product to the investigations of a large number of microfilms, I have been able to identify at least two new manuscripts: first, a Gospel-lectionary uncial from the 8th century which I discovered in the binding of L1126 (Athos, Vatopediu 866);[6] secondly, an unidentified minuscule bound together with

---

[3] Klaus Junack, "Zu den griechischen Lektionarien und ihrer Überlieferung der Katolischen Briefe," in *Die alten Übersetzungen des Neuen Testaments, die Kirchenväterzitate und Lektionare* (ed. Kurt Aland; ANTF 5; Berlin/New York: De Gruyter, 1972), 498-591.

[4] Wayne A. Blakely, "Manuscript Relationships As Indicated by the Epistles of Jude and II Peter" (Ph.D. diss., Emory University, 1964).

[5] Lections from Jude are generally found in the synaxarion in those *Apostolos* lectionaries with readings for all the days of the week (ἑβδομάδες); usually there are two lections (vv. 1-10, 11-25) for Tuesday and Thursday, respectively, in week 36. Furthermore, in a few lectionaries there is a lection from Jude (usually the whole epistle) on June 19 in the menologion (feast-day lectionary) when Saint Jude is celebrated.

[6] An *editio princeps* by the present writer and Klaus Witte is forthcoming in the *Bericht der Hermann Kunst-Stiftung zur Förderung der neutestamentlichen Textforschung*.

2696 (Meteora, Metamorphosis, 302) with parts of the Gospel of John (the same microfilm also contains two different texts of 2 Peter); and, thirdly, in 2736 (Zavorda, Nikanoros, 125), some hitherto unnoticed chapters of the Book of Acts.

I have also discovered that MS 2866 is in fact the same as MS 2483, by comparing my own transcriptions as well as those of Maurice A. Robinson in the Gospel of John (see note below). Finally, I can report that the valuable minuscule 1799 kept in Princeton University Library (see below) is available for examination. Through the willingness of the holder I was able to receive photos of the Epistle of Jude, although the fragile state of the manuscript and its tight binding demanded special procedures.

Table 2: Collated MSS containing the Epistle of Jude (unless otherwise noted)[7]

MS (Gr.-Al. no.)	DATING[1]	LOCATION	NOTES
P72	III/IV	Cologny/Geneva, Bibl. Bodmeriana (*P.Bodmer* VII)	
P74	VII	Cologny/Geneva, Bibl. Bodmeriana (*P.Bodmer* XVII)	
P78[2]	III/IV	Oxford, Sackler Library (P. Oxy. 2684)	
ℵ 01	IV	London, Brit. Libr., Add. 43725	
A 02	V	London, Brit. Libr., Royal 1 D.VIII	
B 03	IV	Rome, Bibl. Vat., Vat. gr. 1209	
C 04	V	Paris, Bibl. Nat., Gr. 9	
K 018	IX	Moscow, Hist. Mus., V. 93, S. 97	
L 020	IX	Rome, Bibl. Angelica, 39	
Ψ 044	IX/X	Athos, Lavra, B' 52	
049	IX	Athos, Lavra A' 88	
056	X	Paris, Bibl. Nat., Coislin Gr. 26	
0142	X	Munich, Bayer. Staatsbibl., Gr. 375	
0251	VI	Paris, Louvre, S.N. 121	Jude 3-5
0316	ca. VII	New York, Pierpont Morgan Libr., M 597 f. II	Jude 18-25; Gr.-Copt.
1 [2 ap]=2815	XII	Basel, Univ. Bibl., A.N.IV.2	
3 [4 ap]=2816	XII	Vienna, Nat. Bibl., Suppl. gr. 52	
5	XIII	Paris, Bibl. Nat. Gr. 84	
6	XIII	Paris, Bibl. Nat. Gr. 106	
18	1364	Paris, Bibl. Nat. Gr. 47	
33	IX	Paris, Bibl. Nat. Gr. 14	
35 [36a]=2818	XI	Paris, Bibl. Nat. Coislin Gr. 199	
38	XII	Paris, Bibl. Nat. Coislin Gr. 200	
42	XI	Frankfurt/Oder, Stadtarchiv, s. n.	
43	XI	Paris, Arsenal 8410	
51	XIII	Oxford, Bodl. Libr., Selden Supra 28	
57	XII	Oxford, Magdalen Coll., Gr. 9	
61	XVI	Dublin, Trinity Coll., Ms. 30	
62	XIV	Paris, Bibl. Nat., Gr. 60	
69	XV	Leicester, Leicestershire Record Office, Cod. 6 D 32/1	Jude 1-7

---

[7] MSS within brackets were not available for collation for various reasons as noted in the table or in the endnotes.

76	XIV	Vienna, Nat. Bibl., Theol. gr. 300	
81	1044	Alexandria, Greek Patriarchate, 59	
82	X	Paris, Bibl. Nat., Gr. 237	
88	XII	Naples, Bibl. Naz., Ms. II. A. 7	
90a[3]	XVI	Amsterdam, Univ. Bibl., Remonstr. 186	90a: fols. 137-39;
90b	XVI	Amsterdam, Univ. Bibl., Remonstr. 186	90b: fols. 250-51
93	X	Paris, Bibl. Nat., Coislin Gr. 205	
94	XIII	Paris, Bibl. Nat., Gr. 202.2	
97	XII	Wolfenbüttel, Herz. Aug. Bibl., Codd. Gud. Graec. 104.2	
102	1444	Moscow, Hist. Mus., V. 412, S. 5	
103	XII	Moscow, Hist. Mus., V. 96, S. 347	
104	1087	London, Brit. Libr., Harley 5537	
105	XII	Oxford, Bodl. Libr., Auct. T.inf. 1.10	
110	XII	London, Brit. Libr., Harley 5778	
131	XIV	Rome, Bibl. Vat., Vat. gr. 360	
133	XI	Rome, Bibl. Vat., Vat. gr. 363	
141	XIII	Rome, Bibl. Vat., Vat. gr. 1160	
142	XI	Rome, Bibl. Vat., Vat. gr. 1210	
149	XV	Rome, Bibl. Vat., Vat. Pal. gr. 171	
172	XIII/XIV	Berlin, Staatsbibl., Phill. 1461	
175	X/XI	Rome, Bibl. Vat., Vat. gr. 2080	
177	XI	Munich, Bayer. Staatsbibl., Gr. 211	
180	1273	Rome, Bibl. Vat., Borg. gr. 18	
181	X	Rome, Bibl. Vat., Reg. gr. 179	
189	XII	Florence, Bibl. Medicea Laur., Plutei VI. 25	
201	1357	London, Brit. Libr., Add. 11837	
203	1111	London, Brit. Libr., Add. 28816	
204	XIII/XIV?	Bologna, Bibl. Univ., 2775	
205	XV	Venice, Bibl. Naz. Marc., Gr. Z. 5 (420)	
205abs	XV	Venice, Bibl. Naz. Marc., Gr. Z. 6 (336)	
206S	XIV	London, Lambeth Palace, 1182	
209	XIV	Venice, Bibl. Naz. Marc., Gr. Z. 10 (394)	
216	1358	London, Lambeth Palace, 1183	
218	XIII	Vienna, Nat. Bibl., Theol. gr. 23	
221	X	Oxford, Bodl. Libr., Canon. Gr. 110	
223	XIV	Ann Arbor, Univ. Libr., Ms. 34	
226	XII	Escorial, Bibl. de El Escorial, X. IV. 17	
234	1278	Copenhagen, Kgl. Bibl., GKS 1322, 4o	
250	XI	Paris, Bibl. Nat., Coislin Gr. 224	
252=[464]	XI	Moscow, Hist. Mus., V. 23, S. 341	
254	XIV	Athen, Nat. Bibl., 490	
(255)	XIV	Krakow, Bibl. Jagiellońska (Fonds der Berliner Hss.), Gr. Qu. 40?	*no film*
256	XI/XII	Paris, Bibl. Nat., Armen. 27 (9)	Gr.-Arm.; with Italian translation
(257)	XIV	Krakow, Bibl. Jagiellońska (Fonds der Berliner Hss.), Gr. Qu. 43? (earlier: Berlin, Staatsbibl., Gr. Qu. 43)	*no film*
263	XIII	Paris, Bibl. Nat., Gr. 61	
296	XVI	Paris, Bibl. Nat., Gr. 123.124	copied from print?
302	XI	Paris, Bibl. Nat., Gr. 103	
307	X	Paris, Bibl. Nat., Coislin Gr. 25	
308	XIV	London, Brit. Libr., Royal 1 B. I	
309	XIII	Cambridge, Univ. Libr., Dd. 11.90	
312	XI	London, Brit. Libr., Add. 5115	
314	XI	Oxford, Bodl. Libr., Barocci 3	
319	XII	Cambridge, Christ's Coll., GG. 1.9 (Ms. 9)	
321	XII	London, Brit. Libr., Harley 5557	

322	XV	London, Brit. Libr., Harley 5620	
323	XII	Geneva, Bibl. publ. et univ., Gr. 20	
325	XI	Oxford, Bodl. Libr., Auct. E.5.9	
326	X	Oxford, Lincoln Coll., Gr. 82	Jude after James
327	XIII	Oxford, New Coll., 59	
328	XIII	Leiden, Univ. Bibl., Voxx. Gr. Q. 77	
330	XII	St. Petersburg, Russ. Nat. Libr., Gr. 101	
(336)	XV	Hamburg, Univ. Bibl., Cod. theol. 1252a	*disappeared*; von Soden refers to the MS cursorily (α500)
337	XII	Paris, Bibl. Nat., Gr. 56	
(339)	XIII	Turin, Bibl. Naz., B. V. 8	fire damaged; *no film*
363	XIV	Florence, Bibl. Medicea Laur., Plutei VI.13	
367	1331	Florence, Bibl. Medicea Laur., Conv. Soppr. 53	
378	XIII	Oxford, Bodl. Libr., E. D. Clarke 4	
383	XIII	Oxford, Bodl. Libr., E. D. Clarke 9	
384	XIII	London, Brit. Libr., Harley 5588	
385	1407	London, Brit. Libr., Harley 5613	
386	XIV	Rome, Bibl. Vat., Ottob. gr. 66	
390	1281/82	Rome, Bibl. Vat., Ottob. gr. 381	
393	XIV	Rome, Bibl. Vallicell., E. 22	
394	1330	Rome, Bibl. Vallicell., F. 17	
398	X	Cambridge, Univ. Libr., Kk. 6.4	
400	XV	Berlin, Staatsbibl., Diez. A Duod. 10	
404	XIII	Vienna, Nat. Bibl., Theol. gr. 313	
421	ca. 1300	Vienna, Nat. Bibl., Theol. gr. 303	
424	XI	Vienna, Nat. Bibl., Theol. gr. 302, fols. 1-353	
425	1330	Vienna, Nat. Bibl., Theol. gr. 221	
429	XIV	Wolfenbüttel, Herz. Aug. Bibl. Codd. Aug. 16.7.4o	
431	XII	Strasbourg, Priestersem., 1	
432	XV	Rome, Bibl. Vat., Vat., gr. 366	
436	XI/XII	Rome, Bibl. Vat., Vat., gr. 367	
440	XII	Cambridge, Univ. Libr., Mm. 6.9	
442	XII/XIII	Uppsala, Univ. Bibl., Gr. 1, pp. 183-440	
444	XV	London, Brit. Libr., Harley 5796	
450	X	Rome, Bibl. Vat., Reg. gr. 29	
451	XI	Rome, Bibl. Vat., Urb. gr. 3	
452	XII	Rome, Bibl. Vat., Reg. gr. Pii II 50	
453	XIV	Rome, Bibl. Vat., Barb. gr. 582	
454	X	Florence, Bibl. Medicea Laur., Plutei IV.1	
456	X	Florence, Bibl. Medicea Laur., Plutei IV.30	
457	X	Florence, Bibl. Medicea Laur., Plutei IV.29	interlinear Latin translation
458	XI	Florence, Bibl. Medicea Laur., Plutei IV.31	
459	1092	Florence, Bibl. Medicea Laur., Plutei IV.32	
460	XIII	Venice, Bibl. Naz. Marc., Gr. Z. 11 (379)	Gr.-Lat.-Arab.
462	XI/XII	Moscow, Hist. Mus., V. 24, S. 346	
(463)	XII	Moscow, Hist. Mus., V. 95, S. 192	commentary only
[464]=252			
465	XI	Paris, Bibl. Nat., Gr. 57	
466	XI	Paris, Bibl. Nat., Gr. 58	
467	XV	Paris, Bibl. Nat., Gr. 59	
468	XIII	Paris, Bibl. Nat., Gr. 101	
469	XIII	Paris, Bibl. Nat., Gr. 102A	
479	XIII	Birmingham, Selly Oak Coll., Cod. Mingana Gr. 3	
(480)	1366	(Metz, Bibl. munic., 4)	*destroyed*
483	1295	Williamstown/Mass., Williams Coll., Chapin Libr., Cod. De Ricci no. 1	

489	1315/16	Cambridge, Trinity Coll., B. X. 16	
491	XI	London, Brit. Libr., Add. 11836	
496	XIII	London, Brit. Libr., Add. 16184	
506	XI	Oxford, Christ Church, Wake 12	
517	XI/XII	Oxford, Christ Church, Wake 34	
522	1515/16	Oxford, Bodl. Libr., Canon. Gr. 34	
547	XI	London, Brit. Libr., Add. 39590	
582[4]	XIV	Ferrara, Bibl. Com., Cl. II, 187, III	Jude is divided in two chapters
592	1289	Milano, Bibl. Ambros., Z. 34 sup.	
601	XIII	Paris, Bibl. Nat., Gr. 104	
602	X	Paris, Bibl. Nat., Gr. 105	
603	XIV	Paris, Bibl. Nat., Gr. 106A	
604	XIV	Paris, Bibl. Nat., Gr. 125	
605	X	Paris, Bibl. Nat., Gr. 216	
606	XI	Paris, Bibl. Nat., Gr. 217	
607	XI	Paris, Bibl. Nat., Gr. 218	
608	XIV	Paris, Bibl. Nat., Gr. 220	
610	XII	Paris, Bibl. Nat., Gr. 221	
(611)	XII	(Turin, Bibl. Naz., C. VI. 19)	*destroyed*
(612)[5]	XII	(Turin, Bibl. Naz., B. V. 19; B. VI. 43)	*partly destroyed*; surviving part does not include Jude
613[6]	XII	Turin, Bibl. Naz., C. V. 1	*partly destroyed*; surviving fragment contains Jude 21-25
614	XIII	Milano, Bibl. Ambros., E. 97 sup.	Jude 1-3
615	XV	Milano, Bibl. Ambros., E. 102 sup.	
616	1434	Milano, Bibl. Ambros., H. 104 sup.	
617	XI	Venice, Bibl. Naz. Marc., Gr. Z. 546 (786)	
618	XII	Modena, Bibl. Est., G. 243, a.F.1.28 (III B 17)	
619	984	Florence, Bibl. Medicea Laur., Conv. Soppr. 191	
620	XII	Florence, Bibl. Medicea Laur., Conv. Soppr. 150	Gr.-Lat.
621	XI	Rome, Bibl. Vat., Vat. gr. 1270	
622	XII	Rome, Bibl. Vat., Vat. gr. 1430	
623	1037	Rome, Bibl. Vat., Vat. gr. 1650	
(624)[7]	XI	Rome, Bibl. Vat., Vat. gr. 1714	Jude not extant (only ὑπόθεσις)
625	XII/XIII	Rome, Bibl. Vat., Vat. gr. 1761	
627	X	Rome, Bibl. Vat., Vat. gr. 2062	
628	XIV	Rome, Bibl. Vat., Ottob. gr. 258	Gr.-Lat. (in Jude only notes to the text in Latin)
629	XIV	Rome, Bibl. Vat., Ottob. gr. 298	Gr.-Lat.
630	XII/XIII	Rome, Bibl. Vat., Ottob. gr. 325	
631	XV	Rome, Bibl. Vat., Ottob. gr. 417	
632	XII-XIV	Rome, Bibl. Vallicell., B. 86	two scribes in Jude; vv. 1-24 (fols. 102-103): XII; v. 25 (fol. 104): XIII
633	XIV	Rome, Bibl. Vallicell., F. 13	
634	1394	Rome, Bibl. Vat., Chis. R V 29 (gr. 23)	
635	XI	Naples, Bibl. Naz, Ms. II. A. 8	
636	XV	Naples, Bibl. Naz, Ms. II. A. 9	
637	XII	Messina, Bibl. Univ., 104	
638	XI	Oxford, Christ Church, Wake 38	
639	XI	Oxford, Christ Church, Wake 37	
641	XI	London, Brit. Libr., Add. 19392a	

642	XIV	London, Lambeth Palace, 1185	
(643)	XII/XIII	London, Brit. Libr., Burney 48, Bd. II, fols. 230-244	Jude not extant (only part of ὑπόθεσις)
656	XII	Berlin, Staatsbibl., Graec. oct. 9	
664	XV	Zittau, Stadtbibl., A1	
665	XIII	Oxford, Bodl., Libr., Auct. F. 6. 24	
676	XIII	Münster, Bibelmus., Ms. 2	
680	XIV	New Haven/Conn., Yale Univ. Libr., ms. 248 (Phillips 7682)	
699	XI	London, Brit. Libr., Add. 28815	
712=[2164]	XI	St. Petersburg, Russ. Nat. Libr., Gr. 320	5 fols. (formerly 2164); Jude 12-25; the rest of MS 712 (240 fols.) is kept in Los Angeles.
720	1138/39	Vienna, Nat. Bibl., Theol. gr. 79	
757	XIII	Athens, Nat. Libr., 150	
796	XI	Athens, Nat. Libr., 160	
801	XV	Athens, Nat. Libr., 130	
808	XIV	Athens, Nat. Libr., 2251	
823⁸	XIII	Krakow, Bibl. Jagiellońska (Fonds der Berliner Hss.), Gr. Oct. 13	
824	XIV	Grottaferrata, Bibl. della Badia, A. α. 1	
832	X	Florence, Bibl. Medicea Laur., Plutei VI. 5	
876	XII	Ann Arbor, Univ. Libr., Ms. 16	
901	XI	Uppsala, Univ. Bibl., Gr. 12	
(909)	1107	(latest known: London, D. A. Smith)	*no film*
910	1009	London, Brit. Libr., Add. 39598	
912	XIII	London, Brit. Libr., Add. 39600	
913	XIV	London, Brit. Libr., Egerton 2787	
914	XIII	Escorial, R. III. 4	
915	XIII	Escorial, T. III. 12	
917	XII	Escorial, X. III. 10	
918	XVI	Escorial, Σ. I. 5	
919	XI	Escorial, Ψ. III. 6	
920	X	Escorial, Ψ. III. 18	
921	1332	Escorial, X. IV. 9	
922	1116	Athos, Grigoriu, 3	
927	1133	Malibu/Calif., The J. Paul Getty Mus., Ludw. II 4	
928	1304	Athos, Dionysiu, 56 (9)	
935	XIV	Athos, Dionysiu, 141 (27)	
941	XIII/XIV	Athos, Dionysiu, 164 (33)	
945	XI	Athos, Dionysiu, 124 (37)	
959	1331	Athos, Dionysiu, 254 (317)	
986	XIV	Athos, Esphigmenu, 186	
996	XIV	Athos, Iviron, 735 (28)	
997	XIII	Athos, Iviron, 679 (29)	
999	XIII	Athos, Iviron, 260 (31)	
1003	XV	Athos, Iviron, 689 (52)	
1022	XIV	Baltimore/Maryland, Walters Art Gall., Ms. W. 533	
1040	XIV	Athos, Karakullu, 121 (268)	
1058	1145	Athos, Kutlumusiu, 90 α'	
1066	X	Athos, Kutlumusiu, 16, fols. 1-145	
1067	XIV	Athos, Kutlumusiu, 57	
1069	1262	Athos, Kutlumusiu, 80	
1070	XIII	Athos, Kutlumusiu, 81	
1072	XIII	Athos, Lavra Γ' 80	
1075	XIV	Athos, Lavra Λ' 51	
1094	XIII	Athos, Panteleimonos, 28	

1099	XIV	Athos, Dionysiu, 135 (68)	
1100	1376	Athos, Dionysiu, 8 (75)	
1101	1660	Athos, Dionysiu, 383 (382)	
1102	XIV	Athos, Dochiariu, 38	
1103	XIII	Athos, Dochiariu, 48	
1104	1702	Athos, Dochiariu, 136	
1105	XV	Athos, Dochiariu, 139	
1106	XIV	Athos, Dochiariu, 147	
1107	XIII	Athos, Esphigmenu, 63	
(1108)	XIII	Athos, Esphigmenu, 64	*no film*
(1109)	XIV	(earlier: Athos, Esphigmenu, 65)	*disappeared*
1115	XII	Athos, Esphigmenu, 66	
1127	XII	Athos, Philotheu 1811 (48)	
(1140)	1242	Athos, Esphigmenu 67	*incomplete film* (not Jude)
1149	XIII	Istanbul, Ecum. Patriarchate 130 (earlier: Chalki, Kamoriotissis 133)	
1161	1280	Patmos, Joannu, 14	
1162	XI	Patmos, Joannu, 15	
1175	X	Patmos, Joannu, 16	
1240	XII	Sinai, St. Catherine's mon., Gr. 259	
1241	XII	Sinai, St. Catherine's mon., Gr. 260	Jude after Colossians
1242	XIII	Sinai, St. Catherine's mon., Gr. 261	
1243	XI	Sinai, St. Catherine's mon., Gr. 262	
1244	XI	Sinai, St. Catherine's mon., Gr. 274	
1245	XII	Sinai, St. Catherine's mon., Gr. 275	
(1246)	?	(earlier: Sinai, St. Catherine's mon., Gr. 265)	*disappeared*
1247	XV	Sinai, St. Catherine's mon., Gr. 266	
1248	XIV	Sinai, St. Catherine's mon., Gr. 267	
1249	1324	Sinai, St. Catherine's mon., Gr. 276	
1250	XV	Sinai, St. Catherine's mon., Gr. 269	
1251	XIII	Sinai, St. Catherine's mon., Gr. 270	
1270	XI	Modena, Bibl. Est., G. 71, α.W.2.7	
[1274b]=2822			
1277	XI	Cambridge, Univ. Libr., Add. Mss. 3046	
(1287)	XIII	?	*disappeared*
1292	XIII	Paris, Bibl. Nat., Suppl. Gr. 1224	
1297	1290	Paris, Bibl. Nat., Suppl. Gr. 1259	
1311	1090	Berlin, Staatsbibl., Ham. 625	
1315	XII	Jerusalem, Orthod. Patriarchate, Taphu 31	
1319	XII	Jerusalem, Orthod. Patriarchate, Taphu 47	
1352[9]=[1352a]	1090/99	Jerusalem, Orthod. Patriarchate, Stavru 94, fols. 1-235	
1354	XIV	Jerusalem, Orthod. Patriarchate, Stavru 101	
1359=[2327]	XII	Paris, Bibl. Nat., Suppl. Gr. 1335	
1360[10]	XII	Athens, Nat. Libr., 207, 321 fols.	Jude 1-16
		Odessa, M. Gorky Libr., 555, 7 fols.	Jude 17-25; *no film*
1367	XV	Athens, Nat. Libr., 1882	
(1382)	XIV	Andros, Nikolau, 26	*no film*
1384	XI	Andros, Panachrantu, 13	
1390	XIV	Athos, Stavronikita, 45	
1398	XIII	Athos, Pantokratoros, 56	
1400	XIII	Athos, Pantokratoros, 58	
1404	XIII	Athos, Pantokratoros, 235	
1405	XV	Athens, Nat. Libr., 208	
1409	XIV	Athos, Xiropotamu, 244 (2806)	
1424	IX/X	Chicago/Ill., Jesuit-Krauss-McCormick Libr., Gruber Ms. 152	
1425	1125	Sofia, "Ivan Dujčev" Research Centre, 358 (earlier: Kosinitza, 216)	

(1433)	XII	Athos, Andreu, 9	*no film*
1448	XII	Athos, Lavra, A' 13	
(1456)	XIII	Athos, Lavra, A' 24	last page (with some text of Jude?) illegible
1482	1304	Athos, Lavra, A' 54	
1490	XII	Athos, Lavra, A' 65	
1495	XIV	Athos, Lavra, A' 73	
1501	XIII	Athos, Lavra, A' 79	
1503	1317	Athos, Lavra, A' 99	
1505	XII	Athos, Lavra, B' 26	
1508	XV	Athos, Lavra, Γ' 30	
1509	XIII	Athos, Lavra, B' 53	
[1518]=1896			
1521	1084	Washington/D.C., Dumbarton Oaks, Ms. 3, acc. no. 62.35	
[1522]=1890[11]			
1523	XIII/XIV	Vienna, Nat. Bibl., Theol. gr. 141	
1524	XIV	Vienna, Nat. Bibl., Theol. gr. 150	
(1525)	XIII	Krakow, Bibl. Jagiellońska (Fonds der Berliner Hss.), Gr. Qu. 57?	*no film*
1548	1359	Athos, Vatopediu, 902	
1563	XIII	Athos, Vatopediu, 929	
1573	XII/XIII	Athos, Vatopediu, 939	
1594	1284	Athos, Vatopediu, 962	
1595	XIII	Athos, Vatopediu, 964	
1597	1289	Athos, Vatopediu, 966	
1598	XIV	Athos, Vatopediu, 967	
1599	XIV	Athos, Vatopediu, 963	
1609	XIII	Athos, Lavra, A' 90	
1610[12]	1364	Athens, Nat. Libr., 209	Act 1:1-Jude 9
	1463		Jude 9-*fin.*
1611	X	Athens, Nat. Libr., 94	
1617	XV	Athos, Lavra, E' 157	
1618	XIV	Athos, Lavra, E' 164	
1619	XIV	Athos, Lavra, E' 175	
1622	XIV	Athos, Lavra, Ω' 1	
1626	XV	Athos, Lavra, Ω' 16	
1628	1400	Athos, Lavra, Ω' 20	
1636	XV	Athos, Lavra, Ω' 139	
1637	1328	Athos, Lavra, Ω' 141	
1642	1278	Athos, Lavra, Λ' 128	
1643	XIV	Athos, Lavra, Λ' 134	
1646	1172	Athos, Lavra, Λ' 173	
1649	XV	Athos, Lavra, Λ' 182	
1652	XVI	Athos, Lavra, Θ' 152	
1656	XV	Athos, Lavra, H' 64	
1661	XIV	Athos, Lavra, H' 163	
1668	XI	Athos, Panteleimonos, 15	
1673	XII	Athos, Panteleimonos, 94	
1678	XIV	Athos, Panteleimonos, 770	
1702	1560	Athos, Konstamonitu, 6	
1704	1541	Athos, Kutlumusiu, 356	
(1706)	XIII-XVI	Tirana, National Archives, Koder-Trapp 18	*no film*; the contents of the MS is uncertain
1717	XIII	Athos, Vatopediu, 850	
1718	XII	Athos, Vatopediu, 851	
1719	1287	Athos, Vatopediu, 852	
1720	X	Athos, Vatopediu, 853	
1721	XVII	Athos, Vatopediu, 863	

1722	XIII	Athos, Vatopediu, 864	
1723	XIV	Athos, Vatopediu, 858	
1724	XI/XII	Athos, Vatopediu, 865	Jude 11-25
1725	1367	Athos, Vatopediu, 859	
1726	XIV	Athos, Vatopediu, 860	
1727	XIII	Athos, Vatopediu, 861	
1728	XIII	Athos, Vatopediu, 862	
1729	XV	Athos, Vatopediu, 968	
1730	XI	Athos, Vatopediu, 972	
1731	XIII	Athos, Vatopediu, 973	
1732	1384	Athos, Lavra, A' 91	
1733	XIV	Athos, Lavra, B' 5	
1734	1015	Athos, Lavra, B' 18	
1735	X	Athos, Lavra, B' 42	
1736	XIII	Athos, Lavra, B' 45	
1737	XII	Athos, Lavra, B' 56	
1738	XI	Athos, Lavra, B' 61	
1739	X	Athos, Lavra, B' 64	
1740	XII	Athos, Lavra, B' 80	
1741	XIV	Athos, Lavra, Γ' 57	
1742	XIII	Athos, Lavra, Γ' 75	
1743	XII	Athos, Lavra, Γ' 78	
1744 [13]	XIV	Athos, Lavra, Ω' 8	
1745	XV	Athos, Lavra, Ω' 49	
1746	XIV	Athos, Lavra, Ω' 114	
1747	XIV	Athos, Lavra, Ω' 128	
1748	1662	Athos, Lavra, Ω' 131	
1749	XVI	Athos, Lavra, Ω' 137	
1750	XV	Athos, Lavra, Λ' 118	
1751	1479	Athos, Lavra, K' 190, fols. 1-168	
1752	XII	Athos, Panteleimonos, 24	
1753	XIV	Athos, Panteleimonos, 66	
1754	XII	Athos, Panteleimonos, 68	
1757	XV	Lesbos, Kalloni, Limonos, 132	
1760	XII	Sofia, "Ivan Dujčev" Research Centre, 176 (earlier: Serres, Prodromu, γ' 23)	
1761	XIV	Athens, Nat. Libr., 2521	
1762	XIV	Athens, Nat. Libr., 2489	
1763	XV	Athens, Nat. Libr., 2450	
1765	XIV	London, Brit. Libr., Add. 33214	
1766	1344	Sofia, "Ivan Dujčev" Research Centre, 279 (earlier: Kosinitza, 54)	
1767	XV	Athos, Iviron, 702 (642)	
1768	1519	Athos, Iviron, 771 (643)	
1769	XIV	Athos, Iviron, 244 (648)	
1780	XIII	Durham/N. C., Duke Univ. Libr., Gr. 1	
(1785)	XIII/XIV	Sofia? (earlier: Drama, Kosinitza, 208)	*disappeared*
1795	XII	Sofia, "Ivan Dujčev" Research Centre, 369 (earlier: Kosinitza, 53)	
1799 [14]	XII/XIII	Princeton/N. J., Univ. Libr., Med. and Ren. Mss., Garrett 8 (earlier: Berlin, Staatsbibl., Gr. Qu. 40)	
(1809)	XIV	(earlier: Trabzon, Sumela, 56)	*disappeared*
[1815]=2127			
1827	1295	Athens, Nat. Libr., 131	
1828	XI	Athens, Nat. Libr., 91	
1829	X	Athens, Nat. Libr., 105	
1830	XV	Athens, Nat. Libr., 129	
1831 [15]	XIV	Athens, Nat. Libr., 119	Jude 1-20

1831S	XVI	Athens, Nat. Libr., 119	Jude 21-25
1832	XIV	Athens, Nat. Libr., 89	
1834	1301	St. Petersburg, Russ. Nat. Libr., Gr. 225	palimpsest (see 025 in Table 3)
1835	XI	Madrid, Bibl. Nac., 4588	
1836	X	Grottaferrata, Bibl. della Badia, A. β. 1	
1837	X	Grottaferrata, Bibl. della Badia, A. β. 3	Jude after James
1838	XI	Grottaferrata, Bibl. della Badia, A. β. 6	
1839	XIII	Messina, Bibl. Univ., 40	
1840	XVI	Rome, Bibl. Casanatense, 1395	
1841	IX/X	Lesbos, Kalloni, Limonos, 55	
1842	XIII/XIV	Rome, Bibl. Vat., Vat. gr. 652	
1843	XIII	Rome, Bibl. Vat., Vat. gr. 1208	
1844	XVI	Rome, Bibl. Vat., Vat. gr. 1227, fols. 256-305	
1845	X	Rome, Bibl. Vat., Vat. gr. 1971	
1846	XI	Rome, Bibl. Vat., Vat. gr. 2099	
1847	XI	Rome, Bibl. Vat., Pal. gr. 38	
1849	1069	Venice, Bibl. Naz. Marc., Gr. II,114 (1107)	
1850	XII	Cambridge, Univ. Libr., Add. Mss. 6678	
1851	X	Linköping, Stiftsbibl., T. 14	
1852	XIII	Uppsala, Univ. Bibl., Gr. 11	
1853	XII	Athos, Esphigmenu, 68	
1854	XI	Athos, Iviron, 231 (25)	
1855	XIII	Athos, Iviron, 404 (37)	
1856	XIV	Athos, Iviron, 362 (57)	
1857	XIII	Athos, Iviron, 424 (60)	
1858	XIII	Athos, Konstamonitu, 108	
1859	XIV	Athos, Kutlumusiu, 82	
1860	XIII	Athos, Kutlumusiu, 83	
1861	XVI	Athos, Kutlumusiu, 275	
1862	IX	Athos, Pavlu, 117 (2)	
1863	XII	Athos, Protatu, 32	
1864	XIII	Athos, Stavronikita, 52	
1865	XIII	Athos, Philotheu, 1801 (38)	
[1866]=L1591			
1867	XII	Alexandria, Greek Patriarchate, 117 (5)	
1868	XII	Istanbul, Ecum. Patriarchate (earlier: Chalki, Triados, 14 [16])	
1869	1688	Istanbul, Ecum. Patriarchate (earlier: Chalki, Theol. School, 9)	
1870	XI	Istanbul, Ecum. Patriarchate (earlier: Chalki, Kamariotissis, 26)	
1871	X	Istanbul, Ecum. Patriarchate (earlier: Chalki, Kamariotissis, 33)	
1872	XII	Istanbul, Ecum. Patriarchate (earlier: Chalki, Kamariotissis, 93 [96])	
1873=[2556]	XIII	Athens, Gennadius Libr., Ms. 1.8	
1874	X	Sinai, St. Catherine's mon., Gr. 273	
1875=[1898]	X	Athens, Nat. Libr., 149	
1876	XV	Sinai, St. Catherine's mon., Gr. 279	
1877	XIV	Sinai, St. Catherine's mon., Gr. 280	
1880	X	Sinai, St. Catherine's mon., Gr. 283	
1881	XIV	Sinai, St. Catherine's mon., Gr. 300	
1882	XV	Paris, Bibl. St. Geneviève, 3399	
1885	1101	Paris, Bibl. Nat., Suppl. Gr. 1262	
1886	XIV	Paris, Bibl. Nat., Suppl. Gr. 1263	
1888	XI	Jerusalem, Orthod. Patriarchate, Taphu, 38	
1889	XII	Jerusalem, Orthod. Patriarchate, Taphu, 43	

1890=[1522]	XIV	Jerusalem, Orthod. Patriarchate, Taphu, 462	
1891	X	Jerusalem, Orthod. Patriarchate, Saba, 107	
1892	XIV	Jerusalem, Orthod. Patriarchate, Saba, 204	
1893	XII	Jerusalem, Orthod. Patriarchate, Saba, 665	
1894	XII	Jerusalem, Orthod. Patriarchate, Saba, 676	
1895	IX	Jerusalem, Orthod. Patriarchate, Stavru, 25	Jude 1-8
1896=[1518]	XIV/XV	Jerusalem, Orthod. Patriarchate, Stavru, 37	
1897	XII/XIII	Jerusalem, Orthod. Patriarchate, Stavru, 57	palimpsest (upper writing)
[1898] =1875			
1899	XIV	Patmos, Joannu, 664	
1902	XIV	Athos, Esphigmenu, 198	
1903	1636	Athos, Xiropotamu, 243 (2805)	
2080	XIV	Patmos, Joannu, 12	
2085	1308	Sinai, St. Catherine's mon., Gr. 277	
2086	XIV	Sinai, St. Catherine's mon., Gr. 278	
(2088)	?	(Zakynthos, Publ. Libr., Katrames κδ')	*destroyed*
(2093)	XIII	Serres, Gymnasium, 5	*no film; destroyed?*
(2115)	XII	(earlier: Athens, G. Burnias)	*disappeared*
2125	X	Modena, Bibl. Est., G. 196, α.V.6.3 (II G 3), fols. 52-321	bound with H (014)
2127=[1815]	XII	Palermo, Bibl. Centrale, Dep. Mus. 4	
2131	XV	Kiev, Vernadsky Centr. Scient. Libr., F. 301 (KDA), 10p	
(2136)	XVII	Moscow, Hist. Mus., V. 26, S. 472	Gr.-Old Church Slav.; *no film*
2138	1072	Moscow, Univ., 2	Jude 1-19
2143	XII	St. Petersburg, Russ. Nat. Bibl., Gr. 211	
2147	XI/XII	St. Petersburg, Russ. Nat. Bibl., Gr. 224	
[2164]=712			
2180	XIII/XIV	St. Petersburg, Russ. Nat. Bibl., Gr. 543	
2186	XII	Athos, Vatopediu, 33, fols. 83-176	
2191	XI	Athos, Vatopediu, 762, fols. 90-330	
2194	1118	Athos, Lavra, A' 58	
2197	XIV	Athos, Vatopediu, 245	
2200	XIV	Elasson, Olympiotissis, 79	
2201	XV	Elasson, Olympiotissis, 6	
2218	XVI	Lesbos, Kalloni, Limonos, 297	
2221	1432	Sparta, Mitropolis, 5	
(2225)	1292	(Kalavgryta, Megalu Spileu, 4)	*destroyed*
(2233)	XII	(Kalavgryta, Megalu Spileu, 27)	*destroyed*
(2239)	XVIII	Athens, Nat. Libr., Taphu 289	commentary; no continuous NT text
2242	XII	Paris, Bibl. Nat., Suppl. Gr. 1299	
2243	XVII	Athens, Nat. Bibl., 222, fols. 144-246	
(2249)[16]	1330	Sofia, "Ivan Dujčev" Research Centre, 193 (earlier: Kosinitza, 221)	*Jude not extant*
2255	XVI	Athos, Iviron, 813 (503)	
2261	XIV	Kalavgryta, Lavra, 31	
2279	XIV	London, Brit. Libr., Add. 37001	
2288	XV	Modena, Bibl. Est., G. 13, α.U.2.14 (II A 13)	
2289	XII	Athos, Vatopediu, 857	Jude 1-12
[2294]=2466			
2298	XII	Paris, Bibl. Nat., Gr. 102	
2318	XVIII	Bukarest, Roman. Akad., 318 (234)	
(2325)	?	New York?	*disappeared*; contents unknown
[2327] =1359			
2344	XI	Paris, Bibl. Nat., Coislin Gr. 18, fols. 170-230	
2352	XV	Meteora, Metamorphosis, 237	

2356	XIV	Sinai, St. Catherine's mon., Gr. 1594	Jude 1-5
(2357)	XIV	Jerusalem, Orthod. Patriarchate, Photiu 48	fragmentary and mostly illegible. Jude not identified
2374	XIII/XIV	Baltimore/Maryland, Walters Art Gall., Ms. W. 524	
2378	1511	Athens, Byzant. Mus., 83	
2400	XIII	Chicago/Ill., Univ. Libr., Ms. 965	
2401	XII	Chicago/Ill., Univ. Libr., Ms. 142	
2404	XIII	Chicago/Ill., Univ. Libr., Ms. 126	
2412	XII	Chicago/Ill., Univ. Libr., Ms. 922	
2423	XIII	Durham/N. C., Duke Univ. Libr., Gr. 3	
2431	1332	Athos, Kavsokalyvia, 4	
(2448)	XII	(earlier: Athens, Mus. Loverdu, Nr. 125)	
2466=[2294]	1329	Patmos, Joannu, 759	
2473	1634	Athens, Nat. Libr., Taphu 545	
2475	XI	Jerusalem, Anastaseos, Skevophylakion, s. n.	
2483=[2866][17]	XIII	Oslo/London, The Schøyen Collection, MS 2932	*same as 2866 (see below)*
2484	1311/12	London, Brit. Libr., Add. 38538	
2492	XIV	Sinai, St. Catherine's mon., Gr. 1342	
2494	1316	Sinai, St. Catherine's mon., Gr. 1991	
2495	XV	Sinai, St. Catherine's mon., Gr. 1992	
2501	XVI	Sinai, St. Catherine's mon., Gr. 2051	
2502	1242	Sinai, St. Catherine's mon., Gr. 2123	
(2505)[18]	X	(Istanbul, Ecum. Patriarchate, 6)	*disappeared*
2508	XIV	Athens, Nat. Libr., 20	
2511	XIV	Athos, Lavra, H' 114a	
2516	XIII	Dimitsana, Publ. Libr., 27	
2523[19]	1453	Orlando/FL., The Scriptorium, VK MS 901	
2527	XIV	Athens, Nat. Libr., 2760	
2541	XII	St. Petersburg, Russ. Nat. Libr., Gr. 694	
2544	XVI	St. Petersburg, Russ. Nat. Libr., Collection of the Kirillo-Belozerskij Monastery 120/125	
2554	1434	Bukarest, Roman. Akad., 3/12610	
2558	XIII	Athens, Mus. Benaki, Ms. 34 (E)	
2587	XI	Rome, Bibl. Vat., Vat. gr. 2503, fols. 1-237	
2625	XII	Ochrid, Nat. Mus., 13	
2626	XIV	Ochrid, Nat. Mus., 14	
2627	1202	Ochrid, Nat. Mus., 15	
2652=[L1306]	XV	Athens, Nat. Libr., 103	
2653	XV	Athens, Nat. Libr., 2925	
2674	1651	Elasson, Olympiotissis, 7	
2675	XIV	Halmyros, Xenias, 5	
2691	XV	Meteora, Metamorphosis, 114	
2696[20]	XIII	Meteora, Metamorphosis, 302	
2704	XV	Meteora, Metamorphosis, 542	
2705	XIV	Meteora, Metamorphosis, 543	
2712	XII	Meteora, Stephanu, 4	
2716	XIV	Meteora, Stephanu, Triados 25	
2723	XI	Trikala, Vissarionos, 4	
(2733)	1227	Zavorda, Nikanoros, 99	*illegible film*
2736[21]	XV	Zavorda, Nikanoros, 125	
2746	XI	Brussels, Bibl. Royale, IV.303	
(2772)[22]	XIII	Sofia, Inst. for Church Hist. and Archives of the Bulg. Patriarchate, 24 (236)	
2774	XIII/XIV	Sofia, Inst. for Church Hist. and Archives of the Bulg. Patriarchate, 23 (852)	
2776	XVII	Athens, Hiera Synodos, s. n.	
2777	XIV	Karditsa, Koronis, s. n.	

(2803)	XIV	Athos, Dimitriu, 53	*no film*
2805	XII/XIII	Athens, Studitu, 1	
2815=[2ap]	XII	Basel, Univ. Bibl., A. N. IV.4	
2816=[4 ap]	XV	Basel, Univ. Bibl., A. N. IV.5	
2818=[36aK]	XII	Oxford, New Coll., 58	
2822=[1274b]	XII	London, Brit. Libr., Add. 11860, fols. 3, 7	Jude 4-15 (fol. 7); palimpsest (underlying text); only one page
(2849)	XIV/XV	Paros, Longovardas, ms. 27 (724), fols. 1-156	*illegible film*
(2853)	X/XI	(latest known: Basel, G. Zakos Library)	*disappeared*
2865	XII	Cambridge/Mass., Harvard Coll. Libr., fMS Typ. 491	
[2866]=2483			
(2874)	1305/06	Athos, Vatopediu, Skevophylakion, 13	*no film*
L6	1265	Leiden, Univ. Bibl., Or. 243	
L62	XII	Moscow, Hist. Mus., V. 22, S. 304	
L145	XII	Paris, Bibl. Nat., Gr. 306	
L147	XII	Paris, Bibl. Nat., Gr. 319	
L156	X	Paris, Bibl. Nat., Gr. 382	
L162	XII	Glasgow, Univ. Libr., Ms. Hunter 406	
L164	1172	Oxford, Christ Church, Wake 33	
L241	1199	Glasgow, Univ. Libr., Ms Hunter 419	
L422	XV	Athens, Nat. Libr., 200	
L427	XIII	Athens, Nat. Libr., 133	
L585	XV	Modena, Bibl. Est., G. 102, α.T.8.7 (II D 3)	
L591	XI	Athens, Nat. Libr., 106	
L593	XV	Athens, Nat. Libr., 102	
L596	1146	Escorial, Ψ. III. 9	
L603	XI	Grottaferrata, Bibl. della Badia, Z. δ. 118, fols. 90-105	
L604	XII	Florence, Bibl. Medicea Laur., S. Marco 704	
L606	XII	Messina, Bibl. Ambros., C. 16. inf.	
L608	XII	Rome, Bibl. Vat., Barb. gr. 478	
L617	XI	Venice, Bibl. Naz. Mar., Gr. II,115 (1058), fols. 1-280	
L623	XII	Athos, Dochiariu, 17	
L740	XI	Athos, Karakullu, 3 (34)	
L809	XII	Sinai, St. Catherine's mon., Gr. 286	
L840	XII	Athos, Konstamonitu, 101	
L884	XIII	Istanbul, Ecum. Patriarchate (earlier: Chalki, Triados, 14)	
L921	XII	Istanbul, Ecum. Patriarchate (earlier: Chalki, Kamariotissis, 59)	
L938	XIII	Istanbul, Ecum. Patriarchate (earlier: Chalki, Kamariotissis, 74)	
L1141	1105	Athos, Vatopediu, 925	
L1178	XI	Patmos, Joannu, 11	
L1196	XVI	Athos, Panteleimonos, 104	
L1279	XI	Athos, Panteleimonos, 86	
L1281	1454	Sinai, St. Catherine's mon., Gr. 296	
L1440	1251	Sinai, St. Catherine's mon., Gr. 290	
L1441	XIII	Sinai, St. Catherine's mon., Gr. 291	
L1505	XI	Rome, Bibl. Vat., Barb. gr. 501	
L1818	XVI	Athens, Nat. Libr., 2726	
L2024	XI	Athens, Mus. Benaki, Ms. 247 (E)	
L2087	XVI	Skopelos, Prodromu, 4	
L2106	XI	Zavorda, Nikanoros, 41	
L2394[23]	XIV	Rhodos, Lindos, Panagias, 4, fols. 167-174	

Table 3 below contains five MSS which could not be collated, but are still included in the study on the basis of evidence in various secondary sources. Codex Porphyrianus, P (025), is included in the main apparatus based on a complete transcription by Tischendorf (see below). MSS 101, 241 and 242 were fully collated by C. F. Matthaei (see note to MS 101). The now lost MS 8a was cited cursorily by Stephanus (see below), and only the known readings are indicated in the appendix to the apparatus.

Table 3: MSS included in the study on the basis of published collation data

MS (Gr.-Al. no.)	DATING	LOCATION	NOTES
P 025[24]	IX	St. Petersburg, Russ. Nat. Libr., Gr. 225	*no film*; palimpsest (upper writing=MS 1834); Jude 1-3, 15-25; Tischendorf, *Mon sac* vol. 5; von Soden α3
8a[25]	?	?	*disappeared*; Stephanus' ια
101[26]	XI	Dresden, Sächs. Landesbibl., A. 104, fols. 37-121	*water damaged*; *no film*; Matthaei (as a)
241	XI	(earlier: Dresden, Sächs. Landesbibl., A 172)	*disappeared*; Matthaei (as k); von Soden δ507
242	XII	Moscow, Hist. Mus., V. 25, S. 407	*no film*; Matthaei (as l); von Soden δ206

Table 4 below is a third list of MSS, which contain various parts of the Catholic Epistles, but not the Epistle of Jude. The latter fact often had to be verified in the individual manuscript, since the exact contents of a manuscript is not always indicated in the standard reference sources. I provide this list for the sake of reference, and in order that the reader may be confident that all extant and available MSS have been considered (it should be noted that there is some overlap with Table 2 above). However, the list does not include lectionary MSS – for these I refer the reader to the *Liste*.

Table 4: MSS containing various parts of the Catholic Epistles except Jude

P9, P20, P23, P54, P81, P100, 048, 093, 0156, 0166, 0173, 0206, 0209, 0232, 0245, 0246, 0247, 0285, 0296, 91, 122, 197, 356, 365, 368, 498, 567, 612, 624, 626, 640, 643, 644, 743, 794[27], 911, 1526, 1758[28], 1759, 1848, 1904, 2130, 2303, 2310, 2385, 2441, 2464, 2718[29], 2731[30], 2741, 2799, 2847.

Endnotes Tables 2-4

[1] If there is more than one date for an MS indicated in the *Liste*, the date in this list refers to the portion with the Epistle of Jude.

[2] According to the entry in the *Liste*, the MS is kept in the Ashmolean Museum, Oxford. However, in 2001 all Ashmolean material in the area of papyrology was transferred to the Sackler Library, Oxford. This has bearing on all the entries of MSS in the Oxyrhynchus collection in the *Liste* and its recent update ("Aktualisierung") available at the homepage of the INTF (see above).

[3] 90a: The manuscript contains two texts of Jude copied by the same scribe (Jacob Faber of Deventer, †1515). 90a (fols. 137-139) was copied from an exemplar of Theodore Hagiopetrites, dated to 1293 C.E., whereas 90b (fols. 250-51) was copied from a different exemplar (Gregory, *Textkritik des Neuen Testaments* [3 vols., Leipzig: J. C. Hinrichs, 1900-1909], 1:149). Only 90b seems to have been collated for *TuT* as inferred from the absence of the reading of 90a in Jude 1, τοις εν τω πατρι, in Teststelle 88 (*TuT*, 1.1:199).

[4] 582: The MS according to the *Liste* (and Gregory's *Textkritik*) is dated to 1334 C.E. However, the MS (Ferrara, Bibl. Com., Cl. II, 187, III) is actually undated, and probably Gregory thought that it was a volume of Cl. II, 188, a Greek OT by the same hand, which is dated to 1334 (thus, the date is at least approximately correct); cf. Norman A. Huffman, "Revised Catalogue Data on Greek Gospel Mss. in Italy," *NovT* 1 (1956):159.

[5] 612: Error in the *Liste* where it is indicated that 33 fols. in B.VI.43 are still extant. There are only three extant folios (28, 29, 72) not including Jude. *TuT* only indicates that the MS has been destroyed.

[6] 613: Error in the *Liste* (and *TuT*) where it is indicated that the MS has been destroyed. Two folios are still extant containing Jude 21-25 (from προσδεχομενοι) followed by a copy of the third century tract, *On the Twelve Apostles: Where Each of Them Preached, and Where He Met His End*, traditionally ascribed to the Church Father Hippolytus (170-236 C.E.).

[7] 624: Error in *TuT* where it is indicated that 3 John is not extant (1.1:6).

[8] 823: The manuscript was not included in *TuT* where it is indicated that the manuscript has disappeared (1.1:7). However, the manuscript is still kept in the Jagiellonian Library in Krakow, from which I received a microfilm copy.

[9] 1352: New dating according to the staff of INTF (earlier dating in the *Liste*: 13th century).

[10] 1360: The part of 1360 kept in Odessa was apparently not available for *TuT* as indicated by the lacunae in the collations of test passages (but not in the list of witnesses).

[11] 1522: F. H. A. Scrivener published a collation by W. Sanderson of this MS in *An Exact Transcript of the Codex Augiensis* (Cambridge: Deighton, Bell & Co., 1859) under siglum "c." His collation deviates slightly from my collation of 1890, but it is clearly the same MS. Albin mistakenly thought that this MS was Greg. 1518 (Judasbrevet, 400). According to the *Liste* the MS is dated to the 14th century and contains 268 pages, whereas Gregory who saw the MS in London in 1883 dates it to the 15th century and indicates 272 pages (*Textkritik*, 1:281; MS 216).

[12] 1610: In the *Liste*, only the date 1463 is indicated.

[13] 1744: The following fols. in the codex were replaced in the 16th century (not Jude): fols. 5-8, 15-16, 98-99, 110-182, 268-269.

[14] 1799: According to the *Liste* the MS is "verbrannt." One may get the impression that this is the reason that the MS has never been photographed. However, in a private correspondence as of 9 May 2005 the curator at Princeton University Libraries, Don Skemer, informed me about the MS: "Garrett MS. 8 is here and can be consulted by visiting researchers. However, it does have a variety of conservation problems and was never microfilmed because of its tight

binding." Through the kind permission of Mr. Skemer the manuscript has now been photographed for the first time, exclusively in the Epistle of Jude.

[15] 1831: Some fols. in this codex were replaced in the 16th century; so fol. 351[r] with Jude 21-25, which has been treated as 1831S (supplement) in accordance with the *ECM*. Cf. Gregory, *Textkritik*, 287 (no. 312).

[16] 2249: Error in the *Liste*; the MS does not seem to contain the Apostolos section. Further, it is bound together with L2418 (see continuous update of the *Liste* at: http://www.uni-muenster.de/NTTextforschung/KgLSGII05_01.pdf). In my own examination, I identified L2418 on fols. 325-372.

[17] 2483: The manuscript originally came from Mount Athos, but later became part of a private collection of René Bonjean in Bulligny, Château de Tumejus (Jean Duplacy, "Manuscrits Grecs du Nouveau Testament émigrés de la Grande Laure de l' Athos," in *Studica Codicologica* [ed. Kurt Treu; TU 124; Berlin: Akademie-Verlag, 1977]: 162). I have found out that it was recently bought by a notorious manuscript dealer, Bruce Ferrini in Ohio, who then sold it to the well-known collector Martin Schøyen, Oslo. Apparently, the INTF did not keep track of these transactions and registered the MS under two different entries (2483; 2866). The institute has been notified, and subsequently they have deleted the entry for 2866. Nevertheless, there were discrepancies between the two entries in terms of dating, numbers of pages and format. My own examination of the manuscript shows that the data in the old entry of 2483 concerning format (21.7 x 15.4 cm) is correct. Therefore I have chosen to retain also this dating (13th century rather than ca. 1300). However, the eight last folios have been detached and are now missing (fols. 341-348).

[18] 2505: Error in *TuT*; the MS is not included in the list of witnesses. In private correspondence Mr. Ivan Yong of the Centre for the Study of New Testament Manuscripts (CSNTM), who has examined the collection of NT MSS at the Ecumenical Patriarchate in Istanbul reports that MS 2505 was not present at his visit there in 2004.

[19] 2523: According to the *Liste* the MS is housed in Athens (Nat. Libr., 2720). However, it is now part of the Van Kampen collection and has been relocated to the Scriptorium in Orlando, Florida.

[20] 2696: At the end of the examined film there seems to be at least one other unidentified manuscript, since at the end of the film there are two pages from the Gospel of John (ch. 1)! In the same film, there are two copies of 2 Peter. The staff at the INTF has been notified of the find, so hopefully the new fragments will be identified and properly registered.

[21] 2736: According to the *Liste*, 2736 does not contain Acts. However, in my own examination I found a couple of chapters from Acts at the very beginning of the MS.

[22] 2772: Error in the *Liste*. The manuscript does not contain the Catholic Epistles.

[23] L2394: In the *ECM* IV (and earlier in *TuT*), the MS is consistently referred to as 2718, but according to the *Liste* 2718 is bound together with L2394 (fols. 167-174), and only the latter contains 1 John-Jude.

[24] P (025): Error in *TuT* indicating the contents of Jude 1-3, 16-25 (*TuT*, 1.1:2); a part of verse 15 is still extant. A collation is available in Constantin von Tischendorf, *Monumenta sacra inedita, nova collectio vol. 5* (Leipzig: Hinrichs, 1865).

[25] 8a: The MS is not included in the *Liste*, but was cited in the apparatus to Stephanus' (Robert Estienne) third edition of the New Testament, *Nouum Iesu Christi D.N. Testamentum. Ex Bibliotheca Regia. Lutetiae* (Paris, 1550). F. H. A. Scrivener stated, "Stephen's ια', now missing, cited about 400 times by that editor, in 276 of which it supports the Latin versions (Mill, N.T., Proleg. § 1171)" (F. H. A. Scrivener, *A Plain Introduction to the Criticism of the New Testament for the Use of Biblical Students* [ed. E. Miller; 2 vols.; 4th ed.; London/New York: Deigton, Bell & Co.,

1894], 1:284). The cited readings in Jude are indicated in a supplement to the apparatus in chapter eight.

26 101: According to the *Liste*, "Die Hs. ist durch Wasserschäden im gegenwärtigen Zustand nicht benutzbar." In a private letter to Albin, the library reports that the MS is "fast völlig unbrauchbar" (*Judasbrevet*, 360). So it seems that the MS should still be examined, to see if it can yield more information. Collations of MSS 101, 241, 242 (=a, k, l) were available in C. F. Matthaei, *Novum Testamentum Graece et Latine* (Riga, 1782).

27 794: In his apparatus, Hermann von Soden cites 794 in Jude, which is somewhat mysterious. Jude is not extant in the MS, and already Gregory stated, "Jud scheint zu fehlen" (*Textkritik*, 1:222). Von Soden also erroneously refers to 614 in Jude 12, 15 (it is only extant in vv. 1-3).

28 1758: In the list of witnesses in *TuT*, 1758 should have been marked with a dagger as in the *Liste*.

29 2718: The MS lacks 1 John-Jude but is bound together with L2394 (see above) containing these books.

30 2731: In the *Liste*, the MS is listed as complete in ap but it is not.

Chapter Seven

Reconstructing the Initial Text of Jude

1. The Initial Text of the Epistle of Jude: Definitions

An important objective of this edition is to reconstruct the initial text of Jude. The term "initial text" refers to a hypothetical, reconstructed text which is something more than an archetype, but something less than an autograph; all surviving witnesses are derived from an archetype, but the precise relationship between the archetype and the autograph remains unknown.[1] The simplest theory must be that there is one single autograph which is identical with the archetype, from which the whole textual tradition derives. However, we do not know how it was in reality—there may have been several autographs, if an author issued more than one version of his work, which, in turn, may be reflected in one or several archetypes. An editor may have revised a writing in various ways, or merged several works of an author into one, perhaps in order to adapt the text(s) for inclusion in a collection. For this reason, I have generally avoided terms like "autograph" and "original text." On the other hand, as soon as we use arguments derived from the supposed intention of the author, we go beyond the archetype(s). For this reason, the term "initial text" is appropriate; what we can reconstruct is less than the autograph but more than the archetype.

In my personal opinion, however, I think there is good reason to assume that the initial text of Jude is identical with the author's text, not least because the individual writings of the Catholic Epistles seem to have a unique textual history. This assumption builds primarily on the results of the CBGM as presented in the *ECM* edition of the Catholic Epistles and elsewhere. The editors of the *ECM* have not yet drawn any explicit conclusions from the fact that the conditions of transmission are so differentiated in regard to the seven writings of this section.[2] One plausible

---

[1] For an extended discussion of these terms, see Gerd Mink, "Problems of a Highly Contaminated Tradition: The New Testament. Stemmata of Variants As a Source of a Genealogy for Witnesses," in *Studies in Stemmatology II* (ed. Pieter van Reenen, August den Hollander and Margot van Mulken; Amsterdam: John Benjamins 2004), 25-27.

[2] Franz-Jürgen Schmitz' examination of the Coptic witnesses to the Catholic Epistles reveals a similar picture of a very complex and differentiated textual tradition: "Die Vergleiche der

reason behind this complexity is that the extant witnesses derive from a time when the writings circulated separately.[3] Evidently, they were collected at some stage, but not in one place at one time; the archetype of the surviving textual tradition of the Catholic Epistles is not necessarily a single manuscript with a seven-letter collection. Significantly, there are no extant witnesses to these epistles that prove the existence of any collection before 300 C.E. The earliest witness to 1 Peter, the Coptic Crosby-Schøyen codex MS 193 (3rd century), lacks 2 Peter. This is not surprising, since the codex is a miscellany organized around the theme of Easter and not a continuous text MS of the New Testament. On the other hand, the *inscriptio* lacks an ordinal number ("The Epistle of Peter"). Perhaps 2 Peter was unfamiliar to the scribe, or simply not extant in the exemplar. The few papyri that are preserved from the 3rd century contain fragmentary portions of individual epistles ($\mathfrak{P}^9$, $\mathfrak{P}^{20}$, $\mathfrak{P}^{23}$, $\mathfrak{P}^{100}$). Thus, the first witness to a collection is $\mathfrak{P}^{72}$ (ca 300 C.E.) with Jude and 1-2 Peter, copied by the same scribe, but with only the two latter writings placed sequentially in a separate section of the codex.[4] Interestingly, the genealogical data of the CBGM for the two Petrine epistles suggest that their mutual textual history is more similar than that of the other Catholic Epistles, which suggests that 1-2 Peter were brought together earlier in the history of transmission.[5] In conclusion, I think the collection of the Catholic Epistles developed gradually and in several places.[6]

---

koptischen Zeugen mit den jeweiligen 'charakteristischen griechischen Zeugen' ergeben in den drei Briefen [James, 1-2 Peter] ein ganz unterschiedliches—jeweils andere Akzente setzendes—Bild" (*Das Verhältnis der koptischen zur griechischen Überlieferung des Neuen Testaments* [ANTF 33; Berlin/New York: de Gruyter, 2003], 595).

[3] Another factor behind the complexity of the tradition is the textual mixture (contamination) which results from the use of multiple exemplars or from the correction of a manuscript from another.

[4] Significantly, the textual character of $\mathfrak{P}^{72}$ seems different for 1-2 Peter and Jude. Kurt and Barbara Aland categorize the text as "normal" in 1-2 Peter but "free" in Jude, "both with certain peculiarities (*The Text of the New Testament: An Introduction to the Critical Editions and to the Theory and Practice of Modern Textual Criticism* [trans. Erroll F. Rhodes; 2d rev. and enl. ed.; Grand Rapids: Eerdmans, 1995], 100). One may also note that in this early witness there are no cases of harmonization between Jude and 2 Peter in $\mathfrak{P}^{72}$ in contrast to many other early witnesses.

[5] It is significant that the CBGM method generates data for the Petrine epistles suggesting a closer textual history of these epistles. In order to test the statistical significance of the CBGM method elsewhere, it would be interesting to compare the results for James 1-2 with 3-5, or 1 John 1-3 with 4-5, respectively.

[6] This assumption is partly in conflict with David Trobisch's "canonical edition" theory; he suggests that all extant MSS are descended from a canonical edition, an *editio princeps*, and that the individual writings did not circulate widely when they were in their initial stages of

This line of inquiry could be pursued in greater detail, but many questions will probably remain unanswered. For example, why are 03 and 1739 the only manuscripts counted among first rank witnesses in all seven epistles, according to the CBGM? Is the method biased in their favor, or were these witnesses copied from manuscripts with seven-letter collections of particularly good overall quality?

2. Method of Reconstruction

The reconstruction of the initial text of Jude is done on the basis of generally accepted principles of textual criticism. More specifically, I use the approach which is commonly referred to as "reasoned eclecticism." This approach takes into account all available evidence in as balanced a manner as possible, giving attention both to the textual witnesses (external evidence), primarily the Greek manuscripts, and to internal considerations regarding the origin of the text (author's style and theology, etc.) and its transmission (scribal habits, tendencies and mistakes, etc.).

In regard to the manuscript evidence, I have taken into account the recent results of the CBGM as applied to Jude, since I consider that to be the best available comprehensive method for the genealogical reconstruction of the textual tradition, in spite of its possible biases and drawbacks.

Significantly, there is no discontinuity between the results of the CBGM and the traditional view of "good witnesses" in Jude. For example, many of the manuscripts among the first rank witnesses in Jude are well-known and traditionally labeled as "Alexandrian" (e.g., $\mathfrak{P}^{72}$, 01, 02, 03, 04, 044, 1739). These manuscripts were already among the "consistently cited witnesses of the first order" in NA[27]. However, the CBGM provides a refined knowledge of the genealogical structure of the tradition and reveals other witnesses that are closely related to the initial text. Admittedly, I have not seen or been able to evaluate the complete data of the CBGM as applied to Jude. However, the available results do concur with my own observations of the manuscripts and my text-critical decisions: the preferred readings in my edition are generally attested by a large number of textual witnesses, including manuscripts well-known for their significance, as well as other closely related, but less familiar witnesses.

---

existence as separate entities (*The First Edition of the New Testament* [Oxford: Oxford University Press, 2000], 21-22). This theory in its most restrictive sense does not explain the wide differentation of transmissional history, which must have taken place in a pre-corpus period. Nevertheless, I think Trobisch's general assumption of an established, archetypical collection is correct, but such an edition is not necessarily the archetype of the extant *textual tradition*, but rather the archetype of the final canonical *collection* which then was able to dominate the transmissional process.

3. The Reconstructed Initial Text of Jude

[[ΙΟΥΔΑ ΕΠΙΣΤΟΛΗ]]

Ἰούδας Ἰησοῦ Χριστοῦ δοῦλος, ἀδελφὸς δὲ Ἰακώβου, τοῖς ἐν θεῷ πατρὶ ἠγαπημένοις καὶ Ἰησοῦ Χριστῷ τετηρημένοις κλητοῖς· **2** ἔλεος ὑμῖν καὶ εἰρήνη καὶ ἀγάπη πληθυνθείη.

3 ἀγαπητοί, πᾶσαν σπουδὴν ποιούμενος γράφειν ὑμῖν περὶ τῆς κοινῆς ἡμῶν σωτηρίας ἀνάγκην ἔσχον γράψαι ὑμῖν παρακαλῶν ἐπαγωνίζεσθαι τῇ ἅπαξ παραδοθείσῃ τοῖς ἁγίοις πίστει. **4** παρεισέδυσαν γάρ τινες ἄνθρωποι, οἱ πάλαι προγεγραμμένοι εἰς τοῦτο τὸ κρίμα, ἀσεβεῖς, τὴν τοῦ θεοῦ ἡμῶν χάριτα μετατιθέντες εἰς ἀσέλγειαν καὶ τὸν μόνον δεσπότην καὶ κύριον ἡμῶν Ἰησοῦν Χριστὸν ἀρνούμενοι.

5 ὑπομνῆσαι δὲ ὑμᾶς βούλομαι, εἰδότας ὑμᾶς ἅπαξ πάντα, ὅτι κύριος λαὸν ἐκ γῆς Αἰγύπτου σώσας τὸ δεύτερον τοὺς μὴ πιστεύσαντας ἀπώλεσεν, **6** ἀγγέλους τε τοὺς μὴ τηρήσαντας τὴν ἑαυτῶν ἀρχὴν ἀλλὰ ἀπολιπόντας τὸ ἴδιον οἰκητήριον εἰς κρίσιν μεγάλης ἡμέρας δεσμοῖς ἀϊδίοις ὑπὸ ζόφον τετήρηκεν, **7** ὡς Σόδομα καὶ Γόμορρα καὶ αἱ περὶ αὐτὰς πόλεις τὸν ὅμοιον τρόπον τούτοις ἐκπορνεύσασαι καὶ ἀπελθοῦσαι ὀπίσω σαρκὸς ἑτέρας, πρόκεινται δεῖγμα πυρὸς αἰωνίου δίκην ὑπέχουσαι.

8 ὁμοίως μέντοι καὶ οὗτοι ἐνυπνιαζόμενοι σάρκα μὲν μιαίνουσιν κυριότητα δὲ ἀθετοῦσιν δόξας δὲ βλασφημοῦσιν. **9** ὁ δὲ Μιχαὴλ ὁ ἀρχάγγελος, ὅτε τῷ διαβόλῳ διακρινόμενος διελέγετο περὶ τοῦ Μωϋσέως σώματος, οὐκ ἐτόλμησεν κρίσιν ἐπενεγκεῖν βλασφημίας ἀλλὰ εἶπεν· ἐπιτιμήσαι σοι κύριος. **10** οὗτοι δὲ ὅσα μὲν οὐκ οἴδασιν βλασφημοῦσιν, ὅσα δὲ φυσικῶς ὡς τὰ ἄλογα ζῷα ἐπίστανται, ἐν τούτοις φθείρονται. **11** οὐαὶ αὐτοῖς, ὅτι τῇ ὁδῷ τοῦ Κάϊν ἐπορεύθησαν καὶ τῇ πλάνῃ τοῦ Βαλαὰμ μισθοῦ ἐξεχύθησαν καὶ τῇ ἀντιλογίᾳ τοῦ Κόρε ἀπώλοντο. **12** οὗτοί εἰσιν οἱ ἐν ταῖς ἀγάπαις ὑμῶν σπιλάδες, συνευωχούμενοι ἀφόβως, ἑαυτοὺς ποιμαίνοντες, νεφέλαι ἄνυδροι ὑπὸ ἀνέμων παραφερόμεναι, δένδρα φθινοπωρινὰ ἄκαρπα δὶς ἀποθανόντα ἐκριζωθέντα, **13** κύματα ἄγρια θαλάσσης ἀπαφρίζοντα τὰς ἑαυτῶν αἰσχύνας, ἀστέρες πλανῆται οἷς ὁ ζόφος τοῦ σκότους εἰς αἰῶνα τετήρηται.

14 προεφήτευσεν δὲ καὶ τούτοις ἕβδομος ἀπὸ Ἀδὰμ Ἐνὼχ λέγων· ἰδοὺ ἦλθεν κύριος ἐν ἁγίαις μυριάσιν αὐτοῦ **15** ποιῆσαι κρίσιν κατὰ πάντων καὶ ἐλέγξαι πάντας τοὺς ἀσεβεῖς περὶ πάντων τῶν ἔργων ἀσεβείας αὐτῶν ὧν ἠσέβησαν καὶ περὶ πάντων τῶν σκληρῶν ὧν ἐλάλησαν κατ' αὐτοῦ ἁμαρτωλοὶ ἀσεβεῖς. **16** οὗτοί εἰσιν γογγυσταὶ μεμψίμοιροι κατὰ τὰς ἐπιθυμίας ἑαυτῶν πορευόμενοι, καὶ τὸ στόμα αὐτῶν λαλεῖ ὑπέρογκα, θαυμάζοντες πρόσωπα ὠφελείας χάριν.

17 ὑμεῖς δέ, ἀγαπητοί, μνήσθητε τῶν ῥημάτων τῶν προειρημένων ὑπὸ τῶν ἀποστόλων τοῦ κυρίου ἡμῶν Ἰησοῦ Χριστοῦ **18** ὅτι ἔλεγον ὑμῖν· ὅτι ἐπ' ἐσχάτου τοῦ χρόνου ἔσονται ἐμπαῖκται κατὰ τὰς ἑαυτῶν ἐπιθυμίας πορευόμενοι τῶν ἀσεβειῶν. **19** οὗτοί εἰσιν οἱ ἀποδιορίζοντες, ψυχικοί, πνεῦμα μὴ ἔχοντες.

20 ὑμεῖς δέ, ἀγαπητοί, ἐποικοδομοῦντες ἑαυτοὺς τῇ ἁγιωτάτῃ ὑμῶν πίστει, ἐν πνεύματι ἁγίῳ προσευχόμενοι, **21** ἑαυτοὺς ἐν ἀγάπῃ θεοῦ τηρήσατε προσδεχόμενοι τὸ ἔλεος τοῦ κυρίου ἡμῶν Ἰησοῦ Χριστοῦ εἰς ζωὴν αἰώνιον. **22** καὶ οὓς μὲν ἐλεᾶτε διακρινομένους, **23** οὓς δὲ σῴζετε ἐκ πυρὸς ἁρπάζοντες, οὓς δὲ ἐλεᾶτε ἐν φόβῳ μισοῦντες καὶ τὸν ἀπὸ τῆς σαρκὸς ἐσπιλωμένον χιτῶνα.

24 τῷ δὲ δυναμένῳ φυλάξαι ὑμᾶς ἀπταίστους καὶ στῆσαι κατενώπιον τῆς δόξης αὐτοῦ ἀμώμους ἐν ἀγαλλιάσει, **25** μόνῳ θεῷ σωτῆρι ἡμῶν διὰ Ἰησοῦ Χριστοῦ τοῦ κυρίου ἡμῶν δόξα μεγαλωσύνη κράτος καὶ ἐξουσία πρὸ παντὸς τοῦ αἰῶνος καὶ νῦν καὶ εἰς πάντας τοὺς αἰῶνας, ἀμήν.

4. Comparison of the Reconstructed Text with the *ECM*

There are only a few differences between my critical text and the critical text of the *ECM*:

v. 5: κύριος (*ECM*: Ἰησοῦς)
v. 13: ἀπαφρίζοντα (*ECM*: ἐπαφρίζοντα)
v. 15: πάντας τοὺς ἀσεβεῖς (*ECM*: πᾶσαν ψυχήν)
v. 18: ὅτι² (*ECM*: omit)

Apart from these differences, I have put the *inscriptio* in square brackets, since, in my opinion, it does not belong to the initial text. Further, I have inserted a comma in v. 5 after πάντα, and I have corrected the accentuation of γογγυσταί (v. 16). The paragraph divisions in my reconstructed text are identical with those of Nestle-Aland in its 27th edition. They have been added here for the sake of convenience and increased readability.

In the *ECM*, a bold dot is used to indicate when a passage calls for special critical consideration (no precise definition is given). There are ten bold dots in Jude. In my textual commentary I use a different system, where the symbol {e=i} is roughly equivalent to the bold dot, indicating that the evidence is balanced (see textual commentary). This symbol occurs at six places in Jude, four of which correspond to the *ECM*:

v. 5:   δέ {e=i} (*ECM* •δε•/•ουν)
v. 5:   κύριος {e=i} (*ECM* •ιησους•/•[ο] κυριος)
v. 18: ἐπ' ἐσχάτου τοῦ χρόνου {e=i} (*ECM* •επ εσχατου χρονου εσονται •/•επ εσχατου του χρονου εσονται)
v. 21: τηρήσατε {e=i} (*ECM* •τηρησατε•/•τηρησωμεν)

At eight places my evaluation differs from the *ECM*:

v. 13: ἀπαφρίζοντα {e=i} (*ECM* επαφριζοντα κτλ.)

v. 14: ἐν ἁγίαις μυριάσιν αὐτοῦ {e+i} (*ECM* •αγιαις μυριασιν αυτου•/ •μυριασιν αγιαις αυτου)

v. 16: ἐπιθυμίας ἑαυτῶν {e<i} (*ECM* •επιθυμιας εαυτων•/•επιθυμιας αυτων)

v. 17: ῥημάτων τῶν προειρημένων {e>i} (*ECM* •ρηματων των προειρημενων•/ •προειρημενων ρηματων)

v. 18: ὅτι {e>i} (*ECM* •omit•/•οτι)

v. 20: ὑμῶν {e+i} (*ECM* •εποικοδομουντες εαυτους τη αγιωτατη υμων πιστει•/• εποικοδομουντες εαυτους τη αγιωτατη ημων πιστει)

v. 24: φυλάξαι ὑμᾶς {e=i} (*ECM* φυλαξαι υμας)

v. 25: τοῦ² {e>i} (*ECM* •προ παντος του αιωνος•/•προ παντος αιωνος)

Chapter Eight

Apparatus

Introduction

1. The Structure of the Apparatus

In many ways the critical apparatus follows the design of the new edition, the *ECM* from the INTF in Münster (with their kind approval), so there is no need for a detailed explanation. The words in the primary line text indicate the adopted text. Every word in the primary line text is assigned an even number indicated below the word, and every space between words is assigned an odd number, reserved for variant readings that represent additions to the text at these specific points. In this way every instance of textual variation is assigned a specific numerical address. Below the primary line, all the variant readings are listed, distinguished by letters (*a* = the primary line reading, *b*, *c*, etc). In the case of an addition to the primary line text (assigned an odd numerical address), the primary line reading *a* will always be indicated as an omission (om.).

The sequence of presentation of the variant readings normally follows the pattern: transposition, substitution/addition, omission, uncertain readings. In some cases, the sequence may differ, in order to improve clarity.

In regard to the variation-units, I generally apply the same division as in the *ECM*, whenever I do not consider the *ECM* to be unclear, misleading or erroneous. Some of these latter cases are noted in the errata list, as well as in the list of differences below.

2. Abbreviations and Symbols in the Apparatus

The following list of abbreviations and symbols follows the standard of the *ECM* unless otherwise noted below:

In the Primary Line Text

[[ ]] The superscription to the epistle has been retained in the primary line text, but enclosed within double square brackets, which indicate that the enclosed words are not part of the initial text proper, although they derive from an early stage of the tradition.

At the Beginning of Each Verse/At the End of Each Unit

– The witnesses cited have a lacuna (in a whole verse; alternatively a whole unit). Note that a witness can be partly lacunose in a variant unit and still be cited in support of a reading (the manuscript number is then followed by the symbol V=*ut videtur*). For the exact extent of lacunae in such cases, the reader is referred to the appropriate list.

After a Numerical Address

↓   the downward arrow marks an address that includes or overlaps with
↑   adresses marked by an upward arrow. When an address includes or
↑↓ overlaps with both previous and subsequent addresses, the symbols are used in conjunction (↑↓).

After a Letter Address of a Reading

f   the defective form represents a reading which cannot be reconstructed with certainty. A reading is considered to be defective when there is not even a remote possibility of its making sense.

0   a possible orthographical or morphological form of the preceding variant reading (e.g., *a, ao*). All orthographica are recorded except for νῦ ἐφελκυστικόν ("movable nu") and the elision of final vowel which in Jude occurs in some prepositions and the word ἀλλά.

Instead of a Letter Address of a Reading

↑   the witnesses listed are not cited because of inclusion or overlap with a numerical address marked by downward arrow.

↔ *a/b/etc* It cannot be determined which of the variant readings is supported. Instead of a letter address, a question mark may be used (e.g., ↔ *a/?*), which indicates that the reading may be unknown in the tradition, or else defective. The text of the witness in question is accounted for in greater detail than otherwise (dots are placed underneath uncertain letters; square brackets indicate lacunae, numbers between square brackets indicate estimated number of letters).

Dots Underneath Uncertain Letters

Dots are placed underneath uncertain letters only in connection with the double arrow when it cannot be determined which variant reading is supported (see above). Otherwise, when it is clear which variant is supported, the symbol V (*ut videtur*) is used after the manuscript number.

In the Witness List

...   the reading is supported by all the Greek MSS except those that are specifically cited in support of other readings (or else uncertain/lacunose).

Instead of a Reading
om. omittit/-unt (followed by the list of witnesses)

After a Manuscript Number
A   alternative reading (coordinate with T)
C   correction (coordinate with *)
f   defective form ("Fehler") which unequivocally supports the reading indicated. All errors are recorded in the apparatus, or in a list of errors in the Greek MSS. Exception has been made for the most frequent kind of vowel interchange (αι-ε, ε-η, ε-ι-η-υ-ι-οι, ο-ω).[1]
(*f)   an originally defective form that was corrected (the defective form is recorded in a subsequent list regarding errors)
(Cf)   an originally correct form of a reading that was erroneously corrected (the defective form is recorded in the errata list of Greek MSS)
K   a reading in the commentary which differs from the lemma
S   supplement (only 1831S; see list of MSS)
T   the reading of the text as distinguished from an alternative reading (A), a reading in a commentary (K) or an additional reading (Z)
V   *ut videtur* (apparently). In some cases, the symbol is used when there are lacunae within a unit; the reader should always consult the list of

---

[1] Chrys C. Caragounis suggests that this process of vowel interchange was initiated already in pre-classical Antiquity as evidenced in Attic inscriptions of the early 6th century B.C.E. where constant confusion of these vowels and diphthongs occurs ("The Error of Erasmus and Un-Greek Pronunciations of Greek," *Filologia Neotestamentaria* 8 [1995]: 159-61). In many of his works, Caragounis has demonstrated convincingly that Greek pronunciation is a vital key to the correct evaluation of many variants (cf. idem, "'To Boast' or 'To Be Burned'? The Crux of 1 Cor 13:3," *SEÅ* 60 [1995]: 115-27; idem, *The Development of Greek and the New Testament: Morphology, Syntax, Phonology, and Textual Transmission* [WUNT 167; Tübingen: Mohr Siebeck, 2004], pt. 3). Therefore, it would have been preferable to indicate the exact spelling of the MSS at every point in the current apparatus, but that would have led to a considerable increase in the number of variants, and would have required much more space at the expense of clarity. For pragmatic reasons, these spelling differences are recorded only in the transcriptions which will be made available separately.

lacunae to see if this is the case. The symbol is also used when one or more letters are uncertain, although it is evident which reading is supported.

Z   an additional reading, interlinear or marginal, that is either a correction or an alternative reading. It should be noted that the definition of Z in this edition is more precise than in the *ECM*: in order to avoid a subjective element of interpretation, I classify all interlinear and marginal readings as additional readings, unless the reading of the text is unequivocally erroneous, or if there is a sign known to be used for corrections. (In the list of differences between this edition and the *ECM*, all cases of different interpretation are noted.)

*   the reading of the first hand (coordinate with C)

/2   lessons from Jude occur in lectionaries of the *synaxarion* in week 36 of the ecclesiastical (movable) year. In a few lectionaries, L427, L585, L1196, L1281, there are lessons from Jude in the second part of the lectionary, the *menologion* with fixed feasts following the civil year (often on June 19). These latter menologion-lessons have been cited consistently under the sigla L427/2, L585/2, L1196/2, and L1281/2. (In the *ECM*, two lessons within the same lectionary are cited separately only when they differ.)

132

[[ΙΟΥΔΑ ΕΠΙΣΤΟΛΗ]]

Inscriptio

1

— P74 P78 04 025 0251 0316 602 610 613 615
712 1668 1724 1730 1831S 1867 1899 2344
2718 2822 L6 L62 L145 L147 L156 L162
L164 L241 L422 L427 L427/2 L585 L585/2
L591 L593 L596 L603 L604 L606 L608 L617
L623 L740 L809 L840 L884 L921 L938
L1141 L1178 L1196 L1196/2 L1279 L1281
L1281/2 L1440 L1441 L1505 L1818 L2024
L2087 L2106

a om. 056 1 61 97 181 205 205abs 254 421
522 620 629 720 919 1066 1070 1107 1115
1247 1367 1400 1404 1405 1828 1834 1839
1846T 1872 2186 2191 2674

b ιουδα επιστολη P72(*f) 02 018 044 5 33 62
81 175 181 241 242 307 326 363 453 458
607 619 623 628 901 1161 1175 1241 1251
1678 1721 1731 1735 1757 1760 1795 1827
1836 1841 1847 1871 1874 1875 1895 2085
2125 2197 2201 2374 2401 2541 2818 2865

c επιστολη ιουδα 177 337 460 618 631 637
876T 1149 1292 1505 1611 1738 1765 1832
1838Z 1843 1873 1893 2138 2298 2495
2527

d ιουδα επιστολης 180 832

e ιουδα καθολικη 1845

f ιουδα επιστολη πρωτη 1875

g ιουδα επιστολη καθολικη 6 38 42 57 69
82 88 90b 110 142 172 221 250 252 256 263
309 314 319 327 393 424 450 452 454 462
467 468 605 606 616 627 633 639 641 699
796 910 915 920 922 941 1022 1058 1103
1244 1245 1277 1352 1360 1424 1448 1509
1573 1642 1722 1739* 1741 1747 1750
1762 1769 1780 1835 1849 1859 1862 1870
1888 2127 2194 2318 2356 2400T 2404
2423 2473 2475 2484 2516 2523 2558 2587
2776 2805

h ιουδα καθολικη επιστολη 18 141 149 201
204 216 226 312 322 323 325 328 385 386
394 404 429 432 440 442 444 456 469 479
517 547 604 608 614V 617 621 634 664 801
913 914 918 921 928 996 999 1100 1101
1105 1240 1242 1249 1250 1384 1482 1490
1508 1548 1599 1609 1610 1649 1661 1702

1704 1719 1723 1725 1726 1727 1732 1733
1737 1742 1748 1749 1752 1761 1763 1766
1767 1768 1799 1830 1831 1853 1855 1856
1857 1858 1865 1876 1886 1897 2080 2131
2180 2218 2221 2255 2261 2288 2378
24122431 2483 2501 2508 2554 2626 2652
2653 2691 2704 2712 2716 2723 2774

i επιστολη ιουδα καθολικη 35 206S 630
757 824 876Z 986 1040 1072 1075 1503
1521 1617 1618 1619 1636 1637 1652 1656
1740 1745 1746 1754 1860 1864 1892 2200
2352 2466 2494 2777

j επιστολη καθολικη ιουδα 321 1850 2143

k καθολικη επιστολη ιουδα 76 378 945
1094 1319 1622 2147 2746

l επιστολη καθολικη τεταρτη 1563Z

m ιουδα επιστολη καθολικη μια 1734

n ιουδα επιστολη καθολικη πρωτη 104

o ιουδα καθολικη επιστολη πρωτη 959
1243

p ιουδα επιστολη καθολικη τη τριτη 103

q ιουδα αποστολου επιστολη καθολικη 457
465 603 622 635 656 1501 1728

r επιστολη καθολικη ιουδα αποστολου 459
1838T 1842

s επιστολη καθολικη ιουδα του αποστολου
302 1390

t καθολικη επιστολη ιουδα του αποστολου
189 1717 2816

u ιουδα αποστολου επιστολη 1837 1882

v ιουδα του αποστολου επιστολη 2544

w επιστολη του αποστολου 1626

x επιστολη ιουδα του αποστολου 0142 436
636 1067 1311 1315 1597 1894 2696

y επιστολη του αγιου αποστολου ιουδα 020
466 625 1523 1524 1844 1851 1877 2502
2705

z του αγιου αποστολου ιουδα επιστολη 049
101 105 131 398 451 997 1643 1646

a' του αγιου ιουδα του αποστολου επιστολη
1852V

b' η του ιουδα καθολικη επιστολη 917

cf' κ επιστολη του αγιου ιουδα καθολικη
2736

133

d' ιουδα του αποστολου επιστολη καθολικη
3 102 496 638 1102 1270 1297 1595 1598
1840 1891 1896

e' ιουδα του αγιου αποστολου επιστολη
καθολικη 383 1880

f' ιουδα του αγιου αποστολου καθολικη
επιστολη 1718

g' επιστολη καθολικη του αγιου αποστολου
ιουδα 330 1069

h' επιστολη του αγιου αποστολου ιουδα
καθολικη 808

i' καθολικη επιστολη του αγιου αποστολου
ιουδα 1248 1495 1743

j' του αγιου ιουδα αποστολου επιστολη
καθολικη 296 1869

k' του αγιου ιουδα αποστολου καθολικη
επιστολη 209

l' του αγιου αποστολου ιουδα επιστολη
καθολικη 90a 133 203 308V 384 425 491
506 642 823 1104 1398 1673 1720 1744
1829 1854 2627

m' του αγιου αποστολου ιουδα καθολικη
επιστολη 218 1127 1359 1425 1885 2815

n' ιουδα του αποστολου επιστολη καθολικη
632f

o' επιστολη του αγιου ιουδα του αποστολου
καθολικη 1903

p' του αγιου αποστολου ιουδα επιστολη
καθολικη πρωτη 93 665

q' του αγιου και πανευφημου αποστολου
ιουδα επιστολη 2625

r' ιουδα επιστολη αδελφος ιακωβου 1106

s' ιουδα επιστολη αδελφου ιακωβου 1099
1354 1736 1889 1890 1902

t' ιουδα αδελφου ιακωβου επιστολη 676

u' επιστολη ιουδα αδελφου ιακωβου 43 489
927

v' επιστολη ιουδα του αδελφου ιακωβου
1729 1868

w' ιουδα επιστολη καθολικη αδελφου
ιακωβου 1881

x' ιουδα αδελφου ιακωβου επιστολη
καθολικη 2086f

y' επιστολη ιουδα του αδελφου του κυριου
94

z' επιστολη ιουδα του αδελφοθεου 431

a'' επιστολη καθολικη ιουδα του
αδελφοθεου 2243

b'' ιουδα επιστολη αλλος αδελφοθεος ταδ
ιουδας ευσεβεεσσιν 2085

c'' ιουδα επιστολη καθολικη αλλος
αδελφοθεος ταδ ιουδας ευσεβεσσιν 2511

d'' ιουδα επιστολη καθολικη αλλος
αδελφοθεος ταδ ιουδας ευσεβεεσσιν 51
223 483 1753 2279

e'' ιουδα καθολικη επιστολη αλλος
αδελφοθεος ταδ ιουδας ευσεβεεσσιν 1594

f'' ιουδα αλλος αδελφοθεος ταδ ιουδας
ευσεβεσιν επιστολη καθολικη 1861

g'' ιουδα αλλος αδελφοθεος ταδ ιουδας
ευσεβεεσσιν επιστολη καθολικη 390 912
1003 1863

h'' ιουδα αλλος αδελφοθεος επιστολη
καθολικη ταδ ιουδας ευσεβεσιν 1739C

i'' αλλος αδελφοθεος ταδ ιουδας
ευσεβεεσσιν 945T 2492

j'' αλλος αδελφοθεος ταδ ιουδας
ευσεβεεσιν επιστολη καθολικη 367

k'' ιουδα επιστολη καθολικη αλλος
αδελφοθεος ταδ ιουδας ασεβεεσσιν 234

l'' ιουδα καθολικη επιστολη αλλος
αδελφοθεος ταδ ιουδας ευσεβεσιν περι
προσευχης της εις χριστον πιστεως δια
την επαναστασιν των ασεβειων και
ασελγων ανδρων 2675

m'' ιουδα επιστολη καθολικη περι προσοχης
της εις χριστον πιστεως δια την
απαναστασιν των ασεβων και ασελγων
ανδρων 601

n'' ιουδα επιστολη προσοχης της εις χριστον
πιστεως δια την απαναστασιν των
ασεβων και ασελγων ανδρων 1162

o'' αλλος ιουδας ου μη δε ο προδοτης την
επιστολην πασιν εθνεσιν γραφει 582

p'' τοισιδ ιουδας ηδυεπης αγορητης
επιστολην γραψας ωπασε πασι βροτοις
1563T

q'' επιστολη ιουδα αποστολου αδελφου
ιακωβου προς τους πιστευσαντας
αδελφους 680

r'' ιουδα τη τριτη και εις τον αποστολον
ιουδαν επιστολη καθολικη 935

s'' αναγνωσμα ιουδα καθολικης 1846Z

t'' καθολικης επιστολης ιουδα
αναγνωσμα 2242

u'' καθολικης επιστολης ιουδα το
αναγνωσμα 1409

v'' επιστολη ιουδα το αναγνωσμα 2400Z

w'' ιουδα 01Z2 03Z2 2289

↔ t''f/u''f: καθολικης επιστολης ιουδα 592
1751

↔ z/a'/k'/m': [του] αγιου [>12] επιστολη 400

1 Ἰούδας Ἰησοῦ Χριστοῦ δοῦλος, ἀδελφὸς
2   4   6   8   10
δὲ Ἰακώβου, τοῖς ἐν θεῷ πατρὶ
12   14   16   18   20   22

---

v. 1

— P74 P78 04 0251 0316 602 610 613 712 1724 1831S 1867 1899 2822

2-34↓

a ιουδας ιησου χριστου δουλος αδελφος δε ιακωβου τοις εν θεω πατρι ηγαπημενοις και ιησου χριστω τετηρημενοις κλητοις ...

b om. 796

4-8↑

a ιησου χριστου δουλος P72 01 02 03 020 044 056 0142 1 3 5 18 33 35 43 61 62 69 81 88 90a 90b 93 94 102 103 105 133 141 149 172 177 189 201 203 204 206S 218 226 241 242 254 263 296 307 309 312 314 321 322 323 326 327 328 337 363 367 378 383 384 386 394 398 425 429 431 432 436 442 444 450 453 454 456 457 458 460 462 465 466 467 479 483 491 496 506 522 547 603 604 606 608 614 618 621 622 623 625 629 630 631 632 633 634 635 636 639 641 656 664 665 676 720 757 801 823 824 832 876 901 910T 913 915 917 918 928 945 959 986 997 999 1040 1058 1066 1069 1070 1072 1075 1094 1100 1101 1102 1104 1105 1106 1107 1162 1241 1242 1243 1244 1247 1248 1249 1250 1251 1270 1292 1297 1311 1315 1352 1359 1367 1384 1390 1398 1400 1404 1409 1425 1448 1482 1490 1503 1505 1508 1509 1521 1523 1524 1548 1563 1595 1597 1598 1599 1610 1611 1617 1618 1619 1628 1636 1637 1642 1649 1652 1656 1673 1678 1702 1704 1717 1718 1720 1723 1725 1726 1727 1728 1731 1732 1733 1735 1737 1738 1739 1740 1741 1745 1746 1747 1748 1749 1750 1752 1754 1761 1762 1763 1765 1766 1767 1768 1799 1827 1828 1830 1831 1832 1834 1836 1837 1838 1840 1842 1843 1844 1845 1846 1850 1852 1853 1854 1855 1856 1858 1864 1865 1869 1874 1875 1876 1877 1880 1882 1885 1891 1892 1894 1896 1897 1902 1903 2080 2131 2138 2143 2147 2180 2186 2197 2200 2218 2221 2242 2243 2255 2261

2289 2298 2318 2344 2352 2378 2401 2404 2412 2431 2466 2473 2492 2494 2495 2501 2523 2527 2544 2554 2558 2587 2626 2652 2653 2691 2696 2704 2723 2774 2776 2777 2805 2815 2816 2818 2865 L147 L427 L585 L585/2 L593 L596 L603 L884 L1196 L1196/2 L1281 L1281/2 L1440 L2087

b χριστου ιησου δουλος 018 025 049 6 38 42 51 57 76 82 97 101 104 110 131 142 175 181 205 205abs 209 216 221 223 234 250 252 302 308 319 325 330 385 390 393 404 421 424 440 451 452 459 468 469 489 517 582 592 601 605 607 615 616 617 619 620 627 628 637 638 642 680 699 808 910Z 912 914 919 920 921 922 927 935 941 996 1003 1022 1099 1103 1115 1127 1149 1161 1175 1240 1245 1277 1319 1354 1360 1405 1424 1495 1501 1573 1594 1609 1622 1626 1643 1646 1661 1668 1719 1721 1722 1729 1730 1734 1736 1742 1743 1744 1753 1757 1760 1769 1780 1795 1829 1835 1839 1841 1847 1849 1851 1857 1859 1860 1861 1862 1863 1868 1870 1871 1872 1873 1886 1888 1889 1890 1893 1895 2085 2086 2125 2127 2191 2194 2201 2279 2288 2356 2374 2400 2423 2475 2483 2484 2502 2508 2511 2516 2541 2625 2627 2674 2675 2705 2712 2716 2718 2736 2746 L6 L62 L145 L156 L162 L241 L422 L427/2 L591 L604 L606 L608 L617 L623 L740 L809 L840 L921 L938 L1141 L1178 L1279 L1441 L1505 L1818 L2024 L2106

c δουλος ιησου χριστου 180 1751 1881 L164

d χριστου δουλος 256 1067

↑ 796

— 400

12↑

a δε ...

b om. 393 1754 2653 L164

↑ 796

— 400 1852

14↑
a ιακωβου ... 680f 1646(*f)
↑ 796
— 1852

16-34↑↓
a τοις εν θεω πατρι ηγαπημενοις και ιησου
χριστω τετηρημενοις κλητοις ... L585Z
L593f
b τετηρημενοις κλητοις L585T
↑ 796

16-24↑↓
a τοις εν θεω πατρι ηγαπημενοις ...
b τοις εν θεω προηγιασμενοις 234f L1818
↑ 796 L585
— 33

16-22↑↓
a τοις εν θεω πατρι P72 01 02 03 018 020
025 044 049 056 0142 1 3 5 18 35 38 42 43
51 57 61 62 69 76 81 82 88 90a 90b 93 94 97
101 102 103 104 105 110 131 133 141 142
149 172 175 177 180 181 189 201 203 204
205 205abs 206S 209 216 218 221 223 226
241 242 250 252 254 256 263 296 302 307T
308 309 312 314 319 321 325 326 327 328
330 337 363 367 383 384 385 386 390 393
394 398 400 404 421 424T 425 429 431 432
436 440 442 444 450 451 452 453 454 456
457 458 459 460 462 465 466 467 468 469
479 483 489 491 496 506 517 522 547 582
592 601 603 604 605 606 607 608 615 616
617 618 619 620 621 622 623 625 627 628
629 630 631 632 633 634 635 636 637 638
639 641 642 656 664 665 676 680 699 720
757 801 808 823 824 832 901 910 912 913
914 915 917 918 919 920 921 922 927 928
935 941 959 986 996 997 999 1003 1022
1040 1058 1066 1067 1069 1070 1072 1075
1094 1099 1100 1101 1102 1103 1104 1105
1106 1107 1115 1127 1149 1161 1162 1175
1240 1242 1244 1245 1247 1248 1249 1250
1251 1270 1277 1297 1311 1315 1319 1352
1354 1359 1360 1367 1384 1390 1398 1400
1404 1405 1409 1424 1425 1448 1482 1490
1495 1501 1503 1508 1509 1521 1523 1524
1548 1563 1573 1594 1595 1597 1598 1599
1609 1610 1617 1618 1619 1622 1626 1628
1636 1637 1642 1643 1646 1649 1652 1656
1661 1668 1673 1678 1702 1704 1717 1718
1719 1720 1721 1722 1723 1725 1726 1727
1728 1729 1730 1731 1732 1733 1734 1735
1736 1737 1738 1740 1741 1742 1743 1744
1745 1746 1747 1748 1749 1750 1751 1752
1753 1754 1757 1760 1761 1762 1763 1766
1767 1768 1769 1780 1795 1799 1827 1828
1829 1830 1831 1834 1835 1836 1837 1838
1839 1840 1841 1842 1843 1844 1845 1846
1847 1849 1850 1851 1853 1854 1855 1856
1857 1858 1859 1860 1861 1862 1863 1864
1865 1868 1869 1870 1871 1872 1873 1874
1875 1876 1877 1880 1882 1885 1886 1888
1889 1890 1891 1892 1893V 1894 1895
1896 1897 1902 1903 2080 2085 2086 2125
2127 2131 2143 2180 2186 2191 2194 2197
2200 2201 2218 2221 2242 2243 2255 2261
2279 2288 2289 2298 2318 2344 2352 2356
2374 2378 2400 2401 2404 2423 2431 2466
2473 2475 2483 2484 2501 2502 2508 2511
2516 2523 2527 2541 2544 2554 2558 2587
2625 2626 2627 2653V 2674 2675 2691
2696 2704 2705 2712 2716 2718 2723 2736
2746 2774 2776 2777 2805 2815 2816 2818
2865 L6 L62 L145 L147 L156 L162 L164
L241 L422 L427 L427/2 L585/2 L591 L593
L596 L603 L604 L606 L608 L617 L623 L740
L809 L840 L884 L921 L938 L1141 L1178
L1196 L1196/2 L1279 L1281 L1281/2
L1440 L1441 L1505 L2024 L2087 L2106
b τοις εν πατρι θεω 2180
c τοις εν θεω πατρασιν 832
d τοις εν θεω πατρι ημων L921
e τοις εν θεω και πατρι 104 459 1838
f τοις εν τω πατρι 90a
g τοις εν χριστω πατρι 205 205abs
h τοις εθνεσιν εν θεω πατρι 307Z 322 323
378 424Z 614 876 945 1241 1243 1292 1505
1611 1739 1765 1832 1852V 1881 2138
2147f 2412 2492 2494 2495 2652
i τοις εθνεσιν πατρι 6
↔ *a/c/d/e:* τοις εν θεω [1384
↑ 234 796 L585 L1818
— 33

ἠγαπημένοις καὶ Ἰησοῦ Χριστῷ
24   26   28   30
τετηρημένοις κλητοῖς· **2** ἔλεος ὑμῖν
32   34   2   4

24↑

a ηγαπημενοις P72 01 02 03 044 5 81 88
101Z 180 326Z 330 385 436 442 451 468
605A 617 621 623 628Z 630 631 876 915
1067 1241f 1243 1292 1409 1505 1611
1643A 1720 1739 1765 1832 1845 1846
2138 2200 2298 2344 2356 2492 2494 2495
2502 2774 2776Z 2805 L585/2 L596 L1441

b ηγιασμενοις 018 020 025 049 056 0142 1 3
6 18 35 38 42 43 51 57 61 62 69 76 82 90a
90b 93 94 97 101T 102 103 104 105 110 131
133 141 142 149 172 175 177 181 189 201
203 204 205 205abs 206S 209 216 218 221
223 226 241 242 250 252 254 256 263 296
302 307 308 309 312 314 319 321 322 323
325 326T 327 328 337 363 367 378 383 384
386 390 393 394 398 400V 404 421 424 425
429 431 432 440 444 450 452 453 454 456
457 458 459 460 462 465 466 467 469 479
483 489 491 496 506 517 522f 547 582 592
601 603 604 605T 606 607 608 614 615 616
618 619 620 622 625 627 628T 629 632 633
634 635 636 637 638 639 641 642 656 664
665 676 680 699 720 757 801 808 823 824
832 901 910 912 913 914 917 918 919 920
921 922 927 928 935 941 945 959 986 996
997 999 1003 1022 1040 1058 1066 1069
1070 1072 1075 1094 1099 1100 1101 1102
1103 1105 1106 1107 1115 1127 1149 1161
1162 1175 1240 1242 1244 1245 1247 1248
1249 1250 1251 1270 1277 1297 1311 1315
1319 1352 1354 1359 1360 1367 1390 1398
1400 1404 1405 1424 1425 1448 1482 1490
1495 1501 1503 1508 1509 1521 1523 1524
1548 1563 1573 1594 1595 1597 1598 1599
1609 1610 1617 1618 1619 1622 1626 1628
1636 1637 1642 1643T 1649 1652 1656
1661 1668 1673 1678 1702 1704 1717 1718
1719 1721 1722 1723 1725 1726 1727 1728
1730 1731 1732 1733 1734 1735 1736 1737
1738 1740 1741 1742 1743 1744 1745 1746
1747 1748 1749 1750 1751 1752 1753 1754
1757 1760 1761 1762 1763 1766 1767 1768
1769 1780 1795 1799 1827 1828 1829 1830

1831 1834 1835 1836 1837 1838 1839 1840
1841 1842 1843 1844 1847 1849 1850 1851
1853 1854 1855 1856 1857 1858 1859 1860
1861 1862 1863 1864 1865 1868 1869 1870
1871 1872 1873 1874 1875 1876 1877 1880
1881 1882 1885 1886 1888 1889 1890 1891
1892 1893 1894 1895 1896 1897 1902 1903
2080 2085 2086 2125 2127 2131 2143 2147
2180 2186 2191 2194 2197 2201 2218 2221
2242 2243 2255 2261 2279 2288 2289 2318
2352 2374 2378 2400 2401 2404 2412 2423
2431 2466 2473 2475 2483 2484 2501 2508
2511 2516 2523 2527 2541 2544 2554 2558
2587 2625 2626 2627 2652 2653 2674f 2675
2691 2696 2704 2705 2712 2716 2718 2723
2736 2746 2776T 2777 2815 2816 2818
2865 L6 L62 L145 L147 L156 L162 L164
L241 L422 L427 L427/2 L591 L593 L603
L604 L606 L608 L617 L623 L740 L809 L840
L884 L921 L938 L1141 L1178 L1196
L1196/2 L1279 L1281 L1281/2 L1440
L1505 L2024 L2087 L2106

c υγιασμενοις 1646 1729
df ηγνησμενοις 1104
↑ 796 L585
— 33 1384 1852

25↑

a om. ...
b και 61
↑ 796 L585
— 33 1384 1852

26-34↑

a και ιησου χριστω τετηρημενοις κλητοις
P72 01 02 03 020 025 056 0142 1 5 6 18 35
42 51 69 76 81 94 97 101 102 103 105 110
141 142 149 172 175 177 180 189 201 204
205 205abs 206S 209 216 218 221 223 226
234 241 242 250 296 307 308 312 314 319
321 322 323 326 327 328 337 363 367 378
383C 385 386 390 393 394 404 421 424 425
429 432 436 440 444 452 453 454 462 465
466 467 468 469 479 483 489 522 547 592
603 604 606 608 614 615f 616 617 618 622
623 625 627 632C 634 635 636Z 638 639

641 642 664 676 680 720 757 801 808 824
901 912 913 918 920 921 927 928 935 941
945 959 986 996 1003 1022 1040 1058 1066
1067 1069 1070 1072 1075 1094 1099 1100
1101 1102 1103 1104 1105 1106 1107 1115
1127 1149 1161 1241 1242 1243 1244 1245
1247 1248 1249 1250 1251 1277 1315 1352
1354 1359 1360 1367 1390 1400 1404 1405
1409 1425 1482 1490 1501 1503 1508 1509
1521 1548 1563 1594 1597 1599 1609 1610
1617 1618 1619 1622 1628 1636 1637 1643
1649 1652 1656 1661f 1678 1702 1704 1717
1718 1719 1721 1722 1723 1725 1726 1727
1728 1730 1732 1733 1736 1737 1738 1739
1740 1742 1743 1744 1745 1746 1747 1748
1749 1750 1751 1752 1753 1754 1760 1761
1763 1766 1767 1768 1795 1799 1828 1830
1831 1837 1839 1840 1841 1842 1845 1847
1849 1851 1853 1855 1856 1857 1858 1859
1860 1861 1862 1863 1864 1865 1868 1871
1876(*f) 1881 1882 1888 1889 1890 1891
1892 1893 1894 1896 1897 1902 2080 2085
2086 2125 2131 2147 2186 2197 2218 2221
2242 2255 2261 2279 2288 2289 2298 2318
2344 2352 2378 2400 2412 2423 2431 2466
2473 2475 2483 2492 2501 2508 2511 2523
2544 2554 2558 2587 2626 2652 2653 2674f
2675 2691 2704 2712 2716 2718 2723 2736
2746 2776 2777 2815 2816 2818 L62 L145
L147 L162 L164 L422 L427 L427/2 L585/2
L593 L603 L606 L608 L623 L740 L809 L840
L921 L938 L1141 L1178 L1196 L1196/2
L1279 L1281 L1281/2 L1440 L1441 L1505
L2024 L2087 L2106

b   και χριστω ιησου τετηρημενοις κλητοις
    203 442 506 621 629 L596

c   και ιησου χριστου τετηρημενοις κλητοις
    018 3 38 43 57 62 82 90a 90bC 131 133 181
    252 254 256 263 302 309 325 330 383* 384
    398 431 450 451 456 457 458 459 460 491
    496 517 582 601 605 607 619 620 632* 633
    637 656 699 823 832 914 917 919 922 997
    999 1162 1175 1240 1311 1319 1398 1424
    1448 1495 1523 1524 1573 1626 1642 1646
    1668 1673 1720 1729 1731 1734 1735 1741
    1757 1762 1769 1780 1827 1829 1834 1835
    1836 1843 1844 1850 1854 1869 1870 1872
    1873 1874 1877 1880 1885 1886 1895 1903
    2127 2143 2180 2191 2194 2201 2356 2374
    2401 2484 2502 2516 2527 2541 2625 2627
    2696 2705 2865 L6 L156 L591 L604 L617
    L884 L1818

d   και χριστου ιησου τετηρημενοις κλητοις
    044 2774 2805

e   και ιησου χριστου κλητοις τετηρημενοις
    93 665 L241

f   και   ιησου   χριστου   τετηρημενοις
    εκλεκτοις 2404

g   και ιησου χριστω τετηρημενοις κλητοις
    αγιοις 628(*f) 1846

h   και κυριου ιησου χριστου τετηρημενοις
    κλητοις 631

i   και ιησου χριστου τετηρημενοις κλητοις
    αγιοις 104 1838

j   και εν χριστω ιησου τετηρημενοις
    κλητοις 61 88 915 1270 1297 1595 1598

k   και ιησου χριστω τετηρημενοις 049

l   κυριου ιησου τετηρημενοις κλητοις 910

m   κλητοις 90b* 630 636T 876 1292 1505
    1611 1765 1832 1875 2138 2200 2243 2494
    2495

↔ a/b/c/d/j: κ̣αι̣ [.... τετηρη]μενοις κλητοις
    400

↔ a/b/c/d/h/j/l: τετη]ρημενοις κλητοις 33

↔ a/g/k:] ιησου χριστω τετηρη[μενοις 1852

↑   796 L585

—   1384

v. 2

—   P74 P78 04 0251 0316 602 610 613 712
    1384 1724 1831S 1867 1899 2822

2-14↓

a   ελεος υμιν και ειρηνη και αγαπη
    πληθυνθειη ...

b   om. 796

2-6↑↓

a   ελεος υμιν και ... 110V 1852V 2516f

b   om. 398

↑   796

4↑

a   υμιν P72 01 02 03 018 020 025 044 049 056
    0142 1 3 5 6 18 33 35 38 42 43 51 57 61 62
    69 76 81 82 88 90a 90b 93 94 97 101 102
    103 104 105 131 133 141 142 149 172 175
    177 180 181 189 201 203 204 205 205abs
    206S 209 216 218 221 223 226 234 241 242
    250 252 254 256 263 296 302 307 308 309
    312 314 319 321 322 323 325 326 327 328
    330 337 363 367 378 383 384 385 386 390
    393 394 400 404 421 424 425 429 431 432
    436 440 442 444 450 451 452 453 454 456
    457 458 459 460 462 465 466 467 468 469
    479 483 489 491 506 517 547 582 592 601
    603 604 605 606 607 608 615 617 618 619
    620 621 622 623 625 627 628 629 630 631

καὶ εἰρήνη καὶ ἀγάπη πληθυνθείη.
6   8   10   12   14

633 634 635 637 638 639 641 642 656 664
665 676 680 699 720V 757 801 808 823 824
876 901 910 912 913 914 915 917 918 919
920 922 927 928 935 941 945 959 986 996
997 999 1003 1022 1040 1058 1067 1069
1070 1072 1075 1094 1099 1100 1101 1102
1103 1104 1105 1106 1107 1115 1127 1149
1161 1162 1175 1240 1241 1242 1243 1244
1247 1248 1249 1250 1251 1270 1277 1292
1297 1311 1319 1352 1354 1359 1360 1367
1390 1398 1400 1404 1405 1409 1425 1448
1482 1490 1495 1501 1503 1505 1508 1509
1521 1523 1524 1548 1573 1594 1595 1597
1598 1599 1609 1610 1611 1617 1618 1619
1622 1626 1628 1636 1637 1642 1643 1646
1649 1652 1656 1661 1668 1673 1678 1702
1704 1717 1718 1719 1720 1721 1722 1723
1725 1726 1727 1728 1729 1730 1731 1732
1733 1734 1735 1736 1737 1738 1739 1740
1741 1743 1744 1745 1746 1747 1748 1749
1750 1752 1753 1754 1757 1760 1761 1762
1763 1765 1766 1767 1768 1769 1780 1795
1827 1828 1829 1830 1831 1832 1834 1835
1836 1837 1838 1839 1840 1841 1842 1843
1844 1845 1847 1849 1850 1851 1852 1853
1854 1855 1856 1857 1858 1859 1860 1861
1862 1863 1864 1865 1868 1869 1870 1871
1872 1873 1874 1875 1876 1877 1880 1881
1882 1885 1886 1888 1889 1890 1891 1892
1893 1894 1895 1896 1897 1902 1903 2080
2085 2086 2125 2127 2131 2138 2143 2147
2180 2186 2191 2194 2197 2200 2201 2218
2221 2242 2243 2255 2261 2279 2288 2289
2298 2318 2344 2352 2356 2374 2378 2400
2401 2404 2412 2423 2431 2466 2473 2475
2483 2484 2492 2494 2495 2501 2502 2508
2511 2516 2523 2527 2541 2544 2554 2558
2587 2625 2626 2627 2652 2653 2674 2675
2691 2704 2705 2716 2718 2723 2736 2746
2774 2776 2777 2805 2815 2816 2818 2865
L6 L62 L145 L147 L156 L164 L241 L422
L427 L427/2 L585 L585/2 L591 L593 L596
L603 L604 L606 L608 L617 L623 L740 L809
L840 L884 L921 L938 L1141 L1178 L1196
L1196/2 L1279 L1281 L1281/2 L1440
L1441 L1505 L1818 L2087 L2106

b   ημιν 496 522 614 616 632 636 832 921
    1066 1245 1315 1424 1563 1742 1751 1799
    1846 2696 2712 L162 L2024
—   110
↑   398 796

6↑
a   και P72 01 02 03 020 025 044 049 1 3 5 6 18
    33 35 38 42 43 51 57 61 62 69 76 81 82 88
    90a 90b 93 94 97 101 102 104 105 131 133
    141 142 149 172 175 177 180 181 189 201
    203 204 205 205abs 206S 209 216 218 223
    226 234 241 242 250 252 254 256 263 296
    302 307 308 309 319 321 322 323 325 326
    328 330 337 363 367 378 383 384 385 386
    390 393 394 400 404 421 424 425 429 431
    432 436 440 442 444 450 451 452 453 456
    457 458 459 460 462 465 466 467 468 469
    479 483 489 491 496 506 517 522 547 582
    592 601 603 604 605 607 608 614 615 616
    617 618 619 620 621 622 623 625 627 628
    629 630 631 632 633 634 635 636 637 638
    639Z 642 656 664 665 676 680 699 720 757
    801 808 823 824 876 901 910 912 913Z 914
    915 917 918 919 920 921 922 927 928 935
    941 945 959 986 996 997 999 1003 1022
    1040 1058 1067 1069 1070 1072 1075 1094
    1099 1100 1101 1102 1103 1104 1105 1106
    1107 1115 1127 1149 1161 1162 1175 1240
    1241 1242 1243 1244C 1245 1247 1248
    1250 1251 1270 1277 1292 1297 1311 1315
    1319 1352 1354 1359 1360 1367 1390 1398
    1400 1404 1405 1409 1424 1425 1448 1482
    1490 1495 1501 1503 1505 1508 1509 1521
    1523V 1524 1548 1563 1573 1594 1595
    1597 1598 1599 1609 1611 1617 1618 1619
    1622 1626 1628 1636 1637 1642 1643 1646
    1649 1652 1656 1661 1668 1673 1678 1702
    1704 1717 1718 1719 1720 1721 1722 1723
    1725 1726 1727 1728 1729 1730 1731 1732
    1733 1734 1735 1736 1737 1738 1739 1740
    1741 1742 1743 1744 1745 1746 1747 1748
    1749 1750 1751 1752 1753 1754 1757 1760
    1761 1762 1763 1765 1766 1767 1768 1769
    1780 1795 1799 1827 1828 1829 1830 1831
    1832 1834V 1835 1836 1837 1838 1839
    1840 1841 1842 1843 1844 1845 1846

1847 1849 1850 1851 1852 1854 1855 1856
1857 1858 1859 1860 1861 1862 1863 1864
1865 1868 1869 1870 1871 1872 1873 1874
1875 1876 1877 1880 1881 1882 1885 1886
1888 1889 1890 1891 1892 1893 1894 1896
1897 1902 1903 2080 2085 2086 2127 2131
2138 2143 2147 2180 2186 2191 2194 2197
2200 2201 2218 2221 2242 2243 2255 2261
2279 2288 2289 2298 2318 2344 2352 2356
2374 2378 2400 2401 2404 2412 2423 2431
2466 2473 2475 2483 2484 2492 2494 2495
2501 2502 2508 2511 2516 2523 2527 2541
2544 2554 2587 2625 2626 2627 2652 2653
2674 2675 2691 2696 2704 2705 2712 2716
2718 2723 2736 2746 2774 2776 2777 2805
2815 2816 2818 2865 L6 L62 L145 L147
L156 L162 L164 L241 L422 L427 L427/2
L585 L585/2 L591 L596 L603 L604 L606
L608 L617 L623 L740 L809 L840 L884 L921
L938 L1141 L1178 L1196 L1196/2 L1279
L1281 L1281/2 L1440 L1441 L1505 L1818
L2024 L2087 L2106

b om. 018 056 0142 103 221 312 314 327 454
606 639T 641 832 913T 1066 1244* 1249
1610 1853 1895 2125 2558 L593

— 110

↑ 796

8-12↑

a ειρηνη και αγαπη P72 01 02 03 018 020
025 044 049 056 0142 1 3 5 6 18 35 38 42 43
51 57 62 69 76 81 82 90a 90b 93 94 97 101
102 103 104 105 110 131 133 141 142 149
172 175 177 180 189 201 203 204 205
205abs 206S 209 216 218 221 223 226 234
241 242 250 252 254 256 263 296 302 307
308 309 312 314 319 321 322 323 325 326
327 328 330 337 363 367 383 384 385 386
390 393 394 398 400 404 421 424 425 429
431 432 436 440 442 444 450 451 452 453
454 456 457 458 459 460 462 465 466 467
468 469 479 483 489 491 496 506 517 522
547 582 592 601 603 604 605 606 607 608
615 616 617 618 620 621 622 623 625 627
628 632 633 634 635 636 637 638 639 641
642 656 664 665 676 680 699 720 757 801
808 823 824 832 901 910 912 918 919 920
921 927 928 935 941 945 959 986 996 997
999 1003 1022 1040 1058 1066 1067 1069
1070 1072 1075 1094 1099 1100 1101 1102
1103 1104 1105 1106 1107 1115 1127 1149
1161 1241 1242 1243 1244 1245 1247 1248

1249 1250 1251 1270 1277 1297 1311 1315
1319 1352 1354 1359 1360 1390 1398 1400
1404 1405 1409 1425 1448 1482 1490 1495
1501 1503 1508 1509 1521 1523 1524 1548
1563 1573 1594 1595 1597 1598 1599 1609
1617 1618 1619 1622 1626 1636 1637 1642
1643 1646 1649 1652 1656 1661 1668 1673
1678 1702 1704 1717 1718 1719 1720 1721
1722 1723 1725 1726 1727 1728 1729 1730
1731 1732 1733 1734 1735 1736 1737 1738
1739 1740 1741 1742 1743 1744 1745 1746
1747 1748 1749 1750 1751 1752 1753 1754
1757 1761 1762 1763 1766 1767 1768 1769
1780 1795 1799 1828 1829 1831 1835 1837
1838f 1839 1840 1841 1842 1843 1844 1845
1846 1847 1849 1850 1853 1854 1855 1856
1857 1858 1859 1860f 1861 1862 1863 1864
1865 1869 1870 1871 1872 1873 1876 1880
1881 1882 1885 1888 1889 1890 1891 1892
1893 1894 1895 1896 1897 1902 1903 2080
2085 2086 2125 2131 2143 2180 2186 2191
2194 2197 2201 2218Z 2221 2242 2255
2261 2279 2288 2289 2298 2318 2344 2352
2356 2374 2378 2400 2401 2404 2423 2431
2466 2473 2475 2483 2484 2492 2501 2502
2508 2511 2516 2523 2527 2541 2544 2554
2558 2587 2625 2626 2627 2653 2674 2675
2691 2696 2704 2705 2712 2716 2718 2723
2736 2746 2774 2776 2777 2815 2816 2818
2865 L6 L62 L145 L147 L156 L162 L164
L241 L422 L427/2 L585 L585/2 L591 L593
L596 L603 L604 L606 L608 L617 L623 L740
L809 L840 L884 L921 L938 L1141 L1178
L1196 L1196/2 L1279 L1281 L1281/2
L1440 L1441 L1505 L1818 L2024 L2087
L2106

b αγαπη και ειρηνη 33V 61 631 1424 1868
c ειρηνη και η αγαπη 2127
d ειρηνη και αγαπη εν κυριω 1367
e ειρηνη εν κυριω και αγαπη 614 630 876
1292 1505 1611 1765 1832 2138 2147 2200
2412 2494 2495 2652
f ειρηνη εν κυριω 378 2243
g ειρηνη 88 181 619 629 913 914 915 917 922
1162 1175 1240 1610 1628 1760 1827 1830
1834 1836 1851 1874 1875 1877 1886
2218T 2805 L427

↔ *a/c/d/e/f/g:* ειρην[η 1852

↑ 796

3 ἀγαπητοί, πᾶσαν σπουδὴν ποιούμενος γράφειν ὑμῖν
　　2　　　4　　　6　　　　8　　　　10　　　12
περὶ τῆς κοινῆς ἡμῶν σωτηρίας
　　14　16　18　　20　　22

14↑
a　πληθυνθειη ... 218f 390f 620Z 1611f
　　1719(*f) 1799(*fV) 2653V L422f
b　πληθειη 620T
cf　πλιν θυ εις 1066
df　π[2-4] 1893
—　33 1852
↑　796

v. 3
—　P78 0316 602 610 613 712 1384 1724 1831S
　　1867 1899 2822

4-6
a　πασαν σπουδην ... 33V 1243f
b　σπουδην πασαν 1270 1297 1390 1595 1598
　　1893 L884
—　P74 0251 1852

8
a　ποιουμενος ... 044(*f) 61V 832V 1880f
　　L608f
b　ποιησαμενος P72 1501
↔　a/b: [5-6]μενος 720
—　P74 0251 1852

10-12
a　γραφειν υμιν 02 03 04 018 020 025 049
　　056 0142 1 3 5 6 18 33V 35 38 42 43 51 57
　　61 62 69 76 81 82 88 90a 90b 94 97 101 102
　　103 104 105 110 131 133 141 142 149 172
　　175 177 180 181 189 201 203 204 205
　　205abs 206S 209 216 218 221 223 226 234
　　241 242 250 252 254 256 263 296 302 307
　　308 309 312 314 319 321 322 323 325 326
　　327 328 330 337 363 367 378 384 385 386
　　390 393 394 398 400V 404 421 424 425 429
　　431 432 436 440 442 444 450 451 452 453
　　454 456 457 458 459 460 462 466 467 468
　　469 479 483 489 491 496 506 517 522 547
　　582 592 601 603 604 605 606 607 608 614
　　615 617 618 619 620 622 623 625 627 628
　　629 630 631f 632 633 634 635 636 637 638
　　639 641 642 656 664 676 680f 699 720 757
　　801 808 823 824 876 901 910 912 913 914

915 917 918 919 920 921 922 927 928 935
941 945 959 986 996 997 1003 1022 1040
1058 1066 1067 1069 1070 1072 1075 1094
1099 1100 1101 1102 1103 1104 1105 1106
1107 1115 1127 1149 1161 1162 1175 1240
1242 1243 1244 1245 1247 1248 1249 1250
1251 1270 1277 1292f 1297 1311 1315 1319
1352V 1354 1359 1360 1367 1390 1398
1400 1404 1405 1409 1424 1425 1448 1482
1490 1495 1501 1503 1505 1508 1509 1521
1523 1524 1548 1563 1573 1594 1595 1597
1598 1599 1609 1610 1611 1617 1618 1619
1622 1626 1628 1636 1637 1642 1643 1646
1649 1652 1656 1661 1668 1673 1678 1702
1704 1717 1718 1719 1720 1721 1722 1723
1725 1726 1727 1728 1730 1731 1732 1733
1734 1735 1736 1737 1738 1739 1740 1741
1742 1743 1744 1745 1746 1747 1748 1749
1750 1752 1754 1757 1760 1761 1762 1763
1765 1766 1767 1768 1769 1780 1795 1799
1827 1828 1829 1830 1831 1832 1834 1835
1836 1837 1839f 1840 1841 1842 1843 1844
1845 1847 1849 1850 1851 1853 1854 1855
1856 1857 1858 1859 1860 1861 1862 1863
1864 1865 1868 1869 1870 1871 1872 1873
1874 1875 1876 1877 1880 1881 1882 1885
1886 1888 1889 1890 1891 1892 1893 1894
1895 1896 1897 1902 1903 2080 2085 2086
2125 2127 2131 2138 2143 2147 2180 2186
2191 2194 2197 2200f 2201 2218 2221 2242
2243 2255 2261 2288 2289 2298 2318 2344
2352 2356 2374 2378 2400 2404 2412 2423
2431 2466 2473 2475 2483 2484f 2492 2494
2495 2501 2502 2508 2511 2516 2523 2527
2541 2544 2554 2558 2587 2625 2626
2627T 2652 2653 2674 2691 2696 2704
2705 2712 2716 2718 2723 2736 2746 2774
2776 2777 2805 2815 2816 2818 2865 L62
L145 L147 L156 L162 L164 L241 L427
L427/2 L585 L585/2 L591 L593 L596 L603
L604 L606 L608 L617 L623 L740 L809 L840
L884 L921 L938 L1141 L1178 L1196
L1196/2 L1279 L1281 L1281/2 L1440
L1441 L1505 L1818 L2024 L2087 L2106

b γραφειν ημιν 383 616 796 1751 1753 1846 2279 2675

c γραφω υμιν 465f 621 1241 1729 1838 L6 L422

d του γραφειν υμιν P72 01 044 2401*V 2627Z

e τουτο γραφειν υμιν 93 665 999 2401C

↔ *a/d/e:* γρ]αφειν υμιν 1852

— P74 0251 832

14-30↓

a περι της κοινης ημων σωτηριας αναγκην εσχον γραψαι υμιν ...

b om. 1241 L604 L1818

14↑

a περι ...

b υπερ 1843

cf περ 1873

↑ 1241 L604 L1818

— P74 0251 33 832 1852

18-22↑

a κοινης ημων σωτηριας P72 02 03 5 43 61f 62 81 88 93 296 307 321 322 323 326 378 431 436 442 453 614 621 623 630 665 720* 915 918 999 1067 1127 1243 1292 1311 1367 1409 1523CV 1524 1678 1720 1735 1739 1837 1845 1846 2147 2197 2200 2344V 2401Z 2412 2652 2818 L6 L596

b κοινης σωτηριας ημων 312 1760 1853 L884 2544Z

c κοινης υμων σωτηριας 6 69 104 254 459 1523*V 1838 1842 1844 1850 1881 2298 2805

d κοινης ημων ζωης 1611 2138

e κοινης υμων ζωης 1505 2495

f κοινης ημων σωτηριας και ζωης 01 044 2627Z

g κοινης σωτηριας 018 020 025 049 056 0142 1 3 18 35 38 42 51 57 76 82 90a 90b 94 97 101 102 103 105 110 131 133 141 142 149 172 175 177 180 181 189 201 203 204 205 205abs 206S 209 216 218 221 223 226 234 241 242 250 252 256 263 302 308V 309 314 319 325 327 328 330 337 363 367 383 384 385 386 390 393 394 398 400 404 421 424 425 429 432 440 444 450 451 452 454 456 457 458 460 462 465 466 467 468 469 479 483 489 491 496 506 517 522 547 582 592 601 603 604 605 606 607 608 615 616 617 618 619 620 622 625 627 628 629 631 632 633 634 635 636 637 638 639 641 642 656 664 676 680 699 720C 757 796 801 808

823 824 876 901 910 912 913 914 917 919 920 921 922 927 928 935 941 945 959 986 996 997 1003 1022 1040 1066 1069 1070 1072 1075 1094 1099 1100 1101 1102 1103 1104 1105 1106 1107 1115 1149 1161 1162 1175 1240 1242 1244 1245 1247 1248 1249 1250 1251 1270 1277 1297 1315 1319 1352 1354 1359 1360 1390 1398 1400 1404 1405 1424 1425 1448 1482 1490 1495 1501 1503 1508 1509 1521 1548 1563 1573 1594 1595 1597 1598 1599 1609 1610 1617 1618 1619 1622 1626 1628 1636 1637 1642 1643 1646 1649 1652 1656 1661 1668 1673 1702 1704 1717 1718 1719 1721 1722 1723 1725 1726 1727 1728 1729 1730 1731 1732 1733 1734 1736 1737 1738 1740 1741 1742 1743 1744 1745 1746 1747 1748 1749 1750 1751 1752 1753 1754 1757 1761 1762 1763 1765 1766 1767 1768 1769 1780 1795 1799 1827 1828 1829 1830 1831 1832 1834 1835 1836 1839 1840 1841 1843 1847 1849 1851 1854 1855 1856 1857 1858 1859 1860 1861 1862 1863 1864 1865 1868 1869 1870 1871 1872 1873 1874 1875 1876 1877 1880 1882 1885 1886 1888 1889 1890 1891 1892 1893 1894 1895 1896 1897(*f) 1902 1903 2080 2085 2086 2125f 2127 2131 2143 2180 2186 2191 2194 2201 2218 2221 2242 2243 2255 2261 2279 2288 2289 2318 2352 2356 2374 2378 2400 2401T 2404 2423 2431 2466 2473 2475 2483 2484 2492 2494 2501 2502 2508 2511 2516 2523 2527 2541 2544T 2554 2558 2587 2625 2626 2627T 2653 2674 2675 2691 2696 2704 2705 2712 2716 2718 2723 2736 2746 2774 2776 2777 2815 2816 2865 L62 L145 L147 L156 L162 L164 L241 L427 L427/2 L585 L585/2 L591 L593 L603 L606 L608 L617 L623 L740 L809 L840 L921 L938 L1141 L1178 L1196 L1196/2 L1279 L1281 L1281/2 L1440 L1441 L1505 L2024 L2087 L2106

h ημετερας σωτηριας L422

i κοινης 1058V

↔ *a/c:* κ[οι]ν[ης] [.μω]ν σωτηριας 04

↔ *a/c/g/h:*] σω[τηριας P74

↑ 1241 L604 L1818

— 0251 33 832 1852

ἀνάγκην ἔσχον γράψαι ὑμῖν παρακαλῶν ἐπαγωνίζεσθαι
  24   26   28   30   32   34
τῇ ἅπαξ παραδοθείσῃ τοῖς ἁγίοις πίστει.
  36   38   40   42   44   46

24↑

a αναγκην ... 0142(*f) 1240 1646(*f) 1719
1831V 1851V 2147f 2675(*f) 2696f
↑ 1241 L604 L1818
— 33 832

26-34↑↓

a εσχον γραψαι υμιν παρακαλων ... L585Z
b εσχον γραψαι υμας παρακαλων 378
L585T
↔ *a/b:* εσχον γραψ[αι .... παρακα]λων 110
↔ *a/b:* εσχον γρα[1852
↔ *a/b:* εσχο[ν .... π]α[ρακαλων P74
↑ 1241 L604 L1818

26-30↑

a εσχον γραψαι υμιν P72 02 03 04 018 020
025 049 056 0142 1 3 5 18 35 38 42 43 51 57
61 62 69 76 81 82 88 90b 93 94 97 101 102
103 104 105 133 141 142 149 172 175 177
180 181 189 201 203 204 205 205abs 206S
209 216 221 223 226 234 241 242 250 252
254 256 263 296 302 307 308 309 314 319
322 323 325 326 327 328 330 337 363 367
383 384 385 386 390 393 394 398 400 404
421 424 425 429 431 432 436 440 442 444
450 451 452C 453 454 457 458 459 460 462
465 466 467 468 469 479 483 489 491 496
506 517 522 547 582 592 601 603 604 605
606 607 608 614 615 617 618 619 620 621
622 623 625 627 628 629 630 632 633 634
635 636 637 638 639 641 642 656 664 665
676 680 699 720 757 796 801 808 823 824
876 901 910 912 913 914 915 917 919 920
921 922 927 928 935 941 945 959 986 996
997 999 1003 1022 1040 1058 1066 1069
1070 1072 1075 1094 1099 1100 1101 1102
1103 1104 1105 1106 1107 1115 1127 1149
1161 1162 1175 1240 1242 1243 1244 1245
1247 1248 1249 1250 1251 1270 1277 1292
1297 1311 1315 1319 1352 1354 1359 1360
1367 1390 1398 1400 1404 1405 1409 1424
1425 1448 1482 1490 1495 1501 1503 1508
1509 1521 1523 1524 1548 1563 1573 1594
1595 1597 1598 1599 1609 1610 1611 1617

1618 1619 1622 1626 1628 1636 1637 1642
1643 1646 1649 1652 1656 1661 1668 1673
1678 1702 1704 1717 1718 1719 1720 1721
1722 1723   1725 1726 1727 1728 1729
1730 1731 1732 1733 1736 1737 1738 1739
1740 1741 1742 1743 1744 1745 1746 1747
1748 1749 1750 1752 1753 1754 1760 1761
1762 1763 1765 1766 1767 1768 1769 1795
1799 1827 1828 1829 1830 1831 1832 1834
1835 1836 1837*f 1839 1840 1841 1842
1843 1844 1845 1847 1849 1850 1851 1854
1855 1856 1857 1858 1859 1860 1861 1862
1863 1864 1865 1868 1869 1870 1871 1872
1873 1874 1875 1876 1877 1880 1881 1882
1885 1886 1888 1889 1890 1891 1892
1893V 1894 1895 1896 1897 1902 1903
2080 2085 2086 2125 2127 2131 2143 2147
2180 2186 2191 2194 2197 2200 2201 2218
2221 2242 2243 2255 2261 2279 2288 2289
2298 2318 2344 2352 2356 2374 2401 2412
2423 2431 2466 2475 2483 2484 2492 2494
2495 2501 2502 2508 2511 2516 2523 2527
2541 2544 2554 2558 2587 2625 2626 2627
2652 2653 2674 2675 2691 2696 2704 2705
2712 2716 2718 2723 2736 2746 2774 2776
2777 2805 2815 2816 2818 2865 L6 L62
L147 L156 L162 L241 L427 L427/2 L585/2
L591V L596 L603 L606 L608 L617 L623
L740 L809 L840 L938 L1141 L1178 L1196
L1196/2 L1279 L1281 L1281/2 L1440
L1441 L1505 L2087C L2106
b εσχον γραφειν υμιν 01 044 1505f 1735
2138
c εσχον γραψαι ημιν 218 616 1846
d εχω γραψαι υμιν 631 918 1780 L422
e εχων γραψαι υμιν 6 90a 321 452* 456
1067 1734 1751 1757 1838 2378 2400 2404
2473 L145 L593 L884 L921 L2024 L2087*
f εχων γραφειν υμιν L164
g εσχον του γραψαι υμιν 312 1853
h γραψαι υμιν 131
↔ *a/c:* εσχον γραψ[αι ....] 110
↔ *a/b/c:* εσχον γρα[1852
↔ *a/b/c/g:* εσχο[ν ....] P74
↑ 378 1241 L585 L604 L1818
— 0251 33 832

32-34

a παρακαλων επαγωνιζεσθαι 01 03 04 018
020 025 044 049 056 0142 3 5 6 18 33 35 38
42 51 57 61 62 69 76 81 82 88 90b 94 97
101 102 103 104 110V 131 133 141 142 149
172 175 177 180 181 189 201 203 204 205
205abs 206S 209 216 218 221 223 226 234
241 242 250 252(*f) 254 256 263 296 302
307 308 312 314 319 321 322 323 325 326
327 328 330 337 363 367 383 385 386 390
393 394 398 400 404 421 424 425 429 431
432 436 440 442 444 450 451 452 453 454
456 457 458 459 460 462 465 467 468 469
479 483 489 491 496 506 517 547 582 592
601 603 604 605 606 607 608 614 615 616
617 618 619 620 621 623 627 628 629 630
632 633 634 637 638 639 641 642 656 664
665 676 699 720 757 796 801 808 823 824
876 901 910 912 913 914 917 918 919 920
921 922 927 928 935 941 945 959 986 997
999 1003 1022 1040 1058V 1066 1067 1069
1070 1072 1075 1094 1099 1100V 1101
1102 1103 1104 1105 1106 1115 1127 1149
1161 1162 1175 1241 1242 1244 1245 1247
1248 1249 1250 1251 1270 1277 1292 1297
1311 1315 1319 1352 1354 1359 1360 1367
1390 1398 1400 1404 1405f 1409 1425 1448
1482 1490 1501 1503 1505 1508 1509 1521
1523*f 1524 1548 1563 1573 1594 1595
1597 1598 1599 1609 1610 1611 1617 1618
1619 1622 1626 1628 1636 1637 1642 1643
1646 1649 1652 1656 1668 1673 1678 1702
1704 1717 1718 1719 1720 1721 1722 1723
1725 1726 1727 1728 1729 1730 1731 1732
1733 1734 1736 1737 1738 1739 1740 1742
1743 1744 1745 1746 1747 1748 1749 1750
1751 1752 1753 1754 1757 1760 1761 1763
1765 1766 1767 1768 1769 1795 1799 1828
1829 1830 1831 1832 1834 1835 1836 1837
1838 1839 1840 1841 1842 1843 1845 1846
1847 1849 1850 1851 1853 1854 1855 1856
1857 1858 1859 1860 1861 1862 1863 1864
1865 1868 1869 1870 1871 1872 1873 1874
1875 1876 1877 1880 1881 1882 1885 1888
1889 1890 1892 1893 1894 1895 1896 1897
1902 1903 2080 2085 2086 2125 2127 2131
2138 2143 2147 2180 2186 2191 2194 2197
2200 2201 2218 2221 2242 2243 2255 2261
2279 2288 2289 2298 2318 2344 2352 2356
2374 2378 2400 2401 2404 2412 2423 2431
2466 2473 2475 2483 2484 2492 2494 2495
2501 2502 2508 2511 2516 2523 2527 2541
2544 2554 2558 2587 2625 2626 2627 2652
2653 2674 2675 2691 2696 2704 2705 2712

2716 2718 2723 2736 2746 2774 2776 2777
2805 2815 2816 2818 L6 L145 L147 L156
L162 L422 L427 L427/2 L585 L585/2 L591
L593 L596 L603 L604 L606 L608 L617 L740
L809 L840 L884 L921 L938 L1141 L1178
L1196 L1196/2 L1279 L1281 L1281/2
L1440 L1441 L1505 L2024 L2087 L2106

b επαγωνιζεσθαι παρακαλων 105

c παρακαλων επαγωνιζεσθε P72 02 93 378
631 1240 1523Cf 1886 L1818f

d παρακαλων επαγωνισασθαι 1 43 309 466
625 636 1107 1424 1495 1735 1780 2865
L241

e παρακαλων επαγωνιζομενος 680

f παρακαλων μεταγωνιζεσθαι 522

g παρακαλων αγωνιζεσθαι 996 1661 1762
1844T

h παρακαλων αγωνιζεσθε 1844Z

i παρακαλω επαγωνιζεσθαι 90a 384 622
635 1243 1827 1891 L62 L164 L623

j παρακαλω επαγωνιζεσθε 915 1741

↔ a/c/d/e/f/g/h/i/j: π]α[P74

↔ a/d/f/g/i:]θαι 1852

— 832

38

a απαξ ... 325V 1850Cf 2127V L164(*f)

b απ αρχη 1850*

— P74 832

40-46

a παραδοθεισ τοισ αγιοισ πιστει P72C 01
02 03 04 018 020 025 044 049 056 0142 1 3f
5 6 18 33 35 38 42 43 51 57 61 62 69 76 81
82 88 90a 90b 93 94 97 101 102 103 104
105 110 131 133 141 142 149 172 175 181
189 201 203 204 205 205abs 206S 209 216
218 221 223 226 234 241 242 250 252 254
256 263 296 302 307 308 309 312 314 319
321 322 323 325C 326 327 328 330 363 367
378 383 384 385 386 390 393 394 398 404
421 424 425 429 432 436 440 442 444 450
451 452 453 454 456 457 458 459 462 465
466 468 469 479 483 489 491 496 506 517
522 547 582 592 601 603 604 605 606 608
615 616 617 619 620 621 622 623 625 627
628T 629 630 631 632 633 634 635 636 637
638 639 641 642 656 664 665Z 676 699 757
796 801 808 823 824 876 901 910 912 913
914 915 917 918 919 920 921 922 927 928
935 941 945 959 986 996 997 999 1003
1022 1040 1058 1066 1067 1069 1070 1072
1075 1094 1099 1100 1101 1102 1103 1104
1105 1106 1107 1127 1149 1161 1162 1175

4 παρεισέδυσαν γάρ τινες ἄνθρωποι, οἱ πάλαι προγεγραμμένοι
  2   *4*   *6*   *8*   *10* *12*   *14*

εἰς τοῦτο τὸ κρίμα, ἀσεβεῖς, τὴν τοῦ θεοῦ ἡμῶν χάριτα
  16 *18* *20* *22*   *24*   *26* *28* *30* *32*   *34*

1240 1241 1242 1243 1244 1245 1247 1248f
1249 1250 1251 1270 1277 1292 1297 1311
1315 1319 1352 1354 1359 1360 1390 1398
1400 1404 1405 1409 1424 1425 1448 1482
1490 1495 1501 1503 1505 1508 1509 1521
1523 1524 1548 1563 1573 1594 1595 1597
1598 1599 1609 1610 1611 1617 1618 1619
1622 1626 1628 1636 1637 1642 1643 1646
1649 1652 1656 1661 1668 1673 1678 1702
1704 1717 1718 1719 1720 1721 1722 1723
1725 1726 1727 1728 1729 1730 1731 1732
1733 1734 1735 1736 1737 1739 1740 1741
1742 1743 1744 1745 1746 1747 1748 1749
1750 1752 1753 1754 1757 1760 1761 1762f
1763 1765 1766 1767 1768 1769 1780 1795
1799 1827 1828 1829 1830 1831 1832 1835
1836 1837 1838 1839 1840 1842 1843 1844
1845 1846 1847 1849 1850 1851 1853 1854
1855 1856 1857 1858 1859 1860 1861 1862
1863 1864 1865 1868 1869 1870 1871 1872
1873 1874 1875 1876 1877 1880 1881 1882
1885 1886 1888 1889 1890 1891 1892 1893
1894 1895 1896 1897 1902 1903 2080 2085
2086 2125 2127 2131 2138 2143 2147 2180
2186 2191 2194 2197 2200 2201 2218 2221
2242 2243 2255 2261 2279 2288 2289 2298
2318 2344 2352 2356 2374 2378 2401 2404
2412 2423 2431 2473 2475 2483 2484 2492
2494 2495 2501 2502 2508 2511 2516
2523Z 2527 2541 2544 2554 2558 2587
2626 2627 2652 2653 2674 2675 2696 2704
2705 2712 2716 2718 2723 2736 2746 2774
2776 2777 2805 2815 2816 2818 2865 L6
L62 L145 L156 L162 L164 L241 L422 L427
L427/2 L585 L585/2 L591 L593 L596 L604
L606 L608 L617 L623 L740 L809 L840 L884
L921f L938 L1141 L1178 L1196 L1196/2
L1279 L1281 L1281/2 L1440 L1441 L1505
L1818 L2024 L2087 L2106

b παραδοθεισα πιστει τοις αγιοις P72*f 177
    180 337 400 460 607 618 1115 1367 1738
    1841 2625
c τοις αγιοις παραδοθεισα πιστει 2466
d περιδοθεισα τοις αγιοις πιστει 431 720

e δοθεισα τοις αγιοις πιστει 467 665T 2400
    2523T L147 L603
f παραδοσει τοις αγιοις πιστει 680
g παραδοθεισα τοις αγιοις τη πιστει 628Z
h παραδοθεισα της πιστεως τοις αγιοις
    1751
i παραδοθεισα αγιοις πιστει 1834
j παραδοθεισα τοις αγιοις 2691
↔ *a/b/g/h/i/j*: παραδοθεισα [614
↔ *a/d/e/i*:] αγιοις πιστει 325*
↔ *a/d/e/f/g/h/i*: π]ισ[τει 0251
— P74 832 1852

v. 4
— P74 0316 602 610 613 614 712 832 1384
    1724 1831S 1867 1899

2
a παρεισεδυσαν ... 110V 309C 398(*f) 642f
    1839C 1844(*f) 1850(*f) 1893V 2502C
    L2087f
ao παρεισεδυησαν 03 04V
bf παρεισεβησαν L2024
c παρεδυσαν 309* 1067 1735 1839* 2502*
    2865
↔ *a/ao/c*:]σαν 2822
— P78

4
a γαρ ... 209Z 2627Z
b δε L884
c om. 3 90b 203 209T 506 796 1642 2627T
    L422
— P78 1852

6
a τινες ... 631(*f)
— P78 1852

8
a ανθρωποι ... 206S(*f)
— P78 110 1852

10
a   οι ... 90b(*f) 0251V 1838f 1893V
b   οι και 01
c   ως 378
d   om. 1834
—   P78 110 1852

14
α   προγεγραμμενοι ... 0251V 94f 110V 636Cf
    1509f 1831V 1852V 1882f 2086Z 2466f
    L162f
b   προγεγυμνασμενοι 918
c   αναγεγραμμενοι 57
d   γεγραμμενοι 2086T L585/2 L1196/2
—   P78

19
a   om. ... 1739(*f)

20
a   το ... P72Z 0251V 90bZ 429Z L585/2C
b   om. P72T 90bT 429T 460 921 1838 2289
    L585/2* L593
—   P78 1852

22
a   κριμα ... P72(*f)
b   κηρυγμα 044
c   κατακριμα 309 2501
—   P78 1852

24
a   ασεβεις ... 1100V 1720f 1831V
b   ασεβειν 044 254 1523 1524 1844 2412
c   ασεβειας 175
d   της ασεβειας 2544
e   προς 616
↔   a/b: ασεβει[.] L884
—   P78 1852 2511

25
a   om. ...
b   και 608
—   P78 1852 2511

26
a   την ... P72(*f) 400V
—   P78 1852 2511

28
a   του ... 0251V
b   om. 1891
—   P78 1852 2511

30
a   θεου ... 0251V 424T 1717V
b   κυριου 424Z 1241
c   σωτηρος 2816
—   P78 2511

32
a   ημων ... 0251V 918CV 1717V
b   υμων 636Z 1241 1678 1729
c   om. 378 496 631 636T 918* 1894 2696
—   P78 2511

34
a   χαριτα P72 02 03 38
ao χαριν 01 04 018 020 025 044 049 056 0142
    0251 1 3 5 6 18 33 35 42 43 51 57 61 62 69
    76 81 82 88 90a 90b 93 94 97 101 102 103
    104 105 110 131 133 141 142 149 172 175
    177 180 181 189 201 203 204 205 205abs
    206S 209 216 218 221 223 226 234 241 242
    250 252 254 256 263 296 302 307 308 309
    312 314 319 321 322 323 325 326 327 328
    330 337 363 367 378 383 384 385 386 390
    393 394 398 400 404 421 424 425 429 431
    432 436 440 442 444 450 451 452 453 454
    456 457 458 459 460 462 465 466 467 468
    469 479 483 489 491 496 506 517 522 547
    582 592 601 603 604 605 606 607 608 615
    616 617 618 619 620 621 622 623 625 627
    628 629 630 631 632 633 634 635 636 637
    638 639 641 642 656 664 665 676 680 699
    720 757 796 801 808 823 824 876 901 910
    912 913 914 915 917 918 919 920 921 922
    927 928 935 941 945 959 986 996 997 999
    1003 1022 1040 1058 1066 1067 1069 1070
    1072 1075 1094 1099 1100 1101 1102 1103
    1104 1105 1106 1107 1115 1127 1149 1161
    1162 1175 1240 1241 1242 1243 1244 1245
    1247 1248 1249 1250 1251 1270 1277 1292
    1297 1311 1315 1319 1352 1354 1359 1360
    1367 1390 1398 1400 1404 1405 1409 1424
    1425 1448 1482 1490 1495 1501 1503 1505
    1508 1509 1521 1523 1524 1548 1563 1573
    1594 1595 1597 1598 1599 1609 1610 1611
    1617 1618 1619 1622 1626 1628 1636 1637
    1642 1643 1646 1649 1652 1656 1661 1668
    1673 1678 1702 1704 1717 1718 1719 1720
    1721 1722 1723 1725 1726 1727 1728 1729
    1730 1731 1732 1733 1734 1735 1736 1737
    1738 1739 1740 1741 1742 1743 1744 1745
    1746 1747 1748 1749 1750 1751 1752 1753
    1754 1757 1760 1761 1762 1763 1765 1766
    1767 1768 1769 1780 1795 1799 1827 1828
    1829 1830 1831 1832 1834 1835 1836 1837

μετατιθέντες εἰς ἀσέλγειαν καὶ τὸν μόνον δεσπότην
36   38   40   42 44 46   48
καὶ κύριον ἡμῶν Ἰησοῦν Χριστὸν ἀρνούμενοι.
50   52   54   56   58   60

1838 1839 1840 1841 1842 1843 1844 1845
1846 1847 1849 1850 1851 1852 1853 1854
1855 1856 1857 1858 1859 1860 1861 1862
1863 1864 1865 1868 1869 1870 1871 1872
1873 1874 1875 1876 1877 1880 1881 1882
1885 1886 1888 1889 1890 1891 1892 1893
1894 1895 1896 1897 1902 1903 2080 2085
2086 2125 2127 2131 2138 2143 2147 2180
2186 2191 2194 2197 2200 2201 2218 2221
2242 2243 2255 2261 2279 2288 2289 2298
2318 2344 2352 2356 2374 2378 2400 2401
2404 2412 2423 2431 2466 2473 2475 2483
2484 2492 2494 2495 2501 2502 2508 2516
2523 2527 2541 2544 2554 2558 2587 2625
2626 2627 2652 2653 2674 2675 2691 2696
2704 2705 2712 2716 2718 2723 2736 2746
2774 2776 2777 2805 2815 2816 2818 2822
2865 L6 L62 L145 L147 L156 L162 L164
L241 L422 L427 L427/2 L585 L585/2 L591
L593 L596 L603 L604 L606 L608 L617 L623
L740 L809 L840 L884 L921 L938 L1141
L1178 L1196 L1196/2 L1279 L1281
L1281/2 L1440 L1441 L1505 L1818 L2024
L2087 L2106
— P78 2511

36-58↓
a μετατιθεντες εις ασελγειαν και τον
   μονον δεσποτην και κυριον ημων ιησουν
   χριστον ...
b om. 102
— P78 2511

36↑
a μετατιθεντες ... 0251V 90b(*f) 1100V
   1104f 1106V 1717V 1869f 1886f 2492C
   L422f
b μεταθεντες 38 2492*
↑ 102
— P78 1852 2511

38↑
a εις ... 0251V 110V 1315f
↑ 102
— P78 1106 1852 2511

40↑
a ασελγειαν ... P78V 628T 1893V
b ασεβειαν 43
c ασελγειαν πορνιαν 628Z
df αγιαν 1838
↔ *a/b/c:*]αν 110
↑ 102
— 1106 1852 2511

44↑
a τον ...
b om. 915
↑ 102
— 2511

46↑
a μονον ... 0251V 110V 1678V
bf νομον P72*
c om. P72C
↑ 102
— 400 2511

48-58↑
a δεσποτην και κυριον ημων ιησουν
   χριστον 01 02 03 04 0251V 6 33 61 81 93
   94 142 216T 218 307 321 322 323 326T
   326Z2 424C 431 436 440 442 453* 467 621
   629 635T 642 720T 808 918 935 1067 1127
   1243 1359 1367 1404 1409 1425 1563 1678
   1718 1722 1739 1760 1840 1845 1846 1894
   2143 2186 2197 2344 2483T 2718 2774
   2805 2818 2822 L6T L145 L427/2 L596
   L604 L606 L623 L809 L840 L921 L938
   L1141 L1279 L2024 L2106
b δεσποτην και κυριον υμων ιησουν
   χριστον 1241
c ημων δεσποτην και κυριον ημων ιησουν
   χριστον L740
d ημων δεσποτην και κυριον ιησουν
   χριστον ημων P72
e δεσποτην θεον και κυριον ημων ιησουν
   χριστον 018 020 044 049 056 0142 1 3 5 18
   35 43 57 62 69 76 82 90b 97 101 103 105
   110 131 133 141 149 172 175 177 180 189
   201 203 204 205 205abs 206S 209 216Z 221

226 241 242 252 254 256 263 296 302 308
309 312 314 319 325 326Z1 327 328 330
337 363 367 384 385 386 394 398 404 421
425 429 432 444 450 451 452 453C 454 456
457 458 460 462 465 466 468 469 479 483
489 491 496 506 517 522 547 582 601 603
604 605 606 607 608 615 617 618 619 620
622 623 625 627 628 630 632 635Z 636 637
639 641 656 664 665 676 680 699 720Z 757
796 801 823 824 876 901Z 910 913 914 917
919 920 921 922 927 928 941 945 959 986
997 999 1022 1040 1058 1069 1070 1072
1075 1094 1099 1100 1101 1102 1103 1104
1105 1107 1115 1149 1161 1162 1175 1240
1242 1244 1245 1247 1248 1249 1250 1251
1270 1277 1292 1297 1311 1315 1319 1352
1354 1390 1398 1400 1424 1448 1482 1490
1495 1501 1503 1505 1508 1509 1521 1523
1524 1548 1573 1595 1597 1598 1599 1609
1610 1611 1617 1618 1619 1626 1628 1636
1637 1642 1643 1646f 1649 1652 1656 1668
1673 1704 1719 1720 1721 1723 1725 1726
1728 1729 1730 1731 1732 1733 1734 1735
1736 1737 1738 1740 1741 1743 1744 1745
1746 1747 1748 1749 1750 1751 1752 1754
1757 1761 1762 1763 1765 1766 1767 1768
1769 1780 1795 1799 1827 1828 1830 1831
1832 1834 1835 1839 1841 1843 1844 1847
1849 1850 1851 1853 1854 1855 1856 1857
1858 1859 1864 1865 1868 1869 1870 1871
1872 1873 1874C 1876 1877 1882 1885
1886 1889 1890 1891 1893V 1895 1897
1903 2080 2086 2125 2127 2138 2180 2191
2194 2200 2201 2218 2221 2242 2243 2255
2261 2288 2289 2298 2318 2352 2356 2374
2378 2400 2401 2404 2412 2423 2431 2466
2473 2475 2483Z 2484 2492 2494 2495
2501 2502 2508 2516 2523 2527 2541 2544
2554 2558 2587 2625 2626 2627 2653 2691
2696 2704 2705 2716 2723 2736 2746 2776
2777 2815 2865 L6Z L62 L147 L156 L162
L164 L241 L427 L585 L585/2 L591 L603
L608 L617 L884 L1178 L1196 L1196/2
L1281 L1281/2 L1440 L1441 L1505 L1818
L2087

f δεσποτην θεον και κυριον ημων χριστον
ιησουν 90a

g δεσποτην ημων θεον και κυριον ιησουν
χριστον 1066

h δεσποτην θεον ημων και κυριον ημων
ιησουν χριστον 1874*

i θεον και δεσποτην τον κυριον ημων
ιησουν χριστον 42 51 223 234 390 912 996
1003 1405 1594 1702 1727 1753 1861 1863
2085 2131 2279 2674 2675

j δεσποτην και θεον και κυριον ημων
ιησουν χριστον 250 383 393 424* 592 616
634 1360 1742 1862 1880 1888 2712

k δεσποτην θεον και δεσποτην τον κυριον
ημων ιησουν χριστον 1661

l δεσποτην θεον και κυριον ιησουν
χριστον 88 104 181 459 631 638 901T 915
1622 1829 1836 1838 1842 1860 1875 1892
1896 L422

m θεον και κυριον ημων ιησουν χριστον
378 2147 2652

n δεσποτην θεον και κυριον ημων ιησουν
633 1902

o δεσποτην και κυριον ημων ιησουν 1837

p δεσποτην και κυριον ιησουν χριστον 1881

q δεσποτην κυριον ημων ιησουν χριστον
P78 38

r δεσποτην θεον και κυριον ημων 1717
2816

s θεον και κυριον ιησουν χριστον L593

↔ *a/c/e/h/j/m:*] και κυριον ημων ιησουν
χριστον 400

↔ *e/f/n/r:* δεσποτην θεον και κυριον η[μων
025

↔ *e/f/n/r:* δεσποτην [.......] κυριον η[μων
1106

↔ *a/b/c/e/g/h/i/j/k/l/m/p/s:*] χριστον 1852

↑ 102

— 2511

60

a αρνουμενοι ... 522f L606f

5 ὑπομνῆσαι δὲ ὑμᾶς βούλομαι, εἰδότας ὑμᾶς
     2   4   6   8   10   12

ἅπαξ πάντα, ὅτι κύριος λαὸν ἐκ γῆς Αἰγύπτου
  14   16   18   20   22 24 26   28

---

v. 5
— P74 025 0316 602 610 613 614 712 832
  1384 1724 1831S 1867 1899 2511 L156
  L427/2 L617 L1818

2-8↓
a υπομνησαι δε υμας βουλομαι ... L585Z
b om. L585T L585/2 L1196/2
— 1852

2↑
a υπομνησαι ... 04fV 665*V 1100V 1241C
  1830(*f) 2816V
b αναμνησαι 665C
c μνησαι 1241*
↔ a/b/c:]αι 0251
↑ L585T L585/2 L1196/2
— 1852

4↑
a δε ... 424T
b ουν 04 044 6 322 323 1241 1243 1501 1739
  2298 2492
c δε ουν 424Z
d om. 1834 1881 2086 2186
↑ L585T L585/2 L1196/2
— 1852

6↑
a υμας ... 110V 378f 1495V 1846C 1862C
b ημας 206S 263 454 489 582 625 629 634
  1646 1649 1729 1846* 1870 1882 2501
  L604
↑ 1852 L585T L585/2 L1196/2
— 400 1678 1852

8↑
a βουλομαι ... 1902f 2086f
↑ L585T L585/2 L1196/2
— 1852 2356

9
a om. ...
b αδελφοι P78V
— 2356

10
a ειδοτας ... 102V 1646(*f) 1728V
b ιδοντας 33
↔ a/b:]ας 1893
— P78 2356

12-20
a υμας απαξ παντα οτι κυριος
b υμας παντα οτι κυριος απαξ 01
c υμας απαξ παντα οτι ιησους 03
d ημας παντα οτι ιησους απαξ 2298
e παντα οτι κυριος απαξ 044
f παντα οτι ο κυριος απαξ 378 630 876 1505
  1611 1765 1832 1842AV 2138 2147 2200
  2243 2412 2494 2495 2652
g απαξ παντα οτι ιησους 02 33C 81 2344
h παντα οτι ιησους απαξ 6 93 322 323 665
  1241 1501 1739T 1881
i παντα οτι ο ιησους απαξ 88 915
j απαξ παντα οτι ο θεος 04C2V 623T 1270
  1297 1598 2805
k παντα οτι ο θεος απαξ 442 621 1243 1845
  1846 2492 L596
l απαξ παντα οτι θεος χριστος P72C
m απαξ παντας οτι θεος χριστος P72*
n παντα απαξ γαρ ιησους 1739A
o υμας απαξ τουτο οτι κυριος 177 180 337
  460 465 468 469 618 628T 633 921 1149
  1649T 1738 1744T 1857T 1875 1894 2674
  2865*
p ημας απαξ τουτο οτι κυριος 1729 1838T
q υμας απαξ τουτο οτι ο κυριος 020 049 1 3
  18 35 38 42 51 57 62 69 76 82 90a 90b 97
  101 102 104 105 110 131 133 141 142 149
  172 175 181 189 201 203 204 205 205abs
  206S 209 216 223 226 234 241 242 250 252
  254 256 296 302 308 309 319 325 326 328
  330 363 367 383 384 385 386 390 393 394
  398 400 404 421 424* 425 429 431 432 440
  444 450 451 456 457 458 459 462 466 467
  479 483 489 491 496 506 517 547*V 592
  601 603 604 605 607 608 615 616(*f) 617
  619 622 625 627 628Z 631 632C 634 635
  636 637 638 656 664 676 680 699 757 796
  801 823 824 901 910 912 914 917 919 920

922 927 928 935 945 959 986 996 997 999
1003 1022 1040 1058 1069 1070 1072 1075
1094 1099 1100 1101 1102 1104 1105 1106
1107 1115 1161 1162 1175 1240 1242 1245
1247 1248 1249 1250 1251 1277 1292 1311
1315 1319 1360 1367 1398 1400 1404 1405
1424 1448 1482 1490 1495 1503 1508 1509
1521 1523 1524 1548 1573 1594 1597 1599
1609 1617 1618 1619 1622 1626 1628 1636
1637 1642 1643 1649Z 1652 1656 1661
1668 1673 1704 1717 1719 1720 1721 1722
1723 1725 1730 1732 1733Z 1734 1737
1740 1741 1742 1743 1744Z 1745 1746
1747 1748 1749 1750 1752 1753 1754 1757
1760 1761 1762 1763 1767 1768 1769 1780
1795 1799 1827 1828Z 1829 1831 1834
1835 1836 1837 1839 1841 1842T 1843
1844 1847 1849 1850 1851 1854 1855 1856
1857Z 1858 1859 1860 1861 1862 1863
1864 1865 1868 1869 1870 1871 1872 1873
1874 1876 1877 1880 1882 1885 1886 1888
1889 1891 1892 1896 1897 1903 2080 2085
2086 2127 2131 2143 2180 2191 2201 2218
2221 2242 2255 2261 2279 2289 2318 2352
2374 2378 2400 2401 2404 2423 2431 2466
2473 2483Z 2484 2501 2502 2508 2516
2523 2527 2541 2554 2587 2625 2626 2627
2653 2675 2691 2696 2704 2705 2712 2716
2718 2723 2736 2746 2776 2777 2815 2816
2822 2865C L6 L62 L145 L147 L162 L422
L427 L585 L585/2 L604 L606 L608 L623
L740 L809 L840 L921 L938 L1141 L1196
L1196/2 L1279 L1281 L1281/2 L1441
L1505 L2024 L2106

r   υμας τουτο απαξ οτι ο κυριος 018 056 103
    221 312 314 327 452 454 606 639 641 913
    941 1066 1103 1244 1352 1610 1830 1853
    1895 2125 2288 2475 2558 L593
s   τουτο υμας απαξ οτι ο κυριος 0142
t   απαξ υμας τουτο οτι ο κυριος 720
u   ημας απαξ τουτο οτι ο κυριος 263 632*
    1646 1726 1731 1838Z L164 L603V L2087
v   υμας απαξ τουτο οτι ο κυριος ιησους L241
    L591 L1178
w   και υμας απαξ τουτο οτι ο κυριος 2544
x   υμας απαξ εις τουτο οτι ο κυριος 2774
y   απαξ τουτο οτι κυριος 582 1828T
z   απαξ τουτο οτι ο κυριος 43 61 94 218 307
    321 436 453 547C 620 629 642 808 918
    1067 1127 1354 1359 1390 1425 1563 1678
    1702 1718 1727 1733T 1736 1751 1840
    1890 1902 2186 2194 2197 2818 L884
    L1440

a' απαξ τουτο οτι ο θεος 5 623Z 1595 1893
b' απαξ τουτο οτι κυριος ιησους 1735
c' υμας απαξ τουτο ο κυριος 522
d' υμας τουτο οτι ο κυριος 1766
e' απαξ οτι ο κυριος 1409
f' οτι ιησους απαξ 424C
g' υμας απαξ 2483T
↔ e/f/h/i/k: παντα οτι [2-3] απαξ 04*
↔ j/?: απαξ παντα οτι ο [..] 33*
↔ g/j/l/m: απαξ παντ[0251
↔ e/f/h/i/k: παντα [1852
↔ a/b/c/o/q/r/v/x/c'/d'/g': υμ[1728
— P78 2356

22-34↓
a   λαον εκ γης αιγυπτου σωσας το δευτερον
    ... 2483Z
b   om. 2483T
—   P78 2356

22-28↑
a   λαον εκ γης αιγυπτου P72f 01 02 03 04
    018 020 049 056 0142 1 3 5 6 18 33 35Z 38
    42 43 51 57 62 69 76 81 82 88 90a 90b 93C
    94 97 101 102 103 104 105 110 131 133 141
    142 149 172 175 177 181 189 201 203 204
    205 205abs 206S 209 216 218 221 223 226
    234 241 242 250 252 254 256 263 296 302
    307 308 309 312 314 319 321 322 323 325
    326 327 328 330 337 363 367 378 383 384
    385 386 390 393 394 398 400 404 421 424
    425 432 436 440 442 444 450 451 452 453
    454 456 457 458 459 460 462 465 466 467
    468 469 479 483 489 491 496 517 547 582
    592Z 601 603 604 605 606 607 608 616 617
    618 619 620 621 622 623 625 627 628 629
    630 631 632 633 634 635 636 638 639 641
    642 656 664 676 680 699 720 757 801 808
    823 824 876 901 910 912 913 914 915 917
    918 919 920 921 922 927 928 935 941 945
    959 996 997 999 1003 1022 1040 1058 1066
    1067 1069 1070 1072 1075 1094 1099 1100
    1101 1102 1103 1105 1106 1107 1115 1127
    1161 1162 1175 1240 1241 1242 1243 1244
    1245 1247 1248 1249 1250 1251 1270 1277
    1292 1297 1311 1315 1319 1352 1354 1359
    1360 1367 1390 1398 1400 1404 1405 1409
    1424 1425 1448 1482 1490 1495 1503 1505
    1508 1509 1521 1523 1524 1548 1563 1573
    1594 1595 1597 1598 1599 1609 1610 1611
    1617 1618 1619 1622 1626 1628 1636 1637
    1642 1643 1646 1649 1652 1656 1661 1668
    1673 1678V 1702 1704V 1717 1718 1719
    1720 1721 1722 1723 1725 1726 1727 1729
    1730 1731 1732 1733 1734 1736 1737 1738

σώσας τὸ δεύτερον τοὺς μὴ πιστεύσαντας
30   32   34   36 38   40
ἀπώλεσεν, **6** ἀγγέλους τε
          42   2   4

1739 1740 1741 1742 1743 1744 1745 1746
1747 1748 1749 1750 1751 1752 1753 1754
1757 1760 1761 1762 1763 1765 1766 1767
1768 1769 1780 1795 1827 1828 1830 1831
1832 1834 1835 1836 1837 1838 1839 1840
1841 1842 1843 1844 1845 1846 1847 1849
1850 1851 1853 1854 1855 1856 1857 1858
1859 1860 1861 1862 1863 1864 1865 1868
1870 1871 1872 1873 1874 1875 1876 1877
1881 1885 1886 1888 1889 1890 1891 1892
1893V 1894 1895 1896 1897 1902 2080
2085 2086 2125 2127 2131 2138 2143 2180
2186 2191 2194 2197 2200 2201 2218 2221
2242 2243 2255 2261 2279 2288 2289 2298
2318 2344 2352 2374 2378 2400 2401 2404
2412 2423 2431 2466 2473 2475(*f) 2484
2492 2494 2495 2501 2502 2508 2516 2523
2527 2541 2544 2554 2558 2587 2625 2626
2627 2652 2653 2674 2675 2696 2704 2705
2712 2716 2718 2723 2736 2746 2774 2776
2777 2805 2815 2816 2818 2822 2865Z L6
L62 L145 L147 L162 L164 L422 L427 L585
L585/2 L591 L593 L596 L603 L604 L606
L608 L623 L740 L809 L840 L884 L921 L938
L1141   L1196   L1196/2   L1279   L1281
L1281/2 L1440 L1441 L1505 L2024 L2087
L2106
b   εκ γης λαον αιγυπτου 1735
c   λαον εκ της αιγυπτου 044 61 93* 180 429
    431 506 522 637 665 1104 1501 1799 1829
    1869 1882 1903
d   λαον εκ της γης αιγυπτου 796
e   λαβων εκ γης αιγυπτου λαον και 615
f   ημων τον λαον εκ γης αιγυπτου 2691
g   λαον εξ αιγυπτου 986
h   εκ γης αιγυπτου 1149 1880 2865T
i   λαον αιγυπτου 35T 592T 2147 L241 L1178
↔ a/b/c/d/e/g/h: α]ιγυπτο[υ 0251
↔ a/b/c/d/g/h: αιγυπτ]ου 1852
↑ 2483
— P78 1728 2356

32↑
a   το ... 1875f 2318f L1196/2f
↑ 2483
— P78 0251 1704 2356

33↑
a   om. ...
b   δε 1838
↑ 2483
— P78 0251 1704 1852 2356

36-40
a   τους μη πιστευσαντας P72 01 02 03 04 018
    020 044 049 056 0142 1 3 5 6 18 33 35 38Z
    42 43 51 57 61 62 69 76 81 82 88 90a 90b 93
    94 97 101 102 103 104 105 110 131 133 141
    142 149 172 175 177 180 181 189 201 203
    204 205abs 206S 209 216 218 221 223 226
    234 241 242 250 252 254 256 263 296 302
    307 308 309 312 314 319 321 322 323 325
    326 327 328 330 337 363 367 378 383 384
    385 386 390 393 394 398 400 404 421 424
    425 429 431 432 436 440 442 444 450 451
    452 453 454 456 457 458 459 460 462 465
    466 467 468 469 479 483 489 491 496 506
    517 522 547 582 592 601 603 604 605 606
    607 608 616 617 618 619 620 621 622 623
    627 628 629 630 631 632 633 634 635 636
    637 638 639 641 642 656 664 665 676 699
    720 757 796 801 808 823 824 876 901 910
    912 913 914 915 917 918 919 920 921 922
    927 928 935 941 945 959 986 996 997 999
    1022Z 1040 1058 1066 1067 1069 1070
    1072 1075 1094 1099 1100 1101 1102 1103
    1104 1105 1106 1115 1127 1149 1161 1162
    1175 1241 1242 1243 1244 1245 1247 1248
    1249 1250 1251 1270 1277 1292 1297 1315
    1319 1352 1354 1359 1360 1367 1390 1398
    1400 1404 1405 1409 1424 1425 1448 1482
    1490 1495 1501 1503 1505 1508 1509 1521
    1523 1524 1548 1563 1573 1594 1595 1597
    1598 1599 1609 1610 1611 1617 1618 1619
    1622 1626 1628 1636 1637 1642 1643 1646
    1649 1652 1656 1661 1668 1678 1702 1704
    1717 1718 1720 1721 1722 1723 1725 1726
    1727 1728 1729 1730 1731 1732 1733 1734
    1735 1736 1737 1738 1739 1740 1741 1742
    1743 1744 1745 1746 1747 1748 1749 1750
    1751 1752 1753 1754 1757 1760 1761 1762
    1763 1765 1766 1767 1768 1769 1780 1795
    1799 1827 1828 1829 1830 1831 1832 1834

1835 1836 1837 1838 1839 1840 1841 1842
1843 1844 1845 1846 1847 1849 1850 1851
1853 1854 1855 1856 1857 1858 1859 1860
1861 1862 1863 1864 1865 1868 1869 1870
1871 1872 1873 1874 1876 1877 1880 1881
1882f 1885 1888 1889 1890 1891 1892 1893
1894 1895 1896 1897 1902 1903 2080 2085
2086 2125 2127 2131 2138 2143 2147 2180
2186 2191 2194 2197 2200 2201(*f) 2218
2221 2242 2243 2255 2261 2279 2288 2289
2298 2318 2344 2352 2374 2378 2400 2401
2404 2412 2423 2431 2466 2473 2475 2483
2484 2492 2494 2495 2501 2502 2508 2516
2523 2527 2541 2544 2554 2558 2587 2625
2626 2627 2652 2653 2674 2675C 2691
2696 2704 2705 2712 2716 2718 2723 2736
2746 2774 2776 2777 2805 2815 2816 2818
2822 2865 L6 L62 L145 L147 L164 L241
L422 L427 L585 L585/2 L591 L596 L603
L604 L606 L608 L623 L740 L809 L840 L884
L921 L938 L1141 L1178 L1196 L1196/2
L1279 L1281 L1281/2 L1440 L1441 L1505
L2024 L2087 L2106

b   τους μη πιστευοντας 205 625 680 1003
   1107 1240 1673 1719 1875 1886 2675*
   L162

c   τους πιστευσαντας 38T L593 1022T

d   μη πιστευσαντας 1311

e   τους εκεινων εχθρους 615

— P78 0251 1852 2356

42

a   απωλεσεν ... 38(*f) 94V 385CV 1573C
   1704V 1765V

b   απωλεσαν 385*V 1573*

— P78 0251 1852 2356

v. 6

— P74 P78 025 0251 0316 602 610 613 614
   712 832 1724 1831S 1867 1899 2356 2511
   L156 L427/2 L617 L1818

2-16↓

a   αγγελους τε τους μη τηρησαντας την
   εαυτων αρχην ...

b   αγγελους δε τους μη τηρησαντας την
   εαυτων αρχην 38C

cf   εαυτων αρχην 38*

2↑

a   αγγελους ... 6f 1704V 1844f L2024V

— 1384 1852

4

a   τε P72 01 03 04 018 020 044 049 056 0142 3
   5 6 18 33 35 42 51 57 61 62 69 76 81 82 88
   90b 93 97 101 102 103 104 105 110 131 133
   141 142 149 175 177 180 189 201 203 204
   205 205abs 206S 209 216 221 223 226 234
   241 242 250 252V 254 256 296 302 307 308
   309 314 319 321 322 323 325 326 327 328
   330 337 363 367 383 384 385 386 390 393
   394 398 400 404 421 424 425 429 432 436
   440 442 444 450 451 452 453 454 456 457
   458 459 460 462 465 467 468 469 479 489
   491 496 506 517 547 582 592 601 603 604
   605 606 607 608 616 617 618 620 622 623
   627 628 629 630 631 632 633 634 635 636
   637 639 641 642 656 664 665 676 680 699
   720 757 796 801 808 823 824 901 910 912
   913 914 915 917 918 919 920 921 922 927
   928 935 941 959 986 996 997 999 1003
   1022 1058 1066 1069 1072 1075 1094 1099
   1100 1101 1102 1103 1104 1105 1106 1107
   1115 1127 1149 1161 1175 1240 1241 1242
   1243 1244 1245 1247 1248 1249 1250 1251
   1270 1277 1297 1311 1315 1319 1352 1354
   1360 1390 1398 1400 1404 1405 1409 1424
   1448 1482 1503 1508 1509 1521 1523 1524
   1548 1573 1594 1597 1598 1599 1609 1610
   1617 1618 1619 1622 1626 1628 1636 1637
   1642 1643 1646 1649 1652 1656 1661 1668
   1673 1702 1704 1717 1719 1720 1721 1722
   1723 1725 1726 1727 1728 1729 1730 1731
   1732 1733 1734 1736 1737 1738 1739 1740
   1741 1742 1743 1744 1745 1746 1747 1748
   1749 1750 1751 1752 1753 1754 1757 1760
   1761 1762 1763 1766 1767 1768 1769 1795
   1799 1827 1828 1829 1830 1831 1834 1835
   1837 1838 1839 1840 1841 1842 1843 1844
   1845 1846 1847 1849 1850 1851 1854 1855
   1856 1857 1858 1859 1860 1861 1862 1863
   1864 1865 1868 1869 1870 1871 1872 1873
   1874 1876 1880 1881 1882 1885 1886 1888
   1889 1890 1891 1892 1893 1894 1895 1896
   1897 1902 1903 2080 2085 2086 2125 2127
   2131 2143 2180 2186 2191 2197 2200 2201
   2218 2221 2242 2255 2261 2279 2288 2289
   2298 2318 2344 2352 2374 2400 2401 2404
   2423 2431 2466 2473 2475 2483 2484 2492
   2501 2502 2508 2516 2523 2527 2541 2544
   2554 2558 2587 2625 2626 2627 2653 2674
   2675 2691 2696 2704 2705 2712 2716 2718
   2723 2736 2746 2774 2776 2777 2805 2815
   2818 2822 2865 L6 L62 L145 L147 L162
   L241 L427 L585 L585/2 L591 L593 L596
   L603 L604 L606 L608 L623 L740 L809 L840

τοὺς μὴ τηρήσαντας τὴν ἑαυτῶν ἀρχὴν ἀλλὰ ἀπολιπόντας
   6   8   10   12   14   16   18   20

L884 L921 L938 L1141 L1178 L1196
L1196/2 L1279 L1281 L1281/2 L1440
L1505 L2024 L2087 L2106

b δε 02 1 43 94 172 181 218 263 312 378 431
466 483 615 619 621 625 638 876 1040
1067 1070 1162 1292 1359 1367 1425 1490
1495 1501 1505 1563 1595 1611 1718 1735
1765 1780 1832 1836 1853 1875 2138 2147
2194 2243 2412 2494 2495 2652 2816 L164
L422 L1441

c τε και 90a

d γαρ 945

e om. 38T 522 1678 1877 2378

↑ 38

— 1384 1852

6-10↑

a τους μη τηρησαντας ... 628Z 641Z 1022(*f)
1245(*f) 1856f 1886f 2186f 2344(*f)V
2400(*f)

b τους μη παρατηρησαντας 1240

c τους τηρησαντας 628T

d τους μαρτυρησαντας L1440

e μη τηρησαντας 2625

f τηρησαντας 641T

↔ a/b/c/d/e/f:]ρησαντας 1384

↔ a/b/c/d/e/f:]ς 1852

↑ 38

12-20↓

a την εαυτων αρχην αλλα απολιποντας ...

b om. L884

12-16↑

a την εαυτων αρχην ... 1852V 2674f

b εαυτων την αρχην L2024

c την εαυτην αρχην 76 1893V 2516 L591

d την αυτων αρχην 2544

e την εαυτου αρχην 1405 L623

f την επ αυτων αρχην 1886

gf την εαυτων 676

↔ a/c/e: την εαυτ[..] [αρ]χην 400

↔ a/g: την εαυτων [1852

↑ 38 L884

— 1704

18-20↑↓

a αλλα απολιποντας ... 1523(*f)

↑ L884

— 1852

18↑

a αλλα ... 6(*f)

↑ 1523 L884

— 1852

20↑

a απολιποντας 01 02 03 04 018 044 056 0142
1 3 6 18 35 42 43 51 57 61 69 76 81 82 90a
90b 93 94 97 101 102 103 105 110 131 133
141 142 149 172 175 177 180 189 201 203
204 205 205abs 206S 209 216 218 221 223
226 241 242 250 252 254 256 263 296 302
307 308 309 312 314 319 321 322 323 325
326 327 328 330 337 363 367 378 383 384
385 386 390 394 398C 400 404 421 424 425
429 432 436 440 444 450 451 452 453 454
457 458 460f 462 465 466 467 468 469 479
483 489 491 496 506 517 522 547 592 601
603 604 605 606 607 608 616 617 618f 622
625 627 628 629 630 632 633 634 635 636
637 638 639 641 642 656 664 665 676 680
699 720 757 796 801 808 823 824 876 901
910 912 913 914 917 918 919 920 921 922
927 928 935 941 945 959 986 996 997 999
1003 1022 1040 1058 1066 1067 1070 1072
1075 1094 1099 1100 1101 1102 1103 1104
1105 1106 1107 1115 1127 1149 1161 1175
1240 1241 1242 1244 1245 1247 1248 1249
1250 1251 1270 1277 1292 1297 1311 1315
1319 1352 1354 1359 1360 1367 1384 1390
1398 1400 1404 1405 1409 1424 1425 1448
1482 1490 1495 1501 1503 1505 1508 1509
1521 1524 1548 1563 1573 1595 1597 1598
1599 1609 1610 1611 1617 1618 1619 1622
1626 1628 1636 1637 1642C 1643 1649
1652 1656 1661 1668 1673 1678 1702 1704
1717 1718 1719 1721 1722 1723 1725 1726
1727 1728 1729 1730 1732 1733 1734 1735
1736 1737 1738 1740 1741 1742 1743 1744
1745 1746 1747 1748 1749 1750 1752 1753
1754 1757 1761 1762 1763 1765 1766 1767
1768 1769 1780 1795 1799 1827 1828 1829
1830 1831 1832 1835 1837 1839 1840 1841
1842 1843 1844 1847 1849 1850 1851 1853
1854 1855 1856 1857 1858 1859 1860 1861

τὸ ἴδιον οἰκητήριον εἰς κρίσιν μεγάλης ἡμέρας
22   24   26   28   30   32   34
δεσμοῖς ἀϊδίοις ὑπὸ ζόφον τετήρηκεν,
      36   38   40   42   44

1862 1863 1864 1865 1868 1869 1870 1871
1872 1873 1875 1876 1877 1880 1882 1885
1886 1888 1889 1890 1891 1892 1894 1895
1896 1897 1902 1903 2080 2085 2086 2127
2131 2138 2180 2186 2191 2194 2197 2200
2201 2218 2221 2243 2255 2261 2279 2288
2289 2298 2318 2344 2352 2374 2378 2400
2404 2412 2423 2431 2466 2473 2475 2483
2484 2492 2494 2495 2501 2502 2508 2523
2527 2541 2544 2554 2558 2587 2625 2626
2627 2652 2653 2674 2675 2691 2704 2705
2712 2716 2718 2723 2736 2746 2774 2776
2777 2815 2816 2818 2822 2865 L62 L145
L147 L162 L241 L422 L427 L585 L585/2
L591 L593 L603 L604 L606 L608 L623 L740
L809 L840 L921 L938 L1141 L1178 L1196
L1196/2 L1279 L1281 L1281/2 L1440
L1441 L1505 L2024 L2087 L2106

b   ἀπολειποντας P72 020 049 5 33 62 88 104
     181 393 398* 431 442 456 459 582 615 619
     620 621 623 631 915 1162 1594 1720 1731
     1739 1760 1834 1836 1838 1845 1846 1874
     1881 1893 2125 2143 2242 2401 2516 2696
     2805 L6 L164 L596
↔ af/bf: απoληποντας 234 1243
↔ af/bf: απολυποντας 1642*
↔ af/bf: απολοιποντας 38 1069 1751 2147
↔ af/bf: απολυποτας 1646
↑   1523 L884
— 1852

22
a το ... 876(*f) 2218Z
b om. 2218T
— 1704 1852

24
a ιδιον ...
b ηδιον 1735
↔ a/b: [..]ιον 1852
— 913 1704

26
a οικητηριον ... 517V 1646f 2718(*f) 2822V
b κατοικητηριον 044 2736 L427
— 913 1704

30
a κρισιν ...
b κρησιν 38 1066
cf κριμασιν 901
↔ a/b: κρ[....] 1678
↔ a/b: κ̣[.....] 2774
— 1852 L6

31
a om. ...
b δε 2194
— 1852 L6

32-34
a μεγαλης ημερας ... 312Z 400Z 432f 1066f
   2704f
b ημερας μεγαλης 1735
c μεγαλης 312T
↔ a/c: μεγαλης [1704
— 1852 L6

36-38
a δεσμοις αιδιοις ... 522f 1405Z 1673f L593f
ao δεσμιοις αιδιοις 637 1311 1521 L604
b δεσμοις ιδιοις 1405T
c δεσμιοις αιδιοις 2746
df δεσμην αιδιους 460 618
e δεσμοις αλυτοις 621
f δεσμοις αει διοις 2147
g δεσμοις αλυτοις και αιδιοις 33 2344
hf δε εσμοις δε αιδιοις 1106V
↔ a/b/e/f: δεσμοις [......]ς 1893
↔ a/b/e/f: δεσ[913
— 1704 L6

40-42
a υπο ζοφον ... 1106V 2822V
b υπο ζοφου 327 454 680 1834 1838 2627 2704
c εις ζοφον 1735 L593
d επι ζοφω 1751
e υπο ζοφον κρισεως 629
↔ a/b: υπο ζοφ[..] L422
↔ a/b: υπο [.....] 2774
↔ a/c: [...] ζοφ[ο]ν 110
↔ a/c:]φον 1704
— 1852 L6

7 ὡς Σόδομα καὶ Γόμορρα καὶ αἱ περὶ αὐτὰς

2   4   6   8   10 12 14   16

πόλεις τὸν ὅμοιον τρόπον τούτοις ἐκπορνεύσασαι

18   20   22   24   26   28

---

v. 7
— 025 0251 0316 610 613 614 712 720 832 1724 1831S 1867 1899 2356 2511 L6 L156 L427/2 L617 L1818

2-4
a   ως σοδομα ... 400V 913V 1311f 1678V 1852V
bf   ω οδομα 466
c   ως και σοδομα 2495
d   σοδομα 38
↔   a/c: ως [1704
— P74 P78 602

7
a   om. ...
b   ως 241 363 378 547
— P74 P78 1704 2653

8
a   γομορρα ... 913V 1360C 1729Z 1753C 2289C 2675C
ao   γομορα P72 393 496 522 618 631 876 1241 1243 1311 1315 1360* 1524 1729T 1753* 1765 1769 1832 1840 1852 2186 2289* 2344 2494 2675* 2696 L604
ao2   γομμορα 462 1162 1874*
ao3   γομμορρα 1874C
— P74 P78 1704 2653

12
a   αι ... 1106V 632f 1871V
bf   τας 0142Z 1367 1409
c   om. 056 0142T 1066 1398 1849 2818 L593
— P74 P78 1852 2653

16
a   αυτας ... 1609C L585Z
bf   αυταις 104 436 459 1609* 1838
c   αυτους 1245 L585T
d   αυτων 1311
— P74 P78 69 1852 2653 2774

18-26↓
a   πολεις τον ομοιον τροπον τουτοις ...
b   πολεις τον ομοιον τουτοις τροπον 421Z
c   om. 421T
— P74 P78 69 2653

22↑
a   ομοιον ...
b   ιδιον 1649
↑   421
— P74 P78 69 620 913 1704 2653 2774

24-28↑
a   τροπον τουτοις εκπορνευσασαι P72(*f) 01 02 03 04 5 33 35* 61 81 93 218 322 323 326 431 442 621 623 630 665 1241 1243 1292 1359 1425 1448 1505 1563 1611 1718 1735 1739 1837 1881 2138 2200 2298 2344 2374 2492 2495 2527 2805 L596
b   τουτοις τροπον εκπορνευσασαι 018 020 049 056 1 3 6 18 35C 42 51 57 62 76 82 90a 90b 94 97 101 102 103 104 105 110V 131 133 141 142 149 172 175 177 180 189 201 203 204 205 205abs 206SC 209 216 221 223 226 234 241 242 250 252 254 256V 263 296 302 307 308V 312 314 319 321 325 327 328 330 337 363 367 378 383 384 385 386 390 393Z 394 398 404 421Z 424 425 429 432 436 440 444 450 451 452 453 454 456 457 458 459 460 462 465 467 468 469 479 483 496 506 517 522 547 582 592 601 602 603 604 605 606 607 608 616 617 618 619 622 625 627 628 629C 631 632 633 634 635 636 637 638 639 641 642 656 664 676 680 699 757 796 801 808 823 824 876 901 910 912 914 917 918 919 920 921 922 928 935 941 945 959 986 996 997 999 1003 1022 1040 1058 1067 1070f 1072 1075 1094 1099 1100 1101 1102 1103C 1104 1105 1107 1115 1127 1149 1161 1162 1175 1240 1242 1244 1245 1247 1248 1249 1250 1251 1270 1277 1297 1311 1315 1319 1352 1354 1360 1367 1384 1390 1398 1400 1404 1405 1424 1482 1490 1495 1501 1503 1508 1509 1521 1523

καὶ ἀπελθοῦσαι ὀπίσω σαρκὸς ἑτέρας,
30   32   34   36   38

1524 1548 1573 1594 1595 1597 1598 1599
1609 1610 1617 1618 1619 1622 1626 1628
1636 1637 1642 1643 1646 1649 1652 1656
1661 1668 1673 1678 1702 1717 1719 1720
1721 1722 1723 1725 1726 1727 1728 1730
1731 1732 1733 1734 1736 1737 1738 1740
1741 1742 1743 1744 1745 1746 1747 1748
1749 1750 1751f 1752 1753 1754 1757 1760
1761 1762 1763 1765 1766 1767 1768 1769
1780 1795 1799 1827 1828 1829 1830 1831
1832 1834 1835 1838 1839 1840 1841 1842
1843 1844 1846 1847 1849 1850 1851 1853
1854 1855 1856 1857 1858 1859 1860 1861
1862 1863 1864 1865 1869 1870 1871 1872
1873 1874 1876 1877 1880 1882 1885 1886
1888 1889 1890 1891 1892 1893 1894 1896
1897 1902 1903 2080 2085 2086 2125 2127
2131 2147 2180 2186 2194 2197 2201 2218
2221 2242 2243 2255 2261 2279 2288 2289
2318 2352 2378 2400 2401 2404 2412 2423
2431 2466 2473 2475 2483 2484 2494 2501
2502 2508 2516 2523 2541 2544 2554 2558
2587 2625 2626 2627 2652 2674 2675 2691
2696 2704 2705 2712 2716 2718 2723 2736
2746 2776 2777 2815 2816 2818 2822 2865
L62 L147 L162 L241 L422 L427 L585
L585/2 L591 L593 L603 L604 L606 L608f
L623 L740 L809 L840 L884 L921 L938
L1141   L1178   L1196   L1196/2   L1281
L1281/2 L1440 L1441 L1505 L2087 L2106

c   τουτοις εκπορνευσασαι τροπον 489 927
1069 1868 2143 L2024

d   τουτον τροπον εκπορνευσασαι 43

e   τουτοις τροπον εκπορευσασαι 393T 491
L145 L1279

ff   τουτων εκπορνευσασαι τροπον 1729

g   τροπον αυτοις εκπορνευσασαι 044

h   αυτοις τροπον εκπορνευσασαι 0142Z 38
206S* 309 466 1066C 1895 L164

i   αυτοις τροπον εκπορευσασαι 0142T

j   εαυτοις τροπον εκπορνευσασαι 1066*V

k   αυτοις τροπον ακολουθησασαι 1409

l   τροπον εκπορνευσασαι 88 181 615 915
1106 1836 1845 1875

mf   τουτοις εκπορνευσασαι 629*V 2191

nf   εκπορνευσασαι 421T 1103*

↔   b/e: τουτοις τροπον [9-10]σαι 2774

↔   b/d/e/h/l:] τροπον εκπορνευσασαι 913
1704

↔   a/g/l: τροπον [1852

↔   a/b/d/e/g/h/j:] εκπορνευσασαι 400

↔   a/b/c/d/e/g/h/i/j/l:]ευ[P74

—   P78 69 620 2653

30
a   και ... P74V 308V
b   om. 1066 2218
—   P74 P78 69 620 913 1704 2653

32
a   απελθουσαι ... 62(*f) 181f 1895(*f)
b   om. 2218
—   P78 69 620 913 1704 2653

34-38
a   οπισω σαρκος ετερας P72f 01 02 03 04 018
020 044 049 056 0142 1 3 5 6 18 33 35 38 42
43 51 57 61 62 76 81 82 88 90a 90b 93 94 97
101 102 103 104 105 131 133 141 142 149
172 175 177 180 181 189 201 203 204 205
205abs 206S 209 216 218 221 223 226 234
241 242 250 252 254 256 263 296 302 307
308 309 312 314 319 321 322 323 325 326
327 328 330 337 363 367 378 383 384 385
386 390 393 394 398 400V 404 421 424 425
429 431 432 436 440 442 444 450 451 452
453 454 456 457 459 460 462 465 466 467
468 479 483 489 491 496 506 517 522 547
582 601 602 603 604 605 606 607 608 615
616 618 619 621f 622 623 625 627 628 629
630 631 632 633 634 635 636 637 638 639
641 642 656 664 665 676 680 699 757 796
801 808 823 824 901 910 912 913 914 915
917 918 919 920 921 922 927 928 935 941
945 959 986 996 997 999 1003 1022 1040
1058 1066 1067 1069 1070 1072 1075 1094
1099 1100 1101 1102 1103 1104 1105 1106
1107 1115 1127 1149 1161 1162 1175 1240
1241 1242 1243 1244 1245 1247 1248 1249
1250 1251 1270 1277 1292 1297 1311 1315
1319 1352 1354 1359 1360 1367 1384 1390
1398 1400 1404 1405 1409 1424 1425 1448
1482 1490 1495 1501 1503 1505 1508 1509
1521 1523 1524 1548 1563 1573 1594 1595
1597 1598 1599 1609 1610 1611 1617 1618

πρόκεινται δεῖγμα πυρὸς αἰωνίου δίκην
40   42   44   46   48
ὑπέχουσαι. **8** ὁμοίως μέντοι καὶ οὗτοι
50   2   4   6   8

1619 1622 1628 1636 1637 1642 1643 1646
1649 1652 1656 1661 1668 1673 1678 1702
1704 1717 1718 1719 1720 1721 1722 1723
1725 1726 1727 1728 1729 1730 1731 1732
1733 1734 1735 1736 1737 1738 1739 1740
1741 1742 1743 1744 1745 1746 1747 1748
1749 1750 1751 1752 1753 1754 1757 1760
1761 1762 1763 1766 1767 1768 1769 1780
1795 1799 1827 1828 1829 1830 1831 1834
1835 1836 1837 1838 1839 1840 1841 1842
1843 1844 1845 1846 1847 1849 1850 1851
1853 1854 1855 1856 1857 1858 1859 1860
1861 1862 1863 1864 1865 1868 1869 1870
1871 1872 1873 1874 1875 1876 1877 1880
1881 1882 1885 1886 1888 1889 1890 1891
1892 1893 1894 1895 1896 1902 1903 2080
2085 2086 2125 2127 2131 2138 2143 2147
2180 2186 2191 2194 2197 2200 2201 2218
2221 2242 2243 2255 2261 2279 2288 2289
2298 2318 2344 2352 2374 2378 2400 2401
2404Z 2412 2423 2431 2466 2473 2475
2483 2484 2492 2495 2501 2502 2508 2516
2523 2527 2541 2544 2554 2558 2587 2627
2652 2674 2675 2691 2696 2704 2712 2718
2723 2736 2746 2776 2777 2805 2815 2816
2818 2822 2865 L62 L145 L147 L162 L164
L241 L427 L585 L585/2C L591 L593
L596CV L603 L604 L606 L608 L623 L740
L809 L840 L884 L921 L938 L1141 L1178
L1196 L1196/2 L1279 L1281 L1281/2
L1440 L1441 L1505 L2024 L2087 L2106
b σαρκος οπισω ετερας 876 1765 1832 2494
c σαρκος ετερας οπισω L596*
d οπισω σαρκος και ετερας 2625
e οπισω σαρκος εταιρας 592 617 1626 2705
   L585/2*
f οπισω σαρκος 2404T
g σαρκος ετερας 458 469 1897 2626 2716
   L422
↔ *a/d/e:* οπισω σαρκος [110
↔ *a/e:* [ο]πισω σαρκος [2774
↔ *a/d/e:* οπισω [1852
↔ *a/d/e/f:* [..... σαρκ]ος [P74
— P78 69 620 2653

40
a προκεινται ... 04V 256fV 321f 322f 323f
   606C 623(*f) 913V 1106V 1719(*f) 2718f
b προσκεινται P72 81 522 606* 641
cf προκειντο 37
↔ *af/bf:* προ[..]κεινται 1902
— P74 P78 69 110

42
a δειγμα ... 01f 04V 42(*f) L593f
b δογμα 2818
c δειγματα 429 522
— P74 P78 69 913

44
a πυρος ... 1319f 1404V 2736V
— P74 913 1831

46-48↓
a αιωνιου δικην ...
b om. L422
— P74 69

46↑
a αιωνιου ... 1847f 2404f
↑ L422
— P74 69 1831

48↑
α δικην ... 400V 1893V 2653V
b δικης 633
c δικας 90a 384
d om. 1836 1877
↔ *a/b/c:* δι[...] 2774
↔ *a/b/c:* δ[....] 102
↑ L422
— P74 69 1852

50

a υπεχουσαι P72 03 04 018 020 044 049 056
0142 1 3 5 6 18 33 35 38 42 43 51 57 61 62
76 81 82 88 90a 90b 93 94 97 101 102 103
104 105 131 133 141 142 149 172 175 177
180 189 201 203 204 205 205abs 206S 209
216 218 221 223 226 234 241 242 250 252
254 256V 263 296 302 307 308 309 312 314
319 321 322 323 325 326 327 328 330 337
363 367 383 384 385 386 390 393 394 398
404 421 424 425 429 431 432 436 440 442
444 450 451 452 453 454 456 457 458 459
460 462 465 466 467 468 469 479 483 489
491 506 517 522 547 582 592 601 602 603
604 605 606 607 608 615 617 618 619 620
621 622 623 625 627 628 629 632 633 634
635 637 638 639 641 642 656 664 665 676
680 699 757 796 801 808 823 824 901 910
912 914 915 917 918 919 920 921 922 927
928 935 941 945 959 986 996 997 999 1003
1022 1040 1058 1066 1067 1069 1070 1072
1075 1094 1099 1100 1101 1102 1103 1105
1106 1107 1115 1127 1149 1161 1162 1175
1240 1241 1242 1243 1244 1245 1247 1248
1249 1250 1251 1270 1277(*f) 1292 1297
1311 1315 1352 1354 1359 1360 1367 1384
1390 1398 1400 1404 1405 1409 1424 1425
1448 1482 1490 1495 1501 1503 1508 1509
1521 1523 1524 1548 1563 1573 1594 1595
1597 1598 1599 1609 1610 1617 1618 1619
1622 1626 1628 1636 1637 1642 1643 1646
1649 1652 1656 1661 1668 1673 1678 1702
1717 1718 1719 1720 1721 1722 1723 1725
1726 1727 1728 1729 1730 1731 1732 1733
1734 1735 1736 1737 1738 1739 1740 1741
1742 1743 1744 1745 1746 1747 1748 1749
1750 1751 1752 1753 1754 1757 1760 1761
1762 1763 1766 1767 1768 1769 1780 1795
1799 1827 1828 1829 1830 1831 1834(*f)
1835 1836 1837 1838 1839 1840 1841 1842
1843 1844 1847 1849 1850 1851 1853 1854
1855 1856 1857 1858 1859 1860 1861 1862
1863 1864 1865 1868 1869 1870 1871
1872V 1873 1874 1875 1876 1877 1880
1881 1882 1885 1886 1888 1889 1890 1891
1892 1894 1895 1896 1897 1902 1903 2080
2085 2086 2125 2127 2131 2143 2147 2180
2186 2191 2194 2197 2201 2218 2221 2242
2255 2261 2279Z 2288 2289 2298 2318
2344 2352 2374 2378 2400 2401 2404 2412
2423 2431 2466 2473 2475 2483 2484 2492
2501 2502 2508 2516 2523 2527 2541 2544
2554 2558 2587 2625 2626 2627 2652 2674
2675 2691C 2704 2705 2712 2716 2723

2746 2776 2777 2805 2815 2816 2818 2822
2865 L62 L145 L147 L162 L164 L241 L427
L585 L585/2 L591 L593 L596 L603 L604
L606 L608 L623 L740 L809 L840 L884 L921
L938 L1141 L1178 L1196 L1196/2 L1279
L1281 L1281/2 L1441 L1505 L2024 L2087
L2106

b υπερεχουσαι 02 2718
c επεχουσαι P78 378f 630 876 1104 1505
1611 1765 1832 2138 2200 2243 2494 2495
L422 L1440
d απεχουσαι 181 1319
e υπεχουσιν 01C2 616 2279T
f υπαρχουσαι 496 631f 636 1845 1846 2696
gf υπεχουσμενος 2691*V
h ουκ εχουσιν 01*
↔ af/ef: υπεχωσ[..] 2736
↔ a/e: υπεχο[....] 913
↔ a/c/d: [.]πεχουσαι 1893
↔ a/c/d: [.....]υσαι 1704 2774
↔ a/c/d/e: [..]ε̱χ[110
↔ a/c/d/e: [...]χ̱[400
— P74 69 1852 2653

v. 8
— P74 025 0251 0316 69 613 614 712 720 832
1724 1831S 1867 1899 2356 2511 L6 L156
L427/2 L617 L1818

2

a ομοιως ... 110V 400V 506(*f) 1704V 1717V
1831V 1852V L604f
b ομως 02
— 610 913

4

a μεντοι ... 2197Z 2653V
b μεν 94 203 307 321 453 506 918 1241 1678
2197T 2818
c δε 1751
d om. 1106
— 610 913

6-8

a και ουτοι ... 517V 913V 1646C 1885Z
2653V
b και αυτοι P78 1735 1885T
cf και τουτοι 1646*
d και 142 1404
e om. 2186 L241
↔ a/b/c/d: και [1852
↔ a/b/c:]τοι 1115
— 610

ἐνυπνιαζόμενοι σάρκα μὲν μιαίνουσιν κυριότητα
    10   12   14   16   18
δὲ ἀθετοῦσιν δόξας δὲ βλασφημοῦσιν.
   20   22   24 26   28

10
a ενυπνιαζομενοι ... P78f 110V 256V 307f 400V 522f 629C 1646(*f)
b εξυπνιαζομενοι 205 205abs
c om. 629* L241
↔ a/b: [..]υπνιαζομενοι 2816
↔ a/b: ε[..........]οι 1678
— 610 1852

12
a σαρκα ... 33V 110V 1704V
b σαρκας 431 1741
cf σαρκαν 1070
— 610 913

14
a μεν ... 110V 203(*f)
b om. P72 631 1245 2344 L603 L1440 L1441
— 610 913 1115

16
a μιαινουσιν ... 61(*f) 110V 256V 308V 400V 1106V 1839f L884f
— 610 913 1115

18
a κυριοτητα ... 1704V
b κυριοτητας 01 044 922 1744V 1845 1846 1886f 2805
cf κυριοτηταν L164
df κυριοτα 1702
— 610 1852

20
a δε ... 256V 1704V 1852V 2653V 2774V
b om. 1175
— 610 1704 1852

22
a αθετουσιν ... 1852V 1893V 2473f 2774V
— 1704

24-28
a δοξας δε βλασφημουσιν P72f 01 02 03 04 018 020 044 049 056 0142 6 18 33 35 38 42

51 57 61 62 76 81 82 88 90a 93f 94 97 101
102 103 104 105 110V 131 133 141 142 149
172 175 177 180 181 189 201 203 204 205
205abs 206S 209 216 218 221 223 226 234
241 242 252 254 256V 263 296 302 307 308
312 314 319 321 322 323 325 326 327 328
330 337 363V 367 378 383 384 385 386 390
393 394 398 400V 404 421 424Z 425 429
431 432 436 440 442 444 450 451 452 453
454 456 457 459 460 462 465 467 468 469
479 483 489 491 506 517 522 547 582 592
601 602 603 604 605 606 607 610 615 617
618 619 620 621 622 623 627 628 629 630
632 634 635 637 638 639 641 642 656 664
665 676 680f 699 757 801 808 823 824 876
901 910 912 914 915 917 918 919 920 921
922 927 928 935 941 945 959 986 996 997Z
999 1003 1022 1040 1058 1066 1067 1070
1072 1075 1094 1099 1100 1101 1102 1103
1104 1105 1106V 1115V 1127 1149 1161
1162 1175 1240 1241 1242 1243 1244 1245
1247 1248 1249 1250 1251 1270 1277 1292
1297 1311 1319 1352 1354 1359 1360 1367
1384 1390 1398 1400 1404 1405 1409 1424
1425 1448 1482 1495 1501 1503 1505 1508
1509 1521 1523 1524 1548 1563 1573 1594
1595 1597 1598 1599 1609 1610 1611 1617
1618 1619 1622 1628 1636 1637 1643
1646(*f) 1649 1652 1656 1661 1668 1673
1702 1704 1718 1719 1720 1721 1722 1723
1725 1726 1727 1728 1729f 1730 1731 1732
1733 1734 1735 1736 1737 1738 1739 1740
1741 1742 1743 1744 1745 1746 1747 1748
1749f 1750 1751f 1752 1753 1754 1757
1760 1761 1762 1763 1765 1766 1767 1768
1769 1780 1795 1827 1828 1829 1830 1832
1834 1835 1836 1837 1838 1839 1840 1841
1842 1843 1844 1845 1847 1849 1851
1852V 1853 1854 1855 1856 1857 1858
1859 1860 1861 1862 1863 1864 1865 1868
1870 1871 1872 1873 1874 1875 1876 1877
1880 1881 1882 1885 1886 1888 1889 1890
1891 1892 1893 1894 1895 1897 1902 1903
2080 2085 2086 2125 2127 2131 2138 2143
2147 2180 2186 2191 2194 2197 2200 2201

9 ὁ δὲ Μιχαὴλ ὁ ἀρχάγγελος, ὅτε τῷ διαβόλῳ
  2 4   6   8   10   12 14 16

διακρινόμενος διελέγετο περὶ τοῦ Μωϋσέως σώματος,
  18   20   22 24   26   28

2218 2221 2242 2243 2255 2261 2279 2288
2289 2298 2318 2344 2352 2374 2378
2401Z 2404 2412 2423 2431 2466 2473
2475 2483 2484 2492 2494 2495 2501 2502
2508 2516 2523 2527 2541 2544 2554 2558
2587 2625 2626 2627 2652 2674 2675 2691f
2704 2712 2716 2718 2723 2736 2746 2774
2776 2777 2805 2815 2818 2822 L62 L145
L147 L162 L164 L241 L422 L427 L585
L585/2 L591 L593 L596 L603 L604 L606
L608 L623 L740 L809 L840 L884 L921 L938
L1141 L1178 L1196 L1196/2 L1279 L1281
L1281/2 L1441 L1505 L2024 L2087 L2106

b δοξαν δε βλασφημουσιν P78V 3 5 90b 496
608 631 636 796 1315 1490 1642 1799 1831
1896 2696 2865

c δοξας δε αθετουσιν και βλασφημουσιν
1869

d δοξας ου βλασφημουντες 1069T

e δοξας ου τρεμουσιν βλασφημουντες 309
633 1069Z 1717 2816

f δοξας βλασφημουσιν 43 250 424T 458 616
997T 1626 1846f 1850 2400 2401T 2705
L1440

g om. 1 466 625 1107

↔ a/b: δοξ[..] δε βλασφημουσιν 1678

— 913 2653

29
a om. ...

bf ομοιως μεν και ουτοι ενυπνιαζομενοι
σαρκα μεν μιαινουσιν κυριοτητα δε
αθετουσι δοξας δε βλασφημουσιν 307

v.9
— P74 P78 025 0251 0316 69 613 614 712 720
832 1724 1831S 1867 1895 1899 2356 2511
L6 L156 L427/2 L617 L1818

2-4
a ο δε ...
b οτε 03
cf δε 1827
— 256 1852

6
a μιχαηλ ... P72f
— 1852

8
a ο ... 1704V
b om. 1744 2501
— 1852

10
a αρχαγγελος ...
b αγγελος 1243 2492

12
a οτε ... 256V 913V 921f
b τοτε 03
c ο τοτε 582 620
— 256 913 2653

18
a διακρινομενος ... 02(*f) 256V 400V 631f
699(*f) 1704V
b ανακρινομενος 1523ZV 1524
c κρινομενος 1523TV 2494
d om. 2675
↔ a/b:]ακρινομενος 2653
↔ a/b/c:]ενος 1852

20
a διελεγετο ... L2087f
b ελεγεν 1836

24-28
a του μωωσεως σωματος P72 01 03 04 020 1
5 33 38 42 43 51 57 61 76 81 93 94 97 101
102V 104 105 110 133 175 181 218 223
226* 234 242 254 256V 263 296 302 307
308 321 326 330 383 385 390 404 421 429Z
431 436 442 451 452 453 456 460f 466 467
468 469 491 517 522 605 607 610 617 618f
619 621 623 625 627 629 642 656 665 676
808 823 901 912 917 918 920 921 941 996
997Z 1003 1022 1067 1069 1070 1094 1103
1104 1107 1127 1149 1162 1175 1243 1244
1245 1277 1352 1359 1398 1405 1409 1425

160

οὐκ ἐτόλμησεν κρίσιν ἐπενεγκεῖν
30　　　32　　　　34　　　36
βλασφημίας ἀλλὰ εἶπεν· ἐπιτιμήσαι σοι
38　　　　40　　　42　　　44　　　46

1501 1521 1523 1524 1563 1594 1622 1643
1646 1661 1673 1702 1718 1719 1721*
1727 1735 1741 1743 1744 1751 1753 1762
1769 1780 1795 1799 1834 1836 1837 1838
1839 1840 1841 1844 1845 1846 1849 1851
1857* 1859 1860 1861 1863 1869f 1871
1874 1875 1880 1881 1885Z 1886 1891
1894 2085 2127 2180 2186 2194 2197
2200* 2201 2242 2279 2344 2374 2475
2492 2502 2544 2625 2627 2674 2675 2705
2716 2746 2776 2805 2818 2865 L585
L585/2 L596 L1141 L1196 L1196/2 L1281
L1281/2 L1441 L2087

ao του μωσεως σωματος 02 018 044 049 3Z 6
18 35 62 82 88 90a 90b 103 141 142 149
172 177f 180 189 201 203 204 205 205abs
206S 209 216 221 226C 241 250 252 309
312 314 319 322 323 325 327 328 337f 363
367 384 386 393 394 398 400 424 425 429T
432 440 444 450 454 457 458 459 462 465
479 483 489 496 506 547 582 592 601 602
603 604 606 608 615 616 620 622 628 630
631 634 635 636 637 638 639 641 664 680
699 757 796 801 824 876 910 914 915 919
922 927 928 935 945 959 986 997T 999
1040 1058 1072 1075 1099 1100 1101 1102
1105 1161 1240 1241 1242 1247 1248 1249
1250 1251 1270 1292 1297 1311 1315 1319
1354 1360 1367 1384 1390 1400 1404 1424
1448 1482 1490 1495 1503 1505 1508 1509
1548 1573 1595 1597 1598 1599 1609 1610
1611 1617 1618 1619 1626 1628 1636 1637
1642 1649 1652 1656 1668 1704 1717 1720
1721C 1722f 1723 1725 1726 1728 1729
1730 1731 1732 1733 1734 1736 1737 1739
1740 1742 1745 1746 1747 1748 1749 1750
1752 1754 1757 1760 1761 1763 1765 1766
1767 1768 1827 1828 1829 1830 1831 1832
1835 1842 1843 1847 1850 1853 1854 1855
1856 1857C 1858 1862 1864 1865 1868
1870 1872 1873 1876 1877 1882 1885T
1888 1889 1890 1892 1893 1896 1897 1902
1903 2080 2086 2125 2131 2138 2143 2191
2200C 2218 2221 2243 2255 2261 2288

2289 2298 2318 2352 2378 2400 2401 2404
2412 2423 2431 2466 2473 2483 2484 2494
2495 2501 2508 2516 2523 2527 2541 2554
2558 2587 2626 2691 2696 2704 2712 2718
2723 2736 2774 2777 2815 2822 L62 L145
L147 L162 L164 L241 L422 L427 L591 L593
L603 L604 L606 L608 L623 L740 L809 L840
L884 L921 L938 L1178 L1279 L1505 L2024
L2106
b του σωματος μωυσεως 378 632* L1440
bo του σωματος μωσεως 056AV 0142AV
632C 2147 2652 2816
c το του μωυσεως σωμα 1738
d του μωυσεως 0142T
do του μωυσεως 056T 3T 633 1066
e μωυσεως σωματος 131
↔ *a/ao:* του [6-7] σωματος 1678
↔ *a/ao/d/do:* τοῠ μ[1115
↔ *a/ao/e:*]σεως σωματος 2653
↔ *a/ao/e:*] σωματος 913 1106
↔ *a/ao/e:*]τος 1852

30-32
a ουκ ετολμησεν ... 256V 469f 491f 1384V
2186f 2716f
bf ου και τολμησεν 1838

34
a κρισιν ...
b κρησιν 1735
c ρησιν 1893
— 913 1106 1852

36
a επενεγκειν P72 01 02 03 04 018 020 049
056 0142 1 3 5 6 18 33 35 38 42 43 51 57 61
62 76 81 82 88 90a 90b 93 94 97 101 102
104 110 131 133 141 149 172 175 177 181T
189 201 204 205 205abs 206S 209 218 223
226 234 242 252 254 263 296 302 307 308
309 312 319 321 322 323 325 326 328 330
337 367 383 384 385 386 390 394 398 400
404 421 425 429 431 432 436 442 444 450
451 452 453 456 457 458 459 460 462 465
466 467 469 479 483 489 491 517 522 547

582 592 601 602 603 604 605 607 608 610
615 617 618 619 620 621 622 623 627 628
629 630 632 634 635 637 638 642 656 664
665 680 699 757 796 801 808 823 824 876
901(*f) 910 912 914 915 917 918 919 920
921 922 927 928 941 945 959 986f 996 997
1003 1022 1040 1058 1066 1067 1069 1070
1072 1075 1094 1100 1101 1102 1103 1104
1105 1107 1115 1127 1149 1161 1175 1240f
1241 1242 1243 1244 1245 1247 1248 1249
1250 1270 1277 1292 1297 1311 1319 1352
1359 1367 1384 1390 1398 1400 1405 1409
1424 1425 1448 1482 1490 1495 1501 1503
1505 1508 1509 1521 1523 1524 1548 1563
1573 1594 1595 1597 1598 1599 1610 1611
1617 1618 1619 1622 1626 1628 1636 1637
1642 1643 1646 1649 1652 1656 1661 1668
1673 1678 1702 1704 1717 1718 1719 1720
1723 1725 1726 1727 1728 1729 1730 1731
1732 1733 1734 1735 1737 1738 1739 1740
1741 1743 1745 1746 1747 1748 1749 1750
1751 1752 1753 1754 1757f 1760 1762 1763
1765 1766 1767 1768 1769 1780 1795 1799
1827 1828 1830 1831 1832 1834 1835 1836
1837 1838 1839 1840 1841 1842 1843 1844
1845 1846 1847 1849 1850 1851 1853 1854
1855 1856 1857 1858 1859 1860 1861 1863
1864 1865 1868 1869 1870 1871 1872 1873
1874 1875 1876 1877 1880 1881 1882 1885
1886 1891 1892 1893 1894 1896 1897 1902
2080 2085 2086 2127 2131 2138 2143 2147
2180 2186 2191 2194 2197 2200 2201 2218
2221 2242 2255 2261 2279 2288 2289 2298
2318 2344 2352 2374 2378 2400 2404 2412
2423 2431 2466 2473 2475 2484 2492 2494
2495 2501 2502 2516 2523 2527 2541 2544
2554 2558 2587 2625 2626 2627 2652 2674
2691 2704 2705 2716 2718 2723 2736 2746
2774 2776 2777 2805 2815 2816 2818 2822
2865 L62 L145 L147 L162 L241 L422 L427
L585 L585/2 L591 L593 L596 L603 L604
L606 L608 L623 L740 L809 L840 L884 L921
L938 L1141 L1178 L1196 L1196/2 L1279
L1281 L1281/2 L1440 L1441 L1505 L2024
L2087 L2106
b υπενεγκειν 044 103 105 142 180 181Z 216
221 241 250 314 327 363 378 393 424 440
454 468 496 606 616 625 631 636 639 641
676 935 999 1099 1162 1251 1315 1354
1360 1404 1609 1721 1722 1736 1742 1744
1761 1829 1862 1888 1889 1890 1903 2125
2243 2401 2483 2508 2675 2696 2712 L164
c εξενεγκειν 203 506

d επαγαγειν 633
↔ *a/b/c:* [....]εγκειν 256
↔ *a/b/c:* [......]κειν 2653
— 913 1106 1852

38
a βλασφημιας ... 1704V
b βλασφημον 1424

42
a ειπεν ... 102V
b ειπον 625
↔ *a/b:* ει[...] 1106 1852

44-48↓
a επιτιμησαι σοι κυριος ...
b επιτιμησαι σοι ο κυριος 1874Z
c om. 1874T
— 913 1106 1852

44-46↑
a επιτιμησαι σοι P72 01 02 03C2 04 018 020
049 056 0142 1 3 6 18 33 35 38 43 51 57 61
62 76 81 82 88 90a 90b 93 94 97 101 102
103 104 105 110 131 133 141 142 149 172
175 177 180 181 189 201 203 204 205
205abs 206S 209 216 218 221 223 226 241
242 250 252 254 263 296 302 307 308 309
312 314 319 321 325 326 327 328 330 337
363 367 378 383 384 385 386 393 394 398
400V 404 421 424 425 429 431 432 436 440
442 444 450 451 452 453 454 456 457 459
460 462 465 466 467 468 469 479 483 489
491 496 506 517 547 582 592 601 602 603
604 605 606 607 610 615 616 617 618 619
620 621 622 625 627 628 629 630 631 632
633 634 635 636 637 638 639 641 656 664
665 676 680 699 757 796 801 808 823 824
876 901 910 914 915 917* 918 919 920 921
922 927 928 935 941 945 959 986 997 999
1003 1022 1040 1058 1066 1067 1069 1070
1072 1075 1094 1099 1100 1101 1102 1103
1104 1105 1107 1115 1127 1149 1161 1162
1175 1240 1242 1243 1244 1245 1247 1248
1249 1250 1251 1270 1277 1292 1297 1311
1315 1319 1352 1354 1359 1360 1367 1398
1400 1404V 1405 1409 1424 1425 1448
1482 1490 1495 1501 1503 1505 1508 1509
1521 1523 1524 1548 1563 1573 1595 1597
1598 1599 1609 1610 1611 1617 1618 1619
1622 1626 1628 1636 1637 1642 1643 1646
1649 1652 1656 1668 1673 1678 1704 1717
1718 1719(*f) 1720 1721 1722 1723 1725
1726 1728 1730 1731 1732 1733 1734 1735
1736 1737 1738 1740 1741 1742 1743 1744

κύριος. **10** οὗτοι δὲ ὅσα μὲν
48   2   4   6   8

1745 1746 1747 1748 1749 1750 1752 1753
1754 1757 1760 1761 1762 1763 1765 1766
1767 1768 1769 1780 1795 1799 1827 1828
1829 1830 1831 1832 1834 1835 1836 1837
1838 1839 1840 1841 1842 1843 1844 1845
1846 1847 1849 1850 1851 1853 1854 1855
1856 1857 1858 1859 1860 1862 1864 1865
1868 1869 1870 1871 1872 1873 1875 1876
1877 1880 1882 1885 1886f 1888 1889 1890
1891 1892 1894 1896 1897 1902 1903 2080
2086 2125 2127 2131 2138 2143 2147 2180
2186 2191 2194 2197 2200 2201 2218 2221
2242 2243 2255 2261 2279 2288 2289 2298
2318 2344 2352 2374 2378 2400 2401 2404
2412 2423 2431 2473 2475 2483 2484 2492
2494 2495 2501 2508 2516 2523 2527 2541
2544 2554 2587 2625 2626 2627 2652 2674
2675 2691 2696 2704 2705 2712 2716 2718
2723 2736 2746 2774 2776 2777Z 2805
2815 2816 2818 2822 2865 L62 L145 L147
L162 L241 L427 L585 L585/2 L591 L593
L596 L603 L604 L606 L608 L623 L740 L809
L840 L884 L921 L938 L1141 L1178 L1196
L1196/2 L1279 L1281 L1281/2 L1440
L1441 L1505 L2024 L2087 L2106
b   επιτιμηςει σοι 5 623 917C 1751
c   επιτιμηςαι σε 42 234 390 458 608 912 996
    1390 1594 1661 1702 1727 1729 1861 1863
    1893 2085 2502 2777T L164 L422
d   επιτιμηςει σε 522(*f) 642 2558
e   επιτιμηςαι εν σοι 03*V 044 322 323 1241
    1739 1881
f   επιτιμηςαι 2466
↔   a/b: επιτιμη[σ.. ..]ι 256
↔   a/b/c/d: επιτι[μησ.. 2-3] 2653
↔   a/b/c/d/e: επι[τιμησ.. 1384
↑   1874
—   913 1106 1852

48↑
a   κυριος P72 02 03 04 018 020 044 049 056
    0142 3 5 6 18 33 35 38 42 43 51 57 61 76 81
    82 88 90a 90b 93 94 97 101 102 103 104
    105 110 131 133 141 142 149 172 175 177
    180 181 189 201 203 204 205 205abs 206S
    209 216 218 221 223 226 234 241 250 252
    254 256 263 296 302 307 308 312 314 319
    321 325 326 327 328 330 337 363 367 383

384 385 386 390 393 394 398 400 404 421
424 425 429 431 432 436 440 444 450 451
452 453 454 456 457 458 459 460 462 465
466 467 468 469 479 483 489 491 496 506
517 522 547 582 592 601 602 603 604 605
606 607 608 610 615 616 617 618 619 620
622 623 627 628 629 631 632 633 634 635
636 637 638 639 641 642 656 664 665 676
680 699 757 796 801 808 823 824 876 901
910 912 914 915 917 918 919 920 921 922
927 928 935 941 945 959 986 996 997 999
1003 1022 1040 1058 1066 1067 1069 1070
1072 1075 1094 1099 1100 1101 1102 1103
1104 1105 1115 1127 1149 1161 1162 1175
1240 1242 1243 1244 1245 1247 1248 1249
1250 1251 1270 1277 1297 1315 1319 1352
1354 1359 1360 1367 1390 1398 1400 1404
1405 1409 1424 1425 1482 1490 1495 1501
1503 1508 1509 1521 1523 1524 1548 1563
1573 1594 1595 1597 1598 1599 1609 1610
1617 1618 1619 1622 1626 1628 1636 1637
1642 1643 1646 1649 1652 1656 1661 1668
1673 1678 1702 1704 1717 1718 1719 1721
1722 1723 1725 1726 1727 1728 1729 1730
1731 1732 1733 1734 1736 1737 1738 1740
1741 1742 1743 1744 1745 1746 1747 1748
1749 1750 1751 1752 1753 1754 1757 1760
1761 1762 1763 1765 1766 1767 1768 1769
1795 1799 1827 1828 1829 1830 1831 1832
1835 1836 1837 1838 1839 1840 1841 1842
1843 1844 1845 1846 1847 1849 1851 1853
1854 1855 1856 1857 1858 1859 1860 1861
1862 1863 1864 1865 1868 1869 1870 1871
1872 1873 1875 1876 1880 1882 1885 1886
1888 1889 1890 1891 1892 1893 1894 1896
1897 1902 1903 2080 2085 2086 2125 2127
2131 2143 2180 2186 2191 2194 2197 2201
2218 2221 2242 2243 2255 2261 2279 2288
2289 2318 2344 2352 2374 2378 2400 2401
2404 2423 2431 2466 2473 2475 2483 2484
2492 2494 2501 2502 2508 2516 2523 2527
2541 2544 2554 2558 2587 2625 2626 2627
2653 2674 2675 2691 2696 2704 2705 2712
2716 2718 2723 2736 2746 2774 2776 2777
2815 2816 2818 2822 L62 L145 L147 L162
L164 L241 L422 L427 L585 L585/2 L591
L593 L603 L604 L606 L608 L623 L740 L809
L840 L884 L938 L1141 L1178 L1196

L1196/2 L1279 L1281 L1281/2 L1440 L1441 L1505 L2024 L2087 L2106
b ο κυριος 01C2 1 62 242 309 378 442 621 625 630 1107 1292 1311 1448 1505 1611 1720 1735 1780 1834 1850 1877 2138 2147 2200 2412 2495 2652 2805 2865 L596 L921
c ο θεος 01* 322 323 1241 1739 1881 2298
d κυριος ο θεος 1501
↑ 1874
— 913 1106 1852

49
a om. ... 1717V
b διαβολε 104 181 459 460 917 1646 1836 1838 1842 1846 1875 2502 2523
— 913 1106 1704 1852

v. 10
— P74 P78 025 0251 0316 69 613 614 712 720 832 1724 1831S 1867 1895 1899 2356 2511 L6 L156 L427/2 L617 L1818

2
a ουτοι ...
b αυτοι 442 2242
— 913 1704 1717

4-8
a δε οσα μεν P72 01 02 03 04 018 020 044 049 056 0142 1 3 5 6 18 33 35 38 42 43 51 57 61 62 76 81 82 88 90a 90b 94 97 101 103 104 105 110 131 133 141 142 149 172 175 177 180 189 201 203 204 205 205abs 206S 209 216 218 221 223 226 234 241 242 250 252 254Z 256V 263 296 302 307 308 312 314 319 321 322 323 325 326C 327 328 337 363 367 378 383 384 385 386 390 393 394 398 400 404 421 424 425 429 431 432 436 440 442 444 450 451 452 453 454 456 457 458 459 460 462 465 466 467 468 469 479 483 491 496 506 517 522 547 582 592 601 602 603 604 605 606 607 608 610 615 616 617 618 619 620 621 622 623 625 627 628 629 632 633 634 635 636 637 638 639 641 642 656 664 676 680 699 757 796 801 808 823 824 824 876 901 910 912 913 914 915 917 918 919 920 921 922 927 928 935 941 945 959 986 996 997 999 1003 1022 1040 1058 1066 1067 1069 1070 1072 1075 1094 1099 1100 1101 1102 1103 1105 1107 1115 1127 1149 1161 1162 1175 1240 1241 1242 1243 1244 1245 1247 1248 1249 1250 1251 1270 1277 1292 1297 1311 1315 1319 1352 1354 1359 1360 1367 1384 1390 1398 1400 1404 1405 1409 1424 1425 1448 1482 1490

1495 1501 1503 1505 1508 1509 1521 1523 1524 1548 1573 1594 1595 1597 1598 1599 1609 1610 1611 1617 1618 1619 1622 1626 1628 1636 1637 1642 1643 1646 1649 1652 1656 1661 1668 1673 1678 1702 1717V 1718 1719 1720 1721 1722 1723 1725 1726 1727 1728 1729 1730 1731 1732 1733 1734 1736 1737 1738 1739 1740 1741 1742 1743 1744 1745 1746 1747 1748 1749 1750 1751 1752 1753 1754 1757 1760 1761 1763 1765 1766 1767 1768 1769 1780 1795 1799 1828Z 1829 1830 1831 1832 1834 1835 1837 1838 1839 1840 1841 1842 1843 1844 1845 1846 1847 1849 1850 1851 1852 1853 1854 1855 1856 1857 1858 1859 1860 1861 1862 1863 1864 1865 1868 1869 1870 1871 1872 1873 1874 1876 1877 1880 1881 1882 1885 1886 1888 1889 1890 1891 1892 1893 1894 1896 1897 1902 1903 2080 2085 2086 2125 2127 2131 2138 2143 2147 2180 2186 2191 2197 2200 2201 2218 2221 2243 2255 2261 2279 2288 2289 2298 2318 2344 2352 2378 2400 2401 2404 2412 2423 2431 2466 2473 2475 2483 2484 2492 2494 2495 2501 2502 2508 2516 2523 2527 2541 2544 2554 2558 2587 2625 2626 2627 2652 2653 2674 2675 2691 2696 2704 2705 2712 2716 2718 2723 2736 2746 2774 2777 2805 2815 2816 2818 2865 L62 L145 L147 L162 L164 L241 L427 L585 L585/2 L591 L593 L596 L603 L604 L606 L608 L623 L740 L809 L840 L884 L921 L938 L1141 L1178 L1196 L1196/2 L1279 L1281 L1281/2 L1440 L1505 L2024 L2087 L2106
b δε μεν οσα 2242
cf μεν οσα δε 630 L422
d δε οσα δε 631
e δε οσοι μεν 1563
f μεν οσα μεν 93 102 181 309 326*V 665 1104 1875
gf μεν δε οσα δε μεν 2776
h δε οσα 254T 330 1762 2194
i δε μεν 489
j οσα μεν 1828T
k μεν οσα 1735 1827 2374 L1441
l ουν οσα 1836
↔ *a/d/h:* δε οσα [1106
↔ *a/b/d/e/h/i:* δε [2822
↔ *a/e/f/i/j:*] μεν 1704

οὐκ οἴδασιν βλασφημοῦσιν, ὅσα δὲ φυσικῶς ὡς τὰ ἄλογα
   10   12   14   16 18   20   22 24   26
ζῷα ἐπίστανται, ἐν τούτοις φθείρονται. **11** οὐαὶ αὐτοῖς,
   28   30   32   34   36   2   4

10
a ουκ ... 1828Z 1852V
b om. 131 1828T 2653
— 1106 1852 2822

11
a om. ...
bf ετολμησε κρισιν επενεγκειν βλασφημιας
     αλλα ειπεν επιτιμησαι σοι κυριος ουτοι
     δε οσα μεν ουκ 1104

14
a βλασφημουσιν ... P72(*f) 76f 757V 1852V
b βλασφημωσιν 2378
— 913 1106 2822

19
a om. ... 582C
bf ουκ οιδασιν 582*
— 1384 2822

20
a φυσικως ... 33f
b φυσικα 1505 1609 2495
c om. 1424 1838
↔ a/b: φυ[256
— 1384 2822

22
a ως ... 252f 1099Z
b εις L422
c om. 321 1099T
— 1106 1384 1852 2822

24
a τα ...
b om. 177 337 460 618 1738 1875 L164
— 1106 1384 1852 2822

26
a αλογα ... 1661f
b αλλα 522 L2087
— 913 1106 1384 1852 2822

28
a ζωα ... 256V 2473f

b om. 43 1736 1877 1890 1891
— 913 1106 1384 1852 2822

30
a επιστανται ... 38Z 1106V 2652f
b εστανται 38T
— 913 1384 2822

31
a om. ...
b και 1837
— 913 1106 1384 2822

32-36↓
a εν τουτοις φθειρονται
b om. 1751
— 1106 1384 2822

32↑
a εν ... 1704V
b om. 431 621 1390
↑ 1751
— 1106 1384 2822

34↑
a τουτοις ... 42f 256V 400V 1646Z 1649Z
     1704V 1765V 2516f 2653V
bf τοις 1646T 1649T
cf τοις τοις 996
↑ 1751
— 1106 1384 2822

36↑
a φθειρονται ... 018(*f) 1617(*f)
b φθειρεται 1762
c διαφθειρονται 044
d δε φθειρονται L623
↑ 1751
— 1106 1384 1852 2822

v. 11
— P78 025 0251 0316 69 613 614 712 720 832
    1831S 1867 1895 1899 2356 2511 2822 L6
    L156 L427/2 L585/2 L617 L1281/2 L1818

1

a om. P72 01 02 03 04 018 020 044 049 056
0142 1 3 5 6 18 33 35 38 42 43 51 57 61 62
76 81 82 88 90b 93 94 97 101 102 103 104
105 110 131 133 141 142 149 172 175 177
180 181 189 201 203 204 205 205abs 206S
209 216 218 221 223 226 234 241 242 250
252 254 256 263 296 302 307 308 309 312
314 319 321 322 323 325 326 327 328 330
337 363 367 378 383 385 386 390 393 394
398 400 404 421 424 425 429 431 432 436
440 442 444 450 451 452 453 454 456 457
458 459 460 462 465 466 467 468 469 479
483 489 491 496 517 522 547 582 592 601
602 603 604 605 606 607 608 610 615 616
617 618 619 620 621 622 623 625 627 628
629 630 631 633 634 635 636 637 638 639
641 642 656 664 665 676 680 699 757 796
801 808 823 824 876 901 910 912 913V 914
915 917 918 919 920 921 922 927 928 935
941 945 959 986 996 997 999 1003 1022
1040 1058 1066 1067 1069 1070 1072 1075
1094 1099 1100 1101 1102 1103 1104 1105
1107 1115 1127 1149 1161 1162 1175 1240
1241 1242 1243 1244 1245 1247 1248 1249
1250 1251 1270 1277 1292 1297 1311 1315
1319 1352 1354 1359 1360 1367 1384 1390
1398 1400 1404 1405 1409 1424 1425 1448
1482 1490 1495 1501 1503 1505 1508 1509
1521 1523 1524 1548 1563 1573 1594 1595
1597 1598 1599 1609 1610 1611 1617 1618
1619 1622 1626 1628 1636 1637 1642 1643
1646 1649 1652 1656 1661 1668 1673 1678
1702 1704 1717 1718 1719 1720 1721 1722
1723 1724 1725 1726 1727 1728 1729 1730
1731 1732 1733 1734 1735 1736 1737 1738
1739 1740 1741 1742 1743 1744 1745 1746
1747 1748 1749 1750 1752 1753 1754 1757
1760 1761 1762 1763 1765 1766 1767 1768
1769 1795 1799 1827T 1828 1829 1830
1831 1832 1834 1835 1836 1837 1838 1839
1840 1841 1842 1843 1844 1845 1846 1847
1849 1850 1851 1852 1853 1854 1855 1856
1857 1858 1859 1860 1861 1862 1863 1864
1865 1868 1869 1870 1871 1873 1874 1875
1876 1877 1880 1881 1882 1885 1886 1888
1889 1890 1891 1892 1893 1894 1896 1897
1902 1903 2080 2085 2086 2125 2127 2131
2138 2143 2147 2180 2186 2191 2194 2197
2200 2201 2218 2221 2242 2243 2255 2261
2279 2288 2289 2298 2318 2344 2352 2374
2378 2400 2401 2404 2412 2423 2431 2466
2473 2475 2483 2484 2492 2494 2495 2501
2502 2508 2516 2523 2527 2541 2544 2554
2558 2587 2625 2626 2627 2652 2653 2674
2675 2691 2696 2704 2705 2712 2716 2723
2736 2746 2774 2776 2777 2805 2815 2816
2818 2865 L1196/2

b και 631

c αδελφοι 90a 384 1751 L1440 L2024 L2087

d αγαπητοι 506 1780 1827Z 2718 L62 L145
L147 L162 L241 L422 L427 L585 L591 L593
L596 L603 L604 L606 L608 L623 L740 L809
L840 L884 L921 L938 L1141 L1178 L1196
L1279 L1281 L1441 L1505 L2106

e αγαπητε L164

f καθολικης επιστολης ιουδα αγαπητοι
ουαι τοις ασεβεσιν 632V

— P74 1106

2-4↓

a ουαι αυτοις ...

b ου εαυτοις 1762

— P74 1106

2↑

a ουαι ... 256V 913V 1106V 1852V 2558V

b ου και 633

↑ 1762

— P74 913 1106

4↑

a αυτοις P72(*f) 01 02 03 04 018 020 044 049
056 0142 1 3 5 6 18 33 35 38 42 43 51 57 61
62 76 81 82 88 90b 93 94 97 101 102 103
104 105 110 131 133 141 142 149 172 175
177 180 181 189 201 203 204 205 205abs
206S 209 216 218 221 223 226 234 241 242
250 252 254 256 263 296 302 307 308 309
312 314 319 321 322 323 325 326 327 328
330 337 363 367 378 383 385 386 390 393
394 398 400 404 421 424 425 429 431 432
436 440 442 444 450 451 452 453 454 456
457 458 459 460 462 465 466 467 468 469
479 483 489 491 496 506 517 522 547 582
592 601 602 603 604 605 606 607 608 610
615 616 617 618 619 620 621 622 623 625
627 628 629 630 631 632 633 634 635 636
637 638 639 641 642 656 664 665 676 680
699 757 796 801 808 823 824 876 901 910
912 913V 914 915 917 918f 919 920 921
922 927 928 935 941 945 959 986 996 997
999 1003 1022 1040 1058 1066 1067 1069
1070 1072 1075 1094 1099 1100 1101 1102
1103 1104 1105 1106V 1107 1115 1127
1149 1161 1162 1175 1240 1241 1242 1243
1244 1245 1247 1248 1249 1250 1251 1270
1277 1292 1297 1311 1315 1319 1352 1354
1359 1360 1367 1384 1390 1398 1400

ὅτι τῇ ὁδῷ τοῦ Κάϊν ἐπορεύθησαν καὶ τῇ πλάνῃ
6   8   10   12   14   16   18 20   22
τοῦ Βαλαὰμ μισθοῦ ἐξεχύθησαν καὶ τῇ ἀντιλογίᾳ
24   26   28   30   32 34   36

1404V 1405 1409 1424 1425 1448 1482
1490 1495 1501 1503 1505 1508 1509 1521
1523 1524 1548 1563 1573 1594 1595 1597
1598 1599 1609 1610 1611 1617 1618 1619
1622 1626 1628 1636 1637 1642 1643 1646
1649 1652 1656 1661 1668 1673 1678 1702
1704 1717 1718 1719 1720 1721 1722 1723
1724 1725 1726 1727 1728 1729 1730 1731
1732 1733 1734 1735 1736 1737 1738 1739
1740 1741 1742 1743 1744 1745 1746 1747
1748 1749 1750 1752 1753 1754 1757 1760
1761 1763 1765 1766 1767 1768 1769 1780
1795 1799 1827 1828 1829 1830 1831 1832
1834 1835 1836 1837 1838 1839 1840 1841
1842 1843 1845 1846 1847 1849 1850 1851
1852 1853 1854 1855 1856 1857 1858 1859
1860 1861 1862 1863 1864 1865 1868 1869
1870 1871 1872 1873 1874 1875 1876 1877
1880 1881 1882 1885 1886 1888 1889 1890
1891 1892 1893 1894 1896 1897 1902 1903
2080 2085 2086 2125 2127 2131 2138 2143
2147 2180 2186 2191 2194 2197 2200 2201
2218 2221 2242 2243 2255 2261 2279 2288
2289 2298 2344 2352 2374 2378 2400 2401
2404 2412 2423 2431 2466 2473 2475 2483
2484 2492 2494 2495 2501 2502 2508 2516
2523 2527 2541 2544 2554 2558 2587 2625
2626 2627 2652 2653 2674 2675 2691 2696
2704 2705 2712 2716 2723 2736 2746 2774
2776 2777 2805 2815 2816 2818 L1440
b   δε αυτοις 1844
c   τοις απιστοις 90a 384
d   τοις ασεβεσιν 1751 2318 2718 L62 L145
      L147 L162 L164 L241 L422 L427 L585 L591
      L596 L603 L604 L606 L608 L623 L740 L809
      L840 L884 L921 L938 L1141 L1178 L1196
      L1196/2 L1279 L1281 L1441 L1505 L2024
      L2087 L2106
ef τοις ασε ασεβεσιν αυτοις L593
↑   1762
—   P74

6
a   οτι ... 1070f
b   τι 1292 1799 2502

c   om. 1175 1405
—   P74

8-10
a   τη οδω ... 1106V 1241Cf 2653V L62f
bf του οδου 1241*
c   την οδον 631
d   εν τη οδω 1319
e   οδω L591
—   P74

12
a   του ... 256V 2279f
b   om. 2127
—   P74

16
a   επορευθησαν ... 90bf
b   επλανηθησαν 2508
—   P74 913 1106 1384 1852

18-30↓
a   και τη πλανη του βαλααμ μισθου
      εξεχυθησαν ... 915Z
b   om. 915T
—   P74

18↑
a   και ... 256V 308V 1704V L593f
b   om. 1896
↑   915
—   P74 913 1106 1852

20-32↑↓
a   τη πλανη του βαλααμ μισθου
      εξεχυθησαν και ... 88Z
b   om. 88T
↑   915
—   P74

20-22↑
a   τη πλανη ... 1642Z 1704V L603Z L884(*f)
b   την πλανην L164
c   οτι πλανη 2502V
d   πλανη 1104 1642T 2194 L603T
↔   a/d: πλα]νη 913
↑   88 915
—   P74

24↑
a του ... 254Z
b om. 254T 1523 1524 1844
↑ 88 915
— P74

26↑
a βαλααμ ... 38Z 256V 432C 619(*f) 927C
   1105(*f) 1875C L809V
ao βαλαμ 429 927* 1523 1719 1754 1875*
ao2 βαλλαμ P72*V
b βαλαακ P72C 432*
c βααλ 38T 378 615 914 1240 1595 1886
   L164 L884
↔ *a/b:* βαλα[1-2] 1852
↑ 88 915
— P74

27↑
a om. ...
b και 1795 1896
↑ 88 915
— P74 913

28↑
a μισθου ... 628(*f) 1424Z 1846Z
b μισθων 431(*f) 522 2242 2412 L145 L884
c om. 1424T 1751 1840 1846T
↔ *a/b:* μισθ[..] 1724
↔ *a/b:* μισ[...] 1106
↑ 88 915
— P74 913

30-42↑↓
a εξεχυθησαν και τη αντιλογια του κορε
   απωλοντο ... 04C2V
b εξεχυ[04*
↑ 88 915

34-36↑
a τη αντιλογια P72 01 02 03 018 020 044 049
   056 0142 1 3 5 6 18 33 35 38 42 43 51 57 61
   62 76 81 82 88 90a 90b 93 94 97 101 102
   103 104 105 110 131 133 141 142 172 175
   177 180 181 189 203 204 205 205abs 206S
   209 216 218 221 223 226 234 241 242 250
   252 254 256 263 296 302 307 308 309 312
   314 319 321 322Z 323 325 326 327 328 330
   337 363 367 378 383 384 385 386 390 393
   394 398 400 404 421 424 425 429 431 432
   436 440 442 444 450 451 452 453 454 456
   457 458 459 460 462 465 466 468 469 479
   483 489 491 496 506 517 522 547 582 592
   601 602 603 604 605 606 607 608 610 615
   616 617 618 619 620 621 622 623 625 627
   628 629 630 631 632 633 634 635f 636 637
   638 639 641 642 656 664 665 676 680 699
   757 796 801 808 823 824 876 901 910 912
   914 915 917 918 919 920 921 922 927 928
   935 941 945 959 986 996 997 1003 1022
   1040 1058 1066 1067 1069 1070 1072 1075
   1094 1099 1100 1101 1102 1103 1104 1105
   1106V 1107 1115 1127 1149 1161 1162
   1175 1240 1241 1242 1243 1244 1245 1247
   1248 1249 1250Z 1251 1270 1277 1292
   1297 1311 1315 1319 1352 1354 1359 1367
   1390 1398 1400 1404 1405 1409 1424 1425
   1448 1482 1490 1495 1501 1503 1505 1508
   1509 1521 1523 1524 1548 1563 1573 1594
   1595 1597 1598 1599 1609 1611 1617 1618
   1619 1622 1626 1628 1636 1637 1642 1643
   1646 1649 1652 1656 1661 1668 1673 1678
   1702 1704 1717 1718 1720 1721 1722 1723
   1724V 1725 1726 1727 1728 1729 1730
   1731 1732 1733 1734 1735 1736 1737 1738
   1739 1740 1742 1743 1744 1745 1746 1747
   1748 1749 1750 1751 1752 1753 1754 1757
   1760 1761 1762 1763 1765 1766 1767 1768
   1769 1780 1795 1799 1827 1828 1830 1831
   1832 1835 1836 1837 1838 1839 1840 1841
   1842 1843 1844 1845 1846 1847(*f) 1849
   1850 1851 1852 1853 1854 1855 1856 1858
   1859 1860 1861 1862 1863 1864 1865 1868
   1869 1870 1871 1872 1873 1875 1876 1877
   1880 1881 1882f 1885 1886 1888 1889 1890
   1891 1892 1893 1894 1896 1897 1902 1903
   2080 2085 2086 2125 2127 2131Z 2138
   2143 2147 2180 2186 2191 2194 2197 2200
   2201 2218 2221 2242 2243 2255 2261 2279
   2288 2289 2298 2318 2344 2352 2374
   2378Z 2400 2404 2412 2423 2431 2466
   2473 2475 2483 2484 2492 2494 2495 2501
   2502 2508 2516 2523 2527 2541 2544 2554
   2558 2587 2625 2626 2627 2652 2653 2674
   2675 2691 2696 2704 2705 2712 2716 2718f
   2723 2736 2746 2774 2776 2777 2805 2815
   2816 2818 L62 L145f L162 L241 L422 L427
   L585 L591 L593f L596 L603 L604 L606 L608
   L623(*f) L740 L809 L840 L884 L921 L938
   L1141 L1178 L1196 L1196/2 L1279 L1281
   L1440 L1441 L1505 L2024 L2106
b αντιλογια τη 999 2401
c τη απολογια 149 201 913V 1610 L2087
d τη αλογια 1829 2131T
e την αντιλογιαν L164
f εν τη αντιλογια 1384
g τη αντιλογια τη 1741
h αντιλογια 322T 467 1250T 1719 1834 1857
   1874 2378T L147

τοῦ Κόρε ἀπώλοντο. **12** οὗτοί εἰσιν οἱ ἐν ταῖς ἀγάπαις ὑμῶν

38	40	42	2	4	6 8	10	12	14

↔ a/b/c/d/e/f/g/h:]ọ[P74V
↑ 04

40↑
a κορε ... 1831*V 2674f
b κοσμου 1831C
↑ 04
— P74 1852

42↑
a απωλοντο ... P74V 1106V L427f
↑ 04
— 1852

v. 12
— P78 025 0251 0316 69 613 614 720 832
1831S 1867 1895 1899 2356 2511 2822 L6
L156 L427/2 L585/2 L617 L1281/2 L1818

2-34↓
a ουτοι εισιν οι εν ταις αγαπαις υμων
σπιλαδες συνευωχουμενοι αφοβως
εαυτους ποιμαινοντες νεφελαι ανυδροι
υπο ανεμων παραφερομεναι ... 2197ZV
b om. 2197T

2-4↑↓
a ουτοι εισιν ... 04C2
↑ 2197
— P74 04*

2↑
a ουτοι ... 1704V
b ου 496
↑ 04 2197
— P74 1831

5↑
a om. ... 01C2b
b γογγυσται μεμψιμοιροι κατα τας
επιθυμιας αυτων πορευομενοι 01C2a
1827
bf γογγυσται μεμψιμοιροι κα τας επιθυμιας
αυτων πορευομενοι 01*
c γογγυσται μεμψιμοιροι κατα τας ιδιας
επιθυμιας αυτων πορευομενοι 04C2V
1270 1297

6↑
a οι P72 01C2 02 03 020 044 5 6 33 35* 61 76
81 88 93 94 104 296 307 321 322 323 326
378 424Z 431 442 453 456 459 621 623 629
630 665 915 918 999 1127 1241 1243 1292
1448 1505 1611 1626 1678 1735 1739 1743
1837 1838 1840 1842 1845 1846 1852 1881
2138 2147 2186 2200 2242 2298 2344 2374
2401 2412 2473 2492 2495 2652 2746 2805
2818 L427 L585 L596 L1196/2 L1281 L1440
b om. 01* 018 049 056 0142 1 3 18 35C 38 42
43 51 57 62 82 90a 90b 97 101 102 103 105
110 131 133 141 142 149 172 175 177 180
181 189 201 203 204 205 205abs 206S 209
216 218 221 223 226 234 241 242 250 252
254 256 263 302 308 309 312 314 319 325
327 328 330 337 363 367 383 384 385 386
390 393 394 398 400 404 421 424T 425 429
432 436 440 444 450 451 452 454 457 458
460 462 465 466 467 468 469 479 483 489
491 496 506 517 522 547 582 592 601 602
603 604 605 606 607 608 610 615 616 617
618 619 620 622 625 627 628 631 632 633
634 635 636 637 638 639 641 642 656 664
676 680 699 757 796 801 808 823 824 876
901 910 912 914 917 919 920 921 922 927
928 935 941 945 959 986 996 997 1003
1022 1040 1058 1066 1067 1069 1070 1072
1075 1094 1099 1100 1101 1102 1103 1104
1105 1106V 1107 1115 1149 1161 1162
1175 1240 1242 1244 1245 1247 1248 1249
1250 1251 1270 1277 1297 1311 1315 1319
1352 1354 1359 1360 1367 1384 1390 1398
1400 1404V 1405 1409 1424 1425 1482
1490 1495 1501 1503 1508 1509 1521 1523
1524 1548 1563 1573 1594 1595 1597 1598
1599 1609 1610 1617 1618 1619 1622 1628
1636 1637 1642 1643 1646 1649 1652 1656
1661 1668 1673 1702 1704 1717 1718 1719
1720 1721 1722 1723 1724 1725 1726 1727
1728 1729 1730 1731 1732 1733 1734 1736
1737 1738 1740 1741 1742 1744 1745 1746
1747 1748 1749 1750 1751 1752 1753 1754
1757 1760 1761 1762 1763 1765 1766 1767
1768 1769 1780 1795 1799 1827 1828 1829
1830 1832 1834 1835 1836 1839 1841 1843
1844 1847 1849 1850 1851 1853 1854 1855
1856 1857 1858 1859 1860 1861 1862 1863

1864 1865 1868 1869 1870 1871 1872 1873
1874 1875 1876 1877 1880 1882 1885 1886
1888 1889 1890 1891 1892 1893 1894 1896
1897 1902 1903 2080 2085 2086 2125 2127
2131 2143 2180 2191 2194 2201 2218 2221
2243 2255 2261 2279 2288 2289 2318 2352
2378 2400 2404 2423 2431 2466 2475 2483
2484 2494 2501 2502 2508 2516 2523 2527
2541 2544 2554 2558 2587 2625 2626 2627
2653 2674 2675 2691 2696 2704 2705 2712
2716 2718 2723 2736 2774 2776 2777 2815
2816 2865 L62 L145 L147 L162 L164 L241
L422 L591 L593 L603 L604 L606 L608 L623
L740 L809 L840 L884 L921 L938 L1141
L1178 L1196 L1279 L1441 L1505 L2024
L2087 L2106
↑ 2197
— P74 04 913 1831

8↑

a εν ... 1106V 1404V
b om. L2106
↑ 2197
— 04 1831

10↑

a ταις ... P74V 378f 1523Z
b om. 1523T
↑ 2197
— 04 1831

12↑

a αγαπαις P72 01 03 018 020 044 049 056
0142 1 3 5 18 33 35 38 42 43 51 57 61 62 76
81 82 90a 90b 93 94 97 101 102 103 105
110 131 133 141 142 149 172 175 177C 180
181 189 201 203 204 205 205abs 206S 209
216 218 221 223 226 234 241 242 250 252
254 256 263 296 302 307 308 309 312 314
319 321 322 323 325 326 327 328 330 363
367 378 383 384 385 386 390 393 394 398
400 404 421 424T 425 429 431 432 436 440
442 444 450 451 452 453 454 456 457 458
462 465 466 467 468 469 479 483 489 491
496 506 517 522 547 582 592 601 602 603
604 605 606 607 608 610 615 616 617 619
620 621 622 623 625 627 628 629 630 631
632 633 634 635 636 637 638 639 641 642
656 664 665 676 680 699 712 757 796 801
808 823 824 876 901 910 912 913 914 917
918 919 920 921 922 927 928 935 941 945
959 986 996 997 999 1003 1022 1040 1058
1066 1067 1069 1070 1072 1075 1094 1099
1100 1101 1102 1103 1104 1105 1107 1115
1127 1149 1161 1162 1175 1240 1241 1242

1244 1245 1247 1248 1249 1250 1251 1270
1277 1292 1297 1311 1315 1319 1352 1354
1359 1360 1367 1384 1390 1398 1400 1404
1405 1409 1424 1448 1482 1490 1495 1501
1503 1505 1508 1509 1521 1523 1524 1548
1563 1573 1594 1595 1597 1598 1599 1609
1610 1611 1617 1618 1619 1622 1626 1628
1636 1637 1642 1643 1646 1649 1652 1656
1661 1668 1673 1678 1702 1704 1717 1718
1719 1720 1721 1722 1723 1724 1725 1726
1727 1728 1729 1730 1731 1732 1733 1734
1735 1736 1737 1739 1740 1741 1742 1743
1744 1745 1746 1747 1748 1749 1750 1751
1752 1753 1754 1757 1760 1761 1762 1763
1765 1766 1767 1768 1769 1780 1795 1799
1827 1828 1829 1830 1832 1834 1835 1836
1837 1838 1839 1840 1841 1843 1844 1847
1849 1850 1851 1853 1854 1855 1856 1857
1858 1859 1860 1861 1862 1863 1864 1865
1868 1869 1870 1871 1872 1873 1874 1875
1876 1877 1880 1881 1882 1885 1886 1888
1889 1890 1891 1892 1893 1894 1896 1897
1902 1903 2080 2085 2086 2125 2127 2131
2138 2143 2147 2180 2186 2191 2194 2200
2201 2218 2221 2242 2243 2255 2261 2279
2288 2289 2298 2318 2344 2352 2374 2378
2400 2401 2404 2412 2423 2431 2466 2473
2475 2483 2484 2494 2495 2501 2502 2508
2516 2523 2527 2541 2544 2554 2558 2587
2625 2626 2627 2652 2653 2674 2675 2691
2696 2704 2705 2712 2716 2718 2723 2736
2746 2774 2776 2777 2805 2815 2816 2818
2865 L62 L145 L147 L162 L164 L241 L422
L427 L585 L591 L593 L596 L603*/T L604
L606 L608 L623 L740 L809 L840 L884 L921
L938 L1141 L1178 L1196 L1196/2 L1279
L1281 L1440 L1441 L1505 L2024 L2087
L2106

b απαταις 02 04V 88 104 177*V 337 459 460
618 915 1243 1425 1738 1842 1845 1846
2492 L603C
cf αγαταις L603Z
d ευωχιαις 6 424Z
↑ 2197
— P74 1106 1831 1852

14↑

a υμων ... 02*V 400V 2815T
b ημων 330 451 517 615 1066 1243 1646
1762 1838 2147 2180 2675 2815Z L591
c υμιν 180
d αυτων 02C 105 582 1626
↔ a/b: [.]μων 308
↑ 2197
— P74 913 1831 1852

σπιλάδες, συνευωχούμενοι ἀφόβως, ἑαυτοὺς ποιμαίνοντες,
  16   18   20   22   24
νεφέλαι ἄνυδροι ὑπὸ ἀνέμων παραφερόμεναι,
   26   28   30   32   34

16↑

a   σπιλαδες ... P74V 049(*f) 43(*f) 400V 1704V 1831V 1852V 2527Z 2675(*f)

b   om. 2527T

↑   2197

—   913 1106 2378

17↑

a   om. ...

b   δε 180

↑   2197

—   P74 913 1106 2378

18↑

a   συνευωχουμενοι ... 489(*f) 680f 1846C 1875*V 2131C 2674C

b   συνευωχουμεναι 33V 177 180 203 337 460 506 607 618 1099 1424 1661 1724 1730 1736 1828 1841 1869 1889 1890V 2423 2508 2625

c   συνευχομενοι P72

df   συνευχουμενοι 1846* 2131* 2674* L884

ef   συνεβοχουμενοι 1646 2675C

ff   συνεβοσκομεν 2675*

g   ευωχουμενοι 1735 1799

h   συνερχομενοι 1875C

if   συνεχουμενοι L593

↑   2197

—   P74 913 1106 2378

19↑

a   om. P72 01 02 03 018 020 044 049 056 0142 1 3 5 18 33 35 38 43 57 61 62 76 81 82 90a 90b 94 97 101T 102 103 104 105 110 131 133 141 142 149 172 175 177 180 181 189 201 203 204 205 205abs 206S 209 216 218 221 226 241 242 250 254 256 263 296 307 308 309 312 314 319 321 326 327 328 330 337 363 367 378 383 384 385 386 393 394 398 400 404 421 424 429 431 432 436 440 442 444 450 451 452 453 454 456 457 458 459 460 462 465 466 468 469 479 483 489 491 496 506 522 547 582 592 601 602 603 604 605 606 607 608 610 615 616 617 618 619 620 621 622 623 625 627 629 630 631 633 634 635 636 637 638 639 641 642 656

664 676 680 699 712 757 796 801 808 823 824 876 901 910 914 917 918 919 920 921 927 928 941 945 959 986 997 999 1040 1058 1066 1067 1069 1070 1072 1075 1094 1099 1100 1101 1102 1103 1104 1105 1107 1115 1127 1149 1162 1175 1240 1242 1244 1248 1249 1250 1251 1277 1292 1311 1315 1319 1352 1354 1359 1360 1384 1390 1398 1400 1404 1409 1424 1425 1448 1482 1490 1495 1503 1505 1508 1509 1521 1523 1524 1548 1563 1573 1597 1598 1599 1610 1611 1617 1618 1619 1622 1626 1628 1636 1637 1642 1643T 1649 1652 1656 1668 1673 1678 1704 1717 1718 1719 1720 1721 1723 1724 1725 1726 1728 1729 1730 1731 1732 1733 1734 1735 1736 1737 1738 1740 1741 1742 1743 1744 1745 1746 1747 1748 1749 1750 1751 1752 1754 1760 1761 1762 1763 1765 1766 1767 1768 1769 1780 1795 1799 1827 1828T 1829 1830 1832 1834 1835 1836 1837 1838 1839 1840 1841 1842 1843 1844 1849 1850 1851 1853 1854 1855 1856 1857 1858 1859 1860 1862 1864 1865 1868 1869 1870 1871 1872 1873 1874 1875 1876 1877 1880 1882 1885 1886 1888 1889 1890 1891 1892T 1893 1894 1896 1897 1902 1903 2080 2086 2125 2127 2131 2138 2143 2147 2180 2186 2191 2194 2200 2201 2218 2221 2242 2243 2255 2261 2288 2289 2318 2344 2352 2374 2400 2401 2404 2412 2423 2431 2466 2473 2475 2483 2484 2494 2495 2501 2502 2508 2516 2523 2527 2541 2544 2554 2558 2587 2625 2626 2627 2652 2653 2691 2696 2704 2705 2712 2716 2723 2736 2746 2774 2776 2777 2805 2815 2816 2818 2865 L585 L596 L884 L1196 L1196/2 L1281 L1441 L2087

b   υμιν 04 6 42 51 88 93 101Z 223 234 252 302 322 323 325 390 425 467 517 628 632V 665 912 915 922 935 996 1003 1022 1161 1241 1243 1245 1247 1270 1297 1367 1405 1501 1594 1595 1609 1643Z 1646 1661 1702 1722 1727 1739 1753 1757 1828Z 1845 1846 1847 1861 1863 1881 1892Z 2085 2279 2298 2492 2674 2675 2718 L62 L145 L147 L162 L164 L241 L422 L427 L591

L593 L603 L604 L606 L608 L623 L740 L809
L840 L921 L938 L1141 L1178 L1279 L1440
L1505 L2024 L2106
↑ 2197
— P74 913 1106 1852 2378

20↑
a αφοβως ... 468V 489f
b αφοβους 1838
↔ *a/b:* αφο[468
↑ 2197
— P74 1106 1852 2378

22↑
a εαυτους ... P72C 631f 1106V 1636V 1739V
1769C
b εαυτοις 378 1828
c αυτους P72* 1769*
↔ *a/b:* εαυτο[.ς] 913
↑ 2197
— P74 1852 2378

24↑
a ποιμαινοντες ... 326(*f) 1067(*f) 1830(*f)
b επιμενοντες 1367
↑ 2197
— P74 913 2378

28↑
a ανυδροι ... 43f 917f
↑ 2197
— P74 1106 1852 2378

30-32↑
a υπο ανεμων ... 1748Z
b υπο νεμων 1748T
c υπο ανομων 43 917
d απο ανεμων 321
e παντι ανεμω 01 104 459 1842
↔ *a/c:* υπο [....]ων 1702
↔ *a/c:* υπο α[.....] 913
↔ *a/c:* υπο [......] 1384
↔ *a/d:* [...] ανεμων 1636
↔ *a/b/c/d:*]ων 1852
↑ 2197
— P74 1106 2378

34↑
a παραφερομεναι P72C 01 02 04 018 020 049
1 3 5 18 33 38 42 57 61 62 76 81 82 88 90a
90b 93 94 97 101 102 103 105 110 133 141
142 149 172 175 177 181 189 201 203 204
205 205abs 206S 209 216 218 221 223 226
234 241 242 250 252 254 256 263 302 307
308 309 312 314 319 321 322 323 325 326

327 328 330 337 363 367 378 383 384 385
386 390 393 394 398 404 421 424 425 429
431 432 436 440 444 450 451 452 453 454
456 457 458 460 462 465 466 467 468 479
483 491 496 506 517 522 547 582 592 601
602 603 604 605 606 607 608 610 615 616
617 618 619 620 622 623 625 627 628 629*
630 631 632 634 635 636 637 638 639 641
642 656 664 665 676 680 699 712 757 796
801 808 823 824 876 901 910 912 915 917
919 920 921 922 928 935 941 945 959 986
996 997 1003 1022 1040 1058 1067 1069
1070 1072 1075 1094 1099 1100 1101 1102
1103 1105f 1107 1115 1149 1161 1162 1175
1241 1242 1243 1244 1245 1247 1248 1249
1250 1251 1270 1277 1292 1297 1311 1315
1319 1352 1354 1359 1360 1367 1390 1398
1400 1404 1409 1424 1425 1448 1482 1490
1495 1503 1505 1508 1521 1523 1524 1548
1563 1573 1594 1595 1597 1598 1599 1609
1610 1611 1617 1618 1619 1622 1628 1636
1637 1643 1646 1649 1652 1656 1668 1673
1678 1702 1704 1717 1718 1719 1720 1721
1722 1723 1725 1726 1727 1728 1730 1731
1732 1733 1734 1735 1736 1737 1738 1739
1740 1741 1742 1743 1744 1745 1746 1747
1748 1749 1750 1751 1752 1753 1754 1757
1760 1761 1762 1763 1765 1766 1767 1768
1769 1780 1795 1799 1827 1828 1829 1830
1831 1832 1834 1835 1836 1837 1840 1841
1844 1847(*f) 1849 1850 1853 1854 1855
1856 1857 1858 1859 1860 1861 1862 1863
1864 1865 1870 1871 1872 1874 1876 1877
1880 1881 1885 1888 1889 1890 1891 1892
1893 1894 1896 1897 1903 2080 2085 2086
2125 2127 2131 2138 2143 2147 2180 2186
2191 2194 2200 2218 2221 2242f 2243 2255
2261 2279 2288 2289 2298 2344 2352 2374
2400 2404 2412 2423 2431 2466 2473
2475V 2483 2484 2492 2494 2495 2501
2502 2508 2516 2523 2541 2544 2554 2558
2587 2625 2626 2627 2652 2653 2675 2691
2696 2704 2712 2718 2723 2736 2746 2777
2805 2816 2818f 2865 L145 L147 L162 L585
L591 L593 L603 L604 L606 L608 L623 L740
L809 L840 L884 L921 L938 L1141 L1178
L1196 L1196/2 L1279 L1281 L1440 L1441
L1505 L2024 L2087 L2106
b παραφερομενοι P72* 03 044 43 131 442
469 621 633 999 1127 1845 1846 1851 1852
2401 2674 2716 2774 L164 L241 L596
c προφερομεναι 1509
d περιφερομεναι 6 35 51 180 629C 914 918
1104 1106 1240 1384 1501 1642 1661 1724
1839 1842T 1869 1882 1886 1902 2318

δένδρα φθινοπωρινὰ ἄκαρπα δὶς ἀποθανόντα
36   38   40   42   44
ἐκριζωθέντα, **13** κύματα ἄγρια θαλάσσης
46   2   4   6

2776 2815 L62 L422 L427
e περιφερομενοι 104 459 1842Z
f περιφαινομεναι 296
g διαφερομεναι 1875
h φερομεναι 056 0142 489 927 1405 1626
1729 1838 1843 1868 1873 2201 2527 2705
i φερομενοι 1066
↔ *a/b*: παραφερο[μεν..] 400
↑ 2197
— P74 913 2378

36
a δενδρα ... 680(*f)
— P74 913 1106 2378

38
a φθινοπωρινα ... 01C2 400V 421f 467f 913V
1245(*f) 1573f 1828f 1872(*f) 2516f L593f
b φθινοπωρικα 01* 1243 2473
cf φθινοπονηρα 1315 2127
df φθινοπωρα 1837
↔ *a/b*: φθιν[.......] 1702
↔ *a/b*: φ[.........]α 04
— P74 1106 2378

40
a ακαρπα ... 18(*f) 915f 1702V 1721*f
1721Cf
b om. 049 1840 2344
— P74 1106 2378

42-46
a δις αποθανοντα εκριζωθεντα P72 01 02
03 04 018 020 044 049 056 0142 1 3 5 6 18
33 35 38Zf 42 43*V 51 62 81 82 88 90a 90b
93 94 97 101 103 104 105 110 131 133 141
149 175 177 181 201 204 205 205abs 206S
209 218 221 223 226 234 241 242 250 252
254 256 302 308 309 312 314 319 322 323
325 326 327 328 330 337 363 383 384 385
386 390 393 394 398 404 421 424 425 429
431 432 436 442 444 450 451 452 454 456
457 458 459 460 462 465 466 468 479 483
491 517 522 547 592 601 602 603 604 605
606 607f 608 615 616 617 618 619 620 621

622 623 627 628 630 632C 633 634 635 637f
638 639 641 642 656 664 665 676 680 699
712 757 796 801 808 823 824 876 901 910
912 915 917 919 920 921 922 928 941 959
986 1003 1040 1058 1066 1067 1069 1070
1072 1075 1094 1099 1100 1101 1103 1105
1115 1127 1149 1161 1162 1175 1241 1242
1243 1244 1247 1248 1249 1250 1251 1270
1277 1292 1297 1311 1319 1352 1354 1359
1384 1390 1398 1400 1405 1409 1424 1425
1448 1482 1490 1495 1503 1505 1508 1521
1523 1524 1548 1563 1573 1594 1595 1598
1599 1610 1611 1617 1618 1619 1622 1626
1628 1636 1637 1643 1646 1649 1652 1656
1668 1673 1702 1704 1717 1718 1719 1720
1721 1723 1724 1725 1726 1727 1728 1730
1731 1732 1733 1734 1735 1736 1737 1739
1740 1741 1742 1744 1745 1746 1747 1748
1749 1750 1751 1752 1753 1754 1757
1760T 1761 1762 1763 1765 1766 1767
1768 1769 1780f 1795 1799 1827 1829 1830
1831 1832 1834 1835 1836 1837 1838 1841
1842 1845 1846 1847 1849 1850 1851 1852
1853 1854T 1855 1856 1857 1858 1859
1860 1861 1862 1863 1864 1865 1870 1871
1872 1874 1875 1876 1877 1880 1881 1882
1885 1888 1889 1890 1891 1892 1894 1896
1897 1902 2080 2085 2086 2125 2127 2131
2138 2143 2180 2191 2194(*f) 2200 2218
2221 2242 2255 2261 2279 2288 2298 2318
2344 2352 2374 2400 2401 2404 2423 2431
2466 2473 2475 2484 2494 2495 2502 2508
2516 2523 2527 2541 2544 2554 2558 2587
2625 2626 2627 2653 2674 2675 2691 2704
2712 2723 2736V 2777 2805 2816 2865
L241 L422 L427 L585 L591 L596 L884
L1178 L1196 L1196/2 L1281
b διο αποθανοντα εκριζωθεντα 38Tf 2705
c δις αποθανοντα εκριζωθησονται 1509
d διο αποθανοντα εκριζωθησονται 945
e δις αποθανοντα εκριζωντα L593
ff δις αποθανοντα εκ ριζωματα 1642
g δις αποθανοντα και εκριζωθεντα 57 61 76
142 172 180 189 203 216 296 307 321 367
378 440 453 467 469 489 496 506 625 629

631 632* 636(*f) 914 927 935 996V 997 999
1022 1102 1104 1107 1240 1245 1315 1360
1367 1404V 1501 1597 1609 1661 1678
1722 1729 1738 1743 1760Z 1828 1840
1843 1854Z 1868 1869 1873 1886 1893
1903 2147 2186 2197 2201 2243 2412 2483
2492 2501 2652 2696 2716 2718 2746 2774
2776 2815 L62 L145 L147 L162 L164 L603
L604 L606 L608 L623 L740 L809 L840 L921
L938 L1141 L1279 L1440 L1441 L1505C
L2024 L2087 L2106

hf δις αποθανοντες και εκριζωθεντα L1505*
i διο αποθανοντα και εκριζωθεντα 102
2818
j δις αποθανοντα ακαρπα εκριζωθεντα
1844
k δις αποθανοντα 263 918
l δις εκριζωθεντα 582
↔ *a/b:* δι[.] αποθανοντα εκριζωθεντα 610
↔ *a/b:* δ[..] αποθανοντα εκριζωθεντα 1839
↔ *a/c/e/g:* δις αποθανοντα [913
↔ *a/g:* δις [10-13] εκριζωθεντα 43C
↔ *a/c/e/g:* δις αποθα[400
↔ *a/c/e/g/j/k/l:* δις [2289
— P74 1106 2378

v. 13
— P74 P78 025 0251 0316 69 613 614 720 832
1831S 1867 1895 1899 2289 2356 2378
2511 2822 L6 L156 L427/2 L585/2 L617
L1281/2 L1818

2-8↓
a κυματα αγρια θαλασσης επαφριζοντα …
b om. 1762 L593

2-6↑
a κυματα αγρια θαλασσης P72(*f) 02 03 018
020 044 049 056 0142 1 3 5 6 18 33 35 38 42
43 51 57 61 62 76 81 82 88 90a 90b(*f) 93
94 97 101 102 103 104 105 110 131 133 141
142 149 172 175 177 180 181 189 201 203
204 205 205abs 206S 209 216 218 221 223
226 234 242 250 252 254 256 263 296 302
307 308V 309 312 314 319 321 322 323 325
326 327 328 330 337 367 383 384 385 386
390 393 394 398 400V 404 421 424 425 429
431 432 436 440 442 444 450 451 452 453
454 456 457 458 459 460 462 465 466 467
468 469 479 483 489 491 496 506 517 522
547 582 592 601 602 603 604 605 606 607
608 610 616 617 618 619 620 621 622 623
625 627 628 630 631 632 633 634 635 636
637 638 639 641 642 656 664 665 676 680

699 712 757 796 801 808 823 824 876 901
910 912 913 914 915 917 918 919 920 921
922 927 928 935 941 945 959 986 996 997
999 1003 1022 1040 1058 1066 1067 1069
1070 1072 1075 1094 1100 1101 1102 1103
1104 1105 1107 1115 1127 1149 1161 1162
1175(*f) 1240 1241 1242 1243 1244 1245
1247 1248 1249 1250 1270 1277 1292 1297
1311 1315 1319 1352 1359 1360 1367
1384V 1390 1398 1400 1404 1405 1409
1424 1425 1448 1482 1490 1495 1501 1503
1505 1508 1509 1521 1523 1524 1548 1563
1573 1594 1595 1597 1598 1599 1609 1610
1611 1617 1618 1619 1622 1626 1628 1636
1637 1642 1643 1646 1649 1652 1656 1661
1668 1673 1678 1702 1704 1717 1718 1719
1720 1721 1722 1723 1724 1725 1726 1727
1728 1729(*f) 1730 1731 1732 1733 1734
1735 1737 1738 1739 1740 1742 1743 1744
1745 1746 1747 1748 1749 1750 1751 1752
1753 1754 1757 1760 1761 1763 1765 1766
1767 1768 1769 1780 1795 1799 1827 1828
1830 1831f 1832 1834 1835 1836 1837 1838
1839 1840 1841 1842 1843 1844 1845 1846
1847 1849 1850 1851 1852 1853 1854 1855
1856 1857 1858 1859 1860 1861 1862 1863
1864 1865 1868 1869 1870 1871 1872 1873
1874 1875 1876 1877 1880 1881 1882 1885
1886 1888 1891 1892 1893 1894 1896 1897
1902 1903 2080 2085 2086 2125 2127 2131
2138 2143 2147 2180 2186 2191 2194 2197
2200 2201 2218 2221 2242 2243 2255 2261
2279 2288 2298 2318 2344 2352 2374 2400
2401 2404 2412 2423 2431 2466 2473 2475
2483 2484 2492 2494 2495 2501 2502f 2516
2523 2527 2541 2544 2554 2558 2587 2625
2626f 2627 2652 2653 2674 2675 2691f
2696 2704 2705 2712 2716 2718 2723 2736
2746 2774 2776 2777 2805 2815 2816 2818
2865 L62 L145 L147 L162 L164 L241 L422
L427 L585 L591 L596 L603 L604 L606 L608
L623 L740 L809 L840 L884 L921 L938
L1141 L1178 L1196 L1196/2 L1279 L1281
L1440 L1441 L1505 L2024 L2087 L2106
b αγρια κυματα θαλασσης 01
c κυματα θαλασσης αγρια 378 629 1741
1829
d κυματα αγια θαλασσης 04V
e κυματα αγρια 241 363 1099 1251 1354
1736 1889 1890 2508
f κυματα θαλασσης 615
↔ *a/e:* κυματα αγρια [1106
↑ 1762 L593

ἀπαφρίζοντα τὰς ἑαυτῶν αἰσχύνας, ἀστέρες πλανῆται οἷς
    8   10   12   14   16   18   20

ὁ ζόφος τοῦ σκότους εἰς αἰῶνα τετήρηται. **14** προεφήτευσεν
22   24   26   28   30   32   34   2

8↑

α απαφριζοντα P72 04 5 33 61* 81 93 254 322 323 326 431 442 621 623 630 665 945 1241 1243 1292 1359 1448 1505 1523 1524 1563 1611 1718 1735 1739 1837 1838Z 1844 1852 1881 2138 2200 2298 2344 2495 2805 L596

b επαφριζοντα 01 02 03 018 020 044 049 056 0142 1 3 6 18 35 38 42 43 51 57 61C 62 76 82 88 90a 90b 94 97 101 102 103 104 105 110 131 133 141 142 149 172 175 177 180 181 189 201 203 204 205 205abs 206S 209 216 218 221 223 226 234 241 242 250 252 256 263 296 302 307 308 309 312 314 319 321 325 327 328 330 337 363 367 378 383 384 385 386 390 393 394 398 400 404 421 424 425 429 432 436 440 444 450 451 452 453 454 456 457 458 459 460 462 465 466 467 468 469 479 483 489 491 496 506 517 522 547 582 592 601 602 603 604 605 606 607 610 615 616 617 618 619 620 622 625 627 628 629 631 632 633 634 635 636 637 638 639 641 642 656 664 676 680 699 712 757 796 801 808 823 824 876 901 910 912 914 915 917 918 919 920 921 922 927 928 935 941 959 986 996 997 999 1003 1022 1040 1058 1066 1067 1069 1070 1072 1075 1094 1099 1100 1101 1102 1103 1104 1105 1107 1115 1127 1149 1161 1162 1175 1240 1242 1244 1245 1247 1248 1249 1250 1251 1270 1277 1297 1311 1315 1319 1352 1354 1360 1367 1384 1390 1398 1400 1404 1405 1409 1424 1425 1482 1490 1495 1501 1503 1508 1509 1521 1548 1573 1594 1595 1597 1598 1599 1609 1610 1617 1618 1619 1622 1626 1628 1636 1637 1642 1643 1646 1649 1652 1656 1661 1668 1673 1678V 1702V 1704 1717 1719 1720 1721f 1722 1723 1724 1725 1726 1727 1728 1729 1730 1731 1732 1733 1734 1736 1737 1738 1740 1741 1742 1743 1744 1745 1746 1747 1748 1749 1750 1751 1752 1753 1754 1757 1760 1761 1763 1765 1766 1767 1768 1769 1780 1795 1799 1827 1828 1829 1830 1832 1834 1835 1836 1838T 1839 1840 1841 1842 1843 1845 1846 1847 1849 1850 1851 1853 1854 1855 1856 1857 1858 1859 1860 1861 1862 1863 1864 1865 1868 1869 1870 1871 1872 1873 1874 1875 1876 1877 1880 1882 1885 1886 1888 1889(*f) 1890 1891 1892 1893 1894 1896 1897 1902 1903 2080 2085 2086 2125 2127 2131 2143 2147 2180 2186 2191 2194 2197 2201 2218 2221 2242 2243 2255 2261 2279 2288 2318 2352 2374 2400 2401 2404 2412 2423 2431 2466 2473 2475 2483 2484 2492 2494 2501 2502 2508 2516 2523 2527 2541 2544 2554 2558 2587 2625 2626 2627 2652 2653 2674 2675 2691 2696 2704 2705 2712 2716 2718 2723 2736 2746 2774 2776 2777 2815 2816 2818 2865 L62 L145 L147 L162 L164 L241 L422f L427 L585 L591 L603 L604 L606 L608 L623 L740 L809 L840 L884 L921 L938 L1141 L1178 L1196 L1196/2 L1279 L1281 L1440 L1441 L1505 L2024 L2087 L2106

c και επαφριζοντα 608

↔ *a/b*: [.]παφριζοντα 1831

↔ *a/b*: [.]παφρι[ζοντα] 913

↑ 1762 L593

— 1106

10-14

a τας εαυτων αισχυνας ... 450V 913V 1668V 1702V 1831V 2288f 2558V 2675f

b τας αυτων αισχυνας 436 L241 L591 L1196/2

c ταις εαυτων αισχυναις 263

d τους εαυτων αυχενας 1501 1751f

e τους αυτων αυχενας L1178f

↔ *a/b/c*: τα[3-5]των αισ[400

— 1106

16

a αστερες ... 1731f 1882(*f) 2344(*f) 2674f 2816(*f)V L623(*f)V L2024V

— 1106

18

a πλανηται ...

b πλανητες 03

— 308 400 1106

20

a οις … 458f 1678V 1834V
− 913 1106

22-34↓

a ο ζοφος του σκοτους εις αιωνα
τετηρηται …
b ο ζοφος εις τον αιωνα τετηρηται του
σκοτους 1311

22-28↑

a ο ζοφος του σκοτους … 110V 218f 263(*f)
400V 1241f 1384V 1702V 1717V 1869f
2344(Cf) 2558V L2087*f L2087Cf
b ζοφος του σκοτους P72 1844
c ζοφος σκοτους 03
↔ a/b/c:]τους 913
↑ 1311
− 1106 1404

30-34↑

a εις αιωνα τετηρηται P72 01 02 03 04 020 1
5 18 33 35 38 42 43 51 61 76 81 88 93 97
101 102 104 105 141 149 175 177 181 201
203 204 205abs 209C 223 226 234 241 254f
256 296 307 309 321 322 323 326 328 337
363 367 378* 386 390 394 400V 404 421
429 431 432 436 444 450 453 456 457 459
460 462 465 466 467 468 469 483 489 506
522 547 582 603 604 618 619 620 621 622
623 625 630 632C 633 635C 642 665 676
757 801 808 824 901 910 912 915 917 918
921 922 927 928 945 986 996 1003 1040
1058 1067 1072 1075 1099 1100 1101 1102
1106 1107 1162 1175 1240 1243 1248 1249
1250 1251 1270 1292 1297 1319 1354 1359
1390 1400 1405 1409 1424 1425 1448 1482
1490 1503 1505 1508 1509 1523 1524 1548
1563 1573 1594 1595 1598 1611 1618 1619
1622 1628 1637 1643 1652 1656 1661
1668V 1678 1702 1704 1718 1723 1725
1726 1727 1728 1729 1731 1732 1733 1735
1736 1737 1738 1739 1740 1745 1748 1749
1751 1752 1753 1754 1760 1761 1763 1767
1768 1795 1799 1827 1831 1834V 1836
1839 1842 1843 1845 1846 1851 1852 1855
1856 1858 1860 1861 1863 1864 1865 1868
1873 1874 1875 1876 1877 1882 1885 1889
1890 1891 1892 1893 1894 1896 1897 1902
1903 2080 2085 2127 2131 2138 2147 2180
2186 2194 2197 2200 2201 2218 2221 2255
2279 2298 2344 2352 2374 2400V 2412
2431 2466 2495 2508 2527 2554 2587 2626
2652 2653 2674 2675 2704 2716 2723 2736

2776 2777 2805 2818 2865 L164 L596 L603
L608 L884 L1196 L1196/2 L1440 L2087
b τετηρηται εις αιωνα 629
c εις τον αιωνα τετηρηται 018 049 056 0142
3 6 57 62 82 90bf 94 103 110V 131 133 142
172 180 189 205 209* 216 218 221 250 263
302 308 312 314 319 325 327 330 383 385
393 398 424 440 451 452 454 479 491 496
517 592 602 605 606 607 608 610 615 616
617 627 631 632* 636 637 638 639 641 656
680 699 712 796 823 876 913V 914 919 920
935 941 997 999 1022 1066 1069 1070 1094
1103 1104f 1105 1115 1149 1244 1245 1277
1315 1352 1360 1384V 1398 1495 1501
1521 1597 1599 1609 1610 1617 1626 1642
1646f 1673 1717 1719 1720 1722 1724 1730
1734 1741 1742 1743 1744 1762 1765 1769
1780 1828 1829 1830 1832 1835 1840 1841
1849 1850 1853 1854 1857 1859 1862 1870
1871 1872 1880 1886 1888 2086 2125 2143
2191 2242 2288 2318 2401 2404 2423 2473
2475 2483 2484 2492 2494 2502 2516 2523
2558 2625 2627 2696 2705 2712 2718 2746
2774 2815 2816 L62 L145 L147 L162 L241
L585 L591 L593 L604 L606 L623 L740 L809
L840 L921 L938 L1141 L1178 L1279 L1281
L1441 L1505 L2024 L2106
d εις αιωνας τετηρηται 044 90a 206S 242
252 378C 384 425 442 458 601(*f) 628 634
635* 664 959 1127 1161 1241 1242 1247
1367 1636 1649 1721 1746 1747 1750 1757
1766 1837 1838 1844 1847 1869 1881 2243
2261 2501 2541 2544 2691f L422 L427
↔ a/c/d:] τετηρηται 1404
↑ 1311

v. 14

− P74 P78 025 0251 0316 69 613 614 720 832
1831S 1895 1899 2289 2356 2378 2511
2822 L6 L156 L427/2 L585/2 L617 L1281/2
L1818

2

a προεφητευσεν … 496f 631(*f) 1066(*f)
1717V 1867V 2404f 2558V 2675f L147(*f)
ao επροφητευσεν P72 03*
b προεφητευεν 1104 1903
c προεφυτευσεν 181 491 901 1751 1834
1838 2242 L1441
d προεφησεν 1311
↔ af/aof: επροεφητευσεν 03C2
↔ af/aof: προεπροφητευσεν 01
− 913

δὲ καὶ τούτοις ἕβδομος ἀπὸ Ἀδὰμ Ἑνὼχ λέγων·
4　6　　8　　　10　　12　　14　　16　　18
ἰδοὺ ἦλθεν κύριος ἐν ἁγίαις μυριάσιν αὐτοῦ
20　　22　　24　　26　　28　　　30　　　32

4-8

a　δε και τουτοις P72 01 03 04 018 020 044
049 056 0142 1 3 5 18 33 35 38 42 43f 51 57
61 62 76 81 82 88 90a 90b 93 94 97 101 102
103 104 105 131 133 141 142 149 172 175
177 180 181 189 201 203 204 205 205abs
206S 209 216 218 221 223 226 234 241 242
250 252 254 256 263 296 302 307 308 312
314 319 321 325 326 327 328 330 337 363
367 378 383 384 385 386 390 393 394 398
400 404 421 424* 425 429 431 432 436 440
442 444 450 451 452 453 454 456 457 458
459 460 462 465 466 467 468 469 479 483
489 491 496 506 517 522 547 582 592 601
602 603 604 605 606 607 610 615 616 617
618 619 620 621 622 623 625 627 628 629
630 631 632 633 634 635 636 637 638 639
641 642 656 664 665 676 680 699 7.12 757
796 801 808 823 824 876 901 910 912 914
915 917 918 919 920 921 922 927 928 935
941 945 959 986 996 997 999 1003Z 1022
1040 1058 1066 1067 1069 1070 1072 1075
1094 1099 1100 1101 1102 1103 1105 1106
1107 1115 1127 1149 1161 1162 1175 1240
1242 1243 1244 1245 1247 1248 1249 1250
1251 1270 1277 1292 1297 1311 1315 1319
1352 1354 1359 1360 1367 1384 1390 1398
1400 1404 1405 1409 1424 1425 1448 1482
1495 1501 1503 1505 1508 1509 1521 1523
1524 1548 1563 1573 1594 1595 1597
1598 1599 1609 1610 1611 1617 1618 1619
1622 1626 1628 1636 1637 1642 1643 1646
1649 1652 1656 1661 1668 1673 1678V
1702 1704 1718 1719 1720 1721 1722 1723
1724 1725 1726 1727 1728 1729 1730 1732
1733 1734 1735 1736 1737 1738 1740 1741
1742 1743 1745 1746 1747Z 1748 1749
1750 1751 1752 1753 1754 1757 1760 1761
1762 1763 1765 1766 1767 1768 1769 1780
1795 1827 1828 1829 1830 1832 1834 1835
1836 1837 1838 1839 1840 1841 1842 1843
1844 1845 1846 1847 1849 1850 1851 1852
1853 1854 1855 1856f 1857 1858 1859 1860
1861 1862 1863 1864 1865 1867 1868 1869
1870 1871V 1872 1873 1874 1875 1876

1877 1880 1882 1885 1886 1888 1889 1890
1891 1892 1894 1896 1897 1902 1903 2080
2085 2086 2125 2127 2131 2138 2143 2147
2180 2186 2191 2194 2197 2200 2201 2218
2221 2243 2255 2261 2279 2288 2318 2344
2352 2374 2400 2401 2404 2412 2423 2431
2466 2473 2475 2483 2484 2492 2494 2495
2502 2508 2516 2523 2527 2541 2544 2554
2558 2587 2625 2626 2627 2652 2653 2674
2675 2691 2696 2704 2705 2712 2716 2718
2723 2736 2746 2774 2776 2777 2805 2815
2818 2865 L62 L145 L147 L162 L164 L241
L422 L427 L585 L591 L593 L596 L603 L604
L606 L608 L623 L740 L809 L840 L884 L921
L938 L1141 L1178 L1196 L1196/2 L1279
L1281 L1440 L1441 L1505 L2024 L2087
L2106

b　δε και ουτος εν τουτοις 1104

c　δε τουτοις 6 322 323 424C 608 1003T 1241
1490 1717 1731 1739 1747T 1799 1881
1893 2242 2298 2816

d　και τουτοις 02 1744 2501

e　τουτοις 309 1831

↔　*a/b*: δε και [110

↔　*a/b/c/d/e*:] τουτοις 913

9

a　om. ...
b　και 1893
—　110

10

a　εβδομος ... 103f 206Sf 421f 496f 615f 917f
996f 1066f 1243f 1311f 1315f 1384V 1523f
1661f 1717V 1734f 1751f 1753f 1780f 1827f
1877f 1881f 1886f 2147f 2502f 2674f 2696f
L164f L591f L2087f

b　εβδομαδος 1846
c　ο εβδομος 631f
— 110

12

a　απο ...
b　om. 2180

14
a αδαμ ... 1106V
b του αδαμ 622 1728 1827

16-18
a ενωχ λεγων ... 90b(*f) 1505f L164(*f)
b λεγων ενωχ 2344

22-24
a ηλθεν κυριος P72 02 03 04 018 020 044
   049 056 0142 1 3 5 6 18 33 35 42 43 51 57
   62 76 81 82 88 90a 90b 93 94 97 101 102
   103 104 105 131 133 141 142 149 172 175
   180 189 201 203 204 205 205abs 206S 209
   216 218 221 223 226 234 241 242 250 252
   254 256 263 296 302 307 308 309 312 314
   319 321 322 323 325 327 328 330 363 367
   383 384 385 386 390 393 394 398 400V 421
   424T 425 429 431 432 440 442 444 450 451
   452 453 454 456 457 458 459 462 465 466
   467 468 469 479 483 489 491 496 506 517
   522 547 582 592 601 602 603 604 605 606
   608 610 615 616 617 619 620 621 622 623
   627 628 629 630 631 632 633 634 635 636
   637 638 639 641 642 656 664 665 676 680
   699 712 757 796 801 808 823 824 876 901
   910 912 913 914 915 917 918 919 920 921
   922 927 928 935 945 959 986 996 997 999
   1003 1022 1040 1058 1066 1069 1070 1072
   1075 1094 1099 1100 1101 1102 1103 1104
   1105 1106 1115 1127 1149 1161 1162 1175
   1240 1241 1242 1243 1244 1245 1247 1248
   1249 1250 1251 1270 1277 1292 1297 1315
   1352 1354 1359 1360 1367 1384 1398 1400
   1405 1424 1425 1448 1482 1490 1495 1501
   1503 1505 1508 1509 1521 1523 1524 1548
   1563 1573 1594 1595 1597 1598 1599 1609
   1610 1611 1617 1618 1619 1622 1626 1628
   1636 1637 1643 1646 1649 1652 1656 1661
   1668 1673 1678 1702 1704 1717 1718 1719
   1720 1721 1722 1723 1724 1725 1726 1727
   1728 1729 1730 1731 1732 1733 1734 1735
   1736 1737 1739 1740 1741 1742 1743 1744
   1745 1746 1747 1748 1749 1750 1752 1753
   1754 1757 1760 1761 1762 1763 1765 1766
   1767 1768 1780 1795 1799 1827 1828 1829
   1830 1831 1832 1835 1836 1837* 1838
   1839 1840 1841 1842 1843 1844 1845 1846
   1847 1849 1850 1851 1852 1853 1854 1855
   1856 1857 1858 1859 1860 1861 1862 1863
   1864 1865 1867 1868 1869 1870 1871 1872
   1873 1875 1876 1880 1881 1882 1885 1886
   1888 1889 1890 1891 1892 1893 1894 1896
   1897 1902 1903 2080 2085 2086 2125 2127
   2131 2138 2143 2147 2186 2191 2194 2197
   2200 2201 2218 2221 2242 2243 2255 2261
   2279 2288 2298 2318 2344 2352 2374 2400
   2401 2404 2412 2423 2431 2466 2473 2475
   2483 2484 2492 2494 2495 2501 2502 2508
   2516 2523 2527 2541 2544 2554 2558 2587
   2625 2626 2627 2652 2653 2674 2675 2691
   2696 2704 2705 2712 2716 2718 2723 2736
   2746 2774 2776 2777 2805 2815 2816 2818
   2865 L62 L145 L147 L162 L164 L241 L422
   L591 L593 L596 L603 L604 L606 L608 L623
   L740 L809 L840 L921 L938 L1141 L1178
   L1196 L1196/2 L1440 L1441 L1505 L2024
   L2087 L2106
b κυριος ηλθεν L427
c ηλθεν ο κυριος 01 38 61 177 181 326 337
   378 404 424Z 436 460 607 618 625 941
   1067 1107 1311 1319 1390 1409 1738 1751
   1769 1834 1837C 1874 1877 2180 L585
   L1279 L1281
d ηλθεν ο θεος L884
ef κυριος 1642
↔ a/c/d: ηλθεν [110
— 1404

26-32
a εν αγιαις μυριασιν αυτου 02 03 018 020
   049 056 0142 1 3 5 6 18 33 35 38*/T 38Z 42
   43 51f 57 62 76 81 82 90b 94 97 101 102
   103 105 133 141 142 149 172 175 177 180
   189 201 203 204 205 205abs 206S 209 216
   218f 221 223f 226 234 241 242 250 252f
   254 256 263 296 302 307 308V 309 312 314
   319 321 325 327 328 330f 337 363 367 383
   385 386 390 393 394 398 400 404 421 424
   425 429 431 432 436 440 444f 450 451f 452
   453 454 456 457 460 462 465 466 467 468
   469 479 483 489 491 496 506f 517 522 547
   582f 592 601 602 603 604 605 606 607 608
   610 615 617 618 619 620f 622 623 625 627
   628 629 632 633 635 636 637 638 639 641
   642 656 664 676 680 699 712 757 796 801
   808 823 824 876 901 910 912 914 917 918
   919 920 921 922 927 928 935 941 945 959
   986 996 997 999 1022 1040 1058 1066 1067
   1069 1070 1072 1075 1094 1099 1100 1101
   1102 1103 1104 1105 1106 1107 1115 1127
   1149 1161 1162 1175 1240 1242 1244 1245
   1247 1248 1249 1250 1251 1270 1277 1297
   1311 1315 1319 1352 1354 1359 1360 1367
   1384V 1390 1398fV 1400 1405 1409 1424
   1425 1482 1490 1495 1501 1503 1508 1509
   1521 1523 1524 1548 1563 1573 1594 1595
   1597 1598 1599 1609 1610 1617 1618 1619

15 ποιῆσαι κρίσιν κατὰ πάντων καὶ ἐλέγξαι

| | 2 | | 4 | | 6 | | 8 | | 10 | | 12 | |

1622 1626 1628 1636 1637 1642 1643 1646
1649fV 1652 1656 1661 1668 1673 1678
1702 1704 1717 1718 1719f 1720 1721 1722
1723 1724 1725 1726 1727 1728 1729 1730
1731 1732 1733 1734 1735 1736 1737 1738
1740 1741 1742 1743 1744 1745 1746 1747
1748 1749 1750 1751 1752 1753 1754 1757
1760 1761 1762 1763 1765 1766 1767 1768
1769 1780 1795 1799 1827 1829 1830 1831
1832 1834 1835 1839 1840 1841 1843 1844
1847 1849 1850 1851 1853 1854 1855 1856
1857f 1858 1859 1860 1861 1862 1863 1864
1865 1867 1868 1869 1870 1871 1872 1873
1874 1876 1877 1880 1882 1885 1886 1888
1889 1890 1891 1892 1893 1894 1896 1897
1902 1903 2080 2085 2086 2125 2127 2131
2143 2180 2186 2191 2194 2197 2201 2218
2221 2243 2255 2261 2279 2288 2344 2352
2374 2400 2401 2404 2423 2431 2466 2475
2483 2484 2492 2494 2501 2502 2508 2523
2527 2541 2554 2558 2587 2625 2626 2627
2653 2674 2675(*f) 2691 2696 2704 2705
2712 2716 2718 2723 2736 2746 2774 2776
2777 2805 2815 2816f 2818 2865 L62 L145
L147 L162 L164 L241 L427f L591 L593f
L603 L604 L606 L608 L623 L740 L809 L840
L884 L921 L938 L1141 L1196 L1196/2
L1279 L1281 L1440 L1441 L1505 L2024
L2087 L2106

b εν μυριασιν αγιαις αυτου 04 322 323 378f
630 631 634 1003 1241 1243 1292 1448f
1505 1611 1739 1828 1881 2138 2147 2200
2298 2318 2412 2473 2495 2652 L1178

c αγιαις εν μυριασιν αυτου 131

d εν αγιαις μυριασιν λεγων 616

e εν αγιαις μυριασιν αγγελων 044

f εν αγιων αγγελων μυριασιν P72

g εν μυριασιν αγιων αγγελων 01

h εν αγιαις μυριασιν αγγελων αυτου 61 93f
181 326 665f 1836 1837 2242 2544 L422
L585

i εν μυριασιν αγιων αγγελων αυτου 88 104
442 459 915 1838 1842 1845 1846 L596

j εν μυριασιν αγγελων αυτου αγιων 621

k εν μυριασιν αγγελων 38C 1852 2516f

l εν μυριασιν αυτου 458

m αγιαις μυριασιν αυτου 90af 384

↔ a/d/e/h/k: εν αγιαις μυριασιν [1875f

↔ a/d/e/h/k: εν αγιαις μυ[913
↔ a/c/h/i/l:]ασιν αυτου 110
— 1404

v. 15

— P74 P78 0251 0316 69 613 614 720 832
1831S 1895 2289 2356 2378 2511 2822 L6
L156 L427/2 L585/2 L617 L1281/2 L1818

1

a om. P72 01 02 03 04 018 020 044 049 056
0142 1 3 5 18 33 35 38 42 43 51 57 61 62 76
81 82 88 90a 90b 94 97 101 102 103 104
105 110 131 133 141 142 149 172 175 177
180 181 189 201 203 204 205 205abs 206S
209 216 218 221 223 226 234 241 242 250
252 254 256 263 296 302 307 308 309 314
319 321 325 326 327 328 330 337 363 367
378 383 384 385 386 390 393 394 398 400
404 421 424T 425 429 431 432 436 440 442
444 450 451 452 453 454 456 457 458 459
460 462 465 466 467 468 469 479 483 489
491 506 517 522 547 582 592 601 602 603
604 605 606 607 608 610 615 616 617 618
619 620 621 622 623 625 627 628 629* 630
632 633 634 635 637 638 639 641 642 656
664 676 680 699 712 757 796 801 808 823
824 876 901 910 912 913V 914 915 917 918
919 920 921 922 927 928 935 941 945 959
986 996 997 999 1003 1022 1040 1058 1066
1067 1069 1070 1072 1075 1094 1099 1100
1101 1102 1103 1104 1105 1106 1107 1115
1127 1149 1161 1162 1175 1240 1242 1243
1244 1245 1247 1248 1249 1250 1251 1270
1277 1292 1297 1311 1319 1352 1354 1359
1360 1367 1384 1390 1398 1400 1404V
1405 1409 1424 1425 1448 1482 1490 1495
1501 1503 1505 1508 1509 1521 1523 1524
1548 1563 1573 1594 1595 1597 1598 1599
1609 1610 1611 1617 1618 1619 1622 1626
1628 1636 1637 1642 1643 1646 1649 1652
1656 1661 1668 1673 1678 1704 1717 1718
1719 1720 1721 1722 1723 1724 1725 1726
1727 1728 1729 1730 1731 1732 1733 1734
1735 1736 1737 1738 1740 1741 1742 1743
1744 1745 1746 1747 1748 1749 1750 1751
1752 1753 1754 1757 1760 1761 1762 1763
1765 1766 1767 1768 1769 1780 1795 1799

1827 1828 1829 1830 1831 1832 1834 1835
1836 1837 1838 1839 1840 1841 1842 1843
1844 1845 1846 1847 1849 1850 1851 1852
1854 1855 1856 1857 1858 1859 1860 1861
1862 1863 1864 1865 1867 1868 1869 1870
1871 1872 1873 1874 1875 1876 1877 1880
1882 1885 1886 1888 1889 1890 1891 1892
1893 1894 1896 1897 1902 1903 2080 2085
2086 2125 2127 2131 2138 2143 2147 2180
2186 2191 2194 2197 2200 2201 2218 2221
2242 2243 2255 2261 2279 2288 2318 2344
2352 2374 2401 2404 2412 2423 2431 2466
2473 2475 2483 2484 2492 2494 2495 2501
2502 2508 2516 2523 2527 2541 2544 2554
2558 2587 2625 2626 2627 2652 2653 2674
2675 2691 2704 2705 2712 2716 2718 2723
2736 2746 2774 2776 2777 2805 2815 2816
2818 2865 L62 L145 L147 L162 L241 L422
L427 L585 L591 L593 L596 L603 L604 L606
L608 L623 L740 L809 L840 L884 L921 L938
L1141 L1178 L1196 L1196/2 L1279 L1281
L1440 L1441 L1505 L2024 L2087 L2106
b   του 6 93 312 322 323 424Z 496 629CV 631
636 665 1241 1315 1702V 1739 1853 1881
2298 2400 2696 L164
—   025 1899

2-4
a   ποιησαι κρισιν ... 056f 400V 941(*f) 1106V
1717V 2255f
b   om. 1875f
—   025 1899

6-16↓
a   κατα παντων και ελεγξαι πασαν ψυχην ...
b   om. 056 1359 1425
—   025 1106 1899

6-8↑
a   κατα παντων ... 326V 2086*
b   περι παντων 0142 1066 1563 1718
c   μετα παντων 81
d   κατα παντα 496 631 636 1127 1315 2696
L422
e   κατα παντων των εργων 1107 2086C
↔   a/b/c/d/e: [....] πα[400
↑   056 1359 1425
—   025 1106 1384 1899

9↑
a   om. ...
b   αυτου 1837
—   025 1106 1384 1899

10-20↑↓
a   και ελεγξαι πασαν ψυχην περι παντων ...
b   om. 0142 1066 1563 1718
↑   056 1359 1425
—   025 1106 1899

10-16↑↓
a   και ελεγξαι πασαν ψυχην ...
b   om. 2627
↑   056 0142 1066 1359 1425 1563 1718
—   025 1106 1899

10↑
a   και ... 110V 1058V 1828Z
b   om. 314 1828T
↑   056 0142 1066 1359 1425 1563 1718 2627
—   025 1106 1899

12↑
a   ελεγξαι P72 01 02 03 04 018 020 044 049 5
6 18 33 35 38 42 51 57 61 62 76 81 82 88
90af 93 94 97 102 103 104 105 110V 133
141 142 149 175 177 180 181 189 201 204
206S 216 218 221 223 226 234 241 242 250
252 254 256 263 302 307 309 312 314 319
321 322 323 325 326V 327 328 337 363 367
378f 383 384 385 386 390 393 394 404 421
424 425 429 431 432 440 442 444 450 452
453 454 456 457 458 459 460 462 465 467
468 469 479 483 489 491 496 517 522 547
582 592 601 602 603 604 605 606 607 608
610 616 617 618 619 621 622 623 627 628
629 630 631 632 633 635 636 637 638 639
641 642 656 664 665 676 680 699 712 757
801 808 823 824 876 901 910 912 915 917
918 919 920 921 922 927 928 935 941 945
959 986 996 997 999 1022 1040 1069 1070
1072 1075 1094 1099 1100 1101 1102 1103
1105 1115 1127 1149 1161 1162 1175f 1241
1242 1243 1244 1245 1247 1248 1249 1250
1251 1270 1277 1292 1297 1311 1315C
1319 1352 1354 1360 1367 1384 1398 1400
1404 1405 1424 1448 1482 1490 1495 1501
1503 1505 1508 1509 1521 1523 1524 1548
1573 1594 1595 1597 1598 1599 1609 1610
1611 1617 1618 1619 1622 1626 1628 1636
1637 1643 1646f 1649 1652 1656 1661 1668
1673 1678 1702 1704 1717 1719 1720 1721
1722 1723 1724 1725 1726 1727 1728 1729
1730 1732 1733 1734 1735 1736 1737 1738
1739 1740 1741 1742 1743 1744 1745 1746
1747 1748 1749 1750 1751 1752 1753 1754
1757 1760 1761 1762 1763 1765 1766 1767f
1768 1769 1795 1799 1827 1829 1830 1831
1832 1834f 1835 1836 1837 1838 1839 1840

πάντας τοὺς ἀσεβεῖς περὶ πάντων τῶν ἔργων
14 16 18 20 22 24 26
ἀσεβείας αὐτῶν ὧν ἠσέβησαν καὶ
28 30 32 34 36

1841 1842 1843 1844 1845 1846 1847 1849
1850 1852 1853 1854 1855 1856 1857 1858
1859 1860 1861 1862 1863 1864 1865 1867
1868 1870 1871 1872 1873 1874 1875 1876
1877 1880 1881 1888 1889 1890 1891 1892
1893 1894 1896 1897 1902 2080 2085 2086
2127 2131 2138 2143 2147 2186 2194 2197
2200 2201 2218 2221 2242 2243 2255 2261
2279 2288 2298 2344 2352 2374 2401 2404
2412 2423 2431 2466 2475 2483 2484 2492
2494 2495 2501 2508 2516 2523 2527 2541
2544 2554 2558 2587 2625 2626 2652 2653
2674f 2675 2691 2696 2704 2705 2712 2716
2718 2723 2746 2774 2777 2805 2815 2816
2818 2865 L62 L145 L147 L162 L164 L241
L427 L585 L591 L593 L596 L603 L604 L606
L608 L623 L740 L809 L840 L921 L938
L1141 L1178 L1196 L1196/2 L1279 L1281
L1440 L1441 L1505 L2024 L2087 L2106
b εξελεγξαι 1 3 43 90b 101 131 172 203 205
205abs 209 296 308 330 398 436 451 466
506 615 620 625 634 796 914f 1003 1058V
1067 1104 1107 1240f 1390 1409 1642 1731
1780 1828(*f) 1851 1869 1882 1885 1886
1903 2125 2180 2191 2318 2400 2473 2502
2736 2776 L422 L884
cf εκλεξαι 1315*V
↔ a/b:]ξαι 400
↑ 056 0142 1066 1359 1425 1563 1718 2627
— 025 913 1106 1899

14-18↑
a παντας τους ασεβεις 02 03 04 044 5 33 61
81 93 94 101 142 216T 307 321 326 330 378
431 436 440 451 453 468 496 623 629 630
631 642 665 676 808 918 935 999 1067
1127 1243 1292 1315 1367 1404 1409 1448
1501 1505 1611 1678 1722 1735 1751
1828C 1837 1838V 1840 1845 1846 1902
2086 2138 2147 2186 2191C 2197 2200
2344 2374 2401 2412 2483 2495 2502 2544
2652 2696 2718 2774 2805 2818 L62 L145
L147 L162 L603 L604 L606 L623 L740 L809
L840 L921 L938 L1141 L1279 L2024 L2106
b παντας τους ασεβεις αυτων 018 020 049 1

3 18 35 38 42 43 51 57 62 76 82 88 90a 90b
97 102 103 104 105 110 131f 133 141 149
172 175 177 180 181 189 201 203 204 205
205abs 206S 209 216Z 218 221 223 226 234
241 242 250 252 254 256 263 296 302 308
309 312 314 319 325 327 328 337 363 367
383 384 385 386 390 393 394 398 400 404
421 424* 425 429 432 444 450 452 454 456
457 458 459 460 462 465 466 467 469 479
483 489 491 506 517 522 547 582 592 601
602 603 604 605 606 607 608 610 615 616f
617 618 619 620 622 625 627 628 632 633
634 635 636 637 638 639 641 656 664 680
699 712 757 796 801 823 824 876 901 910
912 913V 914 915 917 919 920 921 922 927
928 941 945 959 986 996 997 1003 1022
1040 1058 1069 1070 1072 1075 1094 1099
1100 1101 1102 1103 1104 1105 1107 1115
1149 1161 1162 1175 1240 1242 1244 1245
1247 1248 1249 1250 1251 1270 1277 1297
1311 1319 1352 1354 1360 1390 1398 1400
1405 1424 1482 1490 1495 1503 1508 1509
1521 1523 1524 1548 1573 1594 1595f 1597
1598 1599 1609 1610 1617 1618 1619 1622
1626 1628 1636 1637 1642 1643 1646C
1649 1652 1656 1661 1668 1673 1704 1717
1719 1720 1721 1723 1724 1725 1726 1727
1728 1729 1730 1731 1732 1733 1734 1736
1737 1738 1740 1741 1742 1743 1744 1745
1746 1747 1748 1749 1750 1752 1753 1754
1757 1760 1761 1762 1763 1765 1766 1767
1768 1769 1780 1795 1799 1827 1828*
1829 1830 1831 1832 1834 1835 1836 1839
1841 1842 1843 1844 1847 1849 1850 1851
1853 1854 1855 1856 1857 1858 1859 1860
1861 1862 1863 1864 1865 1867 1868 1869
1870 1871 1872 1873 1874 1875f 1876 1877
1880 1882 1885 1886 1888 1889 1890 1891
1892 1893 1894 1896 1897 1903 2080 2085
2125 2131 2143 2180 2194 2201 2218 2221
2242 2243 2255 2261 2279 2288 2318 2352
2400 2404 2423 2431 2466 2473 2475 2484
2492 2494 2501 2508 2516 2523 2527 2541
2554 2558 2587 2625 2626 2653 2674f 2675
2691 2704 2705 2712 2716 2723 2736 2746

2776 2777 2815 2816 2865 L164 L241 L422
L585 L591 L593 L884 L1178 L1196 L1196/2
L1281 L1440 L1441 L2087
c πάντας τους ασεβείς εαυτών 1702V
df πάντων τους ασεβείς αυτών 1646*
e πάντας ασεβείς 6 322 323 424C 1241 1739
1881 2298 L427 L608 L1505
f τους ασεβείς αυτών 2127
g τους ασεβείς 442 621 L596
h πασαν ψυχην P72 01 1852
↔ b/c: πάντας τους [10-13] 2191*
↑ 056 0142 1066 1359 1425 1563 1718 2627
— 025 1106 1384 1899

19↑
a om. ...
b και 383
↑ 0142 1066 1563 1718
— 025 1106 1384 1899

20-36↑↓
a περι παντων των εργων ασεβειας αυτων
ων ησεβησαν και ...
b om. P72 L591
↑ 0142 1066 1563 1718
— 1106 1384

20-34↑↓
a περι παντων των εργων ασεβειας αυτων
ων ησεβησαν ...
bf αυτων ων ησεβησαν περι παντων των
εργων αυτων 1838V
c ων ησεβησαν και περι παντων των
εργων ασεβειας αυτων ων ηθετησαν
393Z
d ων ησεβησαν 393T
↑ P72 0142 1066 1563 1718 L591
— 1106 1384

20-30↑
a περι παντων των εργων ασεβειας αυτων
02 03 018 020 049 0142 1 3 5 18 33 35 38 42
43 51 57 76 81 82(*f) 88 90a 90b 93 97 101
102 103 104 105 110 131 133T 141 142 149
172 175 177 180 181 189 201 203 204 205
205abs 206S 209 216 218 221 223 226 234
241 242 250 252 254 256 296 302 308V 309
312 314 319 325 327 328 330 337 363 367
383 384 385 386 390 394 398 400 404 421
424* 425 429 431 432 436 440 444 450 451
452 454 456 457 458 459 460 462 465 466
467 468 469 479 483 489 491 496 506 517
522 547 592 601 602 603 604 605 606 607
608 610 615 616 617 618 619 620 622 623

625 627 628 632 633 634 635 636 637 638
639 641 642 656 664 665 676 680 699 712
757 796 801 808 823 824 901 910 912 914
915 917 919 920 921 922 927 928 935 941
945 959 986 996 997 999 1003 1022 1040
1058 1067 1069 1070 1072 1075 1094 1099
1100V 1101 1102 1103 1104 1105 1107
1127 1149 1161 1175 1240 1244 1245 1247
1248 1249 1250 1251 1270 1277 1297 1315
1319 1352 1354 1359f 1390 1398 1400 1404
1405 1409 1424 1448 1482 1490 1495 1501
1503 1508 1509 1521 1523 1524 1548 1563
1573 1594 1595 1597 1598 1599 1609 1610
1617 1618 1619 1622 1626 1628 1636 1637
1642 1643 1646 1649 1652 1656 1661 1668
1673 1702 1704 1717 1718 1719 1720 1721
1722 1723 1724 1725 1726 1727 1728 1730
1731 1732 1733 1734 1735 1736 1737 1738
1740 1741 1742 1743 1744 1745 1746 1747
1748 1749 1750 1752 1753 1754 1757 1760
1761 1762 1763 1766 1767 1768 1769 1780
1795 1799 1827 1828 1829 1830 1831 1835
1836 1839 1841 1842 1843 1844 1847 1849
1851 1853 1854 1855 1856 1857 1858 1859
1860 1861 1862 1863 1864 1865 1867 1868
1869 1870 1871 1872 1873 1875 1876 1880
1882 1885 1886 1889 1890 1891 1892Z
1894 1896 1897 1902 1903 2080 2085 2125
2127 2131 2143 2180 2194 2201 2218 2221
2242 2255 2261 2279 2288 2318 2344 2352
2400 2401 2404 2423 2431 2466 2473
2475V 2483 2492 2501 2508 2516 2523
2527 2541 2544 2554 2558 2587 2625 2626
2627 2653 2675 2691 2696 2704 2712 2716
2718 2723 2736 2746 2774V 2776 2777
2815C 2816 2865 L62 L145 L147 L162 L164
L241 L422 L427 L585 L593 L603 L604 L606
L608 L623 L740 L809 L840 L884 L921 L938
L1141 L1178 L1196 L1196/2 L1279 L1281
L1440 L1441 L1505 L2024 L2087 L2106
b περι παντων των εργων αυτων ασεβειας
582 1751
c περι παντων των εργων της ασεβειας
αυτων 62 133Z 1162 1729 1834 1850 1874
1877 2502 2674 2815*
d περιπατουντων των εργων της ασεβειας
αυτων 2086Z
e περι παντων εργων ασεβειας αυτων 61
326 1242C 1425f 1837 1893 2191C
f περι παντων των εργων ασεβειας 1367
1892T 2705
g περι παντων εργων ασεβειας 1242*V
h περι παντων εργων των ασεβειων αυτων
629 2186

περὶ πάντων τῶν σκληρῶν ὧν

38	40	42	44	46

i περι παντων των εργων των ασεβειων αυτων 044Z 630 1292 1505 1611 1765 1832 1840 2138 2147 2200 2243 2412 2494 2495 2652

j περι παντων των εργων των ασεβων αυτων 378

k περι παντων εργων ασεβειων αυτων 1852

l περι παντων των εργων αυτων 04 94 307 321 442 453 621 631C 918 1243 1678 1838 1845 1846 2197 2484 2818 L596

m περι παντων των εργων αυτου 631*

n περι παντων των ασεβειων αυτων 044T 876

o περι παντων των εργων 01 6 322 323 424C 1241 1739 1881 2298 2374 2805

p αυτων 2086T

q om. 263 1115 1311 1360 1888 2191*V

↔ a/c/e/h/i/j/k: περι παντων [>12 αυ]των 913

↔ a/c/d/e:]βειας αυτων 1899

↑ P72 393 1838 L591

— 025 1106 1384

32-44↑↓

a ων ησεβησαν και περι παντων των σκληρων ...

b om. 1721

↑ P72 393 1838 L591

— 025 1384

32-34↑

a ων ησεβησαν 01 02 03 04 018 020 025V 044 049 056 0142 1 3 5 6 18 33 35 38 42 43 51 57 61 62 76 81 82 88 90a 90b 93 94f 102 103 104 105 101 110 131 133 141 142 149 175 177 180 181 189 201 203 204 205 205abs 206Sf 209 216 221 223 226 234 241 242 250 252 254 256 263 296 302 307 308 309 312 314 319 321 322 323 325 326 327 328 330 337 363 367 378 383 384 385 386 390 394 398 400 404 424 425 429 431 432 436 440 442 444 450 451 453 454 456 457 458 459 460 462 465 466 467 468 469 479 483 489 491 496 506 517 522 547 582 592 601 602 603 604 605 606 607 610 615 616 617 618 619 620 621 622 623 627 628 629 630 631 632 633 634 635 636 637 638 639 641 642 656 664 665 676 680 699 712 757

796 801 808 823 824 876 901 910 912 913 914 915 917 918 919 921 922 927 928 935 945 959 986 996 997 999 1003 1022 1040 1058 1066 1067 1069 1070 1072 1075 1094 1099 1100 1101 1102 1104 1105 1115 1127 1161 1162 1175 1240 1241 1242 1243 1245 1247 1248 1249 1250 1251 1270 1292 1297 1311 1315 1319 1354 1359 1360(*f) 1367 1390 1398 1400 1404 1405 1409 1424 1425 1448 1482 1490 1495 1501 1503 1505 1508 1509 1523 1524 1548 1563 1573 1594 1595 1597 1598 1599 1609 1610 1611 1617 1618 1619 1626 1628 1636 1637 1642 1643 1646 1649 1652 1656 1661 1668 1673 1678 1702 1704 1717 1718 1720 1722 1723 1725 1726 1727 1728 1729 1730 1731 1732 1733 1734 1735 1736 1737 1738 1739 1740 1741 1742 1743 1745 1746 1747 1748 1749 1750 1751 1752 1753 1754 1757 1760 1761 1762 1763 1765 1766 1767 1768 1769 1780 1795 1799 1827 1829 1830 1831 1832 1834 1835 1836 1837 1839 1840 1841 1842 1843 1844 1845 1846 1847 1849 1850 1851 1852 1853 1854 1855 1856 1858 1861 1862 1863 1864 1865 1867 1868 1869 1870 1873 1874 1875 1876 1877 1880 1881 1882 1885 1886 1888 1889 1890 1891 1892 1893 1894 1896 1897 1899 1902 1903 2080 2085 2086 2125 2127 2131 2138 2143 2147 2180 2186 2191 2194 2197 2200 2201 2218 2221 2242 2243 2255 2261 2279 2298 2318 2344 2352 2374 2400 2404 2412 2423V 2431 2466 2473 2483 2484 2492 2494 2495 2501 2502 2508 2516 2523 2527 2541V 2544 2554 2558 2587 2625 2626 2627 2652 2653 2674 2675 2691f 2696 2704 2705 2712 2716 2718 2723 2736 2746 2776 2777 2805 2815 2816 2818 2865 L62 L145 L147 L162 L164 L241 L422 L427 L585 L593 L596 L603 L604 L606 L608 L623(*f) L740 L809 L840 L938 L1141 L1178 L1196 L1196/2 L1279 L1281 L1440 L1441 L1505 L2024 L2087 L2106

b ων ηθετησαν 97 218 421 452 608 920 941 1103 1149 1244 1277 1352 1521 1622 1719 1724 1744 1828 1857 1859 1860 1871 1872 2288 2475V

c ων εποιησαν και ησεβησαν 172 625 1107

d om. L884 L921

↔ af/bf: ων [.....]σαν σαν 2401*

↔ *a/b:* ων [........]ν 2774
↑ P72 393 1721 1838 L591
— 1106 1384

36↑
a και ... 308V
b om. L884
↑ P72 1721 L591
— 308 1106 1384

38↑
a περι ... 308V
b om. 383 656 1880
↑ 1721
— 308 913 1384 1404

40↑
a παντων ... 1646(*f)
↑ 1721
— 913 1384 1404

42↑
a των ... P72Z
b om. P72T 664 680 2691
↑ 1721
— 913 1384 1404

44↑
a σκληρων ... 38(*f) 404(*f) 757(*f) 876(*f)
   913V 1834f 2186f 2242(*f) 2423V L1141C
b κηρων L1141*V
c ληρων 1827
d εργων των σκληρων 616 L884
↑ 1721
— 1384 1404

45↑
a om. P72 02 03 018 020 025 044 049 056
   0142 1 3 5 18 35 38 42 43 51 57 61 62 82
   90a 90b 97 101 103 105 110 131 133 141
   142 149 172 175 177 180 181 201 203 204
   205 205abs 206S 209 216 218 221 223 226
   234 241 242 250 252 254 256 263 296 302
   308 309 312 314 319 325 326 327 328 330
   337 363 367 383 384 385 386 390 393 394
   398 400 404 421 424 425 429 431 432 436
   440 444 450 451 452 454 456 457 458 460
   462 465 466 467 468 469 479 483 489 491
   496 506 517 522 547 582 592 601 602 603
   604 605 606 607 608 610 615 616 617 618
   619 620 622 623 625 627 628T 631 632 633
   634 635 636 637 638 639 641 642 656 664
   676 680 699 712 757 796 801 808 823 824
   901 910 912 913 914 917 919 920 921 922
   927 928 935 941 945 959 986 996 997 1003

   1022 1040 1058 1066 1067 1069 1070 1072
   1075 1094 1099 1100 1101 1103 1104 1105
   1107 1115 1127 1149 1161 1162 1175 1240
   1242 1244 1245 1247 1248 1249 1250 1251
   1277 1311 1315 1319 1352 1354 1359 1360
   1390 1398 1400 1405 1409 1424 1425 1482
   1490 1495 1503 1508 1509 1521 1523 1524
   1548 1563 1573 1594 1599 1609 1610 1617
   1618 1619 1622 1626 1628 1636 1637 1642
   1643 1646 1649 1652 1656 1661 1668 1673
   1678 1702 1704 1717 1718 1719 1720 1722
   1723 1724 1725 1726 1727 1728 1729 1730
   1731 1732 1733 1734 1735 1736 1737 1738
   1740 1741 1742 1744 1745 1746 1747 1748
   1749 1750 1751 1752 1753 1754 1757 1760
   1761 1762 1763 1766 1767 1768 1769 1780
   1795 1799 1827 1828 1829 1830 1831 1834
   1835 1836 1837 1839 1841 1843 1844 1847
   1849 1850 1851 1853 1854 1855 1856 1857
   1858 1859 1860 1861 1862 1863 1864 1865
   1867 1868 1869 1870 1871 1872 1873 1874
   1875 1876 1877 1880 1882 1885 1886 1888
   1889 1890 1891 1892 1893 1894 1896 1897
   1899 1902 1903 2080 2085 2086 2125 2127
   2131 2143 2180 2191 2194 2201 2218 2221
   2242 2255 2261 2279 2288 2318 2352 2400
   2401T 2404 2423 2431 2466 2473 2475
   2483 2484 2492 2501 2502 2508 2516 2523
   2527 2541 2554 2558 2587 2625 2626 2627
   2653 2674 2675 2691 2696 2704 2705 2712
   2716 2718 2723 2736 2774 2776 2777 2815
   2816 2865 L62 L145 L147 L162 L164 L241
   L422 L427 L585 L591 L593 L603 L604 L606
   L608 L623 L740 L809 L840 L884 L921 L938
   L1141 L1178 L1196 L1196/2 L1279 L1281
   L1440 L1441 L1505 L2024 L2087 L2106
b λογων 01 04 6 33 76 81 88 93 94 102 104
   189 307 321 322 323 378 442 453 459 621
   629 630 665 876 915 918 999 1102 1106
   1241 1243 1270 1292 1297 1367 1448 1501
   1505 1595 1597 1598 1611 1739 1743 1765
   1832 1838 1840 1842 1845 1846f 1852 1881
   2138 2147 2186 2197 2200 2243 2298 2344
   2374 2401Z 2412 2494 2495 2652 2746
   2805 2818 L596
c ρηματων 628Z
d λογων αυτων 2544
↑ 1721
— 1384 1404

46
a ων ... 61(*f)
b ως 458
— 1384

ἐλάλησαν κατ᾿ αὐτοῦ ἁμαρτωλοὶ ἀσεβεῖς. **16** οὗτοί εἰσιν γογ-
48   50   52   54   56   2   4

γυσταὶ μεμψίμοιροι κατὰ τὰς ἐπιθυμίας ἑαυτῶν πορευόμενοι,
6   8   10 12   14   16   18

48
a ελαλησαν ... 393V 1405V 1780V 1849(*f)
b ελαλησεν 110
↔ *a/b:* ελαλησ[..] 610
↔ *a/b:* [ε]λ[αλησ..] 308
— 1384 2774

50-56↓
a κατ αυτου αμαρτωλοι ασεβεις ...
b αμαρτωλοι κατ αυτου ασεβεις 2404
↔ *a/b:*]βεις 1106
— 1384

50-52↑
a κατ αυτου ... 308V 1767Z
b κατ αυτων 1757
c κατα θεου 1881
d κατα τα του θεου 629
e αυτου 1767T
f om. 918 1067 1852
↔ *a/b:* κατ αυτ[..] 1678 2400
↔ *a/b:* κατ [.....] 1834
↔ *a/b/c:* [........] 1831
↔ *a/b/c/d:* κα[τ 913
↑ 2404
— 1106 1384

54-56↑
a αμαρτωλοι ασεβεις ... 90b(*f) 631f 1741f
   L921(*f)
b ασεβεις αμαρτωλοι 458 1891* L623
c αμαρτωλοι και ασεβεις 1834 1874 1877
d αμαρτωλοι 2523 L422
↔ *a/c:* ασε]βεις 913 1106
↑ 2404
— 1384

v. 16
— P78 0251 0316 69 613 614 720 832 1831S
   1895 2289 2356 2378 2511 2822 L6 L156
   L427/2 L585/2 L617 L1281/2 L1818

2-4↓
a ουτοι εισιν γογγυσται ... 1599Z
b om. 1599T
— P74 1384

2↑
a ουτοι ...
b αυτοι 2627
cf ειτοι 1067V
↔ *a/b:* [..]τοι 308
↑ 1599
— P74 1384 1831 2774

4-6↑
a εισιν γογγυσται ... 049(*f) 308V 400V
   1831V 1846(*f) 2242C 2774V L591(*f)
b εισιν οι γογγυσται 2242*
c εισιν αμαρτωλοι γογγυσται L593
df εις κρισιν γογγυσται 263
e εισηγουνται 522
↔ *a/b/c:* εισιν [913
↑ 1599
— P74 1384

7
a om. ...
b και 1718
— P74 913 1384 1799 2627

8
a μεμψιμοιροι ... 62f 308V 421f 602f 606f
   608V 680f 712f 927f 1100V 1106V 1319f
   1360f 1646f 1678V 1734 1751f 1831V
   1854(*f) 1869f 2125f 2625f L164f L740f
   L1279(*f) L1281f
— P74 1384 1799 2627

10-18↓
a κατα τας επιθυμιας εαυτων πορευομενοι ... P72CfV
b om. P72* 680 L593
— P74 1384 1799 2627

10↑
a κατα ... 913V 1106V 1646(*f) 1678V 2475V
↑ P72 680 L593
— P74 1384 1799 2627

14-18↑↓
a επιθυμιας εαυτων πορευομενοι ...
b εαυτων πορευομενοι επιθυμιας 1741
↑ P72 680 L593
— P74 1799 2627

14-16↑
a επιθυμιας εαυτων 04 020 025 049 1 6 18
35 76 90a 101 105 110 131 141 149Z 175
177 201 204 206S 226 241 242 252 254Z
256 319 322 323 330 337 363 384 385 386
394 400 404 424Z 425 429 432 436 442 444
450Z 451Z 456 457 458 460Z 462 465 466
467 469 479 483 522 547 582 601 603 604
605 607 610V 615 617 618 619 620 621 622
625 627 628 632 634 635 638 642 664 676
699 757 808 824 901 910 914 917 921 928
959 986 1022 1040 1058 1067 1070 1072
1075 1099 1100 1101 1105 1107 1161 1175
1241 1242 1243 1245 1247 1248 1249 1251
1270C 1292Z 1297 1354 1390 1400 1409C
1448 1482 1490C 1495 1503 1508 1509
1523 1524 1548 1595 1599 1609 1610 1617
1618 1619 1628 1636 1637 1643 1649 1652
1656 1668 1704 1720 1721 1723 1725 1726
1728 1730 1732 1733 1736 1737 1738 1739
1740 1743 1744 1745 1746 1747 1748 1749
1750 1751 1752 1754 1757 1760 1761 1763
1766 1767 1768 1769 1780 1795 1829 1830
1835 1838* 1841 1844 1845 1846 1847
1849 1851 1852 1854 1855 1856 1864 1865
1870 1874 1876 1886 1889 1890 1891f 1892
1893 1896 1897 1902 2080 2086 2131 2180f
2191 2197C 2218 2221 2255 2261 2298
2352 2404 2423 2431 2466 2483Z 2484
2492 2508 2516 2523 2541 2554 2625 2626
2653 2704 2718 2723 2746 2774 2777 L62
L145 L147 L162 L596C L603 L604 L606
L623 L740 L809 L840 L938 L1141 L1279
L1441Z L2106
ao επιθυμιας αὐτων 03C2
b επιθυμιας αυτων 01 02 03* 018 044 056
0142 3 5 33(*f) 42 43 51 57 61 62 81 88 90b
93 97 103 104 133 142 149T 172 180 181
203 205 205abs 209 216 218 221 223 234
250 254T 263 296 302 307 309 312 314 321
325 326 327 328 367 378 383 390 393 398
421 424T 431 440 450T 451T 452 453 454
459 460T 468 489 491 496 506 517 592 602

606 608 616 623 629 630 631 633 636 637
639 641 656 665 712 796 801 823 876 912
915 918 919 920 922 927 935 941 945 996
997 1003 1066 1069 1094 1103 1104 1106
1115 1127 1149 1162 1240 1244 1250
1270* 1277 1292T 1311 1315 1352 1359
1360 1367 1398 1404 1405 1409* 1424
1425 1490* 1501 1505 1521 1563 1594
1598 1611 1622 1626 1642 1646 1661 1673
1678 1702 1717 1718 1719 1722 1724 1727
1729 1734 1735 1742 1753 1762 1765V
1827 1828 1831 1832 1834 1836 1837
1838C 1839 1840 1842 1843 1850 1853
1857 1858 1859 1860 1861 1862 1863 1867
1868 1869 1871 1873 1875 1877 1880 1882
1888 1894 1899 1903 2085 2125 2138 2143
2147 2186 2194 2197* 2200 2201 2242
2243 2279 2288 2318 2344 2374 2400 2412
2473 2475 2483T 2494 2495 2501 2502
2527 2544 2558 2587 2652 2674 2675 2691
2696 2705 2712 2716 2736 2776 2815 2816
2818 2865 L164 L241 L422f L427 L585 L591
L596* L608 L884 L921 L1178 L1196
L1196/2 L1281 L1440 L1441T L1505 L2024
L2087
c εαυτων επιθυμιας 38 94 999 1319 1573
1731 2127 2401
d επιθυμιας των εαυτων 82
e ιδιας επιθυμιας εαυτων 189
f ιδιας επιθυμιας αυτων 102 1102 1597
1881 2805
g ασεβειας αυτων 1872 1885
↔ *a/b/d:* επιθυμιας [913
↔ *a/d/e:*] εαυτων 1384
↔ *a/b/d:* [επ]ιθυμιας [308
↑ P72 680 1741 L593
— P74 1799 2627

18-28↑↓
a πορευομενοι και το στομα αυτων
λαλει ...
b λαλει 104
↑ P72 680 1741 L593
— 1799 2627

18↑
a πορευομενοι ... 42* 607V 1100V 1762V
1831V 1881(*f)
b ποργευομενοι 42C
c εισπορευομενοι 1149
↔ *a/b/c:*]ενοι 308
↑ P72 104 680 1741 L593
— P74 1799 2627

καὶ τὸ στόμα αὐτῶν λαλεῖ ὑπέρογκα, θαυμάζοντες
20 22   24   26   28   30   32
πρόσωπα ὠφελείας χάριν. **17** ὑμεῖς δέ, ἀγαπητοί,
    34   36   38   2   4   6

19ꜙ
a   om. ... 1846T 2544T
b   τη ασεβεια και τη παρανομια   459 1838
     1842 1846ZV
c   τη ασεβεια και παρανομια 467
d   εν ασεβεια και ανομια 2544Z
↑   104
−   P74 308 1799 2627

20ꜙ
a   και ... 1106V
b   om. 1241
↑   104
−   P74 308 1799 2627

22-28ꜙ
a   το στομα αυτων λαλει 01 03 04 018 020
     025 044 049 1 3 5 6 18 33 35 38 42 43 51 57
     61 62 76 81 82 88 90a 90b 93 94 101 102
     103 105 110 131 133 141 142 149 172 175
     177 180 181 189 201 203 204 205 205abs
     206S 209 216 221 223 226 234 241 242 250
     252 254 256 263 296 302 307 309 312 314
     319 321 322 323 325 326 327 328 330 337
     363 367 378 383 384 385 386 390 393 394
     398 400 404 424* 425 429 431 432 436 440
     442 444 450 451 453 454 456 457 458 459
     460 462 465 466 467C 468 469 479 483 489
     491 496 506 517 522 547 582 592 601 602
     603 604 605 606 607 610 615 616 617 618
     619 620 621 622 623 625 627 629 630 631
     632 633 634 635 636 637 638 639 641 642
     656 664 665 676 699 712 757 796 801 808
     823 824 876 901 910 912 913 914 915 917
     918 919 921 922 927 928 935 945 959 986
     996 997 999 1003 1022 1040 1058 1067
     1069 1070 1072 1075 1094 1099 1100 1101
     1102 1104 1105 1106V 1107 1115 1127
     1149 1161 1162 1175 1240 1241 1242 1243
     1244* 1245 1247 1248 1249 1250 1251
     1270 1292 1297 1311 1315 1319 1354 1359
     1360 1384 1390 1398 1400 1404 1405 1424
     1425 1448 1482 1490 1495 1501 1503 1505
     1508 1509 1523 1524 1548 1563 1573 1594
     1595 1597 1598 1599 1609 1610 1611 1617
     1618 1619 1626 1628 1636 1637 1642 1643

     1646 1649 1652 1656 1661 1668 1673 1678
     1702 1704 1717 1718 1720 1721 1722 1723
     1725 1726 1727 1728 1729 1730 1731 1732
     1733 1734 1735 1736 1737 1738 1739 1740
     1741 1742 1743 1744 1745 1746 1747 1748
     1749 1750 1751 1752 1753 1754 1757 1760
     1761 1762 1763 1765 1766 1767 1768 1769
     1780 1795 1827 1828 1829 1830 1831V
     1832 1834 1835 1836 1837 1838 1839 1840
     1841 1842 1843 1844 1845 1846 1847 1849
     1850 1851 1852 1853 1854 1855 1856
     1857C 1858 1861 1862 1863 1864 1865
     1867 1868 1869 1870 1873 1874 1875 1876
     1877 1880 1881 1882 1885 1886 1888 1889
     1890 1891 1892 1893 1894 1896 1897 1899
     1902 1903 2080 2085 2086 2125 2127 2131
     2138 2143 2180Z 2186 2191 2194 2197
     2200 2201 2218 2221 2242 2243 2255 2261
     2279 2288 2298 2318 2344 2352 2374 2400
     2401 2404 2412 2423C 2431 2466 2473
     2475 2483 2484 2492 2494 2495 2501 2502
     2516 2523 2527 2541 2544 2554 2558 2587
     2625 2626 2652 2653 2674 2675 2691(*f)
     2696 2704 2705 2712 2716 2718 2723 2736
     2746 2774 2776 2777 2805 2815 2816 2818
     2865 L62Z L145 L147 L162 L164 L241 L422
     L427 L585 L591 L596 L603 L604 L606 L608
     L623 L740 L809 L840 L884 L938 L1141
     L1178 L1196 L1196/2 L1279 L1281 L1440
     L1441 L1505 L2024 L2106
b   το στομα αυτω λαλει 02
c   το στομα αυτων λαλουν L921
d   το στομα αυτων αλει 467*
e   το στομα αυτου λαλει L2087
f   τα στοματα αυτων λαλει 97 218 421 452
     608 680 920 941 1103 1244C 1277 1352
     1367 1521 1622 1719 1724 1857* 1859
     1860 1871 1872 2147 2423*V
g   το στομα λαλει 2508
h   στομα αυτων λαλει P72 056 0142 424C
     628 1066 1409 2180T L62T L593
↔   *a/b/c/d/f/h:* αυτ]ω[P74
↑   104
−   308 1799 2627

μνήσθητε τῶν ῥημάτων τῶν προειρημένων
8   10   12   14   16

30
a υπερογκα ... P74V 3f 90bf 103f 133f 254f
263f 308V 378f 400f 429V 489f 582f 608f
615f 616f 680f 913V 915T 927f 1106V
1240f 1398f 1404V 1425f 1448f 1523f
1524(*f) 1610f 1718f 1724f 1729f 1736f
1765f 1831f 1832f 1834f 1844f 1881f 1886f
1890f 1896f 2147f 2194f 2243f 2400(*f)
2404f 2484f 2502f 2508f 2516f 2523f 2527f
2544f 2674V 2774V L422f L623f
↔ a/?: υπερ[915ZV
— 1799 2627

32
a θαυμαζοντες ... 43* 43Cf 308V 467f 631f
913V 1100V 1728V 1834V 1839V
— P74 1730 1799 2627 2653

34
a προσωπα ... 43* 61f 468V 996f 1106V
1834V 2288f 2716V
b προσωπον 2127 L608 L1505
cf ανασωπα 57
↔ af/bf: προσωπω 43C 1448
↔ a/b: προσ[1834
↔ a/b:]ρο[P74
↔ a/b: π[1106
— 308 1730 1799 2627 2653

36
a ωφελειας ... 308V 386f 633f 913V 2344f
L1279(*f)
bf αφελειας 801 2691
— P74 1730 1799 2627 2653

38
a χαριν ... 308V 913V
b om. 378
— P74 308 1730 1799 2627 2653

v. 17
— P74 P78 0251 0316 69 172 613 614 720 832
1360 1799 1831S 1895 2289 2356 2378
2511 2627 2653 2822 L6 L156 L427/2 L617
L1818

2
a υμεις ... P72(*f) 629*V 876V
b ημεις 321 629C
↔ a/b: [.]μεις 308 1292 1730
— 913 1831

6
a αγαπητοι ... P72(*f) 5(*f) 1241f 2473C
L2024f
b αδελφοι 2473*
c αδελφοι αγαπητοι 629
d αγαπητοι αδελφοι 1872

8
a μνησθητε ... 218f 468V 1448V 1573f 1728V
1831V L1279f
b μεμνησθε 1501
c μνημονευετε 322 323 1241 1739 1881 2298
2544
— 308

10
a των ... 1831V 2523Z
b om. 2523T
— 308 913

12-16
a ρηματων των προειρημενων P72 01 03 04
018 020 025 044 049 056 0142 1 3 5 18 33
35 38 42 43 51 61 76 81 82 88 90a 90b 93 94
97 101 102 103 104 105 110 131 133 141
142 149 175 177 180 181 189 201 204 205
205abs 206S 209 216 218 221 223 226 234
241 242 250 252 254 256 263 296 302 307
309 312 314 319 325 326 327 328 330 337
363 367 383 384 385 386 390 393 394 398
400 404 421 424* 425 429 431 432 436 440
442 444 450 451 452 453 454 456 457 458
459 460 462 465 466 467 468 469 479 483
489 491 496 517 522 547 582 592 601 602
603 604 605 606 607 608 610 615 617 618
619 620 621 622 623 625 627 628 629 631
632 634 635 636 637 638 639 641 642 656
664 665 676 680 699 712 757 796 801 808
823 824 901 910 912 914 915 917 918 919
920 921 927 928 935 941 945 959 986 996
997 999 1003 1022 1040 1058 1066 1067

ὑπὸ τῶν ἀποστόλων τοῦ κυρίου ἡμῶν Ἰησοῦ Χριστοῦ
18   20   22   24   26   28   30   32

18 ὅτι ἔλεγον ὑμῖν· ὅτι ἐπ᾽ ἐσχάτου τοῦ χρόνου ἔσονται
  2   4   6   8   10   12   14   16   18

1069 1072 1075 1094 1099 1100 1101 1102
1103 1104 1105 1107 1115 1127 1149 1161
1162 1175 1240 1242 1243 1244 1245 1247
1248 1249 1250 1251 1277 1315 1319 1352
1354 1359 1367 1384 1390 1398 1400 1405
1409 1424 1425 1482 1490 1495 1503 1508
1509 1521 1523 1524 1548 1563 1573 1594
1597 1599 1609 1610 1617 1618 1619 1622
1626 1628 1636 1637 1642 1643 1646 1649
1652 1656 1661 1668 1673 1678 1702 1704
1717 1718 1719 1720 1721 1722 1723 1724
1725 1726 1727 1728 1729 1730 1731 1732
1733 1734 1735 1736 1737 1738 1740 1741
1742 1743 1745 1746 1747 1748 1749 1750
1751 1752 1753 1754 1757 1760 1761 1762
1763 1766 1767 1768 1769 1780 1795 1827
1828 1829 1830 1831V 1834 1835 1836
1837 1838 1839 1840 1841 1842 1843 1844
1845 1846 1847 1849 1851 1852 1853 1854
1855 1856 1857 1858 1859 1860 1861 1862
1863 1864 1865 1867 1868 1869 1870 1871
1872 1873 1874 1875 1876 1877 1880 1882
1885 1886 1888 1889 1890 1891 1892 1893
1894 1896 1897 1899 1902 1903 2080 2085
2086 2125 2127 2131 2180 2186 2191 2194
2197 2201 2218 2221 2242 2255 2261 2279
2288 2318 2344 2352 2400 2401 2404 2423
2431 2466 2473 2475 2483 2484 2492 2501
2502 2508 2516 2523 2541 2544 2554 2558
2587 2625 2626 2674 2675 2691 2696 2704
2705 2712 2716 2718 2723 2736 2746 2774
2776 2777 2805 2815 2816 2818 2865 L62
L145 L147 L162 L164 L241 L422 L427 L585
L585/2 L591 L593C L596 L603 L604 L606
L608 L623 L740 L809 L840 L884 L921 L938
L1141 L1178 L1196 L1196/2 L1279 L1281
L1281/2 L1440 L1441 L1505 L2024 L2087
L2106
b ρηματων των προειμενων 1070
c ρηματων των πορευομενων 633
d ρηματων των ανειρημενων 57
e ρηματων των ειρημενων 203 506
f ρηματων των προειρημενων ρηματων 1598
g ρηματων των πρωην ειρημενων 321

h προειρημενων ρηματων 02 6 62 322 323 378 424C 630 876 922 1241 1270 1292 1297 1311 1448 1501 1505 1595 1611 1739 1744 1765 1832 1850 1881 2138 2143 2147 2200 2243 2298 2374 2412 2494 2495 2527 2652
i ρηματων προειρημενων L593*
j ρηματων 616
↔ *a/b/c/d/e/f/g*: ρηματων των [1106
↔ *a/b/c/d/e/f/g/i/j*: ρηματων [1404
↔ *a/d/e/g/i*:]ημενων 913
– 308

18-20↓
a υπο των ... 2143Z
b om. 2143T
– 308 1106

18↑
a υπο ... 1404V 1503V 2816Z
b απο 1642 2255V 2816T
↑ 2143
– 308 1106

19
a om. ...
b αγιων 605A 610 617 1495 1839 2400 L164 L585 L585/2 L921 L1281 L1281/2
– 308 1106

28
a ημων ...
b om. 93 665
– 913

29
a om. ...
b [.....] 2776

32
a χριστου ... 1448V
b om. 1881
– 913

v. 18

— P74 P78 0251 69 172 613 614 720 832 1360 1799 1831S 1895 2289 2356 2378 2511 2627 2653 2822 L6 L156 L427/2 L617 L1818

2-4

a οτι ελεγον ... 1642(*f) 1768f 1852V
b οτι ελεγεν 018 456 656 2473 L422
c οτε ελεγον 88 915 1846
d οιτινες ελεγον 629
e οι ελεγον 383Z
f ελεγον γαρ 43
g ελεγον 383T
↔ *a/b*: οτι ελεγ[..] 2475
↔ *a/b*: οτι ελε[γ..] 1106
— 0316

6

a υμιν P72 01 02 03 04 020 025 044 049 056 0142 1 3 5 6 18 33 35 38 42 43 51 57 61 62 76 81 82 88 90a 90b 93 94 97 101 102 104 105 110 131 133 141 142 149 175 177 180C 181 189 201 203 204 205 205abs 206S 209 216 218 223 226 234 241 242 252 254 256 263 296 302 307 308 309 312 314 319 321 322 323 325 326 328 330 337 363 367 378 383 384 385 386 390 394 398 400 404 421 424 425 429 431 432 436 440 442 444 450 451 452 453 456 457 458 459 460 462 465 466 467 468 469 479 483 489 491 496 506 517 522 547 582 592 601 602 603 604 605 607 608 610 615 616 617 618 619 620 621 622 623 625 627 628 629 630 631 632 634 635 636 637 638 642 656 664 665 676 680 699 712 757 796 801 808 823 824 876 901 910 912 913 914 915 917 918 919 920 921 922 927 928 935 941 945 959 986 996 997 999 1003 1022 1040 1058 1066 1067 1069 1070 1072 1075 1094 1099 1100 1101 1102 1103 1104 1105 1107 1115 1127 1149 1161 1162 1175 1240 1241 1242 1243 1244 1245 1247 1248 1249 1250 1251 1270 1277 1292 1297 1311 1315 1319 1352 1354 1359 1367 1384 1390 1398 1400 1404 1405 1409 1424 1425 1448 1482 1490 1495 1501 1503 1505 1508 1509 1521 1523 1524 1548 1563 1573 1594 1595 1597 1598 1599 1609 1610 1611 1617 1618 1619 1622 1626 1628 1636 1637 1642 1643 1646f 1649 1652 1656 1661 1668 1673 1678 1702 1704 1717 1718 1719 1720 1721 1722 1723 1724 1725 1726 1727 1728 1729 1730 1731 1732 1733 1734 1735 1736 1737 1738 1739 1740 1741 1743 1744 1745 1746 1747 1748 1749 1750 1751 1752 1753 1754 1757 1760 1761 1763 1765 1766 1767 1768 1769 1780 1795 1827 1828 1829 1830 1831 1832 1834 1835 1836 1837 1838 1839 1840 1841 1842 1843 1844 1845 1846 1847 1849 1850 1851 1852 1853 1854 1855 1856 1857 1858 1859 1860 1861 1863 1864 1865 1867 1868 1869 1870 1871 1872 1873 1874 1875 1876 1877 1880 1881 1882 1885 1886 1889 1890 1891 1892 1893 1894 1896 1897 1899 1902 1903 2080 2085 2086 2127 2131 2138 2143 2147 2180 2186 2191 2194 2197 2200 2201 2218 2221 2242 2243 2255 2261 2279 2288 2298 2318 2344 2352 2374 2400 2401 2404 2412 2423 2431 2466 2473 2475 2483 2484 2492 2494 2495 2501 2502 2508 2516 2523 2527 2541 2544 2554 2587 2625 2626 2652 2674 2691 2696 2704 2705 2716 2718 2723 2736 2746V 2774 2776 2777 2805 2815 2816C 2818 2865 L62 L145 L147 L162 L241 L427 L585 L585/2 L591 L593 L596 L603 L604 L606 L608 L623 L740 L809 L840 L884 L921 L938 L1141 L1178 L1196 L1196/2 L1279 L1281 L1281/2 L1440 L1441 L1505 L2024 L2087 L2106
b ημιν 018 103 180* 221 250 327 393 454 606 633 639 641 1742 1762 1862 1888 2125 2558 2675 2712 2816* L164 L422
— 0316 1106

8

a οτι ... 020Z 400V 1448V
b om. 01 03 020T 044 61 1872 2344 2736
— 0316 913 1106

10-18

a επ εσχατου του χρονου εσονται 01T 254 630 1292 1505 1523 1524 1611 1844 1845 1846 1852 2138 2200 2495
b επ εσχατου των χρονων εσονται 252 1678
c επ εσχατου χρονου εσονται P72 03 04* 1243
d επ εσχατω χρονω εσονται 1390 1880 L840
e επ εσχατου του χρονου ελευσονται 01Z2 02 33 61 312 431 436 1067 1409 1837 1853
f επ εσχατω του χρονου ελευσονται 326T
g επ εσχατου χρονου ελευσονται 04C2 5 623
h επ εσχατου χρονου αναστησονται 044
i επ εσχατου των χρονων ελευσονται 6 81 94 307 322 323 424Z 453 629* 918 1241 1739 1751 1840 2186 2197 2298 2805 2818

ἐμπαῖκται κατὰ τὰς ἑαυτῶν ἐπιθυμίας
20   22   24   26   28
πορευόμενοι τῶν ἀσεβειῶν.
30   32   34

---

j επ εσχατου των ημερων ελευσονται 1881

k επ εσχατων των χρονων εσονται 425 442
479 628 1161 1270T 1297 1384 1595 1598
1599 1757 1839 1847 2404 L422 L884

l επ εσχατων των χρονων ελευσονται 93
321 378 383 605A 610 617 629C 665 2147
2344 2412 2652 L585T L585/2 L1196/2
L1281/2

m επ εσχατω των χρονων ελευσονται 326Z

n επ εσχατων του χρονου εσονται 621 L596

o επ εσχατων του χρονου ελευσονται 1735

p εν εσχατω τω χρονω εσονται 025 656 914
2400

q εν εσχατω χρονω εσονται 018 020 049 3
18 35 38 42ZV 43 51 57 62 76 82 88 90a
90b 97 101 102 103 104 105 110 131 133
141 142 149 175 177 180 181 189 201 203
204 205 205abs 206S 209 216 218 221 223
226 234 241 242 250 256 263 302 308V 309
314 319 325 327 328 330 337 363 367 384
386 390 393 394 398 400 404 421 424T 429
432 440 444 450 451 452 454 456 457 458
459 460 462 465 466 467 468 469 483 489
491 496 506 517 522 547 582 592 601 602
603 604 605T 606 607 608 615 618 619 620
622 625 627 632 633 634 635 636 637 638
641 642 664 680 699 712 757 796 801 808
823 824 876 901 910 912 915 917 919 920
921 922 927 928 935 941 945 959 986 996
997 999 1003 1022 1040 1058 1069 1070
1072 1075 1094 1099 1100 1101 1102 1103
1105 1107 1115 1149 1162 1175 1242 1244
1245 1247f 1248 1249 1251 1270A 1277
1311 1315 1319 1352 1354 1359 1398 1400
1404 1405 1424 1425 1448 1482 1490 1495
1503 1508 1509 1521 1548 1563 1573 1594
1597 1609 1610 1617 1618 1619 1622 1626
1628 1636 1637 1642 1643 1649 1652 1656
1661 1668 1673 1702 1704 1717 1718 1719
1720 1721 1722 1723 1724 1725 1726 1727
1728 1729 1730 1731 1732 1733 1734 1736
1737 1738 1740 1741 1742 1743 1744 1745
1746 1747 1748 1749 1750 1752 1753 1754
1760 1761 1762 1763 1765 1766 1768 1769
1780 1795 1827 1828 1829 1830 1831V
1832 1834 1835 1836 1838 1841 1842 1843

1849 1850 1851 1854 1855 1856 1857 1858
1859 1860 1861 1862 1863 1864 1865 1867
1868 1869 1870 1871 1872 1873 1874 1875
1877 1882 1885 1888 1889 1890 1891 1892
1893 1894 1896 1897 1899 1902 1903 2080
2085 2086 2125 2127 2131 2143 2180 2191
2194 2201 2218 2221 2242 2243 2255 2261
2279 2318 2352 2374 2401 2423 2431 2466
2473 2475 2483 2484 2492 2494 2501 2502
2508 2516 2527 2541 2544 2554 2558 2587
2625 2626 2674 2675 2691 2696 2704 2705
2712 2716 2723 2736 2746 2774 2776 2777
2815 2816 L147 L162 L164 L241 L427
L585Z L591 L593 L603 L608 L623 L809
L921 L1141 L1178 L1196 L1281 L1441
L2024 L2087f L2106

r εσοντai εν εσχατω χρονω 1127

s εν εσχατω χρονων εσονται 056 0142 1066

tf εν εσχατων χρονων εσονται 616

u εν τω̣ [ε]σχατω χρονω εσονται 2288

v εν εσχατω χρονω ελευσονται 296 385 639
1501 L1440

w εν εσχατω καιρω εσονται 1250 1876

x εν εσχατω καιρω̣ χρονω̣ν εσονται 1767

y εν εσχατοις χρονοις εσονται 676

z εν εσχαταις ημεραις εσονται 631 1646f
2523

a'f εν επεσχατω τω χρονω εσονται 1886

b'f εν επ εσχατω τω χρονω εσονται 1240

c' τω εσχατω χρονω εσονται 1367

d' εσχατω χρονω εσονται 1 2718 L62 L145
L604 L606 L740 L938 L1279 L1505

e' χρονω εσονται 1104

↔ *df/qf*: εν επ εσχατω χρονω εσονται 2865

↔ *q/s/v*: εν εσχατω χρο[......] 42TV

↔ *a/b/c/d/e/f/g/h/i/j/k/l/m/n/o/p/q/s/u/v/
w/x/y/z/c'/d'/e'*:]ται 913

— 0316 1106

19

a om. ... 1617(*f)

20

a εμπαικται ... 020f 307f 1069(*f) 1573f
1877*f 1877Cf 2191f L591f

— 0316 1106

22
a κατα ... 0316V 33fV 621fV
— 913 1106

24-34
a τας εαυτων επιθυμιας πορευομενοι των
ασεβειων P72(*f) 02 03 04 018 020 025 049
056 0142 0316 1 3 5 6 18 33V 35 38 43 57
62 76 81 82 93 94 97 101 102 103 104 105
110 131 133 141 142 149 175 181 189 201
203 204 205 205abs 206S 209 216 221 226
242 250 252 254 256 263 296 302 307 308
309 312 314 319 321 322 323 325 326 327f
328 330 367 378 383 384 385 386 393 394
398 400V 404 421 424 429 431 432 436 440
442 444 450 451 453 454 456 457 458 459
462 465 466 467 468 469 479 489 491 496
506 517V 522 547 582 592 601 602 603 604
605 606 607 608 610 615 616 617 619 620
621V 622 623 625 627 628 629 632 633 634
635 636 637 638 639 641 642 656 664 665
676 680 699 712 757 796 808 823 824 876
901 910 914 917 918 919 920 921 927 928
935 945 959 986 997 999 1022 1040 1058
1066 1067 1069 1070 1072 1075 1094 1099
1100 1101 1102 1104 1105 1115 1127 1149
1161 1162 1175C 1240 1242 1243 1245
1249 1270 1277 1297 1311 1315 1319 1354
1359 1367 1384 1390 1398 1400 1404 1409
1424 1425 1482 1490 1495 1503 1508 1509
1521 1523 1524 1548 1563 1573 1595 1597
1598 1599 1609 1610 1617 1618 1619 1622
1626 1628 1636 1637 1643 1649 1652 1656
1668 1673 1678 1704 1717 1718 1720 1721
1722 1723 1724 1725 1726 1728 1729 1730
1731 1732 1733 1734 1736 1737 1739 1740
1741 1742 1743 1744 1745 1746 1747 1748
1749 1750 1751 1752 1754 1757 1760 1761
1762V 1763 1765 1766 1767 1768(*f) 1769
1780 1795 1827C 1828 1829 1830 1831
1832 1834 1835 1836 1837 1838 1839 1840
1841 1842 1843 1844 1845 1846 1847 1849
1850 1851 1852 1853 1854 1855 1856 1857
1858 1859 1860 1862 1864 1865 1868 1869
1870 1871 1873 1874 1877 1880 1881 1882
1885 1888 1889 1890 1891 1892 1893 1894
1897 1899 1902 1903 2080 2086 2125 2127
2131 2143 2147 2180 2186 2191 2194 2197
2201 2218 2221 2242 2243 2255 2261 2288
2298 2318 2344 2352 2374 2400 2401
2412Z 2423C 2431 2466 2473 2475 2483*
2484 2492 2494 2501 2502 2508 2516 2527
2541 2554 2558 2587 2625 2652 2674f 2696
2704 2705 2712 2716 2723 2736 2746 2774
2776 2777 2805 2815 2816 2865 L62 L145
L147 L162 L241 L427 L585 L585/2 L591f
L596 L603 L604 L606 L608 L740 L809 L840
L884 L921 L938 L1141 L1178 L1196
L1196/2 L1279 L1281 L1281/2 L1440
L1441 L1505 L2024 L2087 L2106
b τας επιθυμιας εαυτων πορευομενοι των
ασεβειων 01Z2 42Z 51 90b 177 223 234
241 337 363 390 460 483 618 912 941 1003
1251 1594V 1727 1738 1753f 1861 1863
2085 2279 2523 2675
c τας επιθυμιας πορευομενοι των εαυτων
ασεβειων 1501
d τας εαυτων επιθυμιας πορευσομενοι των
ασεβειων 631
e τας εαυτων επιθυμιας πορευομενοι των
ασεβων 88 90a 915 1241 1827*V 1896
2818
f τας επιθυμιας εαυτων πορευομενοι των
ασεβων 42T 2412T
g τας αυτων επιθυμιας πορευομενοι των
ασεβειων 044 218 452 801 922 1107
1175*V 1244 1250 1352 1719 1872 1876
2404 2423*V 2483C 2544 2626 2691 L164
h τας επιθυμιας αυτων πορευομενοι των
ασεβειων 01T 180 630 996 1103 1292 1405
1448 1505 1611 1661 1702 1735 2138 2200
2495 2718 L623
i τας εαυτων επιθυμιας πορευομενοι των
ασεβων ασεβειων 61
j τας εαυτων επιθυμιας πορευομενοι των
ασεβειων αυτων 425 1247 1867
k τα εργα αυτων επιθυμιαις πορευομενοι
των ασεβειων 1875
l τας εαυτων επιθυμιας πορευομενοι
ασεβειων 1886
m τας επιθυμιας πορευομενοι των ασεβειων
1642 1646
n τας εαυτων επιθυμιας L422
o τας εαυτων ασεβειων 1248
pf τας ε L593
↔ a/b/c/e/f/g/h/i/j/k/m:] πορευομενοι των
[913
— 1106

19 οὗτοί εἰσιν οἱ ἀποδιορίζοντες, ψυχικοί,

	2	4	6	8		10

v. 19

— P74 P78 0251 69 172 613 614 720 832 1106 1360 1799 1831S 1895 2289 2356 2378 2511 2627 2653 2822 L6 L156 L427/2 L617 L1818

1
a om. ...
b καὶ L422
— 913

2
a ουτοι ... 451f L921V
b αυτοι L593
↔ af/bf: τοι 1594

3
a om. ...
b δε 61
— 913

6-8↓
a οι αποδιοριζοντες ...
b om. L422

6↑
a οι ... 3Z
b om. 0316 3T 131
↑ L422
— 913

8↑
a αποδιοριζοντες P72 01* 01C2b 02 03 018 020 025 044 049 056 0142 0316 1 3 18 33 35C 38 42 43 57 61 62 76 81 82 90a 90b 93 94 97 101T 102 103 105 110Tf 131 133 141 149 175 177 180 181 189 201 203 204 205 205abs 206S 209 221 226 234 241 242 250 254 256 263 302 307 308 309 312 314 319 321 325 326 327 328 330 337 363 384 386 390 393 394 398 400 404 421 424 425 429 431 432 436 442 444 450 451 453 454 456 457 458 460 462 465 466 468 469 483 489 491 506 517 522 547 582 592 601 602 603 604 605 606 607 608 610 615 616 617 618 619 620 621 622 625 627 628 633 634 635 637 638 641 656 664 665 676 680 699 712 757 796 801 823 824 901 910 912 914 917 918 919 920 921 922 927 928 945 959 986 996 997 1003 1040 1058 1066 1067 1069 1070 1072 1075 1094 1099 1100 1101 1102 1104 1105 1107 1115 1149 1161 1162 1175 1240 1241 1244* 1247 1248 1249 1251 1270 1277 1297 1311 1319 1354 1390 1398 1400 1405 1409 1424 1448 1482 1490 1495 1501 1503 1508 1509 1523 1524 1548 1573 1595 1597T 1598 1610 1617 1618 1619 1622 1628 1636 1637 1642 1652 1656 1661 1668 1673 1678 1702 1704 1717 1719 1720 1721 1723 1724 1725 1726 1727 1728 1729 1730 1731 1732 1733 1734 1735 1736 1737 1738 1739T 1740 1741 1742 1743 1745 1746 1748 1749 1751 1752 1753 1754 1757 1760 1761 1762 1763 1766 1767 1768 1769 1780 1795 1827 1828T 1829 1830 1831 1834 1835 1836 1837 1839 1840 1841 1843 1844 1845 1847 1849 1850 1851 1852 1853 1854 1855 1856 1857 1858 1859 1860 1861 1862 1863 1864 1865 1867 1868 1869 1870 1871 1872 1873 1874 1875 1876T 1877 1880 1882 1885 1886 1888 1889 1890 1891 1892 1893 1894f 1896 1897 1899 1903 2080 2085 2086 2125 2127 2131 2143 2180 2186 2191 2194 2197 2201 2218 2221 2242 2255 2261 2279 2318 2344 2352 2400 2401 2404 2423 2431 2466 2473 2484 2492 2501 2502 2508 2516 2523 2527 2541 2544 2554 2558 2587 2625 2626 2674 2675 2691 2704 2705 2712 2723 2736 2746 2776 2777T 2815 2816 2818 2865 L164 L427 L585 L585/2 L593 L596 L1196 L1196/2 L1281 L1281/2 L1441 L2087

b διοριζοντες 01C2a
c αποδιοριζοντες εαυτους 04 5 6 35* 51 88 101Z 104 110Z 142 216 218 223 252 322 323 367 378 383 440 452 459 467 479 496 623 629 630 631 636 642 808 876 915 935 941 999 1022 1103 1127 1242 1243 1244C 1245 1250 1292 1315 1352 1359 1367 1384 1404 1425 1505 1521 1563 1597Z 1599 1609 1611 1626 1643 1646 1649 1718 1722 1739Z 1744 1747 1750 1765 1828Z 1832 1838 1842 1876Z 1881 1902 2138 2147 2200 2243 2288 2298 2374 2412 2475 2483 2494f 2495 2652 2696 2718 2774 2777Z

πνεῦμα μὴ ἔχοντες. **20** ὑμεῖς δέ, ἀγαπητοί,
   12   14   16   2   4   6
ἐποικοδομοῦντες ἑαυτοὺς τῇ ἁγιωτάτῃ ὑμῶν πίστει,
     8   10   12   14   16   18

    2805 L62 L145 L147 L162 L241 L591 L603
    L604 L606 L608 L623 L740 L809 L840 L884
    L921 L938 L1141 L1178 L1279 L1505 L2106
d εαυτους αποδιοριζοντες L1440
e αποδιοριζοντες αυτους 1846
f αποδιοριζοντες εαυτοις 296
g αποδιοριζοντες εαυτων 385 639 L2024
↔ c/e/f/g: αποδιοριζοντες [6-7] 632
↔ a/b:]διοριζοντες 913
↑ L422
- 1594

12
a πνευμα ... 0316V 308V 400V 450C 915f
b πνευματα 450* 1844
- 1594

16
a εχοντες ... 0316V 1448V
b κατεχοντες 1509
- 1594 2138

17
a om. ... 1840TV
b θειον 1840KV
- 1594 2138

v. 20
- P74 P78 0251 69 172 613 614 720 832 1106
    1360 1799 1831S 1895 2138 2289 2356
    2378 2511 2627 2653 2822 L6

2
a υμεις ... 308V 421V 2127(*f) L884C L921V
b ημεις 04 1099 1829 1844 1852 L884*
↔ a/b: [..]εις 1594
↔ a/b: [.μεις] 913
- 1717

6
a αγαπητοι ... 2674(*f)
b αδελφοι 2344
- 1717

8-18
a εποικοδομουντες εαυτους τη αγιωτατη
    υμων πιστει 01 02 03 044 0316V 5 33 61 81
    88Z 93 104 326 436 442 459 467 621f 623
    630 642 665 808 876 915 1067 1127 1243
    1292 1359 1425 1448 1505 1563 1611 1718
    1735 1765 1832f 1837 1838 1842 1845 1846
    1881 2200 2344 2374 2494 2495 2805 L596
b τη αγιωτατη υμων πιστει εποικοδο-
    μουντες εαυτους 018 020 025 049 056
    0142 1 18 35 38 42 43 51 57 76 82 90a 97
    101 102 103 105 110 131 133 141 142 149
    175 180 181 189 201 203 204 205 205abs
    206S 209 216 218 221 223 226 234 241 242
    250 252 254 256 263 296 302 308V 309 312
    314 319 325 327 328 330 363 367 384 385
    386 390 393 394 398 400 404 421 424T 425
    429 432 440 444 450 451 452 454 456 457
    458 462 465 466 468 479 483 489 491 496
    506 517 522 547 582 592 601 602 603 604
    605 606 607 608 610 615 616 617 619 620
    622 625 627 628 631 632 634 635Z 636
    637Z 638 639 641C 656 676 680 699 712
    757 796 801 823 824 901 910 912 914 917
    919 920 922 927 928 935 941 945 959 986
    996 997 999 1003 1022 1040 1058 1069
    1070 1072 1075 1094 1099 1100 1101 1102
    1103 1104 1105 1107 1115 1149 1161 1162
    1175 1240 1242 1244 1245 1247 1248 1249
    1250 1251 1270 1277 1297 1311 1315 1319
    1352 1354 1384 1390 1398 1400 1404 1405
    1424 1482 1490 1495 1501 1503 1508 1509
    1521 1523 1524 1548 1573 1595 1597 1599f
    1609 1610 1617 1618 1619 1622 1626 1628
    1636 1637 1642 1643 1649 1652 1656 1661
    1668 1673 1678 1702 1704 1719 1720 1721
    1722 1723 1724 1725 1726 1727 1728 1730
    1731 1732 1733 1734 1736 1737 1740 1741
    1742 1743 1744 1745 1747 1748 1749 1750
    1751 1752 1753 1754 1757 1760 1761 1762
    1763 1766 1767 1768 1769 1780 1795 1828
    1829 1830 1831 1834 1835 1836 1839 1841
    1843 1844 1847 1849 1850 1851C 1853
    1854 1855 1856 1857 1858 1859 1860 1861
    1862 1863 1864 1865 1867 1868 1869 1870

ἐν πνεύματι ἁγίῳ προσευχόμενοι, **21** ἑαυτοὺς
20   22   24   26   2

ἐν ἀγάπῃ θεοῦ τηρήσατε προσδεχόμενοι
4   6   8   10   12

1871 1872 1873 1874 1875 1876 1880 1882
1885 1886f 1888 1889 1890 1891 1892 1893
1894 1896 1897 1899 1903 2080 2085 2086
2125 2127 2131 2143 2180 2191 2194 2201
2218 2221 2242 2255 2261 2279 2288 2352
2400C 2401 2423 2431 2466 2473 2475
2483 2484 2492 2501 2502 2508 2516 2527
2541 2544 2554 2558 2587 2625 2626 2674
2675 2691 2696 2704 2705 2712 2718 2723
2746 2774 2776 2777 2815 2816 2865 L62
L145 L147 L156 L162 L241 L422 L427
L427/2 L585 L585/2 L591 L593f L603 L604
L606 L608 L617 L623 L740 L809 L840 L921
L938 L1141 L1178 L1196 L1196/2 L1279
L1281 L1281/2 L1505 L2024 L2087 L2106

c ἐποικοδομουντες εαυτους τη αγιωτατη
ημων πιστει 04 322 323 431 1409 1739
1852 2147 2243 2298 2412 2652

d ἐποικοδομουντες εαυτους τη αγιοτητι
ημων εν πιστει 1241

ef ἐποικοδομουντες εαυτους τη αγια ταυτη
ημων πιστει 378

f ἐποικοδομουντες αυτους τη αγιωτατη
υμων πιστει 88T

g ἐποικοδομουντες υμεις εαυτους τη
αγιωτατη ημων πιστει 629

h τη αγιωτατη υμων πιστει οικοδομουντες
εαυτους 1746

if τη αγιωτατη υμιν πιστει εποικοδομουντες εαυτους 3 62 90b 1646

j τη αγιωτατη ημων πιστει εποικοδομουντες εαυτους 6 94 307 321 383 424Z
453 469 633 641* 664 918 921 1066 1367
1598 1729 1840 1851* 1877 2186 2197
2318 2400* 2404 2523 2716V 2736 2818
L164 L884 L1440 L1441 L1818

k την αγιωτατην υμων πιστιν
εποικοδομουντες εαυτους 1827

l τη αγιωτατη πιστει εποικοδομουντες
εαυτους 177 337 460 618 635T 1738

m τη αγιωτατη υμων εποικοδομουντες
εαυτους 637T

nf τη εαυτων αγιοτητι πιστει ανοικοδο-
μεισθε P72

↔ b/j: τη αγιωτατη [.]μων πιστει εποικοδομουντες εαυτους 1902

↔ b/h/j: τη αγιωτα[>12]μομουντες εαυτους
1594

↔ b/h/j: τη [>12]ομουντες εαυτους 913

↔ b/j/l] πιστει εποικοδομουντες [1717

20-26↓
a εν πνευματι αγιω προσευχομενοι ... 910Z
b om. 910T 1248 2675
— 913 1717

20↑
a εν ... 2466(*f)
b om. 1311
↑ 910 1248 2675
— 913 1717

22-24↑
a πνευματι αγιω ...
b αγιω πνευματι 2131
↑ 910 1248 2675
— 913 1717

26↑
a προσευχομενοι 01 02 03 04 020 025 044
056 0142 0316V 3 5 6 18 33 35 42 43 51 57
61 62 76 81 82 88 90a 90b 93 94 97 101 102
104 105 131 133 141 142 149 175CV 177
180 181 189 201 203 204 205 205abs 206S
209 216 218 223 226 234 241 252 254 256
263 296 307 308 312 319 321 322 323 326
327 328 337 363 367 378 383 384 385 386
390 394 398 400 404 421 424 425 429 431
432 436 440 442 444 450 452 453 457 459
460 462 465 466* 467 468 469 479 483 489
491 496 506 517 522 547 582 592 603 604
605 607 608 610 615 617 618 620 621 622
623 628 629 630 631 632 633 634 635 636
638 639 642 656 664 665 676 680 699 757
796 801 808 823 824 876 901 912 914 915
918 919 920 921 922 927 928 935 941 945
959 986 996 997 999 1003 1022 1040 1058
1066 1067 1069 1070 1072 1075 1094 1099
1100 1101 1102 1103 1104 1105 1107 1115
1127 1149 1161 1240 1241 1242 1243 1244
1245 1247 1249 1250 1251 1277 1292 1311
1315 1319 1352 1354 1359 1367 1384 1390

1398 1400 1404 1405 1409 1424C 1425
1448 1482 1490 1501 1503 1505 1508 1509
1521 1523 1524 1548 1563 1573 1594V
1597 1599 1609 1610 1611 1617 1618 1619
1622 1626 1628 1636 1637 1642 1643 1649
1652 1656 1661 1673 1678 1702 1704 1718
1719 1720 1721 1722 1723 1724 1725 1726
1727 1728 1729 1730 1731 1732 1733 1736
1737 1738 1739 1740 1741 1742 1743 1744
1745 1746 1747 1748 1749 1750 1751 1752
1753 1754 1757 1761 1762 1763 1765 1766
1767 1768 1795 1827 1828 1829 1830 1831
1832 1834 1835 1836 1837 1838 1839f 1840
1841 1842 1843 1844 1845 1846 1847 1849
1850 1851 1852 1853 1854 1855 1856 1857
1858 1859 1860 1861 1863 1864 1865 1867
1868 1869 1870 1871 1872 1874 1875 1876
1877 1880 1881 1882 1885 1886 1889 1890
1891 1892 1893 1894 1896 1897 1899 1902
1903 2080 2085 2086 2127 2131 2147 2180
2186 2191 2194 2197 2200 2218 2221 2242
2243 2255 2261 2279 2288 2298 2318 2344
2352 2374 2400 2401 2404 2412 2423 2431
2466 2473 2475 2483 2484 2492 2494 2495
2501 2502 2508 2523 2541 2544 2554 2558
2587 2625 2626 2652 2674 2691 2696 2704
2712 2716 2718 2723 2736 2746 2774 2776
2777 2805 2815 2816 2818 2865 L62 L145
L147 L156 L164 L241(*f) L422 L427 L585
L585/2 L591 L593 L596 L603 L604 L606
L608 L617 L623 L740 L809 L840 L884 L921
L938 L1141 L1178 L1196 L1196/2 L1279
L1281 L1281/2 L1440 L1441 L1505 L1818
L2024 L2087 L2106
bf προσευχομενος L162
c προσερχομενοι 38
d πορευομενοι 1270 1297 1595 1598
e προσευχομενοι εαυτοις P72Z 018 049 1
103 110 175*V 221 242 250 302 309 314
325 330 393 451 454 456 458 466C 601 602
606 616 619 625 627 637 641 712 917 1162
1175 1424* 1646 1668 1734 1735 1760
1769 1780 1862 1873 1888 2125 2143 2201
2516 2527 2705
f προσεχομενοι εαυτοις P72T
g om. 1495 L427/2
↑ 910 1248 2675
— 913 1717

v. 21
— P74 P78 0251 69 172 614 720 832 913 1106
1360 1799 1895 2138 2289 2356 2378 2511
2627 2653 2822 L6

2-12↓
a εαυτους εν αγαπη θεου τηρησατε
προσδεχομενοι ... 1857Z L1279Z
b om. 181 1240 1390 1857T L593 L1279T
L1505
— 1717

2-10↑
a εαυτους εν αγαπη θεου τηρησατε 01 02
020 025 056 0142 0316V 3 5 6 18 33 35 38
42 51 57 61 76 81 82 88 90a 90b 93 94 97
101 102 105 131 133 141 142 149 175CV
177 180 189 201 203 204 205 205abs 206S
209 216 218 223 226 234 241 252 254 256
263 307 308 312 319 321 322 323 326 327
328 337 363 367 378 383 384 385 386 390
394 398 400 404 421 424 425 429 432 436
440 442 444 450 452 453 457 460 462 465
466* 468 469 479 483 489 491 496 506 517
522 547 582 592 603 604 605 607 608 610
615 617 618 620 622 623 628 629 630 633
634 635 636Z 638 639 642 656 664f 665 676
680 699 757 796 801 808 823 824 876 901
910Z 912 915 918 919 920 921 922 927 928
935 941 945 959 986 996 997 1003 1022
1040 1058 1066 1067 1069 1070 1072 1075
1094 1099 1100 1101 1102 1103 1104 1105
1107 1115 1127 1149 1161 1241 1242 1244
1245 1247 1249 1250 1251 1277 1315 1319
1352 1354 1359 1367 1384 1398 1400
1404V 1409 1424C 1425 1482 1490 1495
1501 1503 1508 1509 1521 1523 1524 1548
1563 1573(*f) 1594 1597 1599 1609 1610
1617 1618 1619 1622 1626 1628 1636 1637
1642 1643 1649 1652 1656 1661 1673 1678
1702 1704 1718 1719 1720 1721 1722 1723
1725 1726 1727 1728 1729 1730 1731 1732
1733 1736 1737 1738 1739 1740 1741 1742
1743 1744 1745 1746 1747 1748 1749 1750
1751 1752 1753 1754 1757 1761 1762 1763
1765 1766 1767 1768 1795 1827 1828 1829
1830f 1831 1832 1834 1835 1836 1837 1840
1841 1842 1843 1844 1846 1847 1849 1850
1851 1853 1854 1855 1856 1858 1859 1860
1861 1863 1864 1865 1867 1868 1869 1870
1871 1872 1874 1875 1876 1877 1880 1881
1882 1885 1889 1890 1891 1892 1893 1894
1896 1897 1899 1902 1903 2080 2085 2127
2131 2147 2180 2186 2191 2194 2197 2200
2218 2221 2242 2243 2255 2261 2279 2288
2298 2318 2344 2352 2374 2400 2404 2412
2423 2431 2466 2473 2475 2483 2484 2492
2494 2501 2502 2508 2523 2541 2544 2554

195

τὸ ἔλεος τοῦ κυρίου ἡμῶν Ἰησοῦ Χριστοῦ εἰς ζωὴν αἰώνιον.
14   16   18   20   22   24   26   28   30   32
22 καὶ οὓς μὲν ἐλεᾶτε διακρινομένους,
2   4   6   8   10

2558 2587 2625 2626 2652 2674 2691 2696
2704 2712 2716 2718 2723 2736 2746 2774
2776 2777 2805 2815 2816 2818 2865 L62
L145 L147 L156 L162 L164 L241 L422 L427
L585 L585/2 L591 L596 L603 L604 L606
L608 L617 L623 L740 L809 L840 L884f L921
L938 L1141 L1178 L1196 L1196/2 L1281
L1281/2 L1440 L1441 L1818 L2024 L2087
L2106

b εν αγαπη θεου εαυτους τηρησατε 2086
c εν αγαπη θεου τηρησατε εαυτους 999
   2401
df εαυτους εν αγαπη θεου τηρησητε 04C2
e εαυτους εν αγαπη θεου τηρησαντες 431
   621 632 1405 1724V
f εαυτους εν αγαπη θεου τηρησωμεν P72
   03 1292 1448 1505 1611 1845 1852 2495
g εαυτους εν αγαπη θεου τηρησομεν 1243
hf εαυτους εν αγαπη θεου τηρησονται 43
i εαυτους εν αγαπη του θεου τηρησωμεν
   044
j εαυτους εν αγαπη του θεου τηρησατε 104
   459
k εαυτους εν αγαπη του θεου τηρησαντες
   1838
l εαυτους εν τη αγαπη θεου τηρησατε 296
   1839
m εαυτους εν τη αγαπη του θεου τηρησατε
   467
n εαυτους αγαπη θεου τηρησατε 62 636Τ
   914 1311 1886
o εαυτους εν αγαπη τηρησατε 631
p εν αγαπη θεου τηρησατε 018 049 1 103
   110 175*V 221 242 250 302 309 314 325
   330 393 451 454 456 458 466C 601 602 606
   616 619 625 627 637 641 712 910T 917
   1162 1175 1248 1270 1297 1424* 1595
   1598 1646 1668 1734 1735 1760 1769 1780
   1862 1873 1888 2125 2143 2201 2516 2527
   2675 2705
↔ *f/g:* εαυτους εν αγαπη θεου
   τηρη[σ.]μ[ε]ν 04*
↑ 181 1240 1390 1857 L593 L1279 L1505
— 613 1717 1831S

12-30↑↓
a προσδεχομενοι το ελεος του κυριου ημων
   ιησου χριστου εις ζωην ...
b εις ζωην 922
↑ 181 1240 1390 1857 L593 L1279 L1505

12↑
a προσδεχομενοι ... 0316V 393V 1405f 1448f
   1524f 1872V 2674f
b προσευχομενοι L156
↔ *a/b:* προσ[..χο]μενο[ι] 400
↔ *a/b:* πρ[οσ..χομεν]οι 2400
↑ 922
— 1717

13↑
a om. ... 1610C
b εαυτους 915 1869
c εαυτοις 625 1107
↔ *af/bf:* εαυ 1610*
↑ 922
— 1717

16↑
a ελεος ... 33f 637(*f) 2191V 1837(*f) 2086f
   2652f
b τελος 462
c ευαγγελιον 1751
↑ 922
— 1717

20↑
a κυριου ... 635(*f)
b θεου και κυριου 131
c θεου 1409 1495
↑ 922
— 1717

22-30↑
a ημων ιησου χριστου εις ζωην ... 0316V
   42V 1769V 2716V
b εις ζωην ημων ιησου χριστου P72
c ημων κυριου ιησου χριστου εις ζωην 61V
d ημων και κυριου ιησου χριστου εις ζωην
   1495

e ημων ιησου εις ζωην 1070
f ιησου χριστου εις ζωην 1241
g ιησου εις ζωην 1735
h ημων εις ζωην 613
↑ 922

32
a αιωνιον ... 6f

v. 22
— P74 P78 0251 69 172 614 720 832 913 1106
1360 1799 1831 1895 2138 2289 2356 2378
2511 2627 2653 2822 L6

2-23,22↓
a και ους μεν ελεατε διακρινομενους ους
δε σωζετε εκ πυρος αρπαζοντες ους δε
ελεατε εν φοβω ...
b ους μεν εκ πυρος αρπασατε διακρινομενους δε ελεειτε εν φοβω P72

2-10↑
a και ους μεν ελεατε διακρινομενους 01 03
04C2V 044 88 101A1 442 621 915 1243
1643A1 1845 1846 L596
b και ους μεν ελεειτε διακρινομενους 018K
1751 1842Z 1852 1888f 2242
c και ους μεν ελεειτε διακρινομενοι 018T
020 025 049 056 0142 1 3 18 35 38 43 51 57
62 76 82 90a 90b 94 97 101T 102 103 104
105 110 131 133 141 142 149 175 177 180
189 201 203 204 205 205abs 206S 209 216
218 221 223 226 234 241 242 250 252 254
256 263 296 302 307 308 309 312 314 319
321 325 327 328 330 337 363 367 378 383
384 385 386 390 393 394 398 400 404 421
424*V 425 429 431 432 440 444 450 451
452 453 454 456 457 458 459 460 465 466
467 468 469 479 483 489 491 496 506 517
522 547 582 592 601 602 603 604 605T 606
607 608 613 615 616 618 619 620 622 625
627 628 630 631 632 633 634 635 636 637
638 639 641 642 656 664 676 680 699 712
757 796 808 823 824 876 901 910 912 914
917 918 919 920 921 922 927 928 935 941
945 959 986 996 997 1003 1022 1040 1058
1066 1069 1070 1072 1075 1094 1099 1100
1101 1102 1103 1104 1105 1107 1115 1127
1149 1161 1162 1175 1240 1242 1244 1245
1247 1248 1249 1250 1251 1270 1277 1292
1297 1311 1315 1319 1352 1354 1359 1367
1384 1390 1398 1400 1404 1405 1424 1425
1448 1482 1490 1495 1501 1503 1505V
1508 1509 1521 1523 1524 1548 1563 1573

1594 1595 1597 1598 1599 1609 1617 1618
1619 1622 1626 1628 1636 1637 1642
1643T 1646 1649 1652 1656 1661 1668
1673 1678 1702 1704 1717 1718 1719 1720
1721 1722 1723 1724 1725 1726 1727 1728
1729 1730 1731 1732 1733 1734 1736 1737
1738 1740 1741 1742 1743 1744(*f) 1745
1746 1747 1748 1749 1750 1752 1753 1754
1757 1760 1761 1762 1763 1765 1766 1767
1768 1769 1780 1795 1827 1828 1829 1830
1831S 1832 1834 1835 1838 1840A 1841
1842T 1843 1844 1847 1849 1850 1851
1853 1854 1855 1856 1857 1858 1859 1860
1861 1862 1863 1864 1865 1867 1868 1869
1870 1871 1872 1873 1874 1876 1877 1880
1882 1885 1886 1889 1890 1891 1892 1894
1896 1897 1899 1902 1903 2080 2085 2086
2125 2127 2131 2143 2147 2180 2191 2194
2197 2200 2201 2218 2221 2243 2255 2261
2279 2288 2318 2352 2401*V 2404 2412
2423 2431 2466 2473 2475 2483 2484 2492
2494 2495 2501 2502 2508 2516 2523 2527
2541 2554 2558 2587 2625 2626 2652 2674
2675 2696 2705 2712 2716 2718 2723 2736
2746 2774 2776 2777 2815 2816 2818 2865
L62 L145 L147 L156 L162 L164 L241 L427
L427/2 L585Z L591 L593 L603 L604 L606
L608 L617 L623 L740 L809 L840 L884 L921
L938 L1141 L1178 L1196 L1279 L1281
L1440 L1441 L1505 L1818 L2024 L2087
L2106
d και ους μεν ελεγχετε διακρινομενους 02
04*V 0316V 5 6 33 61 81 93 101A2 322 323
326 424C 436 462 605A 610 617 623 665
999 1067 1241 1409 1611 1643A2 1735
1739 1836 1837 1839 1875 1881 2298 2344
2374 2401C 2544 2805 L422 L585T L585/2
L1281/2
e και ους μεν ελεγχετε διακρινομενοι 629
1840T 1893 2186 L1196/2
f και ους μεν ελεγετε διακρινομενους 181
g και ους δε ελεειτε διακρινομενοι 1610
h και ους ελεειτε διακρινομενοι 801 2691
i και 2704
↔ *c/e:* και ους μεν ελ[3-4]τε διακρινομενοι
42
↔ *c/g:* και [5-6] ελεειτε διακρινομενοι 2400
↑ P72

23 οὓς δὲ σῴζετε ἐκ πυρὸς ἁρπάζοντες, οὓς δὲ ἐλεᾶτε ἐν φόβῳ
　　2　4　　6　　8　　10　　　12　　　　14　16　18　　20　22
μισοῦντες καὶ τὸν ἀπὸ τῆς σαρκὸς ἐσπιλωμένον χιτῶνα.
　　24　　26　28　　30　32　　34　　　　36　　　　38

---

v. 23

— P74 P78 0251 69 172 614 720 832 913 1106
1360 1799 1831 1895 2138 2289 2356 2378
2511 2627 2653 2822 L6

2-12↑↓

a ους δε σωζετε εκ πυρος αρπαζοντες ...
　424C1V
b ους δε εν φοβω σωζετε εκ πυρος
　αρπαζοντες 424*V 424C2V
↑ P72

14-22↑↓

a ους δε ελεατε εν φοβω ... 424Z
b om. 424T
↑ P72

2-22↑

a ους δε σωζετε εκ πυρος αρπαζοντες ους
　δε ελεατε εν φοβω 01C1V 02 044 6 33 81
　93 181 322 323 326(*f) 605A 610* 617*V
　623 665 1735 1739 1836 1837 1839 1875
　1881 2298 2374 2805 L585 L585/2 L1196/2
　L1281/2
bf ους δε σωζετε εκ πυρος αρπαζετες ους δε
　ελεατε εν φοβω 01*
c ους δε σωζετε εκ πυρος αρπαζοντες ους
　δε ελεειτε εν φοβω 5 436 462 610C 617C
　1067 1241 1409 1643A 2344
d ους δε σωζετε εκ πυρος αρπαζοντες τους
　δε ελεειτε εν φοβω 0316
e ους δε εν φοβω σωζετε εκ πυρος
　αρπαζοντες ους δε ελεατε εν φοβω 999
　1611 2401Z
f ους δε εν φοβω εκ πυρος αρπαζοντες
　σωζετε ους δε ελεειτε εν φοβω 2544
g ους δε εν φοβω σωζετε εκ πυρος
　αρπαζοντες ετερους δε ελεειτε εν φοβω
　θεου 629C
h ους δε σωζετε εκ πυρος αρπαζοντες ους
　δε ελεγχετε εν φοβω 94 104 307 321 378T
　442 453 467 621 918* 1678 1838 1846 2147
　2197 2652 2818 L596
i ους δε σωζετε εκ πυρος αρπαζοντες ους
　δε ελεγετε εν φοβω 2412

j ους δε εν φοβω σωζετε εκ πυρος
　αρπαζοντες ους δε ελεγχετε εν φοβω 76
　88 250Z 378Z 459 489 915 918CV 927 945
　1509 1729 1731 1743 1842 1843 1845Z
　1868 1873 2143 2201Z 2527 2746 L1281
k ους δε σωζετε εκ πυρος αρπαζοντες ους
　δε ελεγχετε διακρινομενους ους δε
　ελεειτε εν φοβω 385 639
l ους δε εν φοβω σωζετε εκ πυρος
　αρπαζοντες και ους μεν ελεγχετε
　διακρινομενους ους δε σωζετε εκ πυρος
　αρπαζοντες ους δε ελεατε εν φοβω 2242f
m ους δε σωζετε εκ πυρος αρπαζοντες ους
　δε εν φοβω 61Cf
n σωζετε εκ πυρος αρπαζοντες ους δε
　ελεατε εν φοβω 03
o ους δε εν φοβω σωζετε εκ πυρος
　αρπαζοντες 018 020 025 049 056 0142 1 3
　18 35(*f) 38 57 62 82 90a 90b 97 101 102
　103 105 110 131 133 141 149 175T 177 180
　189 201 203 204 205 205abs 206S 209 218
　221 226 241 242 250T 252 254 256 263 296
　302 308 309 312 314 319 325 327 328 330
　337 363 383 384 386 393 394 398 400 404
　421 425 429 431f 432 444 450 451 452 454
　457 458 460 465 466 468 479 491 506 522
　547 582 592 601 602 603 604 605T 606 607
　608 613 615 616 618 619 620 622 625 627
　632 633 634 635 638 641 656 664 676 680
　699 712 757 796 801 823 824 876 901 910
　914f 917 919 920 921 922 928 941 959 986
　997 1022f 1040 1058 1066 1069 1072 1075
　1094 1099 1101 1102 1103 1104 1105 1107
　1115 1149 1161 1162 1175 1240 1242 1244
　1245f 1247 1248 1249 1250 1251 1270 1277
　1297 1319 1352 1354 1384 1390 1398 1400
　1424 1448 1482 1490 1495 1503 1508 1521
　1523 1524 1548 1573 1595 1597 1598 1599
　1617 1618 1619 1622 1628 1636 1637 1642
　1643T 1646f 1652 1656 1668 1704 1717
　1719 1720 1721 1723 1724 1725 1726 1728
　1730 1732 1733 1734 1736 1737 1738 1740
　1741 1742 1745 1746 1747 1748 1749 1750
　1752 1754 1757 1760 1761 1762 1763 1765
　1766 1767f 1768 1769 1780 1795 1827 1828
　1830 1831S 1832 1834 1835 1840 1841

1844 1847 1849 1850 1851 1853 1854 1855
1856 1857 1858 1859 1860 1862 1864 1865
1867 1869 1870 1871 1872 1874(*f) 1876
1877 1880 1882 1885 1886 1888 1889 1890
1891 1892T 1893 1894 1896 1897 1899
1902 1903 2080 2086 2125 2127 2131 2180
2186 2191 2194 2201T 2218 2221 2255
2261 2288 2352 2400 2401T 2404 2423
2431 2466 2475 2484 2492 2494 2501 2502
2508 2516 2523 2541 2554 2558 2587 2625
2626 2674 2691 2704 2705 2712 2716 2723
2736 2776 2777 2815 2816 2865 L147 L593
L603 L884 L1196 L1441 L2087

p ους δε εν φοβω εκ πυρος σωζετε
αρπαζοντες 175Z

q ους δε σωζετε εκ πυρος αρπαζοντες εν
φοβω 04 630 1243f 1292 1505 1845T 1852
2200 2495

r ους δε σωζετε εκ χειρος αρπαζοντος εν
φοβω L1440

s ους δε σωζοντες εκ πυρος αρπαζοντες εν
φοβω 1751

t ους δε εν φοβω σωζεσθε εκ τινος
αρπαζοντες 43 142

u ους δε εκ φοβου σωζετε εκ πυρος
αρπαζοντες 1829

v ους μεν εν φοβω σωζετε εκ πυρος
αρπαζοντες 1610

w ους δε εν φοβω σωζετε εκ του πυρος
αρπαζοντες 42 216 234 367 390 440 456
483 496 517 628 631 636 637 912 935 996
1003 1070 1100 1315 1367 1404 1501 1594
1609 1626 1649 1661 1673 1702 1722 1727
1753 1861 1863 1892Z 2085 2243 2279
2318 2473 2483 2675C 2696 2718 2774 L62
L145 L164 L427 L427/2 L591 L604 L606
L608 L740 L809 L840 L921 L938 L1141
L1178 L1279 L1505 L2024 L2106

x ους δε εν φοβω σωζεσθε εκ του πυρος
αρπαζοντες 2675*

y ως δε εν φοβω σωζετε εκ του πυρος
αρπαζοντες L623

z ους δε εν φοβω σωζετε εκ του πυρος
αφαρπαζοντες 1311

a' ους δε εν φοβω θεου σωζετε εκ του πυρος
αρπαζοντες 1405

b' ους δε εν φοβω σωζετε ως εκ του πυρος
αρπαζοντες 51 223 469

c' ους δε εν φοβω σωζετε εκ πυρος
αρπαζοντες τον εαυτων αμαρτιων
κεκηλιδωμενον βιον 1744

d' ους δε φοβω σωζετε εκ του πυρος
αρπαζοντες L162 L241

e' ους δε σωζετε εκ του πυρος αρπαζοντες
L617

f ους δε σωζετε εκ πυρος αρπαζοντες 642
808 1127 1359 1425 1563 1718 L156(*f)
L422 L1818

? ους δε εν φοβω σωζετε εκ πυρος
αρπαζοντες ους δε ελε[6-9]τες εν φοβω
θεου 629*

↔ *a/c/h/i:* ους δε σωζετε εκ πυρος
αρπαζοντες ους δε [6-10] εν φοβω 61*f

↑ P72 424

23

a om. ...

b και 680

24

a μισουντες ... 1270f 1869V 2401Z 2501f
2774f

b μισησαντες 1311

c αιτουντες 680

d om. 2401T

↔ *a/b/c:* [5-6]ντες 458

26

a και ... 1869f

b om. 1881 L422

— 2716

28-30

a τον απο ... 0316V 131Z 631f

bf απο τον L884

c τον εκ 2544

d τον 131T L164

e απο 1066 1642 2776

— 2716

32-34

a της σαρκος ... 613V 656f 1384V 1839f
L606f

b σαρκος 203 506 L1440

36

a εσπιλωμενον ... P72f 0142f 0316fV 180f
458V 1115V 1831Sf 2288V L2087f

bf επιλωμενον 632Z 1241

cf επιμελουμενον 1673

d επιμενων 632T

— 1384

38

a χιτωνα ... 876f 1594(*f)

24 τῷ δὲ δυναμένῳ φυλάξαι ὑμᾶς
2　4　　6　　　8　　　10
ἀπταίστους καὶ στῆσαι κατενώπιον
12　　14　16　　18

---

v. 24

— P78 0251 69 172 614 720 832 913 1106
1360 1799 1831 1895 2138 2289 2356 2378
2511 2627 2653 2822 L6

2-6

a　τω δε δυναμενω ... 04V 0316V 935V 1521f
1780Z 1827f
b　τω δυναμενω δε 1270 1595
cf　των δε δυναμενων 459 616
d　τω δυναμενω 1297 1598 1780T
— P74

8-26↓

a　φυλαξαι υμας απταιστους και στησαι
κατενωπιον της δοξης αυτου αμωμους
b　στηριξαι ασπιλους αμωμους αγνευομενους απεναντι της δοξης αυτου P72
— 2492

8-14↑↓

a　φυλαξαι υμας απταιστους και 01 03 020
044 056 0142 0316V 5 33 61 81 88 101T
102 103 181 189 218 296 308 312 326 429
436(*f) 452 460 462 483 522 547 592 605A
606 610 617 622 623 641 642 676 808 876
901 915 941 1003 1022 1066 1067 1102
1103 1127 1244C 1245 1270 1297 1352
1359 1390 1404V 1409 1425 1448 1490
1563 1597 1599Z 1610f 1643T 1718 1728
1735 1760 1765 1828 1830C 1831S 1832
1836 1837 1853 1875 1894 2131 2191Z
2194 2243 2318 2374 2475 2494 2527 2544
2805 L164 L585 L585/2 L884 L1196/2
L1281 L1281/2 L2087
b　φυλαξαι υμας ασπιλους και 1830*
c　φυλαξαι υμας απταιστως και 2344
d　υμας φυλαξαι απταιστως και 2242
e　φυλαξαι ημας απταιστους και 02 1595
2816Z
f　φυλαξαι αυτους απταιστους και 018 025
049 1 3 18 35 38 42 51 57 62 82 90a 90b 97
105 110 133 141 142 149 175 180 201 203
204 205 205abs 206S 209 216 221 223 226
234 241 242 250 252 256 263 302 309 314

319 325 327 328 330 363 383 384 386 390
393 394 398 400 404 421 425 432 440 444
450 451 454 456 457 465 466 469 479 491
506 517 582 601 602 603 604 605T 607 608
613 615 616 619 620 627 628 629 632 634
635 636Z 637 638 656 664 680 699 712 757
796 801 823 824 910 912 914 917 919 920
921 928 935 959 986 997 1040 1058 1069
1070 1072 1075 1094 1099 1100 1101 1104
1105 1107 1115 1149 1161 1162 1175 1240
1244*V 1247 1248 1249 1250 1251 1277
1315 1354 1367 1384 1398 1400 1424 1482
1495 1503 1508 1521 1548 1573 1594 1598
1599T 1609 1617 1618 1619 1622 1626
1628 1636 1637 1643A 1646 1652 1656
1668 1673 1702 1704 1719 1720 1721 1722
1723 1724 1725 1726 1727 1730 1731 1732
1733 1734 1736 1737 1740 1741 1742 1745
1746 1748 1749 1752 1753 1754 1757 1761
1762 1763 1766 1767 1768 1769 1780 1795
1827 1834 1835 1839 1840 1841 1847 1849
1850 1851 1854 1855 1856 1857 1858 1859
1860 1861 1862 1863 1864 1865 1867 1869
1870 1871 1872 1874 1876 1877 1880 1882
1885 1888 1889 1890 1891 1892 1893 1896
1897 1899 1903 2080 2085T 2086 2125(*f)
2127 2143 2180 2186 2191T 2218 2221
2255 2261 2279 2352 2400 2404 2423 2431
2466 2473 2483 2484 2501 2502 2508 2516
2523 2541 2554 2558 2587 2625 2626 2674
2675 2691 2704 2705 2712 2716 2718 2723
2736 2774 2776 2777 2815 2865 L62 L145
L147 L156 L162 L241 L422 L427 L427/2
L591 L603 L604 L606 L608 L617 L623f L740
L809 L840 L921f L938 L1141 L1178 L1196
L1279 L1441 L1505 L1818f L2024 L2106
g　φυλαξαι απταιστους αυτους και 177 337
618 1738
h　αυτους φυλαξαι απταιστους και 1642
1829
i　φυλαξαι αυτους απταιστως και 131f 496
625 631 636T 922 1242 1311 1319 1405
1649f 1747 1750 1902 2696 L593
j　φυλαξαι αυτους αμεμπτους και 43

k φυλαξαι ημας αμεμπτους και 431
l διαφυλαξαι αυτους απταιστως και 459 1842
m φυλαξαι τους απταιστους και 1661
n φυλαξαι υμας αυτους απταιστους και 385 639
o φυλαξαι υμας απταιστους ασπιλους και 94 2201
p φυλαξαι υμας απταιστους και ασπιλους 04 254 442 467 621 945 1243 1292 1505 1523 1524 1611 1844 1845 1846 1852 2495 L596
q φυλαξαι ημας απταιστους και ασπιλους 367
r φυλαξαι αυτους απταιστους ασπιλους και 2085Z
s φυλαξαι υμας απταιστους και ασπιλους και 6 76 93 104 307 321 378 453 468 489 630 665 918 927 999 1678V 1743 1751 1838 1843 1868 1873 2147 2197 2200 2401Z 2412 2652 2746 2818
t υμας φυλαξαι απταιστους και ασπιλους και 322 323 1241 1501 1739 1881 2298
u φυλαξαι ημας απταιστους και ασπιλους και 1729
v φυλαξαι αυτους απταιστους και ασπιλους και 101Z 1509(*f) 1744 L1440
w φυλαξαι αυτους απταιστους 1886
x φυλαξαι απταιστους και 633 1717 2816T
↔ a/e/f/m: φυλαξαι [4-6] απταιστους και 996 2288
↔ c/i/: φυλαξ[αι 4-6] απ[ταιστω]ς και 458TV
↔ a/e/f/m: φυλαξ[αι 4-6] απ[ταιστ]ους και 458Z
↔ f/g/i/j/r/v: φυλαξαι α[>12] και 2401T
↔ a/b/c/d/e/f/g/h/i/j/k/l/m/n/o/r/s/t/u/v:]κα[ι P74
↑ P72
↓ 424
− 2492

8-10↑
a φυλαξαι υμας ... 424C
b φυλαξαι αυτους 424*
↑ P72
− P74 2492

12-14↑
a απταιστους και ... 424T
b απταιστους και ασπιλους και 424Z
↑ P72
− 2492

16↑
a στησαι ... 102f 610V 1738f L606(*f) L1279(*f)
b στησεται L623
c στηριξαι 0316 5 623 2805
d καταστησαι 263 1886
↑ P72
− P74 2492

18↑
a κατενωπιον 01 02 03 018 020 025 044 049 056 0142 0316V 1 3 5 6 18 33 35 38 42 43 51 57 61 62 76 81 82 90a 90b 93 94 97 102 103 104 105 110 131 133 141 142 149 175 177 180 181 189 201 203 204 205 205abs 206S 209 216 218 221 223 226 234 241 242 250 252 256 263 296 302 307 308 309 312 314 319 321 322 323 325 326 327 328 330 337 363 367 378 383 384 385 386 390 393 394 398 400 404 421 424 425 429 431 432 436 440 442 444 450 451 452 453 454 456 457 458V 459 460 462 465 466 467 468 469 479 483 489 491 496 506 517 522 547 582 592 601 602 603 604 605 606 607 608 610 613 615 616 617 618 619 620 621 622 623 625 627 628 629 631 632 633 634 635 636 637 638 639 641 642 656 664 665 676 680 699 712 757 796 801 808 823 824 876 901 910 912 914 917 918 919 920 921 922 927 928 935 941 945 959 986 996 997 999 1003 1022 1040 1058 1066 1067 1069 1070 1072 1075 1094 1099 1100 1101 1102 1103 1104 1105 1107 1115 1127 1149 1161 1162 1175 1240 1241 1242 1244 1245 1247 1248 1249 1250 1251 1270 1277 1297 1311 1315 1319 1352 1354 1359 1367 1384 1390 1398 1400 1404 1405 1409 1424 1425 1448 1482 1490 1495 1501 1503 1508 1509 1521 1548 1563 1573 1594 1595 1597 1598 1599 1609 1610 1617 1618 1619 1622 1626 1628 1636 1637 1642 1646 1649 1652 1656 1661 1668 1673 1678 1702 1704 1717 1718 1719 1720 1721 1722 1723 1724 1725 1726 1727 1728 1729 1730 1731 1732 1733 1734 1735 1736 1737 1738 1739 1740 1741 1742 1743 1744 1745 1746 1747 1748 1749 1750 1751 1752 1753 1754 1757 1760 1761 1762 1763 1765 1766 1767 1768 1769 1780 1795 1827 1828 1829 1830 1831S 1832 1834 1835 1836 1837 1838 1839 1840 1841 1842 1843 1847 1849 1850 1851 1853 1854 1855 1856 1857 1858 1859f 1860 1861 1862 1863 1864 1865 1867 1868 1869 1870 1871 1872 1873 1874 1875 1876 1877 1880 1881 1882 1885 1886 1888

τῆς δόξης αὐτοῦ ἀμώμους ἐν ἀγαλλιάσει,
20   22   24   26   28   30
25 μόνῳ θεῷ σωτῆρι ἡμῶν
2   4   6   8

1889 1890 1891 1892 1893 1894 1896 1897
1899 1902 1903 2080 2085 2086 2125 2127
2131 2143 2147 2180 2186 2191 2194 2197
2201 2218 2221 2242 2243 2255 2261 2279
2288 2298 2318 2344 2352 2374 2400 2401
2404 2412 2423 2431 2466 2473 2475 2483
2484 2494 2501 2502 2508 2516 2523 2527
2541 2544 2554 2558 2587 2625 2626 2652
2674 2675 2691 2696 2704 2705 2712 2718
2723 2736 2746 2774 2776 2777 2805 2815
2816 2818 2865 L62 L145 L147 L156 L162
L164 L241 L422 L427 L427/2 L585 L585/2
L591 L593 L596 L603 L604 L606 L608 L617
L623 L740 L809 L840 L884 L921 L938
L1141 L1178 L1196 L1196/2 L1279 L1281
L1281/2 L1440 L1441 L1505 L1818 L2024
L2087 L2106

b   ενωπιον 04 101 254 630 1243 1292 1505
1523 1524 1611 1643 1844 1845 1846 1852
2200 2495

c   κατεναντι 88 915

↔   *a/b*:]πιϙ[ν P74

↑   P72

—   2492 2716

20-24↑
a   της δοξης αυτου ... 0316V 88fV 458V
628(*f) 629C 1646C 1115V 2288V 2473f
2865Z
b   αυτου της δοξης 2400
c   της αγιας δοξης αυτου 1243
d   δοξης αυτου 629*V
e   αυτου 309 922 1245 2865T
?   της δοξης [...] θ̄ῡ 1646*
↑   P72
—   P74 1404 2492 2716

26↑
a   αμωμους ... 0316V
b   αμεμπτους 02
c   απταιστους 2298
d   om. 489 613 927 1424 1729 1843 1868 1873
2527
↔   *a/b*: αμ[P74

↑   P72
—   2492 2716

27
a   om. ...
b   ασπιλους 88 915
—   P74 2492

v. 25
—   P74 P78 0251 69 172 614 720 832 913 1106
1360 1799 1831 1895 2138 2289 2356 2378
2492 2511 2627 2653 2822 L6

2-8↑↓
a   μονω θεω σωτηρι ημων ...
b   μονω σοφω θεω σωτηρι ημων 629C
c   μονω θεω σοφω σωτηρι ημων 440
d   [>12] ημων 629*

2↑
a   μονω ... 458V
b   om. 1626 2705
↑   440 629

3↑
a   om. P72 01 02 03 04 044 0316 6 33 81 88
93 181 322 323 424C 436 442 621 623T 630
665 915 1067 1241 1243 1292 1409 1505
1611 1739 1836 1845 1852 1875 1881 2200
2298 2344 2495 2805 L596
b   σοφω 018 020 025 049 056 0142 1 3 5 18 35
38 42 43 51 57 61 62 76 82 90a 90b 94 97
101 102 103 104 105 110 131 133 141 142
149 175 177 180 189 201 203 204 205
205abs 206S 209 216 218 221 223 226 234
241 242 250 252 254 256 263 296 302 307
308 309 312 314 319 321 325 326 327 328
330 337 363 367 378 383 384 385 386 390
393 394 398 400 404 421 424* 425 429 431
432 444 450 451 452 453 454 456 457 458
459 460 462 465 466 467 468 469 479 483
489 491 496 506 517 522 547 582 592 601
602 603 604 605 606 607 608 610V 613 615
616 617 618 619 620 622 623Z 625 627 628
631 632 633 634 635 636 637 638 639 641
642 656 664 676 680 699 712 757 796 801

808 823 824 876 901 910 912 914 917 918
919 920 921 922 927 928 935 941 945 959
986 996 997 999 1003 1022 1040 1058 1066
1069 1070 1072 1075 1094 1099 1100 1101
1102 1103 1104 1105 1107 1115 1127 1149
1161 1162 1175 1240 1242 1244 1245 1247
1248 1249 1250 1251 1270 1277 1297 1311
1315 1319 1352 1354 1359 1367 1384 1390
1398 1400 1404 1405 1424 1425 1448 1482
1490 1495 1501 1503 1508 1509 1521 1523
1524 1548 1563 1573 1594 1595 1597 1598
1599 1609 1610 1617 1618 1619 1622 1626
1628 1636 1637 1642 1643 1646 1649 1652
1656 1661 1668 1673 1678 1702 1704 1717
1718 1719 1720 1721 1722 1723 1724 1725
1726 1727 1728 1729 1730 1731 1732 1733
1734 1735 1736 1737 1738 1740 1741 1742
1743 1744 1745 1746 1747 1748 1749 1750
1751 1752 1753 1754 1757 1760 1761 1762
1763 1765 1766 1767 1768 1769 1780 1795
1827 1828 1829 1830 1831S 1832 1834
1835 1837 1838 1839 1840 1841 1842 1843
1844 1846 1847 1849 1850 1851 1853 1854
1855 1856 1857 1858 1859 1860 1861 1862
1863 1864 1865 1867 1868 1869 1870 1871
1872 1873 1874 1876 1877 1880 1882 1885
1886 1888 1889 1890 1891 1892 1893 1894
1896 1897 1899 1902 1903 2080 2085 2086
2125 2127 2131 2143 2147 2180 2186 2191
2194 2197 2201 2218 2221 2242 2243 2255
2261 2279 2288 2318 2352 2374 2400 2401
2404 2412 2423 2431 2466 2473 2475 2483
2484 2494 2501 2502 2508 2516 2523 2527
2541 2544 2554 2558 2587 2625 2626 2652
2674 2675 2691 2696 2704 2705 2712 2716
2718 2723 2736 2746 2774 2776 2777 2815
2816 2818 2865 L62 L145 L156 L164
L241 L422 L427 L427/2 L585 L585/2 L591
L593 L603 L604 L606 L608 L617 L623 L740
L809 L840 L884 L921 L938 L1141 L1178
L1196 L1196/2 L1279 L1281 L1281/2
L1440 L1441 L1505 L1818 L2024 L2087
L2106

↑   440 629

4-8↑

a   θεω σωτηρι ημων 01 02 03 04 018 020 025
044 049 056 0142 1 3 5 18 33 35 38 43 51 57
62 76 81 82 88 90a 90b 93 94 97 101 103
104 105 110 131 133 141 142 149 175 177
180 181 189 201 203 204 205 205abs 206S
209 216 218 221 223 226 242 250 252 254
256 263 296 302 307 308 312 314 319 321

322 323C 325 327 328 330 337 367 378 383
384 385 386 393 394 398 400 404 421 424T
425 429 431 432 436 442 444 451 452 453
454 457 458 459 460 462 465 466 467 468
469 479 483 489 491 496 506 517 547 582
592 601 602 603 604 605 606 607 608 610
613 615 616 617 618 620 621 622 623 625
627 628 630 631 632 633 634 635 636 637
638 639 641 642 656 664 665 676 680 699
712 757 796 801 808 823 824 876 901 910
914 915 918 919 920 921 922 927 928 935
941 945 959 986 996Z 997 999 1022 1040
1058 1066 1067 1069 1070 1072 1075 1094
1099 1100 1101 1102 1103 1104 1105 1107
1115 1127 1149 1161 1240 1242 1243f 1244
1245 1247 1248 1249 1250 1277 1292 1311
1315 1352 1354 1359 1367 1398 1400 1404
1409 1424 1425 1448 1482 1490 1495 1501
1503 1505 1508 1509 1521 1523 1524 1548
1563 1573 1594V 1597 1599 1609 1610
1611 1617 1618 1619 1622 1626 1628 1636
1637 1642 1643 1646f 1649 1652 1656 1668
1673 1678 1704 1717 1718 1719 1720 1721
1722 1723 1724 1725 1726 1728 1729 1730
1731 1732 1733 1734 1735 1736 1737 1738
1739(Cf) 1740 1741 1742 1743 1744 1745
1746 1747 1748 1749 1750 1751 1752 1754
1757 1761 1762 1763 1765 1766 1767 1768
1769 1780 1795 1827 1828 1829 1830
1831S 1832 1835 1836 1838 1839 1840
1841 1842 1843 1844 1845 1846 1847 1849
1850 1852 1853 1854 1855 1856 1857 1858
1859 1860 1862 1864 1865 1867 1868 1869
1870 1871 1872 1873 1875 1876 1880 1881
1882 1885 1886 1888 1889 1890 1891 1892
1894 1896 1897 1899 1902 1903 2080 2086
2125 2127 2131 2143 2147 2180 2186 2191
2194 2197 2200 2201 2218 2221 2242 2243
2255 2261 2298 2344 2352 2374 2400 2401
2404 2412 2423 2431 2466 2473 2475 2483
2484 2494 2495 2501 2502 2508 2516 2523
2527 2541 2544 2554 2558 2587 2625 2626
2652 2674 2691 2696 2704 2705 2712 2716
2718 2723 2736 2746 2774 2776 2777 2805
2815 2816 2818 2865 L62 L145 L147 L156
L162 L164 L241 L427/2 L596 L603 L604
L606 L608 L617 L623 L740 L809 L840 L921
L938 L1141 L1178 L1279 L1440 L1441
L1505 L1818f L2024 L2087 L2106

b   σωτηρι θεω ημων 1851 L591

c   σωτηρι ημων θεω 522

d   θεω σωτηρι υμων 323*V 1241

e   θεω πατρι ημων L422 L593

διὰ Ἰησοῦ Χριστοῦ τοῦ κυρίου ἡμῶν δόξα μεγαλωσύνη
10   12   14   16   18   20   22   24
κράτος καὶ ἐξουσία πρὸ παντὸς τοῦ αἰῶνος
26   28   30   32   34   36   38

---

f και σωτηρι ημων L585/2 L1196/2
   L1281/2
g θεω και σωτηρι ημων 6 241 363 424Z
   1251 1270 1297 1595 1598 2318 L585
   L1196 L1281
h θεω ημων και σωτηρι 61 326 1837
i σοφω τω θεω σωτηρι ημων 1319
j θεω σωτηρι 102
k θεω ημων P72 450
l σωτηρι ημων 42 234 309 390 456 619 912
   917 996T 1003 1162 1175 1390 1405 1661
   1702 1727 1753 1760 1834 1861 1863 1874
   1877 1893 2085 2279 2675 L427 L884
↔ a/d: θεω σωτηρι [....] 0316
↔ a/d: θ[εω] σ[ωτηρι .μων] 2288
↔ a/d/e: θεω [.........] 1384
↑ 440 629

9
a om. ...
b αυτω δοξα κρατος τιμη P72

10-20
a δια ιησου χριστου του κυριου ημων
   P72(*f) 01 02V 03 04 020 044 0316V 5 6 33
   61 81 88 93(*f) 94 101 104 175 181 189 252
   254 307 321 322 323 326 378 436 442 453
   462 489 621 623 629 630 665 676 876 915
   918 927 945 999 1067 1102 1270 1292 1297
   1409 1501 1505 1523 1524 1595 1597 1598
   1609 1611 1643 1678 1729 1731 1735 1739
   1751 1765 1827 1832 1836 1837 1840 1843
   1844 1845 1846 1852 1868 1872 1873 1875
   1881 2143 2147 2186 2197 2200 2201 2242
   2243 2298 2318 2344 2374 2401Z 2412
   2494 2495 2527 2544 2652 2805 2818 L164
   L585 L585/2 L596V L1196 L1196/2 L1281
   L1281/2
b δια ιησου χριστου του κυριου υμων 1241
c δια του ιησου χριστου και κυριου ημων
   1509
d δια ιησου χριστου ημων 102
e ιησου χριστου 1838
f om. 018 025 049 056 0142 1 3 18 35 38 42
   43 51 57 62 76 82 90a 90b 97 103 105 110

131 133 141 142 149 177 180 201 203 204
205 205abs 206S 209 216 218 221 223 226
234 241 242 250 256 263 296 302 308 309
312 314 319 325 327 328 330 337 363 367
383 384 385 386 390 393 394 398 400 404
421 424 425 429 431 432 440 444 450 451
452 454 456 457 458 459 460 465 466 467
468 469 479 483 491 496 506 517 522 547
582 592 601 602 603 604 605 606 607 608
610 613 615 616 617 618 619 620 622 625
627 628 631 632 633 634 635 636 637 638
639 641 642 656 664 680 699 712 757 796
801 808 823 824 901 910 912 914 917 919
920 921 922 928 935 941 959 986 996 997
1003 1022 1040 1058 1066 1069 1070 1072
1075 1094 1099 1100 1101 1103 1104 1105
1107 1115 1127 1149 1161 1162 1175 1240
1242 1243 1244 1245 1247 1248 1249 1250
1251 1277 1311 1315 1319 1352 1354 1359
1367 1384 1390 1398 1400 1404 1405 1424
1425 1448 1482 1490 1495 1503 1508 1521
1548 1563 1573 1594 1599 1610 1617 1618
1619 1622 1626 1628 1636 1637 1642 1646
1649 1652 1656 1661 1668 1673 1702 1704
1717 1718 1719 1720 1721 1722 1723 1724
1725 1726 1727 1728 1730 1732 1733 1734
1736 1737 1738 1740 1741 1742 1743 1744
1745 1746 1747 1748 1749 1750 1752 1753
1754 1757 1760 1761 1762 1763 1766 1767
1768 1769 1780 1795 1828 1829 1830
1831S 1834 1835 1839 1841 1842 1847
1849 1850 1851 1853 1854 1855 1856 1857
1858 1859 1860 1861 1862 1863 1864 1865
1867 1869 1870 1871 1874 1876 1877 1880
1882 1885 1886 1888 1889 1890 1891 1892
1893 1894 1896 1897 1899 1902 1903 2080
2085 2086 2125 2127 2131 2180 2191 2194
2218 2221 2255 2261 2279 2288 2352 2400
2401T 2404 2423 2431 2466 2473 2475
2483 2484 2501 2502 2508 2516 2523 2541
2554 2558 2587 2625 2626 2674 2675 2691
2696 2704 2705 2712 2716 2718 2723 2736
2746 2774 2776 2777 2815 2816 2865 L62
L145 L147 L156 L162 L241 L422 L427
L427/2 L591 L593 L603 L604 L606 L608

L617 L623 L740 L809 L840 L884 L921 L938
L1141 L1178 L1279 L1440 L1441 L1505
L1818 L2024 L2087 L2106

21

a   om. ... 01C2
b   αυτω P72
c   ω 01* 378
—   0316

22

a   δοξα ... 0316V 1751f 2242(*f)
b   η δοξα 378

24-30

a   μεγαλωσυνη κρατος και εξουσια 01 02 03
04 0316V 5 33 81 93 101 175 254 302 322
323 326 400 404 431 436 442 458 489 623
630 665 876 1241 1243 1292 1405 1409
1505 1523 1524 1611 1643 1661 1735 1739
1751 1765 1827 1832 1836 1837 1844 1845
1852 1875 2200 2243 2298 2344 2494 2495
2544 2805 L596 L1440

b   και μεγαλωσυνη κρατος εξουσια 43 1610
1890 2194f L1279

c   και μεγαλωσυνη κρατος και εξουσια 018
020 025 049 056 0142 1 3 6 18 35 38 42 51
57 61 62 76 82 88 90a 90b 94 97 102 103
104 105 110 131 133 141 142 149 177 180
181 189 201 203 204 205 205abs 206S 209
216 218 221 223 226 234 241 242 250 252
256 263 296 307 308 309 312 314 319 321
325 327 328 330 337 363 367 378 383 384
385 386 390 393 394 398 421 424 425 429
432 440 444 450 451 452 453 454 456 457
459 460 462 465 466 467 468 469 479 483
491 496 506 517 522 547 582 592 601 602
603 604 605 606 607 608 610 613 615 616f
617 618 619 620 621 622 625 627 628 632Z
633 634 635 636 637 638 639 641 642 656
664 676 680 699 712 757 796 801 808 823
824 901 910 912 914 915 917 918 919 920
921 922 927 928 935 945 959 986 996 997
999 1003 1022 1040 1058 1066 1069 1070
1072 1075 1094 1099 1100 1101 1102 1103
1104 1105 1107 1115 1127 1149 1161 1162
1175 1240 1242 1244 1245 1247 1248 1249
1250 1251 1270 1277 1297 1311 1315 1319
1352 1354 1359 1367 1384 1390 1398 1400
1404 1424 1425 1448 1482 1490 1495 1501
1503 1508 1509 1521 1548 1563 1573 1594
1595 1597 1598 1599 1609 1617 1618 1619
1622 1626 1628 1636 1637 1642 1646f 1649
1652 1656 1668 1673 1678 1702 1704 1717

1718 1719 1720 1721 1722 1723 1724 1725
1726 1727 1728 1729 1730 1731 1732 1733
1734 1736 1737 1738 1740 1741 1742 1743
1744 1745 1746 1747 1748 1749 1750 1752
1753 1754 1757 1760 1761 1762 1763 1766
1767 1768 1769 1780 1795 1828 1829 1830
1831S 1834V 1835 1838f 1839 1840 1841
1842 1843 1846 1847 1849 1850 1851 1853
1854 1855 1856 1857 1858 1859 1860 1861
1862 1863 1864 1865 1867 1868 1869 1870
1871 1872 1873 1874 1876 1877 1880 1881
1882 1885 1886 1888 1889 1891 1892 1893
1894 1896 1897 1899 1902 1903 2080 2085
2086 2125 2127 2131 2143 2147 2180 2186
2191 2197 2201 2218 2221 2242 2255 2261
2279 2288 2318 2352 2374 2400 2401 2404
2412 2423 2431 2466 2473(*f) 2475 2483
2484 2501 2502 2508 2516 2523 2527 2541
2554 2558 2587 2625 2626 2652 2674 2675
2691 2696 2704 2705 2712 2716 2718 2723
2736 2746 2774 2776 2777 2815 2816 2818
2865 L62 L145 L147 L156 L162 L241 L422f
L427 L427/2 L585 L585/2 L591 L593 L603
L604 L606 L608 L617 L623 L740 L809 L840
L884 L921 L938 L1141 L1178 L1196
L1196/2 L1281 L1281/2 L1441 L1505
L1818 L2024 L2087 L2106

d   και μεγαλοπρεπεια κρατος και εξουσια
632T

e   και μεγαλωσυνη και κρατος και εξουσια
629 631 941 L164(*f)

f   μεγαλωσυνη τε και κρατος και εξουσια
1067

g   μεγαλωσυνη κρατος εξουσια 044

h   και μεγαλωσυνη P72

32-38

a   προ παντος του αιωνος 01 02 03 04 020
044 0316 5 33 61 81 93 101 175 181 203 254
326 404 431 442 467 506 621 623 642 665
808 876 945 1127 1243 1359 1425 1495
1505 1509 1523 1524 1563 1611 1626 1643
1718 1735 1744 1751 1765 1828 1832 1836
1837 1839 1844 1845 1846 1852 1875 2086
2242 2243 2401Z 2494 2495 2544 2805
L164 L596

b   προ παντος αιωνος 6 88 94 104 252 307
321 322 323 378 436 453 459 462 630 915
918 999 1067 1241 1292 1409 1501 1609
1678 1739 1827 1838 1842 1872 1881 2147
2197 2200 2298 2344 2374 2412 2652 2818

c   om. P72 018 025 049 056 0142 1 3 18 35 38
42 43 51 57 62 76 82 90a 90b 97 102 103
105 110 131 133 141 142 149 177 180 189

καὶ νῦν καὶ εἰς πάντας τοὺς αἰῶνας, ἀμήν.

40	42	44	46	48	50	52	54

201 204 205 205abs 206S 209 216 218 221
223 226 234 241 242 250 256 263 296 302
308 309 312 314 319 325 327 328 330 337
363 367 383 384 385 386 390 393 394 398
400 421 424 425 429 432 440 444 450 451
452 454 456 457 458 460 465 466 468 469
479 483 489 491 496 517 522 547 582 592
601 602 603 604 605 606 607 608 610 613
615 616 617 618 619 620 622 625 627 628
629 631 632 633 634 635 636 637 638 639
641 656 664 676 680 699 712 757 796 801
823 824 901 910 912 914 917 919 920 921
922 927 928 935 941 959 986 996 997 1003
1022 1040 1058 1066 1069 1070 1072 1075
1094 1099 1100 1101 1102 1103 1104 1105
1107 1115 1149 1161 1162 1175 1240 1242
1244 1245 1247 1248 1249 1250 1251 1270
1277 1297 1311 1315 1319 1352 1354 1367
1384 1390 1398 1400 1404 1405 1424 1448
1482 1490 1503 1508 1521 1548 1573 1594
1595 1597 1598 1599 1610 1617 1618 1619
1622 1628 1636 1637 1642 1646 1649 1652
1656 1661 1668 1673 1702 1704 1717 1719
1720 1721 1722 1723 1724 1725 1726 1727
1728 1729 1730 1731 1732 1733 1734 1736
1737 1738 1740 1741 1742 1743 1745 1746
1747 1748 1749 1750 1752 1753 1754 1757
1760 1761 1762 1763 1766 1767 1768 1769
1780 1795 1829 1830 1831S 1834 1835
1840 1841 1843 1847 1849 1850 1851 1853
1854 1855 1856 1857 1858 1859 1860 1861
1862 1863 1864 1865 1867 1868 1869 1870
1871 1873 1874 1876 1877 1880 1882 1885
1886 1888 1889 1890 1891 1892 1893 1894
1896 1897 1899 1902 1903 2080 2085 2125
2127 2131 2143 2180 2186 2191 2194 2201
2218 2221 2255 2261 2279 2288 2318 2352
2400 2401T 2404 2423 2431 2466 2473
2475 2483 2484 2501 2502 2508 2516 2523
2527 2541 2554 2558 2587 2625 2626 2674
2675 2691 2696 2704 2705 2712 2716 2718
2723 2736 2746 2774 2776 2777 2815 2816
2865 L62 L145 L147 L156 L162 L241 L422
L427 L427/2 L585 L585/2 L591 L593 L603
L604 L606 L608 L617 L623 L740 L809 L840
L884 L921 L938 L1141 L1178 L1196
L1196/2 L1279 L1281 L1281/2 L1440
L1441 L1505 L1818 L2024 L2087 L2106

40-52

a και νυν και εις παντας τους αιωνας 02 03
04 018 025 044 049 056 0142 1 3 5 6 18 35
38 42 43 51 57 62 81 82 90a 90b 93 101 103
104 105 110 131 133 141 142 149 175 177
201 204 206S 216 218 221 223 226 234 241
250 252 254 256 263 308 309 312 314 319
322 323 325 327 328 330 337 363V 383 384
385 386 390 393 394 398 400 404 424 425
429 440 444 450 451 452 454 456 457 459
460 462 465 466 467 468 479 483 491 496
517 522 547 582 592 601 602 603 604 605
606 610V 615 616 617 618 619 620 622 623
625 627 628 630 631 632 634 635 636 637
638 639 641 642 656 664 665 676 680 699
712 757 796 808 823 824 876 901 910 912
914 917 920 922 928 935 941 945 959 986
996 997 1003 1022 1040 1058 1066 1067
1069 1070 1072 1075 1094 1099 1100 1101
1102 1103 1105 1107 1115 1127 1161 1162
1175 1240 1242 1243 1244 1245 1248 1249
1250 1251 1270 1277 1292 1297 1311 1315
1352 1354 1367 1384V 1390 1398 1400
1404 1405 1409 1424 1482 1490 1495 1501
1503 1505 1508 1509 1521 1523 1524 1548
1573 1594 1595 1598 1599 1609 1611 1617
1618 1619 1626 1628 1636 1637 1642 1643
1646 1652 1656 1661 1668 1673 1702 1704
1717 1719 1720 1721 1722 1723 1725 1726
1727 1728 1730 1731 1732 1733 1735 1736
1737 1738 1739 1740 1742 1743 1744 1745
1746 1748 1749 1752 1753 1757 1761 1762
1765 1767 1769 1780 1795 1827 1828 1829
1831S 1832 1834 1839 1841 1842 1844
1845 1847 1850 1851 1852 1853 1854 1855
1856 1857 1858 1859 1861 1862 1863 1864
1865 1870 1871 1872 1874 1875 1876 1877
1880 1881 1885 1888 1889 1890Z 1891
1892 1893 1896 1897 1899 1902 2080Z
2086 2125 2127 2131 2180 2191 2194 2200
2218 2221 2243 2255 2261 2279 2288 2298
2352 2374 2400 2404 2423 2431 2466 2473
2475 2483 2484 2494 2495 2501 2502 2516
2523Z 2541 2554 2558 2587 2625 2626
2675 2696 2704 2705 2712 2718 2723 2774
2777 2805 2816 2865 L62 L145 L147 L156
L162 L164 L422 L427/2 L585 L585/2 L591
L593f L603 L604 L606 L608 L617 L623

L740 L809 L840 L938 L1141 L1178 L1196 L1196/2 L1279 L1281 L1281/2 L1441 L1505 L1818Z L2087 L2106

b και νυν και εις τους παντας αιωνας P72 1754

c και νυν και εις τους απαντας αιωνας 469 921 1610 1741 1830 2716 L427

d και νυν εις παντας τους αιωνας των αιωνων 613T

e και νυν και εις παντας τους αιωνας των αιωνων 020 88 205 205abs 209Z 367 442 458 607 613Z 621 915 1448 1649 1734 1747 1750 1846 1849 1894 2085 2242 2674 2736 2746 L921 L2024

f και νυν και εις τους απαντας αιωνας των αιωνων 1724

g και νυν και αει εις παντας τους αιωνας 633Z

h και νυν και αει και εις παντας τους αιωνας 431 1678 1840 1867 2186 L884

i και νυν και αει και εις τους παντας αιωνας 326C

j και νυν και αει και εις τους αιωνας παντας 1837

k και νυν και αει και εις τους απαντας αιωνας 326*

l και νυν και αει και εις παντας τους αιωνας των αιωνων 33 2344

m και νυν και αει και εις αιωνας παντας 61

n νυν και εις παντας τους αιωνας 76 97 180 189 203 242 296 302 421 432 489 506 608 801 919 927 999 1149 1247 1319 1597 1622 1729 1763 1766 1768 1835 1843 1860 1868 1869 1873 1882 1886 1903 2080T 2143 2201 2401 2508 2523T 2527 2691 2776 2815

o νυν και εις παντας τους αιωνας των αιωνων 209T 1104

p νυν και αει και εις τους αιωνας 2818 0316V

q νυν και αει εις παντας τους αιωνας 633T

r νυν και αει και εις παντας τους αιωνας 94 307 321 378 453 918 2147 2197 2412 2652

s νυν και αει και εις τους αιωνας των αιωνων L1440

t νυν και αει εις παντας τους αιωνας των αιωνων 629*

u νυν και αει και εις παντας τους αιωνας των αιωνων 629C L596

v και νυν και εις παντας αιωνας 1359 1425 1563 1718 1751

w και νυν και εις τους αιωνας 01 1836 2318 2544

x και νυν εις παντας τους αιωνας 436 1760 1890T L241 L1818T

y και εις τους αιωνας των αιωνων 1241

z νυν και εις τους αιωνας 102

a' και εις παντας τους αιωνας 181

b' om. 1838

54

a αμην ... 424* 1241fV 1768C

b om. 6 424C 467 1311 1319 1735 1768* 1856

208

Subscriptio[1]

— P74 P78 0251 0316 69 172 614 720 832 913 1106 1360 1799 1831 1895 2138 2289 2356 2378 2492 2511 2627 2653 2718 2822 L6 L62 L145 L147 L156 L162 L164 L241 L422 L427 L427/2 L585 L585/2 L591 L593 L596 L603 L604 L606 L608 L617 L623 L740 L809 L840 L884 L921 L938 L1141 L1178 L1196 L1196/2 L1279 L1281 L1281/2 L1440 L1441 L1505 L1818 L2024 L2087 L2106

a om. 056 0142 1 3 33 35 38 43 57 61 76 90a 101 102 105 141 149 175 180 181 189 204 206S 209T 218 226 241 242 263 296 302 308 312 314T 319 321 322 327 337 363 383 384 385 393 394 400 421 431 436 440 442 444 458 467 479 483 489 491 522 547 582 603 607 608 610 615 616 621 622 625 629 630 631 633 634 635 636 639 656 665 676 680 757 808 823 876 901 912 927 941 986 996 997 1003 1040 1058 1066 1067 1070 1072 1075 1094 1100 1101 1102 1103 1104 1105 1107 1115 1149 1161 1241 1244 1247 1248 1249 1251 1270 1292 1311 1315 1319 1354 1359 1367 1384 1390 1400 1404 1425 1495 1509 1563 1573 1598 1599 1609 1610 1611 1617 1618 1619 1622 1626 1628 1636 1637 1646 1649 1652 1656 1661 1668 1702 1717 1720 1721 1722 1723 1727 1728 1729 1730 1731 1733 1735 1736 1737 1740 1741 1742 1743 1745 1746 1747 1748 1750 1752 1754 1757 1761 1763 1765 1767 1827 1830 1832 1834 1838 1839 1840 1842T 1843 1847 1850 1851 1852 1853 1860 1861 1864 1865 1867 1868 1872 1873 1877 1882 1885 1889 1890 1899 1902 1903 2086 2127 2143 2180 2186 2191 2197 2200 2201 2218 2221 2255 2279 2288 2298 2318 2344 2352 2400 2401 2412 2431 2466 2475 2483 2484 2495 2501 2508 2523 2527 2541 2554 2625 2674 2712 2718 2723 2736 2746 2774 2777 2805 2815 2816 2865

b ιουδα επιστολη P72 02 044 81 252 456 466 619 1162 1760 1828 1854 1871 2125

c επιστολη ιουδα 93T 97 221 250 424 452 454 601 605 613f 620 920 1022 1245 1277 1352 1719 1739 1795 1841 1849 1857 1881 1888

d ιουδα επιστολη καθολικη 04 623

e ιουδα καθολικη επιστολη 325 326 517 1766 1837

f επιστολη καθολικη ιουδα 62 1862

g ιουδα επιστολη πρωτη 1243

h εγραφη ιουδα επιστολη 1780

i επιστολη ιουδα αποστολου 025 1448V

j επιστολη αποστολου ιουδα 1734

k η του ιουδα επιστολη 917

l επιστολη του αγιου αποστολου ιουδα 131 1643 1744

m του αγιου αποστολου ιουδα επιστολη 020 049 82 177 181 256 309 398 404 450 459 460 465 602 618 627 637 699 910 919 922 1069 1175 1424 1738 1829 1835 1836 1870 1874 2194 2242

n ιουδα του αγιου αποστολου επιστολη καθολικη 1880

o επιστολη καθολικη του αγιου αποστολου ιουδα 93Z

p του αγιου αποστολου ιουδα επιστολη καθολικη 104 133 203 469 638 921 1398 1673

q του αγιου αποστολου ιουδα καθολικη επιστολη 462

r ιουδα αποστολου αδελφου ιακωβου επιστολη καθολικη 88 915 1842Z 1845

s ιουδας αποστολος αδελφος ιακωβου επιστολη καθολικη 1846

t του αγιου αποστολου ιουδα αδελφου ιακωβου αποστολου επιστολη 1769

u το εν λογοις καλλιστον γραφεν βιβλιον 2404

v του αγιου αποστολου επιστολη 2516

w ιουδα 01 03

x τελος 18 201 712 824 918 1127 1503 1548 1732 2243 2400

y τελος επιστολης 223

z τελος της επιστολης 592 935 1642 1831S 1893

a' τελος της επιστολης τυρινης 1896

b' τελος επιστολης ιουδα 314Z 628f

c' τελος της ιουδα επιστολης 142 367 386 457 468 496 642 1240 1521 1678 1751 1859 1892 2374 2423 2696

d' τελος της επιστολης ιουδα 1724 2558

e' τελος ιουδα καθολικης επιστολης 1704 1753

f' τελος της ιουδα καθολικης επιστολης 51 103 328 432 604 606 641 664 801 928 959 1250 1405 1482 1508 1725 1726 1749 1768 1855 1858 1876 2080 2085 2131 2261 2473 2587 2626 2691 2704 2776

g' τελος της ιουδα καθολικης ειπστολης 1856f 1897f

h' τελος της καθολικης ιουδα επιστολης 42 234 390 1863 1869 2675

i' τελος της ιουδα επιστολης καθολικης 914 1886

j' τελος της καθολικης επιστολης ιουδα 1501

k' τελος της του ιουδα επιστολης καθολικης 90b

l' τελος της επιστολης ιουδα καθολικης επιστολης 429

m' τελος του αγιου αποστολου ιουδα επιστολης 110 506 1762V

n' τελος επιστολης καθολικης του αγιου αποστολου ιουδα 632

o' τελος της επιστολης καθολικης ιουδα του αποστολου 425

p' τελος της επιστολης του αγιου αποστολου ιουδα 330 451 1523 1524 1844 1875 2502

q' τελος της καθολικης επιστολης του αγιου αποστολου ιουδα 1894

r' τελος της επιστολης και του αγιου ιουδα αγιου αποστολου επιστολης καθολικης 2716

s' τελος της επιστολης και του αποστολου 2705

t' τελος της επιστολης και των αποστολων 2494V

u' τελος της επιστολης του αγιου 6V 1242V

v' τελος της εκ του αποστολου 216

w' επιστολη ιουδα τελος των επτα καθολικων επιστολων 796

x' συν θεω τελος των καθολικων επιστολων 307

y' συν θεω τελος των τε πραξεων και των καθολικων επιστολων 453

z' τελος της επιστολης τελος συν θεω αγιω των καθολικων επιστολων 1490

a'' τελος της καθολικης ιουδα επιστολης τελος συν θεω αμην 1594

b'' τελος συν θεω των καθολικων επιστολων 5 2147 2652

c'' τελος συν θεω των επιστολων 1099

d'' τελος συν θεω αμην 94

e'' ετελειωθη συν θεω και η του ιουδα καθολικη επιστολη 018

f'' επληρωθησαν αι επτα καθολικαι επιστολαι 1297

g'' επληρωθησαν επτα καθολικαι επιστολαι 1595f

h'' τελος των καθολικων επιστολων 378 945 999 1505 1891

i'' τελος των επτα καθολικων επιστολων 254 323

j'' τελος των καθολικων επτα επιστολων 2544

k'' τελος των παντων επτα καθολικων επιστολων 1597V

l'' τελος των καθολικων επιστολων ιακωβου πετρου του κεφας ιωαννου του θεολογου και ιουδα 1718

m'' τελος πασων των επιστολων 617

n'' τελος γραφης ενθαδε της εξ ιουδα 205 205absf 209Z

o'' τελος τ[4-6] τελος παντων 1409

[1] This list does not record all subscriptions to the whole section of the *Apostolos* (or Acts and the Catholic Epistles), which are sometimes separate from the subscription to Jude (in 02 e.g.,: ιουδα επιστολη [line break] πραξεις των αγιων αποστολων και καθολικαι).

Appendix

1. Known Readings of MS 8ª (=Stephanus' codex ια)

3,18-22:   *a*   κοινης ημων σωτηριας
5,12-20:   ↔ *j/k/a'*:] οτι ο θεος [
9,44-46:   ↔ *b/d*: επιτιμησει [
12,34:   *a*   παραφερομεναι
14,26-32: *i*   εν μυριασιν αγιων αγγελων αυτου
15,45:   *b*   λογων
16,19:   *b*   τη ασεβεια και τη παρανομια (typo in Stephanus, siglum "α" refers to ια)
18,10-18: *g*   επ εσχατου χρονου ελευσονται
19,8:   *c*   αποδιοριζοντες εαυτους
23,2-22: *h*   ους δε σωζετε εκ [του?] πυρος αρπαζοντες ους δε ελεγχετε εν φοβω
24,8-14: *p*   φυλαξαι υμας απταιστους και ασπιλους

(MS 8ª shares most of the readings above with MS 1846.)

2. List of Lacunae in the Greek MSS
A word is recorded as lacunose below if none of the letters are legible. The writing material is not extant unless otherwise indicated.

Abbreviations
H   nonsensical omissions due to homoioteleuton or homoioarcton[2]
U   illegible ("unleserlich") traces of text on extant writing material
S   system-related lacunae (omissions in the lectionaries due to the character of the lectionary tradition)
P   partly illegible inscriptio/subscriptio (cf. apparatus)
UP illegible traces of text in part of the inscriptio/subscriptio on extant writing material (cf. apparatus)

P74: **Inscr.** 2-**3**,20; 24; 28-30; 34-**7**,26; 30; 34; 38-**11**,34; 38-40; **12**,2-6; 12-14; 18-**16**,24; 28; 32; 36-**24**,12; 16; 20-24, 28-**Subscr.**
P78: **Inscr.** 2-**4**,38; **5**,10-7,44; **8**,28-**Subscr.**
02: **25**,16.
04: **Inscr.** 2-2,14 (U); **5**,20 (U in 04*); **11**, 32-42 (U in 04*); **12**,2-5 (U in 04*); 6-10 (U); **22**,6 (U).
025: **Inscr.** 2-4 (U); **4**,56-**15**,32.
0251: **Inscr.** 2-**3**,44; **4**,2; 10-12; 16-20; 28-32; 38; 56-58; **5**,18-26; 32-**Subscr.**

---

[2] I have been reluctant to impose on the user of this edition any unnecessary interpretations; certainly there will be many more cases of omission due to homoioteleuton/homoioarcton than those noted here.

0316: **Inscr.** 2-**18**,20; **21**,4; 18; 24-26; 32; **22**,4; **24**,14; 30; **25**,8; 40-42; 48-50; **Subscr.**

6: **Subscr.** (UP).

33: **1**,16-30 (U); **2**,10-**3**,4 (U); 14-30 (U); **5**,20 (U in 33*).

43: **12**,44 (U in 43C).

61: **23**,18 (U in 61*)

69: **7**,14-**Subscr.**

110: **2**,4-6 (U); **3**,30 (U); **4**,8-12 (U); 24-26 (U); 38 (U); **6**,40 (U); **7**,38-40 (U); **8**,2 (U); 14 (U); 28 (U); **13**,30 (U); 32 (U); **14**,8-10 (U); 24-28 (U); **15**,10 (U).

172: **17**,2-**Subscr.**

256: **6**,28 (U); **7**,6 (U); **8**,20 (U); 26; **9**,2-4 (U); 12 (U); 24 (U); 30 (U); 40 (U); **10**,8 (U); 28 (U); **11**,2 (U); 12 (U); 18 (U).

308: **Inscr.** (UP); **3**,18 (U); **7**,30 (U); **11**,18 (U); **13**,18 (U); **15**,36-38 (U); 50 (U); **16**,16 (U); 19-28 (U); 34 (U); 38 (U); **17**,4 (U); 8-20 (U); **18**,18 (U); **19**,12-14 (U).

325: **3**,40-42 (U in 325*);

400: **Inscr.** (UP); **1**,4-12 (U); 28-30 (U); **4**,26 (U); 46-48 (U); **5**,6 (U); **7**,2-4 (U); 20 (U); 24-26 (U); **8**,2 (U); **12**,26 (U); 36 (U); 46 (U); **13**,18 (U); **15**,6 (U); 10 (U); **18**,8 (U).

458: **24**,10 (U); 20 (U); **25**,2 (U).

602: **Inscr.** 2-**7**,4.

605: **23**,28 (U in 605A).

610: **Inscr.** 2-**8**,20; **9**,2-4; **25**,3; 50.

613: **Inscr.** 2-**21**,10; **23**,32.

614: **3**,42-**Subscr.**

615: **Inscr.** 2-4 (UP).

620: **7**,20-38 (U).

629: **25**,2-6 (U in 629*).

632: **12**,19 (U in 632*); **13**,19 (U in 632*); **19**,9 (U in 632*

712: **Inscr.** 2-**12**,10.

720: **7**,2-**Subscr.**

832: **3**,10-**Subscr.**

913: **6**,22-26; 38; **7**,6; 20-22; 30-32; 42-44; **8**,2-6; 12-16; 24-28; **9**,12-14; 22-26; 34-36; 44-48; **10**,2; 14-16; 26-30; **11**,2-4; 16-20; 28-34; 42-**12**,6; 14-18; 24-26; 34-36; 46; **13**,10; 20-26; **14**,2-6; 16-18; 32; **15**,2; 10-14; 24-28; 38-42; 52-54; **16**,6-8; 16-18; 30; 38; **17**,2-4; 10-14; 24-32; **18**,8-16; 22-28; 34; **19**,1-6; 12-**20**,2; 14-**Subscr.**

935: **24**,4 (U).

996: **24**,10 (U).

1106: **4**,38-42 (U); 49-50 (U); 56-58 (U); **7**,18 (U); **8**,16 (U); **9**,16 (U); 22-26 (U); 34-36 (U); 44-48 (U); **10**,8-14 (U); 22-28 (U); 32-**11**,4 (U); 10 (U); 16-18 (U); 30-34 (U); 42 (U); **12**,8 (U); 12 (U); 16-20 (U); 28-32 (U); 36-46 (U); **13**,6-28 (U); **14**,2 (U); 14 (U); **15**,6-38 (U); 52-56 (U); **16**,10-12 (U); 20-22 (U); **17**,16-24 (U); **18**,6-**Subscr.** (U).

1115: **8**,6 (U); 14-16 (U); **9**,16 (U); 28 (U); **24**,24 (U).

1244: **24**,10 (U in 1244*).

1277: **7**,49 (U in 1277*).

1360: **17**,2-**Subscr.**

1384: **1**,22-**6**,8 (U); **9**,30 (U); 46-48 (U); **10**,16-36 (U); **11**,14-16 (U); **12**,32 (U); **13**,2 (U); 28 (U); 32-34 (U); **14**,32 (U); **15**,6-8 (U); 14-**16**,14 (U); **23**,32 (U); 36 (U); **25**,6-8 (U); 42 (U).

1404: **11**,4 (U); **12**,8 (U); **13**,22-32 (U); **14**,22-32 (U); **15**,38-44 (U); **17**,14-16 (U); 24-30 (U); **21**,8 (U); **24**,20-24 (U).

1409: **Subscr.** (UP).

1448: **18**,8 (U); **Subscr.** (UP).

1594: **19**,10-16 (U); **20**,16-18 (U); **25**,4 (U).

1617: **10**,35 (U in 1617*); **17**,19 (U in 1617*).

1636: **12**,30 (U).

1646: **24**,23 (U in *).

1668: **Inscr.** 2-4 (UP).

1678: **5**,6 (U); **7**,2 (U); **9**,26 (U); **16**,10-12 (U).

1702: **11**,38-40 (U); **13**,26 (U); **15**,1 (U).

1704: **5**,28-34 (U); 42-**6**,2 (U); 12-16 (U); 22-28 (U); 34-40 (U); **7**,4-10 (U); 18-22 (U); 30-32 (U); **8**,20-22 (U); **9**,2-4 (U); 8 (U); **10**,2-6 (U); 32 (U); **11**,18-20 (U); 32 (U); **12**,2 (U); 16 (U).

1717: **10**,2 (U); 8 (U); **19**,6 (U); **20**,2-6 (U); 10-16 (U); 20-**21**,20 (U).

1724: **Inscr.** 2-**10**,36; **11**,34 (U); **21**,8 (U);

1728: **5**,14-30 (U).

1730: **Inscr.** 2-4; **16**,32-38.

1752: **3**,1 (U in 1752*).

1762: **18**,32; **Subscr.** (P).

1769: **21**,24 (U).

1799: **16**,8-**Subscr.**

1831: **4**,24 (U); **7**,44-46 (U); **12**,4-14 (U); **15**,50-52 (U); **16**,2-4 (U); **17**,2 (U); 10 (U); 14 (U); 24-26 (U); **21**,12-**Subscr.** (U).

1831S: **Inscr.** 2-**21**,10.

1834: **7**,49 (U in 1834Z); **15**,52 (U)

1852: **Inscr.** 2-4 (P); **1**,10-14; 20-26; 34-**2**,2; 10-**3**,8; 14-22; 30-32; 40-46; **4**,4-12; 18-28; 36-40; 48-56; **5**,2-8; 18-26; 34-**6**,8; 16-22; 28-34; 40-**7**,2; 10-20; 26-30; 36-40; 48-50; **8**,8-10; 18-20; **9**,2-8; 14-16; 22-26; 34-36; 44-48; **10**,10-12; 22-28; 36-**11**,2; 14-16; 28-30; 38-42; **12**,12-14; 20-22; 28-30.

1867: **Inscr.** 2-**13**,34.

1871: **14**,4 (U).

1875: **14**,32-**15**,4 (H).

1881: **16**,19 (U in 1881*).

1893: **1**,16 (U); **3**,36 (U); **4**,10 (U); 56-58 (U); **5**,24 (U); **6**,12 (U); **8**,22 (U).

1895: **9**,2-**Subscr.**

1899: **Inscr.** 2-**15**,26.

2138: **19**,14-**Subscr.**

2191: **15**,16-28 (U in 2191*).

2288: **24**,10 (U); 24 (U); **25**,8 (U).

2289: **12**,44-**Subscr.**

2344: **Inscr.** 2-4 (UP); **13**,25 (U in 2344Z).

2356: **5**,8-**Subscr.**

2378: **12**,16-**Subscr.**

2400: **22**,4-6 (U).

2401: **3**,9 (U in 2401*); **24**,10-12 (U in 2401*).

2423: **15**,30 (U).

2475: **15**,30 (U).

2492: **24**,8-**Subscr.**

2511: **4**,24-**Subscr.**

2558: **11**,2 (U); **13**,28 (U).

2627: **16**,8-**Subscr.**

2653: **1**,16-20; **7**,8-38; 50 (U); **8**,4-6 (U); 20 (U); 24-28 (U); **9**,12-16 (U); 22-24 (U); 46 (U); **12**,14 (U); **16**,32-**Subscr.**

2716: **19**,14 (U); **21**,26 (U); **23**,26-30 (U); **24**,2 (U); 18-24 (U).

2718 (= L2394): **Inscr.** (S); **Subscr.** (S).

2774: **6**,42 (U); **7**,14-16 (U); 38 (U); **8**,20 (U); **15**,48 (U); **16**,2-4 (U); **17**,24 (U).

2776: **17**,29 (U).

2822: **Inscr.** 2-3,46; **10**,6-**Subscr.**

L6: **Inscr.** (S); **6**,28-**Subscr.** (S).

L62: **Inscr.** (S); **Subscr.** (S).

L145: **Inscr.** (S); **Subscr.** (S).

L147: **Inscr.** (S); **Subscr.** (S).

L156: **Inscr.** (S); **5**,2-**19**,16 (S); **Subscr.** (S).

L162: **Inscr.** (S); **Subscr.** (S).

L164: **Inscr.** (S); **Subscr.** (S).

L241: **Inscr.** (S); **Subscr.** (S).

L422: **Inscr.** (S); **Subscr.** (S).

L427: **Inscr.** (S); **Subscr.** (S).

L427/2: **Inscr.** (S); **5**,2-**19**,16 (S); **Subscr.** (S).

L585: **Inscr.** (S); **Subscr.** (S).

L585/2: **Inscr.** (S); **11**,2-**16**,32 (S); **Subscr.** (S).

L591: **Inscr.** (S); **Subscr.** (S).

L593: **Inscr.** (S); **Subscr.** (S).

L596: **Inscr.** (S); **25**,14; **Subscr.** (S).

L603: **Inscr.** (S); **Subscr.** (S).

L604: **Inscr.** (S); **Subscr.** (S).

L606: **Inscr.** (S); **Subscr.** (S).

L608: **Inscr.** (S); **Subscr.** (S).

L617: **Inscr.** (S); **1**,34 (U); **5**,2-**19**,16 (S); **Subscr.** (S).

L623: **Inscr.** (S); **Subscr.** (S).

L740: **Inscr.** (S); **Subscr.** (S).

L809: Inscr. (S); Subscr. (S).
L840: Inscr. (S); Subscr. (S).
L884: Inscr. (S); Subscr. (S).
L921: Inscr. (S); Subscr. (S).
L938: Inscr. (S); Subscr. (S).
L1141: Inscr. (S); Subscr. (S).
L1178: Inscr. (S); Subscr. (S).
L1196: Inscr. (S); Subscr. (S).
L1196/2: Inscr. (S); Subscr. (S).
L1279: Inscr. (S); Subscr. (S).
L1281: Inscr. (S); Subscr. (S).
L1281/2: Inscr. (S); 11,2-16,38 (S); Subscr. (S).
L1440: Inscr. (S); Subscr. (S).
L1441: Inscr. (S); Subscr. (S).
L1505: Inscr. (S); Subscr. (S).
L1818: Inscr. (S); 5,2-19,16 (S); Subscr. (S).
L2024: Inscr. (S); Subscr. (S).
L2087: Inscr. (S); Subscr. (S).
L2106: Inscr. (S); Subscr. (S).
L2394 (= 2718): Inscr. (S); Subscr. (S).

3. List of Errors in the Greek MSS

Practically all errors in the manuscripts are recorded; exception has been made for common interchanges of vowels (αι-ε, ε-η, ε-ι-η-υ-ι-οι, ο-ω), the single writing of a double consonant, and the doubling of a single consonant. The list below indicates location, erroneous text, and manuscript siglum. In order to avoid confusion, MSS with common errors are not grouped together below unless they read the same text throughout the complete variant. Note that errors recorded in the main apparatus (*f* after the letter address of a reading) are not repeated here.

Inscr. 1: ιοδα ... (P72*); ... πιστολη ... (632); ... καθολικης (2086); 1,9: ιουδας ιησου χριστου δουλος (1702); 14: ιακω (680); ιακωββου (1646*); 16-34: ... τοις τοις ... (L593); 16-24: ... προ ηγιασμενοις (234); 16-22: ... θεου ... (2147); 24: ηγισαμενοις (522); ηγαποιμενοις (1241); ηγιασμενος (2674); 26-34: ... τιτεμημενοις ... (615); ... κλητοις αγι ... (628*); ... τηρημενοις ... (1661); ... τετημενοις ... (1876*); ... τετηρημενος ... (2674); ... τετηρωμενοις ... (L1196)

2,2-6: ελεους ... (2516); 8-12: ειρηνην ... (1838); ειρη και αγαπη (1860); 14: πληνθυνθειη (218 1719* L422); πληθυνθυνθειη (390); πληθυνθειηι (1611); πλυνθειη (1799*V)

3,4-6: πασιν ... (1243); 8: ποιουμενοι (044* 1880 L608); 10-12: γραφων ... (465); ... υμας (631 1292 2200); γραφαι ... (680); γραειν ... (1839); γραφει ... (2484); 18-22: ημων ημων ... (61); ... σωτηρι (1897*); ... ρ̅ιας (2125); 24: αναγ (0142*); αναγγην (1240

1719 2675*); ανακην (1646*); αναγκη (2147); αγαγκη (2696); 26-30: ... γραφει ... (1505); ... γραφαι ... (1837*); 32-34: πακαλων ... (252*); παρακαλουγ ... (1405); ... εαγωνιζεσθαι (1523*); ... εαγωνιζεσθε (1523C); ... επαγωαγωνιζεσθε (L1818); 38: απ αρ (1850C); α (L164*); 40-46: παραοθειση ... (P72*); ... πιστοι (3 1248); ... πιστειν (1762); ... πιστιν (L921)

4,2: παρειεδυσαν (398*); παρει[..]εδυσαν (642); παρεισεσδυσαν (1844*); παρειδεδυσαν (1850*); παρεισεδωσαν (L2087); 6: τιτινες (631*); 8: ανθρωποι ανθρωποι (206S*); 10: π οι (90b*); οι οι (1838); 14: προσγεγραμμενοι (94); γεγενομενοι (636C); προγεγρασμημενοι (1509); προγεγραμμενοις (1882); προγεγεμημενοι (2466); προς γεγραμμενοι (L162); 19: κρι (1739*); 22: κρικμα P72*; 24: ασεγβεις (1720); 26: τη P72*; 36: μεταθτιθεντες (90b*); μετατιθεντας (1104); μετατεθεντες (1869 1886 L422); 38: ει (1315); 48-58: ... ιησου ... (1646); 60: αρνουμευενοι (522); αρνουμενον (L606)

5,2: υπομνησει (04); υπονησαι (1830*); 6: υμων (378); υμα (1862*); 8: βουλομενοι (2086); 10: ειδοτες (1646*); 12-20: α υμας ... (616*); 22-28: ... εγ (P72); λα[..]ον ... (2475*); 32: τον (1875 2318 L1196/2); 36-40: ... πιστευσαντες (1882); ... [...]στευσαντας (2201*); 42: απω (38*)

6,2: αγγελοις (6); αγγελοι (1844); 6-10: ... ρησαντας (1022* 1245*); τηρησαντους (1856); του ... (1886); τους τους ... (2186); ... τηρησαντες (2344*V); ... τηραισαντας (2400*); 12-16: ... εν αυτων ... (2674); 18-20: αλλα ποντας (1523*); 12: αρ αλλα (6*); 14: απολιποντες (460 618); 16: τον (876*); 20: απολυποτας (1646); 26: οικτηριον (1646 2718*); 32-34: μεγαλην ... (432 1066); μεγαλης ημεγαλης ... (2704); 36-38: ... αδδιοις (522); .. αιδιτοις (1673)

7,2-4: ωσοδα (1311); 12: οι (632); τας (0142Z 1367 1409); 24-28: ... εκπορνευσασθαι (P72*); ... εκπορνευσαι (1070 L608); ... εκπορνευσασα (1751); 32: απελθου (62* 1895*); απελθουσα (181); 34-38: ... τερας (P72); ... εταυρας (621); 40: προκειται (256V 321 322 323 623T 2718); προκενται (1719*); 42: δε δειγμα (01); δειγμα (42*); δειγμαι (L593); 44: τυρος (1319); 46: αι αιωνιου (1847); αινιου (2404); 50: επεχουσα 378; υπαρχουσαν (631); [...] υπεχουσαι (1277* 1834*)

8,2: ομοιωγ (506*); ομοιω (L604); 10: ενυπνειαδομενοι (P78); ενυπναζομενοι (307); ενυπιαζομενοι (522); εξενυπνιαζομενοι (1646*); 14: με[.]ν (203*); 16: μιαν μιαινουσιν (61*); μιαινουου (1839); μιαινουσα (L884); 18: κυριοτητος (1886); 22: ασθνουσι (2473); 24-28: ... βασφημουσιν (P72); ... φλασφημουσιν (93 680); ... [.]βλασφημουσιν (1646*); ... βλαφημουσιν (1729); δοξης ... (1749); ... βλασφημουσας (1751); φλασφημουσιν (1846); ... βαλασφημουσιν (2691)

9,6: μιχαης (P72); 10: οτε τε (921); 18: διεκρινομενος (02*); διακρινομενομενος (631); διακρονομενος (699*); 20: διαλεγετο (L2087); 24-28: ... σωμα (177 337); σωμα (460 618); ... σωμτος (1722); το ... (1869); 30-32: ... ετολμησαι (469 2716); ... ετορμησεν (491); ... ετολπησεν (2186); 36: [...]πενεγκειν (901*); επεν επενεγκειν (986); επενεγγειν (1240); επανεγκειν (1757); 44: επετιμησει ... (522*); επιμησαι ... (1719*); επετιμησαι ... (1886)

10,14: βασφημουσιν (P72*); βλασφημουσιν βλασφημουσιν (76); 20: φρσικως (33); 22: ως ως (252); 26: αλαγα (1661); 28: ζω (2473); 30: επισταται (2652); 34: τοιτοις (42); τουτοι (2516); 36: φθειροντα[.] (018*); [2-3] φθειρονται (1617*)

11,4: αυτοι (P72*); αυαυτοις (918); 6: ο (1070); 8-10: την ... (L62); του οδω (1241C); 12: ου (2279); 16: πορευθησαν (90b); 18: και και (L593); 20-22: τη πανη (L884*); 26:

βααλαμ (619*); βλααμ (1105*); 28: μισθον (431*); μισθος (628*); 34-36: ... α αντιλογια (635); ... αντη αντιλογια (1847* L593); ... αντιλογολια (1882); ... αντολογια (2718 L145); ... ανλογια (L623*); 40: ρε (2674); 42: απωλοντον (L427)

12,10: τοις (378); 16: σπιδες (049 2675*); 18: συνευωχουμεναι (33V 177 180 203 337 460 506 607 618 1099 1424 1661 1724 1730 1736 1828 1841 1869 1889 1890V 2423 2508 2625); συνωευωχουμενοι (489*); συνεαωχουμενοι (680); 20: οφοβως (489); 21: συνευωχουμενοι αφοβως (2712); 22: εαυτω (631); 24: πημαινοντες (326*); ποιμ[..]νοντες (1067*); ποιμεινοντες (1830*); 28: ανυδραι (43 917); 34: παραφορομεναι (1105); παραφερομαι (1847*); παραφυρομεναι (2242); παραφενομεναι (2818); 36: δεινδρα (680*); 38: φινοπωρινα (421 1573); φθινοπωνινα (467); φθινοπ[..]να (1245*); φθιναπωρινα (1828); φθινπρινα (1872*); φθιροπορινα (2516); φθινοπωνοπωρινα (L593); 39: υπο ανεμων φερομεναι (1838*); 40: ακαρπα[..] (18*); ακαρπαι (915); α ακαρπα ακαρπα (1721*); α ακαρπα (1721C); 42-46: ... αποθανεντα ... (38T/Z); διος ... (607); ... αποθανεντα ... (636*); ... αποφθανοντα ... (637); ... αποθανουντα ... (1780); ... απο[.]θανοντα ... (2194*)

13,2-6: κυματα κυματα ... (P72* 2691); κυ[.]ατα ... (90b*); ... αρια ... (1175*); ... αγρα ... (1729*); κ κυματα ... (1831); ... θαλας (2502); κυμτα ... (2626); 8: εφριζοντα (1721); ε[..]φριζοντα (1889*); επαφριζον (L422); 10-14: τας ... αυχενας (1751 L1178); ... αισχαυ[νας] (2288); τους ... αισχυνας (2675); 16: αστερεις (1731 L623*); αστερας (1882*); αστερ[...] (2344*); α αστερες (2674); αστεραι (2816*); 19: [...] (632*); 20: ους (458); 22-28: ... τους σκοτους (218 1241 L2087C); ... το σκοτους (263* L2087*); ... σκοτος (1869); ... ζοφος [2-3] του ... (2344C); 30-34: ... τετηρηνται (90b 1104); ει ... (254); ... τετηρηπεμυ (601*); ... αινα ... (1646); ... τετηται (2691)

14,2: προφητευσεν (496 1066* 2404 2675); προεφησευσεν (631*); προεφητευ (L147*); 4-8: ... τουτους (43 1856); 10: ευδομος (103 206S 421 496 615 917 996 1066 1243 1311 1315 1523 1661 1751 1753 1780 1827 1877 1881 1886 2147 2502 2674 2696 L164 L2087); εδομος (1734); εβδουμος (L591); 16-18: ενοχ λεγων (90b*); ενωλ λεγων (1505); ενω λεγων (L164*); 24-30: ... α[....] (38*); ... αγιοις ... (51 218 223 252 330 444 451 506 582 620 1398V 1649V 1719 1857 2816 L427); αγιας ... (90a); ... αγιοις ... (93 665); ... αγιοις ... (378); ... αγιας ... (1448); ...μυριασιν [(1875; om. due to homoiot.); ... αγιοις ... (2516); ... μυρια[..] ... (2675*); ... μυμυριασιν ... (L593)

15,2-4: ... κρισις (056); ... κρι (941*); om. (1875; om. due to homoiot.); ... κρισει (2255); 12: ελεξαι (90a 378 1175 1646 1767 1834 2674); εξελεξαι (914 1240 1828*); εκλεξαι (1315*); 14-18: ... ασευεις ... (131 616 1595); ... ασεβεισαντων (1875); παν ... (2674); 20-30: ... ασεβεις ... (82*); ... ασεβειαις ... (1359); ... ασεβειαις ... (1425); 32-34: ... ησεβησαν (94 1360*V); ω ... (206S 2691); ως ... (L623*); 37: [πε]ρ[ι π]αντων των εργων ασεβειας αυτων ων ησεβησαν (458); 40: πατων (1646*); 44: [.]ληρων (38*); κληρων (404* 2242*); σκηρων (757* 876* 1834 2186); 45: λολογων (1846); ων [..] (61*); 48: ελαληλησαν (1849*); 54-56: αμαρτ[.]λοι ... (90b*); αμαρτωλοις ... (631) αμαρτωλους ... (1741); ... ασ[..]βεις (L921*)

16,4-6: ... γουγγυσται (049*); ... γγυσται (1846* L591*); 8: μεμφιμεροι (62 680); μεμφιμοροι (421 606 1360 1854* 1869 2625 L740 L1279* L1281); μεμψιμοι (602 712); μιμψιμοιροι (927); μεμψιμωροι (1319 1734); μεψιμοιροι (1646 L164); μυμψιμοιροι (1751); μεμψμωροι (2125); 10-18: ... εαυτω πορεομενοι (P72Z); 10: κατας (1646*); 14-16: επι[3-4]θυμιας αυτων (33*); ε επιθυμιας ... (1891); ... ευατων (2180); ... αυτων αυτων (L422); 18: πορευο[>12]μενοι (1881*); 22-28: στ στομα ... (2691*); 30: υπερογγα

(3 90b 103 133 254 263 378 400 489 582 608 615 616 680 927 1240 1398 1425 1448 1523 1524* 1610 1718 1724 1729 1736 1765 1831 1832 1834 1844 1881 1886 1890 1896 2147 2194 2243 2400* 2404 2484 2502 2508 2516 2523 2527 2544 2674 L422 L623); 32: θαυμαζοντις (43C) θαυμαζοντα (467); θαυμαζον (631); 34: προσωπα προσωπα (61); προσωμα (996); προσωτα (2288); 36: ωφιλειας (386 633); ουφελειας (2344); ωφειας (L1279*)

17,2: υμει (P72*); 6: αγαπητοις (P72*); αγ[..]ητοι (5*); απητοι (1241); αγαιπητοι (L2024); 8: μνησθητι (218 L1279); μνησθε (1573)

18,2-4: ... [1-2]λεγον (1642*); ... εγλεγον (1768); 6: η υμιν (1646); 10-18: ... εσον (1247); ... εσοται (1646); ... εσοται (L2087); 19: [.....] (1617*); 20: εμπαιγκται (020); επεκται (307 1877); εμπικται (1069*); επαικται (1573); εμπακται (1877C); εμπαιγται (2191); ενπαικται (L591); 22: κα (33V 621V); 24-34: ... εαυτω ... (P72*); ... ασε ασεβειων (327); ... ασευειων (1753); ... ασεβαφον (1768*); τας εταυτων ... (2674); ... επιθυμιαις ... (L591);

19,2: οιτοι (451); 8: απυδιοριζοντες (110T); αποδιοριζυντες (1894); ... εατυους (2494); 12: π̄ναμα (915)

20,2: υμειδ̣ (2127*); 6: αγατοι (2674*); 8-18: επωκοδομουντες ... (621); ... εποικοδομουστες ... (1599); ... αγιωτητη ... (1832); ... αγιωτατω ... (1886 L593); 20: ε[..] (2466*); 26: τροσευχομενοι (1839); προσευχονοι (L241*)

21,2-10: ... τητηρησατε (664); ... τητησατε (1573*);... τη ρησατε (1830); επαυτους ... (L884); 12: προδεχομενοι (1405 1524 2674); προσδεδεχομενοι (1448); 16: ελεο[..] (33); ελεος το ελεος (1837* 2086); ελεος του ελεος (637*); ελε̣ (2652); 20: [..] κυριου (635*); 32: αιωνιαν (6)

22,2-10: ... διακρινομενω (1505); ... δ[2-3] διακρινομενοι (1744*); ... διακρινομενος (1888)

23,2-22: ... πυφρος ... (35*); ... ου δε ... (61); ... ουδε ελεατε ... (326*); ... εφοβω ... (431); ... αρπαζοντος (914 1022 1245); ... ε φοβω (1243); ... αρπαζαντες (1646); ... εν εν φοβω ... (1767); ... α αρπαζοντες (1874*); ... αρπαζοντος ... αρπαζοντος (2242); ... μρπαζοντες (L156*); 24: μεσουντες (1270); μισουντες μισουντες (2501); μισοαντες (2774); 26: και και (1869); 28-30: το απο (631); 32-34: τη ... (656); ... σαρκι (1839); ... σαρκοις (L606); 36: εσπιλωμενοι (P72 0142); σπιλωμενον (0316V 180); εσπιλωμενω (1831S L2087); 38: χιτω (876); χιτωναν (1594*)

24,2-6: ωδε δυναμενω (1521); ω δε δυναμενω (1827); 8-14: ... απαιστως ... (131); ... απταιστης ... (436*); ... αυτω ... (1509*); ... απαιστους ... (1610); ... απταστως ... (1649); ... απτ[..]στους ... (2125*); ... και και (L623); ... εαυτους ... (L921); ... αυτοις ... (L1818); 16: στηναι (102 1738 2412); στησι (L606*); στη (L1279*); 18: κατνωπιον (1859); 20-24: ... δοξας ... (88); ... δοξς ... (628*); ... αυτου αυτου (2473)

25,4-8: σωτηρ (1243 1646 1739C L1818); 10-20: ... κυριου ω ημων (P72*); ... τω ... (93*); 22: δοξαν (1751); δοξα δοξα (2242*); 24-30: ... μεγκλωσυνη ... (616); ... κρατο και εξουσι (1646); ... μεγαλοσυνην ... (1838); ... μεγαλωσανη ... (2194); ... μεγαλοπρ[.]η ... (2473*); ... κριτος ... (L164*); ... και και εξουσια (L422); 40-52: ... τους τους ... (L593); 54: ηνμα (1241)

Subscr. : ... αυθαδε ... (205abs); πιστολη ιουδα (613); τελος επιστλολη ... (628); πληρωθησαν ... (1595f); [τελος] ... επιστολη (1762); τελος τελος ... (1856); ... της ... επιστ̣ο̣λη (1897)

4. Errata List to the *ECM* of Jude

The following list corrects some errors and deficiencies in the presentation of Greek manuscript evidence in the *ECM* (left side of arrow).[3] Errors in the list of lacunae in the *ECM* have not been recorded here. Some errors in the patristic and versional evidence of the *ECM* are noted in the textual commentary.

Inscriptio

01C2 ιουδα → 01Z2 ιουδα

03C2 ιουδα → 03Z2 ιουδα

630 om. → 630 επιστολη ιουδα καθολικη

876 επιστολη ιουδα καθολικη → 876T επιστολη ιουδα; 876Z επιστολη ιουδα καθολικη

945 αλλος αδελφοθεος ταδ ιουδας ευσεβεεσσιν → 945T αλλος αδελφοθεος ταδ ιουδας ευσεβεεσσιν; 945Z καθολικη επιστολη ιουδα

1751 om. → 1751 καθολικης επιστολης ιουδα

1799 lacuna (illegible) → 1799 ιουδα καθολικη επιστολη (perfectly legible)

1838 επιστολη καθολικη ιουδα αποστολου → 1838T επιστολη καθολικη ιουδα αποστολου; 1838Z επιστολη ιουδα

1846 ιουδα καθολικη επιστολη → 1846T om.; 1846Z αναγνωσμα ιουδα καθολικη

2718f καθολικης επιστολης ιουδα → L2394 lacuna (system-related)

v. 1

26-34

61 και εν χριστω ... κλητοις → 61f και και εν χριστω ... κλητοις

v. 2

2-4

1563 ελεος υμιν → 1563 ελεος ημιν

8-12

1852 lacuna in unit → 1852 ↔ a/c/d/e (ειρην[η is clearly visible; cf. list of lacuna [B 130], according to which 2/8 is not lacking)

v. 3

10-12

1751 γραφειν υμιν → 1751 γραφειν ημιν

1846 γραφειν υμιν → 1846 γραφειν ημιν

18-22

61 κοινης ημων σωτηριας → 61f κοινης ημων ημων σωτηριας

26-32

218 εσχον γραψαι υμιν παρακαλων → 218 εσχον γραψαι ημιν παρακαλων

1846 εσχον γραψαι υμιν παρακαλων → 1846 εσχον γραψαι ημιν παρακαλων

---

[3] Barbara Aland, Kurt Aland, Gerd Mink and Klaus Wachtel, eds., *Novum Testamentum Graecum Editio Critica Maior.* Vol. IV,4: *The Catholic Letters.* Installment 4: *The Second and Third Letter of John, The Letter of Jude* (1st printing; Stuttgart: Deutsche Bibelgesellschaft, 2005).

34

1523 επαγωνιζεσθαι → 1523*f εαγωνιζεσθαι; 1523Cf εαγωνιζεσθε

40

431 παραδοθεισῃ → 431 περιδοθεισῃ

720 παραδοθεισῃ → 720 περιδοθεισῃ

v. 5

12-20

1852 lacuna in unit → 1852 ↔ g/h/i/y/z/d'/e' (at least ειδοτας παντα is clearly visible; cf. list of lacunae [B 130], according to which 5/10-16 is not lacking)

v. 7

50

2774 ↔ a/b εχο]υσαι → 2774 ↔ a/b/f εχο]υσαι

v. 9

10

1243 αρχαγγελος → 1243 αγγελος

26-28

0142 μωυσεως → 0142T μωυσεως; 0142AV σωματος μωσεως (in mg.: ετεροι σωμα μωσεως; the same note is in the sister MS 056)

2774 σωματος μωσεως → 2774 μωσεως σωματος

30-32

1838 ουκ ετολμησεν → 1838f ου και τολμησεν (new line commences with και)

44-46

5 επιτιμησαι σοι → 5 επιτιμησει σοι

48

1874* κυριος → 1874* omit (the MS reads επιτιμησαι σοι ο κυριος in the margin. In my apparatus I have treated the whole omission as 1874T and the addition as 1874Z; cf below.)

v. 10

22

252 ως → 252f ως ως

30

2652 επιστανται → 2652f επισταται

v. 11

1

1827 om. → 1827T om.; 1827Z αγαπητοι (lectionary incipit)

6

1799f οτι τι → 1799 τι (also in Kenneth W. Clark's edition[4])

22

88 αντιλογια → remove variant

---

[4] Kenneth W. Clark, *Eight American Praxapostoloi* (Chicago: University of Chicago Press, 1941).

26-38

88 om. → remove variant; print instead in *20-32*: 88T (or 88*) om.; 88Z (or 88C) τη πλανη του βαλααμ μισθου εξεχυθησαν και (words in mg. The errors affect subsequent units.)

v. 12

5

01C2(*f) γογγυσται μεμψιμοιροι κατα τας επιθυμιας αυτων πορευομενοι → 01C2a(*f) γογγυσται μεμψιμοιροι κατα τας επιθυμιας αυτων πορευομενοι; 01C2b om. (the words are marked for deletion. In my apparatus I have chosen to account for 01*f, 01C2a, 01C2b for the sake of clarity.)

04C2 γογγυσται μεμψιμοιροι κατα ιδιας επιθυμιας αυτων πορευομενοι → 04C2 γογγυσται μεμψιμοιροι κατα τας ιδιας επιθυμιας αυτων πορευομενοι (= 1270 1297; τας is clearly visible; note that this affects the account of the Sahidic witness. In my apparatus I have chosen to indicate 04C2V, because the two last words are partly illegible.)

18

2423 συνευωχουμενοι → 2423f συνευωχουμεναι

42-46

400 lacuna in unit → 400 ↔ a/b/c/e (the MS reads δις αποθα[; cf. list of lacunae [B 130], according to which 12/42-44 is not lacking)

v. 13

8

1838*V απαφριζοντα; 1838C επαφριζοντα → 1838T επαφριζοντα; 1838Z απαφριζοντα (an *alpha* is in the mg.)

v. 14

28-32

1678 μυριασιν αυτου → 1678 αγιαις μυριασιν αυτου

1875 lacuna in unit → 1875 ↔ a/c/f/i (αγιαις μυριασιν is extant; cf. list of lacunae [B 130], according to which 14/28-30 is not lacking. The omission of αυτου ποιησαι κρισιν is probably due to homoioteleuton.)

v. 15

14-16

1875 παντας τους ασεβεις αυτων → 1875f παντας τους ασεβεισαντων

v. 16

6

049f γουγγυσται → 049*f γουγγυσται; 049C γογγυσται

16

1718 επιθυμιας εαυτων → 1718 επιθυμιας αυτων

61 προσωπα → 61f προσωπα προσωπα

v. 17
2
321 υμεις → 321 ημεις
629 υμεις → 629*V υμεις; 629C ημεις

v. 18
8-14
01* επ εσχατου του χρονου εσονται; 01C2 επ εσχατου του χρονου ελευσονται → 01T επ εσχατου του χρονου εσονται; 01Z2 επ εσχατου του χρονου ελευσονται
20-30
01* τας επιθυμιας αυτων πορευομενοι των ασεβειων; 01C2 τας επιθυμιας εαυτων πορευομενοι των ασεβειων → 01T τας επιθυμιας αυτων πορευομενοι των ασεβειων; 01Z2 τας επιθυμιας εαυτων πορευομενοι των ασεβειων
61 τας εαυτων επιθυμιας πορευομενοι των ασεβειων → 61 τας εαυτων επιθυμιας πορευομενοι των ασεβων ασεβειων

v. 19
8 (no unit in the *ECM*)
01 αποδιοριζοντες → 01* αποδιοριζοντες; 01C2a διοριζοντες; 01C2b αποδιοριζοντες
9
621*V om.; 629C εαυτους → 621 εαυτους (there is no evidence in the Greek column suggesting that the word was not originally written on the line. The Latin side reads *semetipsos*.)

v. 20
2
0316 lacuna → 0316 υμεις
8-18
0316 lacuna in unit → 0316V εποικοδομουντες εαυτους τη αγιωτατη υμων πιστει (the MS reads ϵποικοδομου[ντε]ς εαυτους τη [αγι]ωτατη υμ[ων πι]ϲτει).
621 εποικοδομουντες εαυτους τη αγιωτατη υμων πιστει → 621 επωκοδομουντες εαυτους τη αγιωτατη υμων πιστει
1890f τη αγιωτατην υμων πιστει εποικοδομουντες εαυτους → 1890 τη αγιωτατη υμων πιστει εποικοδομουντες εαυτους (also according to Scrivener's collation[5])
26-21/2
0316 ↔ a/b → 0316 προσευχομενοι εαυτους (in my apparatus I divide the unit differently)

v. 21
8
0316V θεου → 0316 θεου

---

[5] F. H. A. Scrivener, *An Exact Transcript of the Codex Augiensis* (Cambridge: Deighton, Bell & Co., 1859). Apart from the transcript of Codex Augiensis, the publication contains collations of 50 MSS in various sections of the Greek New Testament. Errors in the MSS are recorded in the collations.

10
43 τηρησατε → 43f τηρησονται

v. 22
2-10
0316 lacuna in unit → 0316V και ους μεν ελεγχετε διακρινομενους
442* 442C και ους μεν ελεατε διακρινομενους → 442 και ους μεν ελεατε
διακρινομενους

v. 23
2-22
01 ους δε σωζετε εκ πυρος αρπαζοντες ους δε ελεατε εν φοβω → 01*V ους δε σωζετε
εκ πυρος αρπαζετες ους δε ελεατε εν φοβω; 01C1V ους δε σωζετε εκ πυρος
αρπαζοντες ους δε ελεατε εν φοβω
0316V ους δε σωζετε εκ πυρος αρπαζοντες ους δε ελεειτε εν φοβω → 0316 ους δε
σωζετε εκ πυρος αρπαζοντες τους δε ελεειτε εν φοβω
35 ους δε εν φοβω σωζετε εκ πυρος αρπαζοντες → 35*f ους δε εν φοβω σωζετε εκ
πυφρος αρπαζοντες; 35C ους δε εν φοβω σωζετε εκ πυρος αρπαζοντες
L156 ους δε σωζετε εκ πυρος αρπαζοντες → L156*f ους δε σωζετε εκ πυρος
μρπαζοντες;
L156C ους δε σωζετε εκ πυρος αρπαζοντες
34
0316V εσπιλωμενον → 0316fV σπιλωμενον (σπιλω is clearly visible.)
1241 εσπιλωμενον → 1241f επιλωμενον

v. 24
2-6
0316 ↔ a/c/d → 0316V τω δε δυναμενω (τω δε δυνα is clearly visible.)
1827 τω δε δυναμενω → 1827f ω δε δυναμενω
8-14
0316 ↔ a/b/c/f/k → 0316V φυλαξαι υμας απταιστους και (0316 does not support
b/c/f/k)
94 φυλαξαι υμας απταιστους και ασπιλους και → 94 φυλαξαι υμας απταιστους
ασπιλους και
2344 φυλαξαι υμας απταιστους και → 2344 φυλαξαι υμας απταιστως και
16
0316 ↔ a/b στησαι → 0316 στηριξαι
18
0316 ↔ a/b → 0316 κατενωπιον (the MS reads κ[...]νωπιον)

v. 25
2
0316V om. → 0316 om.
4-8
0316 lacuna in unit → 0316 ↔ a/c (the MS reads θεω σωτηρι [....])

1739 θεω σωτηρι ημων → 1739* θεω σωτηρι ημων; 1739Cf θεω σωτηρ ημων (a corrector apparently removed all *iota adscripts* and accidently deleted this *iota* too)

10-20

93f δια ιησου χριστου τω κυριου ημων → 93*f δια ιησου χριστου τω κυριου ημων; 93C δια ιησου χριστου του κυριου ημων

22

0316 lacuna → 0316V δοξα (*delta* is clearly visible)

40-52

326 και νυν και αει και εις τους παντας αιωνας → 326* και νυν και αει και εις τους απαντας αιωνας; 326C και νυν και αει και εις τους παντας αιωνας

54

1241 αμην → 1241fV ηνμα (word is written on three lines: ην, μ, α)

Subscriptio

6 om. → 6V τελος της ιουδα του αγιου

18 om. → 18 τελος

94 om. → 94 τελος συν θεω αμην

307 om. → 307 συν θεω τελος των καθολικων επιστολων

429 ιουδα καθολικης επιστολης → 429 τελος της επιστολης ιουδα καθολικης επιστολης

915 om. → 915 ιουδα αποστολου αδελφου ιακωβου επιστολη καθολικη

918 om. → 918 τελος

945 om. → 945 τελος των καθολικων επιστολων

1127 om. → 1127 τελος

1409 om. → 1409 τελος τ[4-6] τελος παντων

1490 om. → 1490 τελος της επιστολης τελος συν θεω αγιω των καθολικων επιστολων

1505 om. → 1505 τελος των καθολικων επιστολων

1595 om. → 1595f επληρωθησαν επτα καθολικαι επιστολαι

1678 om. → 1678 τελος της ιουδα επιστολης

1718 om. → 1718 τελος των καθολικων επιστολων ιακωβου πετρου του κεφας ιωαννου του θεολογου και ιουδα

1831S om. → 1831S τελος της επιστολης

1842 om. → 1842T om.; 1842Z ιουδα αποστολου αδελφου ιακωβου επιστολη καθολικη

2544 om. → 2544 τελος των καθολικων επτα επιστολων

2652 om. → 2652 τελος συν θεω των καθολικων επιστολων

5. List of Differences between the *ECM* and This Edition

The following list accounts for some of the differences between the *ECM* (left side of arrow) and this edition (right side of arrow). I do not consider these as "errors" but rather as different interpretations of the manuscript evidence.[6]

Inscriptio
400 lacuna → 400 ↔ q/v (the MS reads [...] αγιου [>12] ε̣π̣ι̣σ̣τ̣ο̣λ̣η)
1739 ιουδα επιστολη καθολικη αλλος αδελφοθεος ταδ ιουδας ευσεβεσιν → 1739 ιουδα αλλος αδελφοθεος επιστολη καθολικη ταδ ιουδας ευσεβεσιν
1852 του αγιου ιουδα του αποστολου επιστολη καθολικη → 1852V του αγιου ιουδα του αποστολου επιστολη καθολικη (several words are defective)

v. 1
24
665*V ηγαπημενοις; 665C ηγιασμενοις → 665 ηγιασμενοις
26-34
400 ↔ a/b/c/d/f] κλητοις (see B 146) → 400 ↔ a/b/c/d/f κ̣α̣ι̣ [.... τετηρη]μενοις κλητοις

v. 2
2-4
1523V ελεος υμιν → 1523 ελεος υμιν
8-12
33 lacuna → 33V αγαπη και ειρηνη (the MS reads αγαπ̣[η)

v. 3
18-22
P74 lacuna in unit → P74 ↔ a/c (the MS reads σ̣ω[; cf. list of lacuna [B 130], according to which 3/22 is not lacking)
1523* κοινης υμων σωτηριας → 1523*V κοινης υμων σωτηριας
1523C κοινης ημων σωτηριας → 1523CV κοινης ημων σωτηριας
24

---

[6] Some of the differences are due to my general reluctance to interpret interlinear and marginal readings as corrections (C). I have rather consistently defined them as additional readings – either corrections or alternative readings (Z) – unless the text is erroneous or if there is a sign known to be used for corrections; see further in the introduction to the apparatus. In the specific cases of MS 252 and MS 1523, the differences reflect the use of different photographic material. For example, the microfilm of 252 which I accessed at the INTF was in poor condition, but when I asked for a microfilm of MS 464 (old registration number) I was presented with a much better film. In regard to the peculiar MS 629 (bilingual Gr.-Lat.) I have given priority to the evidence in the Greek column since there are corrections in both columns, and the corrections in the Greek column sometimes conform the text to the Latin, but at other times move away from the Latin. This MS needs a thorough investigation in the future.

2147 αναγκην → 2147f αναγκη

26-32

P74 lacuna in unit → P74 ↔ a/b/d/e (the MS reads εσχο[ν ; cf. list of lacuna [B 130], according to which 3/26 is not lacking)

400 ↔ a/d εσχον γραψαι [....] παρακαλων → 400 εσχον γραψαι υμιν παρακαλων

2344 ↔ a/e/f] γραψαι υμιν παρακα[λων → 2344 εσχον γραψαι υμιν παρακαλων

34

400 ↔ a/b/c]παγ[→ 400 επαγωνιζεσθαι

v. 4

642 παρεισεδυσαν → 642f παρει[..]εδυσαν

20

0251 lacuna → 0251V om. (no space for το)

22

P72* κριϲμα → P72* κρικμα

24

252 ↔ a/b αϲ[→ 252 ασεβεις

2412f ασεβειη → 2412 ασεβειν

32

252V ημων → 252 ημων

918* om.; 918C ημων → 918* om.; 918CV ημων (an *obelus periestigmenos* [•/•] with reading in mg. as in v. 23 where *ECM* uses T/Z. I have interpreted the sign as a probable correction at both places.)

34

88V χαριν → 88 χαριν

252 χαρ[→ 252 χαριν

46

252V μονον → 252 μονον

48-58

252V δεσποτην θεον και κυριον ημων ιησουν χριστον → 252 δεσποτην θεον και κυριον ημων ιησουν χριστον

326Z δεσποτην θεον και κυριον ημων ιησουν χριστον → 326Z1 δεσποτην θεον και κυριον ημων ιησουν χριστον; 326Z2 δεσποτην και κυριον ημων ιησουν χριστον

1852 ↔ a/b/d/e/g/h/i/l ιησου]ν̣ χριστον → 1852 ↔ a/b/d/e/f/g/h/i/j/k/l] χριστον (errors in the *ECM* concerning possible variants)

60

522f αρνουμενενοι → 522f αρνουμευενοι

v. 5

2

04V υπομνησαι → 04fV υπομνησε̣ι

252V υπομνησαι → 252 υπομνησαι

665* υπομνησαι → 665*V υπομνησαι

6

252V υμας → 252 υμας

1523 ↔ a/b]μας → 1523 υμας

1678V υμας → 1678 lacuna

12-20

04* ↔ y/d' παντα οτι ο [.]ς απαξ → 04* ↔ g/y/z/h/d' παντα οτι [2-3] απαξ (error in the *ECM*; variant reading "g" is still possible with the current interpretation of the evidence, i.e., ↔ g/y/d')

04C2 απαξ παντα οτι ο θεος → 04C2V απαξ παντα οτι ο θεος

33* απαξ παντα οτι ο ιησους → 33* απαξ παντα οτι ο [..] (either ιησους, θεος or κυριος)

252 ↔ a/m/n/o/s/u/w υμας [→ 252 υμας απαξ τουτο οτι ο κυριος

1852 lacuna in unit → 1852 g/h/i/y/z/d'/e' (the MS reads παντα [; cf. list of lacuna [B 130], according to which 5/12-16 is extant)

22-26

35*f λαον; 35C λαον εκ γης → 35T λαον; 35Z λαον εκ γης (the words εκ γης are added supralinearly. I do not define the simple λαον as an error.)

93*V λαον εκ της → 93 λαον εκ της

1735f εκ γης λαον → 1735 εκ γης λαον (I do not define εκ γης λαον as an error)

40

252 ↔ a/b]τας → 252 πιστευσαντας

v. 6

4

252 τε → 252V τε

18

1523 αλλα → 1523* αλλα; 1523C αλλ (in my apparatus this variation is not recorded)

 20 (unnoted unit)

The variation between απολιποντας (aor. ptc) and απολειποντας (pr. ptc) is not noted in the *ECM*. The different readings may reflect itacistic variation but are nevertheless recorded in my apparatus (cf. also textual commentary).

 32-34

252V μεγαλης ημερας → 252 μεγαλης ημερας

1678V μεγαλης ημερας → 1678 μεγαλης ημερας

38

2147 αιδιοις → 2147 αει διοις ("eternally divine;" so also Albin's edition[7])

 40-42

1523 ↔ a/c] ζοφον → 1523 υπο ζοφον

v. 7

16

400V αυτας → 400 αυτας

24-28

43f τουτων τροπον εκπορνευσασαι → 43 τουτον τροπον εκπορνευσασαι

206S*V αυτοις τροπον εκπορνευσασαι → 206S* αυτοις τροπον εκπορνευσασαι

---

[7] C. A. Albin, *Judasbrevet: Traditionen, Texten, Tolkningen* (Stockholm: Natur och Kultur, 1962).

629*V τροπον εκπορνευσασαι → 629*V τουτοις εκπορνευσασαι (the word τροπον in the *ECM* has been inferred from the Latin column that reads *modo*, but the Latin has also been corrected. I give priority to the evidence in the Greek column).

2774 τουτοις τροπον εκπορνευσασαι → 2774V τουτοις τροπον εκπορνευσασαι (the MS reads τουτοις τροπον [9-10]σαι; in my app. the MS could attest either of two possible variant readings)

40

252V προκεινται → 252 προκεινται

50

400 lacuna → 400 ↔ a/b/c/f ..ε]χ[

1523 ↔ a/b]π[ε]χουσαι → 1523 υπεχουσαι

v. 8

18

04 ↔ a/b κυριοτ[→ 04 κυριοτητα (also Tischendorf)

252 ↔ a/b κυριο[→ 252 κυριοτητα

24-28

1678 δοξας δε βλασφημουσιν → 1678 ↔ a/b δοξ[..] δε βλασφημουσιν

29 (no unit in the *ECM*)

307 om. → 307f ομοιως μεν και ουτοι ενυπνιαζομενοι σαρκα μεν μιαινουσιν κυριοτητα δε αθετουσι δοξας δε βλασφημουσιν (albeit a commentary MS, there is no break for a commentary section at this point. The text has just been copied twice for no reason, which I thus perceive as a scribal error.)

v. 9

18

1523*V ανακρινομενος; 1523CV διακρινομενος → 1523TV κρινομενος; 1523ZV ανακρινομενος (ανα is written supralinearly, there is no room for δια on line)

400 ↔ a/b]μενος → 400V διακρινομενος (the MS reads δι[ακριν]ομενος)

36

181* επενεγκειν; 181C υπενεγκειν → 181T επενεγκειν; 181Z υπενεγκειν

642 επιτιμησαι σε → 642 επιτιμησει σε (the MS reads επιτιμησοι σαι; I interpret the itacism differently)

44-46

1874* om.; 1874C επιτιμησαι σοι → 1874T om. ; 1874Z επιτιμησαι σοι (words in mg.)

48

1874* κυριος; 1874C ο κυριος → 1874T om.; 1874Z ο κυριος (words in mg.)

v. 10

2

1523 ↔ a/b]οι → 1523 ουτοι

4-8

330*V μεν οσα; 330C δε οσα → 330 δε οσα

32-26

018 εν τουτοις φθειρονται → 018(*f) εν τουτοις φθειρονται (the MS has been corrected)

996 εν τουτοις φθειρονται → 996f εν τοις τοις φθειρονται

v. 11
18-30

915* om.; 915C και τη πλανη του βαλααμ μισθου εξεχυθησαν → 915T om.; 915Z και τη πλανη του βαλααμ μισθου εξεχυθησαν (words in mg.; the difference affects subsequent units)

26

P72 βαλαακ → P72*V βαλλαμ; P72C βαλαακ

1852 βαλααμ → 1852 ↔ a/ao/b (the MS reads βαλα[)

v. 12
14

400 lacuna → 400V υμων (the MS reads υ[μ]ων)

16

43 σπιλαδες → 43*f σπιξαδες; 43C σπιλαδες

18

33 συνευωχουμενοι → 33V συνευωχουμεναι

400V συνευωχουμενοι → 400 ↔ a/b (the MS reads συνευ[ )

22

P72* αυτους; P72C εαυτους → P72T αυτους ; P72Z εαυτους

30-32

1831 υπ αν[→ 1831 υπο ανεμων

34

629*V παραφερομεναι → 629* παραφερομεναι

1523 παραφερο[→ 1523 παραφερομεναι

2374 παραφερομεν[→ 2374 παραφερομεναι

38

01*V φθινοπωρικα → 01* φθινοπωρικα (clearly so)

04 ↔ a/b/c φ[→ 04 ↔ a/b/c φ[7-9]α

6V φθινοπωρινα → 6 φθινοπωρινα

400 lacuna → 400V φθινοπωρινα (the MS reads]γα)

38-46

918T δις αποθανοντα; 918K δις αποθανοντα εκριζωθεντα → 918 δις αποθανοντα (the commentary reads: την αμαρτιαν εκριζωθεντας δε αυτοις, which I do not consider as adequate evidence for any variant reading at this point)

2818 δις αποθανοντα εκριζωθεντα → 2818V διο αποθανοντα εκριζωθεντα (also Albin's ed.)

v. 13
2-6

400 ↔ a/b] θαλασσης → 400V κυματα αγρια θαλασσης (the MS reads κυ[ματα αγρι]α θαλασσης)

04f κυματα αγια θαλασσης → 04V κυματα αγια θαλασσης

8

629*V απαφριζοντα; 629C επαφριζοντα → 629 επαφριζοντα (the shape of *epsilon* followed by *pi* is similar to other places)

1831 επαφριζοντα → 1831 ↔ a/b (the MS reads]παφριζοντα; also Albin's ed.)

12

400 lacuna → 400 ↔ a/b (the MS reads]των)

22-28

2344V ο ζοφος του σκοτους → 2344(Cf) ο ζοφος του σκοτους (illegible correction ο ζοφος [2-3] του σκοτους)

30-34

400 ↔ a/c αιω]να τετηρηται → 400 ↔ a/d (the MS reads εις ạιω[2-3] τετηρηται)

442 εις αιωνα τετηρηται → 442 εις αιωνας τετηρηται (cf. same abbreviation of αιωνας in v. 25)

v. 14

2

01f επροφητευσεν → 01f ↔ a/o (the MS reads προεπροφητευσεν)

10

206S 996 1243 1523 1661 1751 1827 1881 2147 εβδομος → 206Sf 996f 1243f 1523f 1661f 1751f 1827f 1881f 2147f ευδομος

v. 15

1

629* om.; 629C του → 629*V om.; 629CV του

20-28

0142V 1563V 1718V παντων των εργων ασεβειας αυτων → 0142 1563 1718 παντων των εργων ασεβειας αυτων

1359fV παντων των εργων ασεβειαις αυτων → 1359f παντων των εργων ασεβειαις αυτων

30-32

218f ων ηθετησαν → 218 ων ηθετησαν ("which they ignored;" not defined as error in my edition)

2423 ων ησεβησαν → 2423V ων ησεβησαν

40

P72* om.; P72C των → P72T om.; P72Z των

42

876 σκληρων → 876(*f) σκληρων (the MS has been corrected)

L1141 σκληρων → L1141*V κηρων; L1141C σκληρων

v. 16

8

1751 μεμψιμοιροι → 1751f μυμψιμοιροι

10-18

P72* om.; P72Cf κατα τας επιθυμιας εαυτων πορευομενοι → P72* om.; P72CfV κατα τας επιθυμιας εαυτων πορευομενοι (the unit affects subsequent unit)

14-16

1838 επιθυμιας αυτων → 1838*V επιθυμιας εαυτων; 1838C επιθυμιας αυτων

18 (no unit in the *ECM*)

1881 πορευομενοι → 1881(*f) πορευομενοι (the MS has been corrected)

22-28

467 το στωμα αυτων λαλει → 467* το στομα αυτων αλει; 467C το στομα αυτων λαλει

30

429 υπερογκα → 429V υπερογκα

915 υπερογκα → 915T υπερογκα; 915Z υπερ[(word in mg.; probably cut off; not accounted for in the *ECM*)

1524* υπερογκα; 1524Cf υπερογγα → 1524*f υπερογγα; 1524C υπερογκα

1875*f υπερ; 1875C υπερογκα → 1875 υπερογκα

32

43 θαυμαζοντες → 43* θαυμαζοντες; 43Cf θαυμαζοντις

34

43 προσωπα → 43* προσωπα; 43Cf προσωπω

1448 προσωπα → 1448f προσωπω

v. 17

2

1292 υμεις → 1292 [.]μεις (the MS may read υμεις or ημεις)

1831 υμεις → 1831 lacuna

v. 18

2-4

1852 οτι ελεγον → 1852V οτι ελεγον

7

1448 οτι ελεγον → 1448V οτι (the MS has lacuna but there is space for the word [...])

8-14

104 εν εσχατου χρονω εσονται → 104V εν εσχατω χρονω εσονται

1831 εν εσχατω χρονω εσονται → 1831V εν εσχατω χρονω εσονται

20-30

400 τας εαυτων επιθυμιας πορευομενοι των ασεβειων → 400V τας εαυτων επιθυμιας πορευομενοι των ασεβειων

1523V τας εαυτων επιθυμιας πορευομενοι των ασεβειων → 1523 τας εαυτων επιθυμιας πορευομενοι των ασεβειων

1827 τας εαυτων επιθυμιας πορευομενοι των ασεβειων → 1827*V τας εαυτων επιθυμιας πορευομενοι των ασεβων; 1827C τας εαυτων επιθυμιας πορευομενοι των ασεβειων

v. 20

8-18

88 εποικοδομουντες εαυτους τη αγιωτατη υμων πιστει → 88T εποικοδομουντες αυτους τη αγιωτατη υμων πιστει; 88Z εποικοδομουντες εαυτους τη αγιωτατη υμων πιστει

1827f την αγιωτατην υμων πιστιν εποικοδομουντες εαυτους → 1827 την αγιωτατην υμων πιστιν εποικοδομουντες εαυτους (I do not define this reading as an error; possibly την πιστιν is an accusative of respect)

1831V τη αγιωτατη υμων πιστει εποικοδομουντες → 1831 τη αγιωτατη υμων πιστει εποικοδομουντες

26-21/2

P72* προσεχομενοι εαυτοις εαυτους; P72C προσευχομενοι εαυτοις εαυτους → 1523 P72T προσεχομενοι εαυτοις εαυτους; P72Z προσευχομενοι εαυτοις εαυτους (in my apparatus I divide the unit differently)

v. 21

5

0316 lacuna → 0316V om.

10

04*V τηρησωμεν → 04* ↔ c/e (the MS reads τηρη[σ.]μ[ε]ν

1523V τηρησατε → 1523 τηρησατε

16

2652 ελεος → 2652V ελεος

17

1837*f το ελεος; 1837C om. → I have treated this case of dittography as an error in unit 16. Following the procedure of the *ECM*, it would have been better to treat it in unit 15 since it is the first το ελεος that is corrected in the MS.

23 (no unit)

61 om. → 61V κυριου

v. 22

2-10

1523V και ους μεν ελεειτε διακρινομενοι → 1523 και ους μεν ελεειτε διακρινομενοι

v. 23

2-22

61f ↔ a/b/g ους δε σωζετε εκ πυρος αρπαζοντες ου δε [6-10] εν φοβω → 61*f ους δε σωζετε εκ πυρος αρπαζοντες ου δε [6-10] εν φοβω; 61C ους δε σωζετε εκ πυρος αρπαζοντες ου δε εν φοβω

326CV(*f) ους δε σωζετε εκ πυρος αρπαζοντες ους δε ελεατε εν φοβω → 326(*f) ους δε σωζετε εκ πυρος αρπαζοντες ους δε ελεατε εν φοβω

424*V ους δε εν φοβω σωζετε εκ πυρος αρπαζοντες; 424C ους δε σωζετε εκ πυρος αρπαζοντες ους δε ελεατε εν φοβω; 424C1 ους δε σωζετε εκ πυρος αρπαζοντες; 424C2 ους δε εν φοβω σωζετε εκ πυρος αρπαζοντες → split in two units as follows:

2-12: 424*V ους δε εν φοβω σωζετε εκ πυρος αρπαζοντες; ους δε σωζετε εκ πυρος αρπαζοντες 424C1V; ους δε εν φοβω σωζετε εκ πυρος αρπαζοντες 424C2V

14-22: 424T om. ; 424Z ους δε ελεατε εν φοβω

(In the case of 424, there are changes both on the line and in the margin, but the phrase ους δε ελεατε in the margin has never been deleted.)

629*V ους δε εν φοβω σωζετε εκ πυρου αρπαζοντες ους δε ελεατε εν φοβω θεου → 629*fV ους δε εν φοβω σωζετε εκ πυρος αρπαζοντες ους δε ελε[6-9]τ̣ε̣ς εν φοβω θεου

918T ους δε σωζετε εκ πυρος αρπαζοντες ους δε ελεγχετε εν φοβω; 918Z ους δε εν φοβω σωζετε εκ πυρος αρπαζοντες ους δε ελεγχετε εν φοβω → 918* ους δε σωζετε εκ πυρος αρπαζοντες ους δε ελεγχετε εν φοβω ; 918CV ους δε εν φοβω σωζετε εκ πυρος αρπαζοντες ους δε ελεγχετε εν φοβω (an *obelus periestigmenos* [•/•] with reading in mg. as in v. 4 where *ECM* uses */C. I have interpreted the sign as a probable correction at both places.)

1845* ους δε σωζετε εκ πυρος αρπαζοντες εν φοβω; 1845CV ους δε εν φοβω σωζετε εκ πυρος αρπαζοντες ους δε ελεγχετε εν φοβω → 1845T ους δε σωζετε εκ πυρος αρπαζοντες εν φοβω; 1845Z ους δε εν φοβω σωζετε εκ πυρος αρπαζοντες ους δε ελεγχετε εν φοβω

v. 24

8-14

424* φυλαξαι υμας απταιστους και; 424* φυλαξαι υμας απταιστους και ασπιλους και → 424T φυλαξαι υμας απταιστους και; 424Z φυλαξαι υμας απταιστους και ασπιλους και

20-22

629*V om. → 629* δοξης

88 της δοξης → 88fV της δοξης (the MS reads της δοξας)

629*V εν τη παρουσια του κυριου ημων ιησου χριστου; 629C om. → remove variant (The Greek text in the *ECM* has been inferred entirely from the Latin side—nothing is visible in the Greek column, except that the words from μονω in v. 25 are written very broadly; see below.)

v. 25

2-8 (no unit in the *ECM*)

629*V μονω θεω σωτηρι ημων → [>12] ημων 629*; μονω σοφω θεω σωτηρι ημων 629C (the variant affects subsequent variants)

3

623* om.; 623C σοφω → 623T om.; 623Z σοφω

4-8

323 θεω σωτηρι ημων → 323*V θεω σωτηρι υμων; 323C θεω σωτηρι ημων

Subscriptio

93* επιστολη ιουδα; 93C επιστολη καθολικη του αγιου αποστολου ιουδα → 93T επιστολη ιουδα; 93Z επιστολη καθολικη του αγιου αποστολου ιουδα (there is a second subscript below the first)

Part III

Commentarius

Chapter Nine

Textual Commentary

Introduction

1. The Purpose and Structure of the Commentary

The chief purpose of the textual commentary is to give a detailed account for the reasons that led me to adopt certain variant readings for inclusion in the primary line text (= the proposed initial text), and to relegate others to the apparatus below the primary line. Another important purpose is to discuss variant readings that are interesting from perspectives other than the question of the initial text. Hence, the selection of variants for discussion in the commentary may not always be governed by the relative strength of manuscript support where variation occurs. Another factor is of course the question as to which variants have been discussed by other authors. It is particularly difficult to leave weak arguments unchallenged, and disagreement with another commentator over a textual problem has often functioned as a stimulus to respond.

The numerical address followed by the adopted text indicates the variation-unit under discussion. The adopted text is followed by a rating symbol employed within braces (see below). The primary line text of the *ECM* is indicated in parenthesis when it differs from the primary line text of this edition. Further, all alternative readings to the primary line text of the *ECM* (marked with bold dots) are indicated within parentheses.

In the following, I will describe in detail the basis for the rating system employed in this commentary.

2. Rating Systems in Greek New Testament Editions

As early as 1734, Johann Albrecht Bengel included a letter-rating system in his edition of the Greek New Testament.[1] In more recent years, the United Bible Societies have employed a similar letter-rating system in the four editions of the *Greek New Testament*. By means of the letters A, B, C, and D,

---

[1] See Johann Albrecht Bengel, *Novum Testamentum Graecum* (Tübingen: George Cottae, 1734). Bengel indicated in the margin of his edition the relative value of each variant using the Greek letters α, β, γ, δ, ε.

enclosed within braces { } at the beginning of each set of variants, the editorial committees have sought to indicate "the different degrees of certainty with respect to the form of the original text."[2] The four levels of certainty are defined as follows in UBS[4]:

> The letter A indicates that the text is certain.
> The letter B indicates that the text is almost certain.
> The letter C, however, indicates that the Committee had difficulty in deciding which variant to place in the text.
> The letter D, which occurs only rarely, indicates that the Committee had great difficulty in arriving at a decision.[3]

Ever since this letter rating-system appeared in the UBS editions, it has been severely criticized.[4] In a review article, J. M. Ross states in regard to the first edition of 1966:

> The attempt to indicate by the letters A B C and D the judgment of the editors as to the probability of the printed text represents an important advance on all previous editions, but these markings do not turn out in practice to be as useful as they promised to be at first sight. The scale of four grades from A to D is over-subtle.[5]

In my impression, the arbitrary and over-evaluative rating system has led many users of the editions, including scholars, to take various text-critical decisions for granted, without examining the arguments for the variants in more detail. J. K. Elliott, perhaps the most outspoken critic of the letter-rating system, has strikingly alluded to it as a "patronizing spoon-feeding."[6] The fluctuations in the letters attached to the same variant over the different editions have increased the critique and the recent redefinition of the letter-rating classifications for the fourth edition has not helped much to

---

[2] UBS[4], 3*.

[3] Ibid.

[4] For a summary of the critique, see Kent D. Clarke, "Textual Certainty in the United Bible Societies' *Greek New Testament*," *NovT* 44 (2002): 105-33. Cf. idem, *Textual Optimism: A Critique of the United Bible Societies' Greek New Testament* (Sheffield: Sheffield Academic Press, 1997).

[5] J. M. Ross, "The United Bible Societies' Greek New Testament," *JBL* 95 (1976):117. Ross goes on to suggest another set of symbols (X, Y, Z) with definitions less subtle, but, still indicating various degrees of probability.

[6] J. K. Elliott, "The New Testament in Greek: Two New Editions," *TLZ* 119 (1994): 496. In another review article, Elliott points to the fact that Metzger in his *Textual Commentary* makes no reference to the significance of the ratings in his actual discussions of textual problems, and Elliott concludes: "Those wishing to evaluate the variants in the UBS apparatus are better advised to examine Metzger's comments rather than look at the often arbitrary rating letter attached to the reading selected for the text" ("The Third Edition of the United Bible Societies' Greek New Testament," *NovT* 20 [1978]: 270).

improve the situation. Probably, the current system will be further revised or disappear altogether.

3. A New Descriptive Rating System

In this textual commentary, a new rating system is introduced. In my opinion, a good rating system will make the reader more attentive, careful and curious regarding what lies ahead. It will invite the reader actively to engage with the evidence in order to reach independent conclusions. Therefore, the new system used here is descriptive rather than evaluative, and is offered as a broad summary of the distribution of the evidence from the current editor's perspective. The following symbols are used to describe the evidence:

{e+i}   External and internal evidence unequivocally support the adopted variant reading.

{e>i}   External evidence favors the adopted variant reading, whereas internal evidence is ambiguous.

{e<i}   External evidence is ambiguous, whereas internal evidence favors the adopted variant reading.

{e=i}   External and internal evidence are balanced or, alternatively, external evidence favors one variant reading, internal evidence another.

Naturally, the perceived state of the evidence corresponds to the relative degree of certainty behind the various decisions. If, for example, a variation-unit has rating {e=i} the evidence is ambiguous and the decision highly subjective. Of course, the reader may in many cases come to wholly different conclusions depending on the adopted overall view of the textual transmission, and of the relative weight assigned to external and internal evidence, respectively.

In the new edition from the INTF in Münster, *Novum Testamentum Graecum Editio Critica Maior* (*ECM*), another type of symbol, a bold dot (•), is used to indicate *alternative readings*; a precise definition of the significance of this symbol has not yet been formulated.[7] Nevertheless, the bold dot seems

---

[7] Cf. Barbara Aland, Kurt Aland, Gerd Mink and Klaus Wachtel, eds., *Novum Testamentum Graecum Editio Critica Maior*. Vol. IV: *The Catholic Letters*. Installment 2: *The Letters of Peter*. Part 1: *Text* (Stuttgart: Deutsche Bibelgesellschaft, 1999), 24*: "Its use [the bold dot] was not governed by any absolute or precise definition. Sometimes it signals alternative readings which were considered of equal value. Sometimes the reasons for the reading in the primary line were regarded as superior, but not sufficiently to rule out with complete confidence the claims

to be roughly equivalent to the symbol {e=i} used in this edition. In the textual commentary, I have indicated those places where the *ECM* has a bold dot. In addition, I have indicated places where my preferred text differs from the text printed in the primary line of the *ECM*.

4. The Citation of External Evidence in the Commentary

The Greek manuscript witnesses are cited mainly according to their textual quality, in accordance with the results of the CBGM (see above), and my own estimation. Generally, the following manuscripts of the first and second classes are cited most frequently in the commentary:

1st: 𝔓72, 01, 02, 03, 04, 020, 044, 81, 88, 307, 326, 431, 436, 442, 453, 808, 1739, 2200.

2nd: 18, 33, 35, 323, 621, 623, 630, 665, 915, 1067, 1409, 1836, 1837, 1845, 1852, 1875, 2374.

In addition, the nucleus members of the so-called HK group, MSS 1505, 1611 and 2138, are cited frequently, since, in my opinion, they represent the early stages of the Byzantine text (see above) and thus are important for the reconstruction of the history of the text. Furthermore, the fragmentary MSS 𝔓78, 0316 and 2627 are cited where extant, and MS 424 is cited whenever it has corrections or additional readings (C/Z), which have proven to be of great value.

The Majority Text is cited under the siglum 𝔐, indicating readings supported by the majority of all manuscripts, always including manuscripts of the Byzantine *Koine* text in the narrow sense. When the Majority Text is divided fairly equally between two or more variant readings, the abbreviation *pm* (*permulti*) is used to indicate support from a large number of manuscripts. The abbreviation *pc* (*pauci*) indicates support from a few manuscripts (3-20) other than those mentioned, which differ from the Majority Text, and *al* (*alii*) indicates the support of some manuscripts (>20) other than those mentioned, which differ from the Majority Text. The exact identity and number of manuscripts in support of a given variant can always be deduced from the critical apparatus.

The following witnesses of the third class are cited only occasionally:

3rd: 3, 5, 6, 61, 93, 254, 468, 1243, 1292, 1735, 1846, 1881, 2186, 2298, 2344, 2805, 2818.

---

of the indicated alternative reading. In any event the dot indicates a passage which calls for special critical consideration."

Other witnesses are cited when they support singular or relatively rare readings. The reader is strongly encouraged to use the textual commentary alongside the apparatus in order to see the complete distribution of the manuscript evidence.

The patristic evidence is cited when deemed significant. It has been compiled from the *ECM*, and verified in the best available editions (corrections are noted in the footnotes). In some cases, additional patristic evidence is cited due to its importance. When such significant evidence is absent from the *ECM*, I indicate the complete bibliographic reference.[8]

The versional evidence is likewise cited whenever I find it significant, and it has been compiled from the *ECM* and various other sources.[9] I have indicated when I disagree with other editors concerning the interpretation of the versional evidence, and I have also noted some omissions in the *ECM*. Only the Latin (**L**), Coptic (**K**), and Syriac (**S**) versions are consistently cited, since we lack good critical editions of other versions (Armenian, Georgian, Old Church Slavonic and Ethiopic), and since the relationship of the latter versions to the Greek text is unclear. Furthermore, the versional evidence is generally not cited where it is ambiguous, but in some such cases the potential Greek variants that may be represented are indicated by a double arrow and two or more letter addresses referring to the corresponding Greek variants.

Abbreviations and symbols in the commentary, other than those mentioned in this introduction, follow the *ECM*. Note, however, the

---

[8] The evidence of Theophylact (Thph) is a special case. The commentary on Jude, *Expositio in epistolam S. Judae Apostoli* (PG 126:85-104), ascribed to him has not been considered by the editors of the *ECM*, probably because this commentary is practically identical with a much earlier one by Pseudo-Oecumenius (PsOec), *Catholica epistola Judae Apostoli* (PG 119:703-22), the evidence of which is included in the *ECM*. However, the edition of PsOec, reprinted by Migne, is clearly inferior for our purpose, since the citations from the NT betray heavy influence from Erasmus' *Novum Testamentum* (cf. Jan Krans, *Beyond What Is Written* [NTTS 35; Leiden: Brill, 2006], 131, n. 132), whereas the edition of Theophylact seems more faithful in this regard. Therefore, the evidence from Theophylact's commentary has been included here whenever the citations from Jude in the two commentaries differ. These differences along with the references are indicated in the footnotes.

[9] Apart from the *ECM*, the versional evidence is compiled from the following sources: Latin: Walter Thiele, ed., *Epistulae Catholicae* (Vetus Latina 26/1. Freiburg im Breisgau: Herder, 1956-1969); Syriac (Philoxenian): John Gwynn, *Remnants of the later Syriac versions of the Bible, Part I: New Testament. The Four Minor Catholic Epistles in the Original Philoxenian Version, of the Sixth Century* (Text and Translation Society 5; London/Oxford: Williams & Norgate, 1909); Syriac (Harklean): Joseph White, *Actus apostolorum et epistolas catholicas complectens* (Vol. 1 of *Actuum apostolorum et epistolarum tam catholicarum quam Paulinarum, versio Syriaca Philoxeniana*; Oxford: Clarendon, 1799). White's edition is based on one manuscript (MS New College 333, Oxford). This same MS preserves variant readings in the margin (Harklean apparatus), some of which are not noted in the *ECM*.

different definition of the symbol Z following a manuscript number, as explained in the introduction to the apparatus above.

5. Umlauts in Codex Vaticanus (03)

In 1995, when Philip Payne was studying Codex Vaticanus he discovered the so called "umlauts" or double dots in the margin of the columns next to a line.[10] He concluded that these umlauts were in fact text-critical sigla that indicated textual variations known to the person who wrote them. It turned out that most of the umlauts had been enhanced by a reinforcer, but Payne found some which appeared not to have been traced over, wherefore he concluded that the symbol goes back to the original writing of the codex.[11] Whereas all scholars seem to agree about the function of the umlauts as indicating textual variations, there is some disagreement in regard to the origin and dating of the umlauts; the question remains open, but, in my opinion, no one has yet been able to disprove Payne's original observation concerning the unretouched umlauts.[12]

In Jude, there are eight umlauts in Codex Vaticanus (vv. 1, 4, 5, 16, 22-23, 25 [x3]). The three first umlauts seem to be unenhanced, displaying the original apricot-colored ink. The individual umlauts are indicated in the textual commentary at the end of those variation-units to which each one refers.

---

[10] Philip B. Payne "Fuldensis, Sigla for Variants in Vaticanus and 1 Cor 14.34-5," *NTS* 41 (1995): 240-62.

[11] Ibid., 261.

[12] See further: Curt Niccum, "The Voice of the MSS on the Silence of the Women: The External Evidence for 1 Cor 13:34-35," *NTS* 43 (1997): 242-55; Philip B. Payne and Paul Canart, "The Originality of Text-Critical Symbols in Codex Vaticanus," *NovT* 42 (2000): 105-13; J. Edward Miller, "Some Observations on the Text-Critical Function of the Umlauts in Vaticanus, with Special Attention to 1 Corinthians 14.34-35," *JSNT* 26 (2003): 217-36; Philip B. Payne and Paul Canart, "The Text-Critical Function of the Umlauts in Vaticanus, with Special Attention to 1 Corinthians 14.34-35: A Response to J. Edward Miller," *JSNT* 27 (2004): 105-12.

ΙΟΥΔΑ ΕΠΙΣΤΟΛΗ

Inscriptio: [[ΙΟΥΔΑ ΕΠΙΣΤΟΛΗ]]

The superscriptions of the books of the NT do not originate from the individual writers, but in a way they can be said to represent a certain stage in the manuscript tradition when the various writings were collected together. The earliest superscriptions were short and to the point, so that the reader could identify the place of the individual writing in a collection. In the case of Jude, it is the last book among the Catholic Epistles closing the collection unit of the *Apostolos* (Acts and Catholic Epistles).

The superscriptions of the Catholic Epistles consist of two main elements, the name of the author and the genre description ἐπιστολή. In NA²⁷ we can observe that this genre description is included for the first book of the collection unit only, Ἰακώβου ἐπιστολή (the Epistle of James). In the other epistles, only the name of the authors and numbering, where applicable, are indicated. The same practice is reflected in Codex Vaticanus (03), in which the superscriptions were added later.[13] In my opinion, it is likely that the earliest superscriptions of all the Catholic Epistles included the genre description once the collection unit came in existence, reflecting a homogenous redactional trait (cf. the superscriptions of the other sections).[14] However, I think the reconstruction of the initial text proper can reach further back to the time when the writing circulated separately (see above). Since the superscription derives from an early stage of the tradition, I have chosen to retain it on the primary line within double square brackets.

Since the superscriptions were not part of the authors' text, they became subject to considerable expansion by scribes in the history of transmission. Consequently, they offer interesting insights into the later context of the text. The most common expansion in the MSS is the epithet καθολική. The term probably originated in the latter part of the second century, and came to designate the seven New Testament letters intended for a wider, more "general" (catholic) audience, in contrast to the Pauline Epistles, intended for a specific church or individual.[15] In the manuscript tradition, the

---

[13] Cf. also the inclusion of genre description only in the subscription of James among the Catholic Epistles in 01 and 03 (ἐπιστολὴ Ἰακώβου).

[14] See further David Trobisch, *The First Edition of the New Testament* (Oxford: Oxford University Press, 2000), 39. In chapter seven I briefly assess Trobisch's theory of a "canonical edition."

[15] Near the end of the century Apollonius accused a Montanist named Themiso for having imitated an apostle and composed a "catholic" epistle (Eusebius, *Hist. eccl.* 5.18.5). Clement of

earliest attestation of the term is found in Codex Alexandrinus (02) from the fifth century, in the subscription of the *Apostolos* and in a list of contents.[16]

Other additions in the MSS were motivated by the need to identify the author and increase his status and reputation, ἅγιος, ἀπόστολος, ἀδελφοθεός, ἀδελφὸς Ἰακώβου, πανεύφημος.[17] One scribe apparently saw the need to point out that this Jude was not identical with the betrayer: ἄλλος Ἰούδας οὐ μὴ δὲ ὁ προδότης (582). Further additions identify the addressees as a more or less general group: εὐσεβέσιν, πρὸς τοὺς πιστεύσαντας ἀδελφούς, πᾶσιν ἔθνεσιν, ὥπασε πᾶσι βροτοῖς.

The various descriptions of Jude speaking beautifully, πανεύφημος, ἡδυεπής ἀγορητής, probably echo a comment by Origen who said about the epistle that it was "filled with the healthful words of heavenly grace."[18]

The first of the four summary-headings (τίτλοι) in Jude, περὶ προσοχής κτλ., has also caused significant additions in some MSS. Probably, the numbering of the first heading, "α," caused some scribes to misinterpret it as indicating the *first* (πρώτη) Epistle of Jude (93 104 665 959 1243 1875). The expression ἀνάγνωσμα normally signified the pericope or section of Scripture read in church. In the superscriptions of some MSS, however, the word is used in a wider sense of the text of the writing as a whole.

1,4-8: Ἰησοῦ Χριστοῦ δοῦλος {e+i}

The best MSS, the major part of the Byzantine tradition, and most of the versions support the printed text, although many witnesses read Χριστοῦ Ἰησοῦ δουλος (6 424 808 2374 *pm*). One cannot base a decision about word order on intrinsic grounds by appealing to the examples in vv. 4, 17, 21, 25, since those occurrences are all examples of set expressions.[19] We are left

---

Alexandria described the letter from the Jerusalem council (Acts 15:22-29) as a "catholic epistle" (*Strom.* 4.97.3) and Athanasius called the seven letter collection the "seven catholic epistles" in his 39th *Festal Letter* (39.5).

[16] Landon's invocation of a "theological canon" against those readings which include the term is improper (*Text-Critical Study*, 47); the fact that the writer's theology is not "early Catholic" has little to do with the problem in question, i.e., whether the letter was perceived and described as being generally addressed by the time the superscription was added.

[17] This sort of expansion is not exclusive for Jude as seen in the superscriptions of the other epistles.

[18] The passage in *Comm. Matt.* 10.17 reads: ". . . πεπληρωμένην δὲ τῶν τῆς οὐρανίου χάριτος ἐρρωμένων λόγων"; cf. the subscript of 2404, τὸ ἐν λόγοις κάλλιστον γραφὲν βιβλίον.

[19] Landon admits the fact that most of the examples are set expressions; yet, in the end he prefers Ἰησοῦ Χριστοῦ on an argument from silence, because the opposite word order appears nowhere in Jude (*Text-Critical Study*, 48-49).

with only one other occurrence in v. 1, where there is some textual variation. Thus, stylistic considerations are unhelpful. However, there is another piece of intrinsic evidence; there is much to suggest that our author knew the Epistle of James. There are striking similarities between the two letters in terms of theology, shared traditions, exegetical technique, style and vocabulary, not to mention the fact that the author presents himself as the brother of James, and, implicitly, as the other brother of Jesus.[20] Thus, the intertextual connection is evident right from the start:

’Ιάκωβος θεοῦ καὶ κυρίου ’Ιησοῦ Χριστοῦ δοῦλος (James 1:1)

’Ιούδας ’Ιησοῦ Χριστοῦ δοῦλος, ἀδελφὸς δὲ ’Ιακώβου (Jude 1)

Hence, in addition to external evidence, intrinsic evidence speaks in favor of ’Ιησοῦ Χριστοῦ δοῦλος, since the author seems consciously to allude to James 1:1, where there is no textual variation at this point.

1,16-24: τοῖς ἐν θεῷ πατρὶ ἠγαπημένοις (. . . κλητοῖς) {e+i}

The whole phrase in the dative identifies the recipients of the letter, where the article belongs to κλητοῖς, modified by two parallel participial clauses in intermediate position. The construction speaks against the insertion of the noun ἔθνεσιν after τοῖς in some MSS (323 424Z 1505 1611 1739 1852 2138 *al* **S**:HPh). Nevertheless, the attestation in diverse and important witnesses shows that the word was introduced early on, and that the recipients of the epistle were thought by some to be exclusively Gentiles, which is hardly the case. The same objections apply to the peculiar reading τοῖς ἐν θεῷ πατράσιν (832), which reflects another attempt to narrow down the recipients to the elders of the church.

The two participial clauses present syntactical difficulties. The main problem with the first clause is the awkward combination of ἐν θεῷ πατρί and ἠγαπημένοις. A local sense of the prepositional phrase ("beloved in God") or a dative of agency ("beloved by God") seem tautalogical at first sight.[21] This has led some to suggest that the author or, alternatively, all

---

[20] For a full treatment of the shared features of the two epistles, see J. Daryl Charles, *Literary Strategy in the Epistle of Jude* (Scranton: University of Scranton Press, 1993), 71-81; on intertextuality, see Jörg Frey, "Der Judasbrief zwischen Judentum und Hellenismus," in *Frühjudentum und Neues Testament im Horizont Biblischer Theologie* (ed. Wolfgang Kraus and Karl Wilhelm Niebuhr; WUNT 2.162; Tübingen: Mohr Siebeck, 2003), 203-6.

[21] However, see the passage in LXX Neh 13:26 that reads ἀγαπώμενος τῷ θεῷ ἦν.

Christians are the implied agents ("loved by us in God").[22] This solution, however, leads to an incongruity with the second participle, τετηρημένοις, where God is clearly the agent. The alternative instrumental sense of ἐν is understood by some commentators as a Semitism referring to God as agent.[23] This is still difficult; one would have expected the more natural ὑπὸ θεοῦ (cf. 1 Thess 1:4). Westcott and Hort suspected a "primitive error" and the latter suggested that ἐν is misplaced and should be placed before Jesus Christ.[24]

There are two other possible solutions: Alford interprets the preposition in the sense of "as regards God the Father."[25] The Sahidic translation reflects another interpretation that slightly modifies the local sense, "to the beloved [ones] *who are in* God the Father."[26] The forward position of "in God the Father," supports such an emphasis where the agent is only implied. A local sense is further supported by the author's reference in v. 21, ἐν ἀγάπῃ θεοῦ τηρήσατε.

Regardless of solution, the difficulty apparently prompted scribes to exchange the participle with ἡγιασμένοις (307 323 326T 431 453 665C 808 1836 1837 1875 2374 𝔐 Thph), probably under the influence of Paul's salutation in 1 Cor 1:2, ἡγιασμένοις ἐν Χριστῷ Ἰησοῦ, κλητοῖς ἁγίοις.[27] However, the reading ἠγαπημένοις has overwhelming manuscript support and is more consistent with the writer's style, particularly his abundant use

---

[22] See e.g., Mayor, *The Epistle of St. Jude*, 18. The fact that the author calls his readers ἀγαπητοί throughout the epistle may lend some support to this interpretation.

[23] So e.g., Ernst Kühl, *Die Briefe Petri und Judae* (6th ed.; KEK 12; Göttingen: Vandenheck & Ruprecht, 1897), 299.

[24] In reference to J. Price, Hort suggests the conjecture and says of the printed text: "[It] is without analogy and admits no natural interpretation" (B. F. Westcott and F. J. A. Hort, "Notes on Select Readings," in *The New Testament in the Original Greek* [2 vols.; London: Macmillan, 1881-1882], 2:106); cf. de Zwaan, *II Petrus en Judas*, 134. Hort's appeal to versional evidence in support of the conjecture does not strengthen the case (ibid.). The insertion of prepositions in Syriac and Coptic versions does not prove the presence of an equivalent preposition in the respective Greek Vorlage, since there are no case endings in Syriac and Coptic. Moreover, the reference to Origen is to the Latin translation of his Matthean Commentary, whereas the preserved Greek text actually reads ἐν θεῷ πατρί (*Comm. Matt.* 13.27).

[25] Henry Alford, *The Greek New Testament* (4 vols.; rev. ed.; London/Oxford: Rivingtons; Cambridge: Deighton, Bell & Co., 1871-1877), 4:529. Landon makes a similar interpretation and refers to various grammarians (Moulton, Zerwick, Bauer) who point out that ἐν can also be translated "in someone's judgment." Thus Landon's translation, "beloved in they eyes of God the Father" (*Text-Critical Study*, 51).

[26] Cf. the text of the Vulgate, *his, qui sunt in Deo Patre dilectis* (Augustinus S. J. Merk, ed., *Novum Testamentum graece et latine apparatu critico instructum* [11th ed.; Rome: Biblical Institute Press, 1992]).

[27] PsOec: ἠγαπημένοις (PG 119:705); Thph: ἡγιασμένοις (PG 126:88).

of catchwords from the same stem ἀγαπ- (ἀγάπη, ἀγαπητός, and, thus, ἀγαπάω).[28]

The readings τοῖς ἐν Χριστῷ πατρὶ ἡγιασμένοις (205 205abs) and τοῖς ἔθνεσιν πατρὶ ἡγιασμένοις (6) may represent other peculiar attempts to resolve the problem with the preposition. The addition of ἡμῶν (L921) reflects Pauline greetings (e.g., 2 Thess 1:1). In two MSS the *nomen sacrum* π̅ρ̅ι is confused with the preposition πρό (234 L1818), perhaps under the influence of other compound verbs in the epistle (vv. 4, 7, 14, 17). Other minor variations do not affect the sense much.

Umlaut 1 in Codex Vaticanus (03): this umlaut most probably indicates the knowledge of the variant ἡγιασμένοις on the part of the responsible scribe.

1,26-34: καὶ Ἰησοῦ Χριστῷ τετηρημένοις κλητοῖς {e+i}

The omission of καί . . . τετηρημένοις in some witnesses (630 1505 1611 1875 2138 2200 *pc* **S:H**) is due to homoioteleuton. Even if some of these witnesses are closely related, several scribes probably made the same error independently.[29]

The reading καὶ Ἰησοῦ Χριστῷ τετηρημένοις κλητοῖς has the strongest attestation by far. The difficult phrase Ἰησοῦ Χριστῷ should probably be interpreted as a dative of advantage ("kept for Jesus Christ"). The alternative interpretation is the more common dative of agency ("kept by Christ"). The thought of being kept by Christ is quite familiar in the NT (cf. John 17:12; 2 Thess 3:3; Rev 3:10), but in Jude 24 it is made explicit that God is the one who keeps the addressees. Further, the interpretation of Christ as agent here is incongruent with the first participle where the agent is God. As mentioned above, some MSS supply ἐν with a change in the word order to Χριστῷ Ἰησοῦ under influence of the very common phrase elsewhere in the NT.

The unclear force of the dative may have led to the introduction of the genitive case on the part of some scribes Ἰησοῦ Χριστοῦ (431 665 1836 2374 *al* Or PsOec) or Χριστοῦ Ἰησοῦ (044 *pc*) which conveys much the same sense as the dative of agency. In regard to transmissional likelihood, Landon argues that it is easier to envisage a change from an original dative to the

---

[28] Cf. Charles, *Literary Strategy,* 38-40.

[29] Cf. Klaus Wachtel's account of a number of closely related groups of MSS in the Catholic Epistles on the basis of collations in the Teststellen for the *Text und Textwert* (TuT) (Klaus Wachtel, *Der byzantinische Text der Katholischen Briefe: eine Untersuchung zur Entstehung der Koine des Neuen Testaments* [ANTF 24; Berlin/New York: de Gruyter, 1995], 56-72).

genitive due to the influence of Ἰησοῦ.[30] On the other hand, his main argument for the preferred word order Ἰησοῦ Χριστῷ (and Ἰησοῦ Χριστοῦ earlier in the verse), namely that the opposite order "appears nowhere in Jude where all the MSS agree," is invalid.[31] My own preference for the same word order twice in v. 1 is based mainly on the overwhelming manuscript support.

Finally, some MSS insert κυρίου (631 910), probably under the influence of other passages. The same can be said of the addition of ἁγίοις (104 628* 1838 1846), which occurs twice in Paul's prescripts (Rom 1:7; 1 Cor 1:2), and ἐκλεκτοῖς (2404), which occurs in 1 Peter 1:1.

2,8-12: εἰρήνη καὶ ἀγάπη {e+i}

The printed text has overwhelming manuscript support.[32] Some witnesses insert ἐν κυρίῳ in the greeting (630 1505 1611 2138 2200 *pc* **S:H**). The prepositional phrase is common in Pauline Epistles; it occurs several times in connection with the concluding greetings in Rom 16. A few MSS attest a different word order, ἀγάπη καὶ εἰρήνη (33V 61 631 1424 1868 **K:S**), possibly inspired by other greetings in the NT (2 Cor 13:11; 1 Pet 5:14). Other MSS omit καὶ ἀγάπη (88 181 619 *al*), perhaps occasioned by homoioteleuton, or by harmonization to the salutations in 1 Pet 1:2 and 2 Pet 1:2 (χάρις ὑμῖν καὶ εἰρήνη πληθυνθείη). On intrinsic grounds, Landon aptly refers to the writer's predilection for "triadic illustration as a stylistic device," which speaks against the omission.[33]

3,8: ποιούμενος {e+i}

Two MSS read ποιησάμενος (𝔓72 1501), which is probably the result of independent changes on the part of the scribes. The alternative aorist form

---

[30] Landon, *Text-Critical Study*, 53.

[31] Ibid., 49. The examples from vv. 4, 17, 21, 25, are all set expressions (as Landon acknowledges), and the other occurrence of the phrase exhibits variation.

[32] The *ECM* cites Eusebius, *Hist. eccl.* 4.15.3 in support of εἰρήνη καὶ ἀγάπη. Eusebius' source at this point, however, is the incipit of *Mart. Pol.* Friedrich Spitta says of the passage, "Dagegen ist die Berührung der Grussformel im Martyr. Polyc. . . . mit Jud. 1. 2 so auffallend, dass ich fast glauben möchte, hier finde sich ein Zeugnis für den Gebrauch des Judas-Briefes" (*Der zweite Brief des Petrus und der Brief des Judas* [Halle: Verlag der Buchhandlung des Waisenhauses, 1885], 534).

[33] Ibid., 55; cf. J. Daryl Charles' ample list of such triadic illustration in Jude ("Literary Artifice in the Epistle of Jude," *ZNW* 82 [1991]: 122); and the treatment in D. F. Watson, *Invention, Arrangement, and Style: Rhetorical Criticism of Jude and 2 Peter* (SBLDS 104; Atlanta: Scholar's Press, 1988), 26-42.

of the participle here affects the sense little. Landon explains the variant as an assimilation to Acts 25:17, which is possible.[34] Acts is not included in the miscellaneous codex of which 𝔓[72] (1-2 Peter and Jude) is a part, but other harmonizations on the part of the scribe show his general familiarity with the NT (see above). The same scribe did copy *3 Corinthians* in the same codex, where the Corinthians urge Paul to make haste to come: πᾶσαν εἰσηγήσαι [aor. impv.] σπουδήν παραγενέσθαι (1:16).[35]

In any case, the scribe of 𝔓[72] is known to have produced a large number of singular (and nearly singular) readings, many of which involve grammatical changes without any consequent pattern.[36] Likewise, the scribe of 1501 has produced several unique readings in Jude, in v. 17 involving a modification of the verb form from aorist to perfect (μέμνησθε for μνήσθητε).

3,10: γράφειν {e+i}

The articular infinitive τοῦ γράφειν is supported by a few important witnesses (𝔓[72] 01 044 2401*V 2627Z Cyr).[37] The presence of the article does not affect the sense and, admittedly, it could therefore have been omitted by scribes who saw it as superfluous. On the other hand, this Attic idiom with the genitive article in front of the infinitive occurs mainly in the writings of Luke and Paul in the NT, but became very common in Byzantine Greek and was promoted by the Atticists.[38] The same construction occurs in some MSS in Jude 15 (τοῦ ποιῆσαι), where the article is unquestionably a later addition. In view of external evidence, and the possible Atticistic addition by scribes, the printed text without the article is to be preferred.

Some scribes subsequently corrected or confused the article with the demonstrative pronoun τοῦτο (93 665 999 2401C). The suspension of the

---

[34] Landon, *Text-Critical Study*, 58.

[35] *P.Bodmer* X is the only Greek witness to *3 Corinthians*; *editio princeps* in Testuz, ed., *Papyrus Bodmer X-XII* (Cologny-Geneva: Bibliotheca Bodmeriana, 1959).

[36] For a comprehensive list, see Royse, "Scribal Habits," 483-85.

[37] Interestingly, MS 2627 has another valuable marginal reading in this verse: ἡμῶν σωτηρίας καὶ ζωῆς (actually divided as two separate marginal readings), with which it agrees with 01 and 044. A collation of all marginal readings of this MS would probably yield valuable results.

[38] Antonius N. Jannaris, *An Historical Greek Grammar Chiefly of the Attic Dialect* (London: Macmillan, 1897), 578; Nigel Turner, *Syntax* (vol. 3 [1968] of *A Grammar of New Testament Greek*; ed. James H. Moulton, W. F. Howard and Nigel Turner; 4 vols. Edinburgh: T. & T. Clark, 1908-1976), 140.

finite verb (ἔσχον) in the sentence probably tempted other scribes to write γράφω, and, thus, create two separate sentences.[39]

3,14-30: περὶ τῆς κοινῆς ἡμῶν σωτηρίας ἀνάγκην ἔσχον γράψαι ὑμῖν {e+i}

The lenghty omission in some witnesses (1241 L604 L1818 **L**:VTR **K**:SB **S**:HPh) apparently resulted from haplography (ὑμῖν . . . ὑμῖν).

3,16-22: τῆς κοινῆς ἡμῶν σωτηρίας {e>i}

The external evidence for ἡμῶν is very strong. The various readings with ὑμῶν may have arisen accidently through itacism, or else due to mechanical assimilation to the double ὑμῖν in the sentence. The presence of ὑμῖν could also explain the omission of the pronoun in most witnesses (18 35 468 808 1836 1875 2186 2374 𝔐 PsOec).[40] Metzger thinks the omission reflects "a desire to give the idea a universal character."[41] The pronoun may also have been perceived as unnecessary with κοινῆς. The phrase without the pronoun is attested elsewhere.[42] However, Wachtel views the reading without the pronoun as the *lectio difficilior*, and he finds it difficult to explain why the word would not be reproduced in the Majority Text tradition.[43] The internal evidence for and against the pronoun is rather balanced, but the external evidence speaks in favor of its inclusion.

A few witnesses, including the nucleus HK group, replace σωτηρίας with ζωῆς (1505 1611 2138 **S**:HPh), whereas a few important MSS attest a conflation, τῆς κοινῆς ἡμῶν σωτηρίας καὶ ζωῆς (01 044 2627Z). The attestation of ζωῆς by 01 shows that the substitution is early. Sakae Kubo suggests that a scribe made the change "because σωτηρία did not cover the things which the scribe wrote."[44]

---

[39] One of these MSS (1838) retains a single sentence by substituting ἔχων for ἔσχον. (Cf. v. 21, where the same MS replaces the indicative τηρήσατε with the participle τηρήσαντες.)

[40] PsOec: omit (PG 119:708); Thph: ἡμῶν (PG 126:89).

[41] Bruce M. Metzger, *A Textual Commentary on the Greek New Testament* (2d ed.; Stuttgart: Deutsche Bibelgesellschaft, 1994), 656.

[42] Isocrates, *De pace* 39; idem, *Panegyr.* 85; Jos, *Ant.* X.1.3 (ὑπὲρ τῆς κοινῆς σωτηρίας).

[43] Wachtel comments thus: "Die (möglicherweise spontane) Ergänzung und mehrheitliche Reproduktion von ἡμῶν liegt entschieden näher als die Auslassung" (*Der byzantinische Text*, 345). He also includes this example among untypical Majority Text readings, and says of the omission: "Auslassung ohne erkennbaren Anlaß, weniger glatte Lesart" (ibid., 82).

[44] Kubo, *A Comparative Study*, 226.

3,26-30: ἔσχον γράψαι ὑμῖν {e+i}

A few MSS replace ἔσχον with the more natural ἔχω (631 918 1780 L422).[45] Bauckham interprets the aorist form ἔσχον (with γράψαι) as an epistolary aorist, i.e., that the action (having reason to write) will be past as the letter is read.[46] However, Turner notes that one never finds the equivalent epistolary ἔγραψα in *koine* (the normal form in the NT is γράφω).[47] Bauckham goes on to explain the contrast between the two infinitives in the sentence γράφειν and γράψαι, suggesting that "the distinction is between the general intention of writing [present] . . . and the concrete action actually carried out [aorist]."[48] I would modify this interpretation slightly and interpret the aorist forms in the whole phrase ἀνάγκην ἔσχον γράψαι as ingressive aorist; the author intended to write a letter of a different kind, but received a report of the state of things in the church that gave him reason to start writing this actual letter instead. The difficulties with the aorist forms are evident from the various variant readings where the present intrudes.[49] In regard to the reading ἔσχον γράφειν ὑμῖν (01 044 1505 1735 2138) I agree with Landon who explains the present infinitive as a harmonization to the first γράφειν earlier in the sentence.[50]

3,32-34: παρακαλῶν ἐπαγωνίζεσθαι {e+i}

The various readings with the imperative, ἐπαγωνίζεσθε (𝔓72 02 *pc*), are syntactically and semantically possible (cf. 1 Tim 6:12; Sir 4:28), but the reading is best explained as an itacism.[51] In some witnesses the present has

---

[45] All other instances where the phrase occurs in the NT have the present stem (Luke 14:18; 23:17 in the TR; 1 Cor 7:37; Heb 7:27).

[46] Richard J. Bauckham, *Jude, 2 Peter* (WBC 50; Waco: Word Books, 1983), 28.

[47] Turner, *Syntax*, 73. The interpretation of ἔγραψα as an epistolary aorist here and in some other passages in the NT is a disputed matter. Cf. Daniel B. Wallace, *Greek Grammar Beyond the Basics* (Grand Rapids: Zondervan, 1996), 563.

[48] Bauckham, *Jude, 2 Peter*, 30.

[49] The reading ἔχων, attested in a few minuscules, is syntactically erroneous because the resulting sentence will lack a finite verb. However, MS 1838 has the finite verb γράφω earlier in the sentence and, thus, the syntax is not in error here (contra *ECM*).

[50] Landon, *Text-Critical Study*, 61. For a list of similar harmonizations in 01 and other representatives of the early text in the Catholic Epistles, see Weiss, *Die Katholischen Briefe*, 26-30.

[51] Examples in 𝔓72 and 02 of confusion of ε and αι in Jude include: παλε, υπομνησε, εγυπτου, ε περει, απελθουσε, προσκειντε, εωνιου, πυμενοντες, νεφελε, πλανητε, τετηρητε, ελεγξε, γογγυστε, εμπεκτε, ανυκοδομεισθαι, εωνας (𝔓72); πλανητε, εμπεκται, ελεγχεται, ελεαται (02).

been changed to aorist, ἐπαγωνίσασθαι, in harmony with the other aorist infinitives. However, the present seems to suit the context better—the author is urging the recipients to go on struggling for the faith. The compound verb is a *hapax legomenon*; some MSS attest the more common ἀγωνίζομαι.

4,2: παρεισέδυσαν {e>i}

The aorist passive, παρεισεδύησαν (03 04V), has the same meaning as the aorist active. On transcriptional grounds, it is easy to imagine how the letter η would drop from the longer passive form.[52] There is a tendency in the Hellenistic period to replace intransitive aorist actives with aorist passives, as evident elsewhere in the NT, and so we would expect the author to use the *koine* form.[53] On the other hand, the change to the more common *koine* form may have been introduced by a scribe.[54] Thus, Albin regards the longer form in 03 as an emendation, and, as such, "hardly surprising in the case of B."[55] In conclusion, the internal evidence is rather balanced, but the manuscript evidence clearly favors the aorist active.

4,14: προγεγραμμένοι {e+i}

One MS reads ἀναγεγραμμένοι (57), "recorded" (e.g., in a judgment book). The curious variant originates from this individual scribe who habitually replaces the prepositional morpheme προ- with ἀνα- for some reason, even when the result is nonsensical (v. 16: ἀνάσωπα—nonsensical; v. 17: ἀνειρημένων: "proclaimed").

4,16-24: εἰς τοῦτο τὸ κρίμα, ἀσεβεῖς {e+i}

Two witnesses attest the peculiar reading εἰς τοῦτο τὸ κήρυγμα (044 **K**:S^ms), which is of course secondary, but, nevertheless, very interesting from the

---

[52] Cf. the parallel in 2 Pet 2:1 with the active, παρεισάξουσιν.

[53] See further BDF §76.2. The particular verb was used mostly in the middle (BDAG, s.v. παρεισδύ(ν)ω).

[54] The verb is a *hapax legomenon*, but the simplex form δύνω occurs in Mark 1:32, where 03 05 and a few minuscules replace an Attic second aorist (ἔδυ) with the first aorist (ἔδυσεν) in similar vein (see BDF §75).

[55] Albin, *Judasbrevet*, 597 (my translation). Note, however, that in Albin's days the prevailing view of the recensional nature of the "Alexandrian text-type" (thought to be best represented by 03) had not yet been seriously questioned; cf. C. M. Martini, *Il problema della recensionalità del codice B alla luce del papiro Bodmer XIV* (AnBib 26; Rome: Pontificio Instituto Biblico, 1966), esp. 119-21, 124-28, and 136-37.

perspective of interpretation. Landon explains the reading κήρυγμα, as "a deliberate change introduced to eradicate the contextual difficulty suggested by κρίμα."[56] The difficulty lies in the fact that the writer has not mentioned any condemnation (κρίμα) prior to this verse.

From the paleographical point of view, the reading κήρυγμα could be explained as an accidental misrepresentation of κρίμα. However, in the case of the only Greek witness (044) the meaning and significance of the rare reading κήρυγμα should be considered with attention to the following word, ἀσεβεῖν (044 *pc*). I suggest the following translation of the text of 044: "For certain intruders have stolen in among you, who were long ago designated to continue to act impiously [ἀσεβεῖν] at this message [εἰς τοῦτο τὸ κήρυγμα]." Probably the scribe had in mind Jesus' words in Matt 12:41 (par. Luke 11:32): "The people of Nineveh will rise up [ἀναστήσονται] at the judgment with this generation and condemn it, because they repented at the proclamation [εἰς τὸ κήρυγμα] of Jonah, and see, something greater than Jonah is here!" (NRSV). The exact reference of the prediction (προγεγραμμένοι) as such is a well-known crux.[57] One of the solutions is to connect it with the apostolic prophecy in v. 18. The scribe of 044 seems to have done just that judging from the singular reading in v. 18: ἐπ᾽ ἐσχάτου χρόνου ἀναστήσονται ἐμπαῖκται . . . ἀσεβειῶν. Again we hear echoes of the apostolic prediction of eschatological judgment upon "this (evil) generation" written down by Matthew.

The reading with the infinitive ἀσεβεῖν (044 *pc*) as complement to οἱ προγεγραμμένοι avoids the difficulty with the ambiguous ἀσεβεῖς, which may belong with οἱ πάλαι κτλ. (so e.g., Lm, Td⁷, Weiss), but more probably stands for itself (TR, Tr, Td⁸, WH, NA²⁷, *ECM*).

The omission of the article in some witnesses (𝔓⁷²T *pc*) is probably an accidental slip due to homoioteleuton. The reading κατάκριμα (309 2501) is an amplification on the part of the scribes suggested from the character of the context.

4,28-32: τοῦ θεοῦ ἡμῶν {e+i}

A few witnesses replace θεοῦ with κυρίου (424Z 1241 Did **K:B**), possibly under the influence of the common collocation τοῦ κυρίου ἡμῶν. Didymus the Blind is also cited in support of the reading θεοῦ in the *ECM*. However, a closer examination of the source of this reference reveals an error in the

---

[56] Landon, *Text-Critical Study*, 63.
[57] See Bauckham, *Jude, 2 Peter*, 35-36.

ECM: the citation refers to *De Trinitate* 1.27, and is based on an edition by Jürgen Hönscheid, but in the passage in question, the editor points out that the actual citation from Jude 4 is lacking.[58] Apparently, Hönscheid provided the Greek text himself. This "interpolation" also affects the *ECM* in 4,58, where Didymus is cited in support of the variant reading δεσπότην καὶ κύριον Ἰησοῦν Χριστὸν, attested in one Greek MS (1881); Hönscheid, not Didymus, is responsible for the omission of ἡμῶν.[59]

4,34: χάριτα {e<i}

The reading χάριτα has significant support from early witnesses (𝔓⁷² 02 03) and, interestingly, is now found also in MS 38. This later minuscule is not genealogically related to the ancient witnesses, but it displays a rather eccentric text in Jude. It cannot be excluded that some ancient readings have been preserved in this MS, but the very high number of errors (corrected and uncorrected) and peculiar readings, as observable in Jude, rather points to the general irregularity and originality of the scribe, who may well have created this reading independently.[60]

In any case there is good reason to accept χάριτα as original on transcriptional grounds; the Attic accusative, χάριν, is also the common form in the NT (χάριτα occurs only here and in Acts 24:27).

4,44-58: τὸν μόνον δεσπότην καὶ κύριον ἡμῶν Ἰησοῦν Χριστόν {e>i}

The printed text has strong manuscript support (01 02 03 04 33 81 307 323 326T 326Z2 424C 431 436 442 453* 621 808 1067 1409 1739 1845 *al* Cyr Did **L:VR**). The main problem is the question whether the whole phrase refers to Jesus Christ, or if the first part refers to God. A number of significant witnesses and the Majority Text is unambiguous in this regard, τὸν μόνον δεσπότην θεὸν καὶ κύριον ἡμῶν Ἰησοῦν Χριστόν (044 326Z1

---

[58] "Das folgende Zitat aus Judas kommt im erhaltenen Text nicht vor" (Jörgen Hönscheid, ed., *Didymus der Blinde. De trinitate, Buch I* [Beiträge zur klassischen Philologie 44. Meisenheim am Glan: Hain, 1975], 191, n. 1 (the Greek text including the citation of Jude is on p. 190).

[59] In J.-P. Migne's outdated edition of *De Trinitate*, the text of Jude 4 is cited according to my adopted text, i.e., with θεοῦ (PG 39:408). At the same time, one suspects that the citation of Jude was not intact since the part οἱ πάλαι προγεγραμμένοι εἰς τοῦτο τὸ κρίμα is placed within brackets.

[60] A further examination of MS 38 in regard to the extent of preserved ancient readings is desirable.

453C 623 630 1505 1611 2138 2200 2374 PsOec **S**:HPh 𝔐; 88 915 1836 1875 *pc* without ἡμῶν).

Landon attempts to demonstrate that the word δεσπότης ("Master") does not refer to Jesus Christ, but to God.[61] He rightly questions a mechanical application of the grammatical rule that when one article controls two nouns the writer refers to one person, and he further points out that κύριος is often without the article in the NT.[62] On the other hand, Turner in a similar case (2 Pet 1:1) suggests that the article, "could have been repeated to avoid misunderstanding if separate individuals had been intended."[63]

Landon further appeals to transcriptional evidence, suggesting that the shorter reading (without θεόν) could be the result of deliberate deletion by anti-adoptionist orthodox scribes who did not want God and Jesus to appear as two separate entities.[64] The view that doctrinal alterations have affected the text was first proposed by Johann Jakob Wettstein, who formulated the following canon of criticism: "Of two variant readings that which seems more orthodox is not immediately to be preferred."[65] Interestingly, one of the examples Wettstein appealed to was this passage in Jude 4, where he preferred the reading without θεόν as being the less orthodox reading![66] These paradoxical conclusions demonstrate the bluntness of the instrument in practical application.

A key question is the possible and probable referent of δεσπότης. The title is not among the conventional divine names, but was sometimes used by Greek writers, including Jewish and early Christian authors, to refer to

---

[61] Landon, *Text-Critical Study*, 63-66.

[62] Ibid., 64.

[63] Turner, *Syntax*, 181.

[64] Landon, *Text-Critical Study*, 65. Here and elsewhere, Landon appeals to Bart D. Ehrman's work, *The Orthodox Corruption of Scripture*. The possibility seems to have escaped these writers that if θεόν (= θ͞ν) were really original, the omission could perhaps be due to simple homoioteleuton.

[65] "Inter duas variantes lectiones ea, quae magis orthodoxa videtur, non est protinus alteri praeferenda" (Johann Jakob Wettstein, ed., *Novum Testamentum Graecum* [2 vols.; Amsterdam: Dommerian, 1751-1752], 2:864). The canon in question was formulated already in 1730 in his *Prolegomena ad Novi Testamenti graeci editionem accuratissimam*, which was later republished along with the critical edition. See further, Peter M. Head, "Christology and Textual Transmission: Reverential Alterations in the Synoptic Gospels," *NovT* 35 (1993): 108-9.

[66] In this connection, Wettstein accuses Beza for accepting the "orthodox" reading: "Because this reading [τὸν μόνον θεὸν καὶ δεσπότην τὸν κύριον ἡμῶν Ἰησοῦν Χριστόν] supports orthodoxy, it was, incredibly, accepted by Beza, who says, 'The single article, which is shared by all these epithets, shows beyond doubt that Christ is here called 'sole master, God, and Lord;' even though the ancient translation does not read the name of God, and I have discovered that it is missing in two Greek MSS" (J. J. Wettstein, *Novum Testamentum Graecum*, 2:864; translation P. E. Satterthwaite).

God (in the NT, see Luke 2:29; Acts 4:24; Rev 6:10).[67] The question is whether it could refer to Jesus. As I argue here, the parallel passage in 2 Peter 2:1 is the earliest witness to the text of Jude 4, and it reads καὶ τὸν ἀγοράσαντα αὐτοὺς δεσπότην ἀρνούμενοι. Significantly, the text of 2 Peter attests the shorter reading and interprets δεσπότης as a reference to Jesus.[68] Further, the verb ἀρνέομαι occurs in a similar sense over twenty times in the NT, and then it almost always refers to a denying of Christ; only once to a denying of God the Father (1 John 2:22). Finally, δεσπότης ("Master") is correlative to δοῦλος ("slave"), and the author calls himself the slave of Jesus Christ in the salutation (v. 1). In conclusion δεσπότης in this passage probably refers to Jesus Christ.

Wachtel goes even further; he interprets even the Majority Text as referring to one person, Jesus Christ, appealing to other NT passages and to Pseudo-Oecumenius' commentary, where the Byzantine text is expounded along these lines.[69] Thus, he argues that θεόν was not added to avoid ambiguity, but in order to enhance the Christological standing of Jesus. I do not doubt that Jesus Christ is referred to as God in several places in the NT, although I note that in practically all of the examples to which Wachtel refers, there is ambiguity in terms of punctuation and textual variation.[70] Evidently, the Majority Text was interpreted in this way by Pseudo-Oecumenius and several other authors, but one can hardly deny that the reference of the sole divine title δεσπότης was not perceived as ambiguous in much the same way as κύριος which scribes at times preferred to specify as either Jesus or God (cf. v. 9 below). In fact, the presence of the adjective μόνον increases the ambiguity, in light of its occurrence in v. 25, μόνῳ θεῷ σωτῆρι ἡμῶν διὰ Ἰησοῦ Χριστοῦ τοῦ κυρίου ἡμῶν.

In some witnesses the ambiguity is removed by the omission of the conjunction, so that the title is unequivocally attributed to Jesus: τὸν μόνον δεσπότην κύριον ἡμῶν Ἰησοῦν Χριστόν (𝔓78 38 **L**:T **K**:B).[71] Other witnesses

---

[67] BDAG, s.v. δεσπότης 1b; cf. Metzger, *Textual Commentary*, 656.

[68] See also Luke 13:25 where 𝔓75 replaces οἰκοδεσπότης with δεσπότης, with possible Christological implications. In Eusebius, *Hist. eccl.* 1.7.14 the term δεσπόσυνοι is used to denote the relatives of Jesus.

[69] Wachtel, *Der byzantinische Text*, 347, esp. n. 298.

[70] Cf. I. Moir and J. K. Elliott who state: "The apparent reluctance of the church to equate Jesus and God has affected the textual tradition of virtually all doctrinally sensitive passages in the NT" (*Manuscripts and the Text of the New Testament: An Introduction for English Readers* [Edinburgh: T&T Clark, 1995], 60).

[71] Wachtel is reluctant to see the passage as ambiguous and assumes that this reading in the two Greek MSS (he does not mention the versional evidence) is due to independent scribal

replace the less common δεσπότην with θεόν (378 2147 2652 L593), possibly because of a gloss in the exemplar, or because of omission due to homoioteleuton if the exemplar followed the Majority Text.[72] The text of 𝔓[72] has a different and awkward word order and adds the pronoun ἡμῶν. The scribe is known to have made many additions where he repeats portions of his text, often a single word, and he has also made a number of transpositions, some of which involve a leap followed by a correction where the omitted words are inserted out of order (cf. v. 14, 21; 25).[73] In this case, the scribe was interrupted when copying μόνον as νόμον which he then removed. His eye then probably skipped to ἡμῶν, he realized the mistake and copied the omitted words in the wrong order, including ἡμῶν a second time.

Thus, the accepted reading has the best manuscript support, whereas most of the rejected readings represent various attempts to make the text less ambiguous.

Umlaut 2 in Codex Vaticanus (03): the umlaut certainly refers to the variant reading with θεόν.

5,4: δέ {e=i} (*ECM* •δε•/•ουν)

Several important MSS replace δέ with οὖν (04 044 6 323 1243 1501 1739 2298 *pc*), one MS attests δὲ οὖν (424Z).[74] A few other witnesses omit the word altogether (1834 1881 2086 2186 **K:B**). Nevertheless, the variant reading δέ has the best manuscript support.

As for internal evidence, Landon thinks v. 5 demands a particle denoting a mild contrast to v. 4, which focuses on the opponents, and he points out that the author uses δέ consistently to denote mild contrast (vv. 10, 17, 20, 24).[75] However, the author might have intended to make an inference to the whole context of vv. 3-4, where he explains the intention behind the current letter, to urge (παρακαλέω) his readers to struggle for the faith, specifically caused by the report about the opponents. The inferential

---

error where the eye of the respective scribe has skipped from θ̄ν̄ to κ̄ν̄ (*Der byzantinische Text*, 348). The scribe of MS 38 has evidently produced many errors in Jude, but the manuscript also displays some noteworthy readings. In the case of 𝔓[78], I think the alteration may well have been conscious in view of the consistent pattern of singular readings and the particular usage of the MS (see above).

[72] MSS 378 2147 2652 are closely related (Mink, "Problems," 47).

[73] See further Royse, "Scribal Habits," 477, 480.

[74] In MS 424, δ' οὖν is added supralinearly over δέ.

[75] Landon, *Text-Critical Study*, 68.

particle would fit well in the discourse structure introducing the section in vv. 5-19, with the warning exhortations intertwined with descriptions of the opponents. My interpretation of ἅπαξ in v. 5 (see below) as an adverb of manner further enhances the parallel to v. 3: the faith has been delivered to the saints once and for all, and the author now reminds these saints of the things in their faith of which they have once for all (ἅπαξ) been informed.

Scribes, on the other hand, would be tempted to replace οὖν with δέ in accordance with the examples quoted by Landon, especially passages that contrast the addressees with the opponents; note in particular the second reminder in v. 17: ὑμεῖς δέ, ἀγαπητοί, μνήσθητε τῶν ῥημάτων τῶν προειρημένων. Thus, external and internal evidence are split; in this difficult case, my preference for δέ is based on the stronger manuscript support.

5,9: [omit] {e+i}

𝔓⁷⁸V inserts ἀδελφοί. This address is superfluous—especially if the personal pronoun ὑμᾶς was repeated a second time, which is impossible to say because of the fragmentary state of the MS. The presence of ἀδελφοί at this point may indicate that the manuscript did not contain v. 3, where the author uses the address ἀγαπητοί (as in vv. 17, 20). On the other hand, the scribe could have substituted ἀδελφοί for ἀγαπητοί in that verse under the influence of 2 Pet 1:10, ἀδελφοί, σπουδάσατε and then repeated the address a second time, perhaps in order to create a greater sense of immediacy or gravity to the warnings. In any case, the manuscript contains an eccentric text that may well be connected to its probable usage as an amulet (see above).

5,10-20: εἰδότας ὑμᾶς ἅπαξ πάντα ὅτι κύριος (*ECM* ειδοτας υμας απαξ παντα οτι •ιησους•/•[ο] κυριος)

This is one of the textually most difficult passages in Jude, and in the whole NT. This fact is perhaps best exemplified in the shift from εἰδότας ὑμᾶς ἅπαξ πάντα ὅτι Ἰησοῦς in UBS² to εἰδότας ὑμᾶς πάντα ὅτι ὁ κύριος ἅπαξ in UBS³,⁴ and back again in the new *ECM*.[76] Hence, it has been subject to

---

[76] It is apparent from Metzger's *Textual Commentary*, 657-58, that the members of the UBS Committee had very different opinions concerning the passage, and, hence, it was given a D-rating. Similar disagreement prevails among the editors of the *ECM* (IV, 37*; see further below). The difficulties led Westcott and Hort to assume two primitive errors in the passage, at the word πάντα and at κύριος ("Notes on Select Readings," 2:106).

lengthy discussions among the commentators, including several special studies to which I will refer below. Following the example of Wachtel, I will subdivide the textual problems in the variation-unit in four different sets of variants.[77] Incidentally, the combination of these four different sets of variants in a complex sequence has resulted in the fact that the preferred reading in the variation-unit as a whole is not reflected in any single manuscript, as is evident from the apparatus.[78]

1) The presence and position of the second pronoun ὑμᾶς/ἡμᾶς {e<i}

The pronoun is omitted by significant witnesses (𝔓[72] 02 04C2 044 33C 81 88 307 453 808 1241 1243 1505 1611 1739 2200 *al* Cyr **L**:TV **K**:B **S**:Ph).[79]

Witnesses that include a pronoun are distributed as follows:

υμας παντα οτι κυριος απαξ 01
υμας απαξ παντα οτι ιησους 03
υμας απαξ τουτο οτι κυριος 1875 *al*

---

[77] Wachtel, *Der byzantinische Text*, 349-50. Cf. Eldon J. Epp, "For one thing, at times a multitude of readings will be clustered within a single grammatical or syntactical unit and, upon analysis, will group themselves into two or more subformations of variants, with the sub-formations bearing no relationship to one another" ("Toward the Clarification of the Term 'Textual Variant'," in Eldon J. Epp and Gordon D. Fee, *Studies in the Theory and Method of New Testament Textual Criticism* [SD 45; Grand Rapids: Eerdmans], 49). A warning example in this respect is Landon's treatment of Jude 5, where eventually his argument for the anarthrous κύριος becomes decisive for his acceptance of a particular wording and word order (ibid., 77). In consideration of Landon's eclectic approach, one would have expected a discussion of the stylistic difficulties with the correlation ἅπαξ – τὸ δεύτερον in the reading he prefers.

[78] The fact that my preferred text in the variation-unit has no manuscript support is not surprising, since the sequence of text combines different sub-formations of variants. In fact, Maurice A. Robinson has demonstrated that over 100 complete verses in NA[27] lack manuscript support, and he strongly opposes what he would term "de facto conjecture." This situation he claims to occur when a sequential series of variant units within a short portion of text produces a "zero-support reading," i.e., lacking in the aggregate any support from manuscripts, versions, and fathers (Maurice A. Robinson, "Rule 9, Isolated Variants, and the 'Test-Tube' Nature of the NA27 Text," in *From Text to Translation: The Proceedings of the Bingham Colloquium held at McMaster Divinity College, Hamilton, Ontario, 26-28 May 2005* [ed. Stanley E. Porter and Mark J. Boda; Grand Rapids: Eerdmans, forthcoming 2007]). Robinson's objection needs to be taken seriously. For a preliminary response, see Moisés Silva, "Response," in *Rethinking New Testament Textual Criticism*, 146-48.

[79] The important citation of Jude 5 by Cyril of Alexandria, *Thesaurus de sancta consubstantiali trinitate* 302 (PG 75:513) is lacking altogether in the *ECM*. The citation attests to the reading of 02 33C 81 2344 throughout 5,10-20. Cf. also the citation of Jude 5 in Cyril of Alexandria, *Theot.* 5, indicated in the additional apparatus of the *ECM* (B 145). According to the *ECM*, the Syriac Harklean is ambiguous at this point, but given the close relationship with the Greek MSS 1505 1611 2138, one can safely assume that its Greek Vorlage lacked a pronoun.

υμας απαξ τουτο οτι ο κυριος 020 18 35 2483Z 𝔐 PsOec
υμας τουτο απαξ οτι ο κυριος 018 056 L593 *al*
υμας απαξ τουτο οτι ο κυριος ιησους L241 L591 L1178
υμας απαξ εις τουτο οτι ο κυριος 2774
υμας απαξ τουτο ο κυριος 522
υμας τουτο οτι ο κυριος 1766
υμας απαξ 2483T

ημας παντα οτι ιησους απαξ 2298
ημας απαξ τουτο οτι κυριος 1729 1838T
ημας απαξ τουτο οτι ο κυριος 263 632* 1646 *pc*

τουτο υμας απαξ οτι ο κυριος 0142
απαξ υμας τουτο οτι ο κυριος 720
και υμας απαξ τουτο οτι ο κυριος 2544

We may at once reject ἡμᾶς as an itacism because of its slim manuscript support and contextual inappropriateness (these MSS rather support ὑμᾶς). The external evidence for the presence of ὑμᾶς is balanced, which increases the importance of internal evidence. It is evident that the reading with a second ὑμᾶς is stylistically awkward, since the word seems to be superfluous.[80] For this reason, Matthew Black assumes that it could have been omitted by a scribe, but because of the divided manuscript support he suggests that the word be printed within brackets in a Greek text to indicate that it *may* be original.[81] Wachtel further mentions the possibility that the pronoun was omitted by a scribe due to homoioteleuton (-ας^-ας).[82]

Landon suggests that intrinsic probability speaks strongly against the pronoun, especially in light of the stylistically elaborated composition of the text.[83] He concludes that "the second ὑμᾶς originates rather from an attempt by a scribe to 'improve' the text by manufacturing an example of emphasis by repetition where the original writer did not intend it."[84] Mayor thinks that this very emphasis by repetition contrasting the readers and the "libertines" previously spoken of in v. 4 (ἀσεβεῖς), more probably originates from the author himself, and he draws attention to the similar repetition of ὑμῖν in v. 3.[85]

---

[80] See e.g., Matthew Black, "Critical and Exegetical Notes on Three New Testament Texts: Hebrews xi.11, Jude 5, James i.27," in *Apophoreta: Festschrift für Ernst Haenchen* (ed. W. Eltester; BZNW 30; Berlin: Alfred Töpelmann, 1964), 44; Wachtel, *Der byzantinische Text*, 350.

[81] Indeed, the word was subsequently printed within square brackets in NA[26] (for which Black served in the editorial board), NA[27] and UBS[4]. In the *ECM*, the pronoun is retained and the brackets have been removed.

[82] Wachtel, *Der byzantinische Text*, 350.

[83] Landon, *Text-Critical Study*, 69.

[84] Ibid., 70.

[85] Mayor, *The Epistle of St. Jude*, clxxxiii.

In my opinion, a later insertion by a scribe is more unlikely. Given the different possible reasons for its omission, I regard it as the more difficult reading.[86] The difficulty not only resulted in the omission of the pronoun; in some witnesses it is moved further ahead in the sentence, or a καί is inserted in order to make the text smoother.

2) The position and meaning of ἅπαξ {e<i}

Several important witnesses interpret ἅπαξ as a numerical term ("once," "a first time") and place the word within the ὅτι-clause as a modifier to σώσας (01 04* 044 88 323 424C 442 630 665 1409 1505 1611 1845 1852V 1739T 1881 2138 2200 *al* **L**:T **K**:SB **S**:HPh).[87]

However, the interpretation of ἅπαξ as an adverb of manner ("once and for all"), which modifies εἰδότας outside the ὅτι-clause, is slightly better supported (𝔓[72] 02 03 04C2V 0251 33 81 307 436 453 623 808 1067 1875 *al* 𝔐 Cyr PsOec **L**:V).

In regard to internal evidence, several commentators have suggested that ἅπαξ was moved into the ὅτι-clause attracted by the presence of the difficult adverbial adjective τὸ δεύτερον ("the second occasion"), which seems to demand a corresponding word like πρῶτον ("first time").[88] Carroll D. Osburn thinks the intrusion of the adverb in the ὅτι-clause originates from the late second-century and is due to patristic convention (read freedom).[89] He cites Clement of Alexandria, the marginal comment in MS 1739 attributed to Origen, and Didymus, to this effect, and states that the

---

[86] Cf. Weiss, "so Jud. v. 5, wo das zweite υμας nach ειδοτας . . . so leicht ausfiel, zumal es garnicht vermisst wurde, und daher sicher mit Unrecht von Lchm. [Lachmann] Tisch. [Tischendorf] Treg. [Tregelles] WH. [Westcott & Hort] gestrichen ist, obwohl sich ein Grund seiner Hinzufügung garnicht denken lässt" (*Die Katholischen Briefe*, 87); cf. D. G. Wohlenberg, *Der erste und zweite Petrusbrief und der Judasbrief* (Leipzig: A. Deichert'sche Verlagsbuchhandlung Werner Scholl, 1915), 290, n. 32.

[87] Wachtel points out that Allen Wikgren does not accurately account for the manuscript support for this variant when Wikgren states that it was "an 'improvement' reflected in a comparatively few witnesses ([sic] Ψ C* syr^h and a few minuscules)," not mentioning significant witnesses as 323, 1739 and the HK group (Allen Wikgren, "Some Problems in Jude 5," in *Studies in the History and Text of the New Testament in Honor of Kenneth Willis Clark* [ed. B. L. Daniels and M. J. Suggs; SD 29; Salt Lake City: University of Utah Press, 1967], 147; Wachtel, *Der byzantinische Text*, 351-52, n. 305). Actually, Wikgren did not mention 01 either (although the space in the parenthesis suggests a typo) and both authors fail to cite 04*.

[88] Kühl, *Die Briefe Petri und Judae*, 306, n. 1; Charles Bigg, *A Critical and Exegetical Commentary on the Epistles of St. Peter and St. Jude* (2d ed.; ICC; Edinburgh: T. & T. Clark, 1902), 328; Wohlenberg, *Der erste und zweite Petrusbrief und der Judasbrief*, 290, n. 32; Albin, *Judasbrevet*, 599; Wikgren, "Some Problems in Jude 5," 147. Bauckham, *Jude, 2 Peter*, 43.

[89] Osburn, "The Text of Jude 5," 109-10.

absence of εἰδότας πάντα ὅτι in these citations "precludes any argument for their support of the position of ἅπαξ."[90]

Thus, many commentators take ἅπαξ with εἰδότας suggesting that it refers back to ἅπαξ in v. 3.[91] On the other hand, Mayor thinks that the alternative interpretation—to take ἅπαξ with σώσας—makes the reference to v. 3 even more clear with the warning against unbelief.[92] In this connection, he supplies some examples of the correlative ἅπαξ—τὸ δεύτερον (e.g., Heb 9:27-28).[93] However, Wikgren rejects the interpretation of ἅπαξ as "first in a series" in light of the whole context of vv. 5-7, where "the one common ingredient . . . is not in any sequence of events but in the fact of apostasy from an earlier state"—a point fully elaborated in a subsequent study by A. F. J. Klijn.[94] Furthermore, Wachtel points out that the correlation between ἅπαξ and τὸ δεύτερον, albeit attested elsewhere, is linguistically unsound.[95] He does not see it as original, since it does not supply a strong enough motive for a scribe to move the adverb outside the ὅτι-clause with εἰδότας, whereby the scribe would create other difficulties.[96] Likewise, Tischendorf deemed it incredible that ἅπαξ should have been placed after εἰδότας by some corrector.[97] It is very unlikely that a scribe

---

[90] Ibid., 110. One may note the absence of citations of Clement, Origen and Didymus in the main apparatus of *ECM* at this point (cf. the supplement in B 145), although the marginal comment in MS 1739, ascribed to Origen, is cited as 1739A (cf. Albin "1739schol"). In the supplement (B 145), the reference to Didymus, Did, FrPs: PTS 16,229,22 contains a typo; read PTS 16,259,22. Further, I would add the citation/allusion of Jude 5 in Did, FrPs: PTS 16,57,17-18, Ἰησοῦς γὰρ ἐν Αἰγύπτῳ τὸν λαὸν ἔσωσεν, ὡς ἐν ἐπιστολῇ φησιν ἀποστολικῇ. For the citations of Jude 5 by Cyril of Alexandria, see note 79 above.

[91] Kühl, *Die Briefe Petri und Judae*, 306; Albin, *Judasbrevet*, 599; Wikgren, "Some Problems in Jude 5," 147; Bauckham, *Jude, 2 Peter*, 43.

[92] Mayor, *The Epistle of St. Jude*, 29.

[93] Wikgren questions the example in Heb 9:27-28 "in view of the author's regular use of ἅπαξ to mean 'once for all'" ("Some Problems in Jude 5," 147).

[94] Wikgren, "Some Problems in Jude 5," 147; A. F. J. Klijn, "Jude 5 to 7," in *New Testament Age: Essays in Honor of Bo Reicke* (ed. W. C. Weinrich; 2 vols.; Macon: Mercer University, 1984), 1:237-44.

[95] Wachtel, *Der byzantinische Text*, 351.

[96] In addition to the difficulty of an independent τὸ δεύτερον, Wachtel mentions another problem in moving ἅπαξ to εἰδότας, namely the fact that the participle is transferred from an aorist (σώσας) with punctiliar aspect, to which it would fit better than with the perfect participle with present sense (ibid.). I do not know if this could be a possible cause behind the singular reading ἰδόντας in MS 33, but probably the two (εἰδότας/ἰδόντας) were interchangeable at the time.

[97] Tischendorf says, "[I]ncredibile esset locum post a quopiam correctore nactum esse" (*Novum Testamentum Graece* [3 vols.; 8th ed.; Leipzig: Hinrichs, 1869-1894], 2:354).

would leave the adverb τὸ δεύτερον independent.[98] On the other hand, the author, known for his rich vocabulary and eloquent style, could well have used the rarer meaning of the adverb, "afterwards," which makes perfect sense: "I wish to remind you, although you fully know once and for all, that the Lord saved the people out of Egypt, and afterwards he destroyed those who did not believe."[99]

Thus, the more difficult reading takes ἅπαξ with εἰδότας and this reading also has slightly better manuscript support. The linguistically unsound alternative, ἅπαξ inside the ὅτι-clause, should be rejected in the light of the author's competent Greek style; the reading was probably caused by the difficult τὸ δεύτερον, or, possibly, because of loose quotation habits on the part of Patristic authors.

3) The variation between πάντα, πάντας, and τοῦτο {e+i}

Prior to the finding of 𝔓72, the reading πάντας was known through the Syriac Philoxenian version.[100] On the basis of the Syriac reading, Westcott and Hort assumed a primitive error on the part of a scribe who had dropped the final sigma and so they conjectured πάντας.[101] In this case, the agreement between 𝔓72* and the Philoxenian version is probably accidental, although other textual connections have been noticed which may indicate the mutual preservation of an early tradition.[102] Kubo does prefer this reading and points to the correspondence between the statement as read in 𝔓72T, "though all of you knew once" and v. 3, which speaks of "the faith once delivered to the saints."[103]

Wikgren points out that the reading πάντας may be an accidental assimilation to εἰδότας under the influence of a common collocation, or a conscious avoidance of πάντα, but, at the same time, he does not want to

---

[98] Black's suggestion that a scribal error occurred, where ἅπαξ was displaced for ὑμᾶς by dittography of the first two letters, is not convincing ("Critical and Exegetical Notes," 44).

[99] Cf. F. Maier, "Der Rhytmus des Satzes offenbart unzweideutig die Unabhängigkeit und Selbständigkeit der Stellung des τὸ δεύτερον ("Zur Erklärung des Judasbriefes [Jud 5]," *BZ* 2 [1904]: 395).

[100] Gwynn, *Remnants*, 78, 130.

[101] Westcott and Hort, "Notes on Select Readings," 2:106. The authors think the same error occurred in 1 John 2:20 (. . . καὶ οἴδατε πάντες). Ironically, the reminiscence of this very parallel could have caused a scribe to copy πάντας in Jude.

[102] Cf. Albin, "The connection [of the Philoxenian] with 𝔓72 (primarily in Jude 5, 20-25) is evident" (*Judasbrevet*, 493; my translation). See further J. Neville Birdsall, "The Text of Jude in 𝔓72," *JTS* 14 (1963): 394-99.

[103] Kubo, *𝔓72 and the Codex Vaticanus*, 85-86.

dismiss the reading out of hand, because of its early attestation, and, since "it does have the effect of carrying back an emphasis upon the earlier ὑμᾶς."[104] It should be pointed out that Kubo, Wikgren and many other commentators were unaware of the correction in 𝔓[72], since they imported the error from Michel Testuz' *editio princeps* (possibly via the standard editions), where the correction was not noted.[105] Possibly, they were also unaware of the fact that the two oldest and best Philoxenian MSS actually represent the reading πάντα, as does the Syriac Harklean version.[106] Thus, the manuscript support for πάντας is extremely weak. Moreover, πάντας is unattractive for syntactical and contextual reasons.[107]

As for the reading τοῦτο attested by the Majority Text, it likely represents an attempt by a scribe to improve the text; Wikgren points out that the collocation of εἰδώς with the demonstrative pronoun followed by a ὅτι-clause is very common in Greek literature, especially in argumentative contexts, whereas πάντα may seem ambiguous or even contemptuous at first sight.[108]

However, similar statements about addressees "knowing all things" occur elsewhere in the NT (Rom 15:14; 1 John 2:20 [v.l.], 27).[109] The latter context in 1 John 2 is a particularly significant parallel, where the knowledge of all things on the part of the readers stands in contrast to the threat from the opponents who do not know the truth. In Jude a sharp contrast is drawn between the readers who know all things, and the opponents who are described as irrational animals slandering whatever they do not understand (v. 10).

---

[104] Wikgren, "Some Problems in Jude 5," 149 (with note 9).

[105] Michel Testuz, ed., *Papyrus Bodmer VII-IX* (Cologny-Geneva: Bibliotheca Bodmeriana, 1959), 20. The error was corrected in NA[26] and UBS[4] (surprisingly not in the third corrected ed. of 1983). Besides Kubo and Wikgren, Albin, Birdsall, Wikgren, and Osburn do not mention the correction in 𝔓[72] in their discussions (see above for references). More recently, Landon repeats the error (ibid., 70).

[106] On this basis, the Philoxenian version is cited in support of πάντα in the *ECM*.

[107] Mayor points out that the author hardly expected *all* his readers to have knowledge of the examples that follow throughout the letter, especially not the extracanonical (*The Epistle of St. Jude*, clxxxiv). The syntactical problem is discussed in connection with τοῦτο below.

[108] Wikgren, "Some Problems in Jude 5," 149. While Wikgren cites Mark 12:24 and 2 Pet 1:14, the passages in 1 Tim 1:9 and 2 Tim 1:15 are better examples from the NT of the specific collocation εἰδώς τοῦτο ὅτι . . ..

[109] Bauckham says, "The apostolic faith, in which Jude's readers were thoroughly instructed at the time of their conversion, is definitive and complete; it does not need supplementing" (*Jude, 2 Peter,* 48). Note the similar conception of knowing or understanding everything in *1 En.* 1:2; 25:2, a writing whose influence is manifest throughout Jude.

Furthermore, the reading τοῦτο violates the sentence structure; the subordinate ὅτι-clause depends on ὑπομνῆσαι and not εἰδότας.[110] Hence, the insertion of τοῦτο before ὅτι leaves the main clause dangling without object throughout the long sentence in vv. 5-7. Perhaps it is for this reason some Byzantine witnesses transpose τοῦτο (018 056 0142 *al*) separating it farther from ὅτι, which slightly affects the sense: "I want to remind you— although you know this once and for all—that the Lord . . . "

In conclusion, external and internal evidence speaks in favor of accepting πάντα as original.

4) The subject of ἀπώλεσεν in the ὅτι-clause {e=i} (ECM •ιησους•/•[ο] κυριος)

This is arguably the most difficult point of variation in the passage, mainly because of the presence of the difficult reading Ἰησοῦς, regarded by many commentators as virtually impossible.[111]

The external evidence is distributed as follows:[112]

κυριος 01 044 1875 *al*
ο κυριος 18 35 307 326 424* 431 436 453 630 808 1505 1611 1836 1837 2138 2200 2495 𝔐 PsOec
(ο) κυριος **S**:H
ιησους 02 03 33C 81 323 424C 665 1739 *pc* Cyr **K**:S
ο ιησους 88 915
(ο) ιησους **L**:V
κυριος ιησους 1735
ο κυριος ιησους L241 L591 L1178
ο θεος 04C2V 442 621 623 1845 *pc* **L**:TVmss **S**:Ph
θεος χριστος P72

---

[110] So Wikgren, "Some Problems in Jude," 149; Wachtel rejects πάντας for the same reason (*Der byzantinische Text*, 353). More surprising, in the light of the sentence structure, is the lack of a comma after πάντα in the *ECM*.

[111] Westcott and Hort branded the passage as corrupt and suggested a primitive error ("Notes on Select Readings," 2:106); cf. Metzger, *Textual Commentary*, 657; in the introductory notes to the *ECM* the editors state, "The discussion over the text of 5/12-20 was particularly intense . . ." (*ECM* IV, 37*). The intense discussion over v. 5 in general, and the subject of ἀπώλεσεν in particular, is reflected in the bold dot in the primary line at word 20 (Ἰησοῦς), and below alongside the alternative reading (ο) κυριος. Moreover, it is evident that the editors had adopted ὁ κύριος at an earlier stage, since the numerical addresses of all patristic citations, as indicated in the index (B 134), have not been updated in the subsequent units (5,24-42 instead of 5,22-40).

[112] MS 04* is illegible; MS 33* reads ὁ [..] (contra *ECM*: ὁ ι̅c̅). For the attestation of Ἰησοῦς by Cyril of Alexandria, see note 79.

The reading (ὁ) Ἰησοῦς has strongest support, but (ὁ) κύριος and ὁ θεός are attested in important witnesses, showing that the text suffered corruption early on.[113] The singular reading of 𝔓⁷², θεὸς Χριστός, is interesting, but definitely not original.

If the better attested reading, Ἰησοῦς, is original, one has to account for the idea that Jesus saved the people out of Egypt. The author possibly could have made a typology between Joshua and Jesus (both Ἰησοῦς in LXX) seeing both persons in one. This typology occurs already in the *Epistle of Barnabas* (12:8-10) and became quite common among subsequent patristic authors.[114] Black objects to this interpretation, since it would ascribe to Joshua the destruction of Israel in the wilderness, as well as the keeping of the rebellious angels until the judgment (Jude 5b-6).[115] Bauckham is of the same opinion, but he points out that the potential typology "could have attracted a scribe (who could miss its pitfalls)."[116]

On the other hand, Osburn supplies an example from *1 En.* 69:26-29, where the Son of Man sits in judgment upon the imprisoned angels, and he points out that, regardless of the presence of a Joshua-Jesus typology, the author could still have Ἰησοῦς in mind, referring to the preexistent activity of Christ in OT history (cf. John 12:41; 1 Cor 10:4-5; 9; Heb 11:26).[117] Further, Osburn suggests that Ἰησοῦς could have been altered to κύριος or θεός because of the heated Christological controversies during the third and fourth centuries. He goes far to explain the variation between Χριστόν,

---

[113] Hort thought that the original words, not preserved in any witness, were probably ὅτι ὁ . . . σώσας, without either of the nouns, and that OTIO was read by a copyist as OTIIC or OTIKC (Westcott and Hort, "Notes on Select Readings," 2:106).

[114] Justin (*Dial.* 120.3); Clement of Alexandria (*Paed.* 1.60.3); Origen (*Hom. Exod.* 11.3); Jerome (*Jov.* 1.21). Henning Paulsen points out that this typology was anticipated in Hellenistic Judaism when Philo (*Mut.* 121) interpreted the sum of the names in Num 13:16 as Ἰησοῦς σωτηρία κυρίου (*Der Zweite Petrusbrief und der Judasbrief* [KEK 12/2; Göttingen: Vandenhoeck & Ruprecht, 1992], 60, n. 56).

[115] Black, "Critical and Exegetical Notes," 45; The same objection is raised by J. W. C. Wand, *The General Epistles of St. Peter and St. Jude* (WC; London: Westminster, 1934), 201; J. N. D. Kelly, *A Commentary on the Epistles of Peter and Jude* (BNTC; London: A. & C. Black, 1969), 255; and Bauckham, *Jude, 2 Peter,* 43; cf. the passage in 2 Pet 2:4, where it is God who keeps the rebellious angels until the judgment. E. E. Kellett suggests that the phrase "those who did not believe" could refer to the Amorites who Joshua destroyed (interestingly, MS 615 supports this interpretation, replacing the phrase with "their enemies"), but Kellett admits that a chief objection remains—the subject of τετήρηκεν ("Note on Jude 5," 381).

[116] Ibid. Bauckham develops his treatment of Jude 5 in *Jude and the Relatives of Jesus in the Early Church* (Edinburgh: T. & T. Clark, 1990), 307-12.

[117] Osburn, "The Text of Jude 5," 112-113.

κύριον and θεόν in 1 Cor 10:9 along these lines.[118] Evidently, the passage in 1 Cor 10:9 gave rise to controversy and may have led to modifications of the text.[119] However, the opposite motivation seems to have given rise to the reading ὁ κύριος Ἰησοῦς attested here in Jude by some Byzantine witnesses (L241 L591 L1178; cf. 1735), which is certainly a development of ὁ κύριος (𝔐).[120] Nevertheless, the main question is whether 1 Cor 10:9 can really offer an analogy to Jude 5, since the simple Ἰησοῦς is not attested in the former passage, and the simple Χριστός is lacking in the latter. Nowhere in the NT is the personal name Jesus applied to the pre-existent Christ.

Jarl E. Fossum suggests that the reading Ἰησοῦς refers to "an intermediary figure whose basic constituent is the Angel of the Lord," but, at the same time, he admits that the reference could equally apply to κύριος, especially in light of the Christological confession in v. 4, ("our only Master and Lord, Jesus Christ").[121] This brings us to the next major objection to Ἰησοῦς raised on intrinsic grounds: Wachtel points out that Ἰησοῦς stands in stark contrast to the full formula, ὁ κύριος ἡμῶν Ἰησοῦς Χριστός, used with regularity by the author throughout the epistle (vv. 4, 17, 21, 25 v.l.).[122] I would like to adduce another argument: among all witnesses to the text of *1 En.* 1:9, the author of Jude alone added the subject κύριος to the clause in the citation in vv. 14-15.[123] Undoubtedly, the text in

---

[118] Ibid., 114-115; cf. idem, "The Text of 1 Corinthians 10:9," in *New Testament Textual Criticism: Its Significance for Exegesis—Essays in Honour of Bruce M. Metzger* (ed. Eldon J. Epp and Gordon D. Fee; Oxford: Clarendon, 1981), 201-12.

[119] Note, however, Ehrman who thinks the variant Χριστός in 1 Cor 10:9 is a doctrinal alteration attributing divine characteristics to Jesus Christ (*Orthodox Corruption*, 89-90). Once again the ambiguous nature of Wettstein's theological canon becomes evident. In fact, if a theological tendency in one single direction were possible to detect on the level of individual MSS, one would not expect MSS 02 and 81 (reading Ἰησοῦς in Jude 5) to be among the witnesses that read θεόν in 1 Cor 10:9 (the latter omits ὁ θεός in 1 Cor 10:5, attributing the execution of divine wrath to Christ).

[120] The three lectionaries follow the Majority Text in the whole variation-unit and add Ἰησοῦς, whereas 1735 reads ἅπαξ τοῦτο ὅτι κύριος Ἰησοῦς—a reading which theoretically could have developed from Ἰησοῦς; cf. Didymus who cites or alludes to the passage several times, and on one occasion adds κύριος to Ἰησοῦς in a rather loose citation (*Trin.* 1.19).

[121] Jarl E. Fossum, "Kyrios Jesus as the Angel of the Lord in Jude 5-7," *NTS* 33 (1987): 237. The slightly revised and expanded version of this article, "Kyrios Jesus: Angel Christology in Jude 5-7," in idem, *The Image of the Invisible God: Essays on the Influence of Jewish Mysticism on Early Christology* (NTOA 30; Freiburg: Universitätsverlag Freiburg Schweiz; Göttingen: Vandenhoeck & Ruprecht, 1995), 41-69, adds nothing of substance to the argument in my opinion.

[122] Wachtel, *Der byzantinische Text*, 355-56; cf. Landon, *Text-Critical Study*, 73-74; René Kieffer, *Filemonbrevet, Judasbrevet och Andra Petrusbrevet* (KNT 18; Stockholm: EFS-förlaget, 2001), 54-55.

[123] For a presentation of the various witnesses in Aramaic, Ethiopic, Greek and Latin, see Anton Vögtle, *Der Judasbrief, der 2. Petrusbrief* (EKKNT 22; Solothurn-Düsseldorf: Benziger;

Jude, written for Christians, refers to the Parousia; the same expectation of the "Son of Man" coming with his holy myriads for judgment is reflected in Matt 25:31.[124] Thus, we have another instance where the author consciously uses the simple κύριος in reference to Jesus Christ, in a judgment context.

The reading ὁ θεός has weaker attestation but was defended as original by Friedrich Spitta who thought that an indistinct Θ͞C could have given rise to Ι͞C and Κ͞C.[125] Spitta, who thought that 2 Peter was prior to Jude, referred to the parallel in 2 Pet 2:4 (where God is said to keep the rebellious angels until their judgment) in support of ὁ θεός in Jude.[126] However, in my view Jude is clearly prior, and the author of 2 Peter, like many scribes, changed an original κύριος in Jude to the more natural subject, ὁ θεός.

The singular reading of 𝔓[72], θεὸς Χριστός (Θ͞C Χ͞Ρ͞C), is not a conflation, since no witnesses read Χριστός.[127] The members of the UBS Committee regarded it as a scribal blunder and speculated whether the scribe intended to write θεοῦ Χριστός.[128] Another possible scribal error could have involved the confusion of Κ͞C and Χ͞C.[129] Admittedly, the scribe of 𝔓[72] used another form considered to be older (Χ͞Ρ͞C) but both forms were in use during this time (ca. 300 C.E.) and Κ͞C could have been present in the exemplar (read

---

Neukirchen-Vluyn: Neukirchener Verlag, 1994), 74-75. Bauckham's corresponding presentation is incomplete, since he does not include (or discuss) Ps.-Vigilius (*Jude, 2 Peter*, 95).

[124] Hence, Matthew Black says, "It seems unlikely . . . that the κύριος represents the original. . . . The subject in the present context [in *1 Enoch*] . . . looks back to verse 4, ὁ θεός. 'Behold the Lord cometh' . . . is probably best explained as a Christian interpretation or accommodation of the original, interpreted, of course, of the Lord Jesus' coming" ("The Maranatha Invocation and Jude 14, 15 (1 Enoch 1:9)," in *Christ and Spirit in the New Testament* [ed. Barnabas Lindars and Stephen S. Smalley; Cambridge: Cambridge University Press, 1973], 195. In violation of the principle of Occam's razor, Boudewijn Dehandschutter hypothesizes that the author was citing from a third form (!) of the Greek text of Enoch ("Pseudo-Cyprian, Jude and Enoch: Some Notes on 1 Enoch 1:9," in *Tradition and Re-interpretation in Jewish and Early Christian Literature: Essays in Honour of Jürgen C. H. Lebram* [ed. J. W. van Henten et al.: Leiden: Brill, 1986], 114-20).

[125] Spitta, *Der zweite Brief des Petrus und der Brief des Judas*, 324.

[126] Ibid.

[127] Contra Wikgren who sees a possible conflation, and an indirect witness for Ἰησοῦς ("Some Problems in Jude 5," 148).

[128] Metzger, *Textual Commentary*, 657.

[129] As for the collocation of θεός and κύριος, it is not attested in any Greek MSS, but in Clement's commentary, *Adumbrationes in Epistolas canonicas*, extant in Latin translation, where we find *dominus deus* (GCS 17:207). Interestingly, the marginal comment in 1739 ascribed to Origen (*Hom. Deut. 7*) reads: καὶ ὅτι οὗτός ἐστιν κύριος ὁ θεὸς [κ͞ς ὁ θ͞ς] ἡμῶν ὁ ἐξαγαγὼν ἡμᾶς ἐκ γῆς Αἰγύπτου Χριστὸς Ἰησοῦς [χ͞ς ι͞ς] before the citation of Jude 5; Eduard von der Goltz erroneously cites κ͞ς ι͞ς instead of χ͞ς ι͞ς (*Eine textkritische Arbeit des zehnten bezw. sechsten Jahrhunderts* [TU 17/4; Leipzig: Hinrichs, 1899], 51).

as X̄C̄)—evidently the scribe used alternative forms of *nomina sacra* elsewhere.[130] More significantly, the committee did not consider similar theological or Christological modifications elswhere in 𝔓72.[131] For example, in the passage in 1 Pet 2:3, the scribe explicitly emphasizes the belief that Christ is Lord and God, εἰ ἐγεύσασθε ἐπιστεύσατε ὅτι Χριστός ὁ κύριος. The replacement of χρηστός with Χριστός is shared by other Greek witnesses (018 019 049 33 *al*) as well as the earliest witness to 1 Peter, the Coptic Codex Schøyen, and is in line with a common wordplay in early Christianity, i.e., the referring of LXX quotations in which God is called χρηστός to Christ. 𝔓72 further inserts ἐπιστεύσατε, which specifies the 'tasting' as believing in Christ.[132] In this way the scriptural allusion is now turned into a confessional formula, "Christ is Lord," that is to be believed.[133] Thus, in Jude 5, I think the scribe read the ambiguous κύριος in his exemplar, and associated it to Χριστός (as in 1 Pet 2:3) and θεός in line with such identifications elsewhere (1 Pet 5:1; 2 Pet 1:2); a single Ἰησοῦς in the exemplar is less likely.[134]

In sum, the external evidence is divided and corruption occurred early on. The reading Ἰησοῦς has the best manuscript support and is indeed a difficult reading to the point of impossibility. I find it very unlikely that this early Christian author would write the simple Ἰησοῦς if he had the pre-existent Christ in mind, especially in light of his style, and of the whole context of vv. 5-7.[135] The ambiguous (ὁ) κύριος, on the other hand, could explain all other readings, which may represent conscious alterations or else copying mistakes involving *nomina sacra*. Moreover, the typology Jesus-Joshua which became popular in the patristic era could have led a scribe to supply Ἰησοῦς. I prefer the anarthrous form, κύριος, as original because of the weighty attestation of Ἰησοῦς without the article.

Umlaut 3 in Codex Vaticanus (03): the umlaut can refer to any or all of the four textual problems treated above.

---

[130] In Jude, the scribe consistently abbreviates Ἰησοῦ Χριστοῦ as I̅H̅Y̅ X̅P̅Y̅, but at the opening of 1 Peter the scribe twice offers I̅Y̅ X̅P̅Y̅, then, in the rest of 1-2 Peter, the scribe uses the old forms again.

[131] See the special study on 𝔓72 above.

[132] Cf. F. W. Beare, "The Text of 1 Peter in Papyrus 72," *JBL* 80 (1961): 254.

[133] Note also the use of the *nomen sacrum* in this passage in 𝔓72.

[134] Cf. Wachtel, "Die singuläre Papyruslesart θεὸς Χριστός dagegen vereinigt betont beide Bedeutungsaspekte von (ὁ) κύριος" (*Der byzantinische Text*, 356).

[135] Note the ample use of catchword connections between κύριον, κύριος and κυριοτητα (vv. 4, 5, 8, 9, 14, 17).

5,36-40: τοὺς μὴ πιστεύσαντας {e+i}

The author is referring to the special occasion in the account in Num 14, when the people of Israel "murmured" (γογγύζω—cf. Jude 16) showing their lack of faith. As a result, God decreed that all disbelievers would die in the desert. Some scribes replaced the aorist with the present participle πιστεύοντας (1875 *pc* Did), emphasizing the continuing unbelief reported as ongoing in the accounts of the desert experience. One scribe evidently interpreted the referent of the unbelievers as the enemies of Israel and attempted to clarify the text, τοὺς ἐκεινῶν ἐχθρούς (615), perhaps in order to avoid the offensive thought of God punishing his own people.

6,4: τέ {e+i}

The external support for τέ is very strong, but a few important witnesses attest δέ (02 1505 1611 2138 *al* Ath Did Thph **L**:V **K**:B **S**:H).[136] Landon prefers δέ on intrinsic and transcriptional grounds; he refers to three other examples in Jude where the author could have used δέ, and to Kilpatrick who points out that the word τέ is going out of use in the first century.[137]

However, Landon's examples from Jude are few and misleading. He states that both τέ and δέ "carry the semantic force of 'and' or 'and then'."[138] In Jude 6, however, it is not used to combine single ideas, but in order to connect clauses marking a close relationship between sequential examples ("and likewise").[139] This usage of τέ meets the expectation of the author's good style. In regard to δέ one further notes that the author does not use it twice in a sentence unless it is part of a balanced pair or triplet (vv. 8 and 23).

As for transcriptional probability, it is true that τέ was revived as an atticism, and that many scribes apparently were tempted to introduce τέ at the expense of δέ at various places in the NT.[140] However, in this case it is more probable that a scribe would replace τέ with the common δέ, not acknowledging the particular usage in the context.[141]

---

[136] PsOec: τέ (PG 119:709); Thph: δέ (PG 126:89).

[137] Landon, *Text-Critical Study*, 78-79.

[138] Ibid.

[139] BDF §443.3; BDAG, s.v. τέ 1.

[140] Note that this general rule cannot be applied to Acts where the usage of τέ is a stylistic feature of the author (see further Turner, *Syntax*, 338-39).

[141] Cf. the clear example in Acts 2:40, where 06 has the poorer δέ.

The omission of τέ makes good sense but is poorly attested (522 1678 **K**:B^mss **S**:Ph Did Or), whereas the singular readings τε καί (90a) and γάρ (945 Cyr Did) misunderstand the logic of the passage.

(6,20: ἀπολιπόντας)

The variation between ἀπολιπόντας (aorist) and ἀπολείποντας (present) is not recorded in the *ECM*, probably because the latter may simply represent an itacism, especially in witnesses that retain the aorist accent (ἀπολειπόντας). Only very few witnesses have the proper present accent.[142] However, there is still the possibility that a few scribes did intend the present form, and therefore I have recorded the variation.

6,26: οἰκητήριον {e+i}

A few witnesses read κατοικητήριον (044 2736 L427), which is probably an assimilation to Rev 18:2 where Babylon is described as "a dwelling place of demons and a prison of every unclean spirit."[143] In regard to MS 044, Landon refers to the predilection of introducing compounds on the part of the scribe (cf. vv. 10 and 18), which, in my opinion, is doubtful; the real tendency on the part of this scribe is to assimilate the text to other passages.[144]

6,36-38: δεσμοῖς ἀϊδίοις {e+i}

The description of the chains as "eternal" apparently caused difficulties for some scribes and interpreters (cf. 2 Pet 2:4). At first sight, the idea seems incompatible with the notion of eschatological judgment, but the author's

---

[142] See Albin's apparatus, *Judasbrevet*, 601, where the accent is recorded. According to Albin, only 𝔓^72 049 619 are "without aor-accent." The reference to 𝔓^72 is of course misleading, since accentuation is missing altogether in the witness.

[143] The text of Rev 18:2 reads: ἐγένετο κατοικητήριον δαιμονίων (v.l. δαιμόνων) καὶ φυλακὴ παντὸς πνεύματος. This passage echoes an earlier passage in LXX Jer 9:12 that speaks of the doom of Jerusalem in a similar manner (κατοικητήριον δρακόντων); cf. *1 En.* 15:7, where κατοίκησις is used of the dwelling-place of the spirits of heaven.

[144] Landon, *Text-Critical Study*, 80-81; I have not found examples of the scribe merely favoring compounds in the collations of 044 in Mark, Luke, John and Colossians supplied by Kirsopp Lake, "Texts from Mount Athos," *StudBib* 5 (1902): 89-131. Moreover, the particular choice of ἀναστήσονται in v. 18 probably reflects the influence of the passage in Matt 12:41 (par. Luke 11:32), rather than a predilection for compounds.

terminology probably depends on *1 En.* 10:5.[145] One witness replaces ἀϊδίοις with ἀλύτοις (621), whereas two MSS conflate the two adjectives (33 2344). The adjective ἄλυτος suitably combines the meaning of "indissoluble" and "ceaseless."[146] Possibly, some scribes were familiar with Aeschylus' play, *Prometheus Bound*, in which Zeus punishes the Titan Prometheus by chaining him to a rock where he was tortured every day. In one scene Promethus cries out his wish that he had instead been thrown into Tartarus, fastened "in fetters no hand can loose" (δεσμοῖς ἀλύτοις).[147] In one witness the difficult adjective has instead been divided into two separate words, ἀεὶ δίοις (2147), "eternally divine." Another witness replaces δεσμοῖς with θεσμοῖς (2746), "ordinances."

6,40-42: ὑπὸ ζόφον {e+i}

It is not surprising that the ambiguous and abstract phrase "under darkness" became subject to modification;[148] some MSS offer the more natural "in darkness," εἰς ζόφον (1735 L593) or ἐπὶ ζόφῳ (1751). The peculiar bilingual MS 629 reads ὑπὸ ζόφον κρίσεως, "under judgment of darkness," as related to the Latin column, *sub caligine iudicii* (the latter word is in the margin).[149] In some witnesses, the preposition is followed by the genitive case, marking agency or cause, "by darkness"; the reading is probably the result of an unintentional error occasioned by the similarity of the letters, or attention paid to the *ypsilon* of ὑπό preceding.

In this verse, Landon accepts a variant not attested in any Greek MS, but back-translated and transposed from the Latin in Lucifer (*De non conv.* 15) and Pseudo-Augustine (*Spec.* 33): *eos sanctorum angelorum sub tenebras* (ὑπὸ

---

[145] For the source and meaning of δεσμοῖς ἀϊδίοις in Jude and the relationship to the parallel in 2 Pet 2:4, see chapter four.

[146] LSJ, s.v. ἄλυτος I.

[147] Aeschylus, *Prom.* 155. The notion of unbreakable chains goes back to Homer, and as usual in Greek myth, it is Hephaestus who forges these chains imbued with power (*Od.* 8.274-275; cf. *Il.* 13.37; Pindar, *Pyth.* 4.215).

[148] Cf. the parallel passage in 2 Pet 2:4, σειραῖς ζόφου . . . εἰς κρίσιν τηρουμένους (v.l. σιροῖς ζόφου); see further chapter four.

[149] The MS 629 (*Vat. Ottob.* 432) was first described by J. M. A. Scholz, who expressed his general observation: "Aehnliche Veränderungen [as in 1 John 5:7] und ganze Versetzungen sind auch in vielen anderen Stellen zu Gunsten der lateinischen Uebersetzung vorgenommen worden. Viele von den Abweichungen können jedoch auf Rechnung des nachlässigen Abschreibers kommen" (*Biblisch-kritische Reise in Frankreich, der Schweitz, Italien, Palästina und im Archipel, in den Jahren 1818, 1819, 1820, 1821 nebst einer Geschichte des Textes des NT* [Leipzig, Soran: Friedrich Fleischer, 1823], 105). Thus, the readings of the MS must be carefully evaluated in relation to the Latin text.

ζόφον ἁγίων ἀγγέλων).[150] Clement of Alexandria attests the knowledge of a similar tradition, ὑπὸ ζόφον ἀγρίων ἀγγέλων (*Paed.* 3.44.4). Landon thinks Clement knew the variant ὑπὸ ζόφον ἁγίων ἀγγέλων, "under darkness of holy angels," but saw it as awkward and changed it to ὑπὸ ζόφον ἀγρίων ἀγγέλων, "under darkness of savage angels," and that other scribes omitted it altogether.[151] Landon cites the whole passage in *1 En.* 10:4-8; 11-13, to which he assumes the phrase ἁγίων ἀγγέλων refers; the passage speaks of how the archangels Raphael and Michael executed God's punishment.[152] Whereas this passage *may* explain the interpretative expansion in Lucifer and Pseudo-Augustine, it does not warrant a conjecture in the text of Jude.

As for Clement's text, it too seems a bit awkward. It is of course possible that Clement replaced ἁγίων with ἀγρίων, but a development in the opposite direction cannot be excluded. In fact, an interpretation of ἄγριος in the moral sense, of uncontrolled desires, may in part explain Clement's expression, "under darkness of savage angels."[153] We know from Cassiodorus' translation of Clement's *Hypotyposeis* that Clement interpreted the chains symbolically as signifying the angel's own lust.[154] The express sin of the angels is only hinted at in the passage in Jude. In the next verse, the inhabitants of Sodom and Gomorrah are said to have practiced immorality in the same way as "these" (τούτοις), pursuing unnatural lust. The demonstrative pronoun is ambiguous; it may refer either to the angels in v. 6 (cf. Gen 6:4), to the neighbouring cities of Sodom and Gomorrah, or to the ungodly opponents. In v. 13 the author of Jude uses the same adjective, ἄγριος, to describe the opponents in a metaphor with evident moral implications. Clement perhaps expanded the text of Jude in order to make the sin of the angels more explicit, connecting it to the uncontrolled behaviour of the opponents.[155]

Besides the lack of manuscript support, Landon's conjecture, ὑπὸ ζόφον ἁγίων ἀγγέλων, has other weaknesses; first, it changes the Latin word order on which it is based and, secondly, the particular collocation of ἁγίων

---

[150] Landon, *Text-Critical Study*, 82-84. Note the change from the Latin word order. (Landon does not provide any detailed source apart from the confusing reference to "Lucifer Speculum.") The Latin citations of Lucifer and Ps-Augustine are cited in Thiele, *Epistulae Catholicae*, 418.

[151] Ibid., 82.

[152] Ibid., 83.

[153] See BDAG, s.v. ἄγριος 2; Ign. *Eph.* 10:2.

[154] The passage in *Adumbrationes* reads *cupiditate quippe devincti propria* (GCS 17:207); cf. *Paed.* 3.14.1-2.

[155] See further Clement's comments on Jude 22-23 in *Adumbrationes*, where he says that the stained garment is the garment of the soul and that the spirit is defiled by fleshly passions (GCS 17:208).

ἀγγέλων without the article is unattested in the NT, unless one accepts a reading found in some MSS in Jude 14 (which Landon does not; see below).

7,20-28: τὸν ὅμοιον τρόπον τούτοις ἐκπορνεύσασαι

1) τρόπον τούτοις {e>i}

The external support for the printed word order, τρόπον τούτοις (/αὐτοῖς), is overwhelming, but the alternative word order, τούτοις (/αὐτοῖς) τρόπον, is attested by the Majority Text and some other important witnesses (307 436 453 808 1067 𝔐 AnastS PsOec **L**:V^mssD). From a syntactical viewpoint, both alternatives are possible. Landon, who generally emphasizes intrinsic evidence, especially the author's style, refers to three examples in Jude where the pattern of definite article (DA) + adjective (A) + agreeing substantive (S) occurs (vv. 4, 6, 10) and he concludes that "no words are allowed to come between DA + A + S, nor is there any evidence elsewhere in Jude that the writer would have allowed PN [pronoun] to come between DA + A + S."[156] Thus, Landon rejects the word order of the Majority Text upon an argument from silence. Apparently, he disregards two examples where a pronoun does come between DA + A + S in Jude, namely in v. 3, τῆς κοινῆς ἡμῶν σωτηρίας, and in v. 20, τῇ ἁγιωτάτῃ ὑμῶν πίστει.[157] In the NT (NA^27) in general, I have found that the collocation of DA + A + S + PN occurs 52 times (twice in Jude), whereas DA + A + PN + S occurs 28 times (including the Majority reading of Jude 7). The problem cannot be resolved on intrinsic grounds. However, the external evidence is clear-cut, and the position of the dative demonstrative pronoun in the Majority Text can be explained as the result of attraction by ὅμοιον.

2) τούτοις {e+i}

The second problem concerns the pronoun τούτοις. Again, there is overwhelming support for the printed text. A few witnesses attest αὐτοῖς (044 0142 38 206S* 309 466 1066C 1409 1895 L164). We have already seen that the demonstrative pronoun, τούτοις, is ambiguous, but the personal pronoun, αὐτοῖς, is equally ambiguous. Both are used of the opponents in v. 11 and v. 14, respectively. Here Landon's appeal to the author's style is warranted, since the author consistently uses the

---

[156] Landon, *Text-Critical Study*, 85.

[157] In v. 3, a few witnesses place the pronoun after the noun, and the Majority Text omits the pronoun altogether, which, however, does not affect my point.

demonstrative pronoun as a catchword referring to the opponents, except in v. 11, but there it occurs in a set phrase in a woe oracle (οὐαὶ αὐτοῖς).[158] Therefore, I am inclined to believe that the author is referring to the opponents here, but that some scribes changed it for whatever reason, possibly even in order to de-emphasize the connection to the opponents.

In one witness the difficulty is solved by conformation of the case ending of the pronoun to the adverbial accusative construction, τὸν ὅμοιον τοῦτον τρόπον (43), "in this similar manner." The ambiguous pronoun is omitted altogether in some significant witnesses (88 915 1836 1845 1875 *pc* **L:V**), possibly due to homoioarcton. Perhaps under the influence of the second participle, ἀπελθοῦσαι, one scribe replaced ἐκπορνεύσασαι with ἀκολουθήσασαι (1409). Equally, the second participle perhaps caused some scribes to accidently copy ἐκπορεύσασαι (393T 491 L145 L1279), "making to go out."[159]

7,34-38: ὀπίσω σαρκὸς ἑτέρας {e+i}

The somewhat obscure reference to "strange flesh" may have caused some scribes to copy σαρκὸς ἑταίρας (592 617 1626 2705 L585/2*), "another woman's flesh" (if it is not simply an itacism).

7,40: πρόκεινται {e+i}

Some witnesses read πρόσκεινται (𝔓72 81 522 606* 641), probably due to a scribal error (thus, "Fehler" in the *ECM*). Nevertheless, the resultant text could make sense: "are placed by as a [parallel] example," or, "are added as an example [beside the former]."

7,48-50: δίκην ὑπέχουσαι {e+i}

External evidence strongly speaks in favor of the reading δίκην ὑπέχουσαι. In addition, it best accounts for the origin of the other readings. Landon suggests that unfamiliarity of this *hapax legomenon* (ὑπέχω) on the part of some scribes caused variation at this point.[160] The nature of the variation, however, does not support his conclusion, since most other variants of the

---

[158] Ibid., 86; cf. Bauckham, *Jude, 2 Peter*, 45.
[159] Cf. the common LXX idiom, πορεύεσθαι ὀπίσω θεῶν ἑτέρων (Deut 28:14; Judg 2:12; 3 Kgdms 11:10).
[160] Landon, *Text-Critical Study*, 87. For an example of the idiom δίκην ὑπέχω, see Plutarch, *Thes.* 30.2.

verb are syntactically or contextually difficult in combination with the object δίκην. Thus, readings like δίκην ὑπερέχουσαι (02 2718), "exceeding punishment," or, δίκην οὐκ ἔχουσιν (01*), "they do not have punishment," hardly make sense.[161] The latter reading with negation and main verb was probably influenced by the dittography earlier in 01*, πρόκεινται δε δεῖγμα.

The variant reading δίκην ἐπέχουσαι, attested by several important witnesses (𝔓⁷⁸ 1505 1611 2138 2200 *pc*), seems too difficult; perhaps δίκην could be interpreted as an accusative of respect, "staying, so as to be punished with eternal fire." The reading δίκην ὑπάρχουσαι (1845 1846 *pc*) is just as difficult ("Fehler" in the *ECM*); possibly it could be rendered "beginning punishment."[162]

Apart from ὑπέχουσαι, we are left with two other readings that make reasonable sense: first, δίκην ὑπέχουσιν (01C2 616 2279T Did), which does not affect the sense but presupposes an independent clause, and, finally, ἀπέχουσαι (181 1319), "receiving punishment in full."[163] Nevertheless, these two readings have too slim manuscript support.

8,2-4: ὁμοίως μέντοι {e+i}

The passage in John 12:42, where the adversative particle ὅμως ("nevertheless") is strengthened by μέντοι, may have influenced the scribe of 02 to use the same phrase here, ὅμως μέντοι, if it is not simply due to a slip of the eye.[164] In any case the adversative sense does not fit the context.

8,8: οὗτοι {e+i}

Landon refers to the "midrashic" structure of the text, and he finds that the writer shows an invariable preference for οὗτοι as he refers to his opponents.[165] At the same time, Landon says of the variant reading αὐτοί (𝔓⁷⁸ 1735 1885T) that it could be original, since it too occurs in reference to

---

[161] If the first hand of 01 took δίκη to mean "right" as dependent on law (attested in Homer), the variant could possibly make sense (cf. LSJ, s.v. δίκη II).

[162] Cf. ὑπάρχω εὐεργεσίας (LSJ, s.v. ὑπάρχω I).

[163] Cf. Josephus, *B.J.* 1.596: ἐγὼ μὲν ἀπέχω τῆς ἀσεβείας τὸ ἐπιτίμιον; Matt 6:2: ἀπέχουσιν τὸν μισθὸν αὐτῶν.

[164] ὅμως could have been interpreted as synonym to ὁμοίως ("likewise") were it not for μέντοι (cf. BDF §450.2). D. J. Clark understands the variant reading in 02 in the sense of "likewise," but does not consider the presence of μέντοι here ("Discourse Structure in Jude," *The Bible Translator* 55 (2004): 136 (cf. pp. 128-29, where he discusses ὁμοίως μέντοι).

[165] Landon, *Text-Critical Study*, 88-89. Landon cites MS 92 (from Albin's apparatus), which is only a collection of scholia in Jude, and hence not included in my study.

the opponents in the midrash text at v. 11.[166] As pointed out above, the personal pronoun in v. 11 occurs in the set phrase of a prophetic woe oracle (cf. the LXX: Hos 7:13; 9:12; Nah 3:17; Jer 27:27) and should therefore be rejected both on external and internal grounds.

8,12-14: σάρκα μὲν {e+i}

A few witnesses omit μέν ($\mathfrak{P}^{72}$ *pc* **K**:B^{pt}). The omission was probably accidental due to homoioarcton (μὲν μιαίνουσιν), especially if itacistic spelling was involved in the process (cf. $\mathfrak{P}^{72}$: MEI | ENOYCIN). As for intrinsic evidence, the words σάρκα μέν introduce a typical three-fold witness against the opponents in the description of their negative actions: "[They] defile the flesh, reject authority, and slander the glorious ones" (NRSV).[167] Often, the markers of correlation, μέν . . . δέ, are used to emphasize a contrast, but in this case they merely separate one thought from another.[168] From a rhetorical point of view, the series of three yields a complete condemnation of the opponents' actions.[169]

8,18: κυριότητα {e+i}

A few witnesses attest the plural κυριότητας (01 044 1845 1846 2805 *pc* AnastS Antioch **S**:HPh^{ms}). Bauckham regards the singular κυριότητα as an abstract noun for κύριος, meaning "lordship."[170] If it referred to a class of angels, as in Col 1:16; Eph 1:21, the plural would be more natural forming a synonym with δόξας (with the same case ending).[171] There is of course a

---

[166] Ibid.

[167] For the use of triadic illustration, and three-fold witness against the opponents in Jude, see Charles, *Literary Strategy*, 40-41.

[168] Contra Kühl, *Die Briefe Petri und Judae*, 313. For examples of the correlative particles μέν . . . δέ in sequences without concessive/adversative force, see Matt 13:8; Heb 7:2. In Jude 22-23, the specific interrelationship of the sequence of thoughts is largely dependent on how one regards the textual problems (see below).

[169] Cf. Watson, "The three conjunctions . . . constitute polysyndeton which emphasizes the sins of the sectarians and makes them seem more important and numerous" (*Invention, Arrangement, and Style*, 55).

[170] Bauckham, *Jude, 2 Peter*, 56.

[171] Landon raises the objection that in Eph 1:21 κυριότητος is in the singular (*Text-Critical Study*, 90). However, the context is clear-cut and the wording of the whole passage presupposes the existence of "powers" in the plural (πάσης ἀρχῆς καὶ ἐξουσίας καὶ δυνάμεως καὶ κυριότητος).

possibility that the author used the plural in reference to angels, but that would hardly explain how the reading κυριότητα arose.[172]

More plausible is Bauckham's suggestion that the variant reading κυριότητας arose as an attempt to eliminate the difficult singular, which occurs only here and in the parallel in 2 Pet 2:10.[173] He takes the singular to refer specifically to the lordship of Christ (cf. *Herm. Sim.* 5:6:1), and in light of the author's usage of catchword connections, he links κυριότητα to κύριος in v. 5, thus regarding the statement as parallel to v. 4, where the opponents are said to "deny our only Master and Lord, Jesus Christ."[174]

In view of external evidence and transcriptional probability, there can be no doubt that κυριότητα is original here.

8,24-28: δόξας δὲ βλασφημοῦσιν {e+i}

A few witnesses attest the singular δόξαν (𝔓[78]V 3 5 90b *pc* **L**:V **S**:Ph). Landon suggests that the case for the singular "is that it could be synonymous with κυριότητα."[175] In light of the unequivocal external evidence, a harmonization to κυριότητα on the part of some scribes is far more likely. Moreover, the plural δόξας occurs in the parallel passage in 2 Pet 2:10 without textual variation. Apparently, some scribes harmonized their whole text to this parallel, δόξας οὐ τρέμουσιν βλασφημοῦντες (309 633 1069Z 1717 2816). One witness repeats ἀθετοῦσιν from the previous clause. In some witnesses δέ is absent, probably because of a scribal slip, whereas a few other witnesses omit the whole clause, probably due to homoioteleuton.

---

[172] If one were to disregard the weak manuscript support for δόξαν, there would be a possibility that κυριότητα arose through harmonization. However, the combination of κυριότητας . . . δόξαν does not exist in any manuscript.

[173] Bauckham, *Jude, 2 Peter*, 56; so also Metzger, *Textual Commentary*, 658. Bauckham's reference to Origen as citing the plural is misleading, since the Greek text of Origen attests the singular (*Comm. Matt.* 10.24). The plural is found in Origen's *Letter to Friends in Alexandria* (*Ep. Car.*), of which fragments are preserved in various Latin sources. This particular passage is cited by Jerome (*Ruf.* 2.18; PL 23:462ab). In my opinion, the reference in the apparatus of UBS[4] to Origen[lat] is useless and should be removed.

[174] Ibid., 56-57.

[175] Landon, *Text-Critical Study*, 91. Eventually, Landon opts for the variant with the plural δόξας largely because he accepted ἁγίων ἀγγέλων at v. 6.

9,2-12: ὁ δὲ Μιχαὴλ ὁ ἀρχάγγελος, ὅτε {e+i}

MS 03 replaces ὁ δέ with ὅτε. The singular reading is equivalent to the Latin *quando* (Clement, *Adumb.*; Jerome, *Comm. Tit.* 3.2).[176] The introduction of the temporal particle necessitated the further substitution of the correlative τότε for ὅτε.[177] In that latter case, a pair of MSS (582 620) read ὁ τότε instead of ὅτε, supplying an article to the participle διακρινόμενος. The reading probably arose by accident. Likewise, a scribal slip resulted in the simple ἄγγελος (1243 2492).

9,18: διακρινόμενος {e+i}

Perhaps the notion that an archangel would dispute with the devil caused offense, since some witnesses read ἀνακρινόμενος (1523ZV 1524 Thph), "judge"/"interrogate," or simply κρινόμενος (1523TV 2494) "judge."[178]

9,24-28: τοῦ Μωϋσέως σώματος

1) Μωϋσέως σώματος {e>i}

A few MSS attest a different word order: τοῦ σώματος Μωϋσέως/Μωσέως (056AV 0142AV *pc*). Landon examines the word order tendency in the NT by looking at the articular noun τὸ σῶμα in prepositional phrases with a qualifying genitive; in all nine cases the genitive attribute follows the noun, so Landon concludes that this is an "invariable preference" among NT writers.[179] Landon's search for relevant examples is far too narrow; there are relevant passages in the LXX and NT: ἐν τῇ Μωϋσέως βίβλῳ (1 Esd 5:48); ἐν [γὰρ] τῷ Μωϋσέως νόμῳ (1 Esd 8:3; 1 Cor 9:9); ἐπὶ τῆς Μωϋσέως καθέδρας (Matt 23:2). Hence, we cannot rely upon intrinsic evidence. In fact, transcriptional probability points in the opposite direction, since the more common construction in the NT has the qualifying genitive after the noun. Thus, in addition to strong external evidence, transcriptional probability speaks in favor of the printed word order.

---

[176] The Vulgate reads *cum*, which is a bit ambiguous.

[177] Landon's claim that τότε is supported by the Vulgate is misleading (*Text-Critical Study*, 92).

[178] PsOec: διακρινόμενος (PG 119:709); Thph: ἀνακρινόμενος (PG 126:96). It should be noted that 1523 and 1524 are closely related commentary MSS, so it is likely that the reading ἀνακρινόμενος represents an assimilation to the commentary at this point. This connection was discovered at a point when I did not have an opportunity to control the commentary reading in the manuscripts. Nevertheless, the text of Jude in the two MSS is clearly related to Theophylact's citations of Jude.

[179] Landon, *Text-Critical Study*, 93.

2) Μωϋσέως {e+i}

A second problem is of an orthographical nature, and concerns the variation in spelling between Μωϋσέως and Μωσέως.[180] Although the latter spelling, Μωσέως, is well attested (02 044 6 18 88 323 630 915 1292 1739 2200C 2298 𝔐), the former, Μωϋσέως, predominates in the earliest MSS and is to be preferred.[181]

9,36: ἐπενεγκεῖν {e+i}

The external and internal support for the variant reading ἐπενεγκεῖν leaves little doubt that it is orginal. Yet, the reading ὑπενεγκεῖν is interesting from the perspective of interpretation and reception, and therefore it deserves our attention. At first sight, the clause οὐκ ἐτόλμησεν κρίσιν ἐπενεγκεῖν βλασφημίας seems to suggest that the archangel Michael was tempted to bring "a slanderous judgment" upon the devil. This difficult notion perhaps was avoided by some scribes who interpreted the passage differently and wrote ὑπενεγκεῖν (044 181Z 424 631 *al*), which means "bear," or "submit to."[182] This interpretation of the infinitive changes the agent and attributes the slanderous judgment to the devil.[183] In Cramer's *Catena* we are supplied

---

[180] Landon rules out Μωσέως only because of his favored word order (ibid., 93, n. 151). He does not realize that the two subformations of variants are unrelated; hence, some MSS attest τοῦ σώματος Μωσέως (378 632* L1440). This oft-repeated procedure of Landon reflects badly on his general approach of radical eclecticism.

[181] In the NT as a whole, 𝔓45 always has Μωϋσῆς (17 times). This form is also predominant in 01 03 05, whereas 04 vacillates. In the LXX, Philo and Josephus, the good MSS have -ου-, the inferior ones -ω- (Joachim Jeremias, "Μωϋσέως," *TDNT* 4:848; BDF §38). The orthographical variation between the case endings of the name is a separate issue (cf. Westcott and Hort, "Notes on Orthography," in *The New Testament*, 2:158). Apparently, the Robinson-Pierpont "Byzantine" edition in this case does not go with the nearly 68% numerical "majority" in favor of Μωσέως, but instead considers the 32% minority that read Μωϋσέως as the putative archetype reading at this point (Maurice A. Robinson and William G. Pierpont, eds., *The New Testament in the Original Greek: Byzantine Textform* (Southborough, MA: Chilton Book Publishing, 2005).

[182] The possibility that the verb ὑποφέρω could mean "effect" in this context is probably too farfetched; cf. *1 Clem.* 7:4, τὸ αἷμα τοῦ χριστοῦ . . . παντὶ τῷ κόσμῳ μετανοίας χάριν ὑπήνεγκεν (with v.l. ἐπήνεγκεν).

[183] For a similar reason, the reading παρὰ κυρίου in the parallel passage in 2 Pet 2:11 is the more difficult in that it attributes a "slanderous judgment" to God (cf. chapter four). Because of the lack of complete collation data for 2 Peter, I could not check the readings in 2 Pet 2:11 of all the witnesses that read ὑπενεγκεῖν in Jude 9. However, two of these MSS (044 181) omit the difficult prepositional phrase altogether in 2 Pet 2:11 according to the *ECM* (so also many other significant witnesses).

with a background to the incident in Jude, which may explain both the expression κρίσιν βλασφημίας and the variant reading ὑπενεγκεῖν:

> After the death of Moses, Michael was sent to remove the body, and as the devil began to slander Moses [κατὰ τοῦ Μωϋσέως βλασφημοῦντος] proclaiming him a murderer because he killed the Egyptian, the angel, who did not bear the slander against him [οὐκ ἐνέγκων τὴν κατ' αὐτοῦ βλασφημίαν], said to the devil: "May God rebuke you!"[184]

This Christian source probably preserves some basic traits from the lost ending of the *Testament of Moses*, which is cited in Jude 9.[185] Here it is the devil who slanders Moses. Even if Michael does not tolerate the slander, he does not himself bring judgment but asks the Lord to rebuke the devil. Bauckham suggests that the core tradition reflected in this story explains the difficult phrase κρίσιν βλασφημίας in Jude 9, which in light of its background should be translated, "condemnation for slander," and not "slanderous judgment."[186] In any case, the phrase is difficult, and the latter interpretation is facilitated by the change of agent in the variant reading ὑπενεγκεῖν; Michael did not submit to a slanderous judgment from the devil. Then the sense of ὑπενεγκεῖν would be synonymous to ἐνέγκων in the *Catena*. In conclusion, the variant reading ὑπενεγκεῖν was probably prompted by the difficult phrase, κρίσιν βλασφημίας, and perhaps also by specific knowledge of the background story as recounted in Christian sources. The parallel passage in 2 Pet 2:11 removes this difficulty, and the phrasing ἄγγελοι . . . φέρουσιν . . . βλάσφημον κρίσιν indirectly supports the originality of ἐπενεγκεῖν in Jude.

In addition, the reading ὑπενεγκεῖν eradicates another difficulty with ἐπενεγκεῖν—the apparent contradiction between the statement that the angel did not dare to bring judgment upon the devil, and his subsequent strong rebuke, which is actually an appeal to God's judgment, but may have been perceived by scribes as a judgment de facto.[187] Perhaps the

---

[184] J. A. Cramer, *Catena in Epistolas Catholicas, accerunt Oecumenii et Arethae commentarii in Apocalypsin* (Oxford: Clarendon, 1840), 163 (my translation).

[185] Cf. Bauckham, *Jude and the Relatives of Jesus*, 235-80, esp. 254-55.

[186] Ibid., 273-74. Apparently, the author of 2 Peter was unfamiliar with the source behind Jude 9 and interpreted the phrase in Jude as βλάσφημον κρίσιν (2 Pet 2:11). The same interpretation of βλασφημίας in Jude 9 as a genitive of quality is reflected in many Bible versions: "a railing accusation" (KJV); "a blasphemous judgment" (ESV); "a slanderous accusation" (NIV); "a railing judgment" (NASB); the NRSV is a bit ambiguous: "a condemnation of slander"; better is the circumlocution in NEB Margin: "to charge him with blasphemy."

[187] Note that ἐπιτιμάω has a stronger sense than "reprimand"; in the Gospels it is often used in connection with exorcism (cf. Kee, "The Terminology of Mark's Exorcism Stories," 232-46). A similar interpretation of Jude would imply that the archangel was actively opposing the

variant ἐξενεγκεῖν, attested by two MSS (203 506) and in two loose citations by Photius, is an attempt to remove the tension;[188] Michael did not dare to carry out/accomplish the judgment, but instead appealed to God that he might rebuke (judge) the devil. One witness reads ἐπαγαγεῖν (633), which is synonymous to ἐπενεγκεῖν and occurs in two examples of judgment in 2 Pet 2:1, 5.

9,44-48: ἐπιτιμήσαι σοι κύριος

1) The presence of the preposition ἐν {e>i}

The first main problem concerns the preposition ἐν; some significant witnesses insert the preposition, ἐπιτιμήσαι ἐν σοί (03*V 044 323 1241 1739 1881). As suggested above, the author is probably citing a passage from the lost ending of the *Testament of Moses*, which in turn echoes Zech 3:2 (LXX): εἶπεν κύριος πρὸς τὸν διάβολον ἐπιτιμήσαι κύριος ἐν σοί, διάβολε. Thus, besides the weaker external support for the preposition, transcriptional evidence suggests that its presence in some witnesses is due to scribal assimilation to Zech 3:2.

Nevertheless, Kubo prefers the reading with the preposition for a number of reasons: first, the accomodation of the text to a passage in the LXX is not a typical tendency on the part of the scribe of 03; secondly, Origen, who knew the source behind Jude 9, supports the presence of ἐν; thirdly, the presumed support for harmonization with the OT usually found among Koine MSS is not found here because the quotation is not directly from the OT; fourthly, scribes had every reason to remove the hebraism, since it was not part of a quotation from the LXX.[189]

The first three arguments are weak or even misleading; first, Kubo's reference to the common tendency of the scribe of 03 would have been relevant if the variant in question were a singular reading. However, the reading is attested in a number of witnesses to the Alexandrian tradition, so we can assume that it was in the exemplar of 03 (later to be corrected in 03C2) and that the harmonization to the LXX had occurred at an earlier

---

devil. In fact the passage from Zech 3:2 was used very frequently as a formula in Jewish incantations (Joseph Naveh and Shaul Shaked, *Magic Spells and Formulae* [Jerusalem: The Magnes Press, 1993], 25).

[188] Photius, *Bibliothèque*, 3:158,31; 164,34 (Henry). These two passages (in Photius' *cod.* 222) are loose citations, whereas another passage in *Amphil. 151* is a stricter citation which has ἐπενεγκεῖν (Laourdas and Westerink, 5:193,3). The *ECM* refers to all three passages (B 134), but for some reason Photius is cited only for ἐπενεγκεῖν in the apparatus.

[189] Kubo, *𝔓⁷² and the Codex Vaticanus*, 58-59; Landon follows Kubo, but places most emphasis on Kubo's fourth argument (*Text-Critical Study*, 95-96).

stage; evidently, harmonization to parallels occurred with some frequency in the early stages of the manuscript transmission.[190]

Kubo's appeal to Origen is directly misleading; up to the 25th edition of Nestle's text, Origen was cited in the apparatus as including the preposition. However, this reference does not go back to Origen, but rather to a comment in the inner margin of 1739, which can be read as ωριγ. This might suggest that the text of 1739, ἐπιτιμῆσαι ἐν σοί, at this point was in accordance with the text of Origen. However, Eduard von der Goltz points out that Origen wrote commentaries to Zechariah, which may explain the note in 1739 on the part of the scholiast, who is identified as Ephraim the monk, even if von der Goltz thinks that the note rather goes back to a commentary or homily on Jude.[191]

In his discussion, Kubo instead refers to a passage in Origen's *De Principiis* (Περὶ ἀρχῶν) 3:2.[192] It is true that Origen in that passage states that the incident recounted in Jude 9 is taken from the *Assumption of Moses,* and for Kubo this fact shows that Origen may have been familiar with the very source of Jude and his text is therefore to be considered seriously.[193] However, it is not in that passage Michael's rebuke of the devil is actually cited. The only remaining evidence I have found is a citation found in Origen's *Letter to Friends in Alexandria* (*Ep. Car.*), cited in turn by Jerome:

---

[190] Note e.g., the early attestation of the harmonization to Jude 12 in 2 Pet 2:13, ἀγάπαις αὐτῶν (02C 03 044 623 *pc*). MS 02 is wrongly cited in the *ECM* at this point. For a comprehensive list of examples of harmonization in 01 02 03 and 04, see further Weiss, *Die Katholischen Briefe*, 26-30 (01 02 04); 81-85 (03).

[191] In regard to the note ωριγ at Jude 9, von der Goltz states, "Origenes schrieb, wie Hieronymus berichtet, 2 Bücher zum Propheten Sacharja und da die Lesart ἐν σοί mit LXX Sach 3,2 stimmt, so kann der Scholiast aus dieser Schrift seine Notiz genommen haben; näher liegt aber noch, anzunehmen, dass dem Verf. auch ein Kommentar oder eine Homilie des Origenes zum Judasbrief vorlag, von deren Existenz uns freilich kein Zeugnis vorliegt" (*Eine textkritische Arbeit*, 52). In a recently published monograph, Amy S. Anderson studies another manuscript, 1582, copied by the same scribe, Ephraim the monk (*The Textual Tradition of the Gospels: Family 1 in Matthew* [NTTS 32; Leiden: Brill, 2004]). Anderson suggests that the two MSS are separately descended from a copy of the entire NT furnished with marginalia (ibid., 71-72). A comment on Matt 13:35 in 1582 shows that the scribe did have clear text-critical opinions (ibid., 63-64). However, there are no clear instances of this attitude in 1739. Apparently, the marginal comments in 1582 contain several references to patristic works and in my opinion the obscure reference to Origen in the margin of 1739 is best interpreted thus.

[192] Kubo, *𝔓⁷² and the Codex Vaticanus*, 58, n. 20.

[193] Ibid, 58; Bauckham is probably correct in his assumption that Origen referred to a second-century work which he (and other Alexandrian fathers) knew as the *Assumption of Moses* (*Jude, 2 Peter*, 76).

Unde et Michael cum adversus diabolum disputaret de Moysi corpore, ne tanto quidem malo ausus est iudicium inferre blasphemiae, sed dixit: "Increpet tibi Dominus." Cui quid simile etiam in Zacharia legimus: "Increpet tibi Dominus, diabole; et increpet Dominus in te, qui elegit Jerusalem." (Jerome, *Ruf.* 2.18 [PL 23:462a])

Whatever this passage is worth from the text-critical perspective, it does demonstrate that Origen was well aware of both text forms, in Jude 9 and Zech 3:2, respectively, since a point is made of this in his comment.[194] Interestingly, the presence of the preposition is one of the differences, and it occurs only in the citation of Zech 3:2. Thus, if the citation is to be used for text-critical purposes it can only support the variant without the preposition.[195] In any case, Jerome's citation of Origen sheds new light on the marginal comment in 1739 mentioned above, in that it shows that Origen was familiar with the difference of the two texts.[196]

Kubo's third argument, concerning the lack of manuscript support from Byzantine witnesses for harmonization is simply an argument from silence. In my opinion, the only valid argument is the possibility that scribes were tempted to remove the Hebraism. Landon's appeal to the author's abundant use of Semitic expressions is relevant only if the citation represents his translation from a Semitic source that included the preposition—this is uncertain.[197] In consideration of external and internal evidence as a whole, the arguments for the variant with εν are too weak.

2) κύριος {e+i}

In regard to the subject of ἐπιτιμῆσαι, the adopted reading κύριος has very strong external support, but some significant witnesses read ὁ κύριος (01C2 442 621 630 1505 1611 2138 2200 *al* Olymp^mss). The Latin, Coptic and Syriac versions represent κύριος with or without the article. Other MSS read ὁ θεός (01* 323 1241 1739 1881 2298), whereas a single MS attests the conflation κύριος ὁ θεός (1501). As mentioned above, the referent of

---

[194] The general faithfulness of Jerome's long citations of Origen's letter is confirmed by the fact that his adversary, Rufinus, cites one long passage from the same letter (Rufinus, *De adulteratione librorum Origenis 6-8* [ed. and trans. by Manlio Simonetti; CCSL 20; Turnhout: Brepols, 1961], 11,; cf. with Jerome, *Ruf.* 2.18 [PL 23:462b]).

[195] Kubo's misleading reference to Origen is repeated by Landon (ibid., 96).

[196] Another passage in Jerome's long citations of Origen's letter reads thus: "'Non fuit ausus judicium inferre blasphemiae,' [Jude 9] *quod dicitur de Michaele contra diabolum; et in alio loco:* 'Dominationes quidem reprobant, glorias autem blasphemant'" [Jude 8] (*Ruf.* 2.18 [PL 23:462b]). This confirms that Origen had the passage in Jude in mind. Thus, it is not likely that the marginal comment, ωριγ, in 1739 refers to Origen's text of Jude per se, but rather to a comment similar to that above, or to a work by Origen on Zechariah.

[197] Ibid.

κύριος was sometimes perceived as ambiguous so that scribes would tend to specify with θεός or Ἰησοῦς. Significantly, most of the same MSS that conform the text to the related passage in Zech 3:2 read ὁ θεός here. The support for this variant among MSS 323 1241 1739 1881 indicates a common archetype, since these MSS appear to be closely related.[198] It may seem odd that only two MSS with the preposition ἐν (03 044) follow the text of Zechariah (κύριος) at this point, but, on the other hand, the passage in Zechariah is undoubtedly situated in the throne room of God.[199] In view of external support and transcriptional probability, κύριος is to be preferred. A few MSS add διάβολε (1836 1846 1875 *pc*), assimilating the text to Zech 3:2.

10,20: φυσικῶς {e+i}

A few MSS attest the adjective φυσικά (1505 1609 2495), "natural," instead of the adverb φυσικῶς, "naturally," "by instinct." The reading conforms to ζῷα, as in 2 Pet 2:12, and enhances the repetition of similar case endings. With the adjective, the sense becomes awkward, "natural like irrational animals, they understand."

10,36: φθείρονται {e+i}

The compound διαφθείρονται (044) perhaps reflects an intensification of the sense of φθείρονται here.[200]

11,2-4: οὐαὶ αὐτοῖς {e+i}

In the lectionary system, the second reading from Jude (vv. 11-25) is to be read on Thursday in the 36th week of the ecclesiastical year. This particular lesson is introduced by an incipit in the MSS that provides the

---

[198] According to Wachtel, this group of MSS is closely related in the Catholic Epistles (cf. Wachtel, *Der byzantinische Text*, 65).

[199] Bauckham thinks that the author of Jude actually referred to Jesus in v. 9 (*Jude, 2 Peter*, 62). Origen concludes after citing both passages in Jude 9 and Zech 3:2 that it belongs to God to see whether he will reprimand the devil or not: "*[U]trum increpet, a non increpet Deus diabolum, ipse viderit*" (*Ruf.* 2.18 [PL 23:462a]). If MS 1739 is somehow connected with Origen as suggested by the marginal note (see above), the interpretative ὁ θεός in 1739 seems natural.

[200] Landon suggests that the scribe of 044 has the peculiar habit of altering words to form compounds (*Text-Critical Study*, 98). However, the two other examples he mentions (v. 6: κατοικητήριον; v. 18: ἀναστήσονται) more probably reflect the influence of other passages (Rev 18:32; Matt 12:41; par. Luke 11:32). This could of course be the case here too (cf. the polemic passage in 1 Tim 6:5: διαπαρατριβαὶ διεφθαρμένων ἀνθρώπων τὸν νοῦν καὶ ἀπεστερημένων τῆς ἀληθείας, νομιζόντων πορισμὸν εἶναι τὴν εὐσέβειαν).

hearers with some context: ἀγαπητοί (/ἀδελφοί), οὐαὶ τοῖς ἀσεβέσιν. This incipit occurs with some variation in practically all lectionaries, and has intruded into several continuous text MSS (with variation). In one MS, even a heading related to the liturgical reading has crept into the text, καθολικῆς ἐπιστολῆς Ἰούδα [τὸ ἀνάγνωσμα] (632), "[the reading] of the Catholic Epistle of Jude."

11,26: Βαλαάμ {e+i}

Two MSS read Βαλαάκ (𝔓⁷²C 432*), which is probably due to a scribal slip.[201] Judging from a detailed manuscript image (see plate IV below), I suspect that the scribe of 𝔓⁷² might have intended to write Βαλαάμ, which he spells with two *lambdas* in 2 Pet 2:15 (ΒΑΛΛΑΑΜ). However, the scribe realized the mistake and changed the second *lambda* to an *alpha* and possibly the final *mu* was corrected to a *kappa* (thus ΒΑΛΑΑΚ). In any case, the two characters appear together in the biblical account; the prophet Balaam refused the invitation of the Moabitic king Balak to curse Israel for a monetary reward (Num 22:18; 24:13). However, in Jewish tradition, Balaam was actually described as accepting Balak's proposal, and, when he failed to curse Israel, he advised Balak to entice Israel into sin.[202] Thus, he was remembered as the man who out of greed led Israel into idolatry and promiscuity (cf. Rev 2:14). The charge of greed, hinted at in Jude 11, is accentuated in the parallel passage in 2 Pet 2:15-16 (the parallel supports the reading Βαλαάμ in Jude). Some scribes accidently confused (or intentionally linked!) Βαλαάμ with Βάαλ (38T 378 615 *pc* [**L:R** *Bahal*])— another name associated with idolatry.

11,34-40: τῇ ἀντιλογίᾳ τοῦ Κόρε {e+i}

Some MSS omit the article τῇ (322T 467 1250T *pc*). Landon points out that the "stylistic balance and symmetry" as seen in the juxtaposition of the three examples require the articular dative here (τῇ ὁδῷ . . . τῇ πλάνῃ . . . τῇ ἀντιλογίᾳ).[203] The common meaning of ἀντιλογία is "dispute" (i.e., verbal opposition), but by extension it can refer to rebellion, as in this passage.

---

[201] The spelling βαλαάκ occurs in numerous LXX MSS, and in the present NT variant here in Jude. The normal spelling, however, is Βαλάκ, here unattested.

[202] In particular, the passage in Num 31:16 was developed in haggadaic tradition (see further Bauckham, *Jude, 2 Peter*, 81). For a full treatment of Balaam as a representative leader of wickedness in Jewish tradition, see Geza Vermez, "Deux Traditions sur Balaam," *Cahiers Sioniens* 10 (1955): 289-302.

[203] Landon, *Text-Critical Study*, 101.

Perhaps some scribes were unfamiliar with the extended meaning of the noun, and therefore confused it with the more common ἀπολογία (149 201 913V 1610 L2087) that means "defense" (verbal or written). Two other scribes wrote ἀλογία (1829 2131T), "unreasonable conduct," perhaps under the influence of the related adjective ἄλογος in v. 10.

The opponents were said to commit the same sins as Cain and Balaam, but the notion that they have perished (or will perish) in Korah's rebellion is more difficult.[204] Possibly, a perceived anachronism was avoided by the corrector of 1831 who replaced Κόρε with κόσμου.

12,5: [omit] {e+i}

Following οὗτοί εἰσιν words from v. 16 have been interpolated in some witnesses (01* 01C2a 04C2V 1270 1297 1827). In some Sahidic and Bohairic manuscripts these expansions are written at the end of v. 11.[205] The addition is of course explicable as a dittography due to homoioarcton.[206] However, it cannot be taken for granted that all these scribes made the same error independently;[207] the fact that diverse witnesses, some of which are early, attest an addition of the same, rather long, stretch of text (οὗτοί εἰσιν γογγυσταὶ . . . πορευόμενοι) suggests that the agreement in error is not accidental, but rather that the peculiar addition was introduced early on and is genealogically significant (*Leitfehler*).[208] The natural connection between Korah's "dispute" (ἀντιλογία) in the preceding verse, and the description of the opponents as "complaining grumblers" (γογγυσταὶ μεμψίμοιροι) probably helped ensure its survival in some corners

---

[204] Most likely to be understood as "in the same manner" as Korah.

[205] The interpolation from v. 16 is also attested in other versional MSS, which are only accessible in old critical editions (Armenian: Yovhannes Zōhrapean, ed., *God-Breathed Scriptures of the Old and New Testaments* [original title in Armenian: *Astuacašunč 'matean hin ew norktakaranac '*; Venice: St. Lazar Press, 1805]; Arabic: J. G. Nissel and T. Petraeus, eds., *S. Judae Apostoli epistolae catholicae versio Arabice et Aethiopice* [Leiden, 1654]). In spite of various difficulties (text-critical and linguistic) of reconstructing the Greek behind these versions, they evidence the wide dissemination of the transposition as such. For some reason, these versions were not cited in the *ECM* at this point.

[206] J. Rendel Harris examined Codex Sinaiticus (01) trying to reconstruct its (papyrus-) exemplar, and he suggested that in Jude 12, the scribe's eye had wandered to the side (= *parablepsis*) from the top of a column in the exemplar (with v. 12) to the top of the next column (v. 16) ("New Testament Autographs," *The American Journal of Philology* 3, no. 12 [1882]: 29).

[207] Landon assumes independent errors on the part of the copyists (*Text-Critical Study*, 102).

[208] Most interesting is the fact that the MSS that here read the addition with ἰδίας present (04C2V 1270 1297) are *not* those that read ἰδίας in verse 16 (102 189 1102 1597 1881 2805).

of the manuscript tradition, as long as it was not corrected (as in 01 04).[209] In fact, Moses charged Korah with grumbling (διαγογγύζω) against Aaron (LXX Num 16:11).

12,6-16: οἱ ἐν ταῖς ἀγάπαις ὑμῶν σπιλάδες

1) οἱ {e+i}

The article οἱ is attested by nearly all of the best MSS as well as by the Coptic and Syriac versions. Nevertheless, several significant witnesses omit the article (01* 18 436 1067 1409 1836 1875 𝔐 PsOec). Surprisingly, no commentator seems to consider that the omission of the article in 01* is probably due to homoioteleuton, occasioned by the major interpolation just treated (the article is absent from MSS 1270 1297 1827, whereas 04 is lacunose).[210]

In regard to intrinsic evidence, William Whallon admits that the reading with the article is the *lectio difficilior*, since it does not agree with the feminine σπιλάδες.[211] However, he is not satisfied with any of the proposed explanations (see below), and instead suggests that the text is flawed at this point and that the noun-phrase orginally read αἱ ἐν τοῖς ἀχάταις ὑμῶν σπιλάδες.[212] For Whallon this explains the difficult noun ἀγάπη, which "did not denote a love-feast until later, when this very verse was the authority for its doing so [sic]."[213] This, of course, is a circular reasoning on the part of Whallon—his conjecture does not explain the rise of ἀγάπη in the first place. Furthermore, Whallon's proposed text would surely have resulted in

---

[209] In an examination of a peculiar addition in the Gospel of John, I have demonstrated elsewhere that the history of readings is not synonymous with the history of manuscripts (T. Wasserman, "The Patmos Family of New Testament MSS and Its Allies in the Pericope of the Adulteress and Beyond," *TC: A Journal of Biblical Textual Criticism* [http://purl.org/TC] 7 [2002]: par. 48).

[210] See e.g., Bigg, *A Critical and Exegetical Commentary*, 333; Mayor, *The Epistle of St. Jude*, clxxxv; Bauckham, *Jude, 2 Peter*, 77; William Whallon, "Should We Keep, Omit or Alter the οἱ in Jude 12?," *NTS* 34 (1988): 156; Landon, *Text-Critical Study*, 102; (Bigg, Mayor, Bauckham and Whallon do not even indicate that the corrector of 01 provides οἱ!)

[211] Whallon, "Should We Keep," 156. The parallel passage in 2 Pet 2:12-13 reads οὗτοι δέ . . . φθαρήσονται . . . σπίλοι καὶ μῶμοι ἐντρυφῶντες ἐν ταῖς ἀπάταις αὐτῶν συνευωχούμενοι ὑμῖν. Thus, the article is removed and the rare word σπιλάς is changed to the common σπίλος.

[212] Ibid., 158. Whallon cites a passage from the poem *Lithica* ascribed to Orpheus (line 620), where the gemstone achate (ἀχάτης) is said to have spots (σπιλάδες).

[213] Ibid.

stronger attestation for the feminine συνευωχούμεναι later in the verse (see below).

In conclusion, Whallon's conjecture is unneccesary; several plausible explanations for the difficult article have been offered: it is possible to (1) supply ὄντες or κεκλημένοι (Bigg); (2) read οἱ with συνευωχούμενοι, with σπιλάδες in apposition (Kelly; Bauckham); (3) supply a punctuation mark after οἱ ἐν ταῖς ἀγάπαις ὑμῶν, presupposing an ellipse (Albin).[214] My judgment is that both external and internal evidence speak in favor of the reading with the article.

2) ἀγάπαις {e+i}

A second problem concerns the noun ἀγάπαις ("love-feasts"). The term is unique in the NT and rather striking—Whallon is not the only one to have been puzzled by its occurrence in Jude.[215] However, some light is shed on its use in Christian terminology by Walter Bauer who refers to a "scholion on Pla. 112b" where it is said of such meals among the Lacedaemonians that they were called φιλίτια.[216]

Some important MSS read ἀπάταις (02 04V 88 915 1845 *pc*). In the *ECM*, this variant is marked as an error (f), which is clearly an exaggeration; in fact, G. D. Kilpatrick has argued for its originality, and translates it as "pleasures."[217] The variant could make sense, but, in my opinion, the noun, ἀπάτη, has negative connotations whether it means

---

[214] Bigg, *A Critical and Exegetical Commentary*, 333; Kelly, *A Commentary on the Epistles of Peter and Jude*, 270-71; Bauckham, *Jude, 2 Peter*, 77; Albin, *Judasbrevet*, 665 (a punctuation mark after ὑμῶν occurs in several MSS); cf. Wohlenberg, *Der erste und zweite Petrusbrief und der Judasbrief*, 312, n. 98. G. B. Winer's solution is less satisfactory; he takes the article with σπιλάδες because he thinks the gender was changed or forgotten in late Greek (*A Treatise on the Grammar of New Testament Greek* [trans. idem; 3d rev. ed.; Edinburgh: T. & T. Clark, 1882], 25, 38, 73, 76).

[215] Cf. D. Gregory Dix, "It seems rather remarkable to me that scholars have not been more struck by this name Agape than they appear to be. To call a 'meal' a 'love' has no more sense in Greek than to refer to a 'supper' in English without explanation as a 'hope'" (*Jew and Greek. A Study in the Primitive Church* [London: Dacre Press, 1953], 104).

[216] BDAG, "An Introduction to the Lexicon of the Greek New Testament," xxviii. The work Bauer referred to is *Scholia Platonica* (ed. W. C. Greene; Haverford, Pennsylvania: American Philological Association, 1938). The text reads: τὰ δεῖπνα ἃ κοινῇ ποιοῦνται Λακεδαιμόνιοι. καλεῖται δὲ καὶ φιλίτια, ἐπειδὴ φιλίας συναγωγά ἐστι (112b). Several Greek writers use the word in a similar sense (cf. LSJ, s.v. φιλίτια, φιδίτια, φειδίτια; the unclear ethymology does not affect the subsequent association with φίλος that is evident from the above citation).

[217] G. D. Kilpatrick states, "We suggest . . . that in both passages the original reading was ἀπάταις with the meaning 'pleasures, revels' or the like" ("Ἀγάπη as Love-Feast in the New Testament," in *Parola e spirito: Studi Onore di Settimio Cipriani* [ed. Cesare C. Marcheselli; Brescia: Paideia Editrice, 1982], 160).

"deception" or "pleasure" (i.e., sinful), and therefore is too difficult with ὑμῶν—the author certainly did not mean to characterize the addressees negatively. For the same reason I do not think the word entered the manuscript tradition as a conscious harmonization to the parallel in 2 Peter 2:13, although harmonization could have occurred in individual witnesses (cf. 02 04 88). The parallel passage exhibits variation between the two nouns, but ἀπάταις has stronger external support (𝔓⁷² 01 02* 04 025 33 81 88 307 1175 1448 1735 1852 2295 𝔐 **K**:Sᵐˢˢ**B** **S**:Hᵀ) and is followed by αὐτῶν;[218] only a corrector of 02 changed the pronoun to αὐτῶν in Jude 12 in accordance with the parallel in 2 Pet 2:13.[219] Ironically, a corrector of the same MS changed ἀπάταις to ἀγάπαις in 2 Peter 2:13.[220] In short, ἀπάταις probably entered the manuscript tradition due to a poor transcription of ἀγάπαις and should be rejected.[221]

Two other MSS read εὐωχίαις (6 424Z), "feasts," in Jude 12, which is an adaptation to the verb συνευωχέομαι in the same verse.

12,18: συνευωχούμενοι {e+i}

Some MSS read συνευωχούμεναι (33V 177 180 *al*). Apparently, some scribes assimilated the participle to the feminine σπιλάδες (see above). This could reflect a misunderstanding of the syntax, but if the feminine noun was perceived as personified, the feminine participle could be properly

---

[218] The editors of the *ECM* have indicated with bold dots that they consider the reading ἀγάπαις αὐτῶν (02C 03 044 5 623 1611 1827 2464 2805 *pc* **L**:V **K**:Sᵐˢˢ **S**:PhHᴹ) as of equal value in 2 Pet 2:13; cf. Adolf von Harnack, *Zur Revision der Prinzipen der neutestamentlichen Textkritik* (vol. 7 of *Beiträge zur Einleitung in das Neue Testament*; Leipzig: 1916), 109-10. In any case this does not affect my argument, since αὐτῶν is unequivocally original.

[219] Bauckham regards ἀπάταις αὐτῶν (02C) as "a correction because the presence of the false teachers at the agapes seemed too scandalous" (*2 Peter, Jude*, 77). Apparently, he overlooks that 02* reads ἀπάταις ὑμῶν. Nevertheless, Bauckham's suggestion may be more applicable as an explanation to the modification of the text of Jude in 2 Peter. Landon erroneously cites Syrᵖʰ for ἀπάταις αὐτῶν (*Text-Critical Study*, 105).

[220] The corrections in Jude 12 and 2 Peter 2:13, respectively, could stem from different correctors. MS 02 is wrongly cited in the *ECM* in 2 Pet 2:13.

[221] The variation between the two nouns is attested elsewhere (Mark 4:19 in 037; LXX Eccl 9:6 in Codex Sinaiticus). Curiously, Whallon confuses the two nouns in his reference to Kilpatrick's article: "ἀπάτη [sic] as Love-Feasts in the New Testament" (Whallon, "Should We Keep," 159, n. 6). Since ἀγάπαις is original in Jude, Harnack thinks the author of 2 Peter must have written ἀγάπαις too (because of the significant semantic difference between the two words), and that ἀπάταις entered the MS tradition of 2 Peter as a transcriptional error (in both passages): "Wie oft sind Γ und Π, Π und Τ in den Handschriften verwechselt worden" (*zur Revision*, 110).

conformed to it, and therefore I do not label the reading as an error (contra *ECM*).

In Kim Haines-Eitzen's opinion, the reading of 𝔓⁷², συνευχομένοι ("praying together"), makes perfect sense in the context, and she thinks the substitution might be connected to the ascetic setting in which the text (the codex) was used in order to emphasize prayer rather than feasting, and, at the same time, to avoid the implication that Christians were "feasting together in love-feasts."[222] Although the codex was most probably used in a "proto-orthodox" environment, it is of earlier date than the Pachomian monastic community, and must have entered the monastic library from outside.[223] In the light of other theological modifications in the manuscript, I cannot exclude Haines-Eitzen's assumption, but, in my opinion, the reading is more likely the result of a transcriptional error on the part of the careless scribe (note also the line break after ΣΥΝΕΥ- in 𝔓⁷²).[224]

Two other MSS read εὐωχούμενοι (1735 1799), "feasting." This reading may have been introduced to avoid the notion that the false teachers feasted together with the addressees, which could be implied by συνευωχούμενοι (cf. the secondary reading συνευωχούμενοι ἐν ὑμῖν in 2 Pet 2:13).

The syntactically aberrant reading of 2675*, συνεβόσκομεν ("we tended/fed together"), possibly reflects an influence from the passage to which the author may have alluded in the context, namely Ezek 34:2 (LXX): μὴ βόσκουσιν ποιμένες ἑαυτούς.

12,19: ὑμῖν {e+i}

Several important MSS add the personal pronoun ὑμῖν (04 88 323 665 915 1739 1845 *al*), possibly by way of stylistic improvement prompted by συνευωχούμενοι.[225] The addition may also reflect harmonization to the parallel in 2 Pet 2:13, where practically all MSS read συνευωχούμενοι ὑμῖν or συνευωχούμενοι ἐν ὑμῖν. There is of course a slight possibility that the pronoun was omitted by scribes in order to avoid the difficult notion that the false teachers feasted together with the recipients. If that were the case, however, one would have expected the same development of the textual

---

[222] Haines-Eitzen, *Guardians*, 113.

[223] Wasserman, "Papyrus 72," 139, n.11.

[224] It should be noted that the same scribe wrote συνευωχούμενοι in 2 Peter 2:13.

[225] For examples of similar improvements in the early MSS (in the Catholic Epistles), see Wachtel, *Der byzantinische Text*, 84-87; cf. 1 John 1:4 (addition of ὑμῖν).

tradition in Jude as in 2 Peter, i.e., the introduction of the reading ἐν ὑμῖν ("among you").

12,30-34: ὑπὸ ἀνέμων παραφερόμεναι {e+i}

Some witnesses replace the prepositional phrase ὑπὸ ἀνέμων with παντὶ ἀνέμῳ (01 104 459 1842 **L**:D), which reflects an assimilation to the passage in Eph 4:14, περιφερόμενοι παντὶ ἀνέμῳ, "blown about by every wind"; MSS 104 459 1842Z Isid further attest the same participle in Jude, περιφερόμενοι. Two MSS replace ἀνέμων with ἀνόμων (43 917), which makes good sense but interrupts the metaphor.

The masculine form of the participle, παραφερόμενοι (𝔓⁷²* 03 044 621 1845 1852 *al*), is explicable as a *constructio ad sensum*, referring to the opponents (οὗτοι). However, the combination of the feminine νεφέλαι with παραφερόμενοι is inferior, since it interrupts the metaphor.[226]

Other readings have very weak manuscript support, but are still interesting: some witnesses read περιφερόμεναι with the TR (6 35 *al* PsOec **L**:VTR), which could be translated "blown about."[227] A single Greek MS reads προφερόμεναι (1509), which may simply reflect a misreading of the scribe, but in Homer the verb προφέρω is in fact used of a storm ("sweep away").[228] This reading may explain the Sahidic translation ⲈⲢⲈϨⲈⲚⲦⲎⲨ ϨⲒⲞⲨⲈ ⲚϬⲰⲞⲨ, "the winds driving them [the clouds] away," which is marked with "?" in the apparatus of the *ECM*, since the editors found no equivalent Greek reading.[229] The simplex form φερόμεναι (056 0142 489 *pc*) is of course far more common, whereas the form διαφερόμεναι (1875), "carried hither and yon," normally occurs in nautical context of ships drifting (e.g., Acts 27:27).[230]

---

[226] This collocation does not correspond to the combination of σπιλάδες συνευωχούμεναι, since the latter two are not semantically or syntactically connected (unless personified). Cf. also Rev 11:4.

[227] PsOec: περιφερόμεναι (PG 119:716); Thph: παραφερόμενοι (PG 126:100).

[228] LSJ, s.v. προφέρω III.

[229] Thus, the Sahidic reading is cited in the supplement 5.3 (B 151) in the original language with German and English translation (the latter being erroneous).

[230] Cf. Philo, *Migr.* 148: σκάφος ὑπ᾽ ἐναντίων πνευμάτων διαφερόμενον.

12,38: φθινοπωρινά {e+i}

The rare adjective φθινοπωρικά, "fruitless," is attested in a few MSS (01* 1243 2473).[231] It may have been caused by the neighbouring synonym ἄκαρπα, but is more probably due to a transcriptional error.[232]

The opponents are called δένδρα φθινοπωρινὰ ἄκαρπα, which should probably be translated, "trees in late autumn, without fruit." Whereas one would have expected fruit at the season of late autumn, these trees have not fulfilled their purpose, no more than νεφέλαι ἄνυδροι, "waterless clouds."[233] Thus, the point of the metaphor loses its force with the sequence of two synonyms, φθινοπωρικὰ ἄκαρπα, in much the same way as the inferior interpretation of φθινοπωρινά as referring to the winter.[234]

12,44-46: δὶς ἀποθανόντα ἐκριζωθέντα {e+i}

Some witnesses insert a καί between the two participles (61 307 453 2186 *al* PsOec). The co-ordinating conjunction makes the text smoother (cf. Rom 10:21; 2 Pet 1:8). However, the lists of descriptions given to the opponents are characterized by asyndeton throughout the epistle (vv. 12, 16, 19).

13,2-6: κύματα ἄγρια θαλάσσης {e+i}

MS 01 attests a different word order, ἄγρια κύματα θαλάσσης, where the noun is closer to its genitive attribute within the noun phrase. Generally, the singular readings are numerous in 01.[235] It is impossible to know what was in the exemplar of 01 at this point. There seems to have been a

---

[231] The word is uncommon, but attested in *P.Lille* 1.41,4 (φθινοπωρικὸν σήσαμον).

[232] For examples of similar cases of careless copying resulting in peculiar variants in 01, see Weiss, *Die Katholischen Briefe*, 32-33.

[233] The meaning of φθινοπωρινά is disputed; some commentators think it refers to a time after harvest when the trees are bare, but that would result in a tautology; cf. Mayor who says, "If φθινοπωρινά were equivalent to χειμερινά, denoting the season when the trees are necessarily bare both of leaves and fruit, how could a tree be blamed for being ἄκαρπον? It is because it might have been, and ought to have been a fruit-bearing tree, that it is rooted up" (*The Epistle of St. Jude*, 58). Yet cf. Jesus' cursing of the fig tree, when it was not time for fruit (Mark 11:13-14, 20).

[234] So e.g., Bigg, *A Critical and Exegetical Commentary*, 335 ("trees in winter").

[235] Cf. Westcott and Hort who say of 01, "The singular readings are very numerous, especially in the Apocalypse, and scarcely ever commend themselves on internal grounds. It can hardly be doubted that many of them are individualisms of the scribe himself, when his bold and rough manner of transcription is considered; but some doubtless are older" (Westcott and Hort, *The New Testament*, 1:246-47).

relatively high degree of freedom in the early history of transmission as reflected in the many examples of fluctuating word order elsewhere in 01 and among other early witnesses.[236] In this specific case the word order was possibly occasioned by omission of κύματα through homoioteleuton (-τα^-τα) with immediate restoration after having written ἄγρια. There is also a slight possibility that the scribe was influenced by the passage in Wis 14:1 (ἄγρια . . . κύματα).[237]

13,8-14: ἀπαφρίζοντα τὰς ἑαυτῶν αἰσχύνας {e=i} (*ECM* επαφριζοντα κτλ.)

The manuscript evidence is evenly balanced between ἐπαφρίζοντα (01 02 03 044 18 88 307 436 453 808 915 1067 1409 1836 1845 1875 2374 𝔐) and ἀπαφρίζοντα (𝔓⁷² 04 33 81 323 431 621 623 630 665 1505 1611 1739 1837 1852 2138 2200 *al*). Both forms are attested by patristic witnesses: ἐπαφρίζοντα (Pall Phot PsOec); ἀπαφρίζοντα (Isid).[238] The versions are ambiguous. It cannot be excluded that one of the forms entered the manuscript tradition because of possible phonetic confusion of the two vowels on the part of some scribes, but, in light of the wide attestation of both forms, each form has to be considered seriously. If we look specifically at the earliest witness, 𝔓⁷², the scribe often displays irregularities in spelling.[239] In 𝔓⁷² there are twenty-one singular readings (including errors) in 1-2 Peter and Jude that have arisen from vowel confusion. However, in none of these cases is α taken for ε.[240]

A final decision as to which variant is original must rest on internal grounds. The reading ἐπαφρίζοντα τὰς ἑαυτῶν αἰσχύνας can be translated, "casting up their own shameless deeds as foam (on a watery surface)," or "causing their shameless deeds to foam up," whereas the corresponding phrase with ἀπαφρίζοντα can be rendered, "casting off their own shameless deeds as foam." Both verbs are rare in Greek literature and only ἐπαφρίζω is attested in sources predating Jude, namely in Moschus (2nd century B.C.E.), *Idyll* 5,5, and Nicander (3rd/2nd century B.C.E.), *Alexipharmaca*,

---

[236] For examples in the Catholic Epistles, see Jas 4:4; 1 Pet 2:18; 3:5 (01 singular); 2 Pet 1:4; 1 Joh 2:24; Jud 14.

[237] Cf. *Sib. Or.* 3:778.

[238] For some reason, the *ECM* does not cite Isidorus Pelusiota at this point: τὰ κύματα τὰς ἑαυτῶν ἀπαφρίζουσιν αἰσχύνας κτλ. (*Ep.* 58 in PG 78:1109 [A2, line 20-21]).

[239] Albin thinks that ἐπαφρίζοντα is better attested than ἀπαφρίζοντα, especially in light of the irregular orthography of 𝔓⁷² (*Judasbrevet*, 611).

[240] Royse, "Scribal Habits," 473-74. In one case, ε is taken for α (2 Pet 3:14).

line 32.[241] To my knowledge, the earliest attestation to the verb ἀπαφρίζω is found in a medical text of Galen (2nd century C.E.), *De sanitate tuenda libri vi*.[242] In the context of anatomy, the noun ἀφρός, "foam," and the related verbs ἀφρίζω, "to produce a foam," ἐπαφρίζω, and ἀπαφρίζω normally refer to foam or froth at the mouth. Both ἀφρος and ἀφρίζω are well attested in Greek literature and in the NT (e.g., Matt 9:18, 20; Luke 9:39).

With the passage of Moschus in mind, Bigg finds the language in Jude 13 "tinctured by reminiscences of Greek poetry," but quickly adds that "the image is probably suggested by Isaiah 57:20."[243] That passage reads as follows: "But the wicked are like the tossing sea that cannot keep still; its waters toss up mire and mud" (NRSV). Bauckham agrees with Bigg's judgment, and points out that the author clearly had the Hebrew text before him, since the last clause is missing in the LXX.[244] Bauckham did not consider the presence of the clause in some LXX witnesses, καὶ ἀποβάλλεται τὸ ὕδωρ αὐτῆς καταπάτημα καὶ πηλός.[245] The Greek verb ἀποβάλλω means "throw away," "throw off," and corresponds to the Hebrew, גָּרַשׁ, "cast out," "thrust out" (Qal.). Bauckham draws attention to two other significant passages from the Qumran hymns that echo Isa 57:15: "they have reared like turbulent seas, and their towering waves have *spat out* mud and slime" (1QH 2:27-28); and, "they cast their slime *upon me*" (1QH 8:15) (my italics).[246] It is impossible to conclude safely whether the metaphor in Jude 13 was extended to include the notion of shame cast off on the shore, i.e., on church members; but in any case, the interpretation of the Masoretic version of Isa 57:20, reflected in all of these sources, speaks in favor of ἀπαφρίζοντα in Jude 13.

The metaphor in Jude 13 breaks off somewhat abruptly with αἰσχύνας, "shames." The word may refer to shameful deeds in general, but in the particular context, and in connection with vv. 15-16 the specific reference

---

[241] *Idyll* 5,5 (Gow): ἁ δὲ θάλασσα κυρτὸν ἐπαφρίζῃ; *Alexipharmaca* 32 (Gow and Scholfield): ὡς δ᾽ ὁπότ᾽ ἀγριόεσσαν ὑποθλίψαντες ὀπώρην Σιληνοὶ κεραοῖο Διωνύσοιο τιθηνοὶ πρῶτον ἐπαφρίζοντι ποτῷ φρένα θωρηχθέντες ὄθμασι δινήθησαν ἐπισφαλεροῖσι δὲ κώλοις Νυσαίην ἀνὰ κλιτὺν ἐπέδραμον ἀφραίνοντες.

[242] K. Koch, ed., *Galeni de sanitate tuenda libri vi* (CMG 5.4.2; Leipzig: Teubner, 1923), 120,3; 125,21.

[243] Bigg, *A Critical and Exegetical Commentary*, 335.

[244] Bauckham, *Jude, 2 Peter*, 88.

[245] The second part of Isa 57:20 is attested in what Rahlfs considers *L* (Lucian), and in *O* (Origen's *Hexapla*, marked with an asterisk), and in citations of Theodoret. It is also present in Hebrew witnesses from Qumran, which means it was long available for Greek revisors to use. The variant has strong attestation in "*L*" witnesses (= "Antiochan" text) which frequently attests pre-Christian readings.

[246] Bauckham, *Jude, 2 Peter*, 88,

may be to *shameful words* or *shameful* (i.e., licentious) *teachings*.[247] The anatomic connotation of ἐπαφρίζω/ἀπαφρίζω is consistent with such an interpretation. Interestingly, Alexander Monachus (6th century C.E.) uses ἀπαφρίζω in a manner reminiscent of Jude when he attacks Origen: ὁ δὲ ἐκστατικὸς Ὠριγένης ἐτόλμησε λέγειν πεπερατωμένην εἶναι τὴν τοῦ Θεοῦ δύναμιν, καὶ μυρίας ἑτέρας βλασφημίας ἀπαφρίσας καὶ ὑπέρογκα καὶ δυσεξάγγελτα ἐν τοῖς συντάγμασιν αὐτοῦ ἐκληρήσας κτλ.[248]

In conclusion, this metaphor, possibly based on Isa 57:20, likens the opponents to tumultuous waves that cause dirty foam (i.e., "their own shame") not only to appear on the surface, but, as I suggest, to be cast off from them (in preference of ἀπαφρίζοντα).[249] A similar interpretation of Isa 57:20 is reflected in at least part of the LXX tradition and in other Jewish sources. The strongest argument in favor of the reading ἐπαφρίζοντα from the intrinsic viewpoint is the early attestation of the verb by Moschus and Nicander, whereas the verb ἀπαφρίζω is attested in later sources from the second century onwards and could have been introduced by a later scribe, if not by phonetic error. Nevertheless, the latter verb may well have been in use at the time when the Epistle of Jude was written, especially in light of the established use of ἀφρός/ἀφρίζω in Greek literature and in the NT. In my view, the state of the evidence is ambiguous, but I slightly prefer the variant with ἀπαφρίζοντα in this passage.[250] In any case, I am somewhat surprised that the variant is not marked with a bold dot in the *ECM*.

---

[247] Thus B. Reicke says of the passage, "The waves of the sea pound upon the rocks or against the sides of a ship, but the looming surf is froth and spray without effect. This is equally true of the insolence and 'big words' (cf. vss. 15, 16) which come foaming from the mouths of the heretical teachers as they rave against society and the church" (*The Epistles of James, Peter and Jude* [AB 37; New York: Doubleday, 1964], 207); cf. BDAG, s.v. αἰσχύνη 3.

[248] Alexander Monachus, *Inventio crucis* (PG 87:4021).

[249] Osburn questions the assumption that the metaphor rests upon Isa 57:20, and instead he suggests that it derives from *1 En.* 67:5-7, which speaks about "convulsion of the waters" in connection with the imprisoned angels who had led astray mankind ("1 Enoch 80:2-8 [67:5-7] and Jude 12-13," *CBQ* 47 [1985]: 296-303, esp. 302). Whether correct or not, Osburn effectively dismantles Oleson's argument that the metaphor in Jude depends on the birth of Aphrodite (cf. ἀφρός) in Hesiod's *Theogony* (ibid., 298-99). As for Osburn's main argument that *1 Enoch* provided the essential framework for the metaphors in Jude 12-13, this had already been suggested by Bauckham (*Jude, 2 Peter*, 91).

[250] Landon prefers ἐπαφρίζοντα for two reasons; first, he thinks ἀπαφρίζοντα does not fit the context, since it implies that once the opponents had cast off their deeds of shame, they were free and had abandoned them; secondly, the change to ἀπαφρίζοντα was a reaction to ἐπαφρίζοντα as a *hapax legomenon* (*Text-Critical Study*, 109-10). None of these arguments is valid; in my opinion, the iterative perspective is equally present, or even enhanced, with ἀπαφρίζοντα, the image being of waves constantly casting off their foam upon the shore, and this word is as rare as ἐπαφρίζοντα. The variant μεταφρίζοντα cited by Landon (imported from Kubo, 𝔓⁷² *and the Codex Vaticanus*, 87) does not exist in the textual tradition.

A few MSS read αὐχένας (1501 1751 L1178), which is considered to be an error by the *ECM* editors.[251] However, the reading makes perfect sense; αὐχήν can refer either to the throat (of men or animals), or, methaphorically, to a neck of land (isthmus) or a narrow sea.[252] The unexpected interruption of the metaphor may have led some scribes to copy αὐχένας, with the double meaning ("causing their *throats/isthmuses* to foam").

13,16-18: ἀστέρες πλανῆται {e+i}

MS 03 reads ἀστέρες πλάνητες. The noun πλάνης in 03 equally corresponds to the adjective πλανήτης. In fact, the actual expression with the noun (ἀστέρες πλάνητες) is not rare in Greek literature.[253] Nevertheless, the variant in 03 could be explained as an assimilation to the preceding noun with the same ending.[254]

13,20-28: οἷς ὁ ζόφος τοῦ σκότους {e+i}

A few MSS (𝔓⁷² 03 1844) omit the article before ζόφος, which is probably due to a transcriptional error where O in OICO was dropped, or perhaps it was dropped deliberately and stylistically since ζόφος had not been previously mentioned within this particular context. As a consequence, the scribe of 03 also omitted the article before σκότους.[255]

13,30-32: εἰς αἰῶνα {e+i}

The reading εἰς αἰῶνα is attested by the best MSS and by many Byzantine witnesses (𝔓⁷² 01 02 03 04 81 88 307 326 431 436 453 808 1505 1611 1739 2138 2200 *pm*). Other Byzantine MSS attest εἰς τὸν αἰῶνα (018 049 056

---

[251] Hence, the masculine article in 1501 is also marked as an error (f) in the *ECM*.

[252] LSJ, s.v. αὐχήν.

[253] See several examples in BDAG, s.v. πλανήτης (v.l. πλάνης); cf. Theophilus, *Autol.* 2.15: ἐκ τόπου [ἀστέρες], οἱ καὶ πλάνητες καλούμενοι.

[254] For similar cases of assimilation in 03, see Weiss, *Die Katholischen Briefe*, 81-82.

[255] Landon, who treats the two articles as separate units, thinks the omission of the second article is due to homoioteleuton (*Text-Critical Study*, 111). I think the scribe more likely omitted the second article because the first article (or both) was lacking in the exemplar. Cf. the passage in 1 Pet 2:24-25, ἰάθητε. ἦτε γάρ, where 03 omits ἦτε γάρ; ἦτε after ἰάθητε was probably already omitted in the exemplar of 03 (haplography) and γάρ was omitted in a second stage, perhaps by the scribe of 03 (cf. the omission of οὓς δέ in vv. 22-23 after διακρινομένους).

0142 *pm*), whereas the variant εἰς αιῶνας is attested by relatively few MSS (044 442 1837 *al*). The versions are ambiguous at this point.

In the NT, the set expression εἰς τὸν αἰῶνα occurs some thirty times, whereas εἰς αἰῶνα is very rare (only here in the edition of NA[27]) and εἰς αἰῶνας occurs only in Rev 14:11.[256] If we turn to the LXX (including the Apocrypha), εἰς τὸν αἰῶνα occurs over 300 times, εἰς αἰῶνα 20 times and εἰς αἰῶνας only twice. Landon thinks the transcriptional evidence is ambiguous; scribes could either have harmonized the text to the set expression εἰς τὸν αἰῶνα, or else they could have omitted the article in εἰς αἰῶνα(ς), but when he considers intrinsic evidence he finds seven examples of other set expressions in Jude, which leads him to conclude that the author probably used another set expression here.[257] However, Landon's explanation of how the variant εἰς αἰῶνας arose requires two stages (omission and addition) and neglects the basic text-critical rule to prefer that reading which best explains the other readings.

Thus, the reading εἰς αἰῶνα best explains both the rare reading εἰς αἰῶνας (the added sigma could have been influenced from the preceding εἰς) as well as εἰς τὸν αἰῶνα (an assimilation to the set expression, or (less likely) to the collocations in v. 25, πρὸ παντὸς τοῦ αἰῶνος καὶ νῦν καὶ εἰς πάντας τοὺς αἰῶνας).[258] In addition to this evidence, we have the parallel passage in 2 Pet 2:17 (which Landon neglects). Among the many good MSS that import the phrase from Jude, the reading εἰς αἰῶνα has overwhelming manuscript support. In conclusion, the adopted reading εἰς αἰῶνα not only has the best manuscript support, but it also accounts adequately for the rise of all other variant readings in Jude 13 and 2 Pet 2:17.[259]

14,2: προεφήτευσεν {e>i}

A few MSS attest the alternative form ἐπροφήτευσεν (𝔓[72] 03*). MS 01 is ambiguous with προεπροφήτευσεν. Moulton states that according to a "primitive rule" the augment falls between the last preposition in verbs compounded with one or more prepositions, and this occurs also in indirect compounds where there is no real composition (the verb derives from

---

[256] Note that in the Byzantine text, only Jude 13/2 Pet 2:17 have εἰς αἰῶνα but εἰς τὸν αἰῶνα occurs 29 times, and εἰς αἰῶνας only once (Rev 14:11).

[257] Landon, *Text-Critical Study*, 111-12.

[258] Only 11 MSS out of 68 possible MSS actually add τοῦ here and also before αἰῶνος in v. 25.

[259] The deviant word order in the bilingual 629, τετήρηται εἰς αἰῶνα, follows the Latin column, *servata est in eternum*.

προφήτης, whereas φητεύω does not exist), hence προεφήτευ(σ)-.[260] However, sometimes the association with the original noun (προφήτης) was so vividly present that the rule was resisted; thus, ἐπροφήτευ(σ)- is the common form in the LXX (contra Moulton; but cf. Sir 46:20 προεφήτευσεν, which seems to be the only exception), and in the non-Byzantine MSS of the NT, where of course the root word προφήτης was especially well known.[261] Consequently, Landon sees the variant προεφήτευσεν as an "Atticist correction," and questions why the editors of UBS⁴ prefer the "non-Attic variant" ἐπροφήτευσα and its derivatives at Matt 7:22; 11:13; 15:7; Mark 7:6; Luke 1:67 and John 11:51, but not in Jude 14.[262] I suggest that a glance at the external evidence explains just why the editors made a different decision in Jude 14; the manuscript support for the form ἐπροφήτευ(σ)- is stronger in these other passages:[263]

> Matt 7:22: 01 03* 04 019 032 038 *f*¹³ 33 (05 lacunose)
> Matt 11:13: 01 03* 04 05 *f*¹³ 1 33 124 579 788 1346 1582*
> Matt 15:7: 01 03* 04 05 019 038 124 579
> Mark 7:6: 01 03* 05 019 032 037 038 *f*¹³ 1 33 565 579 788 1071 (04 lacunose)
> Luke 1:67: 01* 02 03* 04 019 032 037 038 039 041 044 1 124 1071 (05 ειπεν)
> John 11:51: 𝔓⁴⁵ 𝔓⁶⁶ 01 03 05 038 33 (𝔓⁷⁵ 04 lacunose)
> Acts 19:6: 𝔓⁷⁴ 01 02 03 05 1 88 104 1175 1837 (04 lacunose)

In matters of orthography the proclivities of an individual scribe must be considered.[264] Looking at the above data, we may conclude that the papyri and the great uncials (first hands) *never* attest that form προεφήτευ(σ)- in passages outside Jude.[265] Therefore it comes as no surprise to find that MS 03 and probably MS 01 support ἐπροφήτευσεν in Jude 14.[266] Besides these

---

[260] James H. Moulton, *Accidence and Word Formation* (vol. 2 of *Grammar of New Testament Greek* [1929]; ed. James H. Moulton, W. F. Howard and Nigel Turner; 4 vols. Edinburgh: T. & T. Clark, 1908-1976), 192.

[261] Thus, Moulton regards προεφήτευσεν as "Attic" (ibid.); cf. BDF §69.

[262] Landon, *Text-Critical Study*, 113.

[263] The manuscript evidence is compiled from the *NTGM* volumes (Swanson).

[264] Landon supplies manuscript evidence from the parallels in Tischendorf (ibid.). Although his approach of radical eclecticism prevents him from placing any weight on external evidence, he ought to have considered the predisposition of individual scribes in the light of the evidence he presents.

[265] It should be noted that the bulk of the Byzantine MSS universally read προεφήτευ(σ)- throughout the NT.

[266] The *ECM* editors cite 01f in support of ἐπροφήτευσεν, whereas the same MS is cited in NA²⁷ within parenthesis in support of προεφήτευσεν. In my opinion, it is preferable to account for the ambiguous reading without a definite decision as to which variant it supports, although one should bear in mind the consistent attestation of the form ἐπροφήτευ(σ)- elsewhere in the MS.

two manuscripts only 𝔓⁷² supports the form in Jude. However, in Jude more weight should be assigned to MSS that either attest both forms elsewhere (e.g., 02 044 33 88), or that go against their normal tendency (e.g., 04).

Outside the NT we find that both spelling forms were current; in Josephus' writings, the form προεφήτευ(σ)- dominates completely;[267] in the writings of Philo the internally augmented form occurs only twice, both times προεφήτευ(σ)-.[268] The evidence shows that both forms were current in the time when the Epistle of Jude was written.[269]

In conclusion, external evidence definitely favors προεφήτευσεν in Jude 14, whereas internal evidence is ambiguous; although both forms were in use during the 1st century, the NT authors seem to have preferred the form ἐπροφήτευ(σ)-. The author of Jude, however, known for his competence in Greek, could well have used the other form, which may have caused some scribes to have harmonized it to the form most common in the LXX and in the NT.

14,22-24: ἦλθεν κύριος {e+i}

The adopted reading with anarthrous κύριος has very strong manuscript support, but some important witnesses read ἦλθεν ὁ κύριος (01 326 424Z 436 1409 1837C *al*). The fact that κύριος is absent from every other witness to the text of *1 En.* 1:9 supports the assumption that it was added by the author of Jude himself in reference to the Parousia of the Lord Jesus.[270] Thus, it is significant that the author elsewhere uses the anarthrous κύριος (vv. 5, 9) as I have argued above. The article may have been introduced by scribes under the influence of the near-parallel in Matt 25:31 (ἔλθη ὁ υἱὸς τοῦ ἀνθρώπου).[271]

---

[267] The form προεφήτευ(σ)- is attested in Josephus (ed. B. Niese), *A.J.* 2.58; 3.60; 4.311; 5.348, 351; 6.261, 335; 8.218, 242, 405, 407; 9.26, 119, 206; 10.35, 106, 112, 141; 11.6; 13.68; *B.J.* 1.69, whereas ἐπροφήτευ(σ)- occurs in *A.J.* 9.242.

[268] Philo (ed. L. Cohn et al.), *Mos.* 2.37 ; *Spec.* 2.189.

[269] In *T. 12 Patr.* (probably 2nd-1st century B.C.E.) both forms occur: in *T. Sim.* 5:6 (προεφήτευσεν) and *T. Dan* 7:3 (ἐπροφήτευσεν) (ed. M. de Jonge).

[270] For the witnesses to *1 En.* 1:9, see Vögtle, *Der Judasbrief, der 2. Petrusbrief*, 74-75.

[271] Landon regards the articular κύριος as an "anti-adoptionist alteration" (*Text-Critical Study*, 114).

14,26-32: ἐν ἁγίαις μυριάσιν αὐτοῦ {e+i} (ECM •αγιαις μυριασιν αυτου•/•μυριασιν αγιαις αυτου)

There are several problems present in this variation-unit, two of which are connected, namely the presence or absence of ἀγγέλων and the variation of the word order.

The most important witnesses are distributed as follows:

a	αγιαις μυριασιν αυτου 02 03 18 33 81 307 431 436 453 623 1067 1409 2374 𝔐 Phot PsOec **L**:VT
b	μυριασιν αγιαις αυτου 04 323 630 1243 1505 1611 1739 1881 2138 2200 *al*
e	αγιαις μυριασιν αγγελων 044
f	αγιων αγγελων μυριασιν P72
g	μυριασιν αγιων αγγελων 01
h	αγιαις μυριασιν αγγελων αυτου 61 93f 326 665f 1836 1837 *pc*
i	μυριασιν αγιων αγγελων αυτου 88 442 915 1842 1845 1846 *pc*
j	μυριασιν αγγελων αυτου αγιων 621
k	αγιαις μυριασιν 1852 1875

S:HPh ↔ *a/b*
K:B ↔ *a/b/k*
K:SᵐˢF ↔ *f/g*
K:SᵐˢˢBᵐˢˢ ↔ *i/j*
L:K ? ("with many thousands of his angels"). The Latin version (K) is reconstructed from Ps.-Cyprian at this point, but it is unclear if the latter represents a witness to the text of Jude [cf. note below]. Ps.-Vigilius has "with thousands."

At first sight the external evidence seems balanced in regard to both problems. In his study of Jude 14-15, Osburn is reluctant to dismiss the unique reading of 𝔓⁷².²⁷² Strangely, he does not discuss the word order in the context, but only the presence of the word ἀγγέλων which he thinks is a good rendition of the Aramaic text of *1 En.* 1:9 in 4QEnᶜ.²⁷³ Nevertheless,

---

²⁷² Carroll D. Osburn, "The Christological Use of 1 Enoch 1.9 in Jude 14, 15," *NTS* 23 (1977): 337-38.
²⁷³ Osburn refers in turn to Black who remarked that the 4QEnᶜ fragment (4Q204) agrees closely with 𝔓⁷² and Ps.-Cyprian (ibid., 338; Matthew Black, "The Christological Use of the Old Testament in the New Testament," *NTS* 18 [1971]: 10). Evidently, Black overlooked the presence of ἀγγέλων in other Greek witnesses; in a later article it becomes clear that this is due to his misinterpretation of Tischendorf's apparatus ("Maranatha Invocation," 193; cf. Tischendorf, *Novum Testamentum Graece* [8th ed], 2:357). The other similarity between 𝔓⁷², 4QEnᶜ and Ps.-Cyprian (and Ps.-Vigilius) in Jude 15 (πᾶσαν ψυχήν = *omnem carnem*) is shared by other Greek witnesses (01 1852). Thus, the singling out of 𝔓⁷² on the part of Black and Osburn is misleading.

Textual Commentary

299

the uniqueness of $\mathfrak{P}^{72}$ only concerns the word order. As I have mentioned above, this scribe has made a number of transpositions elsewhere, some of which involve a leap followed by a correction where omitted words are inserted out of order; this is probably what happened here. Thus, it is best to regard $\mathfrak{P}^{72}$ as a parallel witness to the text of 01.

The next thing to consider is whether ἀγγέλων is original. Osburn admits that it may be a scribal alteration influenced by passages like Matt 25:31 and 2 Thess 1:7.[274] In this connection, I think it is relevant to consider what the source in *1 En.* 1:9 *might* have looked like:

4QEn^c (4Q204):

רבו[את קדישו]הי[275]

[When (Behold) he comes with] the myriads of his holy ones[276]

Ethiopic:

And behold! he comes with ten thousand holy ones[277]

Codex Panopolitanus (6th century):

ὅτι ἔρχεται σὺν ταῖς μυριάσιν αὐτοῦ καὶ τοῖς ἁγίοις αὐτοῦ[278]

Bauckham suggests that the separation of μυριάσιν from ἁγίοις in Greek *Enoch* reflects the combination of two early Christian interpretations of Zech 14:5.[279] I agree with Bauckham that the expansion in Codex Panopolitanus reflects a Christian interpretation on the part of the translator or a scribe who was unfamiliar with the Jewish meaning of οἱ ἅγιοι which referred to angels—in Christian usage it came to signify Christians (cf. 1 Thess 4:16-17; *Did.* 16:7; *Ascen. Isa.* 4:14). In effect, this speaks against the originality of ἀγγέλων in the manuscript tradition of Jude, in which the addition represents the same type of interpretation, not

---

[274] Ibid., 338. To these passages one might add Heb 12:22 (μυριάσιν ἀγγέλων).

[275] The Aramaic text is from J. T. Milik and Matthew Black, *The Books of Enoch: Aramaic Fragments of Qumrân Cave 4* (Oxford: Clarendon, 1976), 184.

[276] Translation here (and below) follows Milik and Black, *The Books of Enoch*, 185.

[277] Translation here (and below) from Bauckham, *Jude, 2 Peter*, 95.

[278] Text here (and below) from Matthew Black, ed., *Apocalypsis Henochi Graece* (PVTG 3; Leiden: Brill, 1970), 19.

[279] Richard J. Bauckham, "A Note on a Problem in the Greek Version of 1 Enoch 1:9," *JTS* 32 (1981): 136-38.

present in the Semitic source of Jude.[280] The latter fact is also evident from the preserved Aramaic fragment, as well as from the Ethiopic witnesses.[281]

The assumption that the word ἀγγέλων was added at a later stage is confirmed by the reading ἁγίαις μυριάσιν ἀγγέλων αὐτοῦ (61 93f 326 665f 1836 1837 *pc*; 044 sine αὐτοῦ). Osburn erroneously thought these witnesses lacked ἁγίαις and therefore said of the reading that it had "every apperance of being an abbreviation of the (ℵ) 88 104 915 cop^sa text by the omission of ἁγίων."[282] On the contrary, it represents an earlier stage, in which ἀγγέλων was added to ἁγίαις μυριάσιν ("holy myriads of angels"). In a second stage, ἀγγέλων attracted ἁγίαις resulting in a change of the case ending to ἁγίων ("myriads of holy angels"). If ἀγγέλων were added to μυριάσιν ἁγίαις one would expect to find the reading μυριάσιν ἁγίαις ἀγγέλων αὐτοῦ, which is lacking in the manuscript tradition.[283]

The scenario suggested here explains the presence of all readings:

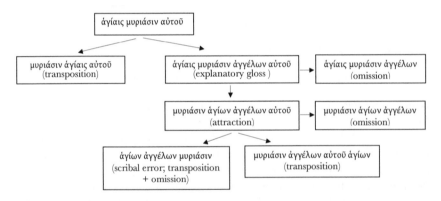

---

[280] Most commentators agree that the author of Jude was using an Aramaic source; for a recent convincing demonstration, see Edward Mazich, "'The Lord Will Come with His Holy Myriads': An Investigation of the Linguistic Source of the Citation of 1 Enoch 1,9 in Jude 14b-15," *ZNW* 94 (2003): 276-81. Note also my new argument below (the elliptic omission of "words" in the citation following the Semitic idiom).

[281] Cf. the presentation of witnesses in Vögtle, *Der Judasbrief, der 2. Petrusbrief*, 74-75. There is disagreement over the question whether the Latin text (K-text) attested in Ps.-Cyprian (*Ad Novatianum* 16.5), *Ecce venit cum multis milibus nuntiorum suorum*, and Ps.-Vigilius (*Contra Varimadum* 1.13), *Ecce venit Dominus in milibus*, offer a citation from Jude or represent a Latin translation of *1 Enoch* (see a full discussion in Dehandschutter, "Pseudo-Cyprian, Jude and Enoch," 116-17). This, however, does not affect my argument, since the presence of *nuntiorum* in the Latin still is explicable as a Christian interpretation; in fact, the complete absence of "holy" (cf. Vg: *sanctis*) in Ps.-Cyprian and Ps.-Vigilius strengthens the impression that "holy ones" was interpreted as "angels" at some point.

[282] Osburn, "Christological Use," 337.

[283] Contra Tischendorf, *Novum Testamentum Graece* (8th ed.), 2:357, whose apparatus is in error.

According to this explanation, the external evidence in favor of ἁγίαις μυριάσιν is considerably stronger than the support for the opposite order, μυριάσιν ἁγίαις, since all manuscript readings to the right side of the chart above presumably support the originality of the adopted word order. At this point we are ready to consider Landon's main argument in favor of μυριάσιν ἁγίαις—the appeal to the grammatical "rule" in Greek which says that an anarthrous adjectival attribute (of quality) *usually* follows its substantive.[284] Landon cites several examples in Jude to show that the author carefully adheres to the "rule," also when there is a preceding preposition.[285] Although I agree with Landon about the author's general preference to place the qualifying adjective before the noun, there is in this particular case an important factor which Landon neglects: the noun μυριάσιν has another qualifier in the pronominal genitive αὐτοῦ. The external evidence for αὐτοῦ is very strong, although the word is lacking in a few important witnesses (𝔓72 01 044 1852 1875), which may partly be explained by the addition of the partitive genitive ἁγίων ἀγγέλων in some of these witnesses (𝔓72 01; 044 ἀγγέλων). With αὐτοῦ present, which Landon accepts as original, both the grammatical rule and the examples of word order in Jude as cited by Landon become irrelevant. In fact, the reading preferred here, ἁγίαις μυριάσιν αὐτοῦ, reflects the common word order. All things considered, the reading ἁγίαις μυριάσιν αὐτοῦ is to be preferred.[286]

15,12: ἐλέγξαι {e+i}

The variant reading ἐξελέγξαι, which found its way into the TR, is attested in some witnesses (436 1067 1409 *al* PsOec).[287] The compound represents an amplification of ἐλέγξαι; the latter form, present in the Greek version of *1 En.* 1:9 (see below), is clearly original.

15,14-18: πάντας τοὺς ἀσεβεῖς {e>i} (*ECM* πασαν ψυχην)

From the 26th edition of Nestle-Aland and onward, the editors have preferred the reading πᾶσαν ψυχήν (𝔓72 01 1852 **K**:SBmss **S**:Phmss), now also printed in the *ECM*. In regard to external evidence, the variant πάντας τοὺς

---

[284] Landon, *Text-Critical Study*, 115 (cf. BDF §474).

[285] Ibid. To Landon's list of six examples we can add δεσμοῖς ἀϊδίοις in v. 6.

[286] Apparently, the editors of the *ECM* are hesitant, since they consider the variant μυριάσιν ἁγίαις αὐτοῦ as being of equal value (marked with bold dot).

[287] PsOec: ἐξελέγξαι (PG 119:717); Thph: ἐλέγξαι (PG 126:100).

ἀσεβεῖς has the support of most of the important witnesses (02 03 04 044 81 307 326 431 436 453 623 630 665 808 1067 1409 1837 1845 2200 2374 *al* Phot), some of which add αὐτῶν with the Majority Text (35 88 915 1836 1875 PsOec). A few MSS read πάντας ἀσεβεῖς (6 323 424C 1241 1739 1881 2298 *pc*), and a few other witnesses support τοὺς ἀσεβεῖς (442 621 L596 **L:**Vmss **S:**Phmss). The main stream of the Latin (V), the Bohairic, the Harklean and some manuscripts of the Philoxenian represent either πάντας τοὺς ἀσεβεῖς or πάντας ἀσεβεῖς. Thus, the main problem is to choose between πᾶσαν ψυχήν and πάντας τοὺς ἀσεβεῖς.

In regard to internal evidence, the first thing is to consider what was in the original source cited in Jude. Unfortunately, the Aramaic fragment has a large lacuna at this point. The witnesses to the text read as follows:

Jude 15:

> . . . ποιῆσαι κρίσιν κατὰ πάντων καὶ ἐλέγξαι <u>πάντας τοὺς ἀσεβεῖς</u> (v.l. <u>πᾶσαν ψυχὴν</u>) περὶ πάντων τῶν ἔργων ἀσεβείας αὐτῶν ὧν ἠσέβησαν καὶ περὶ πάντων τῶν σκληρῶν ὧν ἐλάλησαν κατ' αὐτοῦ ἁμαρτωλοὶ ἀσεβεῖς.

4QEnᶜ (4Q204):

> ב[שרא על עובד]י . . . [. . .] רברבן וקשי[ן
>] <u>flesh</u>, with regard to [all their] works [. . .] the proud and hard [

Codex Panopolitanus (6th century):

> . . . ποιῆσαι κρίσιν κατὰ πάντων καὶ ἀπολέσει <u>πάντας τοὺς ἀσεβεῖς</u> καὶ ἐλέγξει <u>πᾶσαν σάρκα</u> περὶ πάντων ἔργων τῆς ἀσεβείας αὐτῶν ὧν ἠσέβησαν καὶ σκληρῶν ὧν ἐλάλησαν λόγων [. . .] κατ' αὐτοῦ ἁμαρτωλοὶ ἀσεβεῖς.

Ethiopic:

> . . . to execute judgment upon them and to destroy the impious and to contend with <u>all flesh</u> concerning everything which the sinners and the impious have done and wrought against him.

Ps.-Cyprian:

> . . . *facere iudicium de omnibus et perdere omnes impios et arguere <u>omnen carnem</u> de omnibus factis impiorum quae fecerunt impie et de omnibus verbis impiis quae de Deo locuti sunt peccatores.*

Ps.-Vigilius:

> . . . *facere iudicium et perdere omnes impios et arguere <u>omnem carnem</u> de omnibus operibus impietatis eorum.*

The citation of this extended portion of text shows that the author of Jude has adapted and modified that text. Osburn correctly observes that the author has omitted the reference to the destruction (ἀπόλλυμι) in the first clause and the object in the second clause (πᾶσαν σάρκα), and that the remaining elements of the two clauses have been joined into one, applying the prediction to the opponents.[288] There are other signs that the author of Jude has adapted the citation (cf. the discussion concerning κύριος above); so, regardless of which variant is preferred, it is clear that the original source has been rearranged in Jude. Although Osburn, followed by Bauckham, does not consider the variant reading πᾶσαν ψυχήν explicitly, I think he is correct in his main point that the author of Jude was applying the text exclusively to the opponents.[289] In fact, the coming judgment (κρίσιν) of the opponents, characterized as ἀσεβεῖς, is anticipated in v. 4: οἱ πάλαι προγεγραμμένοι εἰς τοῦτο τὸ κρίμα, ἀσεβεῖς. It is not evident that the author is referring exclusively to the prophecy of Enoch in v. 4, but the links are remarkable.[290] We should also note in this connection the author's particular fondness for the word-group ἀσεβ-, with six occurrences in 25 verses.[291]

In regard to stylistic considerations, Landon presents another piece of evidence in favor of πάντας τοὺς ἀσεβεῖς by drawing attention to the author's use of triadic expressions with πᾶς + definite article + adjective or substantive: πάντας τοὺς ἀσεβεῖς, πάντων τῶν ἔργων, πάντων τῶν σκληρῶν.[292] In this connection, Landon compares the three phrases with the text of Codex Panopolitanus, which suggests that the author of Jude himself developed this "stylistically polished formula":[293]

---

[288] Osburn, "Christological Use," 338.

[289] Bauckham, *Jude, 2 Peter*, 94. Perhaps the odd sequence of events in *1 En.* 1:9 also prompted the abbreviation (coming to execute judgment against all; to destroy all the wicked; to convict all flesh); cf. LXX Jer 32:31 (judgment against all flesh; the guilty put to the sword).

[290] Bauckham thinks τοῦτο τὸ κρίμα in v. 4 refers to the condemnation at the Parousia, "prophesied typologically in vv 5-7, 11, and directly in vv 14-15" (*Jude, 2 Peter*, 37); cf. Kühl who says, "[U]m dieses Begriffes [ἀσεβεῖς] willen, mit welchem der Verf. jene Gegner in V. 4 zusammenfassend bezeichnete, hat er gerade diese Henochstelle gewählt" (*Die Briefe Petri und Judae*, 324).

[291] Cf. Mayor's remark: "This word [ἀσεβεῖς] may be almost said to give the keynote to the Epistle (cf. vv. 15, 18) as it does to the Book of Enoch" (*The Epistle of St. Jude*, 26).

[292] Landon, *Text-Critical Study*, 117-18 (cf. 55-56). J. Daryl Charles points out that 20 such triadic sets appear within the 25 verses of the letter, although Charles here prefers πᾶσαν ψυχήν (*Literary Strategy*, 41).

[293] Ibid. David J. Clark questions Landon's preference for a "stylistically polished formula," since it means that the author introduces the root ἀσεβ- a fourth time into one sentence, which is "hardly conducive to stylistic polish" ("Discourse Structure in Jude," 137). On the

1 En. 1:9	Jude 15
πάντας τοὺς ἀσεβεῖς	πάντας τοὺς ἀσεβεῖς
πάντων ἔργων	πάντων τῶν ἔργων
σκληρῶν	πάντων τῶν σκληρῶν

Wachtel instead prefers the reading πᾶσαν ψυχήν, altough he admits that it has relatively weak attestation.[294] His argument that the verb ἐλέγχω does not fit with ἀσεβεῖς is farfetched in my opinion.[295] More importantly, Wachtel thinks πᾶσαν ψυχήν best reflects *1 En.* 1:9—but he does not seriously consider the apparent abbreviation of the source in Jude; in a footnote he briefly dismisses Osburn's suggestion ("Korrektur") of a conscious abbreviation because he thinks it does not explain the reading πᾶσαν ψυχήν.[296] Instead Wachtel suggests that the reading πάντας τοὺς ἀσεβεῖς developed as a more precise specification ("Präzisierung") of πᾶσαν ψυχήν via πάντας ἀσεβεῖς.[297]

I think it is indeed possible to explain πᾶσαν ψυχήν; the reading could either represent a conformation to κατὰ πάντων (so Albin), or an influence from Rom 2:9, where the same collocation occurs (so Kubo).[298] Whereas Wachtel's explanation of the reading πάντας ἀσεβεῖς as a form older than πάντας τοὺς ἀσεβεῖς is necessary for his hypothesis, I think the weakly attested reading is simply the result of scribal deletion of the article, either because it was felt unnecessary, or else by accident due to homoioteleuton.[299] However, I do agree with Wachtel's assessment of the superfluous addition of αὐτῶν by the Majority Text, which was probably meant to clarify and link to the preceding πάντων.

In conclusion, internal evidence is a bit ambiguous, but it slightly favors πάντας τοὺς ἀσεβεῖς, a reading that should be preferred, since it also has the stronger manuscript support.

---

other hand, Clark's observation supports the reading from the point of transcriptional probability.

[294] Wachtel, *Der Byzantinische Text*, 359.

[295] See e.g., LXX Prov 9:7, ἐλέγχων δὲ τὸν ἀσεβῆ; cf. Wis 1:8 where it is said that those who utter unrighteous things will be punished by divine justice (ἐλέγχουσα ἡ δίκη).

[296] Ibid., 359, n. 324.

[297] Ibid., 359.

[298] Albin, *Judasbrevet*, 615; Kubo, *𝔓72 and the Codex Vaticanus*, 88.

[299] The same reasons can explain the omission of ἀσεβείας αὐτῶν in many of the same MSS later in the verse (01 6 323 424C 1241 1739 1881 2298 *pc*). It is also possible that the scribes (or a common scribal archetype) wanted to avoid what was perceived as an excessive repetition of words reflecting the stem ἀσεβ-.

15,20-30: περὶ πάντων τῶν ἔργων ἀσεβείας αὐτῶν {e+i}

The most significant MSS are distributed as follows:

περι παντων των εργων ασεβειας αυτων 02 03 33 81 88 431 436 623 665 808 915 1067
   1409 1836 1875 𝔐 PsOec
περι παντων εργων ασεβειας αυτων 326 1837 *pc*
περι παντων των εργων των ασεβειων αυτων 044Z 630 1505 1611 2138 2200 2495 *pc*
περι παντων εργων ασεβειων αυτων 1852
περι παντων των εργων αυτων 04 307 442 453 621 1845 *pc*
περι παντων των ασεβειων αυτων 044T
περι παντων των εργων 01 323 424C 1739 2374 *pc* **K:**S S:Ph

The Latin text type "V" supports the adopted reading with or without the articles, and so does a manuscript of the Harklean and the Bohairic witnesses, allowing for variation in word order (all Bohairic witnesses construe αὐτῶν with ἔργων; the other manuscript witnesses to the Harklean version support the readings with ἀσεβειῶν). The Fayyumic witness most likely represents περὶ τῶν ἔργων, unattested by Greek MSS. The omission in 𝔓⁷² of a longer stretch of text (περί . . . καί) is a case of haplography.

The adopted reading has the best manuscript support. In regard to intrinsic evidence, we must again consider the possible source text of Jude (see above). A glance at the witnesses to *1 En.* 1:9, especially the Greek version, shows that various elements are omitted in the shorter readings among these witnesses, possibly due to homoioteleuton (-ων^-ων). The remaining problem concerns the choice between ἀσεβείας and (τῶν) ἀσεβειῶν. The Greek version of *1 En.* 1:9 (Codex Panopolitanus) clearly supports the former, whereas the Latin witnesses (Ps.-Cyprian and Ps.-Vigilius) are a bit ambiguous at this point. From the perspective of transcriptional probability, the variant readings with ἀσεβειῶν are likely secondary, since the plural ending conforms to ἔργων and αὐτῶν, making the whole phrase resemble v. 18, τὰς ἑαυτῶν ἐπιθυμίας . . . τῶν ἀσεβειῶν.[300] In conclusion, the adopted reading has the best external and internal support and most clearly explains all other readings.

15,42-44: τῶν σκληρῶν {e<i}

The insertion of λόγων has early and widespread attestation (01 04 33 81 88 307 323 442 453 621 630 665 915 1505 1611 1739 1845 2138 2200

---

[300] Cf. the collocation πασῶν τῶν ἀσεβειῶν that occurs in similar contexts of divine judgment in LXX Ezek 14:6; 18:28, 30 and also may have influenced scribes.

2374 **L**:T^mss **K**:SF **S**:HPh).[301] The Majority Text does not add λόγων, which is somewhat surprising.[302] However, the attestation by the HK group reflects its presence in an early stratum of the Byzantine text.

Many commentators simply regard λόγων as an explanatory gloss.[303] Such an emendation would be equivalent to ῥημάτων attested in 628Z. On the other hand, the noun is present, albeit transposed, in the Greek version of *1 En.* 1:9, σκληρῶν ὧν ἐλάλησαν λόγων, and the Latin witness (Ps.-Cyprian) reads *de omnibus verbis impiis* ("of all wicked words").[304] Unfortunately, the Aramaic witness (4QEn^c = 4Q204) is lacunose at this point (it breaks off with "the proud and hard"). However, the same phrase is repeated in *1 En.* 5:4, of which we have an Aramaic witness (4QEn^a = 4Q201), and it is clear that the expression "proud and hard" in Jude reflects the use of a Semitic idiom (Aram. רברבן וקשין), whereas the explicit λόγων in other witnesses is an emendation to the text of Jude as well as of *1 En.* 1:9 (the Greek version of *1 En.* 5:4 does supply λόγους). This is also another fresh argument for the fact that the author of Jude used a Semitic source.[305]

From the viewpoint of transcriptional probability, the word could have been omitted in Jude due to homoioteleuton on the part of scribes. However, Weiss regards it very unlikely that, out of the five words ending with -ων, scribes would have omitted λόγων, were it original; instead he thinks the noun was added in correspondance with ἔργων, although the word is in fact quite dispensable with the circumlocution σκληρῶν ὧν ἐλάλησαν.[306] One should also note that the same figure of speech occurs in

---

[301] For some reason, the *ECM* does not cite **L**:T^mss in support of λόγων at this point, although several VL MSS read *duris verbis* (or *durisque verbis*). The reading is also found in Ps.-Hilarius and Bede (Thiele, *Epistulae Catholicae*, 427).

[302] Cf. Wachtel who includes a list of "Untypische Mehrheitslesarten," but only selected from the Teststellen; in Jude he includes the omission of ἡμῶν in v. 3 ("weniger glatte Lesart") and αὐτούς for ὑμᾶς in v. 24 ("mit unsinnigem Ergebnis") (*Der byzantinische Text*, 81-82).

[303] So Weiss, *Die Katholischen Briefe*, 53; Bauckham, *Jude, 2 Peter*, 93; Landon, *Text-Critical Study*, 120.

[304] As mentioned above, scholars disagree over whether Ps.-Cyprian offers a citation from Jude or represents an independent Latin translation of 1 *En* 1:9. Thus, in my opinion the Latin text type "K," reconstructed from Ps.-Cyprian, should not be cited in support of λόγων here without qualification (contra *ECM*).

[305] In Bauckham's extensive discussion he compares the phrases including the occurrence in *1 En.* 5:4, but in this connection, he only points out that the adjective "great" (רברבן) is omitted in Jude (*Jude, 2 Peter*, 96). Mazich, on the other hand, is in error when he thinks the equivalent to רברבן is missing in the Greek and Ethiopic versions of *1 En.* 1:9 (which it is not), nor does he refer to other passages like *1 En.* 5:4, which could partly explain Jude 15-16 ("'The Lord Will Come,'" 280-81).

[306] Weiss, *Die Katholischen Briefe*, 53.

Jude 16, καὶ τὸ στόμα αὐτῶν λαλεῖ ὑπέρογκα, where once more no need exists (nor MSS support!) for further specificity.

In conclusion, external evidence is ambiguous, but intrinsic and transcriptional probability speak strongly against λόγων.

(16,8: μεμψίμοιροι)

This rare word and the word ὑπέρογγκα in the same verse are the two most commonly misspelled words in the textual tradition of Jude. Very often the MSS attest the itacistic μεμψίμυροι (itacisms are not recorded in the errata list). Possibly, many transmittors or translators of the text were unfamiliar with the meaning of the word and may have been influenced by μυριάσιν in the context (v. 14). Thus, in a manuscript witness to the Syriac Harklean, the Greek μεμψίμυροι is noted in the margin and erroneously translated "ten thousand."[307]

16,14-16: ἐπιθυμίας ἑαυτῶν {e<i} (*ECM* •επιθυμιας εαυτων•/•επιθυμιας αυτων)

The manuscript support is mainly divided between ἐπιθυμίας ἑαυτῶν (𝔓⁷²CV 04 020 35 323 436 442 621 808 1067 1409C 1739 1845 1852 *pm*) and ἐπιθυμίας αὐτῶν (01 02 03* 33 81 88 307 326 431 453 623 630 665 915 1409*1836 1837 1875 2200 2374 *pm*). The scribe of 𝔓⁷² omitted a long passage probably because of homoioteleuton (μεμψίμοιροι . . . πορευόμενοι), but added the missing portion in the lower margin. A corrector of Vaticanus (03C2) adds a spiritus asper, αὐτῶν, thus indirectly supporting ἑαυτῶν. A few witnesses reverse the word order, ἑαυτῶν ἐπιθυμίας, whereas a few other add ἰδίας in front of ἐπιθυμίας (ἑ)αυτῶν. Two MSS replace ἐπιθυμίας with ἀσεβείας, in harmony with v. 15 (ἀσεβείας αὐτῶν).

Thus, the main choice is between ἑαυτῶν and αὐτῶν. This type of variation in the NT is many times a matter of taste on the part of the individual author.[308] In fact, the aspirated form of the personal pronoun (as in 03C2) and probably also the unaspirated form can have a reflexive

---

[307] This same manuscript (MS New College 333, Oxford) forms the basis of White's edition of the Harklean version, which he erroneously called the "Philoxeniana" (*Actus apostolorum et epistolas catholicas complectens* [vol. 1 of *Actuum apostolorum et epistolarum tam catholicarum quam Paulinarum, versio Syriaca Philoxeniana*; Oxford, 1799]).

[308] Thus, Westcott and Hort comment on the matter in their notes on orthography: "The extent to which simple personal pronouns are replaced by strong reflexive forms is variable in all Greek literature, being partly dependent on individual taste: but in the New Testament reflexive pronouns are certainly employed with unusual parsimony" (Westcott and Hort, "Notes on Orthography," in *The New Testament*, 2:144).

function in the NT, and therefore the editors of UBS³ felt compelled to change several places where UBS² had the rough breathing of the personal pronoun.[309]

The ambiguous nature of the external evidence increases the importance of the internal evidence. Landon appeals to the author's tendency and lists six examples in Jude where the writer uses reflexive rather than personal pronouns with participles (vv. 12, 13, 18, 19, 20, 21).[310] Although there is textual variation in several of these places and even strong external evidence against the reflexive (and personal) pronoun in v. 19, the tendency is real. From the paleographic viewpoint, it is not hard to imagine that *epsilon* would be dropped after *sigma*. On the other hand, the variant with ἑαυτῶν could also represent simply alliteration or a harmonization to the similar phrase in v. 18, κατὰ τὰς ἑαυτῶν ἐπιθυμίας (where αὐτῶν has very slim support). Although one might claim that ἑαυτῶν could reflect a general tendency among scribes to accentuate expressions in the text, such is called into question by 15,18, where the vast majority of scribes read αὐτῶν after ἀσεβείας; one should also compare the strong scribal *exclusion* of ἑαυτῶν in 19,8.

In conclusion, external and transcriptional evidence are ambiguous, whereas I see intrinsic evidence speaking decisively in favor of ἑαυτῶν.

16,19: [omit] {e+i}

A few MSS add τῇ ἀσεβείᾳ καὶ (τῇ) παρανομίᾳ (8a 459 467 1838 1842 1846ZV) or ἐν ἀσεβείᾳ καὶ ἀνομίᾳ (2544Z). The peculiar emendation was possibly influenced by the remotely similar phrase in v. 18, where ἐπιθυμία is further specified: κατὰ τὰς ἑαυτῶν ἐπιθυμίας πορευόμενοι τῶν ἀσεβειῶν, and possibly also by the passage in 2 Pet 2:16, where it is said that Balaam was rebuked for his wrongdoing: ἔλεγξιν δὲ ἔσχεν ἰδίας παρανομίας.

16,22-26: τὸ στόμα αὐτῶν {e+i}

The harder reading with στόμα in the singular is clearly original (cf. *1 En.* 5:4, σκληροὺς λόγους ἐν στόματι ἀκαθαρσίας ὑμῶν), whereas the plural, τὰ

---

[309] See further discussion and references in Bruce M. Metzger, *A Textual Commentary on the Greek New Testament* (1st corr. ed.; London/New York: United Bible Societies, 1975), 615-16. Apparently, the individual members of the UBS Committee were not in agreement over these issues.

[310] Landon, *Text-Critical Study*, 121. Landon's remark in footnote 229, that ἑαυτῶν is "against GNT4," is misleading, since UBS⁴ indeed has ἑαυτῶν—the different word order is not the issue here.

στόματα, attested in some MSS (97 218 2147 *al*) conforms to αὐτῶν. The singular reading τὸ στόμα αὐτῷ (02) is probably accidental perhaps intending αὐτοῦ (cf. L2087), but makes sense, "the mouth (speaks great swelling words) against him."

The omission of the article in some MSS (𝔓⁷² 424C 1409 *pc*) could be accidental, but is reminiscent of the phrase στόμα λαλοῦν μεγάλα in Dan 7:8, 20, echoed in Rev 13:5.

Umlaut 4 in Codex Vaticanus (03): the umlaut probably refers to the variant with plural, τὰ στόματα, or to the omission of the article.

17,8: μνήσθητε {e+i}

The well attested reading μνήσθητε is the aorist tense (imperative) of μιμνήσκομαι. One MS attests the perfect tense of the same verb (indicative), μέμνησθε (1501), used as present. A few MSS read μνημονεύετε (322 323 1241 1739 1881 2298 2544), i.e., the present tense (indicative/imperative) of μνημονεύω. Landon prefers the latter reading because he thinks the writer used present in the midrash commentary.[311] In this connection, he refers to Ellis who first drew attention to the midrashic character of Jude, where each commentary section is marked by a shift in tense (from past to present) and introduced by οὗτοί/οὗτοί εἰσιν.[312] However, Landon clearly overinterprets Ellis when he states, "The aorist is reserved for the midrash texts, and the present is reserved for the midrash commentaries."[313] In my opinion, there is a different discernible pattern, where the aorist tense consistently marks the introduction of exhortations, when the author turns to his audience:

ὑπομνῆσαι δὲ ὑμᾶς (v. 5)

ὑμεῖς δέ, ἀγαπητοί, μνήσθητε (v. 17)

ὑμεῖς δέ . . . ἑαυτοὺς ἐν ἀγάπη θεοῦ τηρήσατε (v. 20-21)

---

[311] Ibid.

[312] Earle. E. Ellis, *Prophecy and Hermeneutic in Early Christianity: New Testament Essays* (WUNT 18; Tübingen: Mohr Siebeck, 1978; repr., Grand Rapids: Eerdmans, 1978), 221-36, esp. 225. Ellis is followed by Bauckham in his commentary (*Jude, 2 Peter*). However, in later works Bauckham prefers to use the term "exegesis" or "commentary" instead of "midrash" (*Jude and the Relatives*, 180, n. 2).

[313] Landon, *Text-Critical Study*, 121.

On transcriptional grounds, it could be argued that the variant with the aorist of μιμνήσκομαι is a scribal harmonization to the parallel passage in 2 Pet 3:2, μνησθῆναι τῶν προειρημένων ῥημάτων (without textual variation), but in this case the parallel can equally be adduced as an argument for the aorist on intrinsic grounds—the author of 2 Peter imported the aorist from Jude. Besides, the form μνήσθητε occurs only here and in Luke 24:6 and is the harder reading, whereas μνημονεύετε is more common (Matt 16:9; Mark 8:18; Luke 17:32; John 15:20; Eph 2:11; Col 4:18; 1 Thess 2:9; 2 Thess 2:5; Heb 13:7). The form of the singular reading μέμνησθε (1501) occurs only in 1 Cor 11:2, but this is too remote to have had any likely influence. In any case, this scribe is rather creative in Jude (cf. vv. 3, 9, 13). In conclusion, external and internal evidence support the reading μνήσθητε.

17,10-16: τῶν ῥημάτων τῶν προειρημένων {e>i} *(ECM •ρηματων των προειρημενων•/•προειρημενων ρηματων)*

The adopted reading has the best manuscript support, but the reading τῶν προειρημένων ῥημάτων is attested by several important witnesses (02 323 424C 630 1505 1611 1739 2138 2200 2374 *al*). Internal evidence is ambiguous; the parallel passage in 2 Pet 3:2 attests to the latter word order without textual variation, which suggests a harmonizing tendency among this minority of MSS, providing compelling intrinsic evidence in the absence of any strong transcriptional evidence. However, my preference for the printed reading is based primarily on external evidence.

The other variant readings have probably arisen through various errors or interpretations on the part of individual scribes. For example, the reading ἀνειρημένων (57), "proclaimed," makes perfect sense, but the scribe is known to substitute ἀν-/ἀνα- for προ- (cf. vv. 4, 16). Curiously, another scribe wrote πρώην εἰρημένων (321), "the recently spoken," instead of προειρημένων, "spoken beforehand." This modification is not surprising, since neither reading requires a long period of time; this is further implied by ὅτι ἔλεγον ὑμῖν. Nevertheless, the author is occupied with the fulfilled predictions regarding the ungodly and their judgment, which encompasses from v. 4 onward in the body of the epistle (cf. προγεγραμμένοι; προεφήτευσεν).

17,19: [omit] {e+i}

Some scribes ascribed the epithet ἁγίων to the apostles, either as a stock epithet or possibly under the influence of 2 Pet 3:2, μνησθῆναι τῶν προειρημένων ῥημάτων ὑπὸ τῶν ἁγίων προφητῶν καὶ τῆς τῶν ἀποστόλων ὑμῶν.

18,2-6: ὅτι ἔλεγον ὑμῖν {e+i}

A few MSS replace the plural ending in ἔλεγον with the singular, ἔλεγεν (018 456 656 2473 L422). The substitution is either due to a misreading, or, as Landon suggests, a misconstrual of the preceding genitive τοῦ κυρίου ἡμῶν Ἰησοῦ Χριστοῦ, which wrongly attributes the prediction to Jesus Christ himself, rather than to the "apostles of Jesus Christ."[314] Some of these same MSS (018 L422 *al*) substitute ἡμῖν for ὑμῖν perhaps through itacism.[315]

18,8 ὅτι {e>i} (*ECM* •omit•/•οτι)

The second οτι was printed within square brackets in NA[27]/UBS[4]. In the *ECM,* it has been removed from the base text, but is marked with a bold dot in the overview of variants. The word is absent from a few witnesses (01 03 020T 044 *pc* **L:R**).[316] The internal evidence is ambiguous; in v. 14 we find the participle λέγων without ὅτι, but this single example says little of the author's habit of introducing quotations—the passage in v. 14 could even have caused scribes to drop the second ὅτι in v. 18. There is a possibility that the word was added in v. 18 by way of harmonization to the parallel passage in 2 Pet 3:2, τοῦτο πρῶτον γινώσκοντες ὅτι ἐλεύσονται. On the other hand, the text in Jude must be one from which 2 Peter has resulted, presuming that Jude is prior, and the syntactical structure (μνησθῆναι . . . τοῦτο πρῶτον γινώσκοντες ὅτι κτλ.) is reminiscent of the corresponding structure in Jude (μνήσθητε . . . ὅτι ἔλεγον ὑμῖν· ὅτι κτλ.).

---

[314] Landon, *Text-Critical Study*, 122-23.

[315] Again Landon treats two separate variants together and states that ὅτι ἔλεγον ἡμῖν is a "conflation" of ὅτι ἔλεγον ὑμῖν and ὅτι ἔλεγεν ἡμῖν (ibid., 123). In the process of combining the two variants, he also creates errors in his apparatus; whereas MSS 639 641 read ἡμῖν they do not read ἔλεγεν; MS 226 reads ὑμῖν (contra Landon).

[316] In the *ECM*, the Syriac versions (HPh) are cited in support of ὅτι. However, according to Gwynn (*apud* Mayor) the presence of the word in these versions "is only in accordance with the Syriac usage in introducing a quotation, and is no evidence as to the Greek reading" (Mayor, *The Epistle of St. Jude*, clxxxv). Gwynn's remark also applies to the Coptic versions.

Perhaps scribes would perceive the second ὅτι as superfluous and drop it; such minor stylistic improvements are not uncommon in the witnesses to the early text. In conclusion, I have chosen to retain ὅτι, primarily on the basis of stronger manuscript support.

18,10-18: ἐπ᾽ ἐσχάτου τοῦ χρόνου ἔσονται (*ECM* •επ εσχατου χρονου εσονται •/•επ εσχατου του χρονου εσονται)

1) ἐπ᾽ ἐσχάτου τοῦ χρόνου {e=i}

The external evidence is mainly divided between ἐπ᾽ ἐσχάτου τοῦ χρόνου (01 02 33 431 436 630 1067 1409 1505 1611 1837 1845 1852 2138 2200 *pc* Cyr Did Thph) and ἐπ᾽ ἐσχάτου χρόνου (𝔓72 03 04 044 623 *pc*). In addition, the reading ἐπ᾽ ἐσχάτου τῶν χρονῶν is attested by some important witnesses (81 307 323 424Z 453 1739 *pc* Cyr **K**:SBA), whereas the majority of witnesses read ἐν ἐσχάτῳ χρόνῳ (18 35 88 808 915 2374 𝔐 PsOec).[317]

The original expression in the Hebrew bible, "in the last days," is rendered in the Septuagint in a variety of ways, with ἐπί or ἐν, always including ἡμέρα in the plural, whereas ἔσχατος is either in singular or plural (cf. Num 24:14; Jos 24:27; Prov 31:26; Isa 2:2; Jer 23:20; 25:19; 37:24; Ezek 38:16; Dan 2:28; 11:20; Hos 3:5). In the Gospel of John, the set expression ἐν τῇ ἐσχάτῃ ἡμέρᾳ occurs six times (6:39, 40, 44; 7:37; 11:24; 12:48). There is no clear pattern elsewhere in the NT (see Acts 2:17; 2 Tim 3:1; Heb 1:2; Jas 5:3; 1 Pet 1:20; 2 Pet 3:3).

Nevertheless, two parallel passages are especially significant for the textual tradition of Jude; in 1 Pet 1:20 we have an attestation of the uncommon χρόνος. Now there is some textual variation in that passage; the reading ἐπ᾽ ἐσχάτου τῶν χρόνων has overwhelming support, whereas 01* and 044 read ἐπ᾽ ἐσχάτου τοῦ χρόνου; 𝔓72 reads ἐπ᾽ ἐσχάτων χρόνων; and the Majority Text reads ἐπ᾽ ἐσχάτων τῶν χρόνων. Thus, the readings in Jude that most likely represent harmonizations to 1 Pet 1:20 are: ἐπ᾽ ἐσχάτου τῶν χρόνων (81 307 323 424Z 453 1739 *al*) and ἐπ᾽ ἐσχάτων τῶν χρόνων (a number of Byzantine witnesses). Harmonization is suspected particularly among those witnesses that have the same expression in both places (e.g., 81 307 323 453 1739). Significantly, MSS 81 307 323 453 also read ἐσχάτου in 2 Pet 3:3 against the best witnesses. As for the adopted and well attested reading in Jude, ἐπ᾽ ἐσχάτου τοῦ χρόνου, only 01* uses the

---

[317] PsOec: ἐν ἐσχάτῳ χρόνῳ (PG 119:720); Thph: ἐπ᾽ ἐσχάτου τοῦ χρόνου (PG 126:100).

exact phrase in 1 Pet 1:20, which of course makes the reading suspect in 1 Pet 1:20 (but not in Jude).

If we turn to the parallel passage in 2 Pet 3:3, the reading ἐπ' ἐσχάτων τῶν ἡμερῶν has almost unequivocal manuscript support. Thus, we see that the author of 2 Peter has changed the text of Jude and used a more common phrase. This increases the probability that readings with ἐσχάτων in the plural (93 665 2344 *al* **K**:B^(mss)) and ἡμερῶν/ἡμέραις (631 1646 1881 2523) in Jude are due to parallel influence.

I agree with Wachtel who sees the Majority Text reading, ἐν ἐσχάτῳ χρόνῳ, as a normalization of the phrase where ἐπί + genitive is replaced with ἐν + dative, possibly under the influence of other passages in the NT; for example, the phrase ἐν τῇ ἐσχάτῃ ἡμέρᾳ occurs often in the Gospel of John.[318] Kubo, followed by Landon, points out that there are no similar changes among MSS from ἐπί to ἐν in Heb 1:2, 1 Pet 1:20, and 2 Pet 3:3.[319] This is an argument from silence that does not disprove ἐν as the normal form. Besides, both authors fail to consider that there are not any opposite changes from ἐν to ἐπί attested in Acts 2:17, 2 Tim 3:1 and Jas 5:3.

Kubo's suggestion is more attractive; namely that the reading ἐπ' ἐσχάτου χρόνου is ambiguous, since ἐσχάτου can be interpreted either as a noun ("in the last of time") or as an adjective ("in the last time"). This ambiguity could explain ἐν ἐσχάτῳ χρόνῳ, but I doubt that scribes, in order to resolve the ambiguity, would add an article and create a more awkward expression, ἐπ' ἐσχάτου τοῦ χρόνου, the Hebrew flavor of which rather speaks for its originality.[320] On paleographic grounds, the article could have been either dropped through haplography or added through dittography. However, Wachtel points to another plausible motive for the omission; the reading with the article presupposes the noun τὸ ἔσχατον, which could have been understood by some scribes as an accentuation of the general expression "the last days" so as to mean "the (very) last day." The problem is that v. 18 does not speak of what happens on the last day (in contrast to vv. 14-15), and, hence, the article would be deleted.[321] On the other hand, the phrase, without direct equivalent in the Septuagint, is explicable as the result of independent translation of Semitic material. In conclusion, the

[318] Wachtel, *Der byzantinische Text,* 361.

[319] Kubo, 𝔓⁷² *and the Codex Vaticanus,* 144. Cf. Landon, *Text-Critical Study,* 124.

[320] Cf. Bauckham: "Again we have evidence of the relatively independent character of Jude's translation. The rather awkward expression ('improved' by those MSS wich omit τοῦ) results from the use of ἐσχάτου as a substantive, equivalent to the Hebrew אחרית ('latter part')" (*Jude, 2 Peter,* 104).

[321] Wachtel, *Der byzantinische Text,* 360-61.

external evidence is ambiguous, but the adopted reading seems to be the more difficult reading from the viewpoint of syntax and context.

2) ἔσονται {e+i}

In regard to the second point of variation, the evidence is mainly divided between ἔσονται (𝔓⁷² 01T 03 04* 18 35 88 442 621 630 808 915 1505 1611 1845 1852 2138 2200 2374 𝔐 PsOec) and ἐλεύσονται (01Z2 02 04C2 33 81 307 323 326 424Z 431 436 453 623 665 1067 1409 1739 1837 *al* Cyr Did). The former reading has the better manuscript support, whereas the latter is clearly the result of harmonization to the parallel passage in 2 Pet 3:3, ἐλεύσονται ἐπ' ἐσχάτων τῶν ἡμερῶν. As I have argued above, the singular reading ἀναστήσονται (044) may reflect an influence from Matt 12:41 (par. Luke 11:32).

18,22-34: κατὰ τὰς ἑαυτῶν ἐπιθυμίας πορευόμενοι τῶν ἀσεβειῶν

1) ἑαυτῶν {e+i}

The external evidence unequivocally supports ἑαυτῶν. I have commented on the similar phrase in v. 16, where the intrinsic evidence became decisive in favor of ἑαυτῶν, i.e., the author's tendency to use reflexive pronouns with participles. Practically all witnesses that read αὐτῶν at this point are among the witnesses to αὐτῶν in v. 16, which strongly suggests conscious harmonization to v. 16 on the part of some scribes. Another piece of evidence is found in the parallel in 2 Pet 3:3, κατὰ τὰς ἰδίας ἐπιθυμίας αὐτῶν πορευόμενοι, where ἰδίας . . . αὐτῶν reflects ἑαυτῶν in Jude 18.

2) τὰς ἑαυτῶν ἐπιθυμίας {e+i}

Some witnesses attest a different word order, τὰς ἐπιθυμίας (ἑ)αυτων (01 630 1505 1611 2138 2200 *al*). Elsewhere the author varies the position of the reflexive pronoun (cf. vv. 6, 13, 16).[322] From the intrinsic viewpoint one could ask why the author would not use the same wording here, especially since he takes up so many elements from v. 16. On the other hand, the author may have had a written source with the apostolic prophecy before him, which more indirectly affected him when writing v. 16.

---

[322] Landon suggests that the word order pattern when a preposition is present is preposition + article + substantive + pronoun; but the argument is based on a single example in v. 16 (*Text-Critical Study*, 125).

In any case, transcriptional evidence is less ambiguous. Landon attempts to explain τὰς ἑαυτῶν ἐπιθυμίας as "internal harmonization to the position of ἑαυτῶν at vv. 6 and 13."[323] I would instead suggest that the variant favored by Landon, τὰς ἐπιθυμίας ἑαυτῶν, represents scribal harmonization to v. 16 in order to make the two phrases identical. Significantly, nearly all of the same witnesses clearly harmonized the phrase to verse 16 in the case of the pronoun (αὐτῶν).

The difficult collocation τὰς ἐπιθυμίας . . . ἀσεβειῶν, "the desire for ungodly deeds"/"ungodly desires," is replaced with τὰς ἐπιθυμίας . . . ἀσεβῶν, "the desires of the ungodly," in a few witnesses (88 915 *pc*), whereas the phrase κατὰ τὰ ἔργα αὐτῶν ἐπιθυμίαις (1875) seems influenced by Rev 20:12-13.

19,8: ἀποδιορίζοντες {e+i}

Many MSS add ἑαυτούς (04 35* 88 323 623 630 808 915 1739Z 2200 2374 *al*). The UBS Committee regarded the addition as an emendation, "clarifying the sense of the verb" in the words of Metzger.[324] The verb ἀποδιορίζω is a *hapax legomenon* which means "marking off by separating," the sense of which is a bit ambiguous. Some commentators take ἀποδιορίζοντες with what follows, ψυχικοί, πνεῦμα μὴ ἔχοντες, i.e., the opponents are accused of making classes in the community by separating *psychikos* from *pneumatikos* (the latter implicit).[325] However, the verb can also be translated "cause division" (in the church), which seems to fit better with v. 20 where the believers are exhorted to "build up themselves."

Likewise, Landon appeals to the antithetical parallel between v. 19 and 20 as an example of a common stylistic feature in Jude, but since ἐποικοδομοῦντες ἑαυτούς is at v. 20, he thinks the parallel becomes "more balanced" with ἀποδιορίζοντες ἑαυτούς ("separate themselves") at v. 19.[326] In my opinion, the balance is superficial; the real problem in this community is not that the opponents separate themselves from others, but that they have crept into the church (note the aorist tense in v. 4,

---

[323] Ibid.

[324] Metzger, *Textual Commentary*, 658. Metzger gives the impression of a weaker manuscript support than is the case at this point: "C and a number of minuscules, followed by the Textus Receptus." (The significance of the minuscules in question have indeed increased through recent research in the Catholic Epistles.)

[325] Weiss, *Die Katholischen Briefe*, 228; Kühl, *Die Briefe Petri und Judae*, 328-29; Mayor, *The Epistle of St. Jude*, clxxxvi. Cf. Paul's use of πνευματικός and ψυχικός in 1 Cor 2:14-15, which may reflect the terminology of his opponents. Also, cf. the use of φυσικῶς in Jude 10.

[326] Landon, *Text-Critical Study*, 127.

παρεισέδυσαν) and that they now participate in the common fellowship-meals (εἰσιν . . . ἐν ταῖς ἀγάπαις ὑμῶν—v. 10, present tense) and that they are causing division (ἀποδιορίζοντες—present). In 2 Pet 2:1, the author speaks in a similar vein about false teachers bringing in "factions of destruction"/"destructive opinions" (αἱρέσεις ἀπωλείας) in the church. In conclusion, I think the pronoun was added by scribes in order to conform the text to v. 20, or else in order to clarify the sense of the ambiguous participle.[327] An omission, on the other hand, is more difficult to explain.

20,8-18: ἐποικοδομοῦντες ἑαυτοὺς τῇ ἁγιωτάτῃ ὑμῶν πίστει

(*ECM* •εποικοδομουντες εαυτους τη αγιωτατη υμων πιστει•/• εποικοδομουντες εαυτους τη αγιωτατη ημων πιστει)

1) ὑμῶν {e+i} (. . . τηρήσατε {e=i} [*ECM* •τηρησατε•/•τηρησωμεν])

Some important witnesses read ἐποικοδομοῦντες ἑαυτοὺς τῇ ἁγιωτάτῃ ἡμῶν πίστει (04 323 431 1409 1739 1852 *pc*). The bold dot in the *ECM* refers to this reading. The problem in question should not be treated in isolation from the context, since the reading is a part of a potential series of "we"-readings in vv. 20-21 that affects several variants in various witnesses:

1.	2.	3.	4.
ἡμεῖς δέ	ἡμῶν πίστει	ἐν ἀγάπῃ θεοῦ τηρήσωμεν	τοῦ κυρίου ἡμῶν
04	04	𝔓72	practically all witnesses
1852	323	03	
L884*	431	04*V	
pc	1409	044	
	1739	1505	
	1852	1611	
	L884	1845	
	pc	1852	
		pc	
		Antioch	
		K:B	
		(431 *pc*: . . . τηρήσαντες)	

It is obvious that the first reading ἡμεῖς has very weak manuscript support. It could simply reflect an itacism, but the presence of all four inclusive readings in 04 and 1852 may be a sign of conscious assimilation on the part of those scribes.

---

[327] K. L. Schmidt points out that the lack of a specific object here is not odd, since any transitive verb can be used thus when emphasis is laid on the point at issue within it ("ὁρίζω, ἀφορίζω, ἀποδιορίζω, προορίζω," *TDNT* 5:456).

The fourth "we"-reading, on the other hand, is unequivocal from the perspective of external evidence. From the intrinsic viewpoint, however, the acceptance of this reading does not presuppose the originality of the other "we"-readings—the author uses the same stock phrase τοῦ κυρίου ἡμῶν Ἰησοῦ Χριστοῦ in the parallel sentence in v. 17 in connection with a 2nd person main verb (aorist imperative as I have argued). On transcriptional grounds, however, the syntactically unrelated pronoun ἡμῶν might still have influenced the first "we"-readings. In regard to the third "we"-reading, the parallel structure of v. 17 and 20-21 actually speaks for the originality of τηρήσατε, whereas the main verb in the sentence may have been changed to the 1st person (τηρήσωμεν) by scribes under the influence of τοῦ κυρίου ἡμῶν, or else because of a desire on their part to make the passage more inclusive to readers. On the other hand, the reading τηρήσωμεν has very strong manuscript support, and the imperatives in the 2nd plural in v. 17 and 22-23 could have caused the opposite change by scribes who substituted τηρήσατε for an original τηρήσωμεν. In the end, internal evidence becomes decisive in this case—the inclusive reading breaks the structure and seems too difficult.

The reading τηρήσαντες (431 *pc*) avoids the interpretation in question but is syntactically difficult and clearly represents a corruption.

As for the second "we"-reading, it too has weak manuscript support. Further, the structure in vv. 19-21 conveys a contrast between the opponents and the addressees: the former are those who cause division (οὗτοί εἰσιν οἱ ἀποδιορίζοντες), whereas the latter are exhorted by the author to build themselves up in their most holy faith. Again, the presence of τοῦ κυρίου ἡμῶν (and τηρήσωμεν/τηρήσαντες in some exemplars) could have caused some scribes to change the pronoun in the phrase τῇ ἁγιωτάτῃ ὑμῶν πίστει to ἡμῶν if not by itacism. It is also possible that the reading represents a harmonization to the similar phrases in v. 3 which speak of the common salvation and faith of (all) saints: τῆς κοινῆς ἡμῶν σωτηρίας; τῇ ἅπαξ παραδοθείσῃ τοῖς ἁγίοις πίστει.

The singular reading of 𝔓⁷², τη ἑαυτῶν ἁγιότητι πίστει ἀνοικοδομεῖσθε, is corrupt at this point and cannot be cited in support of either ὑμῶν or ἡμῶν although the 2p of the verb *may* suggest an original ὑμῶν. The presence of the reflexive pronoun ἑαυτῶν may have to do with the omission of ἑαυτούς. The verb ἀνοικοδομέω, which occurs only in 𝔓⁷² among Greek witnesses, is also attested by the Philoxenian version (in backtranslation: τῇ . . . πίστει ἀνοικοδομεῖτε/ἀνοικοδομεῖσθε ἑαυτούς).[328] Although the reading has rather

---

[328] Cf. Gwynn, *Remnants*, 82; *ECM* IV, B 153.

weak attestation, this and other similar agreements between 𝔓⁷² and the Philoxenian version suggest a common dependence of an early tradition in those cases (see above).

Thus, apart from the fourth "we"-reading only the third "we"-reading above can have a claim to originality on the basis of its strong manuscript support. But all of the three first "we"-readings clearly break the parallel structure of the larger units. Furthermore, these readings are overly difficult in connection with the exhortations that follow in vv. 22-23, with several imperatives in the 2nd person plural.

2) The word order {e>i}

The external evidence strongly supports the word order in ἐποικοδομοῦντες ἑαυτοὺς τῇ ἁγιωτάτῃ ὑμῶν (/ἡμῶν) πίστει. Nevertheless, some important witnesses attest to the word order of the Majority Text, τῇ ἁγιωτάτῃ ὑμῶν (/ἡμῶν) πίστει ἐποικοδομοῦντες ἑαυτούς (18 35 307 424 453 1836 1875 𝔐 PsOec). The peculiar reading of 𝔓⁷², τῇ ἑαυτῶν ἁγιότητι πίστει ἀνοικοδο-μεῖσθε, probably supports the latter word order.

Kubo prefers the majority word order as being the *lectio difficilior*, since it is not as smooth as the former, with the participle nearer the beginning of the sentence, but, at the same time, he admits that the word order of the neighbouring clauses may have tempted scribes to invert the order by moving the participle further ahead.[329] Hence, the internal evidence is ambiguous, but the external evidence in my opinion decisively favors the adopted reading.

20,26-21,2: προσευχόμενοι, ἑαυτοὺς (. . . τηρήσατε) {e+i}

A comma marks off ἑαυτούς, since it belongs to τηρήσατε in v. 21, and not to προσευχόμενοι. Yet, in the apparatus of the *ECM* it stands together with προσευχόμενοι. Thus, the account of the reading of 𝔓⁷², προσε(υ)χόμενοι ἑαυτοῖς ἑαυτούς, inevitably makes the witness look very suspect. The reading is of course not original, but the question is if it represents a scribal error, for example a case of dittography (ἑαυτούς commences a new line in the manuscript).[330] I think that is not the case; it is possible to take the first

---

[329] Kubo, *𝔓⁷² and the Codex Vaticanus*, 146.

[330] Kubo suggests that the intrusion of ἑαυτοῖς is due to the omission of ἑαυτούς in the preceding clause (ibid). Another possible explanation has to do with the fact that the scribe first wrote προσεχόμενοι ("pay attention to," "beware")—a verb often followed by a reflexive pronoun in the dative. But if the scribe realized at a later stage that the reflexive pronoun

pronoun with the preceding προσεχόμενοι (𝔓⁷²T) or προσευχόμενοι (𝔓⁷²Z), "paying attention to yourselves" (𝔓⁷²T)/"praying for (/with) each other" (𝔓⁷²Z) and the second pronoun with τηρήσατε. In fact, a full stop is even clearly visible after the first pronoun suggesting that such is the case. For this reason I have chosen to assign the two pronouns in 𝔓⁷² to different variation-units.

In the other MSS, there is only one pronoun following προσευχόμενοι; normally ἑαυτούς that belongs to τηρήσατε, read by the most important MSS as well as the Majority Text. Nevertheless, some other witnesses read ἑαυτοῖς (018 049 1424* 1735 *al*), which could simply represent a copying mistake; but I am inclined to think that some scribes may have taken the pronoun together with προσευχόμενοι as did the scribe of 𝔓⁷², and therefore I have assigned the MSS reading ἑαυτοῖς to the former variation-unit. Admittedly, this creates a syntactical difficulty in the subsequent unit, since the clause ἐν ἀγάπῃ θεοῦ τηρήσατε will lack an object in these MSS. No matter how one chooses to present the sequence of the two clauses there is an error in the MSS with a simple ἑαυτοίς, since the object to τηρήσατε must be in the accusative.

21,10: τηρήσατε {e=i} (*ECM* •τηρησατε•/•τηρησωμεν)

The variant has been treated above in connection with 20,8-18.

21,16: ἔλεος {e+i}

Interestingly, the marginal reading of the Harklean version representing τέλος is now found in a Greek manuscript witness (462).[331]

21,22-30: ἡμῶν Ἰησοῦ Χριστοῦ εἰς ζωήν {e+i}

Once again 𝔓⁷² has a singular reading, εἰς ζωὴν ἡμῶν Ἰησοῦ Χριστοῦ. Judging from similar transpositions elsewhere (see above), this peculiar reading was likely introduced by the scribe himself due to a misreading.

---

belonged to what follows, one would have expected the pronoun to be corrected (crossed out or marked with dots as in other places).

[331] Theophylact also attests to τέλος in the lemma, but ἔλεος in the commentary (PG 126:101); PsOec: ἔλεος (PG 119:720).

22,2-23,22: καὶ οὓς μὲν ἐλεᾶτε διακρινομένους, οὓς δὲ σῴζετε ἐκ πυρὸς ἁρπάζοντες, οὓς δὲ ἐλεᾶτε ἐν φόβῳ {e<i}

The text of vv. 22-23 has been transmitted in a large number of forms, which makes it "one of the most corrupt passages in NT literature."[332] In order to get an overview of the complex textual tradition, it is proper to first distinguish between two categories: (1) witnesses that attest a two-clause form; (2) witnesses that attest a three-clause form. The most significant MSS are distributed as follows:

1. Two-clause form:[333]

> ους μεν εκ πυρος αρπασατε διακρινομενους δε ελεειτε εν φοβω P72 **L:S K:S S:**Ph
> και ους μεν εκ πυρος αρπαζετε διακρινομενους δε ελεατε Clem
> και ους μεν ελεγχετε διακρινομενους ους δε σωζετε εκ πυρος αρπαζοντες εν φοβω 04*V
> και ους μεν ελεγχετε διακρινομενους ους δε εν φοβω σωζετε εκ πυρος αρπαζοντες 424C2V
> και ους μεν ελεατε (/ελεειτε) διακρινομενους ους δε σωζετε εκ πυρος αρπαζοντες εν φοβω 04C2V 1845T 1852 **S:**H
> και ους μεν ελεειτε διακρινομενοι ους δε σωζετε εκ πυρος αρπαζοντες εν φοβω 630 1505V 2200
> και ους μεν ελεειτε διακρινομενοι ους δε εν φοβω σωζετε εκ πυρος αρπαζοντες 18 424*V 431f 𝔐 PsOec
> και ους μεν ελεειτε διακρινομενοι ους δε σωζετε εκ πυρος αρπαζοντες 808
> και ους μεν ελεγχετε διακρινομενους ους δε σωζετε εκ πυρος αρπαζοντες 424C1V

2. Three-clause form:

> και ους μεν ελεατε διακρινομενους ους δε σωζετε εκ πυρος αρπαζετες ους δε ελεατε εν φοβω 01*
> και ους μεν ελεατε διακρινομενους ους δε σωζετε εκ πυρος αρπαζοντες ους δε ελεατε εν φοβω 01C1V 044
> και ους μεν ελεατε διακρινομενους σωζετε εκ πυρος αρπαζοντες ους δε ελεατε εν φοβω 03
> και ους μεν ελεατε διακρινομενους ους δε σωζετε εκ πυρος αρπαζοντες ους δε ελεγχετε εν φοβω 442 621
> και ους μεν ελεγχετε διακρινομενους ους δε σωζετε εκ πυρος αρπαζοντες ους δε ελεατε (/ελεειτε) εν φοβω 02 33 323 436 623 665 1067 1409 1739 1836 1837 1875 2374 **L:VT K:**B
> και ους μεν ελεγχετε διακρινομενους ους δε σωζετε εκ πυρος αρπαζοντες τους δε ελεειτε εν φοβω 0316

---

[332] Carroll D. Osburn, "The Text of Jude 22-23," *ZNW* 63 (1972): 139.

[333] For some reason, the citation of vv. 22-23 by Clement in *Strom.* 6.8.65 (GCS 52:464,23) is lacking altogether in the *ECM* (in apparatus and supplement), which is very surprising, since it is one of the most significant patristic citations of Jude.

και ους μεν ελεειτε διακρινομενοι ους δε σωζετε εκ πυρος αρπαζοντες ους δε ελεγχετε εν φοβω 307 453

και ους μεν ελεγχετε διακρινομενους ους δε εν φοβω σωζετε εκ πυρος αρπαζοντες ους δε ελεατε εν φοβω 999 1611

και ους μεν ελεατε διακρινομενους ους δε εν φοβω σωζετε εκ πυρος αρπαζοντες ους δε ελεγχετε εν φοβω 88 915 1845Z

In order to reduce the number of variants above, I treat readings with variation between ἐλεᾶτε and ἐλεεῖτε ("have mercy on") together if nothing else distinguishes the variants. The common form of the verb in the NT and the LXX is ἐλεέω, but both forms are attested. With reference to Moulton's grammar, Osburn claims that there is a tendency among "Alexandrian scribes" to write -εω verbs with -αω.[334] Apparently, he has misunderstood Moulton as did Birdsall before him; neither took into account the relevant manuscript evidence in cases of confusion between the paradigms.[335] In fact, there is no clear tendency at all among the Alexandrian scribes as is apparent from the overview in BDF §90.[336] Thus, ἐλεᾶτε is both the rarer and better attested form.[337]

In their treatments of vv. 22-23, Birdsall and Osburn both defend the two-clause format as represented by 𝔓[72] and they attempt to explain the various longer readings as expansions of it.[338] Birdsall thinks there was an intermediate form (no longer extant) that inverted the two verbs of 𝔓[72], i.e., οὓς μὲν ἐλεεῖτε διακρινομένους δὲ ἐκ πυρὸς ἁρπάσατε.[339] According to Birdsall, the reason for this interchange of verbs is found in the ambiguity of the verb διακρίνομαι; here it means either "under judgment" (𝔓[72]) or, in the three-clause forms, "doubting." It is implied in his discusssion that this ambiguity of the participle is further reflected in the transposition of the phrase ἐν φόβῳ: in the original two-clause format the phrase naturally

---

[334] Ibid., 140, n. 5; cf. Moulton, *Accidence and Word Formation*, 195-96.

[335] Birdsall, "The Text of Jude in 𝔓[72]," 398-99.

[336] In regard to this particular verb, the tendency, if any, is the opposite (cf. Rom 9:16, 18). Wachtel, however, goes too far when he says that ἐλεεῖτε is probably an "atticistic improvement" of ἐλεᾶτε (*Der byzantinische Text*, 363; cf. 368, n. 341).

[337] In Landon's discussion of vv. 22-23, he first decides that ἐλεεῖτε is to be preferred and then eliminates all of the readings in the apparatus which preserve ἐλεᾶτε! (*Text-Critical Study*, 132).

[338] Birdsall, "The Text of Jude in 𝔓[72]," 397-99; Osburn, "The Text of Jude 22-23," 139-44. It should be noted that Osburn subsequently changed his position (see further below).

[339] Birdsall does not consider the presence of the prepositional phrase ἐν φόβῳ, but from the subsequent discussion it is clear that he thinks it originally accompanied the participle. Therefore, Wachtel's critique of Birdsall is unjustified: "Spätestens hier wird die Unhaltbarkeit der Überlegungen Birdsalls deutlich, ganz abgesehen davon, daß er die Umstellung von ἐν φόβῳ übergeht" (*Der byzantinische Text*, 368).

accompanies the participle—the merciful treatment of the διακρινομένους (those under judgment) is to be accompanied by fear. In the three-clause format, on the other hand, their rescue is unaccompanied by fear, and therefore "[those] doubting" is a proper rendering of the participle in the latter context. Kubo raises a valid objection to Birdsall's proposed scenario: if ἐν φόβῳ was so troublesome because of the shift in meaning of διακρινομένους, would it not have been easier simply to drop the phrase rather than to reverse the verbs?[340]

Birdsall further assumes that the intermediate form later gave rise to the "Byzantine form with subvariants," and—we may assume—the other two-clause forms.[341] He goes on to suggest that the form of 01 is a conflation of 𝔓[72] and the intermediate form where the syllable -ους was probably duplicated by dittography. The form of 03 "arises from the same conflation but in this case [οὓς] δέ has fallen out."[342] In all of these developed forms, the simple ἁρπάσατε has been expanded to σῴζετε . . . ἁρπάζοντες. Landon attempts to show that this modification is an assimilation to 1 Cor 3:15, where the parallel link between σῴζω and πῦρ is found, but he does not mention the possibility that already the author could have had this passage in mind.[343]

Osburn accepts several of Birdsall's suggestions; first, the reversal of the two verbs because of the ambiguous participle, and, secondly, the expansion of ἁρπάσατε to σῴζετε . . . ἁρπάζοντες (because of "the ambiguity

---

[340] Sakae Kubo, "Jude 22-3: Two-division Form or Three?" in *New Testament Textual Criticism: Its Significance for Exegesis* (ed. Eldon J. Epp and Gordon D. Fee; Oxford: Oxford University Press, 1981), 245.

[341] Birdsall is rather unclear on this point and his later statement seems a bit contradictory: "Forms in which ἐλέγχετε takes the place of one or other ἐλεεῖτε, and some in which διακρινομένους is transposed into the nominative, are evident developments of the conflate text attested by ℵ" ("The Text of Jude in 𝔓[72]," 398).

[342] Ibid.

[343] Landon, *Text-Critical Study*, 133. Landon notes the presence in both passages of a similar idea of people being narrowly saved like an object passing through fire (ibid., 133-34). In fact, there are other contextual and intertextual connections between the two passages: The exhortation in Jude 20 to build up the church (ἐποικοδομέω) instead of dividing it (implied by the disputing in v. 22) corresponds to the context in 1 Cor 3 with divisions in the church (vv. 3-4) and the image of the church as God's building (v. 9). Subsequently, the individual member's building (his works) is put to test by fire in vv. 14-15: εἴ τινος τὸ ἔργον μενεῖ ὃ ἐποικοδόμησεν, μισθὸν λήμψεται · εἴ τινος τὸ ἔργον κατακαήσεται, ζημιωθήσεται, αὐτὸς δὲ σωθήσεται, οὕτως δὲ ὡς διὰ πυρός. In the light of Jude 9, another probable source of the images in vv. 22-23 is the passage in Zech 3:2-4 that speaks of Jerusalem as "a brand plucked from the fire" (ὡς δαλὸς ἐξεσπασμένος ἐκ πυρός) and of "filthy clothes" (ἱμάτια ῥυπαρὰ; cf. ἐσπιλωμένον χιτῶνα in Jude 23). Regardless of possible sources of inspiration, the composition in Jude is independent.

of ἐκ πυρὸς ἁρπάσατε"), but he sligthly modifies the scenario: he thinks διακρίνομαι was interpreted in the sense of "dispute" (as in v. 9) by a scribe who therefore substituted ἐλέγχετε for ἐλεεῖτε and then reversed the verbs, since the logical sequence of events would be first to refute or convict the disputers prior to undertaking more drastic measures, like snatching them out of the fire.[344] According to Osburn, the resultant text is reflected in 04, and, thus, the assumption of an intermediate form is unnecessary. At this crucial point, however, he wrongly cites 04 (without a second οὕς).[345] As a consequence, the subsequent discussion in which he attempts to explain the readings of 03, 01 and 02 as developments of the text of 04 is flawed.[346]

Hence, I disagree with Bauckham who thinks that both Birdsall and Osburn have given "plausible accounts" of how the other readings have originated from the two-clause form, particularly in the case of 01, 03 and 044.[347] Osburn's explanation presupposes an incredible chain of events: (1) the text of 03 is derived from the reading of 04 (wrongly cited) and $\mathfrak{P}^{72}$, affected by some primitive error (à la Hort) where ἐλεᾶτε was inserted mechanically in the first clause from the second clause (ἐλέγχετε removed); (2) the text of 01 (and 044) then arose from the conflate 03 reading; (3) the 02 reading was derived either from the 04 reading by duplication of οὕς by dittography (but 04 already has two instances of οὕς), or from the 01-03 text by an attempt to alleviate the difficulty introduced by the double ἐλεᾶτε, in which case ἐλέγχετε was reintroduced (!); (4) the text of K L P S ($\mathfrak{M}$) is an emended 01 text where the falsely duplicated ἐλεᾶτε has been omitted and ἐν φόβῳ transferred, and the Alexandrian -αω corrected to read the original -εω.[348] Hence, the original two-clause form becomes reversed (04), conflated (03), turned into a three-clause form (e.g., 01), and then changed back into a two-clause form by way of emendation ($\mathfrak{M}$).

---

[344] Osburn, "The Text of Jude 22-23," 141.

[345] Ibid. The discussion contains a number of other errors. For example, Osburn's appeal to ἁρπάζετε in 01* is misleading ("The Text of Jude 22-23," 140, n. 6). The first hand rather wrote ΑΡΠΑΖΕΤΕΣ (ες suspended at the end of the line). The syntax would have been awkward in the exemplar if it had read ἁρπάζετε. Although possible in theory, a scribal error on the part of the first hand of 01 is more likely. At another point, Osburn appeals to Albin "for arguments against the possibility of B giving rise to the form found in $\mathfrak{P}^{72}$ and Clem. Alex." ("The Text of Jude 22-23," 141, n. 10), when in fact Albin's argument has the opposite effect: Albin states that the text of $\mathfrak{P}^{72}$ and Clement are emendations of the B-text, and emphasizes that the "$\mathfrak{P}^{72}$-Clement text" cannot have given rise to the "B-text," which is the text Albin prefers (Albin, *Judasbrevet*, 626).

[346] Cf. Wachtel, *Der byzantinische Text*, 369 (with footnote 342).

[347] Bauckham, *Jude, 2 Peter*, 110; cf. Landon, *Text-Critical Study*, 131-34.

[348] Osburn, "The Text of Jude 22-23," 141-43.

Significantly, Osburn, more than Birdsall, emphasizes the "weight and diversity of the external support" of the two-clause form ($\mathfrak{P}^{72}$, *Liber Comicus*, Philoxenian, Sahidic, Clement, Jerome).[349] Wachtel, however, downplays the significance of the papyrus reading:

> So tut man gut daran, auch auf Jud 22f. die Regel anzuwenden, daß ein früher Papyrus, der von einer schwierigeren, "alexandrinisch" bezeugten Lesart stark abweicht, wahrscheinlich eine individuelle Lösung eines textlichen Problems . . . und nicht den ursprünglichen Text bezeugt. Die sekundäre Bezeugung dieser Lesart zeigt lediglich, daß es sich nicht um eine reine Singulärlesart handelt, sondern daß $\mathfrak{P}^{72}$ hier eine zu seiner Zeit weiter verbreitete Lesart bietet.[350]

Both Kubo and Wachtel argue that the three-division form with the double ἐλεᾶτε/ἐλεεῖτε is original, and that the two-division form arose because of the problem of distinguishing between the first and third groups.[351] For Kubo the ambiguous attestation by Clement to two different two-clause forms in *Strom.* 6.8.65 and *Adumbrationes*, respectively, becomes a crucial piece of evidence of how the two-clause forms evolved because of the difficulty in distinguishing between three groups.[352] In my opinion, the state of the evidence does not permit any safe conclusion as to whether Clement handled the text in different ways—the Latin evidence is of little or no value.[353] Nevertheless, I do agree with Kubo in regard to his general

---

[349] Ibid., 139-40, 144. Note, however, the three differences between the two Greek witnesses to the two-clause form, $\mathfrak{P}^{72}$ and Clement: The absence of καί and the use of the aorist, ἁρπάσατε, in $\mathfrak{P}^{72}$ (none of the variants has survived in the textual tradition, which is surprising should $\mathfrak{P}^{72}$ represent the original form), and the absence of ἐν φόβῳ in Clement's citation.

[350] Wachtel, *Der byzantinische Text*, 369. The notion of an "individual solution" in the case of $\mathfrak{P}^{72}$ is in line with what we know of the text of $\mathfrak{P}^{72}$ in general, and its deviant text towards the end of Jude in particular (cf. also the increasing frequency of errors in this part of the text, commented on above). More likely than a "solution," is the possibility that the two-clause form of $\mathfrak{P}^{72}$ arose through haplography occasioned by homoioteleuton (-ους^-ους) in combination with deviant word order, neither of which is surprising in the case of this scribe.

[351] Kubo, "Jude 22-3," 249 (in an earlier work Kubo defended the two-clause form [$\mathfrak{P}^{72}$ *and Codex Vaticanus*, 139-44], but he subsequently changed his view); Wachtel, *Der byzantinische Text*, 361-73.

[352] Ibid.

[353] Osburn rightly questions whether the Latin citation may truly represent Clement's text, since Cassiodorus, who probably translated the work, explicitly stated that he had made corrections in the original of what he considered to be erroneous ("The Text of Jude 22-23," 143-44). Kubo answers this objection by pointing out that such a general statement cannot automatically be applied to this passage, especially since the Latin citation at this point has no equivalent in the Greek manuscript tradition ("Jude 22-3," 249, n. 19); still, I am inclined to agree with Osburn. In any case, both authors ought to have considered the considerable divergence between Clement's other citations of Jude in the Greek and Latin tradition, respectively (esp. in vv. 5-6).

observation: the key to the solution lies in the difficulty of distinguishing the three groups reflected in the three-clause form with the double ἐλεᾶτε, which is clearly both the *lectio difficilior* and the reading which best explains the origin of all other readings, without demanding any hypothetical intermediate text, let alone a long series of subsequent changes. Further, the attestation of the difficult double ἐλεᾶτε is strong (01 03 044).

Kubo's explanation of how the text developed from the three-clause form is rather convincing in my opinion. If we disregard Kubo's decision to accept Birdsall's (and Osburn's) preference for ἐλεεῖτε over against ἐλεᾶτε, the reading attested by 01C1V and 044 is his preferred initial text:[354]

καὶ οὓς μὲν ἐλεᾶτε διακρινομένους, οὓς δὲ σῴζετε ἐκ πυρὸς ἁρπάζοντες, οὓς δὲ ἐλεᾶτε ἐν φόβῳ

In order to solve the difficulty, scribes either dropped one of the ἐλεᾶτε - clauses (𝔓72 𝔐) or substituted ἐλέγχετε for one of the occurences of ἐλεᾶτε (02 *al* in the first clause; 88 442 621 915 in the third clause).[355] The only exceptions are the readings of 03 and 04*. Kubo thinks the awkward reading of 03 is the result of haplography.[356] The reading of 04* is unusual, since it has only two divisions but no ἐλεᾶτε-clause. For Kubo, however, the awkward position of ἐν φόβῳ (with σῴζετε) shows the secondary character of the reading—in the major witnesses the phrase is connected with ἐλεᾶτε (/ἐλεεῖτε)—which is a sign that an ἐλεᾶτε-clause has dropped out; Kubo thinks this probably happened before ἐλέγχετε replaced the first ἐλεᾶτε (cf. 04C2V 1845T 1852). Wachtel provides a more detailed account of how the various readings developed and slightly modifies some of Kubo's suggestions; for example, Wachtel thinks the reading of 04*

[354] Landon's critique of Kubo, that he has reprimanded others for proposing conjectures when Kubo himself prefers a reading "not to be found in any extant MS," is an exaggeration connected to a general tendency on the part of Landon not to distinguish sub-formations within variation-units (*Text-Critical Study*, 131-32). In any case, Kubo's adopted text cannot be defined as a "conjecture" in the strict sense.

[355] Here Osburn's observation applies, that ἐλέγχετε was possibly introduced as being a more appropriate treatment of "disputers." Bauckham mentions other possibilities: the verb may represent the influence of *Did.* 2:7 or it may reflect ecclesiastical practices of discipline contemporary to the scribes (*Jude, 2 Peter*, 110-11; cf. Matt 18:15-17). Cf. Metzger, *Textual Commentary*, 660.

[356] Kubo, "Jude 22-3," 250. Although Kubo is not explicit on the matter, I think the corruption occurred in two stages: first οὕς was omitted through haplography, and subsequently δέ was dropped; cf. 1 Pet 2:24-25, ἰάθητε. ἦτε γάρ, where 03 omits ἦτε γάρ.

developed from the reading of 02, in which case the ἐλεᾶτε-clause was dropped only after ἐλέγχετε had replaced the first ἐλεᾶτε.[357]

The question remains why the author used a double ἐλεᾶτε and whether he actually meant to distinguish between three groups. Apparently, the three-division arrangement has not only caused scribal modifications, but it has prompted modern commentators to propose various emendations.[358] A crucial point, generally emphasized by commentators who prefer the two-clause division, is that the context seems to presuppose only two groups of people, although there is a considerable disagreement over their identity.[359] Joel S. Allen, on the other hand, presents an original solution suggesting that the three-clause form refers to only one group of persons.[360] He thinks the construction with μέν . . . δέ in the series in vv. 22-23 does not signify a sub-division of groups, as it normally would, but is used here of the same group, described at the outset by the participle διακρινομένους, which he interprets as "those who doubt." Hence, his translation reads: "Have mercy on those who are doubting; save them, seizing them from the fire; have mercy on them with fear, hating even the garment stained by the flesh."[361] Allen admits that the weakness of his proposal is the lack of an analogy of this kind of usage of the construction in the NT, and his attempt to find analogies elsewhere in Biblical and classical texts is unsuccessful.[362]

---

[357] Wachtel, *Der byzantinische Text,* 361-73 (see esp. the figure "Zu Teststelle 94" [ungpaginated]).

[358] For example, Wohlenberg prefers ἐλάσατε instead of ἐλεᾶτε[2] (*Der erste und zweite Petrusbrief und der Judasbrief,* 331, n. 49); Werner Bieder suggests ἐᾶτε ("Judas 22f," *TZ* 6 [1950]:75-77); Hans Windisch proposes ἐκβάλετε (*Die Katholischen Briefe* [HNT 15; Tübingen: Mohr Siebeck, 1930], 47).

[359] Wohlenberg distinguishes two groups influenced to different degrees by the false teachers (*Der erste und zweite Petrusbrief und der Judasbrief,* 331). Bauckham differentiates the two groups rather by the nature of their response to reproof (*Jude, 2 Peter,* 115). Sara C. Winter points out that the letter elsewhere mentions only the false teachers and the addressees ("Jude 22-23: A Note on the Text and Translation," *HTR* 87 [1994]: 217). Landon says that the text, regardless of form, only reckons with "two elements (those upon whom we should have mercy, and those whom we should snatch from the fire)," which, for Landon, also undermines the argument for a triadic arrangement, since it does not fit the context here (*Text-Critical Study,* 133).

[360] Joel S. Allen, "A New Possibility for the Three-clause Format of Jude 22-3," *NTS* 44 (1998): 133-43.

[361] Ibid., 133, 137.

[362] Allen actually states that "the best Biblical support" for his proposal comes from Jude 10, οὗτοι δὲ ὅσα μὲν οὐκ οἴδασιν βλασφημοῦσιν, ὅσα δὲ φυσικῶς ὡς τὰ ἄλογα ζῷα ἐπίστανται, ἐν τούτοις φθείρονται (ibid., 138). Yet, he elsewhere implies the reason why this example cannot function as an analogy to vv. 22-23: "One might conclude that μέν . . . δέ alone could function as an anaphora, but μέν . . . δέ in series had a unique function, and signified some sort of division of categories" (ibid., 137).

Further, the translation of διακρινομένους as "those who doubt" is highly problematic. Peter Spitaler argues persuasively that the concept of a special NT meaning for διακρίνομαι in the sense of "doubt" is based on a circular reasoning, and is lexically unsupportable in light of classical and Hellenistic Greek usage.[363] He suggests that the classical/Hellenistic meaning of the word be retained in both Jude 9 and 22-23; thus, instead of being "a reflexive indicator of an individual's intra-personal conflict" (doubting), the word refers to "an inter-personal, social conflict" (disputing/contesting).[364] Thus, he effectively eliminates one hypothetical subgroup (the doubters).

Spitaler goes on to suggest a solution similar to that of Allen, namely that the relative pronoun οὕς is a grammatical substitute for διακρινομένους throughout vv. 22-23, so that the οὕς μέν . . . οὕς δέ . . . οὕς δέ sequence (he accepts the three-clause form) refers to one group of persons, namely the disputers/separatists/infiltrators.[365] Hence, he proposes the translation: "to these disputers extend mercy; some save by snatching them from the fire; but to these extend mercy, in fear hating also the flesh-stained garment."[366] Spitaler admits in a footnote that his solution suffers from the same weakness as does Allen's.[367] Ironically, the very force behind Spitaler's first argument—the importance of comparative evidence from the larger Greek linguistic environment—exposes the weakness of his second argument; in classic and Hellenistic usage, the οὕς μέν . . . οὕς δέ . . . οὕς δέ structure unequivocally denotes some sort of sub-division of groups.[368] In addition, the very polemic nature of Jude as a whole makes it difficult to accept Spitaler's suggestion that the recipients, towards the end of the epistle, are exhorted to show mercy to the opponents.

The first thing to consider in regard to the οὕς μέν . . . οὕς δέ . . . οὕς δέ sequence is the author's use of μέν . . . δέ in the series in v. 8: οὗτοι ἐνυπνιαζόμενοι σάρκα μὲν μιαίνουσιν κυριότητα δὲ ἀθετοῦσιν δόξας δὲ βλασφημοῦσιν. Here, the text refers to one group of people (the opponents) and the conjunctions are used rhetorically in order to subdivide and

---

[363] Peter Spitaler, "Doubt or Dispute (Jude 9 and 22-23): Rereading a Special New Testament Meaning through the Lens of Internal Evidence," *Bib* 87 (2006): 201-22.

[364] Ibid., 205.

[365] Ibid, 217, 219.

[366] Ibid., 220.

[367] "I agree . . . that Allen's argument is weak due to the scarcity of comparative evidence. However, Allen makes the important point that Jude's particular construct, which is equally rare, ought to be interpreted in a way that does not slavishly follow a one-for-all grammar rule—especially since the literary context contradicts this rule" (ibid., 219, n. 53).

[368] Cf. BDF §250.

enumerate their actions (sins) in a climactic three-fold series.[369] It is to be noted that the two latter actions are practically synonymous in meaning.

Likewise, I think that each of the three clauses creates a similar climactic effect in vv. 22-23, speaking of three parallel actions, each of which implies the separation between the opponents who have crept into the church, influencing the life of the community (vv. 4, 12), and those of God's true people who have been influenced by their sins in various ways. Thus, the exhortation to "keep yourselves in the love of God" (v. 21) is specified in three parallel participial phrases drawing an imperatival function from the finite verb.

I suggest that the participle διακρινομένους may refer to "those who are under judgment," in a juridical setting; those who appear before the throne of God in a legal dispute (cf. v. 9), anticipating the final eschatological judgment.[370] The evident intertextual connections between vv. 22-23 (and v. 9 where the same word occurs) and the heavenly court-room scene in Zech 2:13-3:10 support such an interpretation:

(1) Joshua stands before God's throne and Satan, the adversary, stands on God's right hand to accuse Joshua (Zech 3:2; cf. Jude 9). In Jude, the recipients are exhorted to have mercy on some who are under judgment (v. 22), i.e., God's people. God eventually will judge the adversaries on the final day of judgment (thus, ἐλέγχετε does not suit the context; cf. vv. 9, 14-15; Zech 2:8-9; 3:9-10).

(2) God has chosen Jerusalem (Zech 3:2), the daughter of Zion, not the daughter of Babylon (cf. Zech 2:7, 10). Thus, Joshua, representing God's chosen people, is plucked out of the fire (Zech 3:2). In Jude, the addressees shall pluck the chosen out of the fire (v. 23). The adversaries eventually will be destroyed in the fire of judgment as were Sodom and Gomorrah (v. 7).

(3) The filthy clothes of Joshua are removed and he is given new garments; his guilt is removed (Zech 3:3-5). In Jude, the addressees shall have mercy on the chosen, with fear, hating their garments made filthy by fleshly sin (v. 23; cf. v. 8), whereas the Lord himself will eventually judge all the ungodly for all their wicked words and deeds (vv. 14-16).

The interpretation of vv. 22-23 in an anticipatory eschatological setting before the throne of God is confirmed by v. 24, where it is stated that God

---

[369] Cf. BDF §447.8; BDAG s.v. μέν 1c.

[370] LSJ s.v. διακρίνω III; BDAG s.v. διακρίνω 4, 5; cf. LXX Joel 4:2; LXX Ezek 20:35-36.

has the power to keep his people free from stumbling and to stand them before his throne in glory and joy (cf. Zech 3:8-10). Hence, Osburn, now favoring a three-clause format in vv. 22-23, says concerning the character of the final verses:

> "Guard you from falling" refers . . . to 1 Enoch's preservation from ruin at the judgment. Similarly, "to stand" is to be taken with reference to the shaking of the earth at the advent of God, especially prominent in 1 Enoch 1:5-7 in the context of judgment. . . . The use of the term ["rejoicing"] as eschatological rejoicing . . . continues . . . here in Jude 24. . . . In contrast with the grim depiction of the doom of the intruders of Jude's concern, the masterful doxology reflects great depth of spiritual awareness in denoting the security adhering to those who persist in distinctly Christian ways. The literary function of this lofty doxology, then, is that of a prayer that the faithful may be preserved in their Christian faith rather than be consigned to an inevitable fate due to adopting the decadence of the opponents.[371]

In conclusion, external evidence is ambiguous, but the manuscript support for the double ἐλεᾶτε is rather strong. More importantly, the preferred reading best explains the rise of all other readings. The three-clause form with the double ἐλεᾶτε has caused many difficulties in the history of transmission and interpretation. I have suggested, against the background of Zech 2:13-3:10 and the context of Jude as a whole, that in each of the three parallel clauses, the members are exhorted to take action, thereby separating the opponents (who eventually will be judged by God) from those among God's chosen people who have been influenced by their sins in various ways, but are to be kept within the boundaries of the community. Thus, I propose the following translation of vv. 22-23: "Have mercy on some who are under judgment; save some by snatching them out of the fire; have mercy on some with fear, hating even the clothing that has been soiled by the flesh."

Finally, two peculiar readings demand our attention. First, the bilingual MS 629, which is discussed by Wachtel.[372] The MS has been corrected to conform to the Latin column:

---

[371] Carroll D. Osburn, ("Discourse Analysis and Jewish Apocalyptic in Jude," in *Linguistics and New Testament Interpretation* [eds. David A. Black et al.; Nashville: Broadman Press, 1992], 293-94. In the same treatment, Osburn announced his changed view of vv. 22-23 without going into further details: "[T]he exhortation in verses 22-23 is directed toward what the readers can do for those inclined to defect. Although there is textual uncertainty in these verses, the three-clause text in ℵᶜ . . . is certainly to be preferred. I am honored that Bauckham found my study convincing, but stimulating conversations with Harold Greenlee during a Bible translation workshop in Guatemala in the fall of 1980 have led me to view the three-clause text of ℵᶜ as correct" (ibid., 292).

[372] Wachtel, *Der byzantinische Text*, 373.

ους δε εν φοβω σωζετε εκ πυρος αρπαζοντες ους δε ελε[6-9]τες εν φοβω θεου 629*
ους δε εν φοβω σωζετε εκ πυρος αρπαζοντες ετερους δε ελεειτε εν φοβω θεου (629C)

Wachtel points out that θεοῦ (*dei*), written by the first hand, and ἑτέρους (*alii*), added by the corrector, correspond to the Latin side. However, his assumption that ἐλεεῖτε replaces an original ἐλέγχετε is problematic. The Latin side reads *miseremini* and it is probably for this reason that the *ECM* editors have now cited 629*V in support of ἐλεᾶτε, since it is obvious that the original scribe conforms the Greek text to the Latin. Wachtel argues for the solution that the original scribe had a Greek exemplar with ἐλέγχετε and when he was trying to conform the Greek to the Latin side he neglected ἐλέγχετε, which was then corrected at a later stage.

Whereas this solution is possible, there is another complicating factor— sometimes the corrections move the text away from the Latin. There are many examples of this phenomenon in Jude, but a good illustration of the difficulties is found in the end of v. 24, where many words seem to have been blotted out and replaced with μόνῳ σοφῷ θεῷ σωτῆρι, written very broadly on two lines. In spite of the fact that the original writing is completely invisible, the *ECM* cites 629*V as reading: ἐν τῇ παρουσίᾳ τοῦ κυρίου ἡμῶν Ἰησοῦ Χριστοῦ, as inferred from the Latin side: *in adventum domini nostri Iesu Christi* (an assimilation to 1 Thess 3:13). I am inclined to agree with the editors that this was the original wording of 629, but I cannot be sure. Furthermore, the apparatus does not signal to the reader that the correction involved μόνῳ in v. 25, although it is assumed that 629* omitted σοφῷ. In my opinion, the citation in general of this manuscript in the *ECM* is unsatisfactory. The MS demands a special study of its Latin and Greek side, including a thorough examination of the corrections in both columns. Until such is undertaken, only the Greek (visible) evidence should be taken into account, unless the reader is told exactly what is inferred from the Latin.

Another interesting reading in vv. 22-23 is found in MS 1744: καὶ οὓς μέν ἐλεεῖτε διακρινόμενοι οὓς δὲ ἐν φόβῳ σώζετε ἐκ πυρὸς ἁρπάζοντες τὸν ἑαυτῶν ἁμαρτιῶν κεκηλιδωμένον βίον. This reading is a development of the two-clause form attested by the Majority Text. Interestingly, the interpretative expansion reflects the influence of a patristic comment on χιτών later in the verse, which is ascribed to Maximus the Confessor and transmitted in the *Catena*: [question] τίς ὁ ἀπὸ τῆς σαρκὸς ἐσπιλώμενος χιτών; [answer] ὁ πολλοῖς πλημμέλημα τῶν ἐκ τῆς σαρκὸς παθημάτων κεκηλιδωμένος βίος.[373]

Umlaut 5 in Codex Vaticanus (03): this umlaut is placed before καὶ οὓς μέν in v. 22 and probably refers to the textual variation in the whole passage in vv. 22-23.

24,8-30: φυλάξαι ὑμᾶς ἀπταίστους καὶ στῆσαι κατενώπιον τῆς δόξης αὐτοῦ ἀμώμους ἐν ἀγαλλιάσει {e+i}

Again, there is much to suggest that the reading of 𝔓[72], στηρίξαι ἀσπίλους ἀμώμους ἁγνευόμενος ἀπέναντι τῆς δόξης αὐτοῦ ἐν ἀγαλλιάσει, results from an omission due to homoioteleuton (φυλάξαι . . . στηρίξαι). First, because the text does not make sense without an object (e.g., ὑμᾶς); secondly, because στηρίξαι is attested in the place of στῆσαι by some witnesses (0316 5 623 2805 **L**:S), and is probably an assimilation to Rom 16:25; and, finally, the Old Latin text type "S" would display some striking similarities to such a text without the omission (here with backtranslation):[374]

> *custodire vos sine delicto et confirmare in honorem suum inlibatos inmaculatos*
> φυλάξαι ὑμᾶς ἀπταίστους καὶ στηρίξαι εἰς δόξαν αὐτοῦ ἀσπίλους ἀμώμους
> *castificatos in exultatione ante conspectu(m) eius*
> ἁγνευόμενος ἐν ἀγαλλιάσει ἀπέναντι αὐτοῦ

Landon is impressed by the papyrus reading and accepts it as original.[375] However, his whole discussion of 𝔓[72] is flawed, since the peculiar text is treated in three different variation-units (units 24.1-3).[376] Landon disregards the attestation to στηρίξαι by some witnesses, he treats ἀμώμους as an omission in 𝔓[72] (unit 24.3); and, most importantly, he neglects the wording of the Old Latin altogether.

Albin draws attention to the signs of textual elaboration in the conspicuous alliteration of 𝔓[72], ἀσπίλους ἀμώμους ἁγνευόμενος ἀπέναντι . . . αὐτοῦ ἐν ἀγαλλιάσει, and points out that this reading would hardly have vanished without a trace in the early textual tradition (apart from the OL)

---

[373] Cramer, *Catena in Epistolas Catholicas,* 169. The question (without answer) is preserved in the extant parts of Photius' *Bibliotheca* (R. Henry, *Bibliothèque,* 3:77,6).
[374] Latin text from Thiele, *Epistulae Catholicae.*
[375] Landon, *Text-Critical Study,* 134-35.
[376] Ibid., 134-36.

were it original.[377] It should be noted, however, that two other minuscules may reflect traces of the same tradition: φυλάξαι ὑμᾶς ἀπταίστους καὶ στῆσαι κατέναντι τῆς δοξῆς αὐτοῦ ἀμώμους ἀσπίλους ἐν ἀγαλλιάσει (88 915).[378] In conclusion, the reading of 𝔓[72] is clearly secondary but likely preserves traces of an early tradition.

24,8-10: φυλάξαι ὑμᾶς {e=i} (ΕCM φυλαξαι υμας)

The external attestation for ὑμᾶς is very strong. A few important witnesses attest to ἡμᾶς (02 431 *pc* S:Ph), which may have arisen through itacism. The majority of witnesses read αὐτούς (424* 2186 𝔐 PsOec).[379] Wachtel denotes the latter reading as an "untypical" majority reading, since it does not suit the context of vv. 22-23, but he thinks it is explicable as an error of the eye (αὐτούς—ἀπταίστους).[380] This may be the case, but, in my opinion, and in the light of my interpretation of vv. 22-23, any of the pronouns would fit the context well. In regard to transcriptional evidence, it would have been tempting for a scribe to change the unclear (and more difficult) αὐτούς to ὑμᾶς (cf. Rom 16:25; Col 1:22). Thus, my preference for ὑμᾶς is based on external evidence, whereas the internal evidence supports the Majority Text. The different word order, ὑμᾶς (/αὐτούς) φυλάξαι, has only weak support (323 1739 *pc*).

24,12: ἀπταίστους {e<i}

A significant number of important witnesses add καὶ ἀσπίλους/καὶ ἀσπίλους καί (04 307 323 424Z 442 621 630 1505 1611 1739 1845 1852 2200 *al* Thph K:S^ms S:HPh).[381] Apparently, the reading was early and widespread. However, the addition of the adjective was likely suggested by the context of v. 23 (ἐσπιλωμένον χιτῶνα). Furthermore, the peculiar readings of 𝔓[72] 88 915 L:S in v. 24, in which the adjective stands in direct conjunction with ἀμώμους, support the assumption that the word was attracted early on by the synonym ἄμωμος (first perhaps as a gloss in the margin); the collocation

---

[377] Albin, *Judasbrevet*, 628-29. Cf. the similar alliteration in Col 1:22: παραστῆσαι ὑμᾶς ἁγίους καὶ ἀμώμους καὶ ἀνεγκλήτους κατενώπιον αὐτοῦ.

[378] Since the two adjectives ἄμωμος and ἄσπιλος are synonyms, the Latin word order (*inlibatos inmaculatos*) may reflect either ἀμώμους ἀσπίλους (cf. 1 Pet 1:19) or ἀσπίλους ἀμώμους (cf. 2 Pet 3:14).

[379] PsOec: αὐτούς (PG 119:720); Thph: ὑμᾶς (PG 126:104).

[380] Wachtel, *Der byzantinische Text*, 82, 373. Cf. the reading φυλάξαι ἀπταίστους (633 1717 2816T), where αὐτούς has been omitted due to homoioteleuton.

[381] PsOec: ἀπταίστους (PG 119:720); Thph: ἀπταίστους καὶ ἀσπίλους (PG 126:104).

of the adjectives is attested elsewhere (1 Pet 1:19; 2 Pet 3:14, ἀμώμη-τος/ἄμωμος).

24,16: στῆσαι {e+i}

A few witnesses support στηρίξαι (0316 5 623 2805 **L:S** [cf. 𝔓⁷²]), which is possibly a stock benedictory term in conjunction with δυναμόω, or perhaps a remote assimilation to the doxology of Romans, τῷ δὲ δυναμένῳ ὑμᾶς στηρίξαι (traditionally in Rom 16:25; cf. below).

24,18: κατενώπιον {e>i}

The improper preposition κατενώπιον has overwhelming support in Jude, but is rather unusual elsewhere in the NT (Eph 1:4; Col 1:22; also in the Byzantine text, 2 Cor 2:17; 12:19), whereas the synonym ἐνώπιον, attested in some witnesses (04 630 1505 1611 1845 1852 2200 *pc* Thph), is very common (96 times).[382] The compound form, however, seems always to be used in a context describing a specific act of standing before God himself; if so, it thus becomes quite appropriate in the present context. As part of an elaborated alliteration 𝔓⁷² has another synonym, ἀπέναντι. A pair of other MSS read κατέναντι (88 915), which may reflect the traces of a tradition related to 𝔓⁷² and **L:S** (see above). Landon prefers ἀπέναντι because he thinks κατενώπιον is an assimilation to Eph 1:4 (ἁγίους καὶ ἀμώμους κατενώπιον αὐτοῦ ἐν ἀγάπῃ; cf. Col 1:22) and he regards κατέναντι, preserved by 88 915, as a conflation of κατενώπιον and ἀπέναντι.[383] In my opinion, the external evidence clearly speaks in favor or κατενώπιον, whereas the internal evidence is a bit ambiguous at this point.

25,2-8: μόνῳ θεῷ σωτῆρι ἡμῶν {e+i}

The Majority Text reading, μόνῳ σοφῷ θεῷ σωτῆρι ἡμῶν, probably reflects assimilation to the doxology of Romans (μόνῳ σοφῷ θεῷ κτλ.), which is in turn a "floating passage" that occurs in six different locations (the manuscript evidence strongly supports Rom 16:25-27).[384] A similar

---

[382] PsOec: κατενώπιον (PG 119:720); Thph: ἐνώπιον (PG 126:104).

[383] Landon, *Text-Critical Study*, 135.

[384] Cf. Metzger, *Textual Commentary*, 470-73, 476-77, 661. Landon assumes that μόνῳ σοφῷ θεῷ was original in Jude 25, and that the scribal addition to Romans included the word σοφῷ through harmony with Jude (*Text-Critical Study*, 136). This is very unlikely, since the phrase μόνῳ σοφῷ θεῷ has near-total manuscript support in Romans (including 𝔓⁴⁶ from ca. 200 C.E.), whereas σοφῷ is missing in the early tradition of Jude altogether. It is also absent from

addition of σοφῷ in the Majority Text occurs in 1 Tim 1:17.[385] In my opinion, an omission of the attribute due to homioteleuton (-ω) in both doxologies in Jude and 1 Tim 1:17 is less likely, although such a scenario may explain its omission in parts of the Byzantine tradition.

Some MSS read μόνῳ θεῷ καὶ σωτῆρι ἡμῶν (6 363 424Z *pc*) or μόνῳ θεῷ ἡμῶν καὶ σωτῆρι (61 326 1837). The term σωτήρ for God is traditionally Jewish (see e.g., LXX Pss 23:5; 24:5; 26:1, 9; 61:3, 7; 64:6; 78:9; 94:1). In the NT, the epithet is frequently used of Christ, but a few times also of God (Luke 1:47; 1 Tim 1:1; 2:3; 4:10; Tit 1:3; 2:10; 3:4).[386] Thus, καί was possibly inserted in some witnesses in order to distinguish between God and Christ, so as to reserve the epithet σωτήρ to Christ. The omission of θεῷ in some witnesses (42 234 309 *al*), if not due to homioteleuton, can be explained on the same grounds. The phrase that follows in the best witnesses, διὰ Ἰησοῦ Χριστοῦ τοῦ κυρίου ἡμῶν, causes no contextual difficulty here, since it is absent from all of the 30 MSS that omit θεῷ.

Landon does not discuss these readings, but he thinks that the word σωτήρ was removed by the scribe of 𝔓72 for a similar reason, "because it is linked to God alone, implying a denial of Christ's divinity."[387] In light of similar theological modifications by this scribe I think Landon's assessment is correct. This is further confirmed by the unique addition that follows (see below).

Umlaut 6 in Codex Vaticanus (03): the umlaut probably refers to the variant with σοφῷ.

25,9: [omit] {e+i}

All witnesses except 𝔓72 attest to a single doxology (to God through Christ) in Jude 25 (with textual variation): μόνῳ θεῷ σωτῆρι ἡμῶν διὰ Ἰησοῦ Χριστοῦ τοῦ κυρίου ἡμῶν δόξα μεγαλωσύνη κράτος καὶ ἐξουσία. In 𝔓72, glory

---

the early stratum of the Byzantine text, represented by 1505 1611 **S:H**. (Landon does not consider the doxology in 1 Tim 1:17.)

[385] The phrase has slightly better attestation in 1 Tim 1:17 (01Z2 05C 044 1881 𝔐 **S:H**).

[386] It is interesting to note the common Jewish-Christian terminology of Jude 24-25 and Luke 1:45, 47 (ἐν ἀγαλλιάσει; μόνῳ θεῷ σωτῆρι ἡμῶν/τῷ θεῷ τῷ σωτῆρί μου).

[387] Landon, *Text-Critical Study*, 136-37. In this connection, Landon refers to the passage in 1 Tim 1:1, ". . . of God our Savior and [καί] of Christ Jesus our hope," where Ehrman thinks that some scribes removed καί in order to emphasize the divinity of Christ (Ehrman, *Orthodox Corruption*, 87). Landon's second "transcriptional" argument against the reading of 𝔓72, that the omission of σωτῆρι avoids an awkward attachment to the following prepositional phrase, is invalid, since this is already prevented by the presence of αὐτῷ δόξα κράτος τιμή in 𝔓72.

is ascribed to God and to Christ in a two-fold doxology, accentuating the divine glory and honour of Christ: μόνῳ θεῷ ἡμῶν αὐτῷ δόξα κράτος τίμη διὰ Ἰησοῦ Χριστοῦ τοῦ κυρίου ἡμων αὐτῷ δόξα καὶ μεγαλωσύνη.

The unique addition of αὐτῷ δόξα κράτος τιμή in 𝔓⁷² was perhaps directly or indirectly inspired by the doxology in Rev 5:13, since that is the only place in the NT where these three nouns appear together and in a similar context: τῷ καθημένῳ ἐπὶ τῷ θρόνῳ καὶ τῷ ἀρνίῳ ἡ εὐλογία καὶ ἡ τιμὴ καὶ ἡ δόξα καὶ τὸ κράτος εἰς τοὺς αἰῶνας τῶν αἰώνων. It is also possible that it was influenced by the doxologies in *1 Clem.* 64:1 and 65:2, where the same nouns appear together with μεγαλωσύνη. Nevertheless, similar doxological formulae were used frequently in the church liturgy, which is another important factor behind the considerable textual variation here and elsewhere among the doxologies in the NT.[388]

At this point, the citation of the Sahidic and Philoxenian versions in support of 𝔓⁷² in the *ECM* is misleading in my opinion: apart from the several differences in wording, these versions transpose the location of a *single* doxology, ascribed to God and built up by common liturgical formulae.[389] Thus, it is quite likely that the scribe of 𝔓⁷² once again is responsible for the particular "Christological" modification of the text.[390]

Landon prefers the reading of 𝔓⁷², for three reasons: (1) the triadic juxtaposition of the three nouns is consistent with the author's style; (2) the phrase could have been excluded by all other witnesses in order to avoid a twofold repetition of δόξα; (3) the doxology in 2 Pet 3:18 could be sourced from an original αὐτῷ δόξα in Jude 25.[391] In my opinion, these arguments are too weak; an omission of the triadic expression is equally consistent with the author's style. Moreover, a closer look at the doxology in 2 Peter shows that it is very different from that in Jude, and that it follows a very

---

[388] For a useful overview of the textual variation of liturgical elements in the NT, see Eberhard Güting, "Amen, Eulogie, Doxologie. Eine textkritische Untersuchung," in *Begegnungen zwischen Christentum und Judentum in Antike und Mittelalter: Festschrift für Heinz Schreckenberg* (ed. Dietrich-Alex Koch and Hermann Lichtenberger, et al.; Göttingen: Vandenhoeck & Ruprecht, 1993), 133-62.

[389] The Sahidic manuscripts represent αὐτῷ ἡ δόξα, whereas the Philoxenian attests to αὐτῷ δόξα καὶ κράτος καὶ τιμὴ καί μεγαλωσύνη (*ECM* IV. B 154; cf. Gwynn, *Remnants*, 83). The agreement between 𝔓⁷² and the Philoxenian in Jude 25 is exaggerated in my opinion (cf. *ECM* IV, B 154: "Again the partial agreement with 𝔓⁷² is striking"). In fact, the Philoxenian (single) doxology is more similar to that in *1 Clem.* 64:1: αὐτῷ δόξα καὶ μεγαλωσύνη, κράτος καὶ τιμὴ κτλ..

[390] Cf. Tobias Nicklas, "Der 'lebendige Text' des Neuen Testaments: Der *Judasbrief* in 𝔓⁷² (*P.Bodmer* VII)," *ASE* 22 (2005): 220.

[391] Landon, *Text-Critical Study*, 137.

basic form of early Christian doxologies (cf. Rom 11:36; Eph 3:21; Rev 1:6).[392] In conclusion, neither external nor internal evidence support the singular reading of 𝔓[72].

25,10-20: διὰ Ἰησοῦ Χριστοῦ τοῦ κυρίου ἡμῶν {e>i}

The prepositional phrase has overwhelming manuscript support. However, the phrase is omitted by the Majority Text and a few other important witnesses (35 431 808 𝔐 PsOec **L**:S).[393] Internal evidence is ambiguous; on the one hand the phrase could represent an assimilation to the doxology of Romans (μόνῳ σοφῷ θεῷ, διὰ Ἰησοῦ Χριστοῦ). On the other hand, it could have been omitted due to haplography (ἡμῶν . . . ἡμῶν), or to awkwardness if the expression is understood in attachment to σωτῆρι. Landon suggests that "this awkwardness is apparent rather than real," since the phrase should be taken with the attributes which follow—the glory, majesty, power and authority is mediated to God through Jesus Christ our Lord.[394] With the latter interpretation, however, the well attested phrase that follows, πρὸ παντὸς τοῦ αἰῶνος, becomes difficult. Bauckham acknowledges the ambiguity of the phrase διὰ Ἰησοῦ Χριστοῦ τοῦ κυρίου ἡμῶν, but points out that the doxology of *1 Clem.* 65:2 shows that Christ can be regarded as the mediator of glory before all time, and that the examples in Jude and *1 Clement* (also *1 Clem.* 64:1) could be explained either by the pre-existence of Christ, or, as Kelly suggests, by the lack of precision in passages built up by stereotyped, grandiose-sounding formulae.[395]

Umlaut 7 in Codex Vaticanus (03): this umlaut certainly refers to the omission of the phrase.

---

[392] Cf. Reinhard Deichgräber, *Gotteshymnus und Christushymnus in der frühen Christenheit* (SUNT 5; Göttingen: Vandenhoeck & Ruprecht, 1967), 25.

[393] PsOec: omit (PG 119:720); Thph: διὰ Ἰησοῦ Χριστοῦ τοῦ κυρίου ἡμῶν (PG 126:104).

[394] Landon, *Text-Critical Study*, 138.

[395] Bauckham, *Jude, 2 Peter*, 123; Kelly, *A Commentary on the Epistles of Peter and Jude*, 25; cf. Wachtel: "Daraus, daß bereits eine geprägte Form zugrunde liegt, ist die unklare syntaktische Einbindung der Wendung in Jud 25 und Röm 16,27 zu erklären" (*Der byzantinische Text*, 377); cf. Deichgräber, "Man hat mancherlei Versuche gemacht, dieser Formel διὰ Ἰησοῦ Χριστοῦ einen tiefen Sinn abzugewinnen . . . aber wahrscheinlich ist die Wendung nicht mehr als ein ganz einfacher Versuch, die liturgische Formel zu verchristlichen" (*Gotteshymnus*, 40).

25,21: [omit] {e+i}

The double doxology in 𝔓⁷² has been treated above. The insertion of ᾧ (01*) or ᾧ ἡ (378) in front of δόξα brings the text closer to the standard form of Christian doxology (cf. Rom 16:27; Gal 1:5; 2 Tim 4:18; Heb 13:21).[396]

25,24-30: πρὸ παντὸς τοῦ αἰῶνος

1) The presence of the prepositional phrase {e+i}

The prepositional phrase is omitted by the major part of the Byzantine manuscript tradition and a few other witnesses including 𝔓⁷² 431 808 PsOec **L:S**.[397] From the intrinsic viewpoint, Landon draws attention to the triadic structure, which is evidently logical: (1) πρὸ παντὸς τοῦ αἰῶνος; (2) καὶ νῦν; (3) καὶ εἰς πάντας τοὺς αἰῶνας.[398] His suggestion that the phrase was omitted "through harmony with 2 Pet 3:18," is doubtful; it is safer to say that the phrase in general seems out of place in a doxology.[399] Another possible explanation is the apparent difficulty of combining the two prepositional phrases, as mentioned above. Wachtel remarks that a major part of the witnesses either omit or preserve both of the two prepositional phrases in v. 25 (διὰ Ἰησοῦ Χριστοῦ τοῦ κυρίου ἡμῶν . . . πρὸ παντὸς τοῦ αἰῶνος), but, interestingly, a number of Byzantine witnesses preserve either one of the two phrases in "Mischformen" which shows that both phrases were familiar in the Byzantine tradition.[400] At the same time, the existence of these conflated forms is a sign of the difficulty of combining the two phrases, one had to be dropped, and eventually both fell out.

2) The presence of the article {e>i} (*ECM* •προ παντος του αιωνος•/•προ παντος αιωνος)

Among the witnesses that preserve the prepositional phrase, some significant MSS omit the article (88 307 323 436 453 915 1067 1409 1739 2200 2374 *al*). The internal evidence is ambiguous. The phrase with the article corresponds to the well attested εἰς πάντας τοὺς αἰῶνας; this correspondence could either be original or the result of scribal assimilation. There is no clear pattern in similar phrases in the NT. I have argued

---

[396] Cf. Deichgräber, *Gotteshymnus*, 25.
[397] PsOec: omit (PG 119:720); Thph: πρὸ παντὸς τοῦ αἰῶνος (PG 126:104).
[398] Landon, *Text-Critical Study*, 139.
[399] So Metzger, *Textual Commentary*, 661.
[400] Wachtel, *Der byzantinische Text*, 379.

above, however, that the author independently used the formula πᾶς + definite article + adjective or substantive in v. 15: πάντας τοὺς ἀσεβεῖς, πάντων τῶν ἔργων, πάντων τῶν σκληρῶν, which speaks slightly in favor of the article here, although my decision to include it is primarily based on a consideration of the manuscript evidence.

Umlaut 8 in Codex Vaticanus (03): this umlaut either refers to the omission of the article, or to the omission of the whole phrase.

25,40-52: καὶ νῦν καὶ εἰς πάντας τοὺς αἰῶνας {e+i}

The printed reading has the strongest manuscript support and best explains all other readings. A few witnesses omit καί (180 1729 PsOec), some other MSS omit πάντας (01 1836 2318 2544), and a few other MSS omit τούς (1359 1425 1563 1718 1751), probably due to an error of the eye because of the similar endings.[401] The addition of τῶν αἰώνων in a number of witnesses (020 33 88 442 621 915 *al* **K**:B^mss **S**:H^M) is probably an assimilation to the phrase εἰς τοὺς αἰῶνας τῶν αἰώνων, common in the NT in general and in the doxologies in particular (cf. Gal 1:5; Phil 4:20; 1 Tim 1:17; 2 Tim 4:18; Heb 13:21; Rev 5:13).[402] Another addition of καὶ ἀεί (0316 307 326 431 453 1837 *pc*) reflects an early embellishment on the part of the scribes. The deviant word order of 𝔓^72 is hardly surprising.[403]

25,54: ἀμήν {e+i}

In most cases where an ἀμήν is attested in the manuscript tradition at the end of a book, it is text-critically doubtful because in most cases it reflects the liturgical usage of the text (cf. Matt 28:20; Mark 16:8 [in the added shorter ending] or 16:20; Luke 24:53; Acts 28:31; Rom 16:24, 27; etc.). However, in Jude 25 the concluding ἀμήν has unequivocal manuscript support, only a few MSS omit the word (6 424C 467 1311 1319 1735 1768* 1856). Significantly, in Jude (as in 2 Peter) the final word of the epistle happens to conclude a doxology at this point, and all doxologies in

---

[401] PsOec: νῦν καὶ εἰς πάντας τοὺς αἰῶνας (PG 119:720); Thph: καὶ νῦν καὶ εἰς πάντας τοὺς αἰῶνας (PG 126:104).

[402] Cf. the comment to Rom 16:27 in Metzger, *Textual Commentary*, 477.

[403] Eleven of the singular readings of 𝔓^72 are transpositions, most of which involve small blocks of text; two words: Jude 20, 25; 1 Pet 3:7; three words: Jude 4, 14; 1 Pet 1:25; 3:6; 5:1; five words: Jude 21, 24 (Royse, "*Scribal Habits*," 480).

the NT, irrespectable of their location within a book, conclude with an ἀμήν. [404]

Subscriptio: [omit]

Most of what has been said about the superscriptions to the NT writings apply to the subscriptions too; they do not originate from the author, but rather represent a later stage in the manuscript tradition when the writings had become parts of a collection. The first subscriptions were brief and simple, indicating the closing of the book, e.g., Ἰούδα ἐπιστολή (𝔓⁷² 02 044 81 456 *pc*), or just Ἰούδα (01 03). Just like the superscriptions, the subscriptions became subject to considerable expansion in later centuries; in Jude the expansions in superscriptions and subscriptions are often of similar kind (see further comments above). Since the Epistle of Jude is the last book in the section of the Catholic Epistles or the *Apostolos*, some subscriptions to Jude indicate the closing of the whole section, e.g., τέλος τῶν καθολικῶν ἐπιστολῶν (378 945 999 1505 1891); σὺν θεῷ τέλος τῶν τε πράξεων καὶ τῶν καθολικῶν ἐπιστολῶν (453).

---

[404] Güting, "Amen, Eulogie, Doxologie," 158-59. As Güting points out, this is a very compelling argument for the originality of the word in 2 Pet 3:18, apart from the very strong manuscript support in its favor, and the literary dependence on Jude. The reason for its inclusion within square brackets in NA²⁷ and its placement below the primary line marked with bold dot in the *ECM* is the absence of the word in notable witnesses (03 1241 1739* 1881 *pc*), which is very difficult to explain if the word were original (Metzger, *Textual Commentary*, 637-38). However, Güting thinks it could have been deleted by mistake by a scribe (he mentions B) who had deleted similar cases of ἀμήν elsewhere as he corrected his exemplar (ibid., 159). In this connection, it is interesting to note that the corrector of 424 has deleted the word in Jude.

Bibliography

For a list of the manuscripts included in the study, see chapter six.

1. Primary Sources

1.1 Collations and Editions of New Testament Manuscripts

An Exact Transcript of the Codex Augiensis. Edited by F. H. A. Scrivener. Cambridge: Deighton, Bell & Co., 1859.

Beati Petri Apostoli Epistulae ex papyro bodmeriana VIII transcriptae. Edited by Carlo M. Martini. Milan: ex Hamilcaris Pizzi officina libraria, 1968).

Bibliotheca Bodmeriana: La collection des papyrus Bodmer. Edited by Martin Bircher. 10 vols. Munich: K. G. Saur, 2000.

Catalogue of Coptic Manuscripts in the Pierpont Morgan Library 1 [Text]. Edited by Leo Depuydt. Corpus of Illuminated Manuscripts 4. Leuven: Peeters, 1993. [Incomplete transcription of 0316]

Eight American Praxapostoloi. Edited by Kenneth W. Clark. Chicago: University of Chicago Press, 1941.

"L2435." Edited by Klaus Witte and Tommy Wasserman, forthcoming in *Bericht der Hermann Kunst-Stiftung zur Förderung der neutestamentlichen Textforschung.*

Lake, Kirsopp. "Texts from Mount Athos." *StudBib* 5 (1902): 89-131. [Collation of Codex 044.]

Monumenta sacra inedita, nova collectio vol. 5. Edited by Constantin von Tischendorf. Leipzig: Hinrichs, 1865. (Collation of 025.)

New Testament Greek Manuscripts 1: *Matthew.* Edited by Reuben J. Swanson. Sheffield: Sheffield Academic Press. Pasadena, CA: William Carey International University Press, 1995.

New Testament Greek Manuscripts 2: *Mark.* Edited by Reuben J. Swanson. Sheffield: Sheffield Academic Press. Pasadena, CA: William Carey International University Press, 1995.

New Testament Greek Manuscripts 3: *Luke.* Edited by Reuben J. Swanson. Sheffield: Sheffield Academic Press. Pasadena, CA: William Carey International University Press, 1995.

New Testament Greek Manuscripts 4: *John.* Edited by Reuben J. Swanson. Sheffield: Sheffield Academic Press. Pasadena, CA: William Carey International University Press, 1995.

Papyrus Bodmer VII-IX. Edited by Michel Testuz. Cologny-Geneva: Bibliotheca Bodmeriana, 1959.

The Oxyrhynchus Papyri XXXIV. Edited by L. Ingrams, P. Kingston, P. J. Parsons and J. R. Rea. Graeco-Roman Memoirs 49. London: Egypt Exploration Society, 1968.

1.2 New Testament Editions

Actus apostolorum et epistolas catholicas complectens. Vol. 1 of *Actuum apostolorum et epistolarum tam catholicarum quam Paulinarum, versio Syriaca Philoxeniana.* Edited by Joseph White. 2 vols. Oxford: Clarendon, 1799-1803.

Das Neue Testament auf Papyrus. II.2: *Die Paulinischen Briefe.* Edited by Klaus Wachtel and Klaus Witte. ANTF 22. Berlin/New York: de Gruyter, 1994.

Das Neue Testament in syrischer Überlieferung. I: *Die großen Katholischen Briefe.* Edited by Barbara Aland and Andreas Juckel. ANTF 7. Berlin/New York: de Gruyter, 1986.

Das Neue Testament auf Papyrus. I: *Die Katholischen Briefe.* Edited by Klaus Junack and Winfried Grunewald. ANTF 6. Berlin/New York: de Gruyter, 1986.

Die Schriften des Neuen Testaments in ihrer ältesten erreichbaren Textgestalt hergestellt auf Grund ihrer Textgeschichte. Edited by Hermann von Soden. 2d unchanged ed. 2 parts in 4 vols. Göttingen: Vandenhoeck & Ruprecht, 1911-1913.

Epistula Catholicae. Edited by Walter Thiele. Vetus Latina 26/1. Freiburg im Breisgau: Herder, 1956-1969.

God-Breathed Scriptures of the Old and New Testaments [original title in Armenian: *Astuacašunč 'matean hin ew norktakaranac'*]. Edited by Zōhrapean, Yovhannes. Venice: St. Lazar Press, 1805.

Nouum Iesu Christi D.N. Testamentum. Ex Bibliotheca Regia. Lutetiae. Edited by Robert Estienne (Stephanus). Paris, 1550.

Novum Testamentum Graece, 26 th ed. (Nestle-Aland). Critical apparatus edited by Kurt Aland and Barbara Aland. Stuttgart: Deutsche Bibelstiftung, 1979.

Novum Testamentum Graece, 27 th ed. (Nestle-Aland). Critical apparatus edited by Kurt Aland and Barbara Aland. Stuttgart: Deutsche Bibelgesellschaft, 1993.

Novum Testamentum Graece. Edited by Constantin von Tischendorf. 2 vols. 7th ed. Leipzig: Hinrichs, 1856-1859.

Novum Testamentum Graece. Edited by Constantin von Tischendorf. 3 vols. 8th ed. Leipzig: Hinrichs, 1869-1894.

Novum Testamentum Graece. Edited by Karl Lachmann. Berlin, 1831.

Novum Testamentum Graece et Latine. Edited by C. F. Matthaei. Riga, 1782.

Novum Testamentum graece et latine apparatu critico instructum. Edited by Augustinus S. J. Merk. 11th ed. Rome: Biblical Institute Press, 1992.

Novum Testamentum Graecum Editio Critica Maior. Vol. IV: *Catholic Letters.* Installment 1: *James.* Edited by Barbara Aland, Kurt Aland, Gerd Mink and Klaus Wachtel. Stuttgart: Deutsche Bibelgesellschaft, 1997.

Novum Testamentum Graecum Editio Critica Maior. Vol. IV: *Catholic Letters.* Installment 2: *The Letters of Peter.* Edited by Barbara Aland, Kurt Aland, Gerd Mink and Klaus Wachtel. Stuttgart: Deutsche Bibelgesellschaft, 2000.

Novum Testamentum Graecum Editio Critica Maior. Vol. IV: *The Catholic Letters.* Installment 4: *The Second and Third Letter of John, The Letter of Jude.* Edited by Barbara Aland, Kurt Aland, Gerd Mink and Klaus Wachtel. Stuttgart: Deutsche Bibelgesellschaft, 2005.

Novum Testamentum Graecum. Edited by Johann Albrecht Bengel. Tübingen: George Cottae, 1734.

Novum Testamentum Graecum. Edited by Johann Jakob Wettstein. 2 vols. Amsterdam: Dommerian, 1751-1752.

Remnants of the later Syriac versions of the Bible, Part I: New Testament. The Four Minor Catholic Epistles in the Original Philoxenian Version, of the Sixth Century. Edited by John Gwynn. Text and Translation Society 5. London/Oxford: Williams & Norgate, 1909.

S. Judae Apostoli epistolae catholicae versio Arabice et Aethiopice. Edited by J. G. Nissel and T. Petraeus. Leiden, 1654.

The Greek New Testament. Edited by Henry Alford. 4 vols. Rev. ed. London/Oxford: Rivingtons. Cambridge: Deighton, Bell & Co., 1871-1877.

The Greek New Testament. Edited by Kurt Aland, Matthew Black, Carlo M. Martini, Bruce M. Metzger and Allen Wikgren. 2d ed. New York: United Bible Societies, 1968.

The Greek New Testament. Edited by Kurt Aland, Matthew Black, Carlo M. Martini, Bruce M. Metzger and Allen Wikgren. 3d ed. New York: United Bible Societies, 1975.

The Greek New Testament. Edited by Kurt Aland, Matthew Black, Carlo M. Martini, Bruce M. Metzger and Allen Wikgren. 3d corr. ed. New York: United Bible Societies, 1983.

The Greek New Testament. Edited by Kurt Aland, Matthew Black, Carlo M. Martini, Bruce M. Metzger and Allen Wikgren. 4th rev. ed. Stuttgart: Deutsche Bibelgesellschaft/United Bible Societies, 1993.

The Greek New Testament. Edited by S. P. Tregelles. London: Samuel Bagster & Sons, 1857-72.

The New Testament in the Original Greek. Edited by B. F. Westcott and F. J. A. Hort. 2 vols. London: Macmillan, 1881-1882.

The New Testament in the Original Greek: Byzantine Textform. Edited by Maurice A. Robinson and William G. Pierpont. Southborough, MA: Chilton Book Publishing, 2005.

1.3 Collations and Editions of New Testament Manuscripts and Editions of the New Testament[*]

Aland, Barbara and Andreas Juckel. *Das Neue Testament in syrischer Überlieferung.* I: *Die großen Katholischen Briefe.* ANTF 7. Berlin/New York: de Gruyter, 1986.

Aland, Barbara, Kurt Aland, Gerd Mink and Klaus Wachtel, eds. *Novum Testamentum Graecum Editio Critica Maior.* Vol. IV: *Catholic Letters.* Installment 1: *James.* Stuttgart: Deutsche Bibelgesellschaft, 1997.

——, eds. *Novum Testamentum Graecum Editio Critica Maior.* Vol. IV: *Catholic Letters.* Installment 2: *The Letters of Peter.* Stuttgart: Deutsche Bibelgesellschaft, 2000.

——, eds. *Novum Testamentum Graecum Editio Critica Maior.* Vol. IV: *Catholic Letters.* Installment 4: *The Second and Third Letter of John, The Letter of Jude.* Stuttgart: Deutsche Bibelgesellschaft, 2005.

Aland, Kurt and Barbara Aland, eds. *Novum Testamentum Graece,* 26 th ed. Stuttgart: Deutsche Bibelstiftung, 1979.

Aland, Kurt, Matthew Black, Carlo M. Martini, Bruce M. Metzger and Allen Wikgren, eds. *The Greek New Testament.* 2d ed. New York: United Bible Societies, 1968.

——, eds. *The Greek New Testament.* 3d ed. New York: United Bible Societies, 1975.

---

[*] Listed by modern editor/translator.

———, eds. *The Greek New Testament*. 3d corr. ed. New York: United Bible Societies, 1983.

———, eds. *The Greek New Testament*. 4th rev. ed. Stuttgart: Deutsche Bibelgesellschaft/United Bible Societies, 1993.

Alford, Henry, ed. *The Greek New Testament*. 4 vols. Rev. ed. London/Oxford: Rivingtons. Cambridge: Deighton, Bell & Co., 1871-1877.

Bengel, Johann Albrecht. *Novum Testamentum Graecum*. Tübingen: George Cottae, 1734.

Clark, Kenneth W., ed. *Eight American Praxapostoloi*. Chicago: University of Chicago Press, 1941.

Depuydt, Leo, ed. *Catalogue of Coptic Manuscripts in the Pierpont Morgan Library* 1 [Text]. Corpus of Illuminated Manuscripts 4. Leuven: Peeters, 1993. [Incomplete transcription of 0316]

Estienne, Robert (Stephanus). *Nouum Iesu Christi D.N. Testamentum. Ex Bibliotheca Regia. Lutetiae*. Paris, 1550.

Gwynn, John, ed. *Remnants of the later Syriac versions of the Bible, Part I: New Testament. The Four Minor Catholic Epistles in the Original Philoxenian Version, of the Sixth Century*. Text and Translation Society 5. London/Oxford: Williams & Norgate, 1909.

Ingrams, L., P. Kingston, P. J. Parsons and J. R. Rea, eds. *The Oxyrhynchus Papyri XXXIV*. Graeco-Roman Memoirs 49. London: Egypt Exploration Society, 1968.

Junack, Klaus and Winfried Grunewald, eds. *Das Neue Testament auf Papyrus*. I: *Die Katholischen Briefe*. ANTF 6. Berlin/New York: de Gruyter, 1986.

Lachmann, Karl, ed. *Novum Testamentum Graece*. Berlin, 1831.

Lake, Kirsopp. "Texts from Mount Athos." *StudBib* 5 (1902): 89-131. [Collation of Codex 044.]

Martin, Victor, ed. *Papyrus Bodmer XX*. Cologny-Geneva: Bibliotheca Bodmeriana, 1964.

Martini, Carlo M., ed. *Beati Petri Apostoli Epistulae ex papyro bodmeriana VIII transcriptae*. Milan: ex Hamilcaris Pizzi officina libraria, 1968.

Matthaei, C. F. *Novum Testamentum Graece et Latine*. Riga, 1782.

Merk, Augustinus S. J. ed. *Novum Testamentum graece et latine apparatu critico instructum*. 11th ed. Rome: Biblical Institute Press, 1992.

Nissel, J. G. and T. Petraeus, eds. *S. Judae Apostoli epistolae catholicae versio Arabice et Aethiopice*. Leiden, 1654.

Robinson, Maurice A. and William G. Pierpont, eds. *The New Testament in the Original Greek: Byzantine Texform*. Southborough, MA: Chilton Book Publishing, 2005.

Scrivener, F. H. A. *An Exact Transcript of the Codex Augiensis*. Cambridge: Deighton, Bell & Co., 1859.

Soden, Hermann von. *Die Schriften des Neuen Testaments in ihrer ältesten erreichbaren Textgestalt hergestellt auf Grund ihrer Textgeschichte*. 2 parts in 4 vols. 2d unchanged ed. Göttingen: Vandenhoeck & Ruprecht, 1911-1913.

Testuz, Michel, ed. *Papyrus Bodmer VII-IX*. Cologny-Geneva: Bibliotheca Bodmeriana, 1959.

Thiele, Walter, ed. *Epistula Catholicae*. Vetus Latina 26/1. Freiburg im Breisgau: Herder, 1956-1969.

Tischendorf, Constantin von. *Novum Testamentum Graece*. 2 vols. 7th ed. Leipzig: Hinrichs, 1856-1859.

Tischendorf, Constantin von. *Novum Testamentum Graece.* 3 vols. 8th ed. Leipzig: Hinrichs, 1869-1894.

Tischendorf, Constantin von. *Monumenta sacra inedita, nova collectio, vol. 5.* Leipzig: Hinrichs, 1865.

Tregelles, S. P. *The Greek New Testament.* London: Samuel Bagster & Sons, 1857-72.

Wachtel, Klaus and Klaus Witte, eds. *Das Neue Testament auf Papyrus.* II.2: *Die Paulinischen Briefe.* ANTF 22. Berlin/New York: de Gruyter, 1994.

Westcott, B. F. and F. J. A. Hort. *The New Testament in the Original Greek.* 2 vols. London: Macmillan, 1881-1882.

Wettstein, Johann Jakob. *Novum Testamentum Graecum.* 2 vols. Amsterdam: Dommerian, 1751-1752.

White, Joseph, ed. *Actus apostolorum et epistolas catholicas complectens.* Vol. 1 of *Actuum apostolorum et epistolarum tam catholicarum quam Paulinarum, versio Syriaca Philoxeniana.* 2. vols. Oxford: Clarendon, 1799-1803.

Witte, Klaus and Tommy Wasserman. "L2435." Forthcoming in *Bericht der Hermann Kunst-Stiftung zur Förderung der neutestamentlichen Textforschung.*

1.4 Ancient Texts and Translations

Betz, H. D., ed. *The Greek Magical Papyri in Translation Including the Demotic Spells.* 2 vols. 2d ed. Chicago/London: University of Chicago Press, 1992.

Black, Matthew, ed. *Apocalypsis Henochi Graece.* PVTG 3. Leiden: Brill, 1970.

Daniel, Robert W. and Franco Maltomini, eds. *Supplementum Magicum.* 2 vols. ARWAW PapyCol 16.1-2. Opladen: Westdeutscher Verlag, 1990-1992.

Isaac, E. ed. "1 (Ethiopic Apocalypse of) ENOCH." Pages 5-89 in vol. 1 of *The Old Testament Pseudepigrapha.* Edited by James H. Charlesworth. 2 vols. London: Darton Longman & Todd, 1983-1985.

Isbell, Charles D. *Corpus of Aramaic Incantation Bowls.* Missoula: Scholars Press, 1975.

Kotansky, Roy. *Greek Magical Amulets. The Inscribed Gold, Silver, Copper, and Bronze "Lamellae": Text and Commentary. Part I: Published Texts of Known Provenance.* ARWAW PapyCol 22.1. Opladen: Westdeutscher Verlag, 1994.

Luck, Georg. *Arcana Mundi: Magic and the Occult in the Greek and Roman World. A Collection of Ancient Texts.* Baltimore: Johns Hopkins University, 1985.

Meyer, Marvin W. and Richard Smith. *Ancient Christian Magic: Coptic Texts of Ritual Power.* Princeton: Princeton University Press, 1999.

Milik, J. T. and Matthew Black. *The Books of Enoch: Aramaic Fragments of Qumrân Cave 4.* Oxford: Clarendon, 1976.

Müller-Kessler, Christa. *Die Zauberschalentexte in der Hilprecht Sammlung, Jena.* Wiesbaden: Harrassowitz Verlag, 2004.

Preisendanz, Karl and Albert Henrich, eds. *Papyri Graecae Magicae: Die griechischen Zauberpapyri.* 2 vols. 2d rev. ed. Stuttgart: Teubner, 1973-1974.

Strycker, Émile de. *La Forme la plus ancienne du protévangile de Jacques: Recherches sur Le Papyrus Bodmer 5 avec une édition critique de texte grec et une traduction annotée.* Subsidia Hagiographica 33. Brussells: Société des Bollandistes, 1961.

Testuz, Michel, ed. *Papyrus Bodmer VII-IX.* Cologny-Geneva: Bibliotheca Bodmeriana, 1959.

———, ed. *Papyrus Bodmer XIII.* Cologny-Geneva: Bibliotheca Bodmeriana, 1960.

———, ed. *Papyrus Bodmer X-XII.* Cologny-Geneva: Bibliotheca Bodmeriana, 1959.

Treu, Kurt and Johannes M. Diethart, eds. *Griechische literarische Papyri christlichen Inhalts II*. MPER N.S. 17. Vienna: Hollinek, 1993.

Woude, Adam S. van der. "11QApocryphal Psalms." Pages 181-205 in *Qumran Cave 11. II: 11Q2-18, 11Q20-31*. Edited by Florentino García Martínez, Eibert C. J. Tigchelaar and Adam S. van der Woude. DJD 23. Oxford: Clarendon, 1998.

1.5 Ancient Authors

Aeschylus. *Prometheus vinctus*. Edited by G. Murray in *Aeschyli tragoediae*. 2d ed. Oxford: Clarendon, 1955.

Alexander Monachus. *Inventio crucis* (PG 87).

Augustine. *De doctrina christiana*. In vol. 2 of *A Select Library of The Nicene and Post-Nicene Fathers of the Christian Church*. Series 1. Edited by Philip Schaff. 1886-1889. 14 vols. Repr. Peabody, Mass.: Hendrickson, 1994.

——. *In Evangelium Johannis tractatus*. In vol. 7 of *A Select Library of The Nicene and Post-Nicene Fathers of the Christian Church*. Series 1. Edited by Philip Schaff. 1886-1889. 14 vols. Repr. Peabody, Mass.: Hendrickson, 1994.

Clement of Alexandria. *Adumbrationes in Epistolas canonicas*. Pages 206-9 in *Stromata: Buch VII und VIII, Excerpta ex Theodoto, Eclogae proheticae, Quis dives salvetur, Fragmente*. Edited by Otto Stählin and Ludwig Früchtel. 2d edition. GCS 17. Berlin: Akademie-Verlag, 1970.

——. *Paedagogus*. Edited by H.-I. Marrou, M. Harl, C. Mondésert and C. Matray in *Clement d' Alexandrie: Le pédagogue*. 3 vols. SC 70, SC 108, SC 158. Paris: Cerf, 1960-1970.

——. *Stromata*. Edited by Otto Stählin, Ludwig Früchtel and Ursula Treu. 2 vols. GCS 52 (*Buch I-VI*). GCS 17 (*Buch VII-VIII*). Berlin: Akademie-Verlag, 1970-1985.

Cramer, J. A. *Catena in Epistolas Catholicas, accerunt Oecumenii et Arethae commentarii in Apocalypsin*. Oxford: Clarendon, 1840.

Cyril of Alexandria. *Thesaurus de sancta consubstantiali trinitate* (PG 75).

Didymus the Blind. *De trinitate*. Lib. 2.1-7. Edited by I. Seiler in *Didymus der Blinde. De trinitate, Buch 2, Kapitel 1-7*. Beiträge zur klassischen Philologie 52. Meisenheim am Glan: Hain, 1975.

——. *De trinitate*. Lib. 2.1-7. Edited by I. Seiler in *Didymus der Blinde. De trinitate, Buch 2, Kapitel 1-7*. Beiträge zur klassischen Philologie 52. Meisenheim am Glan: Hain, 1975.

——. *De trinitate*. Lib. 2.8-3 (PG 39).

——. *De trinitate*. Lib. I. Edited by J. Hönscheid in *Didymus der Blinde. De trinitate, Buch I*. Beiträge zur klassischen Philologie 44. Meisenheim am Glan: Hain, 1975.

——. *In Epistulas Catholicas brevis enarratio* (PL 34).

Galen. *De sanitate tuenda libri vi*. Edited by K. Koch. CMG 5.4.2. Leipzig: Teubner, 1923.

Homer. *Ilias*. In vol. 1-2 of *Homeri Opera*. Edited by D. B. Monro and T. W. Allen. 5 vols. Oxford: Clarendon, 1952-1959.

——. *Odyssea*. In vol. 3-4 of *Homeri Opera*. Edited by D. B. Monro and T. W. Allen. 5 vols. Oxford: Clarendon, 1952-1959.

Isidorus Pelusiota. *Epistolarum* (PG 78).

Jerome. *Adversus Jovinianum libri II* (PL 23).

——. *Adversus Rufinum libri III* (PL 23).

——. *Commentariorum in Epistulam ad Titum liber* (PL 26).

——. *De viris illustribus* (PL 23).

John Chrysostom. *Ad populum Antiochenum de statuis*. In vol. 9 of *A Select Library of The Nicene and Post-Nicene Fathers of the Christian Church*. Series 1. Edited by Philip Schaff. 1886-1889. 14 vols. Repr. Peabody, Mass.: Hendrickson, 1994.

——. *Homiliae in epistulam i ad Corinthios*. In vol. 12 of *A Select Library of The Nicene and Post-Nicene Fathers of the Christian Church*. Series 1. Edited by Philip Schaff. 1886-1889. 14 vols. Repr. Peabody, Mass.: Hendrickson, 1994.

Josephus, Flavius. *Antiquitates Judaicae*. In vol. 1-4 of *Flavii Iosephi opera*. Edited by B. Niese. 1899. 6 vols. Repr. Berlin: Weidmann, 1955.

——. *De bello Judaico libri vii*. In vol. 6 of *Flavii Iosephi opera*. Edited by B. Niese. 1899. 6 vols. Repr. Berlin: Weidmann, 1955.

Justin. *Dialogus cum Tryphone*. Pages 90-265 in *Die ältesten Apologeten*. Edited by E. J. Goodspeed. Göttingen: Vandenhoeck & Ruprecht, 1915.

Moschus. *Idyll*. Pages 151-52 in *Bucoli Graeci*. Edited by A. S. F. Gow. Oxford: Clarendon, 1952.

Nicander. *Alexipharmaca*. Pages 94-136 in *Nicander: The Poems and Poetical Fragments*. Edited by A. S. F. Gow and A. F. Scholfield. Cambridge: Cambridge University Press, 1953.

Origen. *Commentarium in evangelium Matthaei*. Lib. 10-11. Edited by R. Girod in *Origène. Commentaire sur l'évangelie selon Matthieu*. Vol. 1. SC 162. Paris: Cerf, 1970.

——. *Commentarium in evangelium Matthaei*. Lib. 12-17. Edited by E. Klostermann in *Origenes Werke*. Vol. 10.1 (1935)-10.2 (1937). GCS 40.1-40.2. Leipzig: Teubner, 1935-1937.

——. *Homilae in Exodum*. Pages 217-218, 221-230 in vol. 6 of *Origenes Werke*. Edited by W. A. Baehrens. GCS 29. Leipzig: Teubner, 1920.

Patrologia graeca. Edited by J.-P. Migne. 162 vols. Paris, 1857-1886.

Patrologia latina. Edited by J.-P. Migne. 217 vols. Paris, 1844-1864.

Philo Judaeus. *De mutatione nominum*. Pages 156-203 in vol. 3 of *Philonis Alexandrini opera quae supersunt*. Edited by L. Cohn, P. Wendland, S. Reiter and H. Leisegang. 1896-1930. 7 vols. Repr. Berlin/New York: de Gruyter, 1962-1964.

——. *De specialibus legibus*. Pages 1-265 in vol. 5 of *Philonis Alexandrini opera quae supersunt*. Edited by L. Cohn, P. Wendland, S. Reiter and H. Leisegang. 1896-1930. 7 vols. Repr. Berlin/New York: de Gruyter, 1962-1964.

——. *De vita Mosis*. In vol. 4 of *Philonis Alexandrini opera quae supersunt*. Edited by L. Cohn, P. Wendland, S. Reiter and H. Leisegang. 1896-1930. 7 vols. Repr. Berlin/New York: de Gruyter, 1962-1964.

Photius. *Bibliotheca*. Edited by René Henry in *Bibliothèque*. 9 vols. *Collection byzantine*. Paris: Société d'édition Les belles lettres, 1959-1991.

——. *Epistulae et Amphilochia*. Edited by Basileios Laourdas and Leendert G. Westerink in *Photii patriarchae Constantinopolitani Epistulae et Amphilochia*. 8 vols. Leipzig: Teubner, 1983-1988.

Pindar. *Pythionikai*. Pages 59-121 in *Pindari carmina cum fragmentis*. Edited by H. Maehler. 5th ed. Leipzig: Teubner, 1971.

Plutarch. *De facie in orbe lunae*. Translated by H. Cherniss and William C. Helmbold in vol. 12 (LCL 406) of Plutarch, *Moralia*. 15 vols. Loeb Classical Library. Cambridge, Mass.: Harvard University press, 1927-1967.

——. *Theseus*. Pages 1-35 in vol. 1.1 of *Plutarchi vitae parallelae*. Edited by K. Ziegler. 4th ed. Leipzig: Teubner, 1969.

Pseudo-Oecumenius. *Catholica epistola Judae Apostoli* (PG 119).

Rufinus. *De adulteratione librorum Origenis 6-8*. Edited and translated by Manlio Simonetti. CCSL 20. Turnhout: Brepols, 1961.

Scholia Platonica. Edited by W. C. Greene. Haverford, Pennsylvania: American Philological Association, 1938.

Testaments of the Twelve Patriarchs. Edited by Marinus de Jonge. 2d ed. PVTG 1. Leiden: Brill, 1970.

The Seven Ecumenical Councils. In vol. 14 of *A Select Library of The Nicene and Post-Nicene Fathers of the Christian Church*. Series 2. Edited by Philip Schaff and Henry Wace. 1886-1889. 14 vols. Repr. Peabody, Mass.: Hendrickson, 1994.

Theophilus of Antioch. *Ad Autolycum*. Edited by Robert M. Grant. Oxford: Clarendon, 1970.

Theophylact. *Expositio in epistolam S. Judae Apostoli* (PG 126).

2. Tools and Lexica

Anchor Bible Dictionary. Edited by David Noel Freedman. 6 vols. New York: Doubleday, 1992.

Bauer, W., F. W. Danker, W. F. Arndt, and F. W. Gingrich. *Greek-English Lexicon of the New Testament and Other Early Christian Literature*. 3d ed. Chicago: University of Chicago Press, 2000.

Blass, F., A. Debrunner, and R. W. Funk. *A Greek Grammar of the New Testament and Other Early Christian Literature*. Chicago: University of Chicago Press, 1961.

Dictionary of the Bible. Edited by James Hastings et al. 5 vols. Edinburgh: T. & T. Clark, 1904-1910.

Dictionnaire de la Bible. Edited by F. Vigouroux. 5 vols. Paris: Letouzey et Ané, 1895-1912.

Encyclopedia of Religion and Ethics. Edited by James Hastings et al. 12 vols. New York: Charles Scribner's Sons, 1908-1926.

Gesenius' Hebrew Grammar. Edited by E. Kautzsch. Translated by A. E. Cowley. 2d rev. ed. London: Oxford University Press, 1910.

Jannaris, Antonius N. *An Historical Greek Grammar Chiefly of the Attic Dialect*. London: Macmillan, 1897.

Liddell, H. G., R. Scott, and H. S. Jones. *A Greek-English Lexicon*. 9th ed. with revised supplement. Oxford: Oxford University Press, 1996.

Mayser, Edwin. *Grammatik der griechischen Papyri aus der Ptolemäerzeit. Band I: Laut- und Wortlehre. 1. Teil: Einleitung und Lautlehre*. 2d ed. Revised by H. Schmoll. Berlin: de Gruyter, 1970.

Moulton, James H. *Accidence and Word Formation with an Appendix on Semitisms in the New Testament*. Vol. 2 (1929) of *Grammar of New Testament Greek*. Edited by James H. Moulton, W. F. Howard and Nigel Turner. Edinburgh: T. & T. Clark, 1908-1976.

Religion in Geschichte und Gegenwart. Edited by K. Galling. 7 vols. 3d ed. Tübingen: Mohr Siebeck, 1957-1965.

Theological Dictionary of the New Testament. Edited by G. Kittell and G. Friedrich. Translated by G. W. Bromiley. 10 vols. Grand Rapids: Eerdmans, 1964-1976.

Turner, Nigel. *Syntax.* Vol. 3 (1963) of *Grammar of New Testament Greek.* Edited by James H. Moulton, W. F. Howard and Nigel Turner. Edinburgh: T. & T. Clark, 1908-1976.

Wallace, Daniel B. *Greek Grammar Beyond the Basics.* Grand Rapids: Zondervan, 1996.

Winer, G. B. *A Treatise on the Grammar of New Testament Greek.* Translated by idem. 3d rev. ed. Edinburgh: T. & T. Clark, 1882.

3. Secondary Literature

Aland, Barbara. "Welche Rolle spielen Textkritik und Textgeschichte für das Verständnis des Neuen Testaments? Frühe Leserperspektiven." *NTS* 52 (2006): 303-18.

Aland, Barbara and Klaus Wachtel. "The Greek Minuscule Manuscripts of the New Testament." Pages 43-60 in *The Text of the New Testament in Contemporary Research: Essays on the Status Quaestionis.* Edited by Bart D. Ehrman and Michael W. Holmes. SD 46. Grand Rapids: Eerdmans, 1995.

Aland, Kurt. "Bemerkungen zu den gegenwärtigen Möglichkeiten text-kritischer Arbeit aus Anlass einer Untersuchung zum Cäsarea-Text der Katholischen Briefe." *NTS* 17 (1970): 1-9.

———, ed. *Repertorium der griechischen christlichen Papyri.* I: *Biblische Papyri: Altes Testament, Neues Testament, Varia, Apokryphen.* PTS 18. Berlin/New York: de Gruyter, 1976.

———, ed. *Text und Textwert der griechischen Handschriften des Neuen Testaments.* I: *Die Katholischen Briefe.* 3 vols. ANTF 9-11. Berlin/New York: de Gruyter, 1987.

Aland, Kurt and Barbara Aland. *The Text of the New Testament: An Introduction to the Critical Editions and to the Theory and Practice of Modern Textual Criticism.* Translated by Erroll F. Rhodes. 2d rev. and enl. ed. Grand Rapids: Eerdmans, 1995.

Aland, Kurt, Michael Welte, Beate Köster and Klaus Junack, eds. *Kurzgefasste Liste der griechischen Handschriften des Neuen Testaments.* 2d rev. and enl. ed. ANTF 1. Berlin/New York: de Gruyter, 1994.

Albin, C. A. *Judasbrevet: Traditionen, Texten, Tolkningen.* Stockholm: Natur och Kultur, 1962.

Albrektson, Bertil. "'Difficilior Lectio Probabilior'—A Rule of Textual Criticism and Its Use in Old Testament Studies." Pages 5-18 in *Remembering All the Way.* Edited by Bertil Albrektsson. Oudtestamentische Studien 21. Leiden: Brill, 1981.

Alexander, Loveday. "Septuaginta, Fachprosa, Imitatio: Albert Wifstrand and the Language of Luke-Acts." Pages 1-26 in *Die Apostelgeschichte und die hellenistische Geschichtsschreibung: Festschrift für Eckhard Plümacher zu seinem 65. Geburtstag.* Edited by Cilliers Breytenbach et al. Leiden/Boston: Brill, 2004.

Allen, Joel S. "A New Possibility for the Three-clause Format of Jude 22-3." *NTS* 44 (1998): 133-43.

Amphoux, Christian-Bernard. "La parenté textuelle du sy[h] et du groupe 2138 dans l'épître de Jacques." *Bib* 62 (1981): 259-71.

———. "Le Texte des épîtres catholiques." Ph.D. diss., Paris Sorbonne University, 1981.

———. "Quelques témoins grecs des formes textuelles les plus anciennes de l'Épître de Jacques: le groupe 2138 (ou 614)." *NTS* 28 (1982): 91-115.

Amphoux, Christian-Bernard and Bernard Outtier. "Les leçons des versions géorgiennes de Jacques." *Bib* 65 (1984): 365-76.

Amundsen, Leiv. "Christian Papyri from the Oslo Collection." *SO* 24 (1945): 121-47.

Anderson, Amy S. *The Textual Tradition of the Gospels: Family 1 in Matthew*. NTTS 32. Leiden: Brill, 2004.

Arzt-Grabner, Peter and Michael Ernst. "*P.Bingen* 16. *Ps.*, 43, 21-24.27 und *Ps.*, 44, 1-2 LXX." Pages 79-84 (+ plate 9) in *Papyri in Honorem Johannis Bingen Octogenarii*. Edited by Henri Melaerts et al. Studia Varia Bruxellensia 5. Leuven: Peeters, 2000.

Aune, David E. "Magic in Early Christianity." *ANRW* 23.2:1507-1557. Part 2, *Principat* 23.2. Edited by H. Temporini and W. Haase. Berlin/New York: de Gruyter, 1980.

Awoniyi, Joel D. "The Classification of the Greek Manuscripts of the Epistle of James." Th.D. diss., Andrews University, 1979.

Bar-Ilan, Meir. "Between Magic and Religion: Sympathetic Magic in the World of the Sages of the Mishnah and Talmud." *Review of Rabbinic Judaism* 5 (2002): 383-99.

Bauckham, Richard J. "2 Peter: An Account of Research." *ANRW* 25.5:3713-52. Part 2, *Principat* 25.5. Edited by H. Temporini and W. Haase. Berlin/New York: de Gruyter, 1988.

——. "A Note on a Problem in the Greek Version of 1 Enoch 1:9." *JTS* 32 (1981): 136-38.

——. *Jude, 2 Peter*. WBC 50. Waco: Word Books, 1983.

——. *Jude and the Relatives of Jesus in the Early Church*. Edinburgh: T. & T. Clark, 1990.

——. "The Letter of Jude: An Account of Research." *ANRW* 25.5:3791-3826. Part 2, *Principat* 25.5. Edited by H. Temporini and W. Haase. Berlin/New York: de Gruyter, 1988.

Beare, F. W. "Some Remarks on the Text of I Peter in the Bodmer Papyrus ($\mathfrak{P}$72)." Pages 263-65 in *Studia Evangelica* 3. Part 2: *The New Testament Message*. Edited by F. L. Cross. TU 88. Berlin: Akademie-Verlag, 1964.

——. "The Text of 1 Peter in Papyrus 72." *JBL* 80 (1961): 253-60.

Benoit, Pierre. "Fragment d'une prière contre les esprits impurs?" *RB* 59 (1951): 549-65.

Bieder, Werner. "Judas 22f." *TZ* 6 (1950):75-77.

Bigg, Charles. *A Critical and Exegetical Commentary on the Epistles of St. Peter and St. Jude*. 2d ed. ICC. Edinburgh: T. & T. Clark, 1902.

Biondi, A. "Le citazione bibliche nei papiri magici cristiani greci." *SPap* 20 (1981): 93-127.

Birdsall, J. Neville. "The Text of Jude in $\mathfrak{P}$72." *JTS* 14 (1963): 394-99.

Black, Matthew. "Critical and Exegetical Notes on Three New Testament Texts: Hebrews xi.11, Jude 5, James i.27." Pages 39-45 in *Apophoreta: Festschrift für Ernst Haenchen*. Edited by W. Eltester. BZNW 30. Berlin: Alfred Töpelmann, 1964.

——. "The Christological Use of the Old Testament in the New Testament." *NTS* 18 (1971): 1-14.

——. "The Maranatha Invocation and Jude 14, 15 (1 Enoch 1:9)." Pages 189-96 in *Christ and Spirit in the New Testament*. Edited by Barnabas Lindars and Stephen S. Smalley. Cambridge: Cambridge University Press, 1973.

Blakely, Wayne A. "Manuscript Relationships As Indicated by the Epistles of Jude and II Peter." Ph.D. diss., Emory University, 1964.

——. "The Text of the Epistle of Jude, A Critical Study." Master Thesis, Emory University, 1958.

Bonner, Campbell. *Studies in Magical Amulets*. Ann Arbor: University of Michigan Press, 1950.

Bouhot, Jean-Paul and Christian-Bernard Amphoux. "Lecture liturgique et critique textuelle des Épitres Catholiques." Pages 283-307 in *La lecture liturgique des Épitres catholiques dans l'Église ancienne*. Edited by Jean-Paul Bouhot and Christian-Bernard Amphoux. HTB 1. Lausanne: Éditions du Zèbre, 1996.

Bremmer, J. N. "The Birth of the Term 'Magic'." *ZPE* 126 (1999): 1-12.

Brown, J. D. M. "The Text of the Epistle of Jude. Studies in Textual Criticism." *Lutheran Church Review* 31 (1912): 53-64, 295-307, 474-84.

Callan, Terrance. "Use of the Letter of Jude by the Second Letter of Peter." *Bib* 85 (2004): 42-64.

Caragounis, Chrys C. *The Development of Greek and the New Testament: Morphology, Syntax, Phonology, and Textual Transmission*. WUNT 167. Tübingen: Mohr Siebeck, 2004.

———. "The Error of Erasmus and Un-Greek Pronunciations of Greek." *Filologia Neotestamentaria* 8 (1995): 151-85.

———. "'To Boast' or 'To Be Burned'? The Crux of 1 Cor 13:3." *SEÅ* 60 (1995): 115-27.

Carder, Muriel M. "A Caesarean Text in the Catholic Epistles?" *NTS* 16 (1970): 252-70.

———. "An Enquiry into the Textual Transmission of the Catholic Epistles." Th.D. diss., Victoria University, 1968.

Charles, J. Daryl. "Literary Artifice in the Epistle of Jude." *ZNW* 82 (1991): 106-24.

———. *Literary Strategy in the Epistle of Jude*. Scranton: University of Scranton Press, 1993.

Christoffersson, Olle. *The Earnest Expectation of the Creature. The Flood Tradition As Matrix of Romans 8:18-27*. CBNTS 23. Stockholm: Almqvist & Wiksell International, 1990.

Clark, David J. "Discourse Structure in Jude." *The Bible Translator* (Technical Papers) 55 (2004): 125-37.

Clarke, Kent D. "Textual Certainty in the United Bible Societies' *Greek New Testament*." *NovT* 44 (2002): 105-33.

———. *Textual Optimism: A Critique of the United Bible Societies' Greek New Testament*. Sheffield: Sheffield Academic Press, 1997.

Collart, Paul. "Psaumes et amulettes." *Aegyptus* 14 (1934): 463-67.

Colwell, Ernest C. "Method in Evaluating Scribal Habits: A Study of $\mathfrak{P}^{45}$, $\mathfrak{P}^{66}$, $\mathfrak{P}^{75}$." Pages 106-24 in Ernest C. Colwell, *Studies in Methodology in Textual Criticism of the New Testament*. NTTS 9. Leiden: Brill, 1969. Repr. from "Scribal Habits in Early Papyri: A Study in the Corruption of the Text," in *The Bible in Modern Scholarship*. Edited by J. Philip Hyatt. Nashville: Abingdon, 1965.

———. "The Significance of Grouping of New Testament Manuscripts." Pages 1-25 in Ernest C. Colwell, *Studies in Methodology in Textual Criticism of the New Testament*. NTTS 9. Leiden: Brill, 1969. Repr. from *NTS* 4 (1958): 73-92 ("The Significance of Grouping of New Testament Manuscripts").

Colwell, Ernest C. and Ernest W. Tune. "The Quantitative Relationships Between MS Text types." Pages 25-32 in *Biblical and Patristic Studies in Memory of Robert Pierce Casey*. Edited by J. Neville Birdsall and Robert W. Thomson. Freiburg/Basel/New York: Herder, 1963.

Dehandschutter, Boudewijn. "Pseudo-Cyprian, Jude and Enoch: Some Notes on 1 Enoch 1:9." Pages 114-20 in *Tradition and Re-interpretation in Jewish and Early Christian Literature: Essays in Honour of Jürgen C. H. Lebram*. Edited by J. W. van Henten et al. Leiden: Brill, 1986.

Deichgräber, Reinhard. *Gotteshymnus und Christushymnus in der frühen Christenheit*. SUNT 5. Göttingen: Vandenhoeck & Ruprecht, 1967.

Deissmann, Adolf. *Light from the Ancient East*. Translated by L. R. M. Strachan. New York: George H. Doran, 1927.

Der Nersessian, Sirarpie. "A Psalter and New Testament Manuscript at Dumbarton Oaks." *Dumbarton Oaks Papers* 19 (1965): 153-83

Dickie, Matthew W. "The Fathers of the Church and the Evil Eye." Pages 9-34 in *Byzantine Magic*. Edited by Henry Maguire. Washington D.C.: Dumbarton Oaks Research Library and Collection, 1995.

Dix, D. Gregory. *Jew and Greek. A Study in the Primitive Church*. London: Dacre Press, 1953.

Duplacy, Jean. "Bulletin de critique textuelle du NT." RSR 50 (1962): 242-63.

———. "Le texte occidental des Épitres Catholiques." *NTS* 16 (1970): 397-99.

———. "Manuscrits Grecs du Nouveau Testament émigrés de la Grande Laure de l' Athos." Pages 159-78 in *Studica Codicologica*. Edited by Kurt Treu. TU 124. Berlin: Akademie-Verlag, 1977.

Duplacy, Jean and Christian-Bernard Amphoux. "À propos de l'histoire du texte de la première épître de Pierre." Pages 155-73 in *Études sur la Première Lettre de Pierre*. Edited by C. Perrot. LD 102. Paris: Cerf, 1980.

Durkheim, Émile. *Les formes élementaires de la vie religieuse: le système totemique en Australie*. Paris: F. Alcan, 1911.

Ehrman, Bart D. "A Problem of Textual Circularity: The Alands on the Classification of New Testament Manuscripts." *Bib* 70 (1989): 377-88.

———. *The Orthodox Corruption of Scripture: The Effect of Early Christological Controversies on the Text of the New Testament*. New York/Oxford: Oxford University Press, 1993.

Elliott, J. K.. "The New Testament in Greek: Two New Editions." *TLZ* 119 (1994): 493-96.

———. Review of Barbara Aland, et al., eds., *Novum Testamentum Graecum Editio Critica Maior. Vol. IV: Catholic Letters. Installment 1: James. Part 1: Text*. NovT 40 (1998): 195-204.

———. "The Petrine Epistles in the *Editio Critica Maior*." *NovT* 42 (2000): 328-39.

———. "The Third Edition of the United Bible Societies' Greek New Testament." *NovT* 20 (1978): 242-77.

Elliott, W. J. "The Need for an Accurate and Comprehensive Collation of all Known Greek NT Manuscripts." Pages 137-43 in *Studies in New Testament Language and Text*. Edited by J. K. Elliott. NovTSup 44. Leiden: Brill, 1976.

Ellis, E. Earle. *Prophecy and Hermeneutic in Early Christianity*. WUNT 18. Tübingen: Mohr Siebeck, 1978. Repr., Grand Rapids: Eerdmans, 1978

Epp, Eldon J. "Issues in New Testament Textual Criticism." Pages 52-70 *in Rethinking New Testament Textual Criticism*. Edited by David A. Black. Grand Rapids: Baker, 2002.

——. "The Claremont Profile Method For Grouping New Testament Minuscule Manuscripts." Pages 211-20 in Eldon J. Epp and Gordon D. Fee, *Studies in the Theory and Method of New Testament Textual Criticism.* SD 45. Grand Rapids: Eerdmans, 1993.

——. "Toward the Clarification of the Term 'Textual Variant'." Pages 47-61 in Eldon J. Epp and Gordon D. Fee, *Studies in the Theory and Method of New Testament Textual Criticism.* SD 45. Grand Rapids: Eerdmans, 1993.

Eshel, Ester. "Genres of Magical Texts in the Dead Sea Scrolls." Pages 394-415 in *Die Dämonen. Demons.* Edited by Armin Lange, Hermann Lichtenberger and K. F. Diethard Römheld. Tübingen: Mohr Siebeck, 2003.

Evans-Pritchard, E. E. *Theories of Primitive Religion.* Oxford: Clarendon, 1965.

Fee, Gordon D. "On the Types, Classification, and Presentation of Textual Variation." Pages 62-79 in Eldon J. Epp and Gordon D. Fee, *Studies in the Theory and Method of New Testament Textual Criticism.* SD 45. Grand Rapids: Eerdmans, 1993.

Filson, Floyd. V. "More Bodmer Papyri." *BA* 25 (1962): 50-57.

Fornberg, Tord. *An Early Church in a Pluralistic Society: A Study of 2 Peter.* CBNTS 9. Lund: CWK Gleerup, 1977.

Fossum, Jarl E. "Kyrios Jesus: Angel Christology in Jude 5-7." Pages 41-69 in Jarl E. Fossum, *The Image of the Invisible God: Essays on the Influence of Jewish Mysticism on Early Christology.* NTOA 30. Freiburg: Universitätsverlag Freiburg Schweiz; Göttingen: Vandenhoeck & Ruprecht, 1995.

——. "Kyrios Jesus as the Angel of the Lord in Jude 5-7." *NTS* 33 (1987): 226-43.

Frazer, James G. *The Golden Bough: A Study in Magic and Religion.* Abr. ed. London: Macmillan, 1922.

Frey, Jörg. "Der Judasbrief zwischen Judentum und Hellenismus." Pages 180-210 in *Frühjudentum und Neues Testament im Horizont Biblischer Theologie.* Edited by Wolfgang Kraus and Karl Wilhelm Niebuhr. WUNT 2.162. Tübingen: Mohr Siebeck, 2003.

Gallagher, J. Tim. "A Study of von Soden's H-Text in the Catholic Epistles." *AUSS* 8 (1970): 97-119.

Geer, Jr., Thomas C. "Analyzing and Categorizing New Testament Greek Manuscripts: Colwell Revisited." Pages 253-67 in *The Text of the New Testament in Contemporary Research: Essays on the Status Quaestionis.* Edited by Bart D. Ehrman and Michael W. Holmes. SD 46. Grand Rapids: Eerdmans, 1995.

Gerdmar, Anders. *Rethinking the Judaism-Hellenism Dichotomy: A Historiographical Case Study of Second Peter and Jude.* CBNTS 36. Stockholm: Almqvist & Wiksell International, 2001.

Gilmour, Michael J. *The Significance of Parallels between 2 Peter and Other Early Christian Literature.* Academia Biblica 10. Atlanta: Society of Biblical Literature, 2002.

Goehring, James E. ed. *The Crosby-Schøyen Codex MS 193 in the Schøyen Collection.* CSCO 521. Leuven: Peeters, 1990.

Goltz, Eduard von der. *Eine textkritische Arbeit des zehnten bezw. sechsten Jahrhunderts.* TU 17/4. Leipzig: Hinrichs, 1899.

Gregory, Caspar René. *Textkritik des Neuen Testaments.* 3 vols. Leipzig: J. C. Hinrichs, 1900-1909.

Guthrie, Donald. *New Testament Introduction.* Leicester: Intervarsity Press, 1970.

Güting, Eberhard. "Amen, Eulogie, Doxologie. Eine textkritische Untersuchung." Pages 133-62 in *Begegnungen zwischen Christentum und Judentum in Antike und Mittelalter:*

Festschrift für Heinz Schreckenberg. Edited by Dietrich-Alex Koch and Hermann Lichtenberger, et al. Göttingen: Vandenhoeck & Ruprecht, 1993.

Haines-Eitzen, Kim. *Guardians of Letters: Literacy, Power, and the Transmitters of Early Christian Literature.* Oxford: Oxford University Press, 2000.

Harnack, Adolf von. *Zur Revision der Prinzipen der neutestamentlichen Textkritik.* Vol. 7 of *Beiträge zur Einleitung in das Neue Testament.* 7 vols. Leipzig: Hinrichs, 1906-1916.

Harris, J. Rendel. "New Testament Autographs." *The American Journal of Philology* 3, no. 12 (1882): 1-54.

Head, Peter M. "Christology and Textual Transmission: Reverential Alterations in the Synoptic Gospels." *NovT* 35 (1993): 105-29.

Heiligenthal, Roman. "Der Judasbrief: Aspekte der Forschung in den letzten Jahrzehnten." *ThR* 51 (1986): 117-29.

Heitmüller, Wilhelm. *Im Namen Jesu: Eine sprach- und religionsgeschichtliche Untersuchung zum Neuen Testament, speziell zur altchristlichen Taufe.* FRLANT 2. Göttingen: Vandenhoeck & Ruprecht, 1903.

Holmes, Michael W. "Reasoned Eclecticism in New Testament Textual Criticism." Pages 336-360 in *The Text of the New Testament in Contemporary Research: Essays on the Status Quaestionis.* Edited by Bart D. Ehrman and Michael W. Holmes. SD 46. Grand Rapids: Eerdmans, 1995.

Horsley, G. H. R. "Reconstructing a Biblical Codex: the Prehistory of MPER *n.s.* XVII. 10 (*P.Vindob.* G 29831)." Pages 473-81 in *Akten des 21. Internationalen Papyrologenkongresses, Berlin, 13.-19.8.1995.* Edited by B. Kramer et al. 2 vols. APF Beihefte 3. Stuttgart/Leipzig: Teubner, 1997.

Hovhanessian, Vahan. "Third Corinthians: Reclaiming Paul for Christian Orthodoxy." Ph.D. diss., Fordham University, 1998.

Hubert, Henri and Marcel Mauss. "Esquisse d'une théorie génerale de la magie." *Année sociologique* 7 (1904): 1-146.

Huffman, Norman A. "Revised Catalogue Data on Greek Gospel Mss. in Italy." *NovT* 1 (1956):156-60.

Judge, Edwin A. "The Magical Use of Scripture." Pages 339-49 in *Perspectives on Language and Text: Essays and Poems in Honor of Francis I. Andersen's Sixtieth Birthday.* Edited by Edgar W. Conrad and Edward G. Newing. Winona Lake: Eisenbrauns, 1987.

Jülicher, A. *Einleitung in das Neue Testament.* 5-6th ed. Tübingen: Mohr Siebeck, 1931.

Junack, Klaus. "Zu den griechischen Lektionarien und ihrer Überlieferung der Katholischen Briefe." Pages 498-591 in *Die alten Übersetzungen des Neuen Testaments, die Kirchenväterzitate und Lektionare.* Edited by Kurt Aland. ANTF 5. Berlin/New York: de Gruyter, 1972.

Kaczynski, Reiner. *Das Wort Gottes in Liturgie und Alltag der Gemeinden des Johannes Chrysostomus.* FThSt 94. Freiburg: Herder, 1974.

Käsemann, Ernst. "Eine Apologie der urchristlichen Eschatologie." *ZTK* 49 (1952): 272-96.

Kee, Howard C. "The Terminology of Mark's Exorcism Stories." *NTS 14* (1968): 232-46.

Kellett, E. E. "Note on Jude 5." *Expository Times* 15 (1903-1904): 381.

Kelly, J. N. D. *A Commentary on the Epistles of Peter and Jude.* BNTC. London: A. & C. Black, 1969.

Kern-Ulmer, Brigitte. "The Depiction of Magic in Rabbinic Texts: The Rabbinic and the Greek Concept of Magic." *JSJ* 27 (1996): 289-303.

Kieffer, René. *Filemonbrevet, Judasbrevet och Andra Petrusbrevet.* KNT 18. Stockholm: EFS-förlaget, 2001.

Kilpatrick, G. D. "Ἀγάπη as Love-Feast in the New Testament." Pages 157-62 in *Parola e spirito: Studi Onore di Settimio Cipriani.* Edited by Cesare C. Marcheselli. Brescia: Paideia Editrice, 1982.

———. "The Bodmer and Mississippi Collection of Biblical and Christian Texts." *GRBS* 4 (1963): 33-47.

King, Marchant A. "Notes on the Bodmer Manuscript." *BSac* 121 (1964): 54-57.

Klijn, A. F. J. "Jude 5 to 7." Pages 237-44 in vol. 1 of *New Testament Age: Essays in Honor of Bo Reicke.* Edited by W. C. Weinrich. 2 vols. Macon: Mercer University, 1984.

Krans, Jan. *Beyond What Is Written.* NTTS 35. Leiden: Brill, 2006.

Kraus, Thomas J. "*P.Oxy.* V 840—Amulett oder Miniaturkodex? Grundsätzliche und ergänzende Anmerkungen zu zwei Termini." *ZAC* 8 (2005): 485-97.

———. "'Pergament oder Papyrus?' Anmerkungen zur Signifikanz des Beschreibstoffes bei der Behandlung von Manuskripten." *NTS* 49 (2003): 425-32.

———. Review of S. J. Kraftchick, *Jude, 2 Peter, n.p. [published 15 May 2004]. Online: http://www.bookreviews.org/pdf/3126_3436.pdf).*

———. "Septuaginta-Psalm 90 in apotropäischer Verwendung: Vorüberlegungen für eine kritische Edition und (bisheriges) Datenmaterial." Paper presented at *The 24th International Congress of Papyrology.* Helsinki, August 2, 2004.

———. *Sprache, Stil und historischer Ort des zweiten Petrusbriefes.* WUNT 2.136. Tübingen: Mohr Siebeck, 2001.

Krüger, Friedrich. *Schlüssel zu von Soden's die Schriften des Neuen Testaments in ihrer ältesten erreichbaren Textgestalt hergestellt.* Göttingen: Vandenhoeck & Ruprecht, 1927.

Kruger, Michael J. "P. Oxy. 840: Amulet or Miniature Codex?" *JTS* 53 (2002): 81-94.

Kubo, Sakae. "A Comparative Study of 𝔓⁷² and the Codex Vaticanus." Ph.D. diss., University of Chicago, 1964.

———. "Jude 22-3: Two-division Form or Three?" Pages 239-53 in *New Testament Textual Criticism: Its Significance for Exegesis.* Edited by Eldon J. Epp and Gordon D. Fee. Oxford: Oxford University Press, 1981.

———. *𝔓⁷² and Codex Vaticanus.* SD 7. Salt Lake City: University of Utah Press, 1965.

———. "Textual relationships in Jude." Pages 276-82 in *Studies in New Testament Language and Text.* Edited by J. K. Elliott. NovTSup 44. Leiden: Brill, 1976.

———. "The Catholic Epistles in the Greek Lectionary: A Preliminary Investigation." *AUSS* 1 (1963): 65-70.

Kühl, Ernst. *Die Briefe Petri und Judae.* 6th ed. KEK 12. Göttingen: Vandenheck & Ruprecht, 1897.

Lake, Kirsopp. "Texts from Mount Athos." *StudBib* 5 (1902): 89-131.

Landon, Charles. *A Text-Critical Study of the Epistle of Jude.* JSNTSup 135. Sheffield: Sheffield Academic Press, 1996.

Lattke, Michael. *Die Oden Salomos in ihrer Bedeutung für Neues Testament und Gnosis.* 4 vols. OBO 25. Göttingen: Vandenhoeck & Ruprecht, 1979-1998.

Lenski, R. C. H. *The Interpretation of The Epistles of St. Peter, St. John and St. Jude.* Columbus: The Wartburg Press, 1945.

Lévy-Bruhl, Lucien. *Les fonctions mentales dans les sociétés inférieures*. Paris: F. Alcan, 1910.

Lichtenberger, Hermann. "Ps 91 und die Exorzismen in 11QpsApᵃ." Pages 416-421 in *Die Dämonen. Demons*. Edited by Armin Lange, Hermann Lichtenberger and K. F. Diethard Römheld. Tübingen: Mohr Siebeck, 2003.

Lövestam, Evald. *Jesus and "this Generation."* CBNTS 25. Stockholm: Almqvist & Wiksell International, 1995.

Maier, F. "Zur Erklärung des Judasbriefes (Jud 5)." *BZ* 2 (1904): 377-97.

Massaux, Edouard. "Le texte de l'épître de Jude du Papyrus Bodmer VII (𝔓⁷²)." Pages 108-25 in *Scrinium Lovaniense: mélanges historiques historische opstellen Étienne van Cauwenbergh*. Edited by Jozef Vergote, et al. Gembloux: J Duculot, 1961.

Mayor, Joseph B. *The Epistle of St. Jude and the Second Epistle of St. Peter*. London: Macmillan, 1907.

Mazich, Edward. "'The Lord Will Come with His Holy Myriads' An Investigation of the Linguistic Source of the Citation of 1 Enoch 1,9 in Jude 14b-15." *ZNW* 94 (2003): 276-81.

Mees, Michael. "Papyrus Bodmer VII (𝔓⁷²) und die Zitate aus dem Judasbrief bei Clemens von Alexandrien." Pages 133-41 in *Miscelánea Patristica; Homenaje al Angel C Vega*. Edited by T. Alonso. Madrid: Real Monasterio de El Escorial, 1968.

——. "𝔓⁷⁸ ein neuer Textzeuge für den Judasbrief." *Orient-Press* 1 (1970): 5-10.

Metzger, Bruce M. "Greek Manuscripts of John's Gospel with Hermeneia'." Pages 162-69 in *Text and Testimony: Essays on New Testament and Apocryphal Literature in Honour of A. F. J. Klijn*. Edited by Tjitze Baarda et al. Kampen: Pharos, 1988.

——. *A Textual Commentary on the Greek New Testament*. 1st corr. ed. London/New York: United Bible Societies, 1975.

——. *A Textual Commentary on the Greek New Testament*. 2d ed. Stuttgart: Deutsche Bibelgesellschaft, 1994.

——. *Manuscripts of the Greek Bible*. New York/Oxford: Oxford University Press, 1981.

——. *The Early Versions of the New Testament*. Oxford: Clarendon, 1977.

Miller, J. Edward. "Some Observations on the Text-Critical Function of the Umlauts in Vaticanus, with Special Attention to 1 Corinthians 14.34-35." *JSNT* 26 (2003): 217-36.

Mink, Gerd. "Problems of a Highly Contaminated Tradition: The New Testament. Stemmata of Variants As a Source of a Genealogy for Witnesses." Pages 13-85 in *Studies in Stemmatology II*. Edited by Pieter van Reenen, August den Hollander and Margot van Mulken. Amsterdam: John Benjamins, 2004.

Moir, Ian and J. K. Elliott. *Manuscripts and the Text of the New Testament: An Introduction for English Readers*. Edinburgh: T&T Clark, 1995.

Moo, Douglas J. *2 Peter and Jude*. NIVAC. Grand Rapids: Zondervan, 1996).

Most, William G. "Did St Luke Imitate the Septuagint?" *JSNT* 15 (1982): 30-41.

Naveh, Joseph and Shaul Shaked. *Magic Spells and Formulae*. Jerusalem: The Magnes Press, 1993.

Neyrey, Jerome H. *2 Peter, Jude*. AB 37C. New York: Doubleday, 1993.

——. "The Form and Background of the Polemic in 2 Peter." Ph.D.diss., Yale University, 1977.

Niccum, Curt. "The voice of the MSS on the Silence of the Women: The External Evidence for 1 Cor 13:34-35." *NTS* 43 (1997): 242-55.

Nicklas, Tobias. "Der 'lebendige Text' des Neuen Testaments: Der *Judasbrief* in $\mathfrak{P}^{72}$ (*P.Bodmer* VII)." *ASE* 22 (2005): 203-22.

——. "Zur historischen und theologischen Bedeutung der Erforschung neutestamentlicher Textgeschichte." *NTS* 48 (2002): 145-58.

Nicklas, Tobias and Tommy Wasserman. "Theologische Linien im *Codex Bodmer Miscellani*?" Pages 161-88 in *New Testament Manuscripts: Their Texts and Their World.* Edited by Thomas J. Kraus and Tobias Nicklas. TENT 2. Leiden: Brill, 2006.

Osburn, Carroll D. "1 Enoch 80:2-8 (67:5-7) and Jude 12-13." *CBQ* 47 (1985): 296-303.

——. "Discourse Analysis and Jewish Apocalyptic in Jude." Pages 287-319 in *Linguistics and New Testament Interpretation.* Edited by David A. Black et al. Nashville: Broadman Press, 1992.

——. "The Christological Use of 1 Enoch 1.9 in Jude 14, 15." *NTS* 23 (1977): 334-41.

——. "The Text of 1 Corinthians 10:9." Pages 201-12 in *New Testament Textual Criticism: Its Significance for Exegesis—Essays in Honour of Bruce M. Metzger.* Edited by Eldon J. Epp and Gordon D. Fee. Oxford: Clarendon, 1981.

——. "The Text of Jude 22-23." *ZNW* 63 (1972): 139-44.

——. "The Text of Jude 5." *Bib* 62 (1981): 107-15.

Paulsen, Henning. *Der Zweite Petrusbrief und der Judasbrief.* KEK 12/2. Göttingen: Vandenhoeck & Ruprecht, 1992.

Payne, Philip B. "Fuldensis, Sigla for Variants in Vaticanus and 1 Cor 14.34-5." *NTS* 41 (1995): 240-62.

Payne, Philip B. and Paul Canart. "The Originality of Text-Critical Symbols in Codex Vaticanus." *NovT* 42 (2000): 105-13.

——. "The Text-Critical Function of the Umlauts in Vaticanus, with Special Attention to 1 Corinthians 14.34-35: A Response to J. Edward Miller." *JSNT* 27 (2004): 105-12.

Perler, Othmar. *Ein Hymnus zur Ostervirgil von Meliton?* Freiburg: Universitätsverlag Freiburg, 1960.

Petersen, William L. "Some Remarks on the First Volume (The Epistle of James) of the Novum Testamentum Graecum Editio Critica Maior." *TC: A Journal of Biblical Textual Criticism* [http://purl.org/TC] 3 (1988): pars. 1-31.

Petrucci, Armando. *Writers and Readers in Medieval Italy: Studies in the History of Written Culture.* New Haven, CT: Yale University, 1995.

Petzer, Jacobus H. "The Latin Version of the New Testament." Pages 113-30 in *The Text of the New Testament in Contemporary Research: Essays on the Status Quaestionis.* Edited by Bart D. Ehrman and Michael W. Holmes. SD 46. Grand Rapids: Eerdmans, 1995.

Pickering, Stuart R. "The Significance of Non-Continuous New Testament Textual Materials in Papyri." Pages 121-40 in *Studies in the Early Text of the Gospels and Acts. The Papers of the First Birmingham Colloquium on the Textual Criticism of the New Testament.* Edited by D. G. K. Taylor. Texts and Studies 3.1. Birmingham: University of Birmingham Press, 1999.

Reicke, Bo. *The Epistles of James, Peter and Jude.* AB 37. New York: Doubleday, 1964.

Richards, W. L. "A Critique of a New Testament Text-Critical Methodology: the Claremont Profile Method." *JBL* 96 (1977): 555-66.

———. "Gregory 1175: Alexandrian or Byzantine in the Catholic Epistles." *AUSS* 21 (1983): 155-68.

———. *The Classification of the Greek Manuscripts of the Johannine Epistles.* SBLDS 35. Missoula, MT: Scholars Press, 1977.

Richardson, Cyril C., ed. *Early Christian Fathers.* New York: Macmillan, 1979.

Roberts, Colin H. "The Codex." *Proceedings of the British Academy* 40 (1954): 198-99.

Robertson, Terry. "Relationships Among the Non-Byzantine Manuscripts of 2 Peter." *AUSS* 39 (2001): 41-59.

Robinson, James M. *The Pachomian Monastic Library at the Chester Beatty Library and the Bibliothèque Bodmer.* Occasional Papers of the Institute for Antiquity and Christianity 19. Claremont: Institute for Antiquity and Christianity, 1990.

Robinson, Maurice A. "Rule 9, Isolated Variants, and the 'Test-Tube' Nature of the NA27 Text." In *From Text to Translation: The Proceedings of the Bingham Colloquium held at McMaster Divinity College, Hamilton, Ontario, 26-28 May 2005.* Edited by Stanley E. Porter and Mark J. Boda. Grand Rapids: Eerdmans, forthcoming 2007.

Ross, J. M. "The United Bible Societies' Greek New Testament." *JBL* 95 (1976):112-21.

Rowston, D. J. "The Most Neglected Book in the New Testament." *NTS* 21 (1975): 554-63.

Royse, James R. "Scribal Habits in Early Greek New Testament Papyri." Th.D. diss., Graduate Theological Union, 1981.

———. "Scribal Tendencies in the Transmission of the Text of the New Testament." Pages 239-52 in *The Text of the New Testament in Contemporary Research. Essays on the Status Quaestionis.* Edited by Bart D. Ehrman and Michael W. Holmes. SD 46. Grand Rapids: Eerdmans, 1995.

Schlosser, Jacques. "Les Jours de Noé et de Lot: A Propos de Luc, XVII, 26-30." *RB* 80 (1973): 13-36.

Schmitz, Franz-Jürgen. *Das Verhältnis der koptischen zur griechischen Überlieferung des Neuen Testaments.* ANTF 33. Berlin/New York: de Gruyter, 2003.

Scholz, J. M. A. *Biblisch-kritische Reise in Frankreich, der Schweitz, Italien, Palästina und im Archipel, in den Jahren 1818, 1819, 1820, 1821 nebst einer Geschichte des Textes des NT.* Leipzig/Soran: Friedrich Fleischer, 1823.

Scrivener, F. H. A. *A Plain Introduction to the Criticism of the New Testament for the Use of Biblical Students.* Edited by E. Miller. 2 vols. 4th ed. London/New York: Deighton, Bell & Co., 1894.

Silva, Moisés. Response. Pages 141-50 in *Rethinking New Testament Textual Criticism.* Edited by David A. Black. Grand Rapids: Baker, 2002.

Skeat, T. C. "An Early Medieval 'Book of Fate': The Sortes XII Patriarcharum. With a Note on 'Books of Fate' in General." *Mediaeval and Renaissance Studies* 3 (1954): 41-54.

Spencer, Matthew, Klaus Wachtel and Christopher J. Howe. "The Greek Vorlage of the Syra Harclensis: A Comparative Study on Method in Exploring Textual Genealogy." *TC: A Journal of Biblical Textual Criticism* [http://purl.org/TC] 7 (2002). Pars. 1-46.

Spitaler, Peter. "Doubt or Dispute (Jude 9 and 22-23): Rereading a Special New Testament Meaning through the Lense of Internal Evidence." *Bib* 87 (2006): 201-22.

Spitta, Friedrich. *Der zweite Brief des Petrus und der Brief des Judas.* Halle: Verlag der Buchhandlung des Waisenhauses, 1885.

Strelan, Rick. "The Fallen Watchers and the Disciples in Mark." *JSP* 20 (1999): 73-92.

Thiele, Walter. "Beobachtungen zum Comma Iohanneum (1 Joh 5, 7f.)." *ZNW* 50 (1959): 61-73.

———. *Die lateinischen Texte des 1. Petrusbriefes.* GLB 5. Freiburg im Breisgau: Herder, 1965.

———. "Probleme der Versio Latina in den Katholischen Briefen." Pages 93-119 in *Die alten Übersetzungen des Neuen Testaments, die Kirchenväterzitate und Lektionare.* Edited by Kurt Aland. ANTF 5. Berlin/New York: de Gruyter, 1972.

Thurén, Lauri. "Style Never Goes Out of Fashion—2 Peter Reconsidered." Pages 341-47 in *Rhetoric, Scripture and Theology.* Edited by Stanley E. Porter and Thomas. H. Olbricht. JSNTSup 131. Sheffield: Sheffield Academic Press, 1996.

———. "The Relationship between 2 Peter and Jude: A Classical Problem Resolved?" Pages 451-60 in *The Catholic Epistles and the Tradition.* Edited by Jacques Schlosser. BETL 176. Leuven: Leuven University Press/Peeters, 2004.

Treu, Kurt. "Christliche Papyri IV." *APF* 22 (1973): 373-77.

Trobisch, David. *The First Edition of the New Testament.* Oxford: Oxford University Press, 2000.

Turner, Eric G. *The Typology of the Codex.* Pennsylvania, PA: University of Pennsylvania Press, 1977.

Tylor, Edward B. *Primitive Culture: Researches into the Development of Mythology, Philosophy, Religion, Language, Art, and Custom.* London: John Murray, 1871.

Vaganay, Leon and Christian-Bernard Amphoux. *An Introduction to New Testament Textual Criticism.* Translated by Jenny Read-Heimerdinger. 2d rev. and enl. ed. New York: Cambridge University Press, 1991.

Van Haelst, Joseph. *Catalogue des papyrus littéraires juifs et chrétiens.* Série "Papyrologie" 1, Université de Paris IV. Paris, Sorbonne: Publications de la Sorbonne, 1976.

Vermez, Geza. "Deux Traditions sur Balaam." *Cahiers Sioniens* 10 (1955): 289-302.

Vögtle, Anton. *Der Judasbrief, der 2. Petrusbrief.* EKKNT 22. Solothurn-Düsseldorf: Benziger; Neukirchen-Vluyn: Neukirchener Verlag, 1994.

———. "Petrus und Paulus nach dem Zweiten Petrusbrief." Pages 223-39 in *Kontinuität und Einheit, Festschrift für Franz Mussner.* Edited by Paul-Gerhard Müller and Werner Stenger. Freiburg: Herder, 1981.

Wachtel, Klaus. *Der byzantinische Text der Katholischen Briefe: eine Untersuchung zur Entstehung der Koine des Neuen Testaments.* ANTF 24. Berlin/New York: de Gruyter, 1995.

Wachtel, Klaus and D. C. Parker. "The Joint IGNTP/INTF Editio Critica Maior of the Gospel of John: Its Goals and Their Significance for New Testament Scholarship." Paper presented at the SNTS meeting. Halle, August 15, 2005.

Wand, J. W. C. *The General Epistles of St. Peter and St. Jude.* WC. London: Westminster, 1934.

Wasserman, Tommy. "Papyrus 72 and the Bodmer Miscellaneous Codex." *NTS* 51 (2005): 137-54.

———. "$\mathfrak{P}^{78}$ (*P.Oxy.* XXXIV 2684): The Epistle of Jude on an Amulet?" Pages 137-60 in *New Testament Manuscripts: Their Texts and Their World.* Edited by Thomas J. Kraus and Tobias Nicklas. TENT 2. Leiden: Brill, 2006.

———. "Some Bibliographic Notes on Greek New Testament Manuscripts." *NovT*, forthcoming.

———. "The Patmos Family of New Testament MSS and Its Allies in the Pericope of the Adulteress and Beyond." *TC: A Journal of Biblical Textual Criticism* [http://purl.org/TC] 7 [2002]: pars 1-59.

Watson, D. F. *Invention, Arrangement, and Style: Rhetorical Criticism of Jude and 2 Peter*. SBLDS 104. Atlanta: Scholar's Press, 1988.

Weiss, Bernhard. *Die Katholischen Briefe*. Textkritische Untersuchungen und Textherstellung 8/3. Leipzig: Hinrichs, 1892.

Whallon, William. "Should We Keep, Omit, or Alter the Hoi in Jude 12." *NTS* 34 (1988): 156-59.

Wifstrand, Albert. "Lukas och den grekiska klassicismen." *SEÅ* 6 (1941): 243-62.

Wikgren, Allen P. "Some Problems in Jude." Pages 147-52 in *Studies in the History and Text of the New Testament in Honor of Kenneth Willis Clark*. Edited by B. L. Daniels and M. J. Suggs. SD 29. Salt Lake City: University of Utah Press, 1967.

Windisch, Hans. *Die Katholischen Briefe*. HNT 15. Tübingen: Mohr Siebeck, 1930.

Winter, Sara C. "Jude 22-23: A Note on the Text and Translation." *HTR* 87 (1994): 215-22.

Wisse, Frederik. *The Profile Method for the Classification and Evaluation of Manuscript Evidence as Applied to the Continuous Greek Text of the Gospel of Luke*. SD 44. Grand Rapids: Eerdmans, 1982.

Wohlenberg, D. G. *Der erste und zweite Petrusbrief und der Judasbrief*. Leipzig: A. Deichert'sche Verlagsbuchhandlung Werner Scholl, 1915.

Wolff, Richard. *A Commentary on the Epistle of Jude*. Grand Rapids: Zondervan, 1960.

Yoo, Kenneth K. "The Classification of the Greek Manuscripts of 1 Peter with Special Emphasis on Methodology." Ph.D. diss., Andrews University, 2001.

Zwaan, J. de. *II Petrus en Judas. Textuitgave met inleidende Studiën en textueelen Commentaar*. Ph.D. diss., University of Leiden, 1909.

———. "Minuskelgruppen in 2 Petri und Judas." *ZNW* 12 (1911): 76-82.

Index of Ancient Authors

Index of Modern Authors

Index of Ancient Literature

For classical and patristic authors, see index of ancient authors. References to the LXX are indicated in the index only where Hebrew and Greek versification differ. The Epistle of Jude is only indexed in chs. 1-5. References to whole books have been omitted.

Plates

PLATE I

Courtesy of the Martin Bodmer Foundation

P.Bodmer VII (Gr.-Al. 𝔓⁷²; ca. 300 C.E.)
Bibliotheca Bodmeriana, Cologny/Geneva
actual size ca. 15.5 x 14 cm
p. 62ᵛ (ancient pag.)
inscriptio; Jude 1-4

Transcription of *P.Bodmer* VII ($\mathfrak{P}^{72}$)

1. *verso* (p. 62): inscriptio; Jude 1-4

ξβ

ϊο^υδα επειστολη

1   ϊουδας ι�︤ηυ χ︤ρ︤υ δουλος αδελφος

       δε ϊακωβου τοις εν θ︤ω︤ π︤ρ︤ι ηγα

       πημενοις και ι︤ηυ χ︤ρ︤ω τετηρη

2   μενοις κλητοις | ελεος υμιν και   5

       ειρηνη και αγαπη πληθυνθιη

3 | αγαπητοι πασαν σπουδην ποι

       ησαμενος του γραφιν υμιν περει

       της κοινης ημων σωτηριας

       αναγ'κην εσχον γραψαι υμιν   10

       παρακαλων επαγωνιζεσθε

       τη απαξ παρα^δοθειση [[πειστι]]

4   τοις αγιοις πειστει | παρεισεδυσα︤

---

12 πειστι: deleted by line

PLATE II

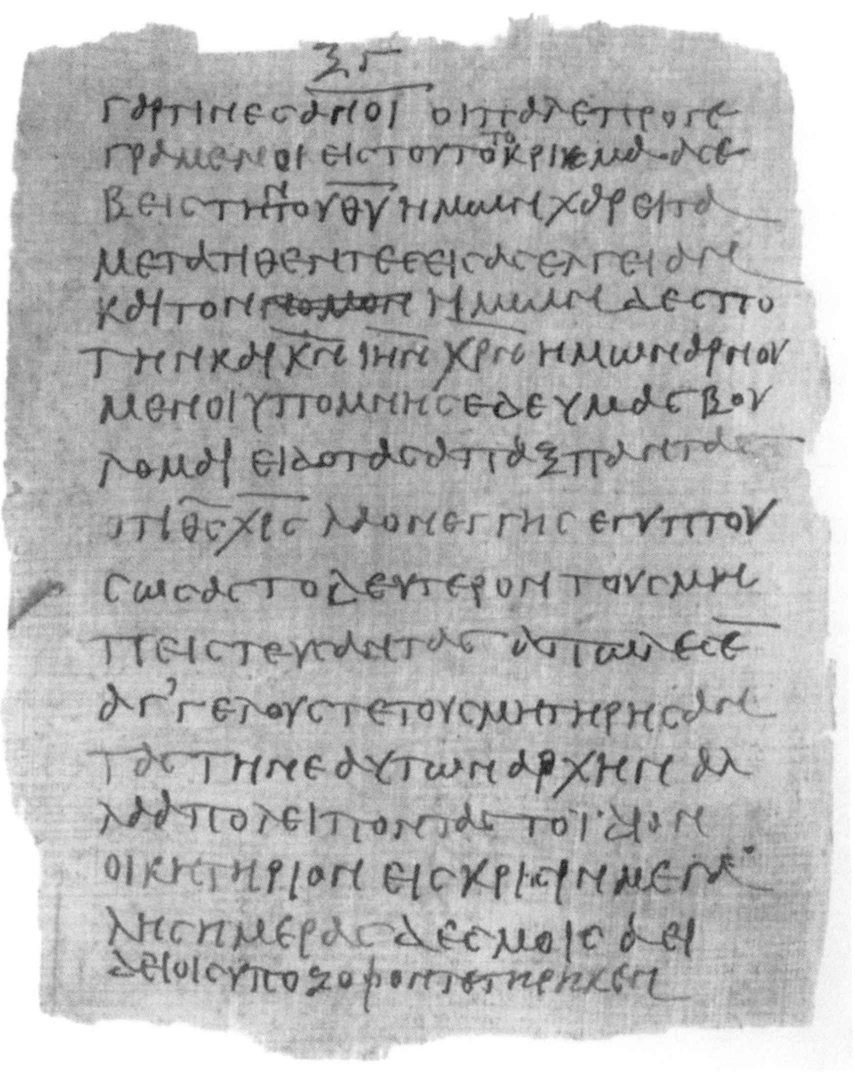

Courtesy of the Martin Bodmer Foundation

P.Bodmer VII ($\mathfrak{P}^{72}$)
p. 63ʳ
Jude 4-6

2. *recto* (p. 63): Jude 4-6

ξγ

γαρ τινες α̅ν̅οι οι παλε προγε
γραμενοι εις τουτο ^{το} κρι[[κ̣]]μα ασε
βεις τη^ν του θ̅υ̅ ημων χαρειτα
μετατιθεντες εις ασελγειαν
και τον [[νομον]] ημων δεσπο   5
την και κ̅ν̅ ι̅η̅ν χ̅ρ̅ν ημων αρνου
5   μενοι | υπομνησε δε υμας βου
λομαι ειδοτας απαξ παντα[[ς]]
οτι θ̅ς̅ χ̅ρ̅ς λαον εγ γης εγυπτου
σωσας το δευτερον τους μη   10
πειστευσαντας απωλεσε̅
6 | αγ'γελους τε τους μη τηρησαν
τας την εαυτων αρχην αλ
λα απολειποντας το ϊδιον
οικητηριον εις κρισιν μεγα   15
λης ημερας δεσμοις αει
δειοις υπο σοφον τετηρηκεν

---

2 κρι[[κ̣]]μα: *ECM* κρι[[σ̣]]μα | *5* νομον: deleted by line | *6* χ̅ρ̅ν: *ed. pr.*: χρν |
8 παντα[[ς]]: *sigma* erased; *ed. pr.*: παντας

PLATE III

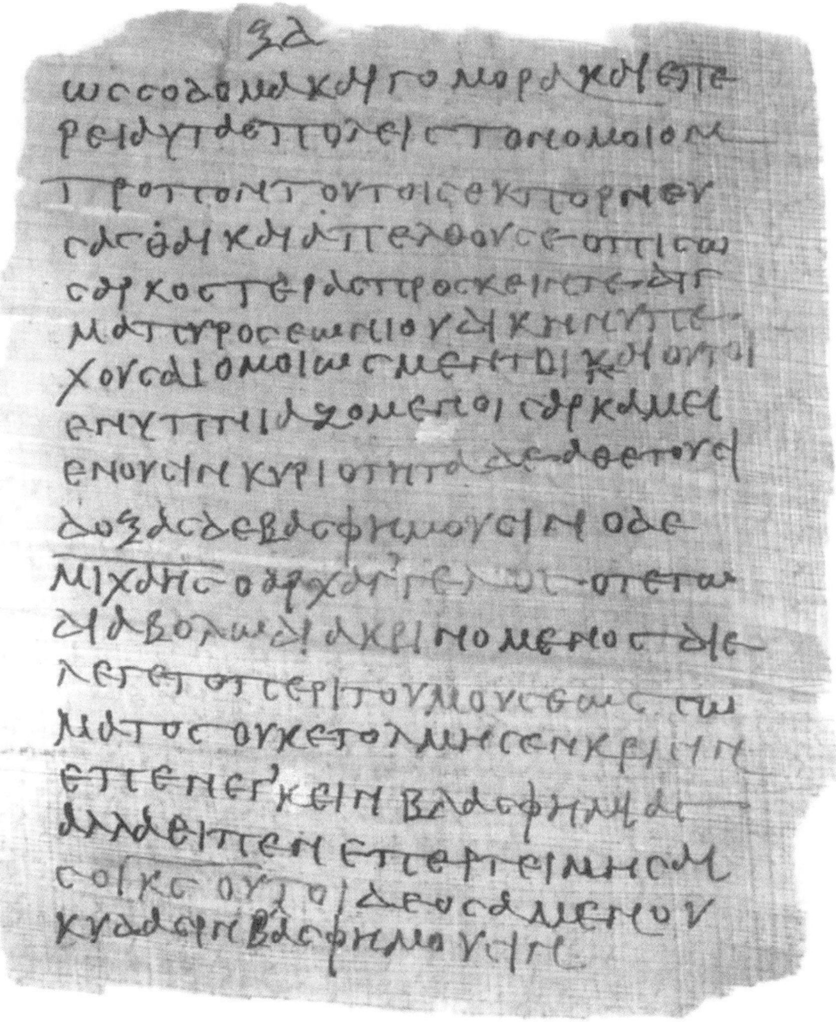

Courtesy of the Martin Bodmer Foundation

P.Bodmer VII ($\mathfrak{P}^{72}$)

p. 64ᵛ

Jude 7-10

3. *verso* (p. 64): Jude 7-10

ξδ

7 | ως σοδομα και γομορα και ε πε
ρει αυτας πολεις τον ομοιον
τροπον τουτοις εκπορνευ
σασ[[θ]]αι και απελθουσε οπισω
σαρκος τερας προσκειντε διγ   5
μα πυρος εωνιου δικην υπε
8 χουσαι | ομοιως μεντοι και ουτοι
ενυπνιαζομενοι σαρκα μει
ενουσιν κυριοτητα δε αθετουσι
9 δοξας δε βασφημουσιν | ο δε   10
μῑχαης ο αρχαγ'γελος οτε τω
διαβολω διακρινομενος διε
λεγετο περι του μουσεως σω
ματος ουκ ετολμησεν κρισιν
επενεγ'κειν βλασφημιας   15
αλλα ειπεν επειτειμησαι
10 σοι κ̄ϲ̄ | ουτοι δε οσα μεν ου
κ υδασιν β^λασφημουσιν

---

3 εκπορνευσασ[[θ]]αι: *theta* deleted by supralinear dot

PLATE IV

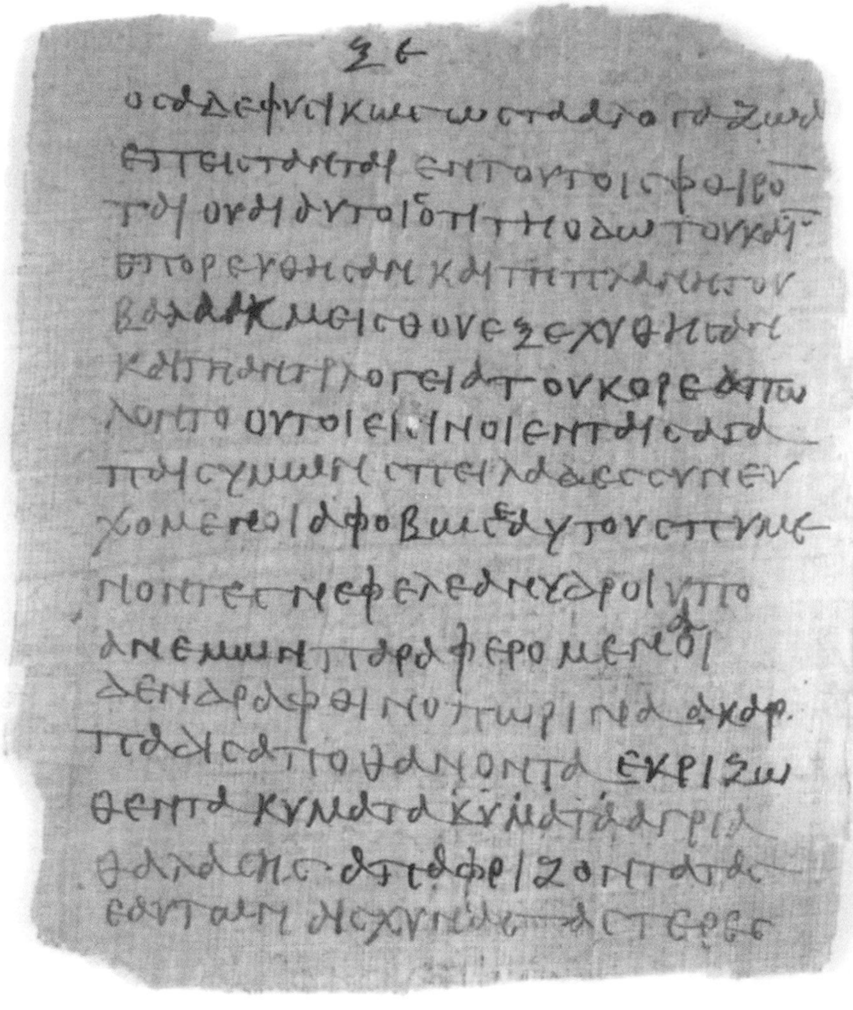

Courtesy of the Martin Bodmer Foundation

P.Bodmer VII ($\mathfrak{P}^{72}$)
p. 65r
Jude 10-13

4. *recto* (p. 65): Jude 10-13

ξε

οσα δε φυσικως ως τα αλογα ζωα
επεισταντai εν τουτοις φθιρο⁻
11 ται | ουαι αυτοιˢ οτι τη οδω του καϊ⁻
επορευθησαν και τη πλανη του
βαλ[[λ]]ααк μεισθου εξεχυθησαν   5
και τη αντιλογεια του κορε απω
12 λοντο | ουτοι εισιν οι εν ταις αγα
παις υμων σπειλαδες συνευ
χομενοι αφοβως ᵉαυτους πυμε
νοντες νεφελε ανυδροι υπο   10
ανεμων παραφερομεν[[o]]ᵃι
δενδρα φθινοπωρινα ακαρ
πα δις αποθανοντα εκριζω
13 θεντα | κυματα [[κυματα]] αγρια
θαλασης απαφριζοντα τας   15
εαυτων αισχυνας αστερες

---

5 βαλ[[λ]]ααк: *prima manus* βαλλαк/βαλλαμ? *lambda* corrected to *alpha* (cf.
βαλλαμ in 2 Pet 2:15): *ed. pr.* and *ECM*: βαλαaκ | *11* παραφερομεν[[o]]ᵃι:
omicron deleted by supralinear dot | *14* [[κυματα]]: deleted by supralinear dots

PLATE V

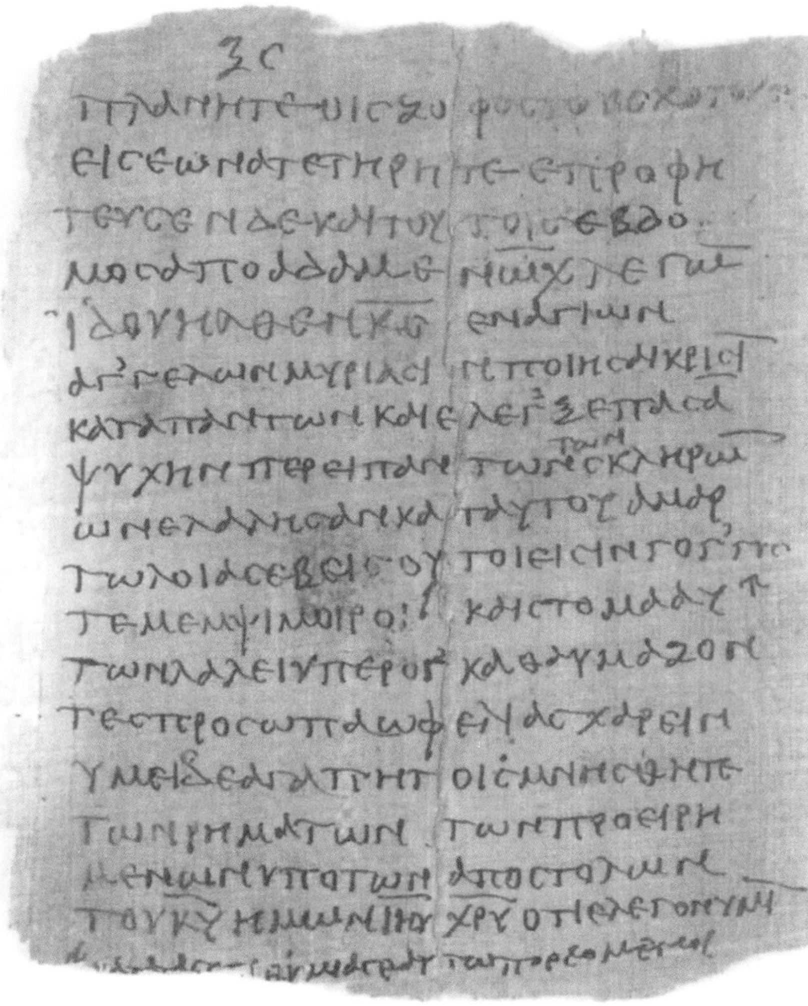

Courtesy of the Martin Bodmer Foundation

P.Bodmer VII ($\mathfrak{P}^{72}$)
p. 66ᵛ
Jude 13-18

5. *verso* (p. 66): Jude 13-18

ξϛ

πλανητε οις ζοφος του σκοτους

14 εις εωνα τετηρητε | επροφη

  τευσεν δε και τουτοις εβδο

  μος απο αδαμ ε̄ν̄ωχ λεγω̄

  ϊδου ηλθεν κ̄ϛ̄ εν αγιων   5

15 αγ'γελων μυριασιν | ποιησαι κρισῑ

  κατα παντων και ελεγ'ξε πασᾱ

  ψυχην περει παντων ᵗʷⁿσκληρω̄

  ων ελαλησαν κατ αυτου αμαρ

16 τωλοι ασεβεις | ουτοι εισιν γογ'γυσ   10

  τε μεμψιμοιροι ¹ και στομα αυ ↑

  των λαλει υπερογ'κα θαυμαζον

  τες προσωπα ωφελιας χαρειν |

17 υμειˢ δε αγαπητοι[[ϛ]] μνησθητε

  των ρηματων των προειρη   15

  μενων υπο των αποστολων

18 του κ̄ῡ ημων ιη̄υ χ̄ρ̄υ | οτι ελεγον υμῑ

  ↑ κ̣ατ̣α τ̣α̣ς ε̣πιθυμιας εαυτω πορεομενοι

---

11 ¹ *et* ↑: ancora in mg. and vertical insert mark in text; insert text in lower mg. after ancora | *14* αγαπητοι[[ϛ]]: *sigma* deleted by supralinear dot | *18* ↑ κ̣ατ̣α κτλ.: no uncertain letters indicated in *ed. pr.*

PLATE VI

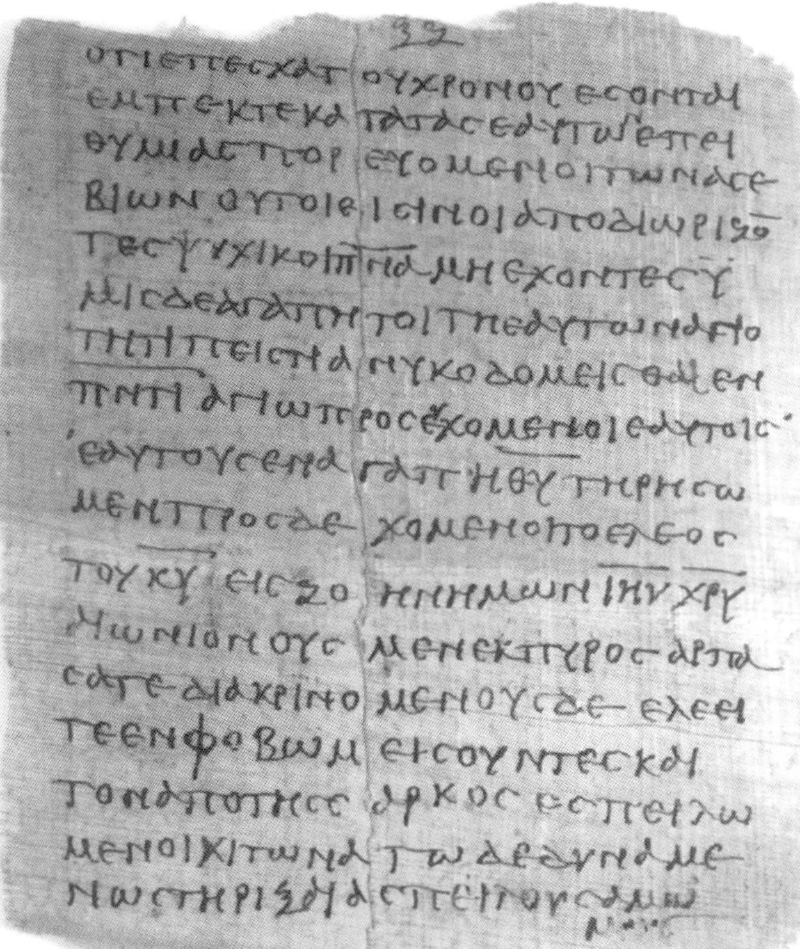

Courtesy of the Martin Bodmer Foundation

P.Bodmer VII ($\mathfrak{P}^{72}$)
p. 67ʳ
Jude 18-24

6. *recto* (p. 67): Jude 18-24

ξζ

     οτι επ εσχατου χρονου εσονται

     εμπεκτε κατα τας εαυτω^ν επει

     θυμιας πορευομενοι των ασε

19   βιων | ουτοι εισιν οι αποδιωριζο⁻

20   τες ψυχικοι π̅ν̅α μη εχοντες | ϋ   5

     μις δε αγαπητοι τη εαυτων αγιο

     τητι πειστι ανυκοδομεισθαι εν

     π̅ν̅τι αγιω προσε^υχομενοι εαυτοις· |

21   εαυτους εν αγαπη θ̅υ̅ τηρησω

     μεν προσδεχομενοι το ελεος   10

     του κ̅υ̅ εις ζοην ημων ι̅η̅υ̅ χ̅ρ̅υ̅

22   αιωνιον | ους μεν εκ πυρος αρπα

     ζατε διακρινομενους | δε ελεει

     τε εν φοβω μεισουντες και

     τον απο της σαρκος εσπειλω   15

     μενοι χιτωνα | τω δε δυναμε

     νω στηριξαι ασπειλους αμω

            μο̣υ̣ς̣

---

9 εαυτους: a raised dot/stroke precedes the word, possibly a smudge. | *17-18* αμωμο̣υ̣ς̣: no uncertain letters indicated in *ed. pr.*

PLATE VII

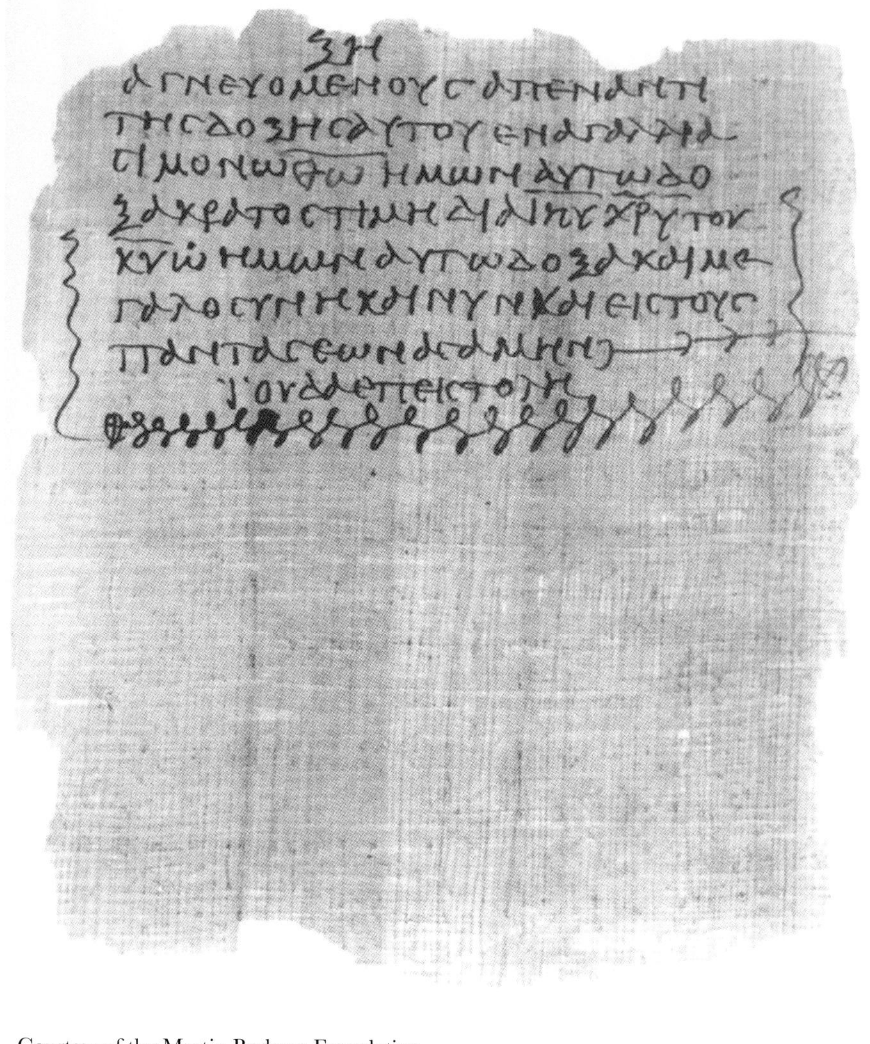

P.Bodmer VII ($\mathfrak{P}^{72}$)

p. 68ᵛ

Jude 24-25; subscriptio

7. *verso* (p. 68): Jude 24-25; subscriptio

ξη

αγνευομενους απεναντι
της δοξης αυτου εν αγαλλια
25   σι | μονω θ$\overline{\omega}$ ημων αυτω δο
ξα κρατος τιμη δια ι$\overline{\eta}$υ χ$\overline{\rho}$υ του
κ$\overline{υ}$ [[ω]] ημων αυτω δοξα και με   5
γαλοσυνη και νυν και εις τους
παντας εωνας αμην
   ϊουδα επειστολη

---

5 [[ω]]: deleted by supralinear dot

PLATE VIII

Courtesy of the Egypt Exploration Society

P.Oxy. XXXIV 2684 (Gr.-Al. 𝔓⁷⁸; III/IV cent. C.E.)
Sackler Library, Oxford
actual size 2.9 x 5.3 cm
fols. 1-2ʳ
Jude 4, 8

PLATE IX

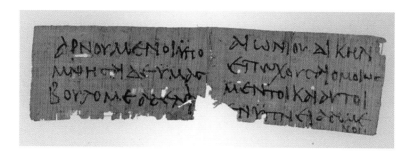

Courtesy of the Egypt Exploration Society

P.Oxy. XXXIV 2684 (𝔓⁷⁸)
fols. 1-2ᵛ
Jude 4-5, 7-8

Transcription of *P.Oxy.* XXXIV 2684 ($\mathfrak{P}^{78}$)

Fol. 1, *recto*: Jude 4

4 γιαν και τον μο   1
   νον δεϲποτην
   κ͞ν ημων ι͞η͞ν χ͞ρ͞ν   3

Fol. 1, *verso*: Jude 4-5

5 αρνουμενοι· | ὑπο   4
   μνηϲαι δε ὑμαϲ
   βουλομε αδελφ[6

Fol. 2, *recto*: Jude 7-8

7 αιωνιου δικην   1
8 επεχουϲαι | ομοιωϲ
   μεντοι και αυτοι
   ενὑπνειαδομε
            νοι·   5

Fol. 2, *verso*: Jude 8

8 ϲαρκα μεν μι   6
   αινουϲιν κυρει
   οτητα δε αθετου
   ϲ̣ιν δοξαν δε̣ [..   9

---

4 δεϲποτην ... ημων: uncertain letters not indicated in *ed. pr.* |
5 αδελφ[: ending is not visible, could be either -οι or -ε (*ed. pr.*: αδελφο̣ι) | *8*
αθετουϲ̣ι̣ν: uncertain letters not indicated in *ed. pr.* | δοξαν: final *nu* is visible
(*ed. pr.*: δοξαν̣) | δε̣[.. : faint traces of one letter; space enough for two letters

PLATE X

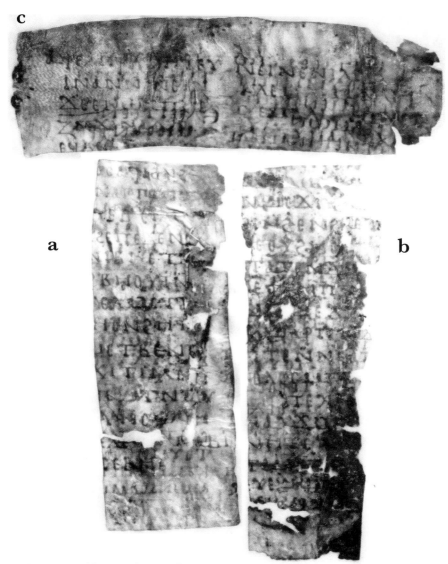

MS M. 597, flyleaf 2ʳ (Gr.-Al. 0316; ca. VII cent.)
The Pierpont Morgan Library, New York
actual size of codex ca. 27 x 21 cm
actual size of fragments a: ca. 19 x 7 cm; b: ca. 18 x 7 cm; c: ca. 7 x 21 cm
Jude 14-18 (Coptic)

Transcription of M. 597 f. II. (0316)*

Fol. 2, *recto*; Jude 14-18

14 ⲁϥⲉⲗ ⲡⲣⲟⲑⲏⲧⲉⲩ
   ⲓⲛ ⲁⲛ ⲛⲛⲉⲓ ⲛ
   ⲭⲉ ⲉⲛⲱⲭ ⲡⲙⲉϩ
   ⲍ̄ ⲛⲭⲓⲛ ⲁⲇⲁⲙ
   ⲉϥⲭⲱ [ⲙⲙⲁⲥ ⲭⲉ]   5
   [ϩⲉⲓ ⲡ]ϭⲥ̄ ⲁϥⲓ ϩⲛ ϩⲉⲛ
   [ⲧⲃⲉ] ⲛⲁⲅⲅⲉⲗⲟⲥ
15 [ⲉⲩⲟ]ⲩⲉⲃ | ⲉⲓⲭⲓ ⲛ
   [ⲟⲩ]ϩⲉⲡ ⲉⲭⲉⲛ ⲟⲩ
   [ⲁⲛ] ⲛⲓⲃⲓ ⲉⲧ[ⲃⲉ]   10
   [ⲛⲉ]ϩⲃⲏⲟⲩⲓ ⲛ[ⲧ]
   [ⲁⲩ]ⲉⲗ ⲙⲉⲧⲁ[ⲥ]
   [ⲉⲃ]ⲏⲥ ⲛϩⲏⲧ[ⲟⲩ]
   [ⲁⲩ]ⲱ ⲉⲧⲃⲉ ⲛⲉ
   [ϣⲉ]ⲭⲓ ⲧⲏⲗⲟ[ⲩ]   15
   [ⲉⲧ]ⲛⲉⲱⲧ ⲛⲧⲁⲩ
   [ⲭⲁⲁ]ⲩ ⲛⲥⲱϥ ⲛ
   [ⲭⲉ ⲛ]ⲉⲗⲉϥⲉⲗⲛⲁⲃⲓ
   ⲛⲁⲥⲉⲃⲏⲥ |

16 ⲛⲉⲓ ⲛⲉ ⲛⲓⲗⲉϥ
   ⲕⲗⲉⲙⲗⲉⲙ ⲛⲗⲉϥ
   ϭⲉⲙⲁⲗⲓⲕⲓ [...]
   [...] ⲉⲩⲙⲁⲁϣⲓ ⲕⲁⲧⲁ
   ⲛⲉⲩ ⲉⲡ̣ⲓ̣ⲑ̣ⲩⲙ̣[ⲓⲁ]   5
   ⲁⲩⲱ ⲗϣⲟⲩ [...]
   ⲛϣⲉⲭⲓ ⲉ[ⲩⲉⲗ ϣⲡⲏ(?)]
   ⲭⲓ ⲛϩⲉⲛϩⲁ ⲉⲧ
   [ⲃ]ⲉ ⲟⲩϩⲟ[ⲩ] |
17 ⲛⲧⲁⲧⲉⲛ ⲇⲉ ⲛ̣ⲁ̣ⲙⲉ   10
   ⲗⲉ† ⲁⲗⲓ ⲡⲙⲉⲉ[ⲩⲉⲓ]
   ⲛⲛϣⲉⲭⲓ ⲛ[ⲧⲁⲩ]
   ⲉⲗ ϣⲁⲣⲡ ⲛⲭ[ⲁⲁⲩ]
   [ϩ]ⲓⲧⲉⲛ ⲛⲉⲁⲡ[ⲟⲥ]
   ⲧⲟⲗⲟⲥ ⲙⲡ[ⲉⲛ̄ϭ̄ⲥ̄   15
   ⲓ̄]ⲏ̄ⲥ̄ ⲡⲉⲭ̄ⲥ̄ | [ⲭⲉ]
18 ⲛⲁⲩⲭⲱ [ⲙⲙⲁⲥ]
   ⲛⲏⲧⲉⲛ [ⲭⲉ]
   [ⲉ]ⲧϩⲁⲏ [...]
   ⲉⲩⲉϣⲱⲡⲓ ⲛ[ⲭⲉ]   20

* For a fuller description of the manuscript, see the *ed. pr.* in Leo Depuydt, *Catalogue of Coptic Manuscripts in the Pierpont Morgan Library* 1 [Text] (Corpus of Illuminated Manuscripts 4; Leuven: Peeters, 1993), 463-64. The transcription of the Coptic side follows the *ed. pr.* However, Depuydt's transcription of the Greek side is highly selective and has been disregarded. There are numerous discrepancies between my transcription of the Greek and the textual data of 0316, recorded in the *ECM* (see errata list of the *ECM* in chapter eight).

PLATE XI

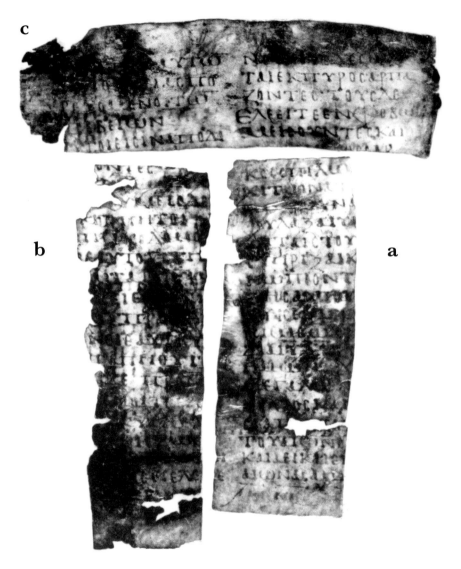

MS M. 597, flyleaf 2ᵛ (0316)
The Pierpont Morgan Library, New York
Jude 18-25

Fol. 2, *verso*; Jude 18-25

18 [κα]τα τας εαυτω‾
    επιθυμιας πο
    ρευομενοι τω‾
    ασεβειων· |

19 ουτοι εισιν αποδι   5
    [οριζ]οντες ψυ[χι
    κοι] π‾ν‾α μη εχ[ον

20 τες] | υμεις δε
    αγαπητοι
    [ε]ποικοδομου[ντε]ς   10
    εαυτους τη
    [αγι]ωτατη υμ[ω‾
    πι]στει εν [π‾ν‾]ι
    [αγι]ω προ[σε]υ[χο

21 με]νοι· | εαυτου[ς   15
    εν] αγαπη θ‾υ‾ τ[η
    ρησ]ατε προσδ[ε
    χομε]νοι το ελ[ε
    ος του] κ‾υ‾ ημων
    [ι‾υ‾ χ‾υ‾] εις ζωη[‾   20

22 αιωνιον | κα]ι
    [ους] μεν ελεγ[χ]ε
    [τε δια]κρινο[με]

23 νους | ους δε σωζε
    ται εκ πυρος αρπα
    ζοντες· τους δε
    ελεειτε εν φοβω
    μεισουντες και   5
    τ[ον α]π̣ο [τ]ης σαρ
    κος σπιλω[μενον]
    χιτωνα : |

24 τω δε δυνα[μενω]
    φυλαξαι υμ[ας]   10
    απταιστου[ς και]
    στηριξαι κ[ατε]
    νωπιον τ[ης δο
    ξ]ης αυτου [αμω

25 μο]υς εν [.... | μο]   15
    νω θ‾ω‾ σ‾ρ‾ι [ημω‾]
    δια ι‾υ‾ χ‾υ‾ το[υ κ‾υ‾]
    ημων δ[οξα]
    μεγαλωσυ[νη]
    κρατος και [εξου]   20
    σια π[ρο] παν[τος]
    του αιωνος [νυν]
    και αει και ει[ς τους]
    αιωνας αμη[ν]

Left column: *19* ημων: traces of letters from the opposite (Coptic) side above ημων | *22* κα]ι: *iota* in left margin of fragment a | *23* ελεγ[χ]ε: final *epsilon* on line 23 in left margin of fragment a | Right column: *15* εν [....: there is hardly enough space for αγαλλιασει (εν δοξα?).

Description of Dumbarton Oaks MS 3 (1521)*

In 1962, the Dumbarton Oaks Collection purchased a Psalter and New Testament MS from a dealer in Europe. The MS had formerly been at the Pantokrator Monastery on Mt Athos (MS 49), but was now incorporated in the Dumbarton Oaks Collection as MS 3. Ever since the MS was first studied and described in the 19th century, its tremendous value for the history of Byzantine and Constantinopolitan art has been acknowledged. Originally the MS consisted of ca. 364 folios on parchment (16.2 x 10.9 cm). The extant portion of the NT (Gregory-Aland 1521) is on fols. 88-340. Fols. 341-362 (beginning with Heb 13:20) are in paper, and were added at a later stage. The MS was copied in 1084, according to the Easter tables starting from 6592 (1084).

The illuminations of the NT section consist mainly of portraits. The Evangelists are depicted in the headpieces of their Gospels. The Apostle Paul is depicted above the Epistle to the Romans, and James, Peter, John and Jude above their Epistles. The illustrations of James and John are typical of the 11th century iconographic types of writing or meditating authors, whereas the portraits of Peter and Jude are derived from the types of prophets, carrying scrolls instead of books. Another interesting feature of the MS is found in the marginal miniatures of the authors that precede each book, in the form of anthropomorphic initials. For example, the initial Π, which commences the Pauline Epistles, is usually formed by Christ and Paul.

---

* This description is partly dependent on the detailed treatment of the manuscript by Sirarpie Der Nersessian, "A Psalter and New Testament Manuscript at Dumbarton Oaks," *Dumbarton Oaks Papers* 19 (1965): 153-83.

Dumbarton Oaks MS 3 (Gr.-Al. 1521; 1084 C.E.)
Dumbarton Oaks Collection, Washington, DC
actual size ca. 16.2 x 10.9 cm
fol. 266v
portrait of Jude; inscriptio; Jude 1-5

PLATE XIII

Dumbarton Oaks MS 3, fol. 266ᵛ, detail of
Christ and Jude

In the Epistle of Jude, the initial I
is represented by Jude (Plate
XIII).

PLATE XIV

The other persons mentioned in
v. 1, Jesus Christ (Plate XIII), and
James (Plate XIV), are depicted in
each margin. Note that Christ is
placed in the left margin above the
two brothers looking at them with
slightly bent head, and they are
turned toward Christ, without
looking directly in his eyes.

Dumbarton Oaks MS 3, foll. 266ᵛ,
detail James

Description of Robert Garrett Collection of Medieval and Renaissance Manuscripts 8 (1799)

MS Garrett 8 (Greg.-Aland 1799) is a parchment MS measuring 13.9 x 10.3 cm. It contains Acts and the Epistles with lacunae. Kenneth W. Clark, who collated the MS, dated it to the 12th century, whereas the *Liste* indicates XII/XIII centuries.[1]

The MS is a curiosity in many ways. It seems to have been copied from several exemplars. In the Pauline Epistles, there are numerous modifications designed for public reading. Lection readings are noted in the margin, and the text itself has been modified. For example, the word ἀδελφοί is added at numerous places. In a similar manner, the addresses τέκνον Τιμόθεε or τέκνον Τίτε have been added at several places in the Pastoral Epistles. Apparently, these insertions stem from the lectionary tradition.

The described feature does not occur in the Catholic Epistles, but in this section the text of the MS is apparently block-mixed; it belongs to the HK group in James-1 John, but reproduces the Byzantine text to a large extent in 2-3 John and Jude.[2]

According to the *Liste* the MS is "verbrannt," and was not collated for *TuT* or the *ECM* (the textual data in the *ECM* builds on Clark's collation). In reality, however, the MS is still preserved, but it does have a variety of conservation problems and has never been microfilmed because of its tight binding. Through the kind permission of the curator Don Skemer at the Princeton University Libraries, the MS has now been photographed for the first time, exclusively in the Epistle of Jude (Plates XII-XIII). The MS has a lacuna after γογγυσταί in Jude 16.

---

[1] Kenneth W. Clark, *Eight American Praxapostoloi* (Chicago: University of Chicago Press, 1941).

[2] Klaus Wachtel, *Der byzantinische Text der Katholischen Briefe: eine Untersuchung zur Entstehung der Koine des Neuen Testaments* (ANTF 24; Berlin/New York: de Gruyter, 1995), 62, n. 18.

PLATE XV

Robert Garrett Collection of Medieval and
Renaissance Manuscripts No. 8 (1799, XII/XIII cent.)
Manuscript Division. Department of Rare Books and Special
Collections. Princeton University Library.
actual size 13.9 x 10.3 cm
fol. 41ʳ
inscriptio; Jude 1-4

PLATE XVI

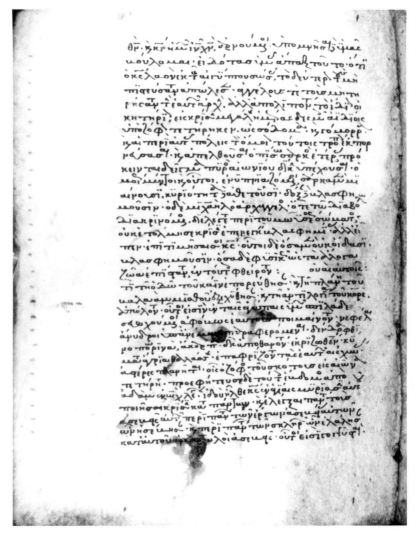

Robert Garrett Collection of Medieval and
Renaissance Manuscripts No. 8 (1799)
fol. 41ᵛ
Jude 4-16

Sammanfattning (Swedish Summary)

Föreliggande arbete, *The Epistle of Jude: Its Text and Transmission*, behandlar Judasbrevets texthistoria. Monografin inleds med en översikt av den textkritiska forskningen på de Katolska Breven i allmänhet och Judasbrevet i synnerhet, från 1800-talet och fram till nutid. Mot bakgrund av det tecknade forskningsläget beskriver så författaren studiens upplägg och syfte, samt antyder några av resultaten (kap. 1). Det handlar främst om två uppgifter.

Den första uppgiften är att fullständigt gå igenom och redovisa källmaterialet, dvs. alla manuskript till Judasbrevet, i en textkritisk apparat. Tidigare har endast en bråkdel av källmaterialet redovisats, genom att handskrifter selekterats bort i stor skala, även i de största textutgåvorna. Den fulla kollationeringen som här redovisas har medfört att talrika hittills okända varianter kommit i dagen, samt att kända och viktiga varianter fått utökat stöd i nya handskrifter. Dessutom har flera nyupptäckta varianter i de grekiska handskrifterna visat sig motsvara ordalydelser som bara varit kända genom de gamla översättningarna (latin, koptiska och syriska).

Den andra uppgiften är att ställa både gamla och nya frågor till källmaterialet. Traditionellt har det allt överskuggande målet för textkritiken varit att söka komma fram till den "ursprungliga texten", och därvid har säregna manuskript och sekundära textvarianter förpassats till historiens bakgård. Även om frågan om den "ursprungliga texten" eller "utgångstexten" (dvs. den text som är möjlig att vetenskapligt rekonstruera) kvarstår, har här hänsyn tagits till andra intressen. Så riktas en tydlig fokus på textvittnena för deras egen skull, såsom fönster in i sin samtid. Manuskripten har sina egna unika historier att berätta om de människor som kopierat, ägt och använt dem. Att detaljerat undersöka enskilda manuskript ur olika aspekter och söka kartlägga skrivarna i möjligaste mån gagnar givetvis även den klassiska uppgiften, att väga olika varianter mot varandra, vilket tar sig tydligast uttryck i textkommentaren (kap. 10).

Två manuskript studeras ingående, nämligen de tidigaste handskriftsvittnena till Judasbrevet, $\mathfrak{P}^{72}$ och $\mathfrak{P}^{78}$ från ca. 300 e.Kr. (kap. 2-3). I undersökningen av dessa två papyrer avtecknar sig två vitt skilda berättelser. $\mathfrak{P}^{72}$ är det enda fullständigt bevarade papyrusvittnet till Petrusbreven och Judasbrevet. Manuskriptet är en del av en samlingskodex vars omfång vuxit över tid, och där dels samlingens beskaffenhet och dels själva textvarianterna pekar på en proto-ortodox miljö. Det andra manuskriptet, $\mathfrak{P}^{78}$, är ett fragment av en miniatyrkodex, som troligen använts som amulett och en intressant fråga är varför man valt Judasbrevet som lämplig text för ett sådant syfte.

När Judasbrevets texthistoria skall undersökas bör man först ta ställning till en grundläggande fråga, nämligen det litterära förhållandet mellan Andra Petrusbrevet och Judasbrevet. Man kan slå fast att den ene författaren varit beroende av den andre, men vilket brev avfattades först? Frågan om litterär prioritet påverkar i sin tur synen på textvarianterna i respektive brev. Om ꞏ Judasbrevet skrivits först måste dess rekonstruerade text kunna förklara uppkomsten av Andra Petrusbrevets texttradition och tvärtom. I behandlingen av det litterära förhållandet mellan de två breven (kap. 4) presenteras nya kriterier för bedömningen av förhållandet mellan breven och en rad argument framförs som pekar på att Judasbrevet har litterär prioritet. I ett angränsande kapitel (kap. 5) påvisas så hur de två texttraditionerna (Judas/2 Petrus) påverkat varandra såsom det tar sig uttryck i sk. harmoniseringar i manuskripten. Resultaten visar att skrivare i relativt liten grad tenderat att harmonisera texten i respektive brev till dess parallelltext. Två viktiga handskrifter visar sig helt sakna sådan harmonisering, $\mathfrak{P}^{72}$ och Codex Vaticanus (B 03).

I följande kapitel (kap. 6) förtecknas de 560 manuskript som ingår i studien, och ett antal av dem har vid behov kompletterats med ytterligare bibliografiska notiser. Efter en kortfattad metodbeskrivning för hur Judasbrevets utgångstext rekonstruerats och en sammanfattande redovisning av denna text och dess förhållande till andra textutgåvor (kap. 7) följer så den textkritiska apparaten där samtliga läsarter redovisas i anslutning till den kritiskt rekonstruerade utgångstexten (kap. 8). I slutet av samma kapitel förtecknas textluckor och fel i handskrifterna som inte framgår av apparaten. Dessutom förtecknas uppenbara fel i och skillnader i förhållande till den textkritiska utgåvan av Judasbrevet, *Editio Critica Maior* (*ECM*), från Institut für neutestamentliche Textforschung (INTF) i Münster.

Det resonemang som ligger bakom textrekonstruktionen redovisas fullödigt i en textkommentar (kap. 9) där över 100 textkritiska problem och intressanta textvarianter kommenteras. En innovation i sammanhanget är det nya rankingsystem som tillämpats i textkommentaren. Det är av mer deskriptiv art än tidigare motsvarigheter och söker ge en samlad bild av bevisläget i fråga och bjuda in läsaren till egen tolkning och värdering av bevisen.

I slutet av boken publiceras för första gången fullständiga bilder (Plates) åtföljda av transkriptioner av papyrushandskrifterna $\mathfrak{P}^{72}$ och $\mathfrak{P}^{78}$, samt majuskelhandskriften 0316. Dessutom publiceras unika bilder på minuskel-handskrifterna 1521 och 1799 tillsammans med korta beskrivningar.